ANCIENT CHRISTIAN COMMENTARY ON SCRIPTURE
Projected & published volumes

Volume editor

Mark Sheridan, OSB, is vice rector and dean of the faculty of theology at the Pontifical Athenaeum of St. Anselm in Rome, Italy. With Jeremy Driscoll he edited *Spiritual Progress: Studies in the Spirituality of Late Antiquity and Early Monasticism.*

General editor

Thomas C. Oden is the Henry Anson Buttz Professor of Theology at The Theological School, Drew University, Madison, New Jersey. In addition to serving as general editor of the Ancient Christian Commentary on Scripture, he is the author of many theological works, including a three-volume systematic theology.

 InterVarsity Press
Downers Grove, Illinois 60515

"Composed in the style of the great medieval *catenae*, this new anthology of patristic commentary on Holy Scripture, conveniently arranged by chapter and verse, will be a valuable resource for prayer, study and proclamation. By calling attention to the rich Christian heritage preceding the separations between East and West and between Protestant and Catholic, this series will perform a major service to the cause of ecumenism."

AVERY CARDINAL DULLES, S.J.
Laurence J. McGinley Professor of Religion and Society
Fordham University

"The initial cry of the Reformation was *ad fontes*—back to the sources! The Ancient Christian Commentary on Scripture is a marvelous tool for the recovery of biblical wisdom in today's church. Not just another scholarly project, the ACCS is a major resource for the renewal of preaching, theology and Christian devotion."

TIMOTHY GEORGE
Dean, Beeson Divinity School, Samford University

"Modern church members often do not realize that they are participants in the vast company of the communion of saints that reaches far back into the past and that will continue into the future, until the kingdom comes. This Commentary should help them begin to see themselves as participants in that redeemed community."

ELIZABETH ACHTEMEIER
Union Professor Emerita of Bible and Homiletics
Union Theological Seminary in Virginia

"Contemporary pastors do not stand alone. We are not the first generation of preachers to wrestle with the challenges of communicating the gospel. The Ancient Christian Commentary on Scripture puts us in conversation with our colleagues from the past, that great cloud of witnesses who preceded us in this vocation. This Commentary enables us to receive their deep spiritual insights, their encouragement and guidance for present-day interpretation and preaching of the Word. What a wonderful addition to any pastor's library!"

WILLIAM H. WILLIMON
Dean of the Chapel and Professor of Christian Ministry
Duke University

"Here is a nonpareil series which reclaims the Bible as the book of the church by making accessible to earnest readers of the twenty-first century the classrooms of Clement of Alexandria and Didymus the Blind, the study and lecture hall of Origen, the cathedrae of Chrysostom and Augustine, the scriptorium of Jerome in his Bethlehem monastery."

GEORGE LAWLESS
Augustinian Patristic Institute and Gregorian University, Rome

"We are pleased to witness publication of the
Ancient Christian Commentary on Scripture. It is most beneficial for us to learn
how the ancient Christians, especially the saints of the church
who proved through their lives their devotion to God and his Word, interpreted
Scripture. Let us heed the witness of those who have gone before us in the faith."

Metropolitan Theodosius
Primate, Orthodox Church in America

"Across Christendom there has emerged a widespread interest
in early Christianity, both at the popular and scholarly level. . . .
Christians of all traditions stand to benefit from this project, especially clergy
and those who study the Bible. Moreover, it will allow us to see how our traditions are
both rooted in the scriptural interpretations of the church fathers while at
the same time seeing how we have developed new perspectives."

Alberto Ferreiro
Professor of History, Seattle Pacific University

"The Ancient Christian Commentary on Scripture fills a long overdue need for scholars and
students of the church fathers. . . . Such information will be of immeasurable
worth to those of us who have felt inundated by contemporary interpreters and novel theories
of the biblical text. We welcome some 'new' insight from the
ancient authors in the early centuries of the church."

H. Wayne House
Professor of Theology and Law
Trinity University School of Law

Chronological snobbery—the assumption that our ancestors working without benefit of
computers have nothing to teach us—is exposed as nonsense by this magnificent
new series. Surfeited with knowledge but starved of wisdom, many of us are
more than ready to sit at table with our ancestors and listen to their holy
conversations on Scripture. I know I am.

Eugene H. Peterson
Professor Emeritus of Spiritual Theology
Regent College

"Few publishing projects have encouraged me as much as the recently announced Ancient Christian Commentary on Scripture with Dr. Thomas Oden serving as general editor. . . . How is it that so many of us who are dedicated to serve the Lord received seminary educations which omitted familiarity with such incredible students of the Scriptures as St. John Chrysostom, St. Athanasius the Great and St. John of Damascus? I am greatly anticipating the publication of this Commentary."

FR. PETER E. GILLQUIST
Director, Department of Missions and Evangelism
Antiochian Orthodox Christian Archdiocese of North America

"The Scriptures have been read with love and attention for nearly two thousand years, and listening to the voice of believers from previous centuries opens us to unexpected insight and deepened faith. Those who studied Scripture in the centuries closest to its writing, the centuries during and following persecution and martyrdom, speak with particular authority. The Ancient Christian Commentary on Scripture will bring to life the truth that we are invisibly surrounded by a 'great cloud of witnesses.'"

FREDERICA MATHEWES-GREEN
Commentator, National Public Radio

"For those who think that church history began around 1941 when their pastor was born, this Commentary will be a great surprise. Christians throughout the centuries have read the biblical text, nursed their spirits with it and then applied it to their lives. These commentaries reflect that the witness of the Holy Spirit was present in his church throughout the centuries. As a result, we can profit by allowing the ancient Christians to speak to us today."

HADDON ROBINSON
Harold John Ockenga Distinguished Professor of Preaching
Gordon-Conwell Theological Seminary

"All who are interested in the interpretation of the Bible will welcome the forthcoming multivolume series Ancient Christian Commentary on Scripture. Here the insights of scores of early church fathers will be assembled and made readily available for significant passages throughout the Bible and the Apocrypha. It is hard to think of a more worthy ecumenical project to be undertaken by the publisher."

BRUCE M. METZGER
Professor of New Testament, Emeritus
Princeton Theological Seminary

ANCIENT CHRISTIAN COMMENTARY ON SCRIPTURE

OLD TESTAMENT
II

GENESIS 12-50

EDITED BY

MARK SHERIDAN

GENERAL EDITOR
THOMAS C. ODEN

InterVarsity Press
Downers Grove, Illinois

InterVarsity Press
P.O. Box 1400, Downers Grove, IL 60515-1426
World Wide Web: www.ivpress.com
E-mail: mail@ivpress.com

InterVarsity Press® is the book-publishing division of InterVarsity Christian Fellowship/USA®, a student movement active on campus at hundreds of universities, colleges and schools of nursing in the United States of America, and a member movement of the International Fellowship of Evangelical Students. For information about local and regional activities, write Public Relations Dept., InterVarsity Christian Fellowship/USA, 6400 Schroeder Rd., P.O. Box 7895, Madison, WI 53707-7895, or visit the IVCF website at <www.ivcf.org>.

Scripture quotations, unless otherwise noted, are from the Revised Standard Version of the Bible, copyright 1946, 1952, 1971 by the Division of Christian Education of the National Council of the Churches of Christ in the U.S.A., and are used by permission.

Selected excerpts from Fathers of the Church: A New Translation, copyright 1947-, used by permission of The Catholic University of America Press.

Cover photograph: Scala/Art Resource, New York. View of the apse. S. Vitale, Ravenna, Italy.

Spine photograph: Byzantine Collection, Dumbarton Oaks, Washington D.C. Pendant cross (gold and enamel). Constantinople, late sixth century.

ISBN 0-8308-1472-8

Printed in the United States of America ∞

Library of Congress Cataloging-in-Publication Data

Genesis 12-50/edited by Mark Sheridan; general editor, Thomas C. Oden.
   p. cm.—(Ancient Christian commentary on Scripture. Old Testament; 2)
   Includes bibliographical references and indexes.
   ISBN 0-8308-1472-8 (alk. paper)
    1. Bible. O.T. Genesis XII-L—Commentaries. I. Title: Genesis twelve through
fifty. II. Sheridan, Mark. III. Series.
   BS1235.53 .G46 2002
   222'.11077'09—dc21

                                           92002027383

P	25	24	23	22	21	20	19	18	17	16	15	14	13	12	11	10	9	8	7	6	5	4	3	2
Y	23	22	21	20	19	18	17	16	15	14	13	12	11	10	09	08	07	06	05	04				

Ancient Christian Commentary Project Research Team

General Editor
Thomas C. Oden

Associate Editor
Christopher A. Hall

Operations Manager
Joel Elowsky

Translations Projects Director
Joel Scandrett

Research and Acquisitions Director
Michael Glerup

Editorial Services Director
Warren Calhoun Robertson

Original Language Version Director
Konstantin Gavrilkin

Graduate Research Assistants

Chris Branstetter	*Sergey Kozin*
Jeffrey Finch	*Hsueh-Ming Liao*
Steve Finlan	*Michael Nausner*
Alexei Khamine	*Robert Paul Seesengood*
Vladimir Kharlamov	*Baek-Yong Sung*
Susan Kipper	*Elena Vishnevskaya*

Administrative Assistant
Judy Cox

CONTENTS

General Introduction

The Ancient Christian Commentary on Scripture has as its goal the revitalization of Christian teaching based on classical Christian exegesis, the intensified study of Scripture by lay persons who wish to think with the early church about the canonical text, and the stimulation of Christian historical, biblical, theological and pastoral scholars toward further inquiry into scriptural interpretation by ancient Christian writers.

The time frame of these documents spans seven centuries of exegesis, from Clement of Rome to John of Damascus, from the end of the New Testament era to A.D. 750, including the Venerable Bede.

Lay readers are asking how they might study sacred texts under the instruction of the great minds of the ancient church. This commentary has been intentionally prepared for a general lay audience of nonprofessionals who study the Bible regularly and who earnestly wish to have classic Christian observation on the text readily available to them. The series is targeted to anyone who wants to reflect and meditate with the early church about the plain sense, theological wisdom and moral meaning of particular Scripture texts.

A commentary dedicated to allowing ancient Christian exegetes to speak for themselves will refrain from the temptation to fixate endlessly upon contemporary criticism. Rather, it will stand ready to provide textual resources from a distinguished history of exegesis that has remained massively inaccessible and shockingly disregarded during the last century. We seek to make available to our present-day audiences the multicultural, multilingual, transgenerational resources of the early ecumenical Christian tradition.

Preaching at the end of the first millennium focused primarily on the text of Scripture as understood by the earlier esteemed tradition of comment, largely converging on those writers that best reflected classic Christian consensual thinking. Preaching at the end of the second millennium has reversed that pattern. It has so forgotten most of these classic comments that they are vexing to find anywhere, and even when located they are often available only in archaic editions and inadequate translations. The preached word in our time has remained largely bereft of previously influential patristic inspiration. Recent scholarship has so focused attention upon post-Enlightenment historical and literary methods that it has left this longing largely unattended and unserviced.

This series provides the pastor, exegete, student and lay reader with convenient means to see what Athanasius or John Chrysostom or the desert fathers and mothers had to say about a particular text for preaching, for study and for meditation. There is an emerging awareness among Catholic, Protestant and Orthodox laity that vital biblical preaching and spiritual formation need deeper grounding beyond the scope of the historical-critical orientations that have governed biblical studies in our day.

Hence this work is directed toward a much broader audience than the highly technical and specialized scholarly field of patristic studies. The audience is not limited to the university scholar concentrating on the study of the history of the transmission of the text or to those with highly focused philological interests in textual morphology or historical-critical issues. Though these are crucial concerns for specialists, they are not the paramount interest of this series.

This work is a Christian Talmud. The Talmud is a Jewish collection of rabbinic arguments and comments on the Mishnah, which epitomized the laws of the Torah. The Talmud originated in approximately the same period that the patristic writers were commenting on texts of the Christian tradition. Christians from the late patristic age through the medieval period had documents analogous to the Jewish Talmud and Midrash (Jewish commentaries) available to them in the *glossa ordinaria* and catena traditions, two forms of compiling extracts of patristic exegesis. In Talmudic fashion the sacred text of Christian Scripture was thus clarified and interpreted by the classic commentators.

The Ancient Christian Commentary on Scripture has venerable antecedents in medieval exegesis of both eastern and western traditions, as well as in the Reformation tradition. It offers for the first time in this century the earliest Christian comments and reflections on the Old and New Testaments to a modern audience. Intrinsically an ecumenical project, this series is designed to serve Protestant, Catholic and Orthodox lay, pastoral and scholarly audiences.

In cases where Greek, Latin, Syriac and Coptic texts have remained untranslated into English, we provide new translations. Wherever current English translations are already well rendered, they will be utilized, but if necessary their language will be brought up to date. We seek to present fresh dynamic equivalency translations of long-neglected texts which historically have been regarded as authoritative models of biblical interpretation.

These foundational sources are finding their way into many public libraries and into the core book collections of many pastors and lay persons. It is our intent and the publisher's commitment to keep the whole series in print for many years to come.

Thomas C. Oden
General Editor

A Guide to Using This Commentary

Several features have been incorporated into the design of this commentary. The following comments are intended to assist readers in making full use of this volume.

Pericopes of Scripture

The scriptural text has been divided into pericopes, or passages, usually several verses in length. Each of these pericopes is given a heading, which appears at the beginning of the pericope. For example, the first pericope in the commentary on Genesis 12—50 is "12:1-3 The Call and the Promise." This heading is followed by the Scripture passage quoted in the Revised Standard Version (RSV) across the full width of the page. The Scripture passage is provided for the convenience of readers, but it is also in keeping with medieval patristic commentaries, in which the citations of the Fathers were arranged around the text of Scripture.

Overviews

Following each pericope of text is an overview of the patristic comments on that pericope. The format of this overview varies within the volumes of this series, depending on the requirements of the specific book of Scripture. The function of the overview is to provide a brief summary of all the comments to follow. It tracks a reasonably cohesive thread of argument among patristic comments, even though they are derived from diverse sources and generations. Thus the summaries do not proceed chronologically or by verse sequence. Rather they seek to rehearse the overall course of the patristic comment on that pericope.

We do not assume that the commentators themselves anticipated or expressed a formally received cohesive argument but rather that the various arguments tend to flow in a plausible, recognizable pattern. Modern readers can thus glimpse aspects of continuity in the flow of diverse exegetical traditions representing various generations and geographical locations.

Topical Headings

An abundance of varied patristic comment is available for each pericope of these letters. For this reason we have broken the pericopes into two levels. First is the verse with its topical heading. The patristic comments are then focused on aspects of each verse, with topical headings summarizing the essence of the patristic comment by evoking a key phrase, metaphor or idea. This feature provides a bridge by which modern readers can enter into the heart of the patristic comment.

Identifying the Patristic Texts

Following the topical heading of each section of comment, the name of the patristic commentator is given. An English translation of the patristic comment is then provided. This is immediately followed by the title of the patristic work and the textual reference—either by book, section and subsection or by book-and-verse references.

The Footnotes

Readers who wish to pursue a deeper investigation of the patristic works cited in this commentary will find the footnotes especially valuable. A footnote number directs the reader to the notes at the bottom of the right-hand column, where in addition to other notations (clarifications or biblical cross references) one will find information on English translations (where available) and standard original-language editions of the work cited. An abbreviated citation (normally citing the book, volume and page number) of the work is provided except in cases where a line-by-line commentary is being quoted, in which case the biblical references will lead directly to the selection. A key to the abbreviations is provided on page xv. Where there is any serious ambiguity or textual problem in the selection, we have tried to reflect the best available textual tradition.

Where original language texts have remained untranslated into English, we provide new translations. Wherever current English translations are already well rendered, they are utilized, but where necessary they are stylistically updated. A single asterisk (*) indicates that a previous English translation has been updated to modern English or amended for easier reading. The double asterisk (**) indicates either that a new translation has been provided or that some extant translation has been significantly amended. We have standardized spellings and made grammatical variables uniform so that our English references will not reflect the odd spelling variables of the older English translations. For ease of reading we have in some cases edited out superfluous conjunctions.

For the convenience of computer database users the digital database references are provided to either the Thesaurus Linguae Graecae (Greek texts) or to the Cetedoc (Latin texts) in the appendix found on pages 353-56.

Abbreviations

ACW	Ancient Christian Writers: The Works of the Fathers in Translation. Mahwah, N.J.: Paulist, 1946-.
ARL	Athanasius. *The Resurrection Letters*. Paraphrased and introduced by Jack N. Sparks. Nashville: Thomas Nelson, 1979.
CCL	Corpus Christianorum. Series Latina. Turnhout, Belgium: Brepols, 1953-.
CG	Augustine. *The City of God*. Translated by Henry S. Bettenson with an introduction by David Knowles. 1972. Reprint, with an introduction by John O'Meara. Harmondsworth, England: Penguin, 1984.
CPG	M. Geerard, ed. *Clavis Patrum Graecorum*. Turnhout, Belgium: Brepols, 1974-1987.
CS	Cistercian Studies. Kalamazoo, Mich.: Cistercian Publications, 1973-.
CSEL	Corpus Scriptorum Ecclesiasticorum Latinorum. Vienna, 1866-.
FC	Fathers of the Church: A New Translation. Washington, D.C.: Catholic University of America Press, 1947-.
LCC	J. Baillie et al., eds. The Library of Christian Classics. 26 vols. Philadelphia: Westminster Press, 1953-1966.
LCL	Loeb Classical Library. Cambridge, Mass.: Harvard University Press; London: Heinemann, 1912-.
LSA	Samuel Rubenson, trans. *The Letters of St. Antony: Origenist Theology, Monastic Tradition and the Making of a Saint*. Studies in Antiquity and Christianity. Minneapolis: Fortress, 1995.
NPNF	P. Schaff et al., eds. A Select Library of the Nicene and Post-Nicene Fathers of the Christian Church. 2 series (14 vols. each). Buffalo, N.Y.: Christian Literature, 1887-1894; reprint, Grand Rapids, Mich.: Eerdmans, 1952-1956; reprint, Peabody, Mass.: Hendrickson, 1994.
OFP	Origen. *On First Principles*. Translated by G. W. Butterworth. London: SPCK, 1936; reprint, Gloucester, Mass.: Peter Smith, 1973.
OSW	*Origen: Selected Writings*. Translated by Rowan A. Greer. Classics of Western Spirituality: A Library of the Great Spiritual Masters. Mahwah, N.J.: Paulist, 1979.
PG	J.-P. Migne, ed. Patrologia Cursus Completus, Series Graeca. 166 vols. Paris: Migne, 1857-1886.
PO	Patrologia Orientalis. Paris, 1903-.
SC	H. de Lubac, J. Daniélou et al., eds. Sources Chrétiennes. Paris: Editions du Cerf, 1941-.
TEG	Traditio Exegetica Graeca. Louvain: Peeters, 1991-.
TTH	G. Clark, M. Gibson and M. Whitby, eds. Translated Texts for Historians. Liverpool: Liverpool University Press, 1985-.
WSA	J. E. Rotelle, ed. *Works of St. Augustine: A Translation for the Twenty-First Century*. Hyde Park, N.Y.: New City Press, 1995.

Introduction to Genesis 12-50

This volume is dedicated to the early Christian exegesis, or interpretation, of the patriarchal history, that is, the stories of Abraham, Isaac, Jacob and Joseph found in Genesis 12—50. Christian authors in the fourth century already used extensively the Greek word *exēgēsis*, meaning to draw out the meaning of a passage, to describe the process by which they interpreted Scripture. From a modern point of view, as we shall see, they were often reading in a new meaning rather than drawing out the original meaning. The Christian interpretation of the history of the patriarchs began already in the writings that came to make up the New Testament. Of these the most important for our subject are the letters of Paul, who makes use of the figure of Abraham in Galatians, Romans and 2 Corinthians.

Interpretation of the Patriarchal History from Paul to Origen

New Testament exegesis. In Galatians, responding to opponents who were insisting on the observance of the Mosaic law, Paul sets up an antithesis between "works of the law" and "hearing by faith" in which Abraham represents the man of faith: "Abraham 'believed God, and it was reckoned to him as righteousness'" (Gal 3:6). Apparently Paul's opponents had also appealed to Abraham as an example of faith and of following the law. Paul is able to separate the faith of Abraham from the question of the law because the promise in Genesis 12 to Abraham responding in his faith precedes the mention of the law of circumcision, a principal point of dispute with the Galatians. In Galatians 3:8-9 Paul argues, "And the scripture, foreseeing that God would justify the Gentiles by faith, preached the gospel beforehand to Abraham, saying, 'In you shall all the nations be blessed.'" For Paul the promise to Abraham anticipates the good news that justification comes through faith in Jesus Christ. Then, citing Deuteronomy 27:26, Habakkuk 2:4 and Leviticus 18:5, Paul argues that doing the works of the law does not bring righteousness. In Galatians 3:13 he states that "Christ redeemed us from the curse of the law, having become a curse for us" by the fact of hanging from a tree (Deut 21:23), showing that the blessing of Abraham has come to the Gentiles apart from the law (Gal 3:14). This blessing, formerly understood as the land and descendants, now becomes "the promise of the Spirit through faith."

Paul then uses an exegetical procedure rather common in ancient Christian interpretation, which might be termed "every detail can be made to count." He argues on the basis of the grammatical singular of the word for "seed" (*sperma* in Greek) in Genesis 12:7 that the promise was not to the Jewish people in general, understood as Abraham's descendants, but "to one, . . . which is Christ" (Gal 3:16). Paul develops this argument by appealing to a number of other texts to explain that the law was a temporary measure, valid only until the fulfillment of the promise in Christ. The promise has now been fulfilled. Paul's real starting point in his argumentation and exegesis is that a new age has thus begun, or rather that the final age (the *eschaton*) has been revealed with the resurrection of Jesus. This interpretation of Abraham and the promise is a new departure destined to have a profound influence on the development of Christian interpretation of the Scriptures.

A radically new departure also is Paul's allegorical interpretation of the story of Sarah and Hagar (Gen 16—21) in Galatians 4:21—5:1. Here Hagar is interpreted to symbolize the covenant of slavery, the law, while Sarah represents the covenant of freedom. "The son of the slave was born according to the flesh, the son of the free woman through promise." Paul states explicitly "this is an allegory" and explains that Hagar represents Mt. Sinai in Arabia (the place where the law was promulgated) and that this corresponds also to the present city of Jerusalem, that is, the center of Judaism. Sarah, by contrast, corresponds to the "Jerusalem above." Implicit is the idea that the "Jerusalem above" has been revealed through the resurrection of Jesus. Paul concludes that the Galatians are children of the promise like Isaac and that they are being persecuted by those born according to the flesh, just as in the time of Isaac and Ishmael. In justification, he cites Genesis 21:10: "Cast out the slave and her son; for the son of the slave shall not inherit with the son of the free woman" (Gal 4:30). Paul's introduction of allegorical interpretation in the interpretation of the Genesis text strongly influenced Origen (see below) and other exegetes of the Alexandrian school, who regarded Paul as the model interpreter of the Old Testament Scriptures.

In Romans, Paul returns to the figure of Abraham. In many respects Romans represents a less polemical and more carefully developed exposition of the argument already found in Galatians. In Romans 3:21-31 Paul argues that all have sinned, whether or not they had the law, and that justification, whether for the Jews or for the Gentiles, comes through "faith in Jesus." In Romans 4 he introduces Abraham as "our forefather according to the flesh." As in Galatians, the principal text being interpreted is Genesis 15:6, "Abraham believed God, and it was reckoned to him as righteousness." Again Paul's argument is based on the precedence of the promise "To your offspring I will give this land" (Gen 12:7) over the law of circumcision in Genesis 17, as well as the statement of Genesis 15:6 that Abraham believed and that it was reckoned to him as righteousness, which Paul interprets to mean that he was justified through faith. In Romans, with the help of Psalm 32:1-2 (where the word *reckon* is also found), Paul explains that Jews and Gentiles are justified by faith and that the promise is to those who share the faith of Abraham.

Abraham is also cited in 2 Corinthians 11:22 in a polemical context where Paul calls himself a descendant of Abraham. Here he is probably claiming not merely descent "according to the flesh" but implying also his Christian identity as justified through faith like Abraham's. Paul's interpretations of the Genesis text weighed heavily in early Christian interpretation, not merely for his particular explanations but also for the style and manner of interpretation.

Another writer who makes use of material from the patriarchal history is the author of the letter to the Hebrews, often attributed also to Paul in antiquity. In Hebrews 7 he draws a parallel between the Son of God and Melchizedek, who is said to resemble the Son of God. Using the silence of the text of Genesis 14:18-19 with regard to the genealogy of Melchizedek, he draws the conclusion that Melchizedek is "without father or mother or genealogy, and has neither beginning of days nor end of life." Like the "Son of God, he continues a priest for ever" (Heb 7:3). Then, with the aid of Psalm 110:4, the only other text of the Old Testament to mention Melchizedek, he is able to explain that Jesus is a priest of an order superior to Aaron. His is the order of Melchizedek, and the author is able to show that Aaron and Levi, through their ancestor Abraham, implicitly acknowledged Melchizedek's superiority when Abraham offered him tithes (Heb 7:7-9; Gen 14:18-20). For the author of this letter, Melchizedek and other figures and institutions of the Old

Testament serve to illustrate the figures and institutions of the new covenant. The latter are the true heavenly realities that the Old Testament figures and institutions resemble. In Hebrews 6:13-18, the author also appeals to the text of Genesis 22:17 to show that God is faithful to his promises (in this case to Abraham), and in Hebrews 11:8-19 he offers Abraham as an example of faith. Various events of his life reflect this faith, such as his migration in response to God's call, his belief that God would be faithful to his promise and his willingness to offer up Isaac (because he believed that God can raise the dead). The other patriarchs, Isaac, Jacob and Joseph, are also cited as examples of faith but without similar detail.

Notable also for the use of the patriarchal history are Peter's and Stephen's speeches in the Acts of the Apostles (Acts 3:25; 7:1-16). In the former the covenant and promise to Abraham (Gen 22:18) are mentioned. Stephen recounted in summary form the whole patriarchal history to illustrate God's providential plan of salvation.

Many other allusions to texts and figures in the patriarchal history are found in the New Testament, including Jacob's ladder (Gen 29) in John's Gospel, but those already mentioned are the most prominent and serve to illustrate the importance of this part of Genesis for the New Testament authors.

By the time of Origen, when we begin to have real commentaries on the books of the Bible, the New Testament existed as a distinct part of the Scriptures for Christians. Thus New Testament interpretations had a significant role in determining further development of Christian exegesis of Genesis. There was never any doubt about it being Scripture. Genesis was held by all to be part of the law of Moses (the Pentateuch), and Moses was held to be the author.

Philo of Alexandria. The development of early Christian exegesis was heavily influenced by the Alexandrian Jewish scholar, Philo. This contemporary of Jesus and Paul came from a wealthy and cultured milieu in a city that was not only a center of commerce but also the principal center of Hellenistic culture in the ancient world. We know little about his life other than what can be gleaned from his numerous works, a large part of which are devoted to the explanation of the Scriptures. It is clear that he had received the best kind of education then available in the Hellenistic world, but he remained a convinced and faithful Jew. He appears to have functioned as a rabbi (an institution then developing) in the Alexandrian Jewish community, then one of the largest and most flourishing in the Diaspora. Philo also defended the Jewish community when the prefect Flaccus instigated the pogrom of 38, and he headed the delegation sent to Rome to appeal to the emperor Caligula in 41.

In Philo's works we find for the first time the encounter on a grand scale of two cultures, the Hellenistic and the Jewish or biblical. Philo speaks of his predecessors in the field of interpretation, but we know of only a few: the author of the Letter of Aristeas, and Aristobulus, whose fragments are preserved in the works of the church historian Eusebius. Philo wrote numerous works, including lives of the patriarchs Abraham, Isaac and Jacob, and also many tracts on particular subjects of the Pentateuch, such as the migration of Abraham, the interpretation of dreams and the three books on the allegorical interpretation of the laws. Through his interpretation of the biblical texts certain key ideas of the Greek philosophical tradition—such as the concept of virtue, the idea of *askēsis* (exercise or practice) and the notion of philosophy itself—enter scriptural exegesis for the first time. All of these ideas will play an important role in the history of early Christian interpretation.

Philo applied to the interpretation of the Scriptures certain interpretive rules and procedures prevalent in the Hellenistic world, the most significant of which is allegory or allegorization. The *Iliad* and the *Odyssey* had long played a role similar to that of Scripture in the Greek-speaking world, and they had formed the basis of Greek education even before the development of Greek philosophy. However, the stories found in these epics, particularly those relating to the behavior of the gods and goddesses, contained elements that later Greeks found unacceptable as models for children. Such behavior was held to be unworthy of the gods, and so the text had to be interpreted in such a way that it acquired an acceptable meaning. Later, by the time of Philo, this method of interpretation came to be called "allegory"; literally, the text says one thing but the meaning is something else.

For Philo, educated as he was in the tradition of the Greek philosophical schools, many things in the Scriptures were unacceptable on a literal level. For example, someone like Philo, who had an exalted notion of a transcendent creator God, could hardly accept all the anthropomorphic language used of God in the Scriptures. Unworthy of God, such language had to be interpreted on an allegorical level. Philo also saw the role of the Scriptures as that of offering instruction on how to live and, accordingly, he interpreted many stories in Genesis in terms of Greek ideas about the ideal philosophical life. Thus, for example, Abraham becomes the person who seeks wisdom through learning. He migrates from Haran, that is, the land of the senses, in the search for wisdom and marries Sarah, who represents virtue. At Sarah's insistence he sends away his servant Hagar, by whom he had begotten a son, Ishmael, because Hagar represents the cycle of preparatory studies (grammar, mathematics, geometry, music, etc.) that must be left behind in the search for wisdom. Jacob is interpreted as the one who seeks wisdom through the ascetic struggle against vice and by exercising virtue. He is called "the ascetic" and "the athlete" because in Greek philosophy the athletic vocabulary had already been applied to the search for wisdom. Through this method of interpretation Philo used a large part of the texts of the Pentateuch, including the dietary and ritual laws, as vehicles for teaching about ethics and morals.

Many of these interpretations will have a long history in Christian preaching and teaching because many of the early Christian preachers and interpreters read Philo directly or because they read others influenced by him. Among those who had direct contact with the writings of Philo must be mentioned Clement of Alexandria, Origen, Eusebius, Didymus the Blind, Gregory of Nyssa, Jerome and Ambrose of Milan. Eusebius and Jerome treat Philo practically as if he were a Christian, and later Christian tradition regarded him as a Christian bishop. In the Catena on Genesis (see below) many passages are attributed to "Philo the bishop."

The development from Paul to Origen. In the period of approximately 150 years between the death of Paul and the appearance of the great commentaries of Origen, many Christian writers continued to interpret the text of Genesis often following the example of Paul. Among the writers and writings that are worthy of note in this period are the *First Letter of Clement, the Letter of Barnabas* and Justin Martyr's *Dialogue with Trypho.* These writers tend to cite Old Testament texts, including figures from the patriarchal history as proof texts in apologetic argument or as examples of virtue to be imitated. In this period we find the first Gnostic writings, produced by writers whom contemporary Christians regarded as Christian heretics. They too made use of the Old Testament Scriptures but with interpretations to support their doctrines.

Similar but different from the Gnostic use of Scripture was the movement launched by Marcion, a Christian teacher from Sinope in Pontus active in Rome about 140. Marcion denied that the God of Jesus Christ was the same as the God of the Old Testament. He found the Old Testament Scriptures too different from the teaching of Jesus to have been produced by the same deity, and so he attributed the Old Testament to the demiurge. The canon of Scripture produced by Marcion included only the Gospel of Luke and the letters of Paul, but these he had to edit in order to remove the interpretations Paul had given of the Old Testament, which tended to validate it. Marcion's radical challenge to the Old Testament was too late to be successful, although Marcionite communities reportedly existed for centuries to come. By this time (140) the Gospels, the letters of Paul and the Acts of the Apostles were all in existence, and all of these had made extensive use of the Old Testament Scriptures. Marcion's doctrine, however, brought forth reactive efforts on the part of Christian writers to show the essential unity of the two Testaments. Especially notable among these are the works of Irenaeus and Tertullian. None of these writers, however, sought to produce detailed running commentaries on any of the books of Scripture.

The Major Christian Interpreters

Origen of Alexandria. Origen of Alexandria was rightly regarded by the church historian Eusebius as the greatest Christian writer and theologian of the early church. Origen's contributions in the fields of textual criticism, biblical interpretation and speculative theology left a lasting imprint on the church. Although his works were the subject of much controversy in later periods and efforts were made to destroy his works and efface his ideas, his influence has remained. Hans Urs von Balthasar has compared the later attempts to wipe out his influence with the attempt to destroy a vase of perfume, which, when the vase is broken, then fills the house with its aroma.

In the area of textual criticism Origen was the first to recognize clearly the problem presented by the many variant readings in the manuscripts through which the Scriptures had been transmitted, as well as in the many translations of the Hebrew Scriptures into Greek. His great work, the *Hexapla*, was an effort to compare all the versions and all the variants in an effort to determine the original or correct reading. Unfortunately, no copy of this work survived beyond the fourth century.

One of Origen's most influential works was known as "On First Principles" (*De principiis*), written while he was the head of the catechetical school in Alexandria in Egypt before moving to spend the last twenty-five years of his life at Caesarea in Palestine. In the fourth book of this work, Origen set forth the principles for the interpretation of Scripture. This first extensive exposition of the methods for the interpretation of Scripture had great influence, even in the West in the Latin-speaking church. While some of Origen's principles of interpretation were later contested, this work remains essential reading for anyone wishing to understand the tradition of Alexandrian biblical interpretation.

Origen was also the first to produce running commentaries on whole books of the Bible, using several literary genres (see below). His *Homilies on Genesis*, preached probably between 239 and 243 in Caesarea, reflect great creativity in relating the text of Genesis to New Testament teaching.

Ephrem the Syrian. Ephrem (c. 306-373), known as the deacon of the church of Edessa, spent most of his life in the city of Nisibis, moving to Edessa some time after the treaty of 363, in which the Romans ceded the territory Nisibis to Persia. Ephrem is generally regarded as the first great writer of the Syrian church, and his voluminous writings reflect a tradition largely independent of the Greek-speaking churches of Alexandria and Antioch. His prose commentary on Genesis, written toward the end of his life, when he lived in Edessa, reflects Jewish as well as Christian exegetical traditions, and it has been suggested that his method of interpretation is closer to Jewish Haggadah than to the schools of Alexandria and Antioch (see below). More than a third of his commentary on Genesis is devoted to the creation and fall narrative; he omitted much of the patriarchal narrative.

Didymus the Blind of Alexandria. One of Origen's most influential successors in the catechetical school of Alexandria was Didymus (d. 398), blind from the age of four. One of the best educated men of his time and one of the most prolific scholars, he was able to cite most of the Scriptures from memory, as well as many pagan, Christian and Jewish sources. In antiquity, reading was generally done aloud; an intelligent and attentive listener could recite the reading he heard in order to fix it in his memory.

Didymus was also a monk in the monastic settlement of Nitria, as well a famous teacher in Alexandria in the middle and later part of the fourth century. Unfortunately, memory of him was damaged by later controversies in the sixth century, and the emperor Justinian condemned his works along with those of Origen and Evagrius of Pontus in 543. As a result, many of his theological works and commentaries on the Scriptures were lost, but about sixty years ago manuscripts containing about two thousand pages of the works of Origen and Didymus were discovered at Tura, south of Cairo. Among these was a large portion of his *Commentary on Genesis*, including some material on the first part of the story of Abraham.

Ambrose of Milan. Ambrose, bishop of Milan from 374 to 397, is held in honor along with Jerome, Augustine and Gregory, as one of the four principal Western church fathers. He was born at Trier, the son of the praetorian prefect, about 339. After a traditional education in the liberal arts, he distinguished himself as a lawyer and an orator, and in 372/3 he was appointed governor of Aemilia-Liguria with headquarters in Milan.

In 374 the Arian bishop of Milan, Auxentius, died, and it fell to Ambrose to maintain the peace between the Arian faction in the church and the supporters of the Nicene definition. When he appeared in this role at the basilica where the election of the new bishop was to take place, Arians and Catholics united in demanding that the governor become the new bishop. Ambrose, without theological training and not yet even baptized, reluctantly accepted and was quickly baptized and ordained bishop.

Ambrose then set to work to remedy his lack of theological knowledge, reading widely and fluently in earlier, especially Greek, exegetes and theologians, including Philo, Origen, Basil, Athanasius and Didymus. He was thus strongly influenced by the Alexandrian tradition of Scriptural interpretation and in turn influenced later Latin authors in this direction. One of the most famous preachers of the age, he published many of his revised sermons as literary compositions, including *On Abraham, On Isaac or the Soul* and *On Joseph*, in all of which he interpreted the texts of Genesis 12—50 allegorically.

Augustine of Hippo. By far the most prolific of early Christian Latin writers, Augustine left an indelible stamp on the theology and spirituality of the Western church. He was born in 354 of a Christian mother and a pagan father in Thagaste in Roman Africa (modern Tunisia). He received a Latin provincial education before going to Rome and Milan to continue his studies. In his search for truth Augustine became for a time a Manichaean and later devoted himself to the study of Neo-Platonism (Plotinus). At Milan the preaching of Ambrose, as well as the influence of his mother, Monica, played a role in his conversion to Catholic Christianity, and Ambrose baptized him in 386. After his return to North Africa, he was ordained priest in 391 and in 395 elected bishop of Hippo, where he continued his activity until his death in 430. Augustine is celebrated for certain works, especially the *Confessions* and *The City of God*, but many of his works were polemical, directed against heretical groups such as the Manichaeans, the Donatists and the Pelagians. He also produced numerous commentaries and homilies on the Scriptures, notably the *Commentary on the Psalms* and that on the Gospel of John. Apart from a few sermons, however, Augustine did not comment directly on the patriarchal history. Nevertheless he often referred to these texts in his other voluminous works.

John Chrysostom. Born at Antioch about 345, John Chrysostom received there a classical education, studying with the most famous rhetorician of the day, Libanius. Due to the influence of the bishop of Antioch, Meletius, John abandoned classical studies and devoted himself to an ascetical life and the study of the Scriptures. He entered a monastic community and later spent time as a hermit before returning to Antioch to serve as lector, deacon and finally (from 386) as priest. In Antioch he quickly became known as the most famous preacher of his day. His commentaries on Scripture are chiefly homilies based on the passages of biblical books read in sequence during the daily liturgy. From 397 Chrysostom was bishop of Constantinople, where conflict with court circles eventually led to his exile and death in 407. He is one of the most revered church fathers in the Western as well as in the Eastern churches.

John Chrysostom preached sixty-seven homilies on Genesis in the year 389, while he was a priest at Antioch, explaining the book verse by verse. From what he says at the beginning of the twenty-third, it appears that he preached the first thirty-two during Lent of that year and the rest after Pentecost of the same year. Chrysostom is a leading representative of the Antiochene school of exegesis, having studied with Diodore of Tarsus, who is often credited as a founder of this tradition. He concentrates on literal interpretation and seeks to avoid allegorical or figurative explanations as far as possible. The result is a commentary heavily weighted with moralism in which the biblical figures provide models of virtue to imitate. This collection of homilies is the most extensive commentary on Genesis to survive from the early church.

Cyril of Alexandria. Cyril of Alexandria (born c. 370) succeeded his uncle Theophilus as patriarch of Alexandria in 412. He is known above all for his vigorous opposition to the teaching of Nestorius, the patriarch of Constantinople, whom he was instrumental in deposing at the Council of Ephesus in 431. Nestorius had denied the legitimacy of applying to Mary the title *theotokos* (mother of God). Cyril's writings in the area of Christology became the norm of orthodoxy for the Egyptian and other Oriental churches. Conflict arose later, however, after Cyril's death (444), when the Council of Chalcedon used a terminology different from that of Cyril in defining the relationship of the divine and the human in Christ (one person in two natures). Cyril wrote extensively on scriptural interpretation, including "elegant treatises" (*glaphyra*) on the patriarchal history, as well as dogmatic and polemical works. Cyril remains to this day one of the principal champions and norms of orthodox faith for the Coptic church.

Caesarius of Arles. Caesarius was born in Burgundy (470) and died at Arles in 542, having served there as bishop for forty years. His episcopal city, near the mouth of the Rhone and close to Marseilles, retained its ancient importance in the social, commercial and industrial life of Gaul, and its bishop held the title of Vicar of the Apostolic See in Gaul. Caesarius shows a thorough knowledge of the Latin tradition of scriptural interpretation. The repeated invasions of Gaul and the collapse of the Roman administration had changed social conditions considerably in the century since the death of Augustine. The shorter and simpler homilies of Caesarius give evidence of changing ecclesiastical concerns, especially for sacramental and church discipline. Caesarius preached a series of homilies on the texts of Genesis, which clearly reflect the influence of Origen, whose works he would have been able to read in a Latin translation.

Bede the Venerable. Bede (673-735) never traveled from his monastery in the north of England but was one of the most learned men of his era. While Bede belongs more to the early Middle Ages than to the patristic period, his thorough acquaintance with the works of Ambrose, Augustine, Gregory and other early Christian authors places him more in continuity with them. Like them, he composed many works on scriptural interpretation, including a commentary on Genesis up to the birth of Isaac, in addition to his better-known historical works.

The catena on Genesis. Sometime in the second half of the fifth century an unknown author set to work to produce a vast compilation of texts relating to the interpretation of Genesis, a kind of synopsis of the exegetical tradition. He selected excerpts from numerous works of authors ranging in time from Philo of Alexandria to Cyril of Alexandria. Texts from Severus of Antioch (d. 538) later were added to the compilation, which has come to be known by the Latin name given to it by later scholars: *catena* (= chain). The author seems to have been interested in furnishing theologians interested in exegesis with an objective instrument for work. The authors selected are not of a single school (Alexandrian or Antiochian), and all the passages are perfectly orthodox. Not only commentaries and homilies but also polemical works are cited. This vast work has recently been critically edited for the first time. The Epitome of Procopius of Gaza on the Pentateuch appears to be dependent on the catena for the part on Genesis.

Among the many authors excerpted are Flavius Josephus (d. after 95); Eusebius of Caesarea (d. 340); Basil the Great (d. 379); Gregory of Nazianzus (d. 389); Gregory of Nyssa (d. 394); Didymus the Blind (d. 398); Epiphanius of Salamis (d. 403); John Chrysostom (d. 407) and Cyril of Alexandria (d. 444). The works cited have also been preserved independently in the original language. In addition, the compiler used works from authors such as Philo of Alexandria (the passages are attributed to Philo the Bishop); Irenaeus of Lyons (d. about 200) and Eusebius of Emesa (d. about 359). Also cited are works that are otherwise unknown or lost from Melito of Sardis (d. about 190); Eustathius of Antioch (d. before 337); Acacius of Caesarea (d. 366); Ephrem (d. 373); Diodore of Tarsus (d. before 394); Severian of Gabala (d. before 408); Theodore of Mopsuestia (d. 428) and Succensus of Diocaesarea (d. about 440).

The Literary Genres Used by Early Christian Commentators

The literary forms used and developed by Origen greatly influenced all later subsequent patristic exegetical work. According to a typology proposed by Jerome and generally accepted, Origen produced three distinct types of exegetical works: brief notes, homilies and books. The first of these consisted of collections of brief notes, in which he dealt succinctly with questions that appeared obscure to him or that contained difficult points of interpretation. This genre may have been based on the example of the *Questiones* of Philo and similar works.

The second type consisted of homilies that he preached at Caesarea and that were taken down by stenographers. In these homilies, Origen adapted himself to a mixed audience containing a majority of unlearned persons in a liturgical setting. Most of these homilies may have been produced within a three-year period in which Origen followed the cycle of liturgical readings. Origen generally follows the traditional division of a public discourse into prologue, body and conclusion. To introduce the first verse to be commented on, he may begin with a general idea, the citation of a work or a story that somehow relates to the text that will follow. A series of quotations from the reading followed by interpretations constitutes the body of the homily. The same text may be quoted several times if different parts of it are to be explained successively or if a series of explanations is to be offered. Origen was highly selective in choosing which chapters and verses to explain, choosing those that lent themselves to interpretations that would edify the listeners. In these homilies the moral and hortatory tone is reduced and concentrated at the end. Origen always concludes his homilies with the same doxology borrowed from 1 Peter 4:11: "To him belong glory and dominion for ever and ever. Amen." Sometimes this is attached to the explanation of the last verse cited, but often it is preceded by a more elaborate conclusion.

The third genre of exegetical work was what Origen called "books" and Jerome called "commentaries." In these, destined for a more select audience, Origen pursued the exegesis of individual books in a more systematic way, passage by passage, without regard to limitations of space or time and often with notable digressions.

Even in the most extensive patristic commentaries, the early Christian commentators were selective and did not feel compelled to explain or use all of the texts. Certain passages lent themselves more obviously to Christian interpretation. Thus an abundance of material exists for certain chapters of Genesis 12—50, such as Genesis 12 (the call of Abraham), Genesis 14 (the sacrifice of Melchizedek) and Genesis 22 (the sacrifice of Isaac), and almost nothing for certain other passages.

These are the principal literary forms used for biblical interpretation in the ancient world, but passages explaining or using the Scriptures can be found in many other types of literature, including letters, catechetical instructions and polemical and apologetic works. The reader should always keep in mind that the nature of the interpretation may be influenced by the literary form and the purpose of the writing. Most of the passages excerpted in this volume are from homiletic works whose purpose was to edify and instruct.

The Rules of Interpretation

Modern methods of scriptural interpretation differ from the rules and procedures used by the ancient authors so strikingly that it is often assumed that patristic commentators operated capriciously and without rules. The modern commentator with the historical critical method seeks above all to establish the original historical setting of each of the biblical books and to explain the text in that historical setting, conveying what the original author intended to say insofar as possible. However, the goals of the ancient writers were quite different. They had surprisingly little interest in the past except as it related to the present.

The Alexandrian and Antiochean schools of interpretation. Two early Christian approaches to biblical interpretation are commonly noted, Alexandrian and Antiochean. The School of Alexandria was in fact a real school, the catechetical school (Didaskaleion), which emphasized allegorical interpretation. Although modern scholars have doubted whether the school had a continuous history, Origen and Didymus seem to have headed it. The school of Antioch, by contrast, was not a physical entity but a school of thought comprising a group of writers with connections to Antioch. The principal members of this group, in chronological order, are Diodorus of Tarsus, John Chrysostom and Theodore of Mopsuestia. The distinguishing characteristic of the Antiochean school was its opposition to the type of allegorical interpretation practiced by the Alexandrian school and its insistence on the Scriptures' literal sense, although not the historical sense as modern authors use the term. The Antiocheans were no more interested in establishing the original historical sense than were the Alexandrians, but they opposed the allegorization of the text, preferring to draw moral lessons from it.

Most influential interpreters belonged to or were shaped by the Alexandrian school. Their rules of interpretation, some of which were shared with the Antiochenes, can most clearly be seen from the point of view of the principal exponent of this tradition, Origen of Alexandria, even though not all used or agreed with all of his rules and procedures.

The influence of Paul. Origen viewed his exegetical work as a continuation of Paul's on the Old Testament and thought that he was employing precisely Paul's principles of exegesis. There is obvious continuity, but his work also contains new ideas not to be found in Paul. At the beginning of his fifth homily on Exodus, Origen states that Paul "taught the church which he gathered from the Gentiles how it ought to interpret the books of the law." According to Origen, Paul was aware of the possibility that the books of the law might be incorrectly interpreted by the Gentile converts because of their lack of familiarity with this literature. The danger from Paul's perspective (and Origen's) was that the Gentile converts would interpret the books of the law literally, as had the Jews. "For that reason," says Origen,

> [Paul] gives some examples of interpretation that we also might note similar things in other passages, lest we believe that by imitation of the text and documents of the Jews we be made disciples. He wishes therefore to distinguish disciples of Christ from disciples of the synagogue by the way they understand the law. The Jews, by misunderstanding it, rejected Christ. We, by understanding the law spiritually, show that it was justly given for the instruction of the church.

In this quotation two phrases in particular should be noted: "examples of interpretation" and "understanding the law spiritually." From Origen's point of view, Paul has given examples of how to interpret the Scriptures. We should analyze these examples and imitate the principles and procedures that Paul used in order to continue the work of interpreting the Scriptures. Second, this program of interpretation can be described as "understanding the law spiritually." The two ideas are united in a similar phrase later in the same homily, where Origen speaks of the "seeds of spiritual understanding received from the blessed apostle Paul." When this program is carried out, then the Scriptures appear in their true light as "given for the instruction of the church." They are not a Jewish but a Christian book, since the Scriptures have been given "for us." This latter idea is an important principle that governs the whole process of spiritual interpretation.

Origen says that Paul has given "examples of interpretation" for us to imitate. Some of the examples that he cites most frequently are 1 Corinthians 10:1-11, 2 Corinthians 3:6-18, Galatians 4:21-24, Hebrews 8:5 and Hebrews 10:1.

The gospel agrees with the law: 1 Corinthians 10:1-11. In the fifth homily on Exodus referred to above, Origen relates briefly the events of Exodus 12—17. The children of Israel departed from Egypt, from Rameses, then from Succoth; they were preceded by the cloud and followed by the rock from which they drank water; and finally they crossed the Red Sea and came to the desert of Sinai. The Jews, he says, accept this simply as a historical narrative. Then he cites 1 Corinthians 10:1-4 to show "what sort of rule of interpretation the apostle Paul taught us about these matters." His conclusion is framed as a question: "Do you not see how much Paul's teaching differs from the literal meaning? What the Jews supposed to be a crossing of the sea, Paul calls a baptism; what they supposed to be a cloud, Paul asserts is the Holy Spirit." His further conclusion is also framed in a question: "Does it not seem right that we apply similarly to other passages this kind of rule which was delivered to us?"

Origen then gives his interpretation of this part of Exodus. He has already established that the exodus from Egypt is to be interpreted spiritually, that is, in terms of the journey of the individual soul. Rameses means, he says, "the commotion of a moth." He then moves, by association with the word *moth*, to the text of Matthew 6:20, "where moth and rust consume" and incorporates this into the Pauline interpretation:

> Depart from Rameses, therefore, if you wish to come to this place that the Lord may be your leader and precede you "in the column of the cloud" and "the rock" may follow you, which offers you spiritual food and "spiritual drink" no less. Nor should you store treasure "there where the moth destroys and thieves dig through and steal." This is what the Lord says clearly in the Gospels: "If you wish to be perfect, sell all your possessions and give to the poor, and you will have treasure in heaven; and come, follow me." This therefore is to depart from Rameses and to follow Christ.

Origen has read here the content of New Testament teaching into an Old Testament text. The use of an etymology generates a meaning, which then serves as a bridge to a New Testament text, using the principle of "interpreting Scripture by Scripture," in this case by association through the hook word *moth*.

Continuing in Exodus to the next place of encampment, Succoth, Origen says that the etymologists understand the name to mean "tents," leading him to cite 2 Corinthians 5:4: "For while we are still in this tent, we sigh with anxiety; not that we would be unclothed, but that we would be further clothed." The next or third encampment is Etham, for which Origen gives the traditional meaning: "signs for them." The fact that this is the third stopping place allows him to associate it with other texts relating to the third day, including Exodus 5:3, Hosea 6:2 and the idea of the resurrection on the third day. This leads him to conclude that on the third day God "went before them by day in a pillar of cloud to lead them along the way, and by night in a pillar of fire" (Ex 13:12). Taking note of Paul's association of this text with baptism (1 Cor 10:2), Origen then cites also Romans 6:3-4 dealing with baptism and resurrection on the third day.

The next three places mentioned in the Exodus journey are Pihahiroth, Migdol and Baalzephon, which are interpreted etymologically as "winding ascent," "tower" and "ascent of a watchtower" respectively. These ideas lead Origen to note that the way to God is "an ascent and a winding ascent." The way to virtue is not downhill, but "it is an ascent, and it is ascended with great difficulty." Then, through association of ideas, Origen brings in the text of Matthew 7:14, "For the gate is narrow and the way is hard, that leads to life, and those who find it are few." Finally he exclaims, "See, therefore, to what extent the gospel agrees with the law. In the law the way of virtue is shown to be a winding ascent; in the Gospels it is said that 'the way which leads to life is straight and narrow.' Cannot even the blind see clearly that one and the same Spirit wrote the law and the Gospels?" In general, Origen moves from meanings generated by etymologies to New Testament texts, allowing him to read the New Testament teachings back into the Old Testament texts. In this way, the Exodus journey can be read as a continuous account of the spiritual journey of the individual Christian.

The special fascination with the meaning of names should be seen as part of the more general Alexandrian conviction that the literal sense of Scripture covered a deeper meaning, which it was the task of the exegete to uncover. The use of etymologies to generate interpretations of scriptural texts was hardly new with Origen. Although Paul does not make use of this procedure, it was well established in his time. Jewish and Greek authors exploited this possibility. Philo seems to have been the first to develop systematically the Old Testament etymologies, but he had predecessors. Although a certain interest in etymology may be detected already in some of the Old Testament accounts of origins, Jewish authors may have been influenced by the use of this procedure in the Hellenistic world, particularly in the interpretation of the Homeric epics. Stoic authors employed this technique and sought to give it philosophical and linguistic justification. Etymology and allegorical interpretation tended to go hand in hand. Christian authors, above all Origen, used the work of Philo and added to the tradition material for the New Testament names. By the third century alphabetical lists of names with these etymologies probably existed as well as lists that followed the order of the biblical books. Most authors under Alexandrian influence made use of the etymologies to generate allegorical or spiritual interpretations of the text.

Origen often cites 1 Corinthians 10 (esp. 1 Cor 10:6, 11) to emphasize that the Scriptures were written "for us" and reach their fulfillment in the present time (the time of the church), which is also understood as the end of the ages. The text is often cited as an introduction to moral exhortation, which is the original Pauline context of 1 Corinthians 10:1-11. Thus, in commenting on the expression "in mortar and bricks" (Ex 1:14), Origen states, "These words were not written to instruct us in history, nor must we think that the divine books narrate the acts of the Egyptians. What has been written 'has been written for our instruction' and admonition." There follows a moral exhortation in which the king of Egypt "who knew not Joseph" is interpreted as the devil.

Similarly, in dealing with the command of the king of Egypt to the midwives to kill the male children of the Israelites, Origen states, "But we, who have learned that all things which are written are written not to relate ancient history but for our discipline and use, understand that these things which are said also happen now not only in this world, which is figuratively called Egypt, but in each one of us also." He then continues the allegorical interpretation, explaining that the passions of the flesh are symbolized by the females but the male represents the rational sense and the intellectual spirit. It is this that the devil (the king of Egypt) wishes to destroy.

The notion of the actuality of the Scriptures seems to be the presupposition for allegorizing. Indeed, the idea of the actuality of Scripture is virtually a corollary of the notion of Scripture itself and the result of the canonization of the texts in the society. The notion that the Scriptures were written "for us," that they are therefore to be interpreted in reference to us and our situation is hardly original with Paul or Origen. It can be detected already in Deuteronomy in the emphasis on today (Deut 4:1-3), which is no longer the time of the events being related but the time when Moses recounted the events once again before the entrance into the Promised Land ("Deuteronomy" means the second giving of the law). In fact, the Deuteronomist had in mind his time many centuries after Moses. The author of the Letter of Aristeas (second century B.C.) shows a similar concern for the actuality of the text, a concern he achieves through allegory. To this general idea of the actuality of the Scriptures Paul has added the concept of the two ages (1 Cor 10:11), which considerably facilitates the possibility of allegorical comparisons between the two ages, then and now, such as is found in 1 Corinthians 10:1-11 and Galatians 4:21-24. While the notion of the two ages helps to specify the content of the allegory, it is not essential to the idea of the actuality of the Scriptures or to the allegorical method.

Allegory of Sarah and Hagar: Galatians 4:21-24. When Origen arrives at Genesis 21:9-10 in his homilies on Genesis, he says that he defers explicit commentary because the apostle has already indicated how these things are to be understood, and he quotes Galatians 4:21-24. He then notes that despite the distinction made by Paul between the flesh and the promise, Isaac was born according to the flesh. Sarah did give birth, and Isaac was circumcised in the flesh. Paul's interpretation is remarkable because he says that these things, which undoubtedly occurred according to the flesh, are to be understood allegorically. Paul teaches in this way, says Origen, so that we may learn how to behave with regard to other things, above all with regard to those passages where the historical narrative does not seem to indicate anything worthy of the divine law. Two points should be noted in this connection. First, Origen, who is often accused of neglecting or denying the literal level of the text, is here insisting on its reality. As he sees it, the interpretation that Paul has offered and that is to serve as a model for others does not obliterate the literal meaning of the historical narrative but is superimposed upon it and presupposes it. Second, the phrase "anything worthy of the divine law" indicates an important exegetical principle for Origen, one that may be detected also in Paul.

Origen makes reference to this text elsewhere, especially when he wishes to emphasize the possibility or need of an allegorical interpretation that does not invalidate the literal meaning of the text. He cites it in the context of a lengthy discussion about the need to distinguish between those texts or prescriptions of the law that are not to be observed in any case according to the letter; those that are not to be completely changed by allegory but are to be observed as formulated in the Scriptures; and those that can stand according to the letter but for which one must also seek an allegorical interpretation. An example of the last is Genesis 2:24, in which it is stated that a man shall leave his father and mother and be united with his wife and the two will become one flesh. Paul has shown that this is to be interpreted allegorically (Eph 5:32), but the teaching of Jesus (Mt 19:5-6) makes it equally clear that it is to be observed according to the letter. Paul's interpretation of Genesis 21:9-10 in Galatians 4:21-24 is to be understood in the same way. The narrative can be understood literally, but it should also be understood allegorically as referring to the two Testaments.

Removing the veil: 2 Corinthians 3:7-18. One of the Pauline texts most frequently cited by Origen not only as an example of Pauline exegesis but as virtually a program of interpretation is that of 2 Corinthians 3:7-18. In commenting on Exodus 34:33-34, where the veil over the glorified face of Moses is mentioned, Origen describes Paul's interpretation as "magnificent." Then he proceeds to dwell especially on the significance of the veil and the question of how it can be removed. Only if one leads a life superior to the common mean can one contemplate the glory on the face of Moses. Moses still speaks with glorified face, but we cannot see it because we lack sufficient zeal. The veil remains over the letter of the Old Testament (2 Cor 3:14). Only if one is converted to the Lord will the veil be removed (2 Cor 3:16). Origen then explains that this veil can be interpreted to mean preoccupation with the affairs of this world, with money, the attraction of riches. To be converted to the Lord means to turn our back on all these things and dedicate ourselves to the Word of God, meditating on his law day and night (Ps 1). He notes that parents who want their children to receive a liberal education do everything to find teachers and books and spare no expense to achieve this goal. The same must be done in pursuit of the understanding of the Scriptures. As for those who do not even bother to listen to the proclamation of the Scriptures but engage in idle conversation in the corners of the church while the Scriptures are being read, not only a veil but also a wall is placed over their hearts.

When the veil is taken away, however, Christ is revealed as already present in the entire Old Testament. In commenting on the verse of the Song of Solomon in which the bridegroom is pictured "leaping upon the mountains, bounding over the hills" (Song 2:8), Origen applies it to the interpretation of the Scriptures:

> This foretelling, of which we read in the Old Testament, has a veil on it, however; but when the veil is removed for the bride, that is, for the church that has turned to God, she suddenly sees him leaping upon those mountains—that is, the books of the law; and on the hills of the prophetical writings. He is so plainly and so clearly manifested that he springs forth, rather than merely appears. Turning the pages of the prophets one by one, for instance, she finds Christ springing forth from them, and, now that the veil that covered them before is taken away, she perceives him breaking out and emerging from individual passages in her reading and bursting out of them in a manifestation that is now quite plain.

The veil as interpreted by Origen is often the literal historical account, or the letter. In order to remove this veil, however, the coming of Christ was indispensable. Origen goes so far as to say that the "divine character" of the prophetic writings and the spiritual meaning of the law of Moses were revealed only with the coming of Christ. Previously it was not possible to bring forth convincing arguments for the inspiration of the Old Testament. The light contained in the law of Moses, covered by a veil, shown forth at the coming of Christ, when the veil was removed and it became possible to have "knowledge of the goods of which the literal expression contained the shadow."

Understanding the law spiritually: Romans 7:14. The phrase "understanding the law spiritually," noted above, is a reference to Romans 7:14, one of the Pauline texts most frequently cited by Origen. In attempting to explain the scandalous story in Genesis in which Abraham gives his wife to Abimelech, saying that she is his sister, Origen tells his listeners, somewhat polemically, that if anyone wants to understand these words literally, that person should gather with the Jews rather than with the Christians. The passage that follows is worth citing at length for the juxtaposition of texts and the insight that it gives into Origen's understanding of the task of interpretation:

> But if he [the hearer] wishes to be a Christian and a disciple of Paul, let him hear Paul saying that "the law is spiritual," declaring that these words are "allegorical" when the law speaks of Abraham and his wife and sons.

And although no one of us can easily discover what kind of allegories these words should contain, nevertheless one ought to pray that "the veil might be removed" from his heart, "if there is anyone who tries to turn to the Lord"—"for the Lord is the Spirit"—that the Lord might remove the veil of the letter and uncover the light of the Spirit and we might be able to say that "beholding the glory of the Lord with open face we are transformed into the same image from glory to glory, as by the Spirit of the Lord."

This passage is of particular interest because it gives us in condensed form almost the entire exegetical program of Origen. For him "spiritual" understanding of the law or of the Scriptures in general is equivalent to allegorical understanding. Origen uses the term *allegory* in the same sense as Paul to denote a text in which one thing is said but another is intended. The text taken literally does have meaning, but there is also another meaning, which is generally the more important one. This discovery of the allegorical meaning can also be described as removing the veil, for which interior conversion and possession of the Spirit of the Lord are required. In this case, by means of an etymology that ascribes the meaning of "virtue" to Sarah, Origen is able to transpose the whole story onto the moral plane and to explain away the scandalous aspects of the story.

In a similar situation in his homilies on Numbers, Origen remarks that if passages from Leviticus or Numbers are read without giving an adequate explanation, this can make the hearers critical of Moses. They begin to ask why such passages having to do with the Jewish ritual or the observance of the sabbath are read in church, because they have nothing to do with the hearers. To avoid such scandals, says Origen, it is necessary to explain that "the law is spiritual." Here again Origen cites 2 Corinthians 3:16 as an exhortation to be converted to the Lord so that he will take away the veil and Moses will appear to us not as deformed but glorious and splendid

Paul's use of the term *type* (or figure) more frequently than *allegory* to indicate Old Testament foreshadowings of Christ and the church has encouraged belief that he wished to avoid the terminology of allegory because of its pagan associations. In the allegorization of the pagan myths the literal sense was destroyed, whereas Paul accepted the literal sense of the Old Testament stories and added new meaning to them to prefigure Christ and the church. Ancient and modern authors are divided on this point. In what might be called the narrow interpretation, typology, that is, seeing a correlation between Old Testament events and New Testament ones, even as further developed in patristic literature, was regarded as legitimate, but further allegorization (by which was often meant moral interpretation) was regarded as illicit. This was the position of the so-called Antiochean school. The Alexandrian school did not so limit the process and did not distinguish between typology and allegory. The modern opposition to allegorical interpretation may be traced back to Martin Luther, who mounted a strong assault on the practice. The eighteenth and nineteenth century reinforced this by the development of the classical-idealist aesthetic. The modern distinction between allegory and typology seems to have developed in the nineteenth century in an effort to rescue Paul and something of patristic exegesis. Some scholars have even suggested that typology is not so much a question of method as it is of a spiritual way of viewing things. This view is firmly rejected by those who insist that typology should be considered methodologically as a subdivision of allegory and who point out, as well, that the same exegetical tools can be used to produce quite different theological contents.

Origen detects two types of spiritual or allegorical sense in the Scriptures, or, put another way, he distinguishes three levels of interpretation. In the fourth book of the *Peri Archon,* having established the necessity of interpreting the Scriptures spiritually, he cites Proverbs 22:20-21 (LXX), in which readers are exhorted to note the concepts three times in their minds and hearts in order to be able to respond with words of truth to those who question them. Origen concludes from this that one must note the concepts of sacred Scripture three times in one's soul, and he unites this threefold division of the sense to the anthropological division of body, soul and spirit. This division in turn is related to the threefold division of believers into the simple, those who have made progress and the perfect (1 Cor 2:6-15). Thus the simple will be able to find edification in the flesh of the Scripture, that is, in the literal sense; those who have progressed will find food for thought in the soul of the Scriptures, and the perfect will find edification in the spiritual law, which contains the shadow of the future goods (see Rom 7:14; Heb 10:1). Here the spiritual sense of the law seems restricted to the perfect and the future.

As an example of the type of interpretation that corresponds to the soul of the Scriptures, Origen cites Paul when he interprets the command of Deuteronomy 25:4, "You shall not muzzle an ox when it treads out the grain," as referring to the rights of the apostles. Origen says that numerous such interpretations in circulation are adapted to those who cannot hear more profound things. The truly spiritual character of the Scriptures is revealed in those interpretations for which the literal sense is but a figure and a shadow (Heb 8:5; Rom 8:5; Heb 10:1). One must seek the wisdom that is veiled in mystery (1 Cor 2:7), says Origen, referring again to Paul. Then he cites again 1 Corinthians 10:11, where, he says, Paul explains in reference to passages from Exodus and Numbers that these things happened to them in symbolic form, but they were written for us at the end of the times.

In commenting on the ark built by Noah, Origen also distinguishes three senses of Scripture but without reference to anthropology or the three classes of persons capable of appreciating the different levels of meaning. According to the text of the Septuagint used by Origen, Noah was instructed to build the ark "with two decks" and "with three decks." The three decks would refer to the historical or literal level of meaning, the mystical meaning refers to Christ and the church, and finally there is the moral meaning. The two decks refer to the situation where there is lacking the historical or literal meaning. This aspect of Origen's theory causes most astonishment to the modern reader schooled in historical-critical methodology. For Origen, however, all Scripture must have a spiritual meaning, because the "law is spiritual," and to him it was clear that not all texts had a literal meaning. In this homily on Genesis he cites as examples the texts "thorns will grow in the hand of a drunkard" (see Prov 26:9) and "the leprosy of a wall and a hide and a cloth is ordered to be examined by the priests and purified" (cf. Lev 13:48; 14:34). In his earlier work, *Peri Archon,* he had expounded the same idea using the expression taken from the Gospel of John, where it is said that the jars used for purification contained two or three measures of water. The three measures refer to the texts where there is a literal meaning capable of edifying.

Origen goes so far as to say that in the law and in the histories, passages have been inserted that are impossible or incongruous in order to alert us to the presence of a more profound meaning. He furnishes an extensive list of passages that cannot be interpreted literally, including the entire creation account as well as specific absurdities such as the command not to eat griffons (Lev 11:13). For Origen this same principle can also be found at work in the New Testament, for example in the mention of a high mountain from which one could view all the kingdoms of the world (Mt 4:8). In expounding this principle, called "the missing literal sense" (*defectus litterae*) in the later Latin tradition, Origen does not appeal to Paul, but he does appeal to a more general principle, not entirely absent from Paul, that we must always search for a meaning that is worthy of God.

Circumcision of the heart. Origen does not appeal to Paul in expounding the principle of *defectus litterae*, although he does appeal to Paul in attempting to deal with the question of circumcision, in which the question of the validity of the literal meaning and the notion of a meaning "worthy of God" come into play. He introduces the subject by asking rhetorically "if the omnipotent God, who holds dominion of heaven and earth, when he wished to make a covenant with a holy man put the main point of such an important matter in this, that the foreskin of his flesh and of his future progeny should be circumcised." The answer that Origen expects from the reader or hearer is clearly negative. Then, after noting that the teachers of the synogogue do hold this implicitly absurd idea, he appeals to Paul:

> We, therefore, instructed by the apostle Paul, say that just as many other things were made in the figure and image of future truth, so also that circumcision of flesh was bearing the form of spiritual circumcision about which it was both worthy and fitting that "the God of majesty" give precepts to mortals.

He then cites Paul's assertion that "we are the true circumcision, who worship God in spirit . . . and put no confidence in the flesh" (Phil 3:2-3) and the statement in Romans 2:28-29: "For he is not a real Jew who is one outwardly, nor is true circumcision something external and physical. He is a Jew who is one inwardly, and real circumcision is a matter of the heart, spiritual and not literal." The introduction of the phrase "circumcision of the heart" permits Origen to note that this is literally impossible. By virtue of the principle of *defectus litterae* it must be interpreted spiritually. However, Ezekiel's employment of the phrase together with circumcision of the flesh (Ezek 44:9) poses a difficulty. The Jew will object, notes Origen, and say, "Behold, the prophet designates both a circumcision of the flesh and heart; no place remains for allegory, where both kinds of circumcision are demanded." To deal with this objection, Origen cites the statement of Jeremiah that the people are uncircumcised in their ears (Jer 6:10) and notes that no one interprets this on the literal level. Then he cites the statement of Moses ("in the Hebrew copies") that he was uncircumcised in lips (Ex 4:10) and observes likewise that this is not interpreted literally but figuratively. His conclusion is "if you refer circumcision of lips to allegory and say no less that circumcision of ears is allegorical and figurative, why do you not also inquire after allegory in circumcision of the foreskin?" Then he is free to exhort his listeners to "take up the circumcision worthy of the word of God in your ears and in your lips and in your heart and in the foreskin of your flesh and in all your members together." There follows an allegorical exposition of these various forms of circumcision on the moral level. The clear governing principle is the need to find a meaning that is "worthy of God" or "worthy of the Word of God."

The letter kills; the Spirit gives life: 2 Corinthians 3:6. Closely related to the necessity of "understanding the law spiritually" is the principle, also derived from Paul, that "the written code kills, but the Spirit gives life" (2 Cor 3:6). At the beginning of his homilies on Leviticus, Origen draws a parallel between the Word of God in the flesh, the knowledge of whose divinity was given only to a few, and the Word of God given through the Law and the Prophets. The veil of the flesh is like the veil of the letter. It is particularly important, according to Origen, to keep this similarity in mind when reading about the sacrificial rites, the diversity of offerings and the ministries of the priests. Otherwise the reader will perceive only "the letter that kills" in these words. Origen has recourse to this text frequently in his later exegetical works in diverse contexts. Sometimes he puts the "letter that kills" in parallel with "types" and "shadows" (Heb 8:5) in order to emphasize the newness of the revelation given by Christ. At other times it functions to urge the believers not to stop at the beauty of the prophetic texts but to penetrate to the meaning that lies beneath them. Still elsewhere he employs it in parallel with Colossians 3:1-2 and 2 Corinthians 4:18 to urge Christians to seek the spiritual meaning of the text in order that they may escape the condition of slaves to become "sons." Finally he uses it to warn that even in the New Testament there is the "letter that kills":

> For if you follow according to the letter that which is said, "Unless you eat my flesh and drink my blood," this "letter kills." Do you want me to bring out of the gospel for you another "letter" that "kills"? He says, "Let the one who does not have a sword sell his tunic and buy a sword." Behold, this is the letter of the gospel, but "it kills." However, if you take it spiritually, it does not kill, but there is in it "a spirit that gives life."

Origen relies on this principle, like others, to press the case for the necessity of finding a meaning in Scripture that is "worthy of God."

Interpreting the Scriptures by Means of the Scriptures

The phrase "spiritual things with spiritual things" denotes a hermeneutical procedure that permeates the exegetical work of Origen as well as that of many other ancient exegetes. In his homily on the ark in Genesis, Origen remarks toward the end: "To be sure, if someone can, at leisure, bring together Scripture with Scripture, and compare divine Scripture and fit together 'spiritual things with spiritual' (1 Cor 2:13), we are not unmindful that he will discover in this passage many secrets of a profound and hidden mystery." For the patristic exegete it is axiomatic that one should seek the explanation of a term or a figure in other texts where the same word is used. To the modern interpreter, conditioned to literary genres and different historical contexts, it seems almost capricious to explain a passage in one book by means of a passage having only a slight verbal similarity from another book of a different literary genre written in a different epoch. To the patristic exegete, or at least the Alexandrian exegete, such a procedure was necessary and absolutely consistent with the basic premise of the unified authorship of Scripture.

Origen invokes this procedure explaining how to discover the meaning of passages that, taken literally, are impossible:

> Accordingly one who reads in an exact manner must, in obedience to the Savior's precept that says, "Search the Scriptures," carefully investigate how far the literal meaning is true and how far it is impossible, and to the utmost of one's power [one] must trace out from the use of similar expressions the meaning scattered everywhere through the Scriptures of that which when taken literally is impossible.

Elsewhere Origen relates a simile that he heard from a rabbi in which the Scriptures are compared with a house with a large number of locked rooms. Each room has a key, but the keys have been mixed up and dispersed throughout the house. The key then to one passage of Scripture is to be found in other passages. We are able to understand obscure passages of Scripture when we take as a point of departure a similar passage from another portion of Scripture, because "the principle of interpretation has been dispersed among them." Origen puts this principle into practice in his commentary on Song of Solomon, where, in order to explain Song 2:9, in which the beloved is compared to a gazelle or young stag, he assembles all references to these animals in other books of Scripture.

This procedure of explaining Scripture by Scripture is based on the fundamental premise that the Holy Spirit is the true author of the whole Bible. In fact, from a formal point of view, the principle is the same as explaining Homer by Homer, a traditional principle of Alexandrian philology, which had been applied to other classical authors such as Plato and Hippocrates.

A similar if not identical procedure can be found already in the New Testament in the writings of Paul. In Galatians 3:16 Paul constructs an exegetical chain using the word for "seed" found in Genesis 13:15 (Gen 17:8; 22:18; 24:7) and 2 Samuel 7:12-14. In Romans 4:1-8 he brings together Genesis 15:6 and Psalm 32:1-2 because of the hook word *reckon*. This exegetical principle was known later in rabbinic literature as *gezera shava*.

However, in justifying his constant use of this procedure, Origen does not appeal so much to the example of Paul as to the principle of "comparing spiritual things with spiritual," which he finds stated in 1 Corinthians 2:13 ("interpreting spiritual truths to those who possess the Spirit"). Origen seems to be the first to interpret this phrase as an exegetical principle. Prior to Origen the verse is found cited only by Clement of Alexandria and in two other works. Clement seems to have interpreted the word *spiritual* as a masculine noun and understood it to mean "spiritual men," that is, initiates, to whom the "spiritual things" could be given. Origen interprets both nouns instead as neuter and equivalent in meaning to "words of Scripture."

Although modern exegetes have tended to read the phrase more in the sense of Clement than in that of Origen, the Jewish schools related texts on the basis of verbal similarities, beginning with the school of Hillel at the end of the first century. Origen could hardly have been ignorant of the fact that this method was employed in the Jewish and pagan schools, but he consistently appeals to Paul as his authority for the method. Thus, for Origen, Paul provided the rule and the example that bound the ancient Scriptures inextricably to the new revelation. Indeed, Origen often understands the phrase "spiritual things with spiritual things" to mean precisely the comparison of passages of the Old and New Testaments respectively.

In keeping with the context of 1 Corinthians 2:13, Origen also insists that only one who is spiritual or perfect is capable of comparing spiritual things with spiritual things. The person who is still spiritually a child (1 Cor 3:1-2), who is nourished "with milk" and "is unskillful in the word of justice" is not able to receive the "solid food" of the divine wisdom and knowledge of the law (cf. Heb 5:13-14) and cannot compare spiritual things with spiritual. Those who do not follow "the letter that kills" but the "spirit that quickens" receive the spirit of adoption, which allows them to penetrate beneath the letter of the law. Applying this same rule further to the story of Hagar and Ishmael, Origen dwells on the fact that Ishmael was given a bottle of water in contrast to a well of living water (Gen 21:14). Bringing together the texts of Genesis 21:14, Genesis 26:14-17, Galatians 4:28 and Proverbs 5:15-16 on this basis, Origen concludes:

The bottle of the law is the letter, from which that carnal people drinks and thence receives understanding. This letter frequently fails them. It cannot extricate itself, for the historical understanding is defective in many things. But the church drinks from the evangelic and apostolic fountains that never fail but "run in its streets" (Prov 5:16), because they always abound and flow in the breadth of spiritual interpretation. The church drinks also "from wells" when it draws and examines certain deeper things from the law.

This method indicated by the phrase "comparing spiritual things with spiritual things" was also combined by Origen with the use of etymologies. An etymology employed in one place to explain a text can be used wherever the same name occurs to introduce the same meaning into the text, even though the texts may be unrelated. Thus Origen interprets Genesis 45:27-28, in which the names Jacob and Israel occur, in such a way that the name Israel represents spiritual intelligence, "he who sees in his mind the true life which is Christ, the true God." He also says that the two names, Jacob and Israel, can be interpreted this way wherever they occur in Scripture and gives a long list of such occurrences.

The Missing Literal Sense in Interpreting What Is Illogical or Impossible

In the fourth book of the *Peri Archon* (4.2.9), Origen raises the question of how one can know whether a passage of Scripture has a literal sense as well as a spiritual one. His answer is that unlikely things, which cause difficulty or scandal because they are unworthy of God, have sometimes been inserted in the law or in the histories. This difficulty is a sign that they are to be interpreted spiritually rather than literally. The same principle holds true for the interpretation of the Gospels and the letters of the apostle, which, he says, do not always present a simple account of the facts on the literal level. Neither these nor the legislation and the precepts of the Old Testament always manifest "reasonableness," the opposite of the word for "illogical" or "absurd."

Origen then offers examples of this principle. First he selects seemingly historical accounts, which lack verisimilitude, such as the tree of the knowledge of good and evil and a mountain sufficiently high that one could see all the kingdoms of the world from its summit (Mt 4:8). Then he says that in the Mosaic legislation as well some things are "illogical" and others are "impossible." Among those that are absurd, he cites the command not to eat griffons (Lev 11:13), since they do not exist. After furnishing numerous similar examples, Origen is careful to avoid the notion that no legislation is to be observed literally simply because some accounts are illogical. The basic assumption is that all Scripture has a spiritual sense and much has a literal as well as a spiritual meaning. The presupposition is that all Scripture is the Word of God, directed to us here and now, and that God would not give us something that has no meaning. If the text does not have a literal meaning, it must have a spiritual one. "Illogicalness" is a key to recognizing when the text is not to be taken literally. It belongs to the more general principle known in the later Latin tradition as *defectus litterae* (the missing literal sense).

In "On First Principles" Origen limits his application of the term *illogical* to specific passages of Scripture, but elsewhere he applies it more generally to the Old Testament. For example, when Zechariah emerges from offering incense in the temple, he can communicate only by signs and remains mute until the birth of John (Lk 1:20-22). Origen explains that the silence of Zechariah is the silence of the prophets among the people of Israel. Zechariah is "the image of that which is carried out among them up to our days." Their institutions are "without reason or sense." They are unable to give an account of their gestures. Origen then asserts that their circumcision is a gesture without meaning. Likewise their Passover and other feasts are gestures rather than truth. Up to this day the people of Israel are deaf and dumb because they have rejected the Word. They are like Moses in Egypt (Ex 4:10), who said to the Lord, "I am not eloquent" ("without word," literally "illogical"). Immediately afterward God explains that he is the source of speech, and he promises to give Moses the words to speak (Ex 4:11-12, 22). Moses therefore both received the word and understood its prior absence. The people of Israel, however, did not understand that they were "without the word." Moreover, they showed by their actions and their silence that they had neither the word or an understanding of its absence. All of these interpretations depend on an elaborate play on the Greek word for "word."

In this interpretation, the Greek term for "without word" or "illogical" has received an additional meaning. That which is illogical or without meaning is also without the Word of God or the Logos, Jesus Christ. The Logos alone gives to the Jewish rites their spiritual sense. The silence of Zechariah signifies that the law, without Christ, no longer has meaning. To refuse the revelation of the Logos, to hold to the ordinances of the old law is to remain a friend of the letter, to be "illogical." Thus the whole Old Testament could be said to be "illogical" when it is not interpreted in the light of the Logos.

The idea that the Old Testament Scriptures are "illogical" or "without sense" when they are not interpreted in the light of the Logos is obviously Christian, but the terminology and the notion of the missing literal sense have a much older history. Already in the Letter of Aristeas (the second-century B.C. account of the origin of the Greek translation of the Pentateuch) we find the admonition "For you must not fall into the degrading idea that it was out of regard to mice and weasels and other such things that Moses drew up his laws with such exceeding care. All these ordinances were made for the sake of righteousness to aid the quest for virtue and the perfecting of character." One cannot avoid the impression that the commentator known as Pseudo-Aristeas feels embarrassed by the text. For him the laws of the Pentateuch are the divinely inspired work of Moses, but he cannot imagine that his God would be interested in making laws about mice and weasels.

With reference to the statement in Genesis 3:8 that the man hid himself from God, Philo comments, "Were one not to interpret it allegorically, it would be 'impossible' to accept the statement, for God fills and penetrates all things and has left no spot void or empty of his presence." Philo makes extensive use of the concepts of the "illogical" and the "impossible" aspects of the text as triggers for allegorical interpretations.

It is evident that a certain conception of God dominates the exegetical practice of these authors. What is inconsistent with this conception must be interpreted allegorically. This approach apparently underlies also Paul's citation of Deuteronomy 25:4 ("You shall not muzzle an ox while it treads out grain") in 1 Corinthians 9:8-10. He then applies this text allegorically to his situation with the comment "Is it for oxen that God is concerned? Does he not speak entirely for our sake?" This echoes the sentiment of Pseudo-Aristeas mentioned above.

The embarrassment of the ancient exegete before a text difficult to reconcile with his notion of God is perhaps expressed most clearly by Origen in commenting on Leviticus:

If, according to this interpretation, we say that the supreme God has promulgated laws to people, I think that the legislation will appear worthy of the divine majesty. If instead we insist on the letter and understand the things written in the law as it seems to the Jews and to the crowd, I am ashamed to say and to profess that God should have given such laws. In that case, human laws, for example those of the Romans or of the Athenians or of the Spartans, will seem more refined and reasonable. If instead the law of God is accepted according to the understanding that the church teaches, then it stands over all human laws, and it will be believed that it is truly the law of God.

For Origen "the understanding that the church teaches" means the tradition of allegorical exegesis or spiritual interpretation found already in the New Testament, particularly in the Pauline letters, which he understood to be his task to continue to elaborate.

Related to the sense of embarrassment that the ancient exegete felt in the presence of these texts was his concern for the ethical and educational effects of the texts. The texts accepted on the literal level were dangerous or, put differently, they were unacceptable to the ancient exegete because their literal content was incompatible with his ethical and theological ideas. Origen expresses this perspective clearly in the same homily:

Recognize that the things written in the divine books are figures and therefore examine and therefore understand the things said as spiritual and not as carnal, since, if you receive them as carnal, they will wound you instead of nourishing you. Even in the Gospels, there is the letter that kills (2 Cor 3:6). . . . It [the Gospel] says, "Whoever does not have a sword should sell his tunic and buy a sword" (Lk 22:36). See, this also is the letter of the gospel, but it kills.

The sense of embarrassment and the concern for the ethical implications of literal readings of the texts have their parallels in the embarrassment and concern felt by Greek writers in the presence of the Homeric epics, which played a role in Greek culture and society similar to the role played by the Scriptures in Jewish and Christian society. This problem is evident already in the classic philosophers and continues to be a concern of philosophers (especially Stoic ones) and educators for many centuries because of the Homeric epics' central role in the Greek educational system. The patristic exegetes, intellectually formed in the traditional Greek schools, undoubtedly learned the traditional methods of interpreting Homer and carried that approach forward to their Scriptural studies.

Summary and Conclusion

I have provided this survey of the principles of interpretation, especially those used by Origen because he is the first Christian exegete to attempt to codify these procedures and his work had enormous influence. Origen thought that he was imitating Paul and applying his rules in interpreting the Scriptures. In fact, some of his principles have other sources. These include the use of etymologies to generate allegorical interpretations and the notion of the missing literal sense. The concern to find a meaning "worthy of God," while it is never raised to the level of a formal exegetical principle, greatly influences ancient exegesis. It may be implicitly present in Paul's use of Deuteronomy 25:4 (1 Cor 9:9) in the sense that it would be unworthy of God to think that he was really concerned with oxen rather than with the situation of the apostles. In any case, the notion is widely diffused in Philo and Origen and in Hellenistic exegesis of Homeric texts as well. It comes into play particularly in efforts to reduce anthropomorphic features attributed to God or the gods.

Needless to say, not all of the patristic interpreters used all of these rules. Some, especially the notion of the missing literal sense, became objects of controversy. The Antiochene authors in particular tried to limit the use of allegory, restricting it to those cases where a parallel, called typology, could be seen between Old and New Testament figures and events.

The early Christian interpreters of the Old Testament Scriptures had many concerns—polemical, apologetic, speculative—but above all they were concerned to provide spiritual nourishment for their congregations. The interpretation of the text was determined by the literary form and by the audience to which it was addressed. The vast majority of the interpretations found in this volume, however, come from homilies in which the preacher was concerned to provide his hearers with correct doctrine and moral teaching. Whenever possible, using the rules explained above, he sought to find such spiritual nourishment in the New Testament and then read it into the Old Testament text. The Antiochene authors, as well as the majority of the Alexandrian interpreters, shared this perspective. Thus the story of the patriarchs becomes a vehicle for teaching New Testament doctrine.

GENESIS 12-50

12:1-3 THE CALL AND THE PROMISE

[1]Now the LORD said to Abram, "Go from your country and your kindred and your father's house to the land that I will show you. [2]And I will make of you a great nation, and I will bless you, and make your name great, so that you will be a blessing. [3]I will bless those who bless you, and him who curses you I will curse; and by you all the families of the earth shall bless themselves."[q]

q Or *in you all the families of the earth shall be blessed*

OVERVIEW: Beginning with Philo, the call and the migration of Abraham came to be interpreted allegorically to represent all those who undertake the spiritual journey (ANTONY THE GREAT). God's command to leave his country is also connected to Jesus' call to "follow me" (DIDYMUS THE BLIND). The direct influence of Philo is evident in the interpretation of Abraham as the mind that is commanded to leave behind the passions (AMBROSE). Abraham is also interpreted as a model of faith (AUGUSTINE). In a later development, the allegorical interpretation of Philo already observed in Ambrose is combined with the sacrament of baptism. The command to leave "your kindred" is then interpreted in the same direction as a command to leave behind vices and sins after baptism, and, using the principle of interpreting the Scriptures by means of the Scriptures (see introduction to this volume, pp. xxxiv-xxxvi), "your father's house" is interpreted to mean the dominion of the devil (CAESARIUS OF ARLES).

The promise to make of Abraham a "great nation" is seen to be fulfilled literally but also spiritually because true greatness lies in virtue (DIDYMUS THE BLIND). The promise to make "your name great" is understood to be fulfilled in the fact that all, including the Jews, claim kinship with Abraham (CHRYSOSTOM). This promise, however, is only an earthly one, while the promise that "all the families of the earth" will be blessed in Abraham is a heavenly one fulfilled in the nation saved in Christ from all the families of the earth. This one man, who abandoned the land of Babel, went forth from it willingly by the order of the Lord, having heard addressed to himself the promise that in one common blessing there would be reunited in him all the peoples divided into various regions and languages (BEDE).

12:1 *The Call from God*

GUIDED BY THE SPIRIT. ANTONY THE GREAT: Some were reached by the Word of God through the law of promise and the discernment of the good inherent in them from their first formation. They did not hesitate but followed it readily as did Abraham, our father. Since he offered himself in love through the law of promise, God appeared to him, saying, "Go from your country and your kindred and from your father's house to the land that I will show you." And he went without hesitating at all but being ready for his calling. This is the model for the beginning of this way of life. It still persists in those who follow this pattern.

Wherever and whenever souls endure and bow to it they easily attain the virtues, since their hearts are ready to be guided by the Spirit of God. LETTER I.[1]

WHY HE LEFT. DIDYMUS THE BLIND: It is not by chance that God orders Abraham to leave his land and his relatives but because he sees in him something that makes him worthy of being the object of divine concern, that is, his faith in God. But it was not fitting that the one who had faith in God should remain among perverse people—the father of Abraham was in fact an idolater—because the company of the wicked often does harm to zealous people, especially to those whose zeal is new. That is why the Savior also proclaims, "If anyone wishes to follow me and does not hate his father, his brothers, his sisters, and even his wife and children, he cannot be my disciple."[2] The Lord did not say that in order to provoke hatred of one's relatives, but if one of them becomes an obstacle to virtue, it is necessary to hate him for virtue's sake. That is what the apostles did, who said, "Look, we have left everything in order to follow you."[3]

Such is the order given now to the patriarch, and God tells him that he will show him a land in which to live, that he will make of him a great nation, that he will bless and magnify his name. ON GENESIS 209.[4]

ABRAHAM REPRESENTS THE MIND. AMBROSE: Abraham represents the mind. In fact Abraham signifies passage. Therefore, in order that the mind, which in Adam had allowed itself to run to pleasure and to bodily attractions, should turn toward the ideal form of virtue, a wise man has been proposed to us as an example to imitate. Actually Abraham in Hebrew signifies "father," in the sense that the mind, with the authority, the judgment and the solicitude of a father, governs the entire person. This mind then was in Haran, that is, in caverns, subject to the different passions. For this reason it is told, "Go from your country," that is, from your body. From this land

went forth the one whose homeland is in the heavens. ON ABRAHAM 2.1-2.[5]

ABRAHAM BELIEVED GOD'S PROMISE. AUGUSTINE: The right thing to do, brothers and sisters, is to believe God before he pays up anything, because just as he cannot possibly lie, so he cannot deceive. For he is God. That's how our ancestors believed him. That's how Abraham believed him. There's a faith for you that really deserves to be admired and made widely known. He had received nothing from him, and he believed his promise. We do not yet believe him, though we have already received so much. Was Abraham ever in a position to say to him, "I will believe you, because you promised me that and paid up"? No, he believed from the very first command given, without having received anything else at all. "Go out from your country," he was told, "and from your kindred, and go into a country which I will give you." And he believed straightaway, and [God] didn't give him that country but kept it for his seed. SERMON 113A.10.[6]

IN BAPTISM OUR LAND IS OUR BODY. CAESARIUS OF ARLES: When the sacred lesson was read just now, we heard the Lord say to blessed Abraham, "Leave your country, your kinsfolk and your father's house." Now everything that was written in the Old Testament, dearly beloved, provided a type and image of the New Testament. As the apostle says, "Now all these things happened to them as a type, and they were written for our correction, upon whom the final age of the world has come."[7] Therefore, if what happened corporally in Abraham was written for us, we will see it fulfilled spiritually in us if we live piously and justly. "Leave your country," the Lord said, "your kinsfolk and your father's house." We believe and perceive all these things fulfilled in us, brothers, through the sacrament of baptism. Our land is our body; we go forth properly from

---

[1]*LSA* 197. [2]Lk 14:26; Mt 16:24. [3]Mk 10:28; cf. Mt 19:27. [4]SC 244:136-38. [5]CSEL 32 1:565. [6]*WSA* 3 4:178*. [7]1 Cor 10:11.

our land if we abandon our carnal habits to follow the footsteps of Christ. Does not one seem to you happily to leave his land, that is, himself, if from being proud he becomes humble; from irascible, patient; from dissolute, chaste; from avaricious, generous; from envious, kind; from cruel, gentle? Truly, brothers, one who is changed thus out of love for God happily leaves his own land. Finally, even in private conversation, if one who is wicked suddenly begins to perform good works we are inclined to speak thus of him: He has gone out of himself. Indeed, he is properly said to have gone out of himself if he rejects his vices and delights in virtue. "Leave your country," says the Lord. Our country, that is, our body, was the land of the dying before baptism, but through baptism it has become the land of the living. It is the very land of which the psalmist relates: "I believe that I shall see the bounty of the Lord in the land of the living."[8] Through baptism, as I said, we have become the land of the living and not of the dying, that is, of the virtues and not of the vices. However, this is true only if after receiving baptism we do not return to the slough of vices, if when we have become the land of the living we do not perform the blameworthy, wicked deeds of death. "And come," says the Lord, "into the land which I will show you." It is certain that then we will come with joy to the land that God shows us if with his help we first repel sins and vices from our land, that is, from our body. SERMON 81.1.[9]

OUR KINSFOLK ARE OUR SINS AND VICES.

CAESARIUS OF ARLES: "Leave your kinsfolk." Our kinsfolk is understood as those vices and sins that are in part born with us in some way and are increased and nourished after infancy by our bad acts. Therefore we leave our kinsfolk when through the grace of baptism we are emptied of all sins and vices. However, this is true only if later we strive as much as we can with God's help to expel vice and to be filled with virtues. If after being freed from all evil through baptism we are willing to be slothful and idle, I fear that what is written in the Gospel may be fulfilled in us:

"When the unclean spirit has gone out of a man, he roams through dry places in search of rest and finds none. If after he returns he finds his house unoccupied, he takes with him seven other spirits more evil than himself; and the last state of that man becomes worse than the first."[10] Therefore let us so go forth from our kinsfolk, that is, from our sins and vices, that we may never again wish to return to them as a dog to its vomit.[11] SERMON 81.2.[12]

THE DEVIL WAS OUR FATHER BEFORE GRACE.

CAESARIUS OF ARLES: "Leave your father's house." This we ought to accept in a spiritual manner, dearly beloved. The devil was our father before the grace of Christ; of him the Lord spoke in the Gospel when he rebuked the Jews: "The father from whom you are is the devil, and the desires of your father it is your will to do."[13] He said the devil was the father of humanity, not because of birth from him but because of imitation of his wickedness. Indeed, they could not have been born of him, but they did want to imitate him. This fact that the devil was our first father the psalmist relates in the person of God speaking to the church: "Hear, O daughter, and see; turn your ear, forget your people and your father's house."[14] SERMON 81.3.[15]

12:2 A Promise of a Great Nation

A HEAVENLY GREATNESS.

DIDYMUS THE BLIND: As for the promise to make of him "a great nation," is it necessary to give a meaning other than the literal one? Because it is clear that it was realized in its historical sense. But, having become a people, it is truly great when it is adorned with virtues. And it is manifest that when the progress becomes more important in the soul, there is established in it a grandeur which is no longer earthly but heavenly. And this soul is a blessing that is not simply offered but realized,

---

[8]Ps 27:13 (26:13 LXX). [9]FC 47:3-4*. [10]Mt 12:43-46. [11]See Prov 26:11. [12]FC 47:4. [13]Jn 8:44. [14]Ps 45:10 (44:11 LXX). [15]FC 47:5.

because the name is made great and becomes celebrated because it is accompanied by virtue and by that beauty which confers a spiritual blessing. It is worth more to have a good name than to have riches.[16] ON GENESIS 210-11.[17]

ABRAHAM'S GOD-FEARING QUALITIES. CHRYSOSTOM: The scope of the promise is extraordinary: "I will make you a great nation; I will bless you and magnify your name." Not only will I place you at the head of a great nation and cause your name to be great, but as well, "I will bless you, and you will be blessed." I will favor you with so much blessing, he says, that it will last for all time. "You will be blessed" to such an extent that everyone will be anxious to thrust themselves into your company in preference to the highest honor. See how God right from the beginning foretold to him the honor he would later confer upon him. "I will make you a great nation," he said; "I will magnify your name; I will bless you, and you will be blessed." Hence the Jews too found in the patriarch grounds for self-importance and endeavored to establish their kinship with him in the words "We are the children of Abraham."[18] For you to learn, however, that on the basis of their evil ways they are in fact unworthy of such kinship, Christ says to them, "If you were children of Abraham, you would do the works of Abraham."[19] John too, the son of Zechariah, when those anxious to be baptized flocked to the Jordan, said to them, "Brood of vipers, who warned you to flee from the wrath to come? Bear fruit that benefits repentance, and don't presume to say, 'We have Abraham for our father.' I tell you, after all, that God can raise up children to Abraham even from these stones."[20] Do you see how great his name was in everyone's estimation? For the time being, however, before the sequel the just man's God-fearing qualities are demonstrated in the way he believed the words coming from God and accepted without demur everything, difficult though it seemed. HOMILIES ON GENESIS 31.13.[21]

12:3 The Extent of the Promise

THE GENERATION OF THE SPIRITUAL ISRAEL. BEDE: The promise of this blessing is greater and more important than the preceding one. That was earthly, this one is heavenly, since that one referred to the generation of the fleshly Israel and this one to the generation of the spiritual Israel; that one to the nation born from him according to the flesh and this one to the generation of the nation saved in Christ from all the families of the earth. Among these saved are included all those born from him according to the flesh, who wished also to imitate the piety of his faith. To all these together the apostle Paul says, "If you are of Christ, you are then the seed of Abraham."[22] Therefore when he says, "In you will be blessed all the families of the earth," it is as if he were saying, "And in your seed will be blessed the families of the earth." Mary, from whom would be born the Christ, was present already when these things were said to him. This is what the apostle meant when he spoke of them [the descendents of Levi] as "in the loins of Abraham." How marvelous was the dispensation of the divine severity and goodness. The multitude of those who had gathered for a work of pride merited to be divided from one another into different languages and races. . . . This one man, who abandoned that region, going forth from it willingly by the order of the Lord, heard addressed to himself the promise that in one common blessing there would be reunited in him all the peoples divided into various regions and languages. ON GENESIS 3.[23]

---

[16]See Prov 22:1. [17]SC 244:141-43. [18]Jn 8:33. [19]Jn 8:39. [20]Mt 3:7-9. [21]FC 82:245-46. [22]Gal 3:29. [23]CCL 118A:169.

12:4-9 MIGRATION FROM HARAN TO BETHEL

⁴*So Abram went, as the LORD had told him; and Lot went with him. Abram was seventy-five years old when he departed from Haran.* ⁵*And Abram took Sarai his wife, and Lot his brother's son, and all their possessions which they had gathered, and the persons that they had gotten in Haran; and they set forth to go to the land of Canaan. When they had come to the land of Canaan,* ⁶*Abram passed through the land to the place at Shechem, to the oak*ʳ *of Moreh. At that time the Canaanites were in the land.* ⁷*Then the LORD appeared to Abram, and said, "To your descendants I will give this land." So he built there an altar to the LORD, who had appeared to him.* ⁸*Thence he removed to the mountain on the east of Bethel, and pitched his tent, with Bethel on the west and Ai on the east; and there he built an altar to the LORD and called on the name of the LORD.* ⁹*And Abram journeyed on, still going toward the Negeb.*

r Or terebinth

OVERVIEW: Abraham's departure is interpreted allegorically to signify the renunciation of the pleasures of the flesh, vices and the world with its father, the devil (BEDE). The appearance of the Lord to Abraham poses the problem of reconciling this text with others, especially New Testament texts that stress God's transcendence, but this is resolved by attributing the appearance to the Son, the "image of the invisible God" (NOVATIAN). Where there is Bethel, that is, the house of God, there is also the altar. The building of an altar at Bethel and calling on the name of the Lord represent spiritual progress (AMBROSE).

12:4 Abraham's Obedience

WE GO FORTH FROM OUR LAND. BEDE: In this, his going forth by divine command from the land, from his kin and from the house of his father, it is clear that all the sons of his promise, among whom are we also, must imitate him. We go forth from our land when we renounce the pleasures of the flesh; from our kin when, in the measure possible for humans, we make an effort to rid ourselves of all the vices with which we are born. We go forth from the house of our father when, for love of the heavenly life, we want to leave the world itself with its head, the devil. All of us, in fact, because of the first disobedience, are born into the world as sons of the devil. But, through the grace of regeneration, all those who belong to the seed of Abraham are made sons of God, because our Father who is in heaven[1] says to us, that is, to his church, "Hear, O daughter, consider, and incline your ear; forget your people and your father's house."[2] ON GENESIS 3.[3]

12:7 The Lord Appears to Abraham

IT WAS THE SON WHO WAS SEEN. NOVATIAN: Please note that the same Moses says in another passage that God appeared to Abraham. Yet the same Moses hears from God that no man can see God and live.[4] If God cannot be seen, how did God appear? If he appeared, how is it that he cannot be seen? For John says similarly, "No one has ever seen God."[5] And the apostle Paul says, "Whom no man has seen or can see."[6] But certainly Scripture does not lie; therefore God was really seen. Accordingly this can only mean that it was not the Father, who never has been seen, that

[1]Mt 6:9. [2]Ps 45:10 (44:11 LXX). [3]CCL 118A:170-71. [4]Ex 33:20. [5]Jn 1:18; 1 Jn 4:12. [6]1 Tim 6:16.

was seen, but the Son, who willed to descend and to be seen, for the simple reason that he has descended. In fact, he is the "image of the invisible God,"[7] that our limited human nature and frailty might in time grow accustomed to see God the Father in him who is the Image of God, that is, in the Son of God. Gradually and by degrees, human frailty had to be strengthened by means of the Image for the glory of being able one day to see God the Father. ON THE TRINITY 18.1-3.[8]

THE ATHLETE OF GOD. AMBROSE: Where there is Bethel, that is, the house of God, there is also the altar. Where there is the altar, there is also the calling on the name of God. It is not by chance that he made such great progress. He hoped in the help of God. The athlete of God exercised and strengthened himself in adversity. He went into the desert. ON ABRAHAM 1.2.6.[9]

12:8 Abraham Called on the Lord

[7]Col 1:15. [8]FC 67:67. [9]CSEL 32 1:505-6.

12:10-16 ABRAHAM GOES TO EGYPT

[10]Now there was a famine in the land. So Abram went down to Egypt to sojourn there, for the famine was severe in the land. [11]When he was about to enter Egypt, he said to Sarai his wife, "I know that you are a woman beautiful to behold; [12]and when the Egyptians see you, they will say, 'This is his wife'; then they will kill me, but they will let you live. [13]Say you are my sister, that it may go well with me because of you, and that my life may be spared on your account." [14]When Abram entered Egypt the Egyptians saw that the woman was very beautiful. [15]And when the princes of Pharaoh saw her, they praised her to Pharaoh. And the woman was taken into Pharaoh's house. [16]And for her sake he dealt well with Abram; and he had sheep, oxen, he-asses, menservants, maidservants, she-asses, and camels.

OVERVIEW: The famine in the land can be interpreted spiritually as the failure to hear the word of God. Following the interpretation of Philo, it is emphasized that Abraham goes down to Egypt, not to dwell there but to "sojourn" there.[1] The story of Abraham passing off his wife as his sister offered a considerable challenge to patristic interpreters. On the literal level, it could be viewed as clever strategy, while on the spiritual level, where Sarah represents virtue, it could be interpreted as modesty and prudence similar to that of Paul in his dealings with diverse peoples. The virtuous do not say that virtue has become their exclusive

privilege in order not to provoke the jealousy of those who do not have it (DIDYMUS THE BLIND). It was also possible to defend Abraham against the charge of lying on the grounds that Sarah was his sister (DIDYMUS THE BLIND, AUGUSTINE). The episode could also be used as vehicle for moral teaching about the desirability of seeking virtue in a wife rather than beauty and riches (AMBROSE). Sarah's experience is also seen as foreshadowing

[1]This is because, beginning with Philo, Egypt comes to represent symbolically the human body as the seat of the passions. See De congressu eruditionis gratia 20; Legum allegoriae 2.77.

the experience of her descendants in Egypt (EPHREM). That Pharaoh dealt well with Abraham is interpreted on the symbolic level to represent the reward of humility (DIDYMUS THE BLIND).

12:10 A Famine

THEY NO LONGER HEARD THE WORD OF THE LORD. DIDYMUS THE BLIND: The content on the literal level is clear. As for the spiritual meaning, it is this. Those who are wise in God are above the earth, since they are not of the earth. A famine then came over the earth, because for those who are concerned about earthly things, there often occurs a famine in this sense, that they no longer hear the word of the Lord. Then, if they are worthy of it, the Word is given back to them one day.

Thus Abraham went to Egypt to "sojourn" there, not to dwell there, because he had sympathy for the victims of the famine. Likewise Daniel and his companions did not come to Babylon because of sins they had committed but to aid the people who had been deported there on account of their own sins. ON GENESIS 225.[2]

12:11-15 Sarah's Beauty

SARAH REPRESENTS VIRTUE. DIDYMUS THE BLIND: On the literal level Abraham made an intelligent compromise with the lustfulness of the Egyptians, being certain that God, who had made him leave his own country, would watch over his marriage. He suggested to his wife that she tell them that she was his sister, because if they were told that and only that at the beginning, they would not have the idea that she was his wife, and by that means he would deceive them. In fact, marriage between brother and sister was practiced in Egypt and in his own country, as he said later, "She really is my sister."[3] It was therefore a clever strategy to suggest to Sarah to say only that at first. As the laws against adultery were probably respected among the Egyptians, Abraham thought in fact that they would kill him in order not to be considered as adulterers.

So much for the literal level. As for the spiritual meaning, those who pass from virtue to vice are said to descend into Egypt. One finds often in the Scriptures, "Woe to those who descend into Egypt." Here it does not say "he descended" but "he entered." His descent is an entrance, because every zealous man condescends to those who fall without falling with them . . . to deliver them from their fall. Just as one becomes Jewish for the sake of the Jews without being a Jew,[4] and ungodly for the sake of the ungodly without being ungodly, so one comes into Egypt without living as an Egyptian.

The others then descend there, but Abraham enters there. It is not their vice that leads him there but the fulfillment of a divine plan. The virtuous man enters into Egypt in the sense that he makes use of foreign culture to draw something useful from it, as Paul the blessed apostle did in citing the verse of Aratus, "for we are indeed his offspring,"[5] in order to behave accordingly, and "to an unknown god" or "Cretans are always liars."[6] He urges us in the same way to "take every thought captive"[7] in order to put it at the service of Christ.

Having entered Egypt, as we have explained it, he imposes restrictions on virtue that she should not say that she is his wife, because the zealous and perfect man does not say that virtue[8] has become his exclusive privilege in order not to provoke the jealousy of those who do not have it. He says that she is his sister, giving himself thus a secondary rank with regard to the union that he enjoys with her, in order to put himself within range of the weak and to inspire in them the desire to receive her as something that is at the disposition of all in common. The fact is that often, when we want to direct the attention of someone to a teaching, we begin by putting it in language common with him, for example the teaching about providence, so that afterward he may receive it personally. The evangelical teaching is thus the gracious spouse of the

---

[2]SC 244:179-80. [3]Gen 20:12. [4]1 Cor 9:20-21. [5]Acts 17:28. [6]Tit 1:12. [7]2 Cor 10:5. [8]Didymus is following Philo in identifying Sarah allegorically as virtue. See *Legum allegoriae* 2.82.

zealous man, but he does not keep her for himself, even if he speaks of her only "among the mature."[9] He places her in common with all, like Paul, who said, "I wish that all were as I myself am,"[10] because, having become such, they might know that this culture is the spouse of the perfect man. "Wisdom begets discernment to a man";[11] and as for me, says the perfect, "I became enamored of her beauty,"[12] that of wisdom, it is understood. But the wise man wishes to share with all that which is his, because in this way they will not become jealous. ON GENESIS 226-27.[13]

TO SAFEGUARD HER HUSBAND, SARAH LIED. AMBROSE: There came a famine, and so he went to Egypt. He knew that in Egypt the dissipation of youth was widespread, characterized by lust, impudent desires and unrestrained passions. He understood that among such men the modesty of his wife would be defenseless and that her beauty would be a danger for him. So he told his wife to say that she was his sister. By this we are taught that it is not so much beauty that one should seek in a wife, for this often leads to the death of the husband. In fact, it is not so much the beauty of the wife but her virtue and her seriousness that make a husband happy. Whoever desires the happiness of marriage should look not for a wealthy woman, who will not be held in check by the obligations of marriage. One looks not for one ornamented with jewels but with good manners. The wife who is conscious of being of a higher social level generally humiliates her husband. These things have a close connection with pride. Sarah was not richer in goods. She was not of more noble origin. Therefore she did not think her husband inferior but loved him as one of equal dignity. She was not held back by riches, by her parents, by her relatives, but she followed her husband wherever he went. She went to a foreign land; she declared herself to be his sister. She was willing, if necessary, to endanger her own modesty rather than the security of her husband. To safeguard her husband, she lied, saying that she was his sister out of fear that those who were

seeking to ensnare her modesty would have killed him as a rival and defender of his wife. The Egyptians, in fact, as soon as they saw her, struck by her uncommon beauty, presented her to the king and treated Abraham with respect, honoring him as the brother of her who was pleasing to the king. ON ABRAHAM 1.2.6.[14]

ABRAHAM DID NOT DENY THAT SARAH WAS HIS WIFE. AUGUSTINE: Having built an altar there and called upon God, Abraham proceeded thence and dwelt in the desert and was compelled by pressure of famine to go on into Egypt. There he called his wife his sister, and he told no lie. For she was this also, because she was near of blood; just as Lot, on account of the same nearness, being his brother's son, is called his brother. Now he did not deny that she was his wife but held his peace about it, committing to God the defense of his wife's chastity and providing as a man against human wiles. If he had not provided against the danger as much as he could, he would have been tempting God rather than trusting in him. We have said enough about this matter against the calumnies of Faustus the Manichaean. At last what Abraham had expected the Lord to do took place. For Pharaoh, king of Egypt, who had taken her to him as his wife, restored her to her husband when faced with severe plague. And far be it from us to believe that she was defiled by lying with another. It is much more credible that, by these great afflictions, Pharaoh was not permitted to do this. CITY OF GOD 16.19.[15]

ABRAHAM GAVE A HUMAN REASON. EPHREM THE SYRIAN: Abraham gave a human reason as human beings do. Nevertheless, because Sarah thought it was Abraham who was sterile, she was taken to the palace. [This happened] first, so that she might learn that it was she who was barren; second, so that her love for her husband might be seen, for she did not exchange [her husband] for a

---

[9]1 Cor 2:6. [10]1 Cor 7:7. [11]Prov 10:23 LXX. [12]Wis 8:2 LXX. [13]SC 244:180-85. [14]CSEL 32 1:506-7. [15]NPNF 1 2:322*.

king while she was a sojourner; and [last], so that the mystery of her descendants might be prefigured in her. Just as she had no love for the kingdom of Egypt, they would not love the idols, the garlic or the onions of Egypt. The entire house of Pharaoh was struck down by Sarah's deliverance. So too would all Egypt be struck down by the deliverance of her descendants.[16] COMMENTARY ON GENESIS 9.3.[17]

12:16 Pharaoh Deals with Abraham

ABRAHAM ENTERED EGYPT. DIDYMUS THE BLIND: The intelligent strategy of the patriarch did not fail. They did not seek to do him harm. Moreover, a way out of it presented itself so that the marriage of the holy man would not be violated, because the Egyptians did not fling themselves on the woman relinquished by him. But the officials, after having seen her, in order to obtain the gratitude of the king, presented her to him as a gift, and thus it happened that they treated Abraham well because of her.

Abraham entered then into Egypt allegorically by adapting himself as one of the perfect to the imperfect in order to do good to them instead of holding on to virtue as a privilege, as has been said above, but in showing her to all as his sister, in humility, so that by contemplating her they might come to love her. But observe how it is said that the officials saw her. There are in fact in the ranks of the allegorically viewed Egyptians some men who are purer, who have a great capacity for perceiving virtue. And they not only perceived her, but they introduced her to their superior, that is, to the reason that governs them, and they praised her. ON GENESIS 228.[18]

[16]Ex 14:26-28. [17]FC 91:149*. [18]SC 244:186.

12:17-20 ABRAHAM DEPARTS FROM EGYPT

[17]But the LORD afflicted Pharaoh and his house with great plagues because of Sarai, Abram's wife. [18]So Pharaoh called Abram, and said, "What is this you have done to me? Why did you not tell me that she was your wife? [19]Why did you say, 'She is my sister,' so that I took her for my wife? Now then, here is your wife, take her, and be gone." [20]And Pharaoh gave men orders concerning him; and they set him on the way, with his wife and all that he had.

OVERVIEW: The affliction visited upon Pharaoh provides the occasion for moral exhortation about chastity in marriage (AMBROSE). Pharaoh's questions to Abraham are seen as the result of grace and the fear of God instilled in him by punishment. His restoration of Sarah to Abraham is evidence of God's providence in difficult situations. Abraham's departure from Egypt with all he had is seen as a demonstration of the rewards for trials and endurance (CHRYSOSTOM).

12:17 The Lord Afflicts Pharaoh

THE NECESSITY OF MAINTAINING CHASTITY. AMBROSE: This passage is a great witness and demonstration of the necessity of maintaining chastity, exhorting everyone to show himself chaste, not to long for the bed of another and not to seduce the wife of another, counting on the hope of not being discovered and of going unpunished. It exhorts all not to let themselves be tempted by neglect . . . or by a prolonged absence. God, the defender of marriage, is present. From him nothing remains hidden, nothing escapes him, and no one can make sport of him. God takes on the task of the absent husband and maintains the sentinels. Indeed, even without sentinels he surprises the guilty before he puts into action what he has premeditated. In the soul of each one, in the mind of all he recognizes the guilt. Adulterer, even if you have deceived the husband, you do not deceive God. Even if you have escaped from the husband, even if you have made sport of the judge of the tribunal, you do not escape from the judge of the whole world. He punishes with greater severity the injury that is done to the weak, the offenses done to an imprudent husband. In fact, the injury is greater when the author rather than the guardian of the marriage is held in contempt and not taken into consideration. ON ABRAHAM 1.2.7.[1]

12:18 Pharaoh Questions Abraham

FEAR QUENCHED THE FIRE OF PHARAOH'S ANGER. CHRYSOSTOM: Note that the severity of the punishment depressed his thinking, to the extent of leading him to offer an excuse to the just man and show signs of every care for him. And yet had God's grace not been active in appeasing his mind and instilling fear into him, the consequence would have been that he would have flown into an even worse temper to the extent of attempting to even the score with his deceiver, the just man, wreaking his vengeance on him and bringing him to the ultimate peril. He did none of this, however. Fear quenched the fire of his anger. His one concern was to show signs of care for the just man. He now knew, you see, that it was impossible that this could be an unimportant man if he enjoyed such marvelous favor from on high. HOMILIES ON GENESIS 32.21.[2]

12:19 Pharaoh Sends Abraham Away

GOD'S PROVIDENCE IS MARVELOUS. CHRYSOS-

TOM: What imagination could adequately conceive amazement at these events? What tongue could manage to express this amazement? A woman dazzling in her beauty is closeted with an Egyptian partner, who is king and tyrant, of such frenzy and incontinent disposition, and yet she leaves his presence untouched, with her peerless chastity intact. Such, you see, God's providence always is, marvelous and surprising. Whenever things are given up as hopeless by human beings, then he personally gives evidence of his invincible power in every circumstance. HOMILIES ON GENESIS 32.22.[3]

12:20 Abraham Leaves Egypt

THE BENEFIT FROM HIS TRIALS. CHRYSOSTOM: You would be right in applying to this just man those words that blessed David used of those who returned from the captivity in Babylon: "Though they sow in tears, they will reap in joy. They went their way and wept as they cast their seed, but in returning they will come in joy, carrying their sheaves aloft."[4] Did you see his downward journey to be beset with worry and fear, with the fear of death heavy upon him? Now see his return marked by great prosperity and distinction! The just man now, you see, was an object of respect to everyone in Egypt and in Palestine. After all, who would have failed to show respect for the one who so enjoyed God's protection and was accorded such wonderful care? Quite likely what befell the king and his household escaped no one's attention. His purpose, you see, in permitting everything and in allowing the just man's trials to reach such a point was that his endurance might appear more conspicuous, his achievement might win the attention of the whole world, and no one would be unaware of the good man's virtue.

Do you see, dearly beloved, the magnitude of the benefit coming from his trials? Do you see the

---

[1]CSEL 32 1:507. [2]FC 82:270-71. [3]FC 82:271. [4]Ps 126:5-6 (125:5-6 LXX).

greatness of the reward for his endurance? Do you see man and wife, advanced in age though they were, giving evidence of so much good sense, so much courage, so much affection for one another, such a bond of love? Let us all imitate this and never become dispirited or consider the onset of tribulations to be a mark of abandonment on God's part or an index of scorn. Rather, let us treat it as the clearest demonstration of God's providential care for us. HOMILIES ON GENESIS 32.24-25.[5]

---

[5]FC 82:273.

13:1-7 ABRAHAM DEPARTS FOR BETHEL

[1]So Abram went up from Egypt, he and his wife, and all that he had, and Lot with him, into the Negeb.
[2]Now Abram was very rich in cattle, in silver, and in gold. [3]And he journeyed on from the Negeb as far as Bethel, to the place where his tent had been at the beginning, between Bethel and Ai, [4]to the place where he had made an altar at the first; and there Abram called on the name of the LORD. [5]And Lot, who went with Abram, also had flocks and herds and tents, [6]so that the land could not support both of them dwelling together; for their possessions were so great that they could not dwell together, [7]and there was strife between the herdsmen of Abram's cattle and the herdsmen of Lot's cattle. At that time the Canaanites and the Perizzites dwelt in the land.

OVERVIEW: On a spiritual or allegorical level, following Philo, Abraham's return from Egypt with his wife can be interpreted to signify the mind that possesses virtue. Abraham's riches of silver and gold represent the word and the mind (AMBROSE), following the interpretation given earlier by Origen and Didymus. His riches reveal God's providence and Abraham's virtue. He calls on the name of the Lord in a desert place, thus revealing that he is a lover of peace and quiet (CHRYSOSTOM). The fact that Lot is mentioned as having flocks, herds and cattle but not silver and gold shows that he lacked Abraham's spiritual riches. An etymological explanation of the name Lot suggests an explanation of why he was at one time joined with Abraham and at another time joined with Sodom. As for the discord that arises, no space is large enough for it (AMBROSE). Dis-

cord among the brethren is the source of all problems (CHRYSOSTOM). By analogy, the cattle represent the senses, and the shepherds are those assigned to keep them in check (AMBROSE).

13:1 Abraham Departs from Egypt

SARAH REPRESENTS VIRTUE. AMBROSE: So Abraham left, taking with him his wife Sarah, which means "sovereign," not "servant." Therefore it was said to Abraham, "Listen to your wife Sarah."[1] In fact, she who is liberated from the slavery of sin obtains sovereignty, not servitude. Therefore a sound mind possesses sovereign virtue, which has dominion over the bodily senses, which is not subject, which has brought back ev-

---

[1]Gen 21:12.

---

erything from Egypt, which has not left there any of the norms that regulate her life. Such a mind is not clothed with intemperance or insolence or shameful immodesty. Nor is it lacking the veil of prudent wisdom, and it is clothed with modesty. ON ABRAHAM 2.5.19.[2]

13:2 Abraham's Wealth

SPIRITUAL RICHES. AMBROSE: "He was very rich," as is natural for one who was not lacking in any good thing, who did not covet the goods of others, because he lacked nothing of what he would have wished to regard as his own. For this is what it means to be rich: to have what is sufficient to satisfy one's own desires. Frugality has a measure. Richness does not. Its measure is in the will of the seeker. He was rich in cattle, in silver and gold. What does this mean? I do not think that the intention is to praise the riches of this world but the righteousness of this man. Thus I understand cattle to be the bodily senses, because they are irrational. Silver represents the word and gold the mind. Abraham was indeed rich, because he was in control of his irrational senses. Indeed, he tamed them and made them docile, so that they might participate in rationality. His word was radiant with the brightness of faith, purified by the grace of spiritual discipline.[3] His mind was full of prudence. And this is why the good mind is compared with gold, because just as gold is more precious than other metals, so the good mind is the best part among those that make up the human substance. So the richness of the wise man consists in these three things: in sensation, in word and in mind. Their order establishes a gradation, as we read also in the apostle: "So faith, hope, love abide, these three; but the greatest of these is love."[4] The mind too, then, is the greatest, because it is the mind that grinds the spiritual grain to purify the senses and the word. The character of the wise man is preserved at every point.

So it is that through the simple facts of Abraham's life great doctrines are expounded and il-

lustrated. Rich indeed is the one who enriches even the arguments of the philosophers, who would formulate their precepts on the basis of his conduct. It was his riches, then, that Scripture had brought to light. ON ABRAHAM 2.5.20-21.[5]

GOD'S PROVIDENCE AND ABRAHAM'S VIRTUE. CHRYSOSTOM: Let us not rush idly by this reading but rather recognize clearly the precision of sacred Scripture in recounting nothing to us as of no importance. "Now Abram was very rich," the text says. Consider first of all this very fact that its habit had been to convey nothing idly or to no purpose. In this case is it not without reason that [the text] calls him rich. Nowhere else had it made mention of his being rich—this was the first time. Why, and to what purpose? For you to learn the inventiveness of God's wisdom and providence displayed in favor of the great man, as well as his boundless and extraordinary power. The man who had gone into exile in Egypt under the pressure of famine, unable to sustain the privations of Canaan, suddenly became rich—and not just rich but very rich, not only in cattle but also in silver and gold. Do you not see the extent of God's providence? Abraham left to find relief from famine and came back not simply enjoying relief from famine but invested with great wealth and untold reputation, his identity well known to everyone. Now the inhabitants of Canaan gained a more precise idea of the good man's virtue by seeing this sudden transformation that had taken place—the stranger who had gone down into Egypt as a refugee and vagabond now flush with so much wealth. HOMILIES ON GENESIS 33.4-5.[6]

13:3 Abraham Calls on the Lord

A LOVER OF PEACE AND QUIET. CHRYSOSTOM: Consider, I ask you, how he was a lover of peace and quiet and was constantly attentive to divine worship. The text says, remember, that he went

---

[2]CSEL 32 1:578. [3]Ps 12:6 (11:7 LXX). [4]1 Cor 13:13. [5]CSEL 32 1:578-79. [6]FC 82:278-79*.

down to that place where he had previously built the altar. By calling on the name of God he right from the very beginning fulfilled in anticipation that saying of David, "I would rather be of no account in the house of my God than take up residence in sinners' dwellings."[7] In other words, solitude turned out to be preferred by him for invoking the name of God, instead of the cities. After all, he well knew that cities' greatness is not constituted by multitude of inhabitants but by the virtue of its residents. Hence too the desert proved to be more desirable than the cities, adorned as it was by the just man's virtue and thus a more resplendent vision than the whole world. HOMILIES ON GENESIS 33.5.[8]

13:5 Lot's Flocks, Herds and Tents

LOT LACKS ABRAHAM'S SPIRITUAL RICHES. AMBROSE: It remains to be seen if Lot too, his nephew, was rich as one who belonged to the same family. But Scripture says only that he had many cattle. In fact, the text reads, "Lot also, who went with Abraham, had flocks, herds and tents." He had no silver, because he was not yet just; in fact, "the tongue of the just man is like silver purified by fire."[9] He had no gold, which was the possession of the one who saw the posterity of Christ, of whom it is written: "And his posterity shines like gold."[10] Abraham saw him, as the Lord testified when he said, "Abraham saw my day and rejoiced."[11] This is why he deserved to shine like gold and to have gold as his endowment. ON ABRAHAM 2.5.24.[12]

WHY LOT WENT WITH ABRAHAM. AMBROSE: It is impossible for me to omit here a discussion of a question that has stumped even the more learned, namely, why the text is worded this way: "Lot also, who went with Abraham," as though we were to understand that there was another Lot who did not go with him. And many believe the problem is as yet unresolved. So to satisfy these and at the same time to abide by the rule of Scripture, we would say that there is one person

who takes on two roles, that in one and the same individual two things are signified. Numerically Lot is a single individual; virtually he is two. In fact, Lot, according to the Latin interpretation, means *declinatio* ("a deviation"). But one can deviate either from the good or from the bad. So when Lot deviated from the bad, that is, from error, from base and criminal behavior, he was joined to his uncle. When he deviated from the good, that is, from what is just, innocent, holy and sacred, he was joined to baseness. This is why it says, "now Lot too, who accompanied Abraham," because he had not yet chosen Sodom, and he was not dwelling among those who are authors of evil. Thereafter he did go to live in Sodom. And so it was that he became alienated from himself; he thought of himself as of another, as of one, that is, who withdraws not only from the just man but even from himself. ON ABRAHAM 2.6.25.[13]

13:6 Great Possessions

NO SPACE LARGE ENOUGH. AMBROSE: In fact, since [Lot] had already deliberately begun to deviate from his uncle, the land could not support both of them dwelling together; indeed, no space can be large enough for those who love discord. . . . Even limited spaces are more than adequate for those who are meek and peace-loving, while for those whose mentality is one of discord even wide open spaces are too restricted. ON ABRAHAM 2.6.24.[14]

13:7 Arguments Between the Herdsmen

THE SOURCE OF ALL PROBLEMS. CHRYSOSTOM: Notice how the abundance of their possessions proved to be a major cause for their separation, creating a division, sundering their harmony and undoing the bond of kinship. "Trouble developed

---

[7]Ps 84:10 (83:11 LXX). [8]FC 82:279. [9]Prov 10:20. [10]Ps 68:13 (67:14 LXX). [11]Jn 8:56. [12]CSEL 32 1:581. [13]CSEL 32 1:581-82. [14]CSEL 32 1:581.

between Abram's herdsmen and Lot's herdsmen. Now the Canaanites and the Pherezites inhabited the land at that time." Notice how the relatives are responsible for the first signs of separation. Invariably this is the source from which springs all sorts of problems—discord among the brethren. The text says, remember, "Trouble developed between the herdsmen." They are the ones who provide the occasion for separation, who sunder the harmony, who give evidence of bad feeling. HOMILIES ON GENESIS 33.6.[15]

CATTLE TYPIFY THE IRRATIONAL SENSES.
AMBROSE: Let us now consider who are the shepherds, and what living creatures they shepherd and what was the nature of the dispute between the shepherds of Abraham and those of Lot. Shepherds are those who govern the flocks. They are diligent and wise when they do not allow their animals to trample the farmlands with their feet or to damage the crops with their teeth. [They are] negligent and lazy when they do not invite their cattle to pasture on grassy fields rather than in planted areas but allow them to wander freely through the various garden crops. These shepherds then should be watchfully attentive so that what has happened through the carelessness of the negligent be not attributed to the diligent. But since we are here not speaking of visible things, let us first of all consider what kind of animal they have to shepherd. We can supply a definition of these shepherds: "they are shepherds of cattle," says the text. Now cattle, as we have said, signify the irrational senses of the body. Who then are the shepherds of the senses, if not their masters and, in a certain sense, their rulers and guides, that is to say, the monitors of a certain way of speaking or the thoughts of our mind? If these are expert and constant in the pastoral exercise, they do not permit the flock of the senses to wander off and to stop to graze in useless or positively harmful pastures, but with wise leadership they call them back and apply the brakes of reason to block their activity when they rebel. But the bad leaders or useless disputes allow the cattle to be carried away by their own impulsiveness, to run toward the precipice, to trample on planted fields and to feed on their produce, so much so that if at present there are still fruits of virtue to be found, they destroy even these. ON ABRAHAM 2.6.27.[16]

---

[15]FC 82:280*. [16]CSEL 32 1:583-84.

13:8-13 ABRAHAM AND LOT SEPARATE

[8]Then Abram said to Lot, "Let there be no strife between you and me, and between your herdsmen and my herdsmen; for we are kinsmen. [9]Is not the whole land before you? Separate yourself from me. If you take the left hand, then I will go to the right; or if you take the right hand, then I will go to the left." [10]And Lot lifted up his eyes, and saw that the Jordan valley was well watered everywhere like the garden of the LORD, like the land of Egypt, in the direction of Zoar; this was before the LORD destroyed Sodom and Gomorrah. [11]So Lot chose for himself all the Jordan valley, and Lot journeyed east; thus they separated from each other. [12]Abram dwelt in the land of Canaan, while Lot dwelt among the cities of the valley and moved his tent as far as Sodom. [13]Now the men of Sodom were wicked, great sinners against the LORD.

OVERVIEW: The decision of Abraham and Lot to separate shows evidence of Abraham's desire to preserve harmony. At the same time the story shows that riches are a cause of strife. On an allegorical level of interpretation, the story is about the preservation of harmony within the individual soul, between the rational part of the soul and the irrational part, the senses (AMBROSE). The story also reveals the extraordinary humility of Abraham (CHRYSOSTOM). Lot, whose name can be interpreted to mean "deviation," is shown to be insolent and one who chooses according to appearances. The mention of the wickedness of the men of Sodom provides the occasion to note that God judges not according to appearances or as people judge but according to the inner conscience (AMBROSE). It also reveals that Lot chose according to his desire for riches rather than uprightness (CHRYSOSTOM).

13:8 No Strife

THE PRESERVATION OF HARMONY. AMBROSE: Rightly, then, devotion has claimed first place for itself. Let us consider now also the adornment of the other virtues. Holy Abraham enjoyed the presence of his nephew, to whom he showed fatherly affection. A conflict occurred between the servants of the nephew and those of the uncle. As a truly wise man Abraham was aware that disagreements among servants often break the peace among their masters. He broke the thread of discord so that the contagion might not spread. He thought it preferable that the two separate than that good harmony among them be broken. This is what you should do whenever you find yourself in a similar situation, to forestall a hotbed of discord. In fact, you are not stronger than Abraham. He thought it best to withdraw from the servants' disputes, not to treat them with contempt. And if you are strong enough, take care lest someone weaker than you gives ear to the whisperings of the servants. It often happens that by their undivided service they sow discord among relatives. Better it is to separate from each other so that

friendship might remain. When two cannot live together in a house with common property, is it not better graciously to withdraw than to live together in discord? ON ABRAHAM 1.3.10.[1]

RICHES THE CAUSE OF STRIFE. AMBROSE: Abraham made the division, because "the territory"—says Scripture—"was insufficient to contain them both," because they were too rich. It is a worldly vice that land is always insufficient for the rich. Nothing satisfies the greed of the rich. The richer one is, the more greedily one desires possessions. The rich man is eager to extend the boundaries of his field, to exclude his neighbor. Is this what Abraham was like? Not at all, although at the beginning he too was imperfect. For where could perfection have come from before the coming of Christ? He had not yet come who was to say, "If you will be perfect, go, sell everything you possess and give it to the poor and come follow me."[2] However, Abraham offers the choice, quite unlike what a greedy person would do. Like a just man he forestalls strife. ON ABRAHAM 1.3.12.[3]

PRESERVING INTERIOR HARMONY. AMBROSE: "Let there be no strife," he says, "between you and me and between your herdsmen and my herdsmen; for we are human beings and brothers." We have seen that Abraham is Lot's uncle and Lot is his nephew. Why then does he call him brother? Notice that the motives invoked by the wise man are those of concord. For this reason he first speaks of their common humanity as "human beings." All human beings are children of a single nature, conceived deep within the inward parts, nourished and brought into this world by one womb. For this reason we are bound to one another by a certain family law, like brothers, begotten of one father and borne into this world by one mother, like uterine brothers. And so, since we are the offspring of a rational nature, we should love one another with a mutual love like brothers and not be fighting with one another and perse-

---

[1]CSEL 32 1:509-10. [2]Mt 19:21. [3]CSEL 32 1:510-11.

cuting one another. But much more properly the term *brothers* refers to the soul which is one, the soul whose rational dimension is joined, as we said above, to the senses of the irrational, but being the rational part it is also united to the virtues. For this reason the vices and the virtues of a person are united by fraternal necessity. In fact, the vices are carnal; the virtues belong to the rational soul. But the flesh and the soul, which are the human components, are united as it were by conjugal law. Humanity therefore must make a treaty of sorts between its component parts and impose a peace on them, as it were. But no one is endowed with such great power as to conquer the flesh. And for this reason came "our peace, who has made us both one and has broken down the dividing wall of hostility, by abolishing in his flesh the law of commandments and ordinances, that he might create in himself one new man in place of two, so making peace, and might reconcile us both to God in one body through the cross, thereby bringing hostility to an end."[4] Rightly then the apostle described himself as "*homo infelix*,"[5] because he had to endure such a great war within himself, the flames of which he was unable to extinguish. Indeed, Solomon, speaking only of one small part of the passions, namely, anger, says, "The wise man is better than the strong, and he who rules his spirit than he who takes a city."[6] Happy then is one who escapes from this war, who is no longer a stranger and a pilgrim but a fellow citizen of the saints and member of the household of God, who though still on earth is not battered by things of the earth. ON ABRAHAM 2.6.28.[7]

THE EXTRAORDINARY DEGREE OF ABRAHAM'S HUMILITY. CHRYSOSTOM: See the extraordinary degree of his humility; see the height of his wisdom. The elder, the senior, addresses his junior and calls his nephew "brother," admits him to the same rank as himself and retains no special distinction for himself. Instead, he says, "Let there be no trouble between you and me, nor between my herdsmen and yours." Nor would it be proper,

after all, for this to happen, he says, since we are brothers. Do you see him fulfilling the apostolic law, which says, "Already, then, the verdict has completely gone against you for having lawsuits with one another. Why not rather suffer wrong? Why not rather be defrauded? Instead, you do wrong and defraud, and this to your own brothers."[8] All these admonitions the patriarch observes in fact by saying, "Let there be no trouble between my herdsmen and your herdsmen, because we are brothers." What could be more peace-loving than such a spirit as this? It wasn't idly, of course, or to no purpose that I mentioned at the outset that his reason for preferring solitude to the whole civilized world was a love for peace and quiet. See him in this case too, when he noticed the herdsmen completely at odds, how right from the beginning he tried to quench the fire that threatened to break out and put a stop to the rivalry. You see, it was important for him in his role of teacher of wisdom sent to the inhabitants of Palestine, far from providing any bad example or offering any encouragement, rather to give them all the clearer instruction through the clarion call of his restraint in manners and to convert them into imitators of his own virtue. HOMILIES ON GENESIS 33.7.[9]

THE JUST PERSON HANDLES EVERYTHING WITH RESTRAINT. CHRYSOSTOM: Notice how he addresses Lot on terms of equality—and yet I have the impression that the outbreak of trouble had no other origin than in the refusal of the patriarch's herdsmen to allow Lot to enjoy the same privileges as they. The just man, however, handles everything with restraint, demonstrating the remarkable degree of his own good sense and teaching not only those present at the time but also every one in the future never to settle their differences with our relatives by feuding. Their squabbling brings great disgrace on us, and instead of trouble being attributed to them, the blame re-

---

[4]Eph 2:14-16. [5]An unhappy person. [6]Prov 16:32. [7]CSEL 32 1:584-86. [8]1 Cor 6:7-8. [9]FC 82:280-81.

verts to us. So what fittingness could there be for brothers, sharing in fact the same nature, the same links of kinship and due at that point to dwell near to each other, to engage in hostilities when it was expected of them to play the role of teaching all these people restraint, gentleness and complete good sense? Let people who believe they are above such reproach give heed to this example when on the grounds of relationship they connive at their relatives' larceny, rapacity, scheming beyond measure, in the city and in the country, confiscation of one person's farm and another's home, and on that basis they show such scoundrels even greater favor. HOMILIES ON GENESIS 33.8.[10]

13:10 Lot Sees a Fertile Valley

LOT WAS RATHER INSOLENT. AMBROSE: Haughtiness is the companion of those who deviate from the truth. In fact, as Abraham was quite humble in that he offered the choice, so Lot was rather insolent in presuming to choose. Virtue humbles itself, whereas wickedness becomes arrogant. Lot should rather have relied on one more wise than he, to be on the safe side. Indeed, he did not have the knowledge to make a choice. ON ABRAHAM 2.6.33.[11]

13:11 Lot Chose for Himself

CHOOSE THAT WHICH IS TRULY BETTER. AMBROSE: How appropriately then Scripture says, "Lot," that is, deviation, "chose for himself." Indeed, God has placed before us good and evil, so that each may choose what he wishes. Let us not then choose that which is more pleasing at first sight but that which is truly better, so that, having been granted the ability to choose what is preferable, we lift up our eyes and be attracted by false beauty while we leave concealed the truth of nature, as one who looks the other way. ON ABRAHAM 2.6.35.[12]

13:13 The People of Sodom Were Wicked

GOD EXAMINES THE CONSCIENCE OF THE MIND. AMBROSE: But the fact that "the men of Sodom were wicked, great sinners in the sight of the Lord" is not a matter of minor importance, in terms of the way God deals with human beings. Rather, its aim is to help us understand that the harsh gravity of sin can compel a gentle God to retaliate. The reason Abraham was unable to obtain pardon for the Sodomites through his prayer is that their malice was beyond all measure. There are many people who the more wicked they are the more sheltered and secure they seem to be. They find ways of escaping human detection, where things are done without supervision or where a just person is indicted through false testimony. The just person remains just before God, even if others condemn him. God does not look at the outcome of trials or judicial actions based on unjust machinations but observes matters in their naked reality. In human trials, however, the error of false opinion often obstructs the force of truth. Susanna remained exceedingly chaste in God's eyes, even when she was convicted of adultery, because God did not make a finding of fact based on the assertions of lying witnesses but directly examined the inner conscience of the mind. ON ABRAHAM 2.6.36.[13]

THE SUMMIT OF BLESSINGS IS UPRIGHTNESS. CHRYSOSTOM: Do you observe Lot having regard only for the nature of the land and not considering the wickedness of the inhabitants? What good, after all, is fertility of land and abundance of produce when the inhabitants are evil in their ways? By contrast, what harm could come from solitude and a simple lifestyle when the inhabitants are more restrained? The summit of blessings, you see, is the uprightness of those who dwell in a place. Lot, however, had eyes for one thing only, the richness of the countryside. Hence Scripture desires to indicate to us the wickedness of those who dwelt there in the words "Now the people of Sodom were very wicked sinners in God's sight." They were not

---

[10]FC 82:281-82 [11]CSEL 32 1:590. [12]CSEL 32 1:591. [13]CSEL 32 1:591-92.

merely "wicked" but also "sinners," and not simply "sinners" but also "in God's sight." That is, the extent of their sins was extreme, and their wickedness superabounded—hence it added as well, "very wicked in God's sight." Do you see the extremity of the evil? Do you see how great an evil it is to usurp pride of place and not to consider what is for the common good? Do you see what a great thing is deference, ceding pride of place, taking second

place? Take note, in fact: As the instruction develops we shall see that the one who took the pick of the best places gained no advantage from it, whereas he who chose the lesser became more resplendent day by day, and, with his wealth increasing, he became the attraction of all eyes. HOMILIES ON GENESIS 33.15.[14]

---

[14]FC 82:286-87.

13:14-18 ABRAHAM MOVES TO HEBRON

[14]The LORD said to Abram, after Lot had separated from him, "Lift up your eyes, and look from the place where you are, northward and southward and eastward and westward; [15]for all the land which you see I will give to you and to your descendants for ever. [16]I will make your descendants as the dust of the earth; so that if one can count the dust of the earth, your descendants also can be counted. [17]Arise, walk through the length and the breadth of the land, for I will give it to you." [18]So Abram moved his tent, and came and dwelt by the oaks[s] of Mamre, which are at Hebron; and there he built an altar to the LORD.

s Or terebinths

OVERVIEW: Continuing the allegorical interpretation of Abraham, the departure of Lot and the promise of the land reveal the progress of the soul embodied in the Stoic maxim that "everything belongs to the wise man" (AMBROSE). The promise of the land is also interpreted as a reward for Abraham's humility. The promise of descendants as numerous as the grains of sand served to increase Abraham's trust in God, since it surpassed all human power (CHRYSOSTOM). The promise includes not only the Israelites born of the flesh but also the Christians born of the Spirit (AUGUSTINE). Abraham's movements from place to place like a stranger or a pilgrim revealed his good sense and God-fearing attitude (CHRYSOSTOM).

13:14 *Look Around You*

THE WISE AND FAITHFUL POSSESS ALL THINGS. AMBROSE: There follows a passage that clearly teaches us how fast the soul progresses once the excesses of the irrational parts have been eliminated and how much evil is produced by an accumulation of vices. Not without reason did Scripture put it this way: "And God said to Abraham, after Lot had separated from him: 'Lift up your eyes and look from the place where you are, northward and southward and eastward and westward: for all the land which you see I will give to you and to your descendants for ever.'" This text is the source from which the Stoic philosophers drew one of their doctrinal maxims: that everything belongs to the wise man. Indeed, north, south, east and west are the parts of the universe: they encompass the entire world. And when God promises that he will give all of this to Abraham, what else is he saying than that the wise and faithful man possesses all things, lacks nothing at all? For which reason Solomon also says in Proverbs, "The whole world of riches belongs to him who is faithful."[1] How much earlier did Solomon live than Zeno the teacher and founder of the Stoic school itself! How much earlier was he than Plato, the very father of philosophy, or Pythagoras, who invented the term *philosophy*. But who is the faithful person if not one who is wise? For "the fool changes like the moon,"[2] but the wise person remains unchanging in faith. ON ABRAHAM 2.7.37.[3]

GOD REWARDS ABRAHAM'S HUMILITY. CHRYSOSTOM: See the promptness of God's providential recompense demonstrated in favor of the good man. Sacred Scripture wants to teach us the extent of the reimbursement the patriarch was accorded for such humility from the loving God. And so after saying that Lot took his leave and went off to the land he had selected on the score of its beauty, [Scripture] immediately added, "The Lord God said to Abram." Then, for our precise realization that he said this by way of rewarding him for what had been done for Lot, it added, "God said to Abram after Lot's parting with him," as if to say the following words to him without demur: You ceded the beautiful region to your nephew on account of your great restraint and thus gave evidence of your eminent humility and showed such concern for peace as to put up with anything for the sake of preventing any rivalry coming between you—accept from me a generous reward. HOMILIES ON GENESIS 34.5.[4]

13:16 Descendants Beyond Number

TRUSTING IN THE POWER OF GOD. CHRYSOSTOM: Then, in case Abraham should have regard only to his own condition, his advanced years and Sarah's sterility, and thus lose confidence in the promise instead of trusting in the power of the One making the promise, he said, "I will make

your descendants as numerous as all the grains of sand in the world. If anyone can number the grains of sand in the world, your descendants too will be numbered." No doubt the promise went beyond human nature. Not only did he promise to make him a father despite so many impediments but also to extend the gift to such a multitude as to be compared with all the grains of sand in the world, and the multitude to be beyond number, wishing as he did to demonstrate the extent of the remarkable increase by the comparison. HOMILIES ON GENESIS 34.10.[5]

THE PROMISE INCLUDES CHRISTIANS. AUGUSTINE: Truly that multitude which was promised to Abraham is not innumerable to God, although it is to the human mind. But to God not even the dust of the earth is so. Further, the promise here made may be understood not only of the nation of Israel but of the whole seed of Abraham, which may be fitly compared with the dust for its multitude. Regarding this seed, there is also the promise of many children, not according to the flesh but according to the spirit. However, the reason why I said that this is not clear from the text is that even the multitude of the one people sprung from Abraham, according to the flesh, through his grandson Jacob, has increased so greatly as to fill almost every region of the world. It is because even the number of this progeny is beyond human power to count that it may, by a hyperbole, be compared with the number of dust particles. What is beyond doubt is that the only land meant is that which is called Canaan. However, some may find a difficulty in the expression "I will give to you and your posterity forever," if the "forever" is taken to mean "eternally." There is no trouble if only they will take this "forever" to mean "to the end of time," which, as we hold on faith, is to be the beginning of eternity. For although the Israelites are expelled from Jerusalem, they still remain in other cities in the land of Canaan and shall re-

---

[1]Prov 17:6. [2]Sir 27:11. [3]CSEL 32 1:592-93. [4]FC 82:292. [5]FC 82:295.

main even to the end. And even when that whole land is inhabited by Christians, they also are the very seed of Abraham. City of God 16.21.[6]

13:18 The Oaks of Mamre

Like a Stranger or a Pilgrim. Chrysostom: Wonderful the extent of the promise; remarkable the depth of generosity of the Lord of us all; extraordinary the degree of the reward conferred by him in his mercy and love on this blessed man and on the descendants destined to be born to him! Hearing this, and amazed at God's unspeakable goodness, the patriarch "struck camp and moved on until settling at the oak of Mamre, which is at Hebron." After accepting the promise . . . and following Lot's parting, he changed his campsite to the vicinity of the oak of Mamre. Notice his sensible attitude, his high sense of responsibility in effecting the transfer with ease and making no difficulty of changing from place to place. You will not find him shackled and hidebound by any custom, something that frequently affects a great number of people, even those considered wise and those generally free of concerns. If the occasion should require them to change and move in a different direction, even in many cases for a spiritual matter, you would find many of them troubled, beside themselves, regretting the change on account of their being prisoners of habit. The just man, on the other hand, wasn't like that. He showed good sense from the very outset. Like a stranger or a pilgrim he moved from here to there and from there to the next place. And in all cases his concern was to give evidence of his God-fearing attitude in his actions. Homilies on Genesis 34.12.[7]

---

[6]FC 14:525-26*; NPNF 1 2:322-23. [7]FC 82:297*.

14:1-12 THE CAMPAIGN OF THE FOUR KINGS

[1]In the days of Amraphel king of Shinar, Arioch king of Ellasar, Ched-or-laomer king of Elam, and Tidal king of Goiim, [2]these kings made war with Bera king of Sodom, Birsha king of Gomorrah, Shinab king of Admah, Shemeber king of Zeboiim, and the king of Bela (that is, Zoar). [3]And all these joined forces in the Valley of Siddim (that is, the Salt Sea). [4]Twelve years they had served Ched-or-laomer, but in the thirteenth year they rebelled. [5]In the fourteenth year Ched-or-laomer and the kings who were with him came and subdued the Rephaim in Ashteroth-karnaim, the Zuzim in Ham, the Emim in Shaveh-kiriathaim, [6]and the Horites in their Mount Seir as far as El-paran on the border of the wilderness; [7]then they turned back and came to Enmishpat (that is, Kadesh), and subdued all the country of the Amalekites, and also the Amorites who dwelt in Hazazon-tamar. [8]Then the king of Sodom, the king of Gomorrah, the king of Admah, the king of Zeboiim, and the king of Bela (that is, Zoar) went out, and they joined battle in the Valley of Siddim [9]with Ched-or-laomer king of Elam, Tidal king of Goiim, Amraphel king of Shinar, and Arioch king of Ellasar, four kings against five. [10]Now the Valley of Siddim was full of bitumen pits; and as the kings of Sodom and Gomorrah fled, some fell into them, and the rest fled to the mountain. [11]So the enemy took all the goods of Sodom and Gomorrah, and all their provisions, and went

their way; ¹²they also took Lot, the son of Abram's brother, who dwelt in Sodom, and his goods, and departed.

OVERVIEW: The account is not without value but gives an example of valor and prepares the way for the account that follows showing God's power and the patriarch's virtue (CHRYSOSTOM). On the allegorical level, the five kings represent our five bodily senses, and the four kings are the seductions of the body and of the world (AMBROSE). Lot learns from his capture not to set his heart on the better material things and what a great good is harmony (CHRYSOSTOM).

14:8 The Battle in the Valley of Siddim

AN EXAMPLE OF VALOR. CHRYSOSTOM: Let us not idly pass these words by, dearly beloved, or consider the account to be of no value. It was of set purpose that sacred Scripture recounted everything to us with precision so that we should learn the might of these barbarians and the degree of valor they displayed and with how much ferocity they involved themselves in war so as to clash even with the giants—that is, men powerful in bodily stature—and put to flight all the peoples dwelling there. You see, just as a swollen torrent sweeps away everything in its path and destroys it, in the same way the barbarians fell on these peoples and destroyed them completely with the result that they put to flight the rulers of the Amalekites and all the others. But perhaps someone may say, "What good is it for me to know about the might of the barbarians?" It was not idly or to no purpose that Scripture mixed these matters in with its account. Nor is it without point that we are now bringing it to your attention and directing you in turn to recall their valor. Rather, our purpose is that from the ensuing instruction you may learn the extraordinary degree of God's power and also the patriarch's virtue. HOMILIES ON GENESIS 35.9.[1]

THE FIVE KINGS ARE OUR FIVE BODILY

SENSES. AMBROSE: We have seen now the progress of the noble mind, which, finding itself in perilous deviation from the path of virtue, immediately arose to search for the reward of wisdom, the inheritance of justice. The readings that follow will show how harmful are the vices connected with frivolity. For those four kings who defeated the five kings and took captive the whole cavalry of the Sodomites captured Lot the son of Abraham's brother as well and went on their way. The five kings are our five bodily senses: sight, smell, taste, touch and hearing. The four kings are the seductions of the body and of the world, because human flesh and the world are composed of four elements. Rightly are they called kings, because sin has a sovereignty of its own, has its own great kingdom. For this reason, the apostle says, "Let not sin reign in your mortal body."[2] Our senses, then, easily yield to the pleasures of the body and of the world and become as it were subject to their dominion. Indeed, the pleasures of the body and the seductions of the world are conquered only by a mind that is spiritual, that clings to God and separates itself totally from earthly things—for every perversion is subjection to these allurements. Hence John says, "Woe to the inhabitants of the world!"[3] He was certainly not referring to every human being living on earth at that time—for there are those who live on earth but whose citizenship is in heaven—but rather to those who had been overcome by attachment to this earthly citizenship and the seduction of the world. We are not then inhabitants of this world but pilgrims. Pilgrims live in hope of finding a temporary lodging, but inhabitants seem to place every hope and every use of their goods where they believe they are living by right. Thus one who is a pilgrim on earth is an inhabitant of heaven, but the inhabitant of earth is an owner of death. ON ABRAHAM 2.7.41.[4]

[1]FC 82:310. [2]Rom 6:12. [3]Rev 8:13. [4]CSEL 32 1:595-97.

14:12 *Lot's Capture*

DIVISION IS A GREAT EVIL. CHRYSOSTOM: Notice that what I said yesterday has come to be true, that Lot, far from being better off for his choice of the better parts, rather had learned from experience not to set his heart on the better parts. You see, not only did no benefit come to him from it, but indeed he was even led away into captivity. He learned the lesson through experience that it was much better for him to enjoy the just man's company than to be parted from him and undergo these great trials even if living independently. I mean, he parted from the patriarch and thought he enjoyed greater independence, had the good fortune to enjoy the better parts and experience great prosperity—and all of a sudden he becomes a captive, dispossessed, without hearth or home. The purpose was for you to learn what a great evil division is and what a great good harmony is, and that we ought not hanker after pride of place but love to take second place instead. "Now, they seized Lot and his accoutrements," the text says, remember. How much better was it to be in the company of the patriarch and accept everything for the sake of not sundering the mutual harmony than be separated and while choosing the better parts be immediately beset with such awful perils and fall into the clutches of barbarians? HOMILIES ON GENESIS 35.11.[5]

---

[5]FC 82:311.

14:13-16 ABRAHAM RESCUES LOT

[13]*Then one who had escaped came, and told Abram the Hebrew, who was living by the oaks[s] of Mamre the Amorite, brother of Eshcol and of Aner; these were allies of Abram.* [14]*When Abram heard that his kinsman had been taken captive, he led forth his trained men, born in his house, three hundred and eighteen of them, and went in pursuit as far as Dan.* [15]*And he divided his forces against them by night, he and his servants, and routed them and pursued them to Hobah, north of Damascus.* [16]*Then he brought back all the goods, and also brought back his kinsman Lot with his goods, and the women and the people.*

s Or *terebinths*

OVERVIEW: The name used to describe Abraham ("the traveler") shows God's loving kindness, foretelling events to happen a long time later (CHRYSOSTOM). Even the number of men (318) has a symbolic value, pointing prefiguratively by a numerological analysis to those whom he judged worthy to belong to the number of the faithful who were to believe in the passion of our Lord Jesus (AMBROSE). The patriarch prevailed against the enemy not by physical strength but through faith in God (CHRYSOSTOM). Abraham prefigures the trained mind that marches into battle against the passions with the cross of Christ and in the name of Jesus. The rout of the enemy and pursuit as far as Hobah also reveal the triumph of the trained mind (AMBROSE). The recovery of Lot shows that Abraham won the victory with aid from on high (CHRYSOSTOM).

14:13 Abraham's Allies

GOD FORETELLS EVENTS DUE TO HAPPEN A LONG TIME LATER. CHRYSOSTOM: How was it that the patriarch had no knowledge that such forces of war were on the rampage? Perhaps he chanced to be at a great distance from the conflict and for that reason knew nothing of it. "Now, someone came and told Abraham the traveler,"[1] the text says, to remind us that he got the news on his return from Chaldea. You see, because he had his camp across the Euphrates, consequently he was described also as traveler. Right from the outset his parents gave him this name, suggesting to him ahead of time his movement from there. In other words, he was also called Abram because he would one day cross the Euphrates and enter Palestine. Notice how his parents, all unaware, and unbelievers to boot, gave the child the name under the influence of God's inventive wisdom, as was also the case when Lamech gave Noah his name. This, after all, is a characteristic of God's loving kindness, oftentimes to foretell—even through unbelievers—of events due to happen a long time later. So, the text says, someone came and told the traveler what had happened, the capture of his nephew, the great power of those kings, the sack of Sodom and the shameful flight. "Now, he was camped near the oak of Mamre the Amorite, brother of Eschol and Aunan, who were confederates of Abram." Perhaps at this point, however, someone might wonder, why was it that the just man Lot, alone of the fugitives from Sodom, was taken into captivity? Far from occurring idly or to no purpose, this was for Lot to learn through the events themselves the patriarch's virtue, and that others might also be saved, and that he might learn not to hanker after pride of place but yield to his elders. HOMILIES ON GENESIS 35.12.[2]

14:14 Abraham Pursues the Kings

THE VALUE OF ELECTION. AMBROSE: "When Abraham learned of this, he counted his servants born in the house" and with 318 men won a victory and liberated his nephew. This shows that the separation had taken place in friendship, since Abraham's love for his nephew was so great that he was willing to confront even the dangers of war on his behalf. What does it mean "he counted"? It means he "chose." So too what Jesus said in the Gospel refers not only to the knowledge of God but also to the grace of the just: "Even the hairs on your head are all counted."[3] Indeed, "the Lord knows those who are his,"[4] but those who are not his he does not deign to know. Abraham, then, counted 318 men. You should understand that it is not numerical quantity that is here expressed but the value of their election. He chose, in fact, those whom he judged worthy to belong to the number of the faithful who were to believe in the passion of our Lord Jesus Christ. Indeed, the letter T in Greek means "three hundred," and the sum IH—ten plus eight—expresses the name of Jesus.[5] So Abraham conquered in virtue of faith, not through the strength of a numerous army. And so it was that with no more than a few house servants he triumphed over those who had defeated the armies of five kings. ON ABRAHAM 1.3.15.[6]

THE PATRIARCH PREVAILED THROUGH FAITH. CHRYSOSTOM: Consider in this case, I ask you, dearly beloved, the greatness of heart exemplified in the just man's virtue. Trusting in the power of God, he was not cowed by the force of the enemy when he learned of the rout they had caused, first by falling upon all the tribes and prevailing against the Amalekites and all the others, and then by engaging the Sodomites, putting them to flight and seizing all their property. The reason,

---

[1]Chrysostom is commenting on the Greek translation, which had rendered the Hebrew root with a word meaning "emigrant" or "traveler." [2]FC 82:312*. [3]Lk 12:7. [4]2 Tim 2:19. [5]This symbolic interpretation of the number 318 is first found in the *Epistle of Barnabas* 9.7-9. In Greek, which expresses numerals by letters, 318 is TIH. IH in Greek are the first letters of the word *Jesus*. The Greek symbol for 300 is T. The number 318 in fact comes from Genesis 14:14; see Clement of Alexandria *Stromateis* 6.85. [6]CSEL 32 1:512-13.

you see, why sacred Scripture described all this to us ahead of time, as well as all they achieved through their bravery, was that you might learn that the patriarch prevailed against them not by physical strength but through faith in God. [He] achieved all this under the protection of help from on high, not by wielding weapons and arrows and spears or by drawing bows or raising shields but with a few retainers of his own household. Homilies on Genesis 35.14.[7]

14:15 Abraham Divides His Forces

The Victory Prefigures the Cross. Ambrose: "Abraham counted 318 servants, born in his house . . . as far as Hobah, which is to the right of Damascus." Even the number is of vital importance. For in that number there is life, if we believe in the passion in the name of the Lord Jesus. In fact, this is the interpretation of the above-mentioned name, Hobah, that is, "life." Appropriately too it is said that Hobah is located to the right of Damascus. For the sheep stand on the right, while the goats are on the left. The trained mind knows how many soldiers to choose to finish the battle, with what arms to supply them, with what banners to lead them. It does not lead its forces with images of eagles or dragons, but it marches into battle with the cross of Christ and in the name of Jesus, deriving courage from this sign, loyal to this banner. Rightly then is that mind called trained which has received the true wisdom of the just man. And justice is quick to correct, and by admonishing it calls back sinners, it stems the assaults of the passions. On Abraham 2.7.42.[8]

14:16 Abraham Brings Back Lot

Victory with Aid from On High. Chrysostom: Why was it, someone may ask, that he called up retainers of his own household to the number of 318? For you to learn that he did not simply take everyone but only retainers of his own household, men raised by Lot, so that they might wreak their vengeance with much relish, like men entering this conflict for their own lord. "He fell upon them by night," the text says, "himself and his retainers, and continued to strike and pursue them." It was, you see, a hand from on high that joined in the attack and assisted in directing the battle. Hence they had no need of weapons or fighting machines. Instead, he had only to heave into sight with his retainers to smite some and cause others to take to flight, doing both in complete security without harassment from anyone. And he recovered the cavalry of the king of Sodom, his nephew Lot, all his accoutrements and the women. Do you see why it was permitted that while the others fled Lot alone should be taken captive? For two reasons: so that the patriarch's virtue should become manifest and that on his account many others also might find deliverance. Then he returns bearing a great prize of distinction, Lot, and parading as well as him the cavalry, women and accoutrements. [He] announces in a clear voice and proclaims more loudly than any trumpet that it was not by human power nor by force of numbers that he had won the prize and achieved victory but had done everything with aid from on high. Homilies on Genesis 35.15.[9]

The Vital Goods of the Soul. Ambrose: "Abraham also recovered the goods." . . . This certainly does not refer to patrimony but to the vital goods of the soul, where the truly valuable riches—not straw, not hay—are to be found, where there is a reliable splendor of eloquence that contains the substance of our hope. These are indeed our true goods, that is, wisdom that abounds in riches; these are the goods that do not perish. Bodily enjoyment and the use of external goods, on the other hand, are of short, not of long, duration. This is why some people rightly regard it as improper to speak of inherited substance. In fact, inheritance is not the basis of our subsistence, since even people who lack money do not, however, lack the substance of life. On Abraham 2.7.44.[10]

---

[7]FC 82:313-14. [8]CSEL 32 1:597. [9]FC 82:314. [10]CSEL 32 1:598.

14:17-24 MELCHIZEDEK BLESSES ABRAHAM

[17]*After his return from the defeat of Ched-or-laomer and the kings who were with him, the king of Sodom went out to meet him at the Valley of Shaveh (that is, the King's Valley).* [18]*And Melchizedek king of Salem brought out bread and wine; he was priest of God Most High.* [19]*And he blessed him and said,*

"Blessed be Abram by God Most High,
maker of heaven and earth;
[20]*and blessed be God Most High,*
who has delivered your enemies into your hand!"

And Abram gave him a tenth of everything. [21]*And the king of Sodom said to Abram, "Give me the persons, but take the goods for yourself."* [22]*But Abram said to the king of Sodom, "I have sworn to the Lord God Most High, maker of heaven and earth,* [23]*that I would not take a thread or a sandal-thong or anything that is yours, lest you should say, 'I have made Abram rich.'* [24]*I will take nothing but what the young men have eaten, and the share of the men who went with me; let Aner, Eshcol, and Mamre take their share."*

Overview: The Christian interpretation of the story of Melchizedek begins with Hebrews 7, where Melchizedek is interpreted with the help of Psalm 110:4 as a figure of Christ the true high priest. Abraham's encounter with the king of Sodom reveals God's providence (Chrysostom). The offering of bread and wine, not mentioned by the author of Hebrews, is seen to increase the resemblance between Melchizedek and Christ (Cyprian). Melchizedek is also identified with Shem, the son of Noah, who had received the priesthood from his father (Ephrem).

Melchizedek resembles Christ in that he had no family history (Chrysostom). With Melchizedek there first appeared the sacrifice now offered by Christians (Augustine). The fact that Abraham offered tithes to Melchizedek shows that he was humble even in victory (Ambrose). Abraham's victory manifests the grace of God (Chrysostom). Abraham's refusal to take the spoils of victory shows that he has his mind set on heavenly things (Ambrose) and shows his contempt for material wealth, so as to anticipate later

apostolic teaching (Chrysostom).

14:17 The King of Sodom

Demonstrating God's Providence. Chrysostom: Do you see here in every event the just man being conspicuous and demonstrating to everyone on every occasion God's providence in his regard? Now you see him also zealous to prove a teacher of reverence for God to the Sodomites. "The king of Sodom," Scripture says, remember, "came out to meet him on his return from the defeat of Chedorlaomer and the kings with him." Notice the extent of his virtue and his enjoyment of assistance from God. The king comes out to meet this stranger, advanced in years, and shows high regard for him. He had learned, you see, that the advantage of kingship is as nothing to the person who lacks assistance from on high and that nothing could be more efficacious than God's hand raised to assist. Homilies on Genesis 35.15.[1]

---

[1]FC 82:314-15*.

14:18 *Melchizedek, King and Priest*

A Priest of the Most High God. Cyprian: Likewise, in the priest Melchizedek, we see the sacrament of the sacrifice of the Lord prefigured according to what the divine Scripture testifies and says: "And Melchizedek, the king of Salem, brought out bread and wine, for he was a priest of the most high God, and he blessed Abraham." But that Melchizedek portrayed a type of Christ, the Holy Spirit declares in the Psalms, saying in the person of the Father to the Son: "Before the day star . . . I have begotten you. . . . You are a priest forever according to the order of Melchizedek."[2] The order proceeds first from the sacrifice and then descends to Melchizedek, a priest of the most high God, because he offered bread, because he blessed Abraham. For who is more a priest of the most high God than our Lord Jesus Christ, who offered sacrifice to God the Father and offered the very same thing that Melchizedek had offered, bread and wine, that is, actually, his body and blood? Letters 63.4.[3]

This Melchizedek Is Shem. Ephrem the Syrian: This Melchizedek is Shem, who became a king due to his greatness; he was the head of fourteen nations.[4] In addition, "he was a priest." He received this from Noah, his father, through the rights of succession. Shem lived not only to the time of Abraham, as Scripture says, but even to [the time of] Jacob and Esau, the grandsons of Abraham. It was to him that Rebekah went to ask and was told, "Two nations are in your womb, and the older shall be a servant to the younger."[5] Rebekah would not have bypassed her husband, who had been delivered at the high place, or her father-in-law, to whom revelations of the divinity came continually, and gone straight to ask Melchizedek unless she had learned of his greatness from Abraham or Abraham's son. Commentary on Genesis 11.2.[6]

Melchizedek, Like Christ, Has No Fam-

ily History. Chrysostom: What is conveyed to us by this comment, "the king of Salem and priest of God the most high"? He was, for one thing, king of Salem, the text says. Blessed Paul, after all, said the same in drawing attention to him when writing to the believers among the Hebrews, calling to mind his name and his city of origin. At the same time he plumbed the significance of his name and employed some degree of etymology in saying, "Melchizedek, king of righteousness." You see, in the Hebrew language the word *Melchi* means "kingdom" and *Sedek* "righteousness." Then, moving on to the name of the city, he says, "king of peace," Salem after all meaning "peace." On the other hand, he was a priest, possibly self-appointed, this being the way with the priests of the time, you see. So in fact his peers had either accorded him the honor on account of his preeminence in age, or he had made it his business to act as a priest, like Noah, like Abel, like Abraham when they used to offer sacrifices. In a particular manner he was to prove a type of Christ. Hence Paul too understands him in this role in the words "With no father, with no mother, with no family history, lacking beginning of days and end of life, he yet resembles the Son of God and remains a priest forever."[7] How, you ask, is it possible for a person to have no father or mother and to lack beginning of days and end of life? You heard that he was a type; well, neither marvel at this nor expect everything to be found in the type. You see, he would not be a type if he were likely to contain every feature that occurs in reality. So what does the saying mean? It means this: Just as Melchizedek is said to have no father or mother on account of there being no mention of his parents and to have no family history on account of there being no history for him, so too Christ, on account of his having no mother in

---

[2]Ps 110:4 (109:4 LXX). [3]FC 51:204*. [4]This identification was present in the Jewish tradition. See *Encyclopedia Judaica* 5:225-26. Epiphanius claims (*Panarion* 55.6) that the Samaritans made the identification of Shem and Melchizedek. [5]Gen 25:22-23. [6]FC 91:151. [7]Heb 7:3.

heaven or father on earth, is said to have no family history and in fact has none. HOMILIES ON GENESIS 35.16.[8]

THE SACRIFICE NOW OFFERED TO GOD BY CHRISTIANS. AUGUSTINE: Having received this oracle of promise, Abraham migrated and remained in another place of the same land, that is, beside the oak of Mamre, which was Hebron. Then, on the invasion of Sodom, when five kings carried on war against four and Lot was taken captive with the conquered Sodomites, Abraham delivered him from the enemy, leading with him to battle 318 of his homeborn servants. [He] won the victory for the kings of Sodom but would take nothing of the spoils when offered by the king for whom he had won them. He was then openly blessed by Melchizedek, who was priest of God most high, about whom many and great things are written in the epistle that is inscribed to the Hebrews, which most say is by the apostle Paul, though some deny this. For then first appeared the sacrifice which is now offered to God by Christians in the whole wide world. Long after the event this sacrifice was said by the prophet to be fulfilled in Christ, who was yet to come in the flesh: "Thou art a priest forever after the order of Melchizedek."[9] That is to say, not after the order of Aaron, for that order was to be taken away when the things shone forth that were intimated beforehand by these shadows. CITY OF GOD 16.22.[10]

ABRAHAM BECAME MORE HUMBLE. AMBROSE: But one who is victorious should not claim the victory for himself; rather, he should attribute it to God. This is the teaching of Abraham, who became more humble, not more proud, in victory. Indeed, he offered a sacrifice and gave tithes; for this reason too, he received the blessing of Melchizedek, which means in translation "king of justice, king of peace." He was indeed the priest of the most high God. Who is the king of justice, the priest of God, but he to whom it is said, "You are a priest forever according to the order of

Melchizedek,"[11] that is, Son of God, priest of the Father, the one who through the sacrifice of his body propitiated the Father for our transgressions? ON ABRAHAM 1.3.16.[12]

14:19-20 Blessed by God

WITHOUT GRACE ABRAHAM COULD NOT HAVE PREVAILED. CHRYSOSTOM: He not only blessed him but also praised God. In the words "blessed be Abraham by God the most high, who created heaven and earth," he also highlighted to us God's power as distinguished from his creatures. If he in fact is God, Creator of heaven and earth, those worshiped by human beings would not be gods; Scripture says, remember, "Let those gods perish who did not make heaven and earth."[13] The text reads, "Blessed be God, who delivered your enemies into your hands." Notice, I ask you, how he not only celebrates the just man but also acknowledges God's assistance. After all, without grace from above he could not have prevailed over the might of those besetting him. "Who delivered your enemies," the text says, namely, he it is who caused everything, he it is who rendered the strong powerless, he it is who brought down the armed hordes through those unarmed. From that source is the grace coming forth that provides you with such power. HOMILIES ON GENESIS 35.17.[14]

14:23 Abraham Takes No Reward

ABRAHAM RAISES HIS MIND TO HEAVENLY THINGS. AMBROSE: It is characteristic of the perfect mind not to take for itself any earthly thing, anything prone to bodily seduction. This is why Abraham says, "I will take nothing of what is yours." He avoids intemperance like the plague. He flees from sensual bodily temptations as from filth. He rejects worldly pleasures to seek those that are above the world. This is what

---

[8]FC 82:315-16. [9]Ps 110:4 (109:4 LXX). [10]NPNF 1 2:323. [11]Ps 110:4 (109:4 LXX). [12]CSEL 32 1:513-14. [13]Jer 10:11. [14]FC 82:316-17*.

it means to raise one's hands to the Lord.[15] The hand that does good is the virtue of the soul. He puts forth his hand not to the fruit of the earthly tree but to the Lord, "who," Scripture says, "made heaven and earth,"[16] that is to say, both intelligible and visible substance. In fact, the invisible *ousia*, or substance, is heaven, while the earth is the visible and sensible substance. The passage then means that Abraham raises the virtue of his mind to heavenly things. From that intelligible substance he might reach the heights of the contemplative life, looking not to the things that are seen but to those that are not seen; not to earthly things, not to bodily things; not to things present but to things that are immaterial, eternal, heavenly. But from that other substance, the visible, he extracts the benefit of a discipline related to the practical order and to civil life. ON ABRAHAM 2.8.46.[17]

THE PATRIARCH'S CONTEMPT FOR MATERIAL WEALTH.

CHRYSOSTOM: The patriarch's contempt for material wealth was intense. Why is it with an oath that he rejects the offer in the words "I will raise my hand to swear before God the most high, who created heaven and earth"? He wants to give the king of Sodom two lessons. First, he is above the gifts offered by him; and this gives evidence of great wisdom. He is ready to prove an instructor for him in reverence, as if to teach him in so many words: I am calling to witness the Creator of all that I will take nothing of yours, so that you may come to know the God over all and not regard as gods the things shaped by human hands. This One in fact is the maker of heaven and earth, who indeed determined the course of this war and was the cause of victory. So don't expect me to be ready to take anything you've offered me. It was not, you see, for a reward that I wreaked vengeance. Instead, in the first instance it was out of love for my nephew, and then from the very nature of a good man that I should wrest from the clutches of barbarians people wrongfully abducted. HOMILIES ON GENESIS 35.18.[18]

NO NEED OF HUMAN RESOURCES.

CHRYSOSTOM: He would not take even a chance item, even something worthless or anything thought beneath contempt, even the shoelace at the tip of the shoe, where it comes to a point. Then he states the reason for his refusal. It is "in case you were to say, 'I gave Abram his wealth.' I have on my side the supplier of countless goods; I enjoy much favor from on high. I have no need of wealth from you. I don't want human resources. I am content with the regard God pays me. I know the generosity of his gifts toward me. Having yielded to Lot worthless scraps, I have been granted great promises beyond telling. Now by not accepting wealth from you I earn for myself greater wealth and enjoy further grace from him." This in my opinion . . . was the reason why he took the oath in the words "I will raise my hand to swear before God the most high"; namely, that the king should not think that he was simply putting up a pretense about what was likely to happen but should rather be quite clear about his not taking the least trinket from him. He was honoring that command given by Christ to the disciples: "Freely you have received, freely give."[19] In other words, he is saying, Surely I have contributed nothing to the course of the war other than consent and encouragement, whereas the victory and the spoils and everything else has been God's work in his invisible might. HOMILIES ON GENESIS 35.19.[20]

14:24 A Share for Abraham's Confederates

AGAIN ABRAHAM FULFILLS THE APOSTOLIC LAW.

CHRYSOSTOM: These I will allow to take a portion, he says, since they have given evidence of deep friendship. "These," you see, the text says, "were Abram's confederates,"[21] that is, they were joined in friendship, willing to share the perils with him. Hence, with the intention of rewarding

---

[15]*Levo manum meam ad Dominum Deum excelsum* (Gen 14:22 Vulgate). [16]Gen 14:22. [17]CSEL 32 1:599-600. [18]FC 82:317-18*. [19]Mt 10:8. [20]FC 82:318*. [21]Gen 14:13.

them, he is even prepared to take some portion, and in this once again he fulfills the apostolic law in the words "the worker deserves his fare."[22] I mean, he lets them take no more than their due: "except what my young men consumed and the portion for the men who accompanied me, Eschol, Aner and Mamre—they will take a portion." Do you see the precision of the patriarch's virtue? He gives evidence as well of good sense in the matter of his disregard and scorn for wealth. And at the same time [he does] everything so as not to appear to have acted from pretense or contempt and thus to have entertained grandiose notions about winning the victory. HOMILIES ON GENESIS 35.20.[23]

THE GRATUITOUS CHARACTER OF A FAVOR.
AMBROSE: How remarkable it is, then, that Abraham did not wish to touch any of the spoil gained by his victory or to take even what was offered him? The fact is that to receive recompense diminishes the joy of a victory and blunts the gratuitous character of a favor. For it makes a great difference whether one has fought for money or for fame. In one case, a person will be regarded as a mercenary. In the other case he will be deemed worthy of fame as a deliverer. The holy patriarch rightly refuses to appropriate any of the spoil, even if it was offered to him, lest the one who gave it say, "I made him rich." He testifies that he is content to receive what had been needed for the upkeep of the young warriors. But someone will say, since he had won the battle, why does he say to the king of the Sodomites, "I will take nothing from you"? Surely the booty belonged to the victor! Abraham is giving instruction for military protocol. Everything should be left to the king. Naturally he affirms that any who might have been enlisted to help in his military engagement should be given a part of the profit in recompense for their effort. ON ABRAHAM 1.3.17.[24]

---

[22]Mt 10:10. [23]FC 82:319*. [24]CSEL 32 1:514.

15:1-6 THE LORD APPEARS TO ABRAHAM IN A VISION

[1]*After these things the word of the LORD came to Abram in a vision, "Fear not, Abram, I am your shield; your reward shall be very great."* [2]*But Abram said, "O Lord GOD, what wilt thou give me, for I continue childless, and the heir of my house is Eliezer of Damascus?"* [3]*And Abram said, "Behold, thou hast given me no offspring; and a slave born in my house will be my heir."* [4]*And behold, the word of the LORD came to him, "This man shall not be your heir; your own son shall be your heir."* [5]*And he brought him outside and said, "Look toward heaven, and number the stars, if you are able to number them." Then he said to him, "So shall your descendants be."* [6]*And he believed the LORD; and he reckoned it to him as righteousness.*

OVERVIEW: The admonition to "fear not" is related to Abraham's rejection of the material gifts offered him in the previous chapter (CHRYSOSTOM). On the moral level, the promise reveals that the Lord is not slow to reward. What Abraham desired was the progeny of the church. The true heir is Jesus Christ, of whom Isaac is a figure (AMBROSE). We believe in the power of the One who promises in order to gain righteousness from faith (CHRYSOSTOM). Abraham is a model because he did not seek the rational explanation but believed with great promptness of spirit. The phrase "he brought him outside" can be interpreted allegorically to signify the need to purify our dwelling (the body) of all uncleanness (AMBROSE). We believe in the power of the One who promises in order to gain righteousness from faith (CHRYSOSTOM).

15:1 *Abraham's Shield*

FEAR NOT, ABRAHAM. CHRYSOSTOM: God said to him, "Don't be afraid, Abram." Notice the extraordinary degree of his care. Why did he say, "Don't be afraid"? Since Abraham had scorned so much wealth by giving little importance to the offerings of the king, God said to him, Have no fear for despising gifts of such value. Do not be distressed on the score of your diminished prosperity. "Don't be afraid." Then to cheer his spirit further, he adds his name to the encouragement by saying, "Don't be afraid, Abram." It proves to be no little help in encouraging a person to invoke the name of the person we are addressing. Then he said, "I am your shield." This phrase is also rich in meaning: I summoned you from the Chaldeans. I led you to this point. I rescued you from the perils of Egypt. I promised once and again to give this land to your descendants. It is I who will be your shield. After daily making you acclaimed by all, I will be your shield—that is, I will struggle in your place. I will be your shield. "Your reward will be exceedingly great." You refused to accept reward for the troubles you suffered in exposing yourself to such risks. You scorned the king and what he offered you. I will provide you with a reward, not to the degree that you would have received but wonderfully, exceedingly great. "Your reward," the text says, remember, "will be exceedingly great." HOMILIES ON GENESIS 36.10.[1]

THE LORD IS NOT SLOW TO REWARD.

AMBROSE: Because Abraham did not seek recompense from man, he received it from God, as we read in Scripture: "After these words the Lord spoke to Abraham in a vision saying, Fear not, Abraham, I will protect you. Your reward will be exceedingly great." The Lord is not slow to reward. He is eager to promise, and he gives in abundance, lest any delay cause weak souls to repent of having despised visible things. He pays back, so to speak, at high interest, rewarding with great abundance the one who has not been seduced by the things of this world that were offered to him. ON ABRAHAM 1.3.18.[2]

15:2-3 *Abraham's Lack of Children*

PASSING ON WITHOUT CHILDREN. CHRYSOSTOM: Since God had promised him a reward, a wonderfully, exceedingly great reward, Abraham revealed his grief of spirit and the disappointment affecting him constantly on account of his childless condition. He says, "Lord, what sort of thing will you give me? After all, you can see, I have reached the height of old age and am to pass on without children." See how from the outset the just man showed his sound thinking in calling his departure from here a "passing on." I mean, people who live an assiduous life of virtue really pass on from struggle, as it were, and are freed from their bonds when they transfer from this life. You see, for people living virtuously it is a kind of transfer from a worse situation to a better, from a temporary existence to an everlasting one that is protected from death and has no end. HOMILIES ON GENESIS 36.11.[3]

A SLAVE FOR AN HEIR. CHRYSOSTOM: These words reveal the extreme degree of the pain in his soul. [It is if he were saying] to God, Far from being granted what my slave was, I am to pass away without child or heir, whereas my slave will inherit the gifts granted me by you, despite the promise received from you more than once in the

[1]FC 82:332-33*. [2]CSEL 32 1:515. [3]FC 82:333-34*.

words "to your descendants I will give this land." Consider, I ask you, the just man's virtue in this case also in the fact that while entertaining these thoughts in his mind he did not protest nor say any harsh words. Instead, driven on in this case by the words spoken to him, he spoke boldly to the Lord, revealed the tumult of his interior thoughts and made no secret of the wound to his spirit. Hence in turn he received instant healing. HOMILIES ON GENESIS 36.11.[4]

AN HEIR WORTHY OF HIS WORK. AMBROSE: Let us also consider what recompense he requests from the Lord. He does not ask for riches, as would a greedy person, nor for a long life in this world, as would one who fears death, nor for power. Rather he asks for an heir worthy of his work. "What will you give me?"—he says—"I am about to depart without children." And then he says, "Because you have not given me posterity, a slave born in my house will be my heir." Let everyone learn therefore not to despise marriage. Let them not unite with disreputable persons, so as not to have children of such a standing that they are unable to be their heirs. In view of the inheritance to be transmitted, if they are not moved by any consideration of decency, they at least should desire a worthy marriage. ON ABRAHAM 1.3.19.[5]

HE DESIRED THE PROGENY OF THE CHURCH. AMBROSE: But the holy and prophetic mind is more concerned with an eternal posterity. What Abraham desires is in fact the offspring of wisdom and the inheritance of faith. This is why he says, "What will you give me, since I am about to depart without children?" What he desired was the progeny of the church. What he was requesting was a descendancy that would be not servile but free, not according to the flesh but according to grace. ON ABRAHAM 2.8.48.[6]

15:4 The Promise of His Own Son

THE LEGITIMATE SON. AMBROSE: But if the

words of Abraham are not enough to correct, consider the word of God, who condemns such a mode of transmitting inheritance. "This man shall not be your heir," he says, "but the other who will come out from you, he will be your heir." Who is this other of whom he speaks? In fact Hagar too bore a son, Ishmael, but he is not speaking of him. Instead, he is speaking of holy Isaac. For this reason he added "who will come out from you." In fact, the one who truly came out of Abraham is the one who was born of a legitimate marriage. But in Isaac, the legitimate son, we can see the One who is the true legitimate son, the Lord Jesus, of whom at the beginning of the Gospel according to Matthew we read that he is the son of Abraham.[7] He was the true heir of Abraham, bringing renown to the descendants of the progenitor. Through him Abraham looked up to heaven and understood that the splendor of his posterity would be no less luminous than the radiance of the stars of heaven. As "one star differs from another in brightness, so it is also for the resurrection of the dead," said the apostle.[8] The Lord, in joining to his resurrection people whom death was accustomed to hide in the ground, made them sharers in the heavenly kingdom. ON ABRAHAM 1.3.20.[9]

15:5 Innumerable Descendants

A REWARD BESTOWED. AMBROSE: What is the meaning then of the expression "he brought him outside"? The prophet is as it were led out, so that he goes outside of the body and sees the limitations imposed by the flesh that is his garment and the infusion of the Holy Spirit who makes a kind of visible descent. We too must exit from the confinement of this our temporary dwelling. We must purify the place where our soul dwells from all uncleanness, throw out every stain of wickedness, if we wish to receive the spirit of wisdom, because "wisdom will not enter a wicked soul."[10]

---

[4]FC 82:334. [5]CSEL 32 1:515. [6]CSEL 32 1:601. [7]Mt 1:1. [8]1 Cor 15:41-42. [9]CSEL 32 1:515-16. [10]Wis 1:4.

Abraham believed, not because he was drawn by a promise of gold or silver but because he believed from the heart. "It was reckoned to him as righteousness." A reward was bestowed that corresponded to the test of his merit.[11] ON ABRAHAM 2.8.48.[12]

15:6 Abraham Believes the Lord

RIGHTEOUSNESS FROM FAITH. CHRYSOSTOM: Accordingly let us learn, I beseech you, a lesson for ourselves as well from the patriarch: Let us believe in the words of God and trust in his promise. Let us not apply the yardstick of our own reasoning but give evidence of deep gratitude. This, you see, will succeed in making us also be seen to be righteous and will quickly cause us to attain to the promise made by him. In Abraham's case, however, the promise was made that a complete multitude would develop from his descendants. The effect of the promise was beyond the limits of nature and human logic. Hence faith in God won righteousness for him. In our case, . . . if we are alert enough to see it, he promised much more. We are able in great measure to transcend human reasoning, provided we believe in the power of the One who promises, in order that we may gain also righteousness from faith and attain to the good things promised. HOMILIES ON GENESIS 36.15.[13]

HE BELIEVED WITH PROMPTNESS OF SPIRIT. AMBROSE: And how did Abraham's progeny spread? Only through the inheritance he transmitted in virtue of faith. On this basis the faithful are assimilated to heaven, made comparable to the angels, equal to the stars. This is why he said, "So will your descendants be. And Abraham," the text says, "believed in God." What exactly did he believe? Prefiguratively he believed that Christ through the incarnation would become his heir. In order that you may know that this was what he believed, the Lord says, "Abraham saw my day and rejoiced."[14] For this reason "he reckoned it to him as righteousness," because he did not seek the rational explanation but believed with great promptness of spirit. ON ABRAHAM 1.3.21.[15]

---

[11]This and the preceding selection from Ambrose illustrate the different character of the two books *On Abraham*, the first being devoted more to the literal and moral explanation, the second more to the spiritual and allegorical sense. [12]CSEL 32 1:602. [13]FC 82:336-37*. [14]Jn 8:56. [15]CSEL 32 1:516-17.

15:7-12 ABRAHAM PREPARES THE SACRIFICE

[7]And he said to him, "I am the LORD who brought you from Ur of the Chaldeans, to give you this land to possess." [8]But he said, "O Lord GOD, how am I to know that I shall possess it?" [9]He said to him, "Bring me a heifer three years old, a she-goat three years old, a ram three years old, a turtledove, and a young pigeon." [10]And he brought him all these, cut them in two, and laid each half over against the other; but he did not cut the birds in two. [11]And when birds of prey came down upon the carcasses, Abram drove them away.

[12]As the sun was going down, a deep sleep fell on Abram; and lo, a dread and great darkness fell upon him.

OVERVIEW: Although various symbolic interpretations of the animals are possible, the fathers had no doubt that spiritual meanings are prefigured by them (AUGUSTINE). The three animals may symbolize the carnal people in the church, while the two birds represent spiritual persons (CAESARIUS OF ARLES). The fact that the birds were not divided shows that spiritual people in general are not divided among themselves (AUGUSTINE). The turtledove represents chastity and the pigeon simplicity; they are not divided because spiritual souls have one heart and one soul (CAESARIUS OF ARLES). The fact that Abraham remained when the birds of prey came down signifies that true believers shall persevere to the end (AUGUSTINE). The dread and darkness that fell upon Abraham signify the ecstasy, the thrill of passing from visible to invisible things (DIDYMUS THE BLIND).

15:9 Bringing Animals and Birds

A SYMBOL WAS GIVEN. AUGUSTINE: Here also, in fine, a symbol was given, consisting of these animals: a heifer, a she-goat, a ram and two birds, a turtledove and pigeon, that he might know that the things which he had not doubted should come to pass were to happen in accordance with this symbol. The heifer may be a sign that the people should be put under the law, the she-goat that the same people were to become sinful, the ram that they should reign. Perhaps these animals are said to be of three years old for this reason: that there are three remarkable divisions of time, from Adam to Noah, and from him to Abraham, and from him to David. David, on the rejection of Saul, was first established by the will of the Lord in the kingdom of the Israelite nation. In this third division, which extends from Abraham to David, people grew up as if passing through the third age of life. Or perhaps it may be that they had some other more suitable meaning. Still I have no doubt whatever that spiritual things were prefigured by them as well as by the turtledove and pigeon. CITY OF GOD 16.24.[1]

A TYPE OF ALL NATIONS. CAESARIUS OF ARLES: Therefore the heifer, the she-goat and the ram of three years, as also the turtledove and the pigeon, presented a type of all nations. They were described as of three years, because all the nations were to believe in the mystery of the Trinity. Now the entire Catholic church has not only spiritual members but carnal ones also, for although some say they believe in the Trinity, they are nevertheless carnal because they neglect to avoid sins and vices. Since there are spiritual souls with the carnal ones, for this reason the turtledove and pigeon were added. In the latter, spiritual people can be meant, but in those other three animals carnal people are understood. SERMON 82.1.[2]

15:10 The Birds Not Divided

CHILDREN OF THE PROMISE. AUGUSTINE: And it is said, "But the birds divided he not," because carnal people are divided among themselves. But those who are spiritual are not divided at all, whether they seclude themselves from the busy conversation of humankind, like the turtledove, or dwell among them, like the pigeon. For both birds are simple and harmless, signifying that even in the Israelite people, to which that land was to be given, there would be individuals who were children of the promise and heirs of the kingdom that is to remain in eternal felicity. CITY OF GOD 16.24.[3]

SPIRITUAL SOULS ARE NOT DIVIDED. CAESARIUS OF ARLES: Now notice carefully Abraham is said to have divided the three animals into two parts and to have placed them one against the other. "The birds," says Scripture, "he did not cut in two." Why is this, brothers? Because in the church catholic, carnal people are divided but spiritual people are not. And, as Scripture says, they are separated one against the other. Why are carnal people divided and set against each other? Because all wicked lovers of the world do

---

[1]NPNF 1 2:324*. [2]FC 47:7. [3]NPNF 1 2:324.

not cease to have divisions and scandals among each other. For this reason they are divided, since they are opposed to one another. However, the birds, that is, spiritual souls, are not divided. Why not? Because they have "one heart and one soul in the Lord."[4] To will and not to will is all one thing to them. Surely the turtledoves and pigeons that we mentioned above are like these souls. In the turtledove chastity is represented, and in the pigeon, simplicity. All God-fearing people in the church catholic clearly are chaste and simple, and with the psalmist they can say, "Had I but wings like a dove, I would fly away and be at rest."[5] And again: "The swallow finds a nest in which she puts her young."[6] Carnal people, who can be divided, are pressed down by the heavy fetters of vice. Spiritual people are raised on high by the wings of various virtues. As if by two wings, that is, the two precepts of love of God and charity toward the neighbor, they are lifted up to heaven. With the apostle they can say, "But our citizenship is in heaven."[7] As often as the priest says, "Lift up your hearts," they can say with assurance and devotion that they have lifted them up to the Lord. However, very few and rare are the people in the church who can say this with confidence and truth. Therefore Abraham did not divide the birds, because spiritual souls who have one heart and soul, as I said, cannot be divided or separated from love of God and of neighbor. They exclaim with the apostle, "Who shall separate us from the love of Christ? Shall tribulation, or distress or persecution?"[8] Other words follow until it is said, "Nor any other creature will be able to separate us from the love of God, which is in Christ Jesus our Lord."[9] Therefore spiritual souls are not separated from Christ by torments. Carnal souls are sometimes separated by idle gossip. The cruel sword cannot separate the former, but carnal affections can remove the latter. Nothing hard breaks down spiritual people, but even flattering words can corrupt the carnal. For this reason Abraham divided those animals into two parts, but the birds he did not divide. SERMON 82.2.[10]

15:11 Birds of Prey

TRUE BELIEVERS PERSEVERE TO THE END.
AUGUSTINE: The fowls coming down on the divided carcasses represent nothing good but [rather] the spirits of this air, seeking some food for themselves in the division of carnal people. But that Abraham sat down with them signifies that even amid these divisions of the carnal, true believers shall persevere to the end. With the going down of the sun great fear fell upon Abraham and a horror of great darkness. This signifies that about the end of this world believers shall be in great perturbation and tribulation, of which the Lord said in the Gospel, "For then shall be great tribulation, such as was not from the beginning."[11] CITY OF GOD 16.24.[12]

15:12 A Deep Sleep

THE FEAR THAT BELONGS TO THE PERFECT.
DIDYMUS THE BLIND: As he contemplated the wonderful things of God, Abraham was struck with fear, the fear that belongs to the perfect. It will be noted . . . that the ecstasy came upon him "toward sunset." The text suggests by this a progression, because the day of the present state has gone by for Abraham so that further progress might follow. Thus the blessing was extended to Abraham which says, "I will fill you with length of days,"[13] a blessing that by no means promised him longevity but, as is quite clear, further advances in illumination.

An ecstasy then fell upon him, not the ecstasy that resembles a loss of reason but that of wonder, the thrill of passing from visible to invisible things. The apostle even says, "Indeed, if we are beside ourselves, it is for God; if we are in our right mind, it is for you."[14] By this he means not "we are out of our minds for God" but "even if we are transported through contemplation beyond the realm of hu-

---

[4]Acts 4:32. [5]Ps 55:6 (54:7 LXX). [6]Ps 84:3 (83:4 LXX). [7]Phil 3:20. [8]Rom 8:35. [9]Rom 8:39. [10]FC 47:7-9*. [11]Mt 24:21. [12]NPNF 1 2:324. [13]Ps 91:16 (90:16 LXX). [14]2 Cor 5:13.

man things, we do this for God." David likewise declares, "I said in my ecstasy: every man is a liar."[15] It was indeed because he was transported out of himself to participate in the divine that he said of people that they are liars, because he was no longer merely a man, by reason of his communion with the Holy Spirit. He was quite different from those of whom it is said, "While there is jealousy and strife among you, are you not of the flesh and behaving like ordinary men?"[16] When Abraham then had been transported out of himself, a "dark fear" fell upon him, dark not by participation in darkness but in the sense of obscurity, of something

whose meaning is not immediately evident. Being a "great" fear, it is not the kind that happens to the mediocre. Remember "darkness" is often used for "obscurity," as according to this saying: "He made darkness around him his canopy."[17] It is indeed true that the contemplation and grasp of supernatural truths produce, even among great people, a divine vertigo and fear, and it is with some trepidation that they apply themselves to such things. On Genesis 230.[18]

---

[15]Ps 116:11 (115:2 LXX). [16]1 Cor 3:3. [17]2 Sam 22:12; Ps 18:11 (17:12 LXX). [18]SC 244:188-90.

15:13-16 EGYPTIAN CAPTIVITY PREDICTED

[13]Then the Lord said to Abram, "Know of a surety that your descendants will be sojourners in a land that is not theirs, and will be slaves there, and they will be oppressed for four hundred years; [14]but I will bring judgment on the nation which they serve, and afterward they shall come out with great possessions. [15]As for yourself, you shall go to your fathers in peace; you shall be buried in a good old age. [16]And they shall come back here in the fourth generation; for the iniquity of the Amorites is not yet complete."

Overview: With regard to the figure of four hundred years, there is no discrepancy with what is written in Exodus (Didymus the Blind, Augustine). The prediction that Abraham would go to his "fathers in peace" means that persons full of zeal will go to be with their spiritual fathers, even if those persons had bad fathers according to the flesh. The saying that "the inquity of the Amorites is not yet complete" shows that God inflicts chastisements with measure and in time, exercising patience until the time of retribution has come (Didymus the Blind). The fourth generation can be interpreted mystically to represent many things, but especially the fullness of wisdom, which comes in fourth place in the ages of humanity (Ambrose).

15:13 Descendants to Be Slaves

No Discrepancy Between Genesis and Exodus. Didymus the Blind: This word anticipates the sojourn of the people in Egypt, for they were to sojourn as it were in a land not their own. They would be reduced to slavery by the Pharaoh and mistreated in many ways by him and by the Egyptians. There is no discrepancy between what is said here and what is written in Exodus. There it is said, "After 430 years, the army of the Lord left the land of Egypt."[1] Here: "After four hundred years." It should be noted that it is not said that they left when four hundred years were com-

---

[1]Ex 12:41.

pleted but rather after four hundred years, which leaves room for the thirty years.

And the promise "I will judge the nation to which you will be enslaved" was realized in the very way described in Exodus: God afflicted the Egyptians with ten plagues, and in the end "they sank as lead in the mighty waters."[2] Finally, they were to leave "with much baggage," as history would show. From this we learn that if God maltreats someone for a time, he does this not as a matter of indifference but only for some good purpose.

Consider too whether this passage might also allude to the sojourn of the saints. ON GENESIS 231.[3]

THE PROPHETIC WORDS PERTAIN TO ISRAEL.

AUGUSTINE: But note what is said to Abraham, "Know of a surety that your seed shall be a stranger in a land not theirs, and they shall reduce them to servitude, and shall afflict them four hundred years." This is most clearly a prophecy about the people of Israel, who were to be in servitude in Egypt. Not that this people was to be in that servitude under the oppressive Egyptians for four hundred years, but it is foretold that this should take place in the course of those four hundred years. It is written of Terah the father of Abraham, "And the days of Terah in Haran were 205 years,"[4] not because they were all spent there but because they were completed there. So it is said here also, "And they shall reduce them to servitude and shall afflict them four hundred years" . . . because that number was completed, not because it was all spent in that affliction. The years are said to be four hundred in round numbers, although they were a little more—whether you reckon from this time when these things were promised to Abraham, or from the birth of Isaac, as the seed of Abraham, of which these things are predicted. For, as we have already said above, from the seventy-fifth year of Abraham, when the first promise was made to him, down to the exodus of Israel from Egypt, there are reckoned 430 years, which the apostle thus mentions: "And this I say, that the covenant confirmed by God, the

law, which was made 430 years after, cannot disannul, that it should make the promise of no effect."[5] So then these 430 years might be called four hundred, because they are not much more, especially since part even of that number had already gone by when these things were shown and said to Abraham in vision, or when Isaac was born in his father's one hundredth year, twenty-five years after the first promise, when of these 430 years there now remained 405, which God was pleased to call four hundred. No one will doubt that the other things that follow in the prophetic words of God pertain to the people of Israel. CITY OF GOD 16.24.[6]

15:15 Abraham to Die in Peace

THE WISE PERSON LEAVES THIS LIFE IN PEACE.

DIDYMUS THE BLIND: Anyone can see that God is here announcing Abraham's departure from this life. As for the anagogical [mystical] sense, one could say the following: The wise person leaves this life in peace, while the sinner does so with troubled thoughts and an agitated soul. And the way death takes one, so is one judged. One who has already attained peace here below takes leave also in peace. But one who has nothing but disturbance and agitation in his or her thoughts will be judged also in this way. This is clear from the saying in Ecclesiastes: "In the place where the tree falls, there it will lie."[7] Things do not occur this way in historical reality, because a tree does not necessarily always lie where it falls. Often it is cleared away. But it is evidently humankind who is symbolically represented by the tree, namely, a person who will be judged as he or she is found.

In peace, then, as is fitting, Abraham will depart to his fathers. Being pleasing to God, he shares in their promise: "First Christ, then those who are of Christ."[8] And for the just themselves, there are different promises and different dwellings, because "there are many mansions"[9] with the

---

[2]Ex 15:10. [3]SC 244:190-92. [4]Gen 11:32. [5]Gal 3:17. [6]NPNF 1 2:324-25*. [7]Eccles 11:3. [8]1 Cor 15:23. [9]Jn 14:2.

Father. The person full of zeal will go to be with his spiritual fathers, whose son he is through a moral likeness, even if, according to the flesh, he had fathers who were bad men. ON GENESIS 231-32.[10]

15:16 *The Fourth Generation*

GOD INFLICTS EVEN CHASTISEMENTS WITH MEASURE AND IN TIME. DIDYMUS THE BLIND: After having said this of Abraham himself, God speaks of the children who will come from him: "In the fourth generation they shall come back here," meaning the generation that would return to the land of inheritance. This is why he says that the return would take place after four hundred years, "because the iniquity of the Amorites is not yet complete"—iniquity for which they will suffer ruin, so that their condemnation will allow the descendants of Abraham to occupy their land. For God inflicts even chastisements with measure and in time, using patience until the time of retribution has arrived. There is a similar and edifying saying in the Gospel: "Then Jesus began to upbraid the cities where most of his mighty works had been done, because they did not repent: Woe to you, Chorazin! Woe to you, Bethsaida! For if the mighty works done in you had been done in Tyre and Sidon, they would have repented long ago in sackcloth and ashes."[11] To which one might object: Why then were the miracles not done in Tyre and Sidon, because they would have repented, but were performed instead in places where the people did not repent? We would respond that the Son of God who acted in this way is Wisdom. As he knew the hidden things, he knew that these people would not have been authentically repentant, even while doing penance, and this is why the miracles did not take place among them. And one could appropriately say about these people: It was better for them not to have known the truth than, having once known it, to return to their former errors. Thus he did not do works in Tyre and Sidon, because their repentance would be fragile. . . . How-

ever, one might also ask whether this was not said by the Savior in a hyperbolic manner, simply to make those people reflect who had seen his miracles and had not repented, for hyperbole is a common teaching device.

The patience and goodness of the judge are shown, then, in the fact that he waits until the sins of the Amorites have reached their full measure. It is only after reproaches, exhortations and everything that can provoke repentance that God inflicts chastisements. The same was true in the case of Pharaoh: often reprimanded and having obtained many reprieves, through his hardness of heart he brought upon himself the final judgment as well. ON GENESIS 232-33.[12]

IN THE FOURTH GENERATION THEY SHALL RETURN. AMBROSE: The history of the Jews, who went down into Egypt and came out from Egypt, seems to accord with this. The years they spent there were 430, but not all of them lived a hundred years and more, as did Moses and Joshua,[13] so that the time of the fourth generation would be appropriate in this context. So let us search rather for a mystical sense. In fact, the number four adapts well to all numbers, and it is in a certain sense the root and base of the decimal. It also represents the midpoint of the number seven. In fact, the ninety-third psalm is entitled "fourth day of the week" because this number is the intermediary between the first three and those that follow. In fact, three days precede it: the first, the second and the third; and three follow: the fifth, the sixth, the seventh. One who sings this psalm is proceeding through the life of this world, so to speak, in accordance with aptly placed numbers, like a quadrangle stable and perfect. In four books the Gospel is complete and perfect. There are four mystical animals;[14] and there are also four parts of the world, from which the assembled children of the church have propagated the most holy kingdom of Christ,

---

[10]SC 244:192-94. [11]Mt 11:20-21. [12]SC 244:194-96. [13]Deut 34:7; Josh 24:29. [14]Ezek 10:14.

coming from east and west and north and south. The holy church, therefore, has arisen with four sides. The decade too derives from this number. For if you total up the numbers from one to four you will have the number ten. Count one, add two to this: this makes three. Add three to three, this makes six. And to six add four, and this makes ten. Four then generates the decade, and the decade includes all numbers. Four is also the number of ages of a man: childhood, adolescence, virility and maturity. He rises gradually, and his wisdom is consolidated. Thus the fullness of wisdom comes, considering the ages, in fourth place. For this reason even if one has formerly been subjected to the king of Egypt, nevertheless with the age of maturity he is freed from his power and acknowledges his duty to follow the law. Then the sea of this life opens up to him. ON ABRAHAM 2.9.65.[15]

---

[15]CSEL 32 1:619-20.

15:17-21 A SMOKING FIRE POT AND A FLAMING TORCH

[17]*When the sun had gone down and it was dark, behold, a smoking fire pot and a flaming torch passed between these pieces.* [18]*On that day the LORD made a covenant with Abram, saying, "To your descendants I give this land, from the river of Egypt to the great river, the river Euphrates,* [19]*the land of the Kenites, the Kenizzites, the Kadmonites,* [20]*the Hittites, the Perizzites, the Rephaim,* [21]*the Amorites, the Canaanites, the Girgashites and the Jebusites."*

OVERVIEW: As fire illuminates and at the same time burns, the gift of the law burns those who abandon it and enlightens those who observe it. The smoking fire pot and the flaming torch allowed the patriarch to see what was happening and to reveal in a more divine manner the mysteries to be searched out (DIDYMUS THE BLIND). The smoking fire pot in the evening can be interpreted to signify the end of the world, when the carnal shall be judged by fire (AUGUSTINE). Let us rather show the simplicity of the pigeon and the chastity of the turtledove, so that we may be raised to heaven on the spiritual wings of virtue (CAESARIUS OF ARLES). Abraham's descendants would sin and be oppressed but would be saved through the prayers of their righteous ones (EPHREM). The promise to give the land to Abraham's descendants is to be understood as a promise to his spiritual posterity, to those who practice gentleness, as promised also by the Savior (DIDYMUS THE BLIND). The mention of the land of the ten peoples indicated that the church was to be constituted from the gathering of pagan peoples who would believe (AMBROSE).

BURNING AND ILLUMINATION. DIDYMUS THE BLIND: What is clearly stated in the text can be expounded as follows. When the sun was already near setting, a flame emerged, and there appeared a smoking oven and fiery torches "that passed between the two parts of the divided animals," burning and lighting up the place, to allow the patriarch to see what was happening and to reveal in a more divine manner the mysteries to be searched out. It should be noted that a fire did not appear only after the covenant had been made, but the gift of the law through Moses took place itself in the midst of a fire. Fire could be seen, and, without being able to see the one who was speaking, the giving of the commandments could be heard. What is suggested here is perhaps something like this. As the law contains rewards and punishments, it was given in the midst of fire to indicate that it brings burning to some and illumination to others. In fact, fire has a twofold power: it illuminates, and at the same time it burns. The gift of the law, then, burns those who abandon it and enlightens those who observe it. So too here, torches and smoke appeared; now smoke is the result and as it were the consequence of a fire that has been lit. Moreover, a flame had appeared first. We conclude, then, that one who is defining what is to be done and what is not to be done in a matter this difficult requires the light of God and also fear, symbolized by the furnace, so as to accomplish everything in accordance with right reason. ON GENESIS 233-34.[1]

15:17 When It Was Dark

THE CARNAL SHALL BE JUDGED BY FIRE.
AUGUSTINE: When it is added, "And when the sun was now setting there was a flame, and lo, a smoking furnace, and lamps of fire, which passed through between those pieces," this signifies that at the end of the world the carnal shall be judged by fire. The affliction of the city of God, such as never was before, which is expected to take place under Antichrist, was prefigured by Abraham's horror of great darkness about the going down of the sun. When the end of the world draws nigh, so at the going down of the sun, that is, at the very end of the world, there is signified by that fire the day of judgment, which separates the carnal who are to be saved by fire from the carnal who are to be condemned in the fire. And then the covenant made with Abraham particularly sets forth the land of Canaan and names eleven tribes in it from the river of Egypt even to the

great river Euphrates. It is not then from the great river of Egypt, that is, the Nile, but from a small one that separates Egypt from Palestine, where the city of Rhinocorura is. CITY OF GOD 16.24.[2]

THAT EVENING SIGNIFIED THE END OF THE WORLD. CAESARIUS OF ARLES: Notice, brothers, that what is called a fiery torch passing between those pieces is also not said to have touched the turtledove and pigeon. That evening signified the end of the world. Those animals, as we already said, showed a type of all the nations who believe in Christ. Because those nations have in them not only spiritual people, as was already said, that is, not only good people but even the wicked, for this reason the animals were divided and the fiery torch passed through them. According to what the apostle says, "The day of the Lord will declare it, since it will be revealed in fire,"[3] and so forth. That burning, smoking oven and fiery torch prefigured the day of judgment, and for this reason fear and a darksome horror settled upon blessed Abraham. Therefore we have realized that "if the just man scarcely will be saved," on the day of judgment, "where will the impious and the sinner appear?"[4] That burning, smoking oven signified judgment day: the day of judgment, I repeat, on which "there will be the weeping and the gnashing of teeth."[5] On that day there will be wailing and lamenting and repentance that is too late, when the foundations of the mountains will be moved and the earth will burn down to hell. SERMON 82.3.[6]

ABRAHAM SOUGHT TO KNOW. EPHREM THE SYRIAN: Abraham thought, "Perhaps these kings will destroy each other, or other peoples might rise up and destroy them and empty out the land for us. Perhaps my seed will become strong and will go and slay its inhabitants and possess it, or maybe the land will swallow [its inhabitants]

---

[1]SC 244:196-98. [2]NPNF 1 2:325*. [3]1 Cor. 3:13. [4]1 Pet 4:18. [5]Mt 8:12. [6]FC 47:9.

because of their deeds. Perhaps the [inhabitants] might go into exile into another land because of hunger or rumor or some such reason." Abraham sought to know which of these [would happen], but he had no doubts whatsoever.

Then God, who knew what he sought, showed him what he did not seek in addition to what he did seek. For by the offering that Abraham made [when] the birds came down and he chased them away, God clearly showed him that his descendants would sin and be oppressed but would be saved through the prayers of their righteous ones. And by the pot of fire that came down, God made known that even if all their righteous ones should come to an end, deliverance from heaven would come to them. By the three-year-old calf and the three-year-old ram and the three-year-old goat [God showed him] that either they would be delivered after three generations or that kings, priests and prophets would soon arise from among his descendants. By the limbs of the animals that Abraham cut in two [God] depicted their many tribes, and by the bird that Abraham did not cut in two [God] signified their unity. COMMENTARY ON GENESIS 12.3.[7]

THAT BURNING, SMOKING OVEN. CAESARIUS OF ARLES: Therefore, in order that we may not come to this torture of soul, let us awake while there is time for correction and like good, profitable servants seek the will of our Lord. Then when that dreadful day of judgment comes, which is dreaded exceedingly even by the good and was signified by that burning, smoking oven, we will not be tormented in hell by avenging flames in company with carnal people. These souls were signified by the animals, because they can be divided by various contentious desires. Let us rather show the simplicity of the pigeon and the chastity of the turtledove, so that we may be raised to heaven on the spiritual wings of virtue. According to the apostle's words, "We shall be caught up together with them in clouds to meet the Lord in the air, and so we shall ever be with the Lord"[8] with the help of our Lord Jesus Christ,

to whom is honor and glory together with the Father and the Holy Spirit world without end. Amen. SERMON 82.3.[9]

15:18-19 *This Land Given to Abraham's Descendants*

THE PROMISE TO THOSE WHO PRACTICE GENTLENESS. DIDYMUS THE BLIND: When the torches had passed over the divided animals, the covenant was made. God said to Abraham, "To your descendants I will give this land," and he described in detail how far the land extended in each direction. But, through an anagogical [mystical] transposition consistent with our above remarks, we must understand that this land is given to the holy man's spiritual posterity. The Savior too promises it to those who practice gentleness. This is a promise that applies to the true children and not to all who descend from Abraham, for "it is not the children of the flesh who are the children of God, but the children of the promise are reckoned as descendants."[10] It is "the one who does the works of Abraham"[11] who is in fact his child.

The phrase "from the river to the river" is also well put, for the promise that belongs to the posterity of the holy man is virtue, which is placed between flowing things. Flowing things, of course, do not make up virtue but are its very borders, in the sense that if one departs from virtue, one encounters them immediately. But it is possible too that the rivers represent the trials that come to virtuous persons, since they are placed among people who oppress them, and yet the virtuous triumph over them. ON GENESIS 234.[12]

THE MYSTERY OF THE CHURCH. AMBROSE: Foreign peoples are given to Abraham as though for education and so that the most scrupulous mind of the just person might cut away their

---

[7]FC 91:153-54. [8]1 Thess 4:17. [9]FC 47:10. [10]Rom 9:8. [11]Jn 8:39. [12]SC 244:198-200.

vices and correct their errors. But what is most evident here is rather the mystery of the church. Through its apostles, "who are Israelites, to whom belong the patriarchs," and from whose patriarchs "Christ was born according to the flesh"[13] under the law, the church was to be constituted from the gathering of pagan peoples who would believe. And it is not by accident that these are

indicated by the number ten but rather to show that these, at first unbelievers, when they had completed the measure of impiety, would certainly obtain the crown of faith. On Abraham 2.10.71.[14]

---

[13]Rom 9:4-5. [14]CSEL 32 1:625.

16:1-6 SARAH AND HAGAR

[1]Now Sarai, Abram's wife, bore him no children. She had an Egyptian maid whose name was Hagar; 2and Sarai said to Abram, "Behold now, the LORD has prevented me from bearing children; go in to my maid; it may be that I shall obtain children by her." And Abram hearkened to the voice of Sarai. 3So, after Abram had dwelt ten years in the land of Canaan, Sarai, Abram's wife, took Hagar the Egyptian, her maid, and gave her to Abram her husband as a wife. 4And he went in to Hagar, and she conceived; and when she saw that she had conceived, she looked with contempt on her mistress. 5And Sarai said to Abram, "May the wrong done to me be on you! I gave my maid to your embrace, and when she saw that she had conceived, she looked on me with contempt. May the LORD judge between you and me!" 6But Abram said to Sarai, "Behold, your maid is in your power; do to her as you please." Then Sarai dealt harshly with her, and she fled from her.

OVERVIEW: This episode posed a challenge to biblical interpreters, Jewish and Christian, because it portrayed the patriarch engaging in extramarital relations. The problem could be resolved by the use of allegorical interpretation, as Philo had done, and Christian interpreters adopted this solution. But the literal sense could also be used for purposes of edification. On the allegorical level Sarah represents virtue while Hagar signifies the introductory sciences or preparatory disciplines (DIDYMUS THE BLIND). Abraham could also be defended on the basis that the law against adultery had not been given in his time. A second defense of Abraham could be made on the grounds that he had only done his duty to society by guaranteeing posterity (AMBROSE). Hagar's

contempt for her mistress and Sarah's reproach to Abraham are also interpreted on the allegorical level to refer to the perfect virtue and the preliminary studies that must be transcended (DIDYMUS THE BLIND). Abraham's response to Sarah's reproach shows that he had acted dispassionately, for the sake of producing progeny and not out of lust (AUGUSTINE).

16:2 Obtaining an Heir

MODERATION AND PASSIONLESSNESS. DIDYMUS THE BLIND: The apostle saw in these women the type of the two covenants, in accordance with the rule of allegory, but since what the text narrates actually took place, the literal sense also deserves consideration. The saints entered the married life not to pursue pleasure but for the sake of children. There is in fact a tradition that says they would go with their wives only when the time was suitable for conception. They would not go with them during the lactation period, when they were nursing their young, or when they were with child, because they regarded neither of these times as suitable for coming together. . . .

When Sarah, therefore, who was wise and holy, had observed for a long time that in spite of coming together with her husband she was not conceiving, she abstained from conjugal relations, and since she knew that it was in the order of things that he should have children, she gave him her slave girl as a concubine. This shows the moderation (*sophrosyne*) and the absence of jealousy of Sarah and the passionlessness (*apatheia*) of Abraham, who chose this solution at his wife's instigation and not on his own initiative and who yielded to her request only in order to give birth to children. The literal sense too, then, is useful according to the considerations offered above. ON GENESIS 235.[1]

SARAH ALSO REPRESENTS VIRTUE. DIDYMUS THE BLIND: As for the anagogical [mystical] teaching, one could explain the text by recalling that Paul allegorically transposed the two women into the two covenants.[2] Philo also used allegory here but giving the text another application: He understood Sarah to represent perfect virtue and philosophy, because she was a free woman and wife, of noble birth and living with her husband in lawful union. Now virtue lives with the wise man in lawful union so that he can give birth from her to a divine progeny: "Wisdom," in fact, "begets a man of discernment."[3] In Scripture the devout and holy man is addressed with the words "your wife is like a fruitful vine. . . . Your children are like olive shoots around the table. So shall the man be blessed who fears the Lord."[4]

Sarah then is allegorically transposed into perfect and spiritual virtue. Hagar, the Egyptian

slave, symbolizes, according to Philo, the preliminary exercises (*progymnasmata*),[5] and, in Paul, "the shadow" [of good things to come].[6] It is not possible, in fact, to understand anything of the spiritual or elevated ideas without the shadow that is the letter or without a preliminary study of the introductory sciences, for one must first bear children from inferior unions. In the era of the shadow, they offered actual animal sacrifices, they celebrated Passover in an external and tangible way, they received physical circumcision, and all of this was preparing them gradually so that eventually they could "offer to God a sacrifice of praise,"[7] which pertains to the free woman. As the zeal of the wise impels them to go on to the higher realities in due order, virtue impels them, by divine intention, to make use first of the introductory sciences and to have children from them. Since it is impossible, in fact, for one who has just recently approached virtue so successfully to attain perfection as to have children through her too, virtue counsels such a one to subject himself first to the preparatory disciplines so that by this path he might perfectly grasp her, if he is able. ON GENESIS 235-36.[8]

ABRAHAM DID NOT VIOLATE THE LAW. AMBROSE: Some might still be struck by the fact that Abraham had a relationship with his slave girl when he was already conversing with God, as it is written: "Sarah said to Abraham, 'See now, the Lord has prevented me from bearing children; go in to my maid to make children from her.'" And this is exactly what happened. But we should consider first of all that Abraham lived prior to the law of Moses and before the gospel; adultery, it seems, was not yet prohibited at this time. The penalty for the crime goes back only to the time of the law, which made adultery a crime.

---

[1]SC 244:200-202. [2]Gal 4:22-31. [3]Prov 10:23 LXX. [4]Ps 128:3-4 (127:3-4 LXX). [5]Philo develops this allegorical interpretation especially in *De Congressu Eruditionis Gratia 1-9*, although he employs it elsewhere as well. Hagar represents the studies preliminary to philosophy in the Greek system of education: grammar, music, mathematics, rhetoric, etc. [6]Heb 10:1. [7]Ps 50:14 (49:14 LXX). [8]SC 244:202-4.

So there is no condemnation for the offense that precedes the law but only one based on the law. Abraham then cannot be said to have violated the law since he came before the law. Though in paradise God had praised marriage, he had not condemned adultery. In fact, he does not wish the death of sinners,[9] and for this reason he promises the reward without exacting the penalty. Indeed, God prefers to stimulate with mild proddings than to terrify with severe threats. If you too sinned, when you were a pagan, you have an excuse. But now you have come to the church and have heard the law, "You shall not commit adultery,"[10] you no longer have an excuse for the offense. However, since this discourse is directed also to those who are inscribed to receive the grace of baptism, if anyone has committed such a grave sin, let him be sure that he will be pardoned, but as one who has committed an offense. Let him know, however, that for the future he is obliged to abstain. Indeed, in the case of the adulterous woman spoken of in the Gospel, whom the scribes and Pharisees presented to the Lord, the Lord forgave her former sins but said, "Go, and from now on be careful not to sin any more."[11] In saying this to her, he says it to you. You have committed adultery as a pagan; you have sinned as a catechumen. The sin is forgiven you, remitted through baptism; go, and in the future, see that you do not sin. Such is the first defense of Abraham. ON ABRAHAM 1.4.23.[12]

16:3-4 Hagar the Egyptian

THE MERIT OF HAVING DONE ONE'S DUTY. AMBROSE: It was not because he was ablaze with the heat of some unbridled passion, not because he was overcome by the charm of seductive beauty that Abraham gave preference to a relationship with a slave girl over the conjugal bed, but through a desire to procure a posterity and to enlarge his progeny. After the flood the human race was still numerically sparse. Hence it was also a matter of moral obligation that no one be seen to have failed to render the debt to nature. For this reason, even the children of holy Lot[13] were inspired by this motive to procure a posterity for themselves so that the human race would not become extinct. Thus the merit of having done one's duty to society excused individual guilt. And it is not without significance that the wife is presented as the instigator of the deed. In [a] sense [this] exculpates her husband, so that no one could believe that he was carried away by some mad perversion. At the same time . . . women might learn to love their husbands, not to allow themselves to be tormented by empty suspicions of infidelity and not to dislike their stepchildren, when they themselves have been childless. That wonderful wife desired only that her husband forgive her sterility, and, wishing to avoid being herself the reason for her husband's not having children, she persuades him to go in to the slave girl. Later on, Leah and Rachel did the same thing.[14] Learn, O woman, to put aside jealousy, which often drives women to madness. ON ABRAHAM 1.4.24.[15]

HAGAR CONCEIVED. DIDYMUS THE BLIND: As we said above, it is a most authentic proof of moderation (sophrosyne) that Sarah gives in offering her slave girl to Abraham without a hint of jealousy, after she had observed that in ten months' time she had not conceived. And we have acknowledged too the passionlessness (apatheia) of the wise man, in that his clear purpose in yielding to his wife's request was to have children.

The anagogical [mystical] sense has already been expounded. It is in accordance with its goal that virtue asks us to first make use of the introductory sciences so as to first have children by them. This does not prevent the works of preparatory education from being themselves children of virtue, since they are engaged for the sake of virtue. By employing these, it was not long before the wise man effected a conception, for progress is spontaneous for the wise man. ON GENESIS 236-37.[16]

---

[9]See Ezek 33:11. [10]Ex 20:14 (20:13 LXX). [11]Jn 8:11. [12]CSEL 32 1:517-18. [13]Gen 19:30-38. [14]Gen 30:1-21. [15]CSEL 32 1:518-19. [16]SC 244:206.

FIXATING ON THINGS PRELIMINARY. DIDYMUS THE BLIND: Virtue's purpose was, as we have said, that the wise man do training exercises first in preliminary education and shadow so that later, with this training behind him, he might arrive at greater things—which is the proper procedural order. It is likewise illogical that after the knowledge of perfect things one should turn back to petty things. This is in fact what the apostle Paul writes to the Galatians, who, after the gospel had been preached to them, wanted to live with the shadow, which is the law. . . . They had been taken in by a certain Ebion,[17] who wanted to practice Judaism after having become a Christian and who was so successful in persuading others that the apostles gave him this surname to show his poverty. Ebion, in fact, means "poor," and he was so called because of the perversion and poverty of his ideas. As for the fact that the Galatians were of pagan origin, Paul writes, "Formerly, when you did not know God, you were in bondage to beings that by nature are not gods, but now you have come to know God, or rather to be known by God."[18] He reproached them, as I said, in these terms (to produce now the text I announced): "Having begun with the Spirit, are you now ending with the flesh?"[19] Indeed, when once they had given a wholly divine beginning to their edifice, they were looking for figures in an inappropriate manner, for they were searching for them when it was no longer their time. For we must understand why the visible circumcision was given and until what time it was appropriate to practice it. If one has understood this, he has had children from the concubine and is able, after this, to comprehend the circumcision of the heart that is effected by the Spirit. This holy man, upon the advice of virtue, went in to the slave girl whom she had placed at his disposal, as we have explained, and the slave girl conceived. But after this, it is inappropriate to remain with her beyond the time of her favor. Many indeed, having made use of the preparatory exercises in view of the perfect teaching, never go beyond this point, thus giving birth to a prog-

eny of slavery, and in a certain sense dishonor virtue. . . . One dishonors virtue, then, who gives other things precedence over it. For if one chooses virtue, not for its own sake but for the sake of something else—praise, for example, or glory—then in a certain sense one is dishonoring the good, which in itself is not susceptible to dishonor. ON GENESIS 237-38.[20]

16:5 May the Wrong Done to Me Be on You

PERFECT WISDOM. DIDYMUS THE BLIND: The words *ek sou*[21] can be understood in two ways: either "by you" or "from the time that." The interpretation "by you" gives the following sense: When one who has engaged the preparatory exercises in view of virtue and perfect wisdom [the promise of faith] remains at that preparatory level [that is, the relation with Hagar], in a sense he wrongs virtue, because he has not properly employed what comes before it. But the translation "from the time that" also yields the same sense, the only difference being the one already mentioned, because in this case too virtue is wronged by one who is eager to have children from the preliminary exercises alone and who makes of this level of child bearing a kind of end in itself. ON GENESIS 240.[22]

16:6 Hagar Flees

THE ZEALOUS MAN ACCEPTS CORRECTION. DIDYMUS THE BLIND: In the literal sense, this statement introduces the beginner to the passionlessness (*apatheia*) of the patriarch, who had received the slave girl from his wife without looking for pleasure and who now yields to his wife and withdraws in accordance with her wishes. As for the spiritual sense, the zealous man, even if he is still at the introductory level, since he is not altogether a stranger to virtue, receives with pleasure

---

[17]Paul does not say this. The information about Ebion is found in Origen *De Principiis* 4.3.8. [18]Gal 4:8-9. [19]Gal 3:3. [20]SC 244:206-8. [21]LXX. [22]SC 244:212.

her reproaches and thus more rapidly abandons the petty things. As one who submits to her, he follows her directions in the use of the preparatory exercises and allows her to control them. Since he is desirous to make virtue the goal of all his words, actions and thoughts, he willingly accepts any corrections that come from her. ON GENESIS 241.[23]

ABRAHAM WAS NOT A SLAVISH LOVER. AUGUSTINE: And here follow the times of Abraham's sons, the one by Hagar the bondmaid, the other by Sarah the free woman, about whom we have already spoken in the previous book. As regards this transaction, Abraham is in no way to be branded as guilty concerning this concubine. For he dealt with her for the begetting of progeny, not for the gratification of lust, and not to insult but rather to obey his wife, who supposed it would be solace of her barrenness if she could make use of the fruitful womb of her handmaid to supply the defect of her own nature. By that law of which the apostle says, "Likewise also the husband has not power of his own body, but the wife,"[24] Sarah could, as a wife, do benefit to him through childbearing by another, when she could not do so in her own person. Here there is no wanton lust, no crude lewdness. The handmaid is delivered to the husband by the wife for the sake of progeny and is received by the husband for the sake of progeny, each seeking not guilty excess but natural fruit. Then the pregnant bondwoman despised her barren mistress, and Sarah, with womanly jealousy, rather laid the blame of this on her husband. Yet even then Abraham showed that he was not a slavish lover but a free begetter of children and that in using Hagar he had guarded the chastity of Sarah his wife and had gratified her will and not his own. He had received her without seeking her, gone in to her without being attached, impregnated without loving her. For he says, "Behold, your maid is in your power; do to her as you please." Here is a man able to treat different women as they require—his wife temperately, his handmaid compliantly, neither intemperately! CITY OF GOD 16.25.[25]

HAGAR FLED FAR. DIDYMUS THE BLIND: There is a kind of maltreatment of the slave girl that we have likened, by anagogy, to the preparatory exercises (*progymnasmata*): the shadow [Hagar] of things to come [the generative promise] is transcended. For one who is hastening toward perfection no longer needs that which is preparatory. This is why it is quite natural that the slave girl should flee, because what belongs to the introductory level no longer remains when progress and perfection have arrived. ON GENESIS 241.[26]

---

[23]SC 244:214. [24]1 Cor 7:4. [25]NPNF 1 2:325*. [26]SC 244:214.

16:7-14 THE ANGEL APPEARS TO HAGAR

[7]*The angel of the LORD found her by a spring of water in the wilderness, the spring on the way to Shur. [8]And he said, "Hagar, maid of Sarai, where have you come from and where are you going?" She said, "I am fleeing from my mistress Sarai." [9]The angel of the LORD said to her, "Return to your mistress, and submit to her."* [10]The angel of the LORD also said to her, "I will so greatly multiply your descendants that they cannot be numbered for multitude." [11]And the angel of the LORD said to her, "Behold, you are with child, and shall bear a son; you shall call his name Ish-*

mael;[t] *because the* LORD *has given heed to your affliction.* [12]*He shall be a wild ass of a man, his hand against every man and every man's hand against him; and he shall dwell over against all his kinsmen."* [13]*So she called the name of the* LORD *who spoke to her, "Thou art a God of seeing"; for she said, "Have I really seen God and remained alive after seeing him?"*[u] [14]*Therefore the well was called Beer-lahai-roi;*[v] *it lies between Kadesh and Bered.*

t That is *God hears*   u Cn: Heb *have I even here seen after him who sees me?*   v That is *the well of one who sees and lives*   *LXX, "humble yourself under her hands," which is the basis for the patristic comments.

OVERVIEW: The dialogue between the angel and Hagar can be interpreted on the allegorical level to represent the relationship between Wisdom and the introductory teaching at the literal level (DIDYMUS THE BLIND). The relationship of Sarah and Hagar also reflects the relationship between the evangelical teaching and the cult of the law (CYRIL OF ALEXANDRIA). The fact that Hagar's descendants are not compared with the stars in number as are Sarah's reflects allegorically the distinction between the introductory exercises and perfect virtue. The details of the description of Ishmael can also be interpreted in this allegorical framework. The fact that the text states that Hagar bore a son "to Abram" can be interpreted allegorically to refer to the process of spiritual paternity. When the person who is making spiritual progress gives birth according to the goal assigned by the master, the child borne is not to be despised (DIDYMUS THE BLIND).

16:7 A Spring of Water

WHY HAGAR IS FOUND BY A SPRING. DIDYMUS THE BLIND: It is well too that Hagar was found "by a spring of water," for beginners find themselves engaged in purifications, which are signified by water.[1] By contrast, those who are more fully matured come into a desert place, no longer needing purifications, having already rid themselves of vices and having been endowed with virtue. ON GENESIS 243.[2]

16:8 Hagar, Sarah's Maid

THE VIRTUE OF HAGAR. DIDYMUS THE BLIND: From this text one gains insight into the virtue of

Hagar as well, and one becomes aware that she is a woman not to be despised since an angel converses with her and shows concern for her that is hardly superficial, for it is evidently by the will of God that [the angel speaks]. It is not at all improbable that Hagar was a person of zeal, because she was chosen by the holy woman Sarah to sleep with Abraham. Her nobility of soul is likewise shown by the fact that she says, "I am fleeing from my mistress, Sarah," without saying anything bad about her. We earlier had hypothesized that Sarah represented virtue and a spiritual understanding of the Scriptures but that Hagar represented the introductory knowledge and the shadow. One who approaches the divine teaching should listen to Scripture in such a way as to understand it first according to the letter, while grasping its spirit gradually and in due order.

Sarah's child therefore requires an introductory course so that by this means he might reach the more perfect things. Similarly it would be said of the Israelites that they were "the first to whom the oracles of God were entrusted,"[3] which were given to them "until the time of correction."[4] No one, in fact, who remains trapped in the letter and at the introductory level can claim Wisdom itself. If then lovers of Wisdom, who make use of what belongs to the introductory level, should remain there, they are in a sense despising virtue, but if they return to better sentiments, they put aside the introductory method so that it makes a kind of flight. For once progress has arrived, the earlier things pass away. That which has been the possession of Hagar the Egyptian is transcended.

[1]See Heb 6:1-2.   [2]SC 244:220.   [3]Rom 3:2.   [4]Heb 9:10.

It is to earthly examples that the introductory teaching appeals for support. . . .

The angel then, having found her fleeing because of the greatness of virtue, makes her retrace her steps. The word of the Master indeed causes even what belongs to the introductory exercises to redound to virtue. . . .

The virtuous one must in fact know the principles and the goal, while the one who is still at the introductory stage often remains at this level under the pretext that virtue is too high. He flees, as it were, the effort required by perfection. This is what is revealed in the statement "I am fleeing from Sarah, my mistress." ON GENESIS 242-43.[5]

THE SHADOW OF THE SPIRITUAL LAW. DIDYMUS THE BLIND: Moreover, when the beauty of the spiritual law is illuminated, that which is no more than shadow flees. Sacrifices that are luminous compared with those of "the shadow"[6] were in fact announced in the transmitted teaching and have been effectively introduced in practice. Likewise too "that which was only partial"[7] is abolished when that which is perfect is present. A case of "fleeing far from the face" is the one who, on hearing the Lord say, you must "be born from above," inquires, "How can a man be born when he is old?"[8] for he is interpreting a divine saying in human terms. ON GENESIS 243.[9]

16:9 Return and Submit

HUMBLE UNDER HER HANDS. DIDYMUS THE BLIND: The literal sense is clear enough. From the point of view of allegory, it is suggested that even in the case of one who has done a purposeless act that he believes to be obligatory for those who revere the shadow of the law and who is in a sense fleeing from its spiritual sense, the Word of the Master brings him back to the original divine intention. And in fact the Lord gradually made it clear that the things in Scripture that were of the shadow would cease to be, when he says, "What to me is the multitude of your sacrifices?"[10] and "Do I eat the flesh of bulls or drink the blood of

goats? Offer to God a sacrifice of thanksgiving, and pay your vows to the Most High."[11]

It is a great thing then to be "under the hands" of the spiritual doctrine, referred to as "mistress," and to be "humble under her hands"; not that the slave girl is of lowly estate in herself, but only with respect to the mistress. For in this matter what is glorified is not really glorified at all, because its glory is transcendent. ON GENESIS 244.[12]

THE SLAVE OF THE EVANGELICAL TEACHINGS. CYRIL OF ALEXANDRIA: As in concrete image, we see here foreshadowed the fact that once the Emmanuel has appeared and his mystery has been shown to the world, the types of the Mosaic cult necessarily disappear, giving way to the evangelical teachings, the better and more perfect precepts. Of what image am I speaking? Because Sarah had not had children, Hagar, after having given birth to Ishmael, began to show arrogant contempt for her owner, the free woman. Sarah was unable to bear that arrogance and began also to mistreat the Egyptian woman. The latter fled from the house and lost her way in the desert. An angel from heaven asked her where she was going and where she had come from. She replied, "I am fleeing from my mistress, Sarah." And the holy angel replied, "Return to your mistress, and humble yourself under her hands." She was ordered then, by the voice of the angel, not to depart from the free woman—from instruction, that is, which summons to the dignity of free persons—and to humble herself instead under the free woman's hands. The cult according to the law, in fact, which takes place through images and types, is as it were the servant of evangelical teachings. In it, obscurely, the beauty of the truth is revealed. At this point in time, the law, which was once established by Moses through the ministry of angels,[13] receives an order from the voice of an angel to

---

[5]SC 244:216-18. [6]Heb 10:1. [7]1 Cor 13:10. [8]Jn 3:3-4. [9]SC 244:218-20. [10]Is 1:11. [11]Ps 50:13-14 (49:13-14 LXX). [12]SC 244:220-22. [13]See Acts 7:53.

bend the neck to the evangelical oracles and to bow and yield, even if unwillingly, to the free woman. This, I maintain, is the spiritual interpretation of Hagar's imposed submission to the rule of Sarah. We should remember, moreover, that even the venerable Paul sees Hagar and Sarah as prefiguring the two Testaments: "One, who bears children for slavery, and corresponds to the present Jerusalem,"[14] and the other—Sarah—who bears for the dignity of the free.[15] GLAPHYRA ON GENESIS, 3.79.9.[16]

16:10 Descendants Multiplied

HAGAR'S DESCENDANTS NOT LUMINOUS.
DIDYMUS THE BLIND: It is not implausible that one who is living the life of a beginner should also be judged worthy of a blessing, for, if his progress continues toward the appropriate goal, he will arrive at perfection. But notice that when the text was talking about virtue—for it is from virtue that the true seed of Abraham comes—after God had led him outside and said to him, "Look toward heaven, and number the stars if you can count them," he had added, "So shall your descendants be."[17] But notice that in the case of Hagar it is not said, "Your descendants will be like the stars," but only "They will not be able to be numbered for their multitude." Can you not conclude from this a difference: that the progeny of that which is perfect is luminous and that which pertains to the introductory level is not? ON GENESIS 244-45.[18]

16:11 Ishmael

GIVING BIRTH COUNTED AS A BLESSING.
DIDYMUS THE BLIND: At that time, giving birth to children was regarded as a matter of great importance in view of the multiplication of human beings, as we have explained—this, moreover, at a time when virginity and the teaching on virtue did not yet have much credibility. This is why even prayers were said for conception and they counted such a thing as giving birth among

the blessings. So much for the literal explanation.

As for the spiritual sense, it could be this: One who has begun to be educated according to God and who is at the introductory stage is like one in a gestation period. The Master's word, however, makes him the promise that he will give birth, for masters who teach are often perspicacious when they see the efforts of their disciples and they acknowledge too their natural gifts. That the fruit of the womb is uncertain one can learn from a Gospel saying, when the Savior remarks, "Alas for those who are with child and for those who give suck in those days!"[19] Such situations in fact are precarious when a trial comes along. This is why, wishing to wean those who are in this situation, the Word says, "Those who are weaned from the milk, those taken from the breast, affliction upon affliction, hope upon hope,"[20] for, as people who are henceforth on a solid diet, they receive affliction upon affliction. But there are imperfect people of whom Paul writes, "I fed you with milk, not solid food; for you were not ready for it; and even yet you are not ready."[21] ON GENESIS 245.[22]

16:12 A Wild Man

A MAN OF THE COUNTRY. DIDYMUS THE BLIND: There are a number of differences that distinguish a man who is studious, sophisticated and urbane from a man who is none of these things. We say then of this latter type that by comparison with one who is a city person and a man of science, he is a simpleton, a rustic or "man of the country,"[23] and that by comparison with an educated and cultivated individual, he is uneducated or at least of low education. The fruit engendered by virtue is a style of life conformed to laws. So the person who does not live as a citizen according to the laws of the "city of the living God,"[24] of the heavenly city,[25] is a man of the

---

[14]Gal 4:24-25. [15]Gal 4:26. [16]PG 69:132-33. [17]Gen 15:5. [18]SC 244:222. [19]Mt 24:19. [20]Is 28:9-10 LXX. [21]1 Cor 3:2. [22]SC 244:224. [23]A more colloquial translation might be "country bumpkin." [24]Heb 12:22. [25]See Rev 21:2.

country. For, since he is not able to live up to the constitution of this city, he lives in the country and not yet in the city.

And it is well that the text says not only that he is "of the country" but also that he is "a man," for a share in the Word of God is not yet given to one who is just beginning. This will not happen until he has made some progress—for those whom Scripture called "godly" are those into whom the Word of God has entered.[26] It is then that he will be a citizen of the heavenly city. Appropriately of such people, in fact, the wise Paul writes these words in the epistle to the Hebrews: "To the mountain of Zion and to the city of the living God, the heavenly Jerusalem."[27] For it is there that they will be inscribed. The Savior indeed says, "Nevertheless do not rejoice in this, that the spirits are subject to you; but rejoice that your names are written in heaven."[28] This is certainly not to be taken in the sense that these names composed of syllables are literally written in heaven. But these are names relative to virtue, and as such they have in heaven an inscription that will perpetuate their memory. Such are the people who are inscribed in heaven, but those who are of contrary mind, who are concerned only with earthly things, have not managed to do more than inscribe their names on earthly things. Jeremiah rightly says in their regard: "Those who turn away from thee shall be written in the earth."[29] ON GENESIS 246.[30]

16:13-14 The God Who Sees

THE ANGEL SPOKE THE WORDS OF GOD. DIDYMUS THE BLIND: In the verses read before, it was an "angel of God" who was speaking with Hagar. Here she names him "Lord" and "God." It is not too much of a stretch to say that the angel was not in the service of his own words but of God's, as are also the prophets. For, in a certain sense, when angels exercise their ministry and when they foretell the future, they do the work of prophets. The name *angel* indicates an activity, not a substance; the same is true of the name *prophet*. [Since] the angel was speaking the words of God, Hagar called him God because of the One who lived in him. Similarly, when Isaiah prophesies, he sometimes speaks in his own person, as a man who has within himself the prophetic spirit, and he sometimes, as it were, makes God the character who speaks, without adding "says the Lord." For example, he writes, "I made the earth and created man upon it,"[31] but (it is he himself speaking) as one sent by the Lord he proclaims, "Hear, O heavens, and give ear, O earth; for the Lord has spoken."[32] We say this to show that the words of Isaiah are not all spoken as though he were merely an intermediary but that participation in God confers also the authority of God; and because of God's dwelling in them, those who share in him are called gods. This is so true that an angel speaking to Moses was also called God. It is written in fact: And the angel of the Lord called him and said to him, "I am the God of Abraham, the God of Isaac and the God of Jacob."[33] If one looks at the minister, these are words of angels, but if one looks at the sense, they are words of God. ON GENESIS 247-48.[34]

BETWEEN KADESH AND BERED. DIDYMUS THE BLIND: It is well too that the vision of the instructing Word was seen "between Kadesh and Bered." Kadesh in fact is interpreted to mean "holy," and Bered, "lightning."[35] It is between these two things that divine education takes place: the holy, on the one hand, to which it belongs (to see the divine things) and the lightning, on the other, which is a luminous state. For "your lightnings lighted up the world."[36] ON GENESIS 249.[37]

---

[26]Jn 10:35. [27]Heb 12:22. [28]Lk 10:20. [29]Jer 17:13. [30]SC 244:226-28. [31]Is 45:12. [32]Is 1:2. [33]Ex 3:4, 6 LXX. [34]SC 244:228-30. [35]This interpretation is based on the supposed Hebrew etymology of the names. See introduction to this volume, p. xxvii. [36]Ps 77:18; 97:4 (76:19; 96:4 LXX). [37]SC 244:232.

16:15-16 THE BIRTH OF ISHMAEL

[15]*And Hagar bore Abram a son; and Abram called the name of his son, whom Hagar bore, Ishmael.* [16]*Abram was eighty-six years old when Hagar bore Ishmael to Abram.*

OVERVIEW: The fact that the text states that Hagar bore a son "to Abram" can be interpreted allegorically to refer to the process of spiritual paternity (DIDYMUS THE BLIND).

16:16 Hagar Bore Ishmael

PROFITABLE SEED. DIDYMUS THE BLIND: It is plausible to say that it was to establish the fact that Hagar was a serious woman and Ishmael an authentic son of Abraham that Scripture went out of its way to remark that Hagar bore a son "to Abram." What follows is clear as to the literal sense, but let us examine too the anagogical [mystical] sense. When the person who is making progress gives birth according to the goal assigned by the master, the child he bears is not to be despised. The verse then applies the metaphorical notion of generation to the master who correctly teaches and who thus provides profitable seed. This is why it is said, "Hagar bore to Abram." The proof that the meaning is indeed what I have indicated according to the terms of Scripture is that, in the following phrase, "And Abram called the name of his son," the Word adds, "whom Hagar bore him." If an idea (like the one I suggested) were not in the background here, the text would simply have said, "And Abram named his son," without adding "whom she bore him." ON GENESIS 249.[1]

[1]SC 244:234.

17:1-8 THE PROMISE TO ABRAHAM AND THE CHANGE OF NAME

[1]*When Abram was ninety-nine years old the LORD appeared to Abram, and said to him, "I am God Almighty;*[w] *walk before me, and be blameless.* [2]*And I will make my covenant between me and you, and will multiply you exceedingly."* [3]*Then Abram fell on his face; and God said to him,* [4]*"Behold, my covenant is with you, and you shall be the father of a multitude of nations.* [5]*No longer shall your name be Abram,*[x] *but your name shall be Abraham;*[y] *for I have made you the father of a multitude of nations.* [6]*I will make you exceedingly fruitful; and I will make nations of you, and kings shall come forth from you.* [7]*And I will establish my covenant between me and you and your descendants after you throughout their generations for an everlasting covenant, to be God to you and to your descendants after you.* [8]*And I will give to you, and to your descendants after*

you, the land of your sojournings, all the land of Canaan, for an everlasting possession; and I will be their God."

w Heb El Shaddai   x That is *exalted father*   y Here taken to mean *father of a multitude*

OVERVIEW: God waited until Abraham was ninety-nine in order to show us his power and the just man's endurance and virtue (CHRYSOSTOM). The command to be blameless means that one must be constantly in training (AMBROSE). The change of Abram's name to Abraham is related to his acceptance of the covenant of God and of circumcision as a sign of faith (ORIGEN). The addition of one letter to his name changes the meaning from "useless father" to "chosen father" (AMBROSE). The name Abraham received its explanation in this world because it was here that he became the father of many nations (AUGUSTINE).

17:1 God Appears to Abraham

ABRAHAM WAS NINETY-NINE YEARS OLD. CHRYSOSTOM: After the tenth year he took Ishmael, his child by the maidservant, and considered that the promises had been fulfilled for him in the child. The patriarch was, you remember, the text tells us, eighty-six years old when Ishmael was born. The loving God, however, exercised the virtue of the just man for a still further period of thirteen years. When God saw that he had been purified like gold in a furnace[1] for a long period of time and had rendered the just man's virtue more conspicuous and resplendent, Scripture says, "When Abram was ninety-nine years old, God appeared to him again."[2] Why did God delay so long? Not simply that we should get to know the just man's endurance and his great virtue, but for us to see as well the extraordinary degree of his power. You see, when nature lost its potency and was now useless for childbearing, his body being wasted and chilled with old age, God put into effect the promise to demonstrate his peculiar power. HOMILIES ON GENESIS 39.5.[3]

BE BLAMELESS. AMBROSE: The words "be

blameless" are addressed to Abraham, to whom had been given the spirit of wisdom, holy, marvelously agile,[4] unpolluted.[5] The soul of the just man, therefore, must be in training night and day, ever on the lookout, never indulging in sleep[6] but on perpetual watch, intent on God, so as to understand the things that are and to comprehend the causes of each. But wisdom is also the interpreter of future things: "She knows the things of old and infers the things to come. She understands turns of speech and the solutions of riddles. She has foreknowledge of signs and wonders and of the outcome of seasons and times."[7] One who has obtained her, therefore, cannot but be good and perfect, because he possesses every virtue and is the very image of goodness. Even the sophists[8] of this world drew from this text a definition of such a wise man: The wise man is (by definition) a good man and an accomplished communicator. ON ABRAHAM 2.10.76.[9]

17:5 Father of Many Nations

YOUR NAME SHALL BE ABRAHAM. ORIGEN: Many responses are given to Abraham by God, but they are not all delivered to one and the same man. For some are to Abram and some to Abraham; that is, some are expressed after the change of name and others while he was still known by his name given at birth. And first indeed, before the change of name, God delivered to Abraham the oracle that says, "Go out from your country and from your kindred and from your father's house," and the rest.[10] But no order is given in this about the covenant of God, no order about

[1]See Wis 3:6. [2]The text of Genesis 17:1 does not contain "again" even in the Septuagint. This is Chrysostom's addition. [3]FC 82:377*. [4]*Bene mobilis,* translating Greek *eukineton.* [5]See Wis 7:22. [6]See Mk 14:37-38. [7]Wis 8:8. [8]Greek for professional teachers skilled in reasoning. [9]CSEL 32 1:628-29. [10]Gen 12:1.

circumcision. For it was not possible while he was still Abram and was bearing the name of his physical birth to receive the covenant of God and the mark of circumcision. But when "he went out from his country and his kindred," then responses of a more sacred kind are delivered to him at this time. First God says to him, "You shall no longer be called Abram, but Abraham shall be your name." Then at once he received the covenant of God and accepted circumcision as a sign of faith that he could not accept while he was still in his father's house and in the relationship of flesh and while he was still called Abram. HOMILIES ON GENESIS 3.3.[11]

HE BECAME FATHER OF A SON. Ambrose: God changes Abraham's name, adding one letter. Instead of Abram he is called Abraham, that is, instead of useless father—such is the interpretation of the name[12]—he is called sublime father, chosen father; or, alternatively, from being simply father he becomes father of a son. He was useless because he did not know God. He was made the chosen one after he had come to know God. He was father when he had had offspring through the slave girl, but he was not father of a son, because he was not truly his son who had not been born of a legitimate marriage. When Sarah gave birth, he became father of a son. ON ABRAHAM 1.4.27.[13]

FROM THAT TIME. AUGUSTINE: However, a question arises here which should not be passed over and which may perhaps also, quite independently, be bothering some of you. What does it mean, that when the name of Abraham, this man Jacob's grandfather, was changed (he was previously called Abram, you see, and God changed his name and said, you shall not be called Abram, but Abraham)? From that time on he was never called Abram. Search in the Scriptures, and you will see that earlier on, before he received another name, he was only called Abram. After he had received the new one, he was only called Abraham. This man Jacob, however, heard the same words when

he received another name: You shall not be called Jacob, but you shall be called Israel. Now search the Scriptures, and see how he was always called either name, both Jacob and Israel. When Abram got another name, he was never called anything but Abraham; when Jacob got another name, he was called Jacob and Israel.

The name Abraham was to receive its explanation in this world, because it was here that he became the father of many nations, from which his name is derived. The name Israel, on the other hand, belongs to the next world, where we will see God. So the people of God, the Christian people, is in this world and this time both Jacob and Israel; Jacob in our actual situation, Israel in our hopeful expectation. SERMON 122.4.[14]

17:6 Nations Descended from Abraham

THE VIRTUOUS MIND ABOUNDS IN ROYAL OFFSPRING. AMBROSE: Let us turn now to the gift of God than which nothing is more pregnant with promise. For what could be better than wisdom, what could be worse than vanity, what could be more degrading than superstition? So it is that as to one to whom he had promised the fullness of perfection, God says, "I will make you exceedingly fruitful; and I will make nations of you, and kings shall come forth from you." For "the whole world of riches belongs to the faithful person,"[15] and he will increase, not diminish like the fool. Abraham is made into nations, that is to say, his faith is transferred to the nations and to kings of the world, who have become believers, submitting to the authority of the Lord Jesus, to whom it is said, "To you will kings offer gifts."[16] Nor is this absurd, because from the stock of Abraham there will be not only kings in rank but also those who are kings in the sense that they are not slaves to sin, people who cannot be overcome by evil because death has no dominion over them.

---

[11]FC 71:91-92*. [12]The name Abraham literally means "father of a great number." [13]CSEL 32 1:522. [14]WSA 3 4:240-41*. [15]Prov 17:6 LXX. [16]Ps 68:29 (67:30 LXX).

We have seen too that the discoveries of the virtuous mind are also regal and sovereign, because, like Abraham, the virtuous mind does not have a lower-class progeny but abounds rather in royal offspring. To it the world is given in full possession, so that it might rule the body, not being captivated by carnal pleasures, but that submissive flesh might cater to the mind in appropriate servitude. But the figure of Abraham clearly conveys the mystery of the church, which through the inheritance of faith takes possession of the whole world. Well is he called "chosen father of the sound,"[17] father of faith, father of the pious confession. ON ABRAHAM 2.10.77.[18]

---

[17]The etymologies used by Ambrose here derive from Philo. [18]CSEL 32 1:629.

17:9-14 THE INSTITUTION OF CIRCUMCISION

[9]And God said to Abraham, "As for you, you shall keep my covenant, you and your descendants after you throughout their generations. [10]This is my covenant, which you shall keep, between me and you and your descendants after you: Every male among you shall be circumcised. [11]You shall be circumcised in the flesh of your foreskins, and it shall be a sign of the covenant between me and you. [12]He that is eight days old among you shall be circumcised; every male throughout your generations, whether born in your house, or bought with your money from any foreigner who is not of your offspring, [13]both he that is born in your house and he that is bought with your money, shall be circumcised. So shall my covenant be in your flesh an everlasting covenant. [14]Any uncircumcised male who is not circumcised in the flesh of his foreskin shall be cut off from his people; he has broken my covenant."

OVERVIEW: True circumcision is the ability to pass beyond worldly things to approach the transcendent realities through understanding ("CYRIL").[1] Bodily circumcision is the sign of spiritual circumcision, which is the salvation of the whole person, body and soul (AMBROSE). Circumcision is best interpreted as the figure and image of future truth, as Paul has done for us (ORIGEN). Circumcision of the flesh means the precept of chastity. The command of circumcision on the eighth day harbors a mystery, because this is the day of resurrection (AMBROSE). The threat to cut off from the people those not circumcised is disturbing, because the infant of eight days cannot be held personally responsible. The text can be understood to refer either to the parents or to those who have reached the age of reason (AMBROSE, PHILO). Circumcision was given as a sign to prevent the Israelites from mingling with other peoples (CHRYSOSTOM).

17:11 A Covenant Sign

TRUE CIRCUMCISION. "CYRIL OF ALEXANDRIA": In what sense is the covenant eternal?[2] One interpretation is that it is eternal according to the One

---

[1]In the Catena on Genesis many attributions are uncertain (only some manuscripts), unidentified or dubious. Names of the alleged authors appear here in quotation marks. [2]See Gen 17:7, 13.

promising, for the things of God are not time conditioned. But relative to us eternal things become time conditioned. Another interpretation is that even when the covenant with Israel was abolished, it was maintained for us, and we are God's [people] in place of them. Circumcision took over a second territory after the faith [came]. For just as the birth of the illegitimate child came first, after the promise of the legitimate one, because the birth of the latter was likewise belated, so now circumcision came first because the time for the spiritual [circumcision] was not yet; but when this new one appears, the other circumcision is thrown out. For "in Christ Jesus," we say, "neither circumcision nor uncircumcision is of any avail."[3] That circumcision was a sign of the covenant, which could be present even in transgressors. But the true circumcision is the perfect observance of the law, the cutting away and removing of everything alien to God and the ability to pass beyond worldly things to approach the transcendent realities through understanding. Of this the eighth day of circumcision is the symbol. For the eighth day is supernatural, even as the Savior, by accomplishing the resurrection on the eighth day, showed the mystery. Likewise appropriate is the text's reference to extermination, whether of those uncircumcised in the flesh or those whose heart has not been circumcised, the uncircumcised of heart,[4] as one would say using Old Testament terminology. CATENA ON GENESIS 3.1026.[5]

A SIGN OF SPIRITUAL CIRCUMCISION. AMBROSE: I know that this part of the text is disturbing to many. Indeed, if circumcision is a good thing, it should be maintained today as well. If it is useless, it never should have been mandated in the first place, particularly not by divine precept. But, inasmuch as the apostle said, "Abraham received the sign of circumcision,"[6] certainly the sign is not the reality itself but points to another reality. That is, it is not the truth but points to the truth. In fact, Paul expounds this teaching in the following terms: "He received the sign of circumcision as a seal of justice and of faith."[7] For

this reason it is not inappropriate for us to understand that bodily circumcision is a sign of spiritual circumcision. Therefore the sign remained until the truth arrived. The Lord Jesus arrived, he who says, "I am the way and the truth and the life,"[8] because he circumcises the whole person in truth, not a minor bodily member in sign. He abolished the sign; he installed the truth, because once that which was perfect arrived, that which was partial was abolished. Thus the circumcision of a part ceased when the circumcision of the whole shone forth. For it is now no longer man in part but the whole man who is saved in body, saved in soul. For it is written, "If any man would come after me, let him deny himself and take up his cross and follow me."[9] This is the perfect circumcision, because through the sacrifice of the body the soul is redeemed, of which the Lord himself says, "Whoever loses his life for my sake, he will save it."[10] ON ABRAHAM 1.4.29.[11]

THE FIGURE AND IMAGE OF FUTURE TRUTH. ORIGEN: We, therefore, instructed by the apostle Paul, say that just as many other things were made in the figure and image of future truth, so also that circumcision of flesh was bearing the form of spiritual circumcision about which it was both worthy and fitting that "the God of majesty" give commands to mortals.[12] Hear, therefore, how Paul, "a teacher of the Gentiles in faith and truth,"[13] teaches the church of Christ about the mystery of circumcision. "Behold," he says, "the mutilation"—speaking about the Jews who are mutilated in the flesh—"for we," he says, "are the circumcision, who serve God in spirit and have no confidence in the flesh."[14] This is one opinion of Paul about circumcision. Hear also another: "For he is not a Jew who is so outwardly; nor is that circumcision which is outwardly in the flesh. But he is a Jew who is one inwardly with circumcision of the heart in the spirit, not in the letter."[15]

---

[3]Gal 5:6. [4]See Jer 9:26 (9:25 LXX). [5]TEG 3:92-93. [6]Rom 4:11. [7]Rom 4:11. [8]Jn 14:6. [9]Mt 16:24. [10]Lk 9:24. [11]CSEL 32 1:524-25. [12]Ps 29:3 (28:3 LXX). [13]1 Tim 2:7. [14]Phil 3:2-3. [15]Rom 2:28-29.

Does it not seem more appropriate to you to speak of such a circumcision among the saints and friends of God than to speak of a pruning of the flesh?

But the novelty of the expression may perhaps deter not only the Jews but even some of our brothers. For Paul, who introduces "circumcision of the heart," seems to assume things that are impossible. For how shall it be possible that a member be circumcised that, covered by the internal viscera, lies hidden even from the view of men? HOMILIES ON GENESIS 3.4.[16]

THE PRECEPT OF CHASTITY. AMBROSE: Abraham is ordered to circumcise himself when he is about to receive the inheritance of a true progeny. Is it not evident that "circumcision of the flesh" is the precept of chastity, that one should remove the passions of the flesh and curb the desires that unbridled lust renders indomitable? Indeed, the very word *circumcision* prescribes this, that every stench of impurity be wiped away and that the stimulus of the passions be removed. ON ABRAHAM 1.4.27.[17]

17:12 Circumcised on the Eighth Day

PERFECT CIRCUMCISION IS THE SPIRITUAL ONE. AMBROSE: And because he is called to what is perfect, Abraham receives the oracle that summons to perfection. "Circumcise," it says, "every male of yours and circumcise your flesh"; but perfect circumcision is the spiritual one. Indeed, Scripture also teaches this when it says, "Circumcise the hardness of your heart."[18] Even here many interpret the text to be saying, "Circumcise every male of yours," that is, your minds; for nothing is more virile than the mind. Moreover, because the male is also holy, it is said, "Every male opening the womb shall be called holy for the Lord."[19] But what is holier than the mind that produces the seeds of good thoughts by which it opens the womb of the soul, which was closed by the sterility that prevented it from childbearing, so that it might give birth to invisible genera-

tions, obviously through that spiritual womb of which Isaiah said, "We have conceived in the womb and given birth to the spirit of salvation"?[20] So what is mandated is the intelligible circumcision of the heart as well as the sensible circumcision of the flesh: the former in truth, the latter in sign. Circumcision then is twofold because it requires the mortification of the mind and the body. The Egyptians in fact circumcise their males in the fourteenth year, and it is said that their women too are circumcised in the same year, because in that year the passion of virility begins to flare up and the menstrual cycles of women commence. But the promulgator of the eternal law requires the mark of carnal circumcision only in males, because in the sexual relationship the man is more impetuous than the woman, and for this reason he wished to check his passionate impulse by the mark of circumcision. Or, because men regard their error as licit, so long as they avoid adultery, and are convinced that the practice of prostitution is in conformity to the natural law, while the truth is that neither men nor woman are permitted to have sexual relationships outside of marriage. But according to a deeper interpretation, the intention is to explain that if the mind has once been purified and circumcised, freed from illicit desires and thoughts, it binds the soul to its own chastity, and, having infused it with purity of the senses, makes it capable of generating good offspring.

The law orders that the baby boy be circumcised on the eighth day: evidently a precept that harbors a mystery, because this is precisely the day of the resurrection. Indeed, the Lord Jesus rose from the dead on Sunday. For this reason, if the day of resurrection finds us circumcised and free from excesses and crimes, purified from every filth, cleansed from bodily vices, if you go forth from this day clean, you will rise clean. ON ABRAHAM 2.11.78-79.[21]

---

[16]FC 71:94. [17]CSEL 32 1 :522. [18]Deut 10:16. [19]Ex 13:2. [20]Is 26:18. [21]CSEL 32 1:630-31.

17:13 *An Everlasting Covenant*

THE COVENANT IN YOUR FLESH. "CYRIL OF ALEXANDRIA": God's covenant is "in the flesh" of the person who "does not fight on the terms of the flesh"[22] and who "always carries about in his body the death of Jesus."[23] CATENA ON GENESIS 3.1027.[24]

17:14 *Uncircumcision Breaks the Covenant*

THE AGE OF REASON. PHILO OF ALEXANDRIA: Nothing done unwittingly is declared punishable by the law, since the law makes allowance even for one who claims to have committed unintentional homicide.[25] Why then is the eight-day-old infant who is uncircumcised menaced as though subject to the penalty of death? Some say that this is to be applied, by way of interpretation, to the parents. They, it is thought, should be punished as having made light of the precept of the law. But others think that by the use of hyperbole, the text expresses anger with respect to the infant child, as much as it appears to do, in order that the inevitable punishment might be brought upon those who have reached the use of reason and who have broken the law. QUESTIONS ON GENESIS 3.52.1.[26]

THE CASE IS NOT CLEAR. AMBROSE: Not without reason or by excessive reaction do many find this passage disturbing, in that the Lord should say, "Any uncircumcised male who is not circumcised in the flesh of his foreskin shall be cut off from his people; he has broken my covenant." Indeed, it is not taken lightly that the negligence of the parents could bring punishment upon an eight-day-old infant, so much so that his soul would perish, while even in the case of homicide—committed, however, by one who had unintentionally killed a man—the law stipulated to what cities the perpetrator might flee to obtain impunity for the shedding of blood.[27] How is it possible, then, that for the case of homicide the involuntary character of the killing is taken into consideration, while here no account is taken of infancy, in which there could have been no fault whatever, whether of negligence or of purpose—unless perhaps some might think that the parents receive an even graver punishment in the death of their son? But it is regarded as unjust when the crime of a wrongdoer is inflicted on an innocent party or when a person is included in the punishment of another when he is not responsible to the same degree. For this reason some think that the passage is saying that the parent is to be exterminated, that it is his soul that should perish, not that of the baby. But the case is not at all clear, even if this opinion seems to be supported by the comment "because he has violated my covenant." This then seems to refer to one who is capable of understanding, not to the infant child. Others maintain that the Lord God is threatening the parents, even if silently, with still graver punishments, so that as adults they will have even greater fear when [they see that] not even children are spared. ON ABRAHAM 2.11.83.[28]

IN CASE THEY SHOULD MINGLE. CHRYSOSTOM: See the Lord's wisdom in knowing how inobservant future generations are likely to be, and so, as though putting a bit in their mouths, he gave them this sign of circumcision, curbing their unrestrained urges in case they should mingle with other peoples. You see, he was aware of their lustful tendencies in not practicing restraint, even though it had been drummed into them countless times to refrain from their irrational impulses. Consequently he gave them a perpetual reminder with this sign of circumcision, as though fastening them with a chain. He set limits and rules to prevent them overstepping the mark instead of staying within their own people and having no association with those other peoples but rather keeping the patriarch's line uncontaminated. In this way even the fulfillment of the promises

---

[22]2 Cor 10:3. [23]2 Cor 4:10. [24]TEG 3.93. [25]Num 35:11; Deut 4:41-43; 19:1-13; Josh 20:1-9. [26]TEG 3.94. [27]Num 35:9-15; Deut 4:41-43; 19:1-13; Josh 20:1-9. [28]CSEL 32 1:634.

could be achieved for their benefit. It is like a man of self-control and good sense having a disobedient child; he puts limits and rules on him not to show his face outside the front door or to be seen by passersby. In fact, he oftentimes ties him up by the feet so as to succeed in this way in getting the better of his extreme indiscipline. Well, in just the same way the loving Lord also placed this sign of circumcision in their flesh, like shackles on their feet, so that with this reminder at home they might have no further need of instruction from others. HOMILIES ON GENESIS 39.14.[29]

---

[29]FC 82:384*.

17:15-21 THE PROMISE OF ISAAC

[15]And God said to Abraham, "As for Sarai your wife, you shall not call her name Sarai, but Sarah shall be her name. [16]I will bless her, and moreover I will give you a son by her; I will bless her, and she shall be a mother of nations; kings of peoples shall come from her." [17]Then Abraham fell on his face and laughed, and said to himself, "Shall a child be born to a man who is a hundred years old? Shall Sarah, who is ninety years old, bear a child?" [18]And Abraham said to God, "O that Ishmael might live in thy sight!" [19]God said, "No, but Sarah your wife shall bear you a son, and you shall call his name Isaac.[z] I will establish my covenant with him as an everlasing covenant for his descendants after him. [20]As for Ishmael, I have heard you; behold, I will bless him and make him fruitful and multiply him exceedingly; he shall be the father of twelve princes, and I will make him a great nation. [21]But I will establish my covenant with Isaac, whom Sarah shall bear to you at this season next year."

z That is he laughs

OVERVIEW: The change of Sarai's name to Sarah is interpreted on the basis of a Hebrew etymology to mean a change from "my ruler" to "ruler." She is the parent of all rightly believing women (BEDE). Abraham's laughter at the announcement of a son was not evidence of doubt on his part but rather of his marveling at what was happening (EPHREM). His laughter, obviously a problem for interpreters, is interpreted also as an expression not of unbelief but of joy (AMBROSE). The etymology of the name Isaac as "laughter" or "joy" also provides the basis for interpreting Isaac as everyone for whom blessed laughter follows upon the weeping here below ("CYRIL").

17:15 Sarai Renamed

THE PARENT OF ALL RIGHTLY BELIEVING WOMEN. BEDE: [God] said, "And you shall not call your wife Sarai but Sarah," that is, "You shall not call her 'my ruler' but 'ruler.'" [This change teaches] clearly that since she had become a companion and sharer of such great faith, he should call her [by a name that expressed what] he understood her to be: not exclusively the ruler of his own house but ruler absolutely, that is, the parent of all rightly believing women. Hence, when blessed Peter was urging believing women from the nations to the virtues of humility, chastity and modesty, he remembered our mother Sarah with due praise, saying, "Just as Sarah was obedient to Abraham, calling him lord, you are her daughters when you do rightly and do not fear any disturbance."[1] HOMILIES ON THE GOSPELS 1.11.[2]

17:17 Abraham Laughs

A MARVEL TO HIM. EPHREM THE SYRIAN: Now Abraham was not guilty of any doubt by his laughter, for he showed his love toward Ishmael in what he said. He had clung to this hope for twenty-five years. Abraham had manifested his faith in every vision that had come to him. However great his contest with barrenness became, he manifested the victory of his faith. But when old age was added to the barrenness, he laughed in his heart. That his Lord would do these two things for him was a marvel to him. COMMENTARY ON GENESIS 14.2.[3]

THE PROGENITOR OF ALL BELIEVERS. AMBROSE: One should consider the fact that Abraham was uncircumcised when God called him, and he was still uncircumcised when he was promised a legitimate son as heir. You are hereby invited to believe that he is not only the father of the Jews, as they claim, but the progenitor, through faith, of all believers. Sarah also, before the circumcision of her husband and by the addition of one letter to her name, receives the blessing of no small gift, so that she might have the primacy of virtue and of grace. God promises that from her nations and kings of peoples will come, so that in her might be established the type not of the synagogue but of the church. The fact that Abraham laughed when he had been promised a

son through her was an expression not of unbelief but of joy. Indeed, he "fell on his face"—in worship, which means he believed. And he added, "Shall a child be born to a man who is a hundred years old? Shall Sarah, who is ninety years old, bear a child?" And he said, "O that Ishmael might live in thy sight!" He is not incredulous with regard to the promises, nor is he greedy in what he asks for in prayer. "I have no doubt that you will come through, granting a son to an old man of a hundred years and that, as the author of nature, you will effectively stretch its limits. Blessed indeed is the one on whom this gift is bestowed; but I will be doubly favored if even this Ishmael here, whom I begot from the household slave, should live in your presence." And so the Lord approved Abraham's sentiments, did not deny his request and confirmed his own promises. ON ABRAHAM 1.4.31.[4]

HE MARVELED. "CYRIL OF ALEXANDRIA": He was not laughing because he did not believe, as some might imagine, but rejoicing because he did. "He laughed" is sometimes put in place of "he rejoiced," as it is also in the Gospels.[5] And for this reason, he also "fell on his face" and marveled in his heart. CATENA ON GENESIS 3.1038.[6]

17:19 Isaac

EVERY PERSON IS ISAAC. ANONYMOUS: Isaac is the first whose name is given by command of God, for it is he who gives his name, by prophecy, to the blessed laughter that follows upon the weeping here below. And in a playful way, you will say that every person is "Isaac" who has attained that promise: they "shall laugh."[7] CATENA ON GENESIS 3.1041.[8]

---

[1]1 Pet 3:6. [2]CS 110:106-7. [3]FC 91:157. [4]CSEL 32 1:526. [5]See Lk 6:21, 25. [6]TEG 3:100. [7]Lk 6:21. [8]TEG 3:101.

17:22-27 THE CIRCUMCISION OF ABRAHAM
AND HIS HOUSEHOLD

^{22}When he had finished talking with him, God went up from Abraham. ^{23}Then Abraham took Ishmael his son and all the slaves born in his house or bought with his money, every male among the men of Abraham's house, and he circumcised the flesh of their foreskins that very day, as God had said to him. ^{24}Abraham was ninety-nine years old when he was circumcised in the flesh of his foreskin. ^{25}And Ishmael his son was thirteen years old when he was circumcised in the flesh of his foreskin. ^{26}That very day Abraham and his son Ishmael were circumcised; ^{27}and all the men of his house, those born in the house and those bought with money from a foreigner, were circumcised with him.

OVERVIEW: The reason why the text mentions Abraham's age is to show the obedience of the just man in meekly submitting to pain (CHRYSOSTOM). The circumcision of Ishmael in his thirteenth year signifies the need for one who is beginning to be sexually active to trim the ardor of his passion (AMBROSE). The number of men circumcised by Abraham that day was 318,[1] a number that symbolically represents Jesus and his cross (PSEUDO-BARNABAS). Our circumcision is the grace of baptism (CHRYSOSTOM).

17:24 Abraham Was Circumcised

THE JUST MAN'S OBEDIENCE. CHRYSOSTOM: Don't think it was without purpose that Scripture indicated to us his age; instead, it was for you to learn from the just man's obedience in meekly submitting to pain despite his extreme old age on account of God's command, and not only he but also Ishmael and all the servants—that was the reason for giving the ages. HOMILIES ON GENESIS 40.14.[2]

17:25 Ishmael Was Circumcised

TO TRIM ARDOR. AMBROSE: Even the fact that Ishmael was circumcised in his thirteenth year is for an obvious reason, because one who is beginning to be sexually active should trim the ardor of

his passion, so as to abstain from illicit unions and limit himself to a legitimate union only. ON ABRAHAM 2.11.91.[3]

17:27 All the Men Were Circumcised

ABRAHAM CIRCUMCISED 318 MEN. PSEUDO-BARNABAS: Learn fully then, children of love, concerning all things, for Abraham, who first circumcised, did so looking forward in the spirit to Jesus and had received the doctrines of the three letters. For it says, "Abraham circumcised from his household eighteen men and three hundred." What then was the knowledge that was given to him? Notice that he first mentions the eighteen, and after a pause the three hundred. The eighteen is I (= 10) and H (= 8)—you have Jesus—and because the cross was destined to have grace in the T he says "and three hundred."[4] So he indicates Jesus in the two letters and the cross in the other. He knows this who placed the gift of his teaching in our hearts. EPISTLE OF BARNABAS 9.7-9.[5]

A REMEDY FREE FROM PAIN. CHRYSOSTOM: Consider, on the other hand, I ask you, dearly beloved, God's loving kindness and his unspeakable

---

[1]Cf. Gen 14:14. [2]FC 82:396. [3]CSEL 32 1:638. [4]See p. 23 n. 5. [5]LCL 24:373.

kindness to us. In that case pain and distress resulted from the action and no benefit came from circumcision, except simply making people recognizable through this sign and separating them from the other peoples. Our circumcision, on the contrary—I mean the grace of baptism—involves a painless medicine and is the means of countless good things for us, filling us with the grace of the Spirit. It has no limited span as in that other case, but rather in early years, in middle age and in the very height of old age can a person receive this circumcision—not the work of human hands[6]—which involves not simply endurance but laying aside sin's burden and finding pardon for the faults of all time. . . . The loving God saw the extraordinary degree of our limitations and the fact that we are suffering from incurable diseases and need a lot of care as well as his ineffable love. [Thus] he is in his provision for our salvation granted us the renewal that comes from the bath of rebirth, so that by setting aside the former person—that is, evil deeds—and putting on the new we may advance along the way of virtue. HOMILIES ON GENESIS 40.16.[7]

---

[6]See Col 2:11. [7]FC 82:397*.

18:1-8 THE APPEARANCE TO ABRAHAM AT MAMRE

[1]And the LORD appeared to him by the oaks[a] of Mamre, as he sat at the door of his tent in the heat of the day. [2]He lifted up his eyes and looked, and behold, three men stood in front of him. When he saw them, he ran from the tent door to meet them, and bowed himself to the earth, [3]and said, "My lord, if I have found favor in your sight, do not pass by your servant. [4]Let a little water be brought, and wash your feet, and rest yourselves under the tree, [5]while I fetch a morsel of bread, that you may refresh yourselves, and after that you may pass on—since you have come to your servant." So they said, "Do as you have said." [6]And Abraham hastened into the tent to Sarah, and said, "Make ready quickly three measures[b] of fine meal, knead it, and make cakes." [7]And Abraham ran to the herd, and took a calf, tender and good, and gave it to the servant, who hastened to prepare it. [8]Then he took curds, and milk, and the calf which he had prepared, and set it before them; and he stood by them under the tree while they ate.

a Or terebinths   b Heb seahs

OVERVIEW: The statement that "God appeared" posed a problem: How could a human being see the invisible God and Creator of all?[1] The more common and earlier solution was based on Genesis 18:3, in which Abraham says, "my Lord," thus appearing to speak to only one of the three visitors, who was then interpreted to be the divine Word of God (EUSEBIUS). The three visitors were also seen as a symbol or prefiguration of the Trinity (AMBROSE) and explained in terms of post-Nicaean terminology. Another interpretation saw the three visitors as angels (EPHREM, AUGUS-

---

[1]See also the comment on Genesis 12:7 (pp. 5-6).

TINE). The oak of Mamre is interpreted etymologically to mean "vision," and, using the principle of interpreting the Scriptures by means of the Scriptures (see introduction, p. xxxiv), this notion can be linked with the Beatitudes, which promise the vision of God to the pure of heart. The contrast between the three men who come to Abraham and the two who visit Lot (Gen 19) permits a comparison between their respective merits (ORIGEN, CAESARIUS OF ARLES). Small details such as the phrase "in front of him" also provide material for edifying comment (ORIGEN, EPHREM, CAESARIUS OF ARLES) based on the principle that Scripture does not waste words or every detail counts (see introduction, p. xvii). The passage also provides an occasion for exhortation to the virtue of hospitality. The reference to three loaves or cakes and to the calf prepared for the visitors is interpreted as foreshadowing the doctrine of the Trinity and the sacrifice of Christ (ORIGEN, AMBROSE, CAESARIUS OF ARLES).

18:1 The Lord Appears by the Oaks of Mamre

THE LORD APPEARED. EUSEBIUS OF CAESAREA: Thus the Lord God is said to have appeared as a common man to Abraham while he was seated by the oak of Mamre. But [Abraham] immediately fell down, although he saw a man with his eyes, and worshiped him as God, besought him as Lord and confessed that he was not ignorant as to who he was, using these very words, "O Lord, judge of all the earth, will you not judge righteously?"[2] For if it should be unreasonable to suppose that the unbegotten and immutable substance of God the Almighty was changed into the form of man and, in turn, that the eyes of the beholders were deceived by the phantasm of something created and that such things were falsely invented by Scripture, who else could be proclaimed God and the Lord who judges all the earth and judges righteously, appearing in the shape of a man—if it be not proper to call him the first cause of all things—than his preexis-

tent Word alone? ECCLESIASTICAL HISTORY 1.2.7-8.[3]

ABRAHAM SAW THE TRINITY TYPIFIED. AMBROSE: Abraham, who was glad to receive strangers, faithful to God and tireless in his service and prompt in fulfilling his duty, saw the Trinity typified. He added religious devotion to hospitality, for although he beheld three, he adored one, and, while keeping a distinction of the persons, yet he called one Lord, thus giving honor to the three but signifying one power. For not knowledge but grace spoke in him. And he believed better what he had not learned than we who have been taught. No one had falsified the type of truth, and therefore he saw three but worshiped their unity. He brought out three measures of meal but slaughtered one calf, believing one sacrifice was sufficient, but a threefold offering; one victim, but a threefold gift. ON HIS BROTHER, SATYRUS 2.96.[4]

THEY WERE ANGELS. AUGUSTINE: God appeared again to Abraham at the oak of Mamre in three men, who it is not to be doubted were angels, although some think that one of them was Christ and assert that he was visible before he put on flesh. Now it belongs to the divine power and invisible, incorporeal and incommunicable nature, without changing itself at all, to appear even to mortals, not by what it is but by what is subject to it. And what is not subject to it? Yet if they try to establish that one of these three was Christ by the fact that although he saw three, he addressed the Lord in the singular, as it is written, "He lifted up his eyes and looked, and behold, three men stood in front of him. When he saw them, he ran from the tent door to meet them, and bowed himself to the earth and said, 'My lord, if I have found favor in your sight.'"[5] Why do they not refer also to this, that when two of them came to destroy the Sodomites, while Abraham still spoke to one, calling him Lord and interceding that he would not destroy the right-

[2]Gen 18:25. [3]FC 19:39-40*. [4]FC 22:239-40. [5]Gen 18:2-3.

eous along with the wicked in Sodom, Lot received these two in such a way that he too in his conversation with them addressed the Lord in the singular? For after saying to them in the plural, "My lords, turn aside, I pray you, to your servant's house,"[6] yet it is afterward said, "So [the angels] seized him and his hand, [because] the Lord [was] merciful to him, and they brought him forth and set him outside the city. And when they had brought them forth, they said, 'Flee for your life; do not look back or stop anywhere in the valley; flee to the hills, lest you be consumed.' And Lot said to them, 'Oh, no, my lords; behold, your servant has found favor in your sight. . . .'"[7] And then after these words the Lord also answered him in the singular, although he was in two angels, saying, "Behold, I grant you this favor. . . ."[8] This makes it much more credible that Abraham in the three men and Lot in the two recognized the Lord, addressing him in the singular number, even when they were addressing men; for they received them as they did for no other reason than that they might minister human nourishment to them as men who needed it. Yet there was about them something so excellent that those who showed them hospitality as men could not doubt that God was in them as he was wont to be in the prophets and therefore sometimes addressed them in the plural, and sometimes God in them in the singular. But that they were angels the Scripture testifies, not only in this book of Genesis, in which these transactions are related, but also in the epistle to the Hebrews, where in praising hospitality it is said, "For thereby some have entertained angels unawares."[9] City of God 16.29.[10]

The Oak of Mamre. Origen: But let us see what this tree represents, under which Abraham stood and provided a meal for the Lord and the angels. "Under the tree of Mamre" the text says. Mamre in our language is translated "vision" or "sharpness of sight." Do you see what kind of place it is where the Lord can have a meal? Abraham's vision and sharpness of sight pleased the

Lord. For he was pure in heart so that he could see God.[11] In such a place, therefore, and in such a heart the Lord can have a meal with his angels. In fact, earlier prophets were called seers.[12] Homilies on Genesis 4.3.[13]

Abraham Was Clean of Heart. Caesarius of Arles: Now where did this happen? "Near the holm-oak of Mamre," which in Latin is interpreted as "vision" or "discernment." Do you see what kind of a place it is in which the Lord can have a feast? The vision and discernment of Abraham delighted him; he was clean of heart, so that he could see God. Therefore in such a place and in such a heart the Lord can have his feast. Of this vision our Lord spoke to the Jews in the Gospel when he said, "Abraham rejoiced that he was to see my day. He saw it and was glad."[14] He saw my day, he says, because he recognized the mystery of the Trinity. He saw the Father as day, the Son as day, the Holy Spirit as day, and in these three one day. Thus the Father is God, the Son is God, the Holy Spirit is God, and these three are one God. For individually each person is complete God, and all three together are one God. Moreover, because of the unity of substance, in those three measures of flour the Father, Son and Holy Spirit are not unfittingly understood. However, this can also be taken in another way by understanding Sarah as the church; the three measures of flour then are faith, hope and charity. In these three virtues all the fruits of the church are contained, so that if one merits to possess the three within oneself, one can with security receive the entire Trinity at the banquet of one's heart. Sermon 83.5.[15]

18:2 Three Men Stand Before Abraham

Three Men Stood in Front of Him. Origen: Let us compare, first of all, if you please, this appearance with that one which Lot experienced.

---

[6]Gen 19:2. [7]Gen 19:16-19. [8]Gen 19:21. [9]Heb 13:2. [10]NPNF 1 2:327-28*. [11]See Mt 5:8. [12]See 1 Sam 9:9. [13]FC 71:106. [14]Jn 8:56. [15]FC 47:14.

"Three men" come to Abraham and stand "before him"; "two" come to Lot and sit "in the street."[16] See if, in the dispensation of the Holy Spirit, these events did not occur as each man deserved. For Lot was far inferior to Abraham. For if he had not been inferior, he would not have been separate from Abraham, nor would Abraham have said to him, "If you go to the right, I will go to the left; if you go to the left, I will go to the right."[17] And if he had not been inferior, the land and habitation of Sodom would not have pleased him.

Three men, therefore, come to Abraham at midday; two come to Lot and in the evening.[18] For Lot could not receive the magnitude of midday light, but Abraham was capable of receiving the full brightness of the light.

Let us see now how Abraham received those who came and how Lot did, and let us compare each man's preparation of hospitality. First, however, observe that the Lord also was present with Abraham with two angels, but two angels alone proceed to Lot. And what do they say? "The Lord has sent us to consume the city and destroy it."[19] He therefore received those who would give destruction. He did not receive him who would save. But Abraham received him who saves and those who destroy. HOMILIES ON GENESIS 4.1.[20]

BEFORE HIM. ORIGEN: But let us now, meanwhile, pursue what Abraham does with the three men who "stood before him." Behold what sort of expression this is itself, that they come "before him," not against him. He had, to be sure, subjected himself to the will of God; therefore God is said to stand "before him." HOMILIES ON GENESIS 4.2.[21]

THREE MEN STOOD OVER HIM. CAESARIUS OF ARLES: Notice, brothers, and see how God appeared to Abraham and how he appeared to Lot. The three men came to Abraham and stood over him; two came to Lot and stayed in the street. Consider, brothers, whether these things did not happen through the dispensation of the Holy Spirit according to their merits. Indeed, Lot was

far inferior to Abraham; if he had not been, he would not have merited to be separated from Abraham, nor would the dwelling of Sodom have pleased him. Now the three men came to Abraham at noon, while the other two came to Lot in the evening for this reason: Lot was unable to endure the power of the noonday sun, but Abraham could stand its full brightness. SERMON 83.2.[22]

SUBJECT TO GOD'S WILL. CAESARIUS OF ARLES: "Three men came to Abraham and stood over him."[23] Observe how it is that they come upon him but not against him. He had subjected himself to God's will, and for this reason God is said to stand over him. "They stood over him," not against him to repulse him but over him for protection. SERMON 83.4.[24]

HE RAN TO MEET THEM. ORIGEN: Now let us see how each man receives his guests. "Abraham saw," the text says, "and ran to meet them." Notice that Abraham immediately is energetic and eager in his duties. He runs to meet them, and when he had met them, "he hastens back to the tent," the text says, "and says to his wife: 'Hasten to the tent.' "[25] Behold in the individual matters how great is his eagerness to receive them. He makes haste in all things; all things are done urgently; nothing is done leisurely. HOMILIES ON GENESIS 4.1.[26]

THE LORD APPEARED IN ONE OF THE THREE. EPHREM THE SYRIAN: Although Abraham ran from the tent toward them as if toward strangers, he ran to receive those strangers with love. His love for strangers was thus proved by the haste with which he ran to meet those strangers. Therefore the Lord, who had just appeared to him at the door of the tent, now appeared to Abraham clearly in one of the three. Abraham then fell down and worshiped him, seeking from

---

[16]Gen 19:1. [17]Gen 13:9. [18]Gen 19:1. [19]Gen 19:13. [20]FC 71:103-4. [21]FC 71:105. [22]FC 47:11. [23]This is a loose translation by Caesarius of Arles based on Genesis 18:2. [24]FC 47:12. [25]Gen 18:6. [26]FC 71:104.

him in whom majesty dwells that he condescend to enter his house and bless his dwelling. "If I have found favor in your sight, do not pass by your servant." God did not oppose him, for he said, "Do as you have said."[27] Then Abraham ran to Sarah [telling her] to make three measures of wheat, and then he ran to the herd to get a fatted calf. COMMENTARY ON GENESIS 15.1.[28]

HOSPITALITY HAS ITS RECOMPENSE.
AMBROSE: Hospitality is a good thing, and it has its recompense: first of all the recompense of human gratitude and then, more importantly, the divine reward. In this earthly abode we are all guests; here we have only a temporary dwelling place. We depart from it in haste. Let us be careful not to be discourteous or neglectful in receiving guests, lest we be denied entrance into the dwelling place of the saints at the end of our life. For this reason, the Savior said in the Gospel, "Make friends for yourselves by means of unrighteous mammon, so that when it fails they may receive you into the eternal habitations."[29]

Moreover, while we are in this body, there often arises the necessity of traveling. Therefore that which you will have denied to others, you will have decided against yourself. You must show yourself worthy of that which you will have offered to others. If all decided not to receive guests, where would those who are traveling find rest? Then we would have to abandon human habitations and seek out the dens of the wild beasts. ON ABRAHAM 1.5.34.[30]

18:4 Abraham's Hospitality

WASH YOUR FEET. ORIGEN: But how does he continue again as if speaking to men: "Let water be received," the text says, "and your feet be washed"?

Abraham, the father and teacher of nations, is indeed teaching you by these things how you ought to receive guests and that you should wash the feet of guests. Nevertheless even this is said mysteriously. For he knew that the mysteries of

the Lord were not to be completed except in the washing of feet.[31] But he was not unaware of the importance of that precept, indeed, in which the Savior says, "If any shall not receive you, shake off even the dust which clings to your feet for a testimony to them. Truly I say to you that it shall be more tolerable for the land of Sodom in the day of judgment than for that city."[32] He wished, therefore, to anticipate that and to wash their feet lest perhaps any dust should remain, which, shaken off, could be reserved "in the day of judgment" for a testimony of unbelief. For that reason, therefore, wise Abraham says, "Let water be received and your feet be washed." HOMILIES ON GENESIS 4.2.[33]

IN CONSIDERATION OF HIS HOSPITALITY.
CAESARIUS OF ARLES: Moreover he adds, as though speaking to the men, "I will bring water, that you may wash your feet." Learn from blessed Abraham, brothers, to receive strangers gladly and to wash their feet with humility and piety. Wash, I repeat, the feet of pious strangers, lest there remain in them some dust that they will be able to shake off of their feet to your judgment. In the Gospel we read, "Whoever does not receive you—go forth and shake off the dust from your feet. Amen, I say to you, it will be more tolerable for the land of Sodom and Gomorrah in the day of judgment than for that town."[34] Abraham foresaw this in spirit and for this reason wanted to anticipate it by washing their feet, lest perchance any dust remain that might be kept and shaken off on judgment day as an evidence of unbelief. Therefore the wise Abraham says, "I will bring water, that you may wash your feet." Carefully listen to this, brothers, if you are unwilling to exercise hospitality and to receive even your enemy as a guest. Behold, while blessed Abraham welcomed those men warmly, he merited to receive God in consideration of his hospitality. Christ further confirmed this in the Gospel when he

---

[27]Gen 18:5. [28]FC 91:158. [29]Lk 16:9. [30]CSEL 32 1:528. [31]See Jn 13:6. [32]Mk 6:11; Mt 10:15. [33]FC 71:105-6. [34]Mt 10:14-15.

said, "I was a stranger, and you took me in."[35] Therefore do not despise strangers, lest perhaps he himself be the one you have rejected. Sermon 83.4.[36]

18:6 Cakes of Fine Meal

Three Measures of Fine Meal. Origen: He serves therefore bread mixed "with three measures of fine wheat flour." He received three men; he mixed the bread "with three measures of fine wheat flour." Everything he does is mystical; everything is filled with mystery. Homilies on Genesis 4.2.[37]

Secret or Hidden Bread. Origen: Therefore he says to his wife Sarah, "Hasten to the tent and mix three measures of fine wheat flour and make bread upon the hearth." The Greek is *enkryphia*, which indicates secret or hidden bread. Homilies on Genesis 4.1.[38]

About the Mystery of the Faith. Ambrose: He says, "Mix three measures of fine flour and make cakes." In Greek these are called *enkryphia*, that is, hidden things, to indicate that every mystery must remain hidden and as if covered by inviolable silence, so that it should not be divulged inconsiderately to profane ears. In this silence the divine majesty is nurtured. With this inner attitude the one who is sober in speech avoids divulging the sacred. In using three measures of flour, Sarah is in fact giving a brief teaching about the mystery of the faith, she who is herself a prefiguration of the church, to whom are addressed the words, "Sing, O barren one, who did not bear; break forth into singing and cry aloud, you who have not been in travail."[39] It is in fact the church that protects the faith in the intimacy of the Spirit when it professes the Trinity of one and the same nature, when it adores in equal measure and with equal veneration the Father, the Son and the Holy Spirit and celebrates them together in the same majesty, distinguishing according to what is proper to each person. Mix your piety with this

profession of faith! On Abraham 1.5.38.[40]

18:7 Preparing a Calf

No One Is Slow in the House of a Wise Man. Origen: "But he ran," the text says, "to the cattle and took a calf." What kind of calf? Perhaps the first one he encountered? Not at all, but "a good and tender" calf. And although he would hasten in all things, nevertheless he knows that what is excellent and great should be offered to the Lord or to angels. He took therefore or chose from the herd a "good and tender" calf and delivered it to his servant. "The servant," the text says, "hastened to slaughter it." He himself runs, his wife hastens, the servant makes haste. No one is slow in the house of a wise man.[41] He serves therefore a calf and at the same time with it bread and fine wheat flour, but also milk and butter. These were the courtesies of hospitality of Abraham and Sarah. Homilies on Genesis 4.1.[42]

A Calf, Tender and Good. Origen: A calf is served; behold, another mystery. The calf itself is not tough but "good and tender." And what is so tender, what so good as that One who "humbled himself" for us "to death" and "laid down his life for his friends"?[43] He is the "fatted calf"[44] which the father slaughtered to receive his repentant son. "For he so loved this world, as to give his only Son"[45] for the life of this world. Nevertheless the wise man is not ignorant of whom he has received. He runs to three men and adores one, and he speaks to the one saying, "Turn aside to your servant, and refresh yourself under the tree."[46] Homilies on Genesis 4.2.[47]

What the Law Represented in a Shadow. Ambrose: The fact that Abraham ran to the herd, took a good and tender calf and served it

---

[35]Mt 25:35. [36]FC 47:13-14. [37]FC 71:105. [38]FC 71:104*. [39]Is 54:1. [40]CSEL 32 1:531. [41]Cf. Philo *De Abrahamo* 109. [42]FC 71:104. [43]Phil 2:6; 1 Jn 3:16; Jn 15:23. [44]Lk 15:23. [45]Jn 3:16. [46]Gen 18:3-4. [47]FC 71:105.

with milk is not without significance. In fact, in Exodus Moses, when he proclaimed the Passover of the Lord, said, "Your lamb shall be without blemish, a male a year old; you shall take it from the sheep or from the goats, and you shall kill it at sunset in the midst of the whole assembly." So also here it is specified that it was midday that Abraham offered hospitality to the Lord. But it was for supper that the calf was immolated and eaten with milk, that is, not with blood but with the purity of the faith. A "good calf" because it should wash away sins. "Tender" because it received the yoke of the law, not with a stiff neck[48] but docilely, and did not refuse the gibbet of the cross. And it is "tender" since nothing of its head, feet or internal organs is thrown away,[49] nor were any of its bones broken,[50] but it was eaten in its entirety by those taking part in the meal. Thus what the law represented in a shadow,[51] the gospel has shown us in reality. ON ABRAHAM 1.5.40.[52]

ANGELS ENTER A HOSPITABLE HOME. CAESARIUS OF ARLES: Lot too received men, but only two, not the whole Trinity; moreover in the evening, not at noon. What did he serve them? "He baked unleavened bread, and they ate."[53] Because he was much inferior to Abraham in merits he did not have a fatted calf. Nor did he recognize the mystery of the Trinity in the three measures of flour. However, since he offered what he could in a kindly spirit, he merited to be freed from the destruction of Sodom. Notice, brothers, that even Lot deserved to receive the angels, because he did not reject strangers. Behold, angels enter a

hospitable home, but houses that are closed to strangers are burned with flames of sulphur. SERMON 83.3.[54]

THE MYSTERY OF THE TRINITY. CAESARIUS OF ARLES: He received the three men and served them loaves out of three measures. Why is this, brothers, unless it means the mystery of the Trinity? He also served a calf; not a tough one, but a "good, tender one." Now what is so good and tender as he who humbled himself for us even unto death? He himself is that fatted calf which the father killed upon receiving his repentant son. "For God so loved the world that he gave his only-begotten Son."[55] For this reason Abraham went to meet the three men and adored them as one. In the fact that he saw three, as was already said, he understood the mystery of the Trinity; but since he adored them as one, he recognized that there is one God in the three persons. SERMON 83.4.[56]

BLESSING DISTRIBUTED. EPHREM THE SYRIAN: The bread and meat, which was in abundance, was not to satisfy the angels but rather so that the blessing might be distributed to all the members of his household. After the angels had washed and sat down beneath a tree, "Abraham brought and set before them what he had prepared"; he did not dare recline with them but like a servant "stood apart from them." COMMENTARY ON GENESIS 15.2.[57]

---

[48]See Ex 32:9. [49]See Ex 12:9-10. [50]Cf. Jn 19:36; Ex 12:46; Num 9:12; Ps 34:20 (33:21 LXX). [51]Heb 10:1. [52]CSEL 32 1:532-33. [53]Gen 19:3. [54]FC 47:12. [55]Jn 3:16. [56]FC 47:13. [57]FC 91:158.

18:9-15 THE PROMISE OF A SON

⁹They said to him, "Where is Sarah your wife?" And he said, "She is in the tent." ¹⁰The LORD said, "I will surely return to you in the spring, and Sarah your wife shall have a son." And Sarah was listening at the tent door behind him [11]*Now Abraham and Sarah were old, advanced in age; it had ceased to be with Sarah after the manner of women.* [12]*So Sarah laughed to herself, saying, "After I have grown old, and my husband is old, shall I have pleasure?"* [13]*The LORD said to Abraham, "Why did Sarah laugh, and say, 'Shall I indeed bear a child, now that I am old?'* [14]*Is anything too hard[c] for the LORD? At the appointed time I will return to you, in the spring, and Sarah shall have a son."* [15]*But Sarah denied, saying, "I did not laugh"; for she was afraid. He said, "No, but you did laugh."*

c Or *wonderful*

OVERVIEW: The scene of Sarah listening in the tent provides material for moral exhortation on different levels: the need to follow a believing husband (ORIGEN); Sarah is seen as an example of modesty; Sarah is rebuked for denying that she laughed (EPHREM).

18:9 Where Is Sarah Your Wife?

LEARNING BY EXAMPLE. ORIGEN: What then does the Lord say to Abraham? "Where," the text reads, "is Sarah your wife?" And he said, "Lo, she is in the tent." But the Lord said, "I will certainly come to you at this time in due season, and Sarah your wife will have a son." But Sarah, standing behind the door of the tent behind Abraham, heard.

Let the wives learn from the examples of the patriarchs; let the wives learn, I say, to follow their husbands. For not without cause is it written that "Sarah was standing behind Abraham," but that it might be shown that if the husband leads the way to the Lord, the wife ought to follow. I mean that the wife ought to follow if she sees her husband standing by God....

But we can also perceive something mystical in this passage if we see how in Exodus "God went before them by night in a pillar of fire and by day in a pillar of a cloud" and the congregation of the Lord followed behind him.[1]

So therefore I understand also Sarah to have followed or stood "behind Abraham."

What is said next? "And they were both," the text says, "presbyters"—that is, old—"and far advanced in their days." So far as pertains to bodily age, many before them lived for more numerous years, but no one was called *presbyter*. It appears that this title is ascribed to the saints not by reason of longevity but of maturity. HOMILIES ON GENESIS 4.4.[2]

THEY ONLY SEEM TO BE MEN. EPHREM THE SYRIAN: After they had eaten, "they inquired about Sarah." She, who even in her old age had preserved her modesty, came out from inside the tent to the door of the tent. From Abraham's haste and from the silence that Abraham imposed on everyone with his gestures, those of his household knew that these who, because of the man of God, allowed their feet to be washed like men were not men. COMMENTARY ON GENESIS 15.2.[3]

A SIGN GIVEN. EPHREM THE SYRIAN: "Then [God] said of Sarah, 'At this time I will return to you, and Sarah will have a son.'" But Sarah, even though Abraham was standing behind her to strengthen her, "laughed and said, 'After I have grown old shall I [again] have youthfulness? My husband is also old.'"[4] A sign would have been given her if she had asked to hear or to see and then believe: first, because she was a woman, old and barren; and second, because nothing like this had ever been done before. God then gave a sign specifically to her who had not asked for a sign, and said, "Why did you laugh, Sarah, and say, 'Am I, who am old, to bear a child?'"[5] But Sarah, in-

---

[1]Ex 13:21. [2]FC 71:106-7. [3]FC 91:158-59. [4]Gen 18:10-12. [5]Gen 18:13.

stead of accepting the sign that was given to her, persisted, by this falsehood, in denying the true sign that had been given to her. Even though she had denied it because she was afraid, nevertheless in order to make her know that a false excuse did not convince him, God said to her, "But you did

laugh in your heart; lo, even your heart is denying the foolishness of your tongue."[6] COMMENTARY ON GENESIS 15.3.[7]

---

[6]Gen 18:15. [7]FC 91:159.

18:16-21 THE OUTCRY AGAINST SODOM AND GOMORRAH

[16]*Then the men set out from there, and they looked toward Sodom; and Abraham went with them to set them on their way.* [17]*The LORD said, "Shall I hide from Abraham what I am about to do,* [18]*seeing that Abraham shall become a great and mighty nation, and all the nations of the earth shall bless themselves by him?[d]* [19]*No, for I have chosen[e] him, that he may charge his children and his household after him to keep the way of the LORD by doing righteousness and justice; so that the LORD may bring to Abraham what he has promised him."* [20]*Then the LORD said, "Because the outcry against Sodom and Gomorrah is great and their sin is very grave,* [21]*I will go down to see whether they have done altogether according to the outcry which has come to me; and if not, I will know."*

d Or *in him all the nations of the earth shall be blessed*   e Heb *known*

OVERVIEW: The phrase "they looked toward Sodom" is used to suggest that Sarah was not told of the coming punishment of Sodom so that she would not grieve for her brother (EPHREM). The principal cause for comment in the passage, however, is the phrases "The outcry . . . is great" and "I will go down to see" because of the need to explain the anthropomorphisms. This is done by suggesting that God is teaching people not to pass judgment before investigating the evidence (EPHREM, CHRYSOSTOM). It is also important not to think of God ascending and descending in spatial terms (ORIGEN).

18:16 The Lord Looks Toward Sodom

HIDING A DECREE OF WRATH. EPHREM THE SYRIAN: After the three men promised Sarah

fruit, "they arose, and they looked toward Sodom." It was not revealed to Sarah that they were going to Sodom lest, on the same day that they had given her joy in the promise that a son was to be hers, she be grieving over her brother on account of that sentence of wrath decreed on Sodom and the nearby villages. They hid this from Sarah lest she never cease weeping, but they revealed it to Abraham so that he not cease praying and so that it be announced to the world that nowhere in Sodom was there found a single just man for whose sake it might be saved. COMMENTARY ON GENESIS 16.1.[1]

18:20-21 The Great Sin of These Cities

---

[1]FC 91:159-60.

The Outcry Is Great. Salvian the Presbyter: The cry of Sodom and Gomorrah is multiplied, he said. Well did he say that sins can cry out. Great surely is the cry of sinners as it mounts from earth to heaven. But why does he say that the sins of people cry out? It is because God says his ears are assaulted by the cries of our sins that the punishment of sinners be not delayed. Truly is it a cry, and the cry is great when the love of God is overpowered by the cries of sins to the extent that he is forced to punish the sinners. The Lord shows how unwilling he is to punish even the gravest sinners when he said that the cry of Sodom ascended to him. This means: My mercy urges me to spare them, but the cry of their sins compels me to punish them. The Governance of God 1.8.[2]

God Descends. Origen: These are the words of the divine Scripture. Let us see, therefore, now what is fitting to be understood in them.

"I have descended," the text says, "to see." When responses are delivered to Abraham, God is not said to descend but to stand before him, as we explained above: "Three men," the text says, "stood before him."[3] But now, because sinners are involved, God is said to descend. Beware lest you think of ascending and descending spatially. For this is frequently found in the sacred literature, as in the prophet Micah: "Behold," Scripture says, "the Lord departed from his holy place and came down and will tread upon the high places of the earth."[4] Therefore God is said to descend when he deigns to have concern for human frailty. This should be discerned especially of our Lord and Savior, who "thought it not robbery to be equal with God but emptied himself, taking the form of a servant."[5] Therefore he descended. For "no other has ascended into heaven, but he that descended from heaven, the Son of man who is in heaven."[6] For the Lord descended not only to care for us but also to bear these things that are ours. "For he took the form of a servant," and although he himself is invisible in nature, inasmuch as he is equal to the Father, nevertheless he took a visible appearance "and was found in appearance as a man."[7]

But also when he descends he is below with some, but he ascends with others and is above. For he goes up with the chosen apostles "into a high mountain and there is transfigured before them."[8] Therefore he is above with those whom he teaches about the mysteries of the kingdom of heaven. But he is below with the crowds and Pharisees, whose sins he reproaches, and he is there with them. . . . He could not, however, be transfigured below, but he ascended above with those who could follow him, and there he is transfigured. Homilies on Genesis 4.5.[9]

An Example Not to Prejudge. Ephrem the Syrian: It was not that God, who had just said, "their sins were very grave," did not know that they had sinned. This was an example to judges not to prejudge a case, even based on very reliable hearsay. For if he who knows all set aside his knowledge lest he exact vengeance without full knowledge before the trial, how much more should they set aside their ignorance and not effect judgment before the case is heard. Commentary on Genesis 16.1.[10]

No Sentence Without Proof. Chrysostom: Then, to teach the whole human race that even if their sins are exceedingly great and confessed to be such, he does not pronounce sentence before proof is manifest, he says, "I am going down to see if their deeds correspond to the outcry reaching me, so as to know if it is true or not." What is meant by the deliberation of the expression? "I am going down to see if their deeds correspond to the outcry reaching me, so as to know if it is true or not." What is meant by the considerateness of the expression? "I am going down to see." I mean, does the God of all move from place to place? No indeed! It doesn't mean this; instead, as I have often remarked, he wants to teach us by the concreteness of the expression that there is

---

[2]FC 3:43-44. [3]Gen 18:2. [4]Mic 1:3. [5]Phil 2:6-7. [6]Jn 3:13. [7]Phil 2:7. [8]Mk 9:2. [9]FC 71:108*. [10]FC 91:160.

need to apply precision and that sinners are not condemned on hearsay nor is sentence pronounced without proof. HOMILIES ON GENESIS 42.12.[11]

TO MAKE THEM WORTHY OF MY KNOWLEDGE. CAESARIUS OF ARLES: Now let us see what he means by saying, "I descended to see whether they have done all that the outcry which has come to me indicates; if not, I will know." Because of this, pagans, and especially the exceedingly foul Manichaeans, are wont to assail us by saying, "Behold, the God of the law did not know what was being done in Sodom." Now we reply with sound understanding and say that God knows the just in one way and sinners in another. What is said concerning the just? "The Lord knows who are his."[12] What is said about sinners? "Depart from me, all you workers of iniquity; I do not know you."[13] Moreover, the apostle Paul says, "If anyone is the Lord's, he knows what I am saying; if anyone ignores this, he shall be ignored."[14] What does it mean, then, "I do not know you"? "I do not recognize you in my pattern; I do not recognize my image in you. My justice knows something to punish in you, but my mercy does not

find anything to crown." For this reason if one's actions are unworthy of God, one is said to be unworthy of his knowledge also. "I descended to see"; not in order to know what they are doing but to make them worthy of my knowledge if I find any of them just, repentant, or such as I should know. SERMON 83.6-7.[15]

ACCORDING TO THE OUTCRY. ORIGEN: So also now, therefore, it is said of these who live in Sodom, that if indeed, on his examination, "their deeds are completed as the cry" that has ascended to God, they would be considered unworthy. But if there is any conversion among them, if even ten just men might be found among them, so, at last, God would know them. And for this reason the text said, "But if not, that I might know." It did not say that I might know what they are doing but that I might know them and make them worthy of knowledge of me, if I should find some among them just, if I should find some repentant, if some such as I ought to know. HOMILIES ON GENESIS 4.6.[16]

---

[11]FC 82:424-25*. [12]2 Tim 2:19. [13]Mt 7:23. [14]1 Cor 14:37-38. [15]FC 47:14-15. [16]FC 71:110.

18:22-33 ABRAHAM INTERCEDES FOR SODOM

[22]*So the men turned from there, and went toward Sodom; but Abraham still stood before the* LORD. [23]*Then Abraham drew near, and said, "Wilt thou indeed destroy the righteous with the wicked?* [24]*Suppose there are fifty righteous within the city; wilt thou then destroy the place and not spare it for the fifty righteous who are in it?* [25]*Far be it from thee to do such a thing, to slay the righteous with the wicked, so that the righteous fare as the wicked! Far be that from thee! Shall not the Judge of all the earth do right?"* [26]*And the* LORD *said, "If I find at Sodom fifty righteous in the city, I will spare the whole place for their sake."* [27]*Abraham answered, "Behold, I have taken upon myself to speak to the Lord, I who am but dust and ashes.* [28]*Suppose five of the fifty righteous are lacking? Wilt thou destroy the whole city for lack of five?" And he said, "I will not destroy it if I*

---

find forty-five there.” [29]*Again he spoke to him, and said, “Suppose forty are found there.” He answered, “For the sake of forty I will not do it.”* [30]*Then he said, “Oh let not the Lord be angry, and I will speak. Suppose thirty are found there.” He answered, “I will not do it, if I find thirty there.”* [31]*He said, “Behold, I have taken upon myself to speak to the Lord. Suppose twenty are found there.” He answered, “For the sake of twenty I will not destroy it.”* [32]*Then he said, “Oh let not the Lord be angry, and I will speak again but this once. Suppose ten are found there.” He answered, “For the sake of ten I will not destroy it.”* [33]*And the LORD went his way, when he had finished speaking to Abraham; and Abraham returned to his place.*

OVERVIEW: Abraham's intercession for Sodom also provides material for moral exhortation: a just person is a powerful bulwark for a country (AMBROSE); God's intercession reveals God's marvelous patience and love of humanity (CHRYSOSTOM), but no one wished to know God's mercy and so God did not know them (ORIGEN).

18:26 For the Sake of Fifty Righteous Men

FIFTY RIGHTEOUS. AMBROSE: And thus, through a sequence of questions and answers, even if ten just are found in the city, [God] promises not to punish the entire populace thanks to the rectitude of a few. From this we should understand what a powerful bulwark a just person can be for the country and how we should not be jealous of saintly persons or criticize them with temerity. In fact their faith saves us; their rectitude preserves us from destruction. Even Sodom, if it had had ten just men, would have been able to save itself. ON ABRAHAM 1.6.48.[1]

18:29 For the Sake of Forty Righteous Men

FORTY RIGHTEOUS. CHRYSOSTOM: Who could worthily praise the God of all for his marvelous long suffering and considerateness or congratulate the good man for enjoying such great confidence? "He continued to speak," the text goes on. " 'But what if only forty can be found there?' He replied, 'For the sake of the forty I will not destroy it.' " Then at that point the good man, while respecting God's ineffable long suffering

and being afraid of ever seeming to go too far and surpass the limit in his entreaty, said, "Pardon me, Lord, if I continue to speak: if only thirty can be found there?"[2] Since he saw God was disposed to kindness, he still did not proceed gradually with his compromise. He sought to rescue not merely five good people but ten in pursuing his request thus, "If only thirty can be found there?" He replied, "I will not destroy it if I find thirty there." Consider the degree of the good man's persistence. As though he personally were due to be liable for sentence, he takes great pains to snatch the people of Sodom from the impending punishment. "He said, 'Since I am able to speak to the Lord, what if there are only twenty there?' He replied, 'For the sake of the twenty I will not destroy it.' "[3] O, the goodness of the Lord beyond all telling and all imagining! I mean, which of us living in the middle of countless evils could ever choose to exercise such wonderful considerateness and loving kindness in executing a sentence against our peers? HOMILIES ON GENESIS 42.19.[4]

18:32 For the Sake of Ten Righteous Men

FOR THE SAKE OF TEN. CHRYSOSTOM: For proof that such persons' good standing is a means of winning long suffering for us, take heed in that very story to what he says to the patriarch: "If I find ten good people, I will not destroy the city." Why do I say ten good people? No one was found there free from lawlessness,

---

[1]CSEL 32 1:535-36. [2]Gen 18:30. [3]Gen 18:31. [4]FC 82:428.

except alone the good man Lot and his two daughters. His wife, you remember, perhaps on his account escaped punishment in the city but paid later the penalty for her own indifference. Now, however, since through God's ineffable love the growth of religion was taking place, there were many people unobtrusively in the heart of the cities capable of appealing to God, others in hills and caves, and the virtue of these few succeeded in canceling out the wickedness of the majority.

The Lord's goodness is immense, and frequently he finds his way to grant the salvation of the majority on account of a few just people. Why do I say on account of a few just people? Frequently, when a just person cannot be found in the present life, he takes pity on the living on account of the virtue of the departed and cries aloud in the words, "I will protect this city for my own sake and the sake of my servant David."[5] Even if they do not deserve to be saved, he is saving. And [they] have no claim on salvation; yet, since showing love is habitual with me and I am prompt to have pity and rescue them from disaster, for my own sake and the sake of my servant David I will act as a shield; he who passed on from this life many years before will prove the salvation of those who have fallen victim to their own indifference. HOMILIES ON GENESIS 42.23-24.[6]

THE LORD WENT HIS WAY. ORIGEN: Finally, because no one besides Lot is found who would repent, no one would be converted. He alone is known; he alone is delivered from the conflagration. Neither his children, having been admonished, nor his neighbors nor his next of kin followed him. No one wished to know the mercy of God; no one wished to take refuge in his compassion. Consequently also no one is known.

These things indeed have been said against those who "speak iniquity on high."[7] But let us give attention to make our acts such, our manner of life such, that we may be held worthy of knowledge of God; that he may see fit to know us; that we may be held worthy of knowledge of his Son Jesus Christ and knowledge of the Holy Spirit; that we, known by the Trinity, might also deserve to know the mystery of the Trinity fully, completely and perfectly, the Lord Jesus Christ revealing it to us. "His is the glory and sovereignty forever and ever. Amen."[8] HOMILIES ON GENESIS 4.6.[9]

---

[5]2 Kings 19:34. [6]FC 82:430-31. [7]Ps 73:8 (72:8 LXX). [8]1 Pet 4:11. [9]FC 71:110-11.

19:1-11 TWO ANGELS VISIT LOT

[1]*The two angels came to Sodom in the evening; and Lot was sitting in the gate of Sodom. When Lot saw them, he rose to meet them, and bowed himself with his face to the earth,* [2]*and said, "My lords, turn aside, I pray you, to your servant's house and spend the night, and wash your feet; then you may rise up early and go on your way." They said, "No; we will spend the night in the street."* [3]*But he urged them strongly; so they turned aside to him and entered his house; and he made them a feast, and baked unleavened bread, and they ate.* [4]*But before they lay down, the men of the city, the men of Sodom, both young and old, all the people to the last man, surrounded the house;* [5]*and they called to Lot, "Where are the men who came to you tonight? Bring them out to us, that we*

may know them." ⁶Lot went out of the door to the men, shut the door after him, ⁷and said, "I beg you, my brothers, do not act so wickedly. ⁸Behold, I have two daughters who have not known man; let me bring them out to you, and do to them as you please; only do nothing to these men, for they have come under the shelter of my roof." ⁹But they said, "Stand back!" And they said, "This fellow came to sojourn, and he would play the judge! Now we will deal worse with you than with them." Then they pressed hard against the man Lot, and drew near to break the door. ¹⁰But the men put forth their hands and brought Lot into the house to them, and shut the door. ¹¹And they struck with blindness the men who were at the door of the house, both small and great, so that they wearied themselves groping for the door.

OVERVIEW: A comparison of the details of the appearances in Genesis 18 and Genesis 19 leads to the conclusion that God takes no pleasure in punishments ("THEODORE OF MOPSUESTIA"). Angels were not mentioned earlier in Scripture so as not to endanger the belief in one God ("SEVERIAN OF GABALA"). The arrival of the angels in the evening illustrates the fervor and vigilance of Lot (CHRYSOSTOM). The fact that he was sitting at the gate shows his desire to offer hospitality (ORIGEN). A number of details in the account of Lot's reception of the visitors illustrate different aspects of the virtue of hospitality (CHRYSOSTOM). The behavior of the Sodomites shows that they were habitually unjust (ANONYMOUS).

19:1 Sodom in the Evening

WHEN THE SUBJECT IS PUNISHMENT. "THEODORE OF MOPSUESTIA": It was "three men" who came to Abraham,[1] and "in the heat of the day"; but in the case of Sodom, "two angels, and in the evening." Good things are likened to light, bad things to evening, since the "sun of justice" has set on them.[2] For the punishment of the wicked is night and darkness, but the righteous "will shine like light."[3] It is significant too that where there was an announcement of good things, the Lord was present.[4] But when the subject is punishment, he does not appear in person, showing that when people have good experiences, it is his pleasure, so that he chooses, as it were, to act directly

in such matters. Since he takes no pleasure in punishments but inflicts them only because of necessity, he makes use of underlings. CATENA ON GENESIS 3.1110.[5]

ANGELS NOT MENTIONED EARLIER. "SEVERIAN OF GABALA": Scripture seems to have made no mention at all of angels before the flood. Only now [does it mention angels], as though seeing fit to have instructed people abundantly, by the length of the time past, to regard as God and Lord of the universe only that one Being who had made the created universe and supplied human beings, beginning with Adam, with the appropriate knowledge. [This knowledge was supplied] by his providence and through a variety of visions, guiding its transmission from the first people to those who followed in order. CATENA ON GENESIS 3.1112.[6]

A FERVENT AND VIGILANT SOUL. CHRYSOSTOM: "Now, the two angels," the text says, "arrived at Sodom in the evening." The time in particular shows us this good man's extraordinary virtue in the fact that even despite the coming of evening he stayed at his post and did not leave it. That is to say, since he realized the advantage accruing to him from that, consequent-

---

[1]Gen 18:1-2. [2]Mal 4:2 (3:20 LXX). [3]Prov 4:18; cf. Mt 13:43. [4]Gen 18. [5]TEG 3:137. [6]TEG 3:138. The first occurrence of the word *angel* is Genesis 16:7, but here it can be interpreted to refer to Christ. The first occurrence in the plural is Genesis 18:1.

ly he was anxious to attain the wealth and brought great vigilance to bear, not even desisting at the end of the day. This, you see, is what a fervent and vigilant soul is like. Far from being impeded by any obstacles from giving evidence of its virtue, it is spurred on to greater heights by the very impediments in particular and burns with a brighter flame of desire. HOMILIES ON GENESIS 43.9.[7]

SITTING AT THE GATE. ORIGEN: Lot was not inside Sodom "but at the gate." I might have said, just as Abraham was sitting outside his tent, out of hospitality, even at an inconvenient time (for it was the middle of the day) on the lookout for travelers, so his relative and the imitator of his morality "was sitting at the gate" ready to invite those passing through the land, even though evening had now come. For he surely knew the impiety of the Sodomites and that there was no rest for the stranger in that place. SELECTIONS ON GENESIS.[8]

LOT'S JOY ON SEEING THE ANGELS. CHRYSOSTOM: "Now, on seeing them," the text goes on, "Lot rose to meet them." Let this be heeded by those who are given to repulsing people who call on them with requests to make and causes to plead and who show them great inhumanity. I mean, see how this good man did not wait until the visitors reached him but like the patriarch, without knowing who the visitors were but presuming that they were travelers of some kind, well nigh jumped for joy on seeing them, as though falling upon his prey and not missing the object of his desire. HOMILIES ON GENESIS 43.9.[9]

19:2 Lot Offers Hospitality

LOT WELCOMES THE VISITORS. CHRYSOSTOM: "On seeing them," the text says, note, "he rose to meet them and prostrated himself on the ground." He gave thanks to God for being found worthy to welcome the visitors. Notice his virtue of soul: he considered it a great kindness on

God's part to encounter these men and by welcoming them to fulfill his private longing. Now don't tell me they were angels; remember, rather, that this good man did not realize that yet but behaved as though receiving unknown travelers. "He said, 'Lo, sirs, break off your journey at your servant's house. Rest and bathe your feet; then rise early and resume your journey.'" These words are sufficient to reveal the virtue residing in the good man's soul. How could you help being amazed at his exceeding humility and the fervor with which he displayed his hospitality? "Lo, sirs," he said, "break off your journey at your servant's house." He addresses them as "sirs" and calls himself their servant. Let us listen precisely, dearly beloved, to these words and learn how we too can do likewise. This man of good name and reputation, enjoying great prosperity, a householder, addresses as master these travelers, these strangers, unknown, unprepossessing wayfarers, no connections of his, and says, "Break off your journey at your servant's house and rest." You see, evening has fallen, he says; accede to my wish and assuage the day's hardship by resting in the home of your servant. I mean, surely I'm not offering you anything wonderful? "Bathe your feet" wearied with traveling, "and rise early and resume your journey." So do me this favor, and don't refuse my entreaty. HOMILIES ON GENESIS 43.10.[10]

HIS HOSPITALITY NOT LIMITED. CHRYSOSTOM: "They replied," the text goes on, "No, instead, we shall rest in the street." Seeing that despite his entreaty they declined, he did not lose heart, he did not give up what he was intent on, he did not have the kinds of feelings we often do. If at any time we want to win someone over and then we see them somewhat reluctant, we immediately desist; this is due to our doing it without ardor and longing and especially to our thinking that we have excuse enough to be able to say that at any rate we did our best. What do you mean, you have done your best? You have let slip the

---

[7]FC 82:440. [8]PG 12:116. [9]FC 82:440. [10]FC 82:440-41.

prey, you have missed the treasure—is this doing your best? Then you would have done your best if you hadn't let the treasure slip through your fingers, if you hadn't bypassed the prey, if your display of hospitality was not limited to a perfunctory remark. HOMILIES ON GENESIS 43.11.[11]

19:3 *The Angels Enter Lot's House*

GENEROSITY OF ATTITUDE. CHRYSOSTOM: When he saw them resisting and bent on resting in the street (the angels did this out of a wish to reveal more clearly the just man's virtue and to teach us all the extent of his hospitality), then he in turn did not stop at making entreaty in words but also applied force. Hence Christ also said, "Men of violence seize the kingdom of heaven."[12] . . . "He compelled them," the text says. It seems to me he drew them in against their will. Then when they saw the just man applying this effort and not desisting until he should achieve the object of his desire, "they turned aside to him and entered his house. He prepared a meal for them,

cooking flat bread for them; they ate before lying down." Do you see here as well hospitality manifested not in richness of fare but in generosity of attitude? I mean, when he succeeded in bringing them into his house, at once he gave evidence of the signs of hospitality. He occupied himself in attending on them, providing something to eat and giving evidence of respect and attention to the visitors in his belief that they were only human beings, travelers of some kind. HOMILIES ON GENESIS 43.12.[13]

19:9 *The Sodomites Pressure Lot*

HABITUAL INJUSTICE. ANONYMOUS: Their habitual injustice to human beings eventually led the Sodomites to violence against angels. . . . Bad morals are therefore a harmful and destructive thing, even if not immediately. CATENA ON GENESIS 3.1122.[14]

---

[11]FC 82:441. [12]Mt 11:12. [13]FC 82:441-42. [14]TEG 3:144.

19:12-14 THE DESTRUCTION OF SODOM THREATENED

[12]*Then the men said to Lot, "Have you any one else here? Sons-in-law, sons, daughters, or any one you have in the city, bring them out of the place;* [13]*for we are about to destroy this place, because the outcry against its people has become great before the LORD, and the LORD has sent us to destroy it."* [14]*So Lot went out and said to his sons-in-law, who were to marry his daughters, "Up, get out of this place; for the LORD is about to destroy the city." But he seemed to his sons-in-law to be jesting.*

OVERVIEW: When the number of evildoers is excessive, the just are removed from the city (ANONYMOUS). Jesus' unfavorable comparison of Capernaum to Sodom leads to the reflection that ne-

glect of the gospel is a worse sin than that of the Sodomites (SALVIAN).

19:13 *Sent to Destroy Sodom*

THE RIGHTEOUS ARE REMOVED. ANONYMOUS: Note that if the multitude of evildoers is excessive, cities are not saved on account of the righteous, but the righteous are removed. CATENA ON GENESIS 3.1125.[1]

THOSE WHO NEGLECT THE GOSPELS. SALVIAN THE PRESBYTER: However, how do we account for the fact that the Savior himself has brought to mind that all who spurned the gospel were worse? Finally to Capernaum he said, "If in Sodom had been wrought the miracles that had been wrought in you, perhaps it would have remained unto this day. But I say unto you that it shall be more tolerable for the land of Sodom in the day of judgment than for you."[2] If he says the people of Sodom are less worthy of damnation than all those who neglect the Gospels, then it is most certainly reasonable that we, who neglect the Gospels in most things, should have all the more fear. This is especially so because we are unwilling to be content with sins to which we are already long accustomed and, as it were, on daily familiarity. THE GOVERNANCE OF GOD 4.9.[3]

---

[1]TEG 3:145. [2]Mt 11:23-24. [3]FC 3:104-5*.

19:15-23 LOT FLEES TO ZOAR

[15]*When morning dawned, the angels urged Lot, saying, "Arise, take your wife and your two daughters who are here, lest you be consumed in the punishment of the city."* [16]*But he lingered; so the men seized him and his wife and his two daughters by the hand, the LORD being merciful to him, and they brought him forth and set him outside the city.* [17]*And when they had brought them forth, they[f] said, "Flee for your life; do not look back or stop anywhere in the valley; flee to the hills, lest you be consumed."* [18]*And Lot said to them, "Oh, no, my lords;* [19]*behold, your servant has found favor in your sight, and you have shown me great kindness in saving my life; but I cannot flee to the hills, lest the disaster overtake me, and I die.* [20]*Behold, yonder city is near enough to flee to, and it is a little one. Let me escape there—is it not a little one?—and my life will be saved!"* [21]*He said to him, "Behold, I grant you this favor also, that I will not overthrow the city of which you have spoken.* [22]*Make haste, escape there; for I can do nothing till you arrive there." Therefore the name of the city was called Zoar.[g]* [23]*The sun had risen on the earth when Lot came to Zoar.*

f Gk Syr Vg: Heb *he* g *That is Little*

OVERVIEW: The angels had concern for their host because of the hospitality he had offered them, but he was not yet perfect enough to ascend the mountain. He was somewhere in the middle between the perfect and the doomed (ORIGEN). Lot's flight from Sodom teaches the spiritual flight from vice through the "passageway of thoughts" (AMBROSE). When one leaves the territory of evil, one is able to converse with God. God's loving kindness is shown in the exhortation to make haste ("CYRIL").

19:15 The Angels Urge Lot to Flee

CONCERN FIRST FOR THEIR HOST. ORIGEN: When the angels who were sent to destroy Sodom desired to expedite the task with which they were charged, they first had concern for their host, Lot, that, in consideration of his hospitality, they might deliver him from the destruction of the imminent fire.

Hear these words, you who close your houses to strangers; hear these words, you who avoid a guest as an enemy. Lot was living in Sodom. We do not read of other good deeds of his. The hospitality alone occurring at that time is mentioned. He escapes the flames, he escapes the conflagration for this reason alone: because he opened his house to strangers. Angels entered the hospitable house; fire entered the houses closed to strangers.

Let us therefore see what the angels say to their host on account of his services of hospitality. "Save your life in the mountain," the text says, "lest perchance you be included."[1] Lot was indeed hospitable. And, as the Scripture has borne testimony to him, he was hidden from destruction when the angels had been hospitably received.[2] But he was not so perfect that immediately on departing from Sodom, he could ascend the mountain; for it belongs to the perfect to say, "I have lifted up my eyes to the mountains, whence help shall come to me."[3] He therefore was neither such that he should perish among the inhabitants of Sodom, nor was he so great that he could dwell with Abraham in the heights. For if he had been such, Abraham would never have said to him, "If you go to the right, I will go to the left, or if you go to the left I will go to the right,"[4] nor would the dwellings of Sodom have pleased him. He was therefore somewhere in the middle between the perfect and the doomed. And knowing that it is not appropriate with his strength to ascend the mountain, he piously and humbly excuses himself saying, "I cannot be saved on the mountain, but, behold, this city is small. Here I shall be saved; and it is not small?"[5] To be sure, when he entered the small city of Zoar he is saved in it.[6] And after this he went up into the mountain with his daughters.[7]

For there was no possibility of ascending from Sodom into the mountain, although it is written of the land of Sodom before it was overthrown, in that time when Lot chose it as his dwelling place, that "it was as the paradise of God and as the land of Egypt."[8] And yet, to digress slightly, what similarity does there appear to be with the paradise of God and the land of Egypt that Sodom should be compared fittingly with these? Now I think it is in this way: before Sodom sinned, when it still preserved the simplicity of the unstained life, it was "as the paradise of God," but when it began to be discolored and to be darkened with the stains of sins it became "as the land of Egypt."

But since indeed the prophet says, "Your sister Sodom shall be restored to her ancient state,"[9] we inquire also whether her restoration also recovers this, that she be "as the paradise of God" or only "as the land of Egypt." I, at least, doubt if the sins of Sodom can be diminished to such an extent and its evils purged to the point that its restoration be so great that it be compared not only with the land of Egypt but also with the paradise of God. Those, however, who wish to establish this will press us especially from that word that appears added to this counterpromise. For the Scripture did not say "Sodom will be restored," and stop, but it says, "Sodom will be restored to its ancient state."[10] And they will assert strongly that its ancient state was not "as the land of Egypt" but "as the paradise of God." HOMILIES ON GENESIS 5.1.[11]

THOSE WHO RENOUNCE THE VICES. AMBROSE: Let us flee like Lot, who feared the crimes of the people of Sodom more than their punishments. A holy man surely, he chose to shut his house to the men of Sodom and flee the contagion of their offenses. When he dwelt with them, he did not come to know them, for he did not know their outrages and turned away from their disgraces. When he fled, he did not look back on them, for he did not desire to associate with them. The one

[1]Gen 19:17. [2]See Heb 13:2. [3]Ps 121:1 (120:1 LXX). [4]Gen 13:9. [5]Gen 19:19-20. [6]Gen 19:23. [7]Gen 19:30. [8]Gen 13:10. [9]Ezek 16:55. [10]Ezek 16:55. [11]FC 71:112-14.

who renounces the vices and rejects the way of life of his fellow citizens is in flight like Lot. Such a person does not look behind himself but enters that city which is above by the passageway of his thoughts, and he does not withdraw from it until the death of the chief priest who bore the sin of the world. He indeed died once, but he dies for each person who is baptized in Christ's death, that we may be buried together with him and rise with him and walk in the newness of his life.[12] Your flight is a good one if your heart does not act out the counsels of sinners and their designs. Your flight is a good one if your eye flees the sight of cups and drinking vessels, so that it may not become envious as it lingers over the wine. Your flight is good if your eye turns away from the woman stranger, so that your tongue may keep the truth. Your flight is a good one if you do not answer the fool according to his folly.[13] Your flight is good if you direct your footsteps away from the countenance of fools. Indeed, one swiftly goes astray with bad guides; but if you wish your flight to be a good one, remove your ways far from their words.[14] FLIGHT FROM THE WORLD 9.55-56.[15]

19:18 Oh, No, My Lords

LEAVING THE TERRITORY OF EVIL. "CYRIL OF ALEXANDRIA": It seems that now, after the exodus from Sodom, the conversation is no longer with angels but with the Lord.[16] For when one leaves the territory of evil he will find God conversing with him, and he will have the courage and confidence to ask for whatever he wishes. CATENA ON GENESIS 3.1139.[17]

19:22 Hurry!

GOD ACCOMMODATES WEAKNESS. "CYRIL OF ALEXANDRIA": Great is the loving kindness of God. He who is all-powerful says, "I can do nothing until you arrive there." He accommodates even the weakness of his servant and tolerates his delay. CATENA ON GENESIS 3.1144.[18]

---

[12]Col 2:12; Rom 6:4. [13]Prov 23:33 LXX; 26:4. [14]Prov 5:8. [15]FC 65:321-22. [16]LXX, "But Lot said to them, 'Please, Lord . . .'" [17]TEG 3:154. [18]TEG 3:156.

19:24-28 THE DESTRUCTION OF SODOM

[24]*Then the LORD rained on Sodom and Gomorrah brimstone and fire from the LORD out of heaven;* [25]*and he overthrew those cities, and all the valley, and all the inhabitants of the cities, and what grew on the ground.* [26]*But Lot's wife behind him looked back, and she became a pillar of salt.* [27]*And Abraham went early in the morning to the place where he had stood before the LORD;* [28]*and he looked down toward Sodom and Gomorrah and toward all the land of the valley, and beheld, and lo, smoke of the land went up like the smoke of a furnace.*

OVERVIEW: Lot represents allegorically "the rational understanding and the courageous soul" while his wife represents the flesh (ORIGEN).[1] The example of Lot's wife shows that God takes into account the inner purpose of a person

(CLEMENT OF ALEXANDRIA).

---

[1]This is a traditional contrast that can be found earlier in Philo of Alexandria, e.g., *Questiones et Solutiones in Genesin* 1.46; 3.3.

19:26 *Lot's Wife Looks Back*

LOT'S WIFE REPRESENTS THE FLESH. ORIGEN: But let us return to Lot, who, fleeing the destruction of Sodom with his wife and daughters after he had received the command from the angels to not look back, was proceeding to Zoar.[2] But his wife became negligent of the command. "She looked back"; she violated the imposed law; "she became a little statue of salt." Do we think there was so much evil in this transgression, that the woman, because she looked behind her, incurred the destruction that she appeared to be fleeing by divine favor? For what great crime was it, if the concerned mind of the woman looked backward whence she was being terrified by the excessive crackling of the flames?

But because "the law is spiritual"[3] and the things that happened to the ancients "happened figuratively,"[4] let us see if perhaps Lot, who did not look back, is not the rational understanding and the courageous soul, and his wife here represents the flesh. For it is the flesh which always looks to vices; when the soul is proceeding to salvation, the flesh looks backward and seeks after pleasures. For concerning that the Lord also said, "No man putting his hand to the plow and look-ing back is fit for the kingdom of God."[5] And he adds, "Remember Lot's wife."[6] But the fact that "she became a little statue of salt" appears to be an open indication of her folly. For salt represents the prudence which she lacked.

Lot therefore pushed on to Zoar. After he had gained strength there for a while, which he could not have in Sodom, he ascended the mountain and dwelt there, as the Scripture says, "he and his two daughters with him."[7] HOMILIES ON GENESIS 5.2.[8]

GOD LOOKS AT THE INNER PURPOSE. CLEMENT OF ALEXANDRIA: For God looks closely at the actual inner purpose, as when Lot's wife was the only one to turn of her own free will toward the wickedness of the world. He left her insensible, giving her the likeness of a pillar of salt and leaving her without the power of forward movement, a statue, yet not one without a useful message but one intended to season and salt the person capable of spiritual perception. STROMATEIS 2.14.61.4.[9]

---

[2]See Gen 19:17. [3]Rom 7:14. [4]1 Cor 10:11. [5]Lk 9:62. [6]Lk 17:32. [7]Gen 19:30. [8]FC 71:114. [9]FC 85:200*.

19:29-38 LOT SEDUCED BY HIS DAUGHTERS

[29]*So it was that, when God destroyed the cities of the valley, God remembered Abraham, and sent Lot out of the midst of the overthrow, when he overthrew the cities in which Lot dwelt.*

[30]*Now Lot went up out of Zoar, and dwelt in the hills with his two daughters, for he was afraid to dwell in Zoar; so he dwelt in a cave with his two daughters.* [31]*And the first-born said to the younger, "Our father is old, and there is not a man on earth to come in to us after the manner of all the earth.* [32]*Come, let us make our father drink wine, and we will lie with him, that we may pre-serve offspring through our father."* [33]*So they made their father drink wine that night; and the first-born went in, and lay with her father; he did not know when she lay down or when she arose.* [34]*And on the next day, the first-born said to the younger, "Behold, I lay last night with my father;*

let us make him drink wine tonight also; then you go in and lie with him, that we may preserve off-spring through our father." ³⁵So they made their father drink wine that night also; and the younger arose, and lay with him; and he did not know when she lay down or when she arose. ³⁶Thus both the daughters of Lot were with child by their father. ³⁷The first-born bore a son, and called his name Moab; he is the father of the Moabites to this day. ³⁸The younger also bore a son, and called his name Ben-ammi; he is the father of the Ammonites to this day.

OVERVIEW: The story of Lot's seduction by his daughters posed a challenge to interpreters. The question of his culpability was one aspect of the problem. Although a variety of typological interpretations existed, Lot can best be interpreted to represent the law and his wife the people of Israel who longed for the comforts of Egypt when they were in the desert (ORIGEN). Another interpretation made the offspring of Lot to represent the two synagogues, Samaria and Judea (IRENAEUS). On a spiritual level, the story shows that the law (Lot), when deprived of its spiritual or allegorical sense, begets only carnal understanding. That is, it does not lead to Christ. The two sisters can also be interpreted to represent vainglory and pride (ORIGEN).

19:33-35 Lot's Daughters Sleep with Him

LOT IS PARTLY CULPABLE AND PARTLY EXCUSABLE. ORIGEN: After these things now that well-known story is related in which it is written that Lot's daughters cunningly lay with their father by stealth.[1] In this matter I do not know if anyone can so excuse Lot as to free him from sin. Nor again do I think he should be so accused that he ought to become party to such serious incest. For I do not find him to have plotted against or to have violently snatched away the chastity of his daughters but rather to have been the victim of a plot and cunningly ensnared. But neither would he have been ensnared by the girls unless he could have been inebriated. Thus he seems to me to be found partly culpable and partly excusable. For indeed he can be excused because he is free of the offense of concupiscence and pleasure, and

because he is shown neither to have wished nor to have consented to those wishing. But he is at fault because he could be trapped, because he indulged in wine too much, and this not once, but he did it a second time.

For instance, even Scripture seems to me to make excuse for him in a certain manner when it says, "For he did not know when he slept with them and when he arose." This is not said of the daughters, who intentionally and cunningly deceive their father. He, however, was so senseless from wine that he did not know that he lay with his older daughter or with the younger.

Hear what drunkenness does. Hear what an outrage intoxication produces. Hear and beware, you who do not hold that evil to be a fault but practice it. Drunkenness deceives him whom Sodom did not deceive. He whom the sulphurous flame did not burn is burned by the flames of women. HOMILIES ON GENESIS 5.3.[2]

19:36 Lot's Daughters Pregnant

WITHOUT KNOWLEDGE OR CARNAL PLEASURE. IRENAEUS: This had happened without Lot's knowledge and without his having been a slave to pleasure; it was accomplished wholly by divine arrangement, through which the two synagogues[3] born from one and the same father, without carnal pleasure, were evoked. For there was no one else who could give them vital seed and the fruit of children, as it was written. AGAINST HERESIES 4.31.1.[4]

---

[1]Gen 19:31-38. [2]FC 71:114-15. [3]Evidently Samaria and Judea, or Jerusalem. [4]TEG 3:172.

NOT THE WILL OF THE LAW. ORIGEN: After these things, therefore, Lot ascends into the mountains, and there "he dwells in a cave," as the Scripture says, "he and his two daughters."[5] The law also should be thought to have ascended, because an embellishment was added to it by the temple built by Solomon, when it became indeed "the house of God, a house of prayer."[6] Evil inhabitants, however, made it "a den of thieves."[7] Therefore "Lot and his two daughters dwelt in a cave."[8] The prophet evidently describes these two daughters saying that Oholah and Oholibah are two sisters, and Oholah indeed is "Judah" and Oholibah is "Samaria."[9] The people therefore divided into two parts made the two daughters of the law. Those daughters, desiring carnal offspring to be preserved and the forces of earthly dominion to be fortified by an abundant posterity, depriving their father of sense and making him sleep, that is, covering and obscuring his spiritual understanding, draw only carnal understanding from him. Then they conceive. Then they give birth to such sons as their father neither perceives nor recognizes. For it was neither the understanding nor the will of the law to beget carnally. But the law is deprived of its sense that such posterity might be begotten that "shall not enter the assembly of the Lord."[10] "For the Ammonites," Scripture says, "and Moabites shall not enter the assembly of the Lord unto the third and fourth generation and forever."[11] HOMILIES ON GENESIS 5.5.[12]

THE SISTERS REPRESENT VAINGLORY AND PRIDE. ORIGEN: As we have been able, we have carved out these explanations according to the spiritual understanding of Lot and his wife and daughters. We pass no judgment on those who have been able to perceive something more sacred from this text.

But above, in the moral sense, we referred Lot indeed to the rational understanding and the courageous soul; but his wife, who looked back, we said to be the flesh given to concupiscence and pleasures. Do not, O hearer, receive these things

carelessly. For you ought to watch lest perhaps even when you have fled the flames of the world and have escaped the fires of the flesh, even when you have risen above "Zoar, the city" that is "small and not small,"[13] which is somewhere in the middle . . . you seem to have ascended to the height of knowledge, as to some mountain peak. Beware lest those two daughters lie in wait for you, who do not depart from you but follow you even when you ascend the mountain. They are vainglory and her older sister, pride. Beware lest with their embraces those daughters constrict you, deprived of sense and sleeping, while you seem neither to perceive nor know. They are called daughters because they do not come upon us from outside but proceed from us and from a kind of innocence, as it were, of our acts. Be vigilant, therefore, as much as you can, and watch lest you beget sons from these daughters, because those who have been born from them "shall not enter the assembly of the Lord."[14] But if you wish to beget, beget in the spirit, since "he who sows in the spirit, of the spirit shall reap life everlasting."[15] If you wish to embrace, embrace wisdom and "say wisdom is your sister,"[16] that Wisdom also may say of you: He "who shall do the will of my Father who is in heaven, he is my brother and sister and mother."[17] Jesus Christ our Lord is this wisdom, "to whom be glory and sovereignty forever and ever. Amen."[18] HOMILIES ON GENESIS 5.5-6.[19]

19:37 Lot Fathered the Moabites

LOT IS A FIGURE OF THE LAW. ORIGEN: But I know that some, so far as the story pertains to a spiritual interpretation, have referred Lot to the person of the Lord and his daughters to the two Testaments. But I do not know if anyone freely accepts these views who knows what the Scripture says about the Ammonites and Moabites

---

[5]Gen 19:30. [6]Is 56:7. [7]Mt 21:13; Lk 19:46; Jer 7:11. [8]Gen 19:30. [9]Ezek 23:4. The LXX has the identification in reverse: "Samaria was Oholah, and Jerusalem Oholibah." [10]Deut 23:3. [11]Deut 23:3; Ex 34:7. [12]FC 71:119*. [13]Gen 19:20. [14]Deut 23:3. [15]Gal 6:8. [16]Prov 7:4. [17]Mt 12:50. [18]1 Pet 4:11. [19]FC 71:120*.

who descend from Lot's race. For how will one be able to apply to Christ the statement that those who descend from his seed "shall not enter the assembly of the Lord" "to the third and fourth generation"?[20]

But we, as we are able to perceive, consider Lot to be a figure of the law. Let not the fact that the word *law is* declined in the feminine gender in Latin appear incongruous, since it preserves the masculine gender in Greek.[21]

We consider his wife to represent the people who, after they had set out from Egypt and had been delivered from the Red Sea and the persecution of Pharaoh, as if from the fires of Sodom, again desiring the meat and "pots of Egypt and onions and cucumbers,"[22] looked back and fell in the desert. Those people too became a memorial of concupiscence in the wilderness.[23] In regard to that first people, therefore, it was there that the law, like Lot, lost and left his wife looking back.

Then Lot comes and dwells in Zoar, about which he says, "This city is small, and my life shall be saved in it; and it is not small."[24] Let us see, therefore, so far as it pertains to the law what "the city" is that is "small and not small." A city is so named from the manner of life of the multitude, because it orders and holds together the lives of many in one place.[25] These therefore who live by the law have a small and petty manner of life as long as they understand the law literally. For there is nothing great in observing sabbaths and new moons and circumcision of the flesh and distinctions between foods in a fleshly manner. But if someone should begin to understand spiritually, these same observances, which in the literal sense were small and petty, in the spiritual sense are not small but great. HOMILIES ON GENESIS 5.5.[26]

---

[20]Deut 23:3; Ex 34:7. [21]This is obviously a gloss by Rufinus, the Latin translator. [22]Num 11:5. [23]Ps 106:14 (105:14 LXX). [24]Gen 19:20. The translation of the Latin quotation of verse 20 (*civitas pusilla et non pusilla*) has been amended to conform to the Latin/LXX text and the sense of Origen's comment. Origen evidently did not read it as a question. [25]See Plato *Republica* 369C. [26]FC 71:117-18*.

20:1-7 ABRAHAM AND SARAH IN GERAR

[1]*From there Abraham journeyed toward the territory of the Negeb, and dwelt between Kadesh and Shur; and he sojourned in Gerar.* [2]*And Abraham said of Sarah his wife, "She is my sister." And Abimelech king of Gerar sent and took Sarah.* [3]*But God came to Abimelech in a dream by night, and said to him, "Behold, you are a dead man, because of the woman whom you have taken; for she is a man's wife."* [4]*Now Abimelech had not approached her; so he said, "Lord, wilt thou slay an innocent people?* [5]*Did he not himself say to me, 'She is my sister'? And she herself said, 'He is my brother.' In the integrity of my heart and the innocence of my hands I have done this."* [6]*Then God said to him in the dream, "Yes, I know that you have done this in the integrity of your heart, and it was I who kept you from sinning against me; therefore I did not let you touch her.* [7]*Now then restore the man's wife; for he is a prophet, and he will pray for you, and you shall live. But if you do not restore her, know that you shall surely die, you, and all that are yours."*

OVERVIEW: The incident in which Abraham passes off his wife Sarah as his sister to Abimelech posed a challenge to interpreters similar to that of Genesis 12, where he had done the same thing with Pharaoh. There was a difference, however, in that it was difficult to find fault with Abimelech, whereas Pharaoh could be represented as an oppressor. The problem could be resolved by allegorizing the passage and interpreting Sarah as virtue, as Philo had done earlier (ORIGEN). Abraham's movements could also be seen to provide examples of a restrained and austere life (CHRYSOSTOM). The innocent Abimelech could be interpreted to represent the studious and wise men of this world (ORIGEN). Abraham could also be excused on the ground that he was a prophet (ANONYMOUS).

20:1 Abraham's Journeys

ABRAHAM ENCOUNTERS ABIMELECH. ORIGEN: We have read from the book of Genesis the story where it is related that after the appearance of the three men, after the destruction of Sodom and the salvation of Lot, either due to his hospitality or because of his kinship to Abraham, "Abraham departed thence," the text says, "to the south" and came to the king of the Philistines.[1] It is related also that he made an agreement with Sarah his wife that she should not say that she was Abraham's wife but his sister.[2] It is also said that King Abimelech took her, but God went in to Abimelech at night and said to him, "You have not touched this woman, and I have not permitted you to touch her, etc."[3] But after this Abimelech gave Sarah back to her husband and at the same time rebuked Abraham for not having told him the truth. It is also related that, as a prophet, Abraham prayed for Abimelech, "and the Lord healed Abimelech and his wife and his handmaids."[4] And the omnipotent God was concerned to heal even the handmaids of Abimelech, "since he had closed up their wombs that they might not bear."[5] But they began to bear because of Abraham's prayer.

If anyone wishes to hear and understand these words literally, he ought to gather with the Jews rather than with the Christians. But if he wishes to be a Christian and a disciple of Paul, let him hear Paul saying that "the law is spiritual,"[6] declaring that these words are "allegorical" when the law speaks of Abraham and his wife and sons.[7] And although no one of us can by any means easily discover what kind of allegories these words should contain, nevertheless one ought to pray that "the veil might be removed" from the heart. "If there is anyone who tries to turn to the Lord"[8]—"for the Lord is Spirit"[9]—the Lord might remove the veil of the letter and uncover the light of the Spirit. [Then] we might be able to say that "beholding the glory of the Lord with open face we are transformed into the same image from glory to glory, as by the Spirit of the Lord."[10] HOMILIES ON GENESIS 6.1.[11]

20:2 Sarah His Sister

SARAH REPRESENTS THE VIRTUE OF THE SOUL. ORIGEN: I think, therefore, that Sarah, which means "princess" or "one who governs empires," represents *aretē*, which is the virtue of the soul. This virtue then is joined to and clings to a wise and faithful man, even as that wise man who said of wisdom, "I have desired to take her for my spouse."[12] For this reason therefore God says to Abraham, "In all that Sarah has said to you, listen to her voice."[13] This saying, at any rate, is not appropriate to physical marriage, since that well known statement was revealed from heaven which says to the woman concerning the man, "In him shall be your refuge, and he shall have dominion over you."[14] If therefore the husband is said to be lord of his wife, how is it said again to the man, "In all that Sarah has said to you, pay attention to her voice"?[15] If anyone therefore has

---

[1]The LXX text says "to the south" instead of "the Negeb." [2]Gen 20:2. [3]Gen 20:3-4, 6. [4]Gen 20:17. [5]Gen 20:18. [6]Rom 7:14. [7]Gal 4:22-24. [8]2 Cor 3:16. [9]2 Cor 3:17. [10]2 Cor 3:18. [11]FC 71:121-22. [12]Wis 8:2. [13]Gen 21:12. [14]Gen 3:16. [15]Gen 21:12.

married virtue, let him listen to her voice in all which she shall counsel him.

Abraham therefore does not now wish that virtue be called his wife. For as long as virtue is called his wife, she belongs to him and can be shared with no one. And it is proper that until we reach perfection, virtue of the soul be within us and personal. But when we reach perfection so that we are capable also of teaching others, let us then no longer enclose virtue within our bosom as a wife but as a sister; let us unite her also with others who desire her. For to those who are perfect the divine Word says, "Say that wisdom is your sister."[16] In this way therefore Abraham too said Sarah was his sister. . . .

Nevertheless Pharaoh too once wished to receive Sarah,[17] but he did not wish with a pure heart; and virtue cannot unite except with purity of heart. For this reason, therefore, Scripture relates that "the Lord afflicted Pharaoh with afflictions which were grievous and most severe."[18] For virtue could not dwell with a destroyer—for this is what Pharaoh means in our language. Homilies on Genesis 6.1-2.[19]

A Restrained, Austere Life. Chrysostom: "Abraham moved from there to the southern land," the text goes on, "and dwelt between Kadesh and Shur, sojourning at Gerar." Moved on from where? From the place where he was camped, where he was given the privilege of hosting the Lord of all with the angels. Moving from there, the text says, "he sojourned in Gerar." Notice the life of these good people, how restrained and austere it was, how they shifted place with ease and conducted their life like pilgrims or nomads, pitching their tent at one time in this place, at another in that, as though living in a strange land.[20] They are unlike us, who live in a strange land as though in our home country, erecting extravagant mansions, porches and covered walks, possessing land, building baths and countless other luxuries.

By contrast see the good man holding all his possessions in his household and flocks alone. [He is] never staying in one place but at one time pitching his tent in Bethel, at another by the oak of Mamre, at another going down to Egypt and now camping at Gerar, submitting to all this with ease and giving clear evidence in every way of gratitude to his own Lord. Despite such wonderful promises and guarantees given him by God, he saw himself beset by such imposing difficulties and encountering such varied and differing trials. Yet he stood unshaken like some piece of steel, showing his godly attitude and proving no less resolute in any of the problems surrounding him. See in the present instance too, dearly beloved, the kind of trial that befell him at Gerar and the wonderful caliber of the just man's virtue. What everyone else found unbearable and could not bring themselves to accept he put up with without complaint and without demanding from the Lord explanation of what happened, as many people do, even though weighed down with countless burdens of sin. When they encounter some difficulties, they become meddlesome and inquisitive, saying, "Why has this or that happened?" The just man, on the contrary, didn't behave like that; hence he enjoyed greater favor from on high. This, after all, is truly the mark of a dutiful servant, not to pry into reasons for what is done by the master but to accept everything in silence and with deep thanks. Homilies on Genesis 45.3-4.[21]

20:4 Abimelech Did Not Touch Sarah

Truly a Divine Gift. Origen: The expression "had not touched" is emphatic, like the statement "it is good for a man not to touch a woman,"[22] which means, even apart from sexual union, in no other way either to gaze at or to touch a woman with passion. God, of course, did not permit Abimelech to touch Sarah, though perhaps too because he had perfect self-control in all matters. Such a quality is truly a divine gift. Selections on Genesis.[23]

---

[16]Prov 7:4. [17]Gen 12:15. [18]Gen 12:17. [19]FC 71:122-23*. [20]Heb 11:9. [21]FC 82:470-72*. [22]1 Cor 7:1. [23]PG 12:117.

20:5 Abimelech Claims Innocence

IN THE INTEGRITY OF MY HEART. ORIGEN: But let us see what Abimelech said to the Lord. "You know, Lord," the text says, "that I have done this with a pure heart." This Abimelech acts very differently from Pharaoh. He is not so ignorant and vile but knows that he ought to prepare a "pure heart" for virtue. And because he wished to receive virtue with a pure heart, therefore God heals him when Abraham prays for him. And God heals not only Abimelech but also his handmaids. HOMILIES ON GENESIS 6.2.[24]

20:6 God Vindicates Abimelech

ABIMELECH REPRESENTS STUDIOUS AND WISE MEN. ORIGEN: But what is the meaning of that which Scripture adds: "And the Lord did not permit him to touch her"? If Sarah represents virtue and Abimelech wished to receive virtue "with a pure heart," why is it said that "the Lord did not permit him to touch her"?

Abimelech means "my father is king." It seems to me therefore that this Abimelech represents the studious and wise men of the world, who by giving attention to philosophy, although they do not reach the complete and perfect rule of piety, nevertheless perceive that God is the Father and King of all things. Those, therefore, so far as it pertains to ethics (that is, moral philosophy), are acknowledged also to have given attention in some respects to purity of heart and to have sought the inspiration of divine virtue with all their mind and zeal. But "God did not permit" them "to touch" her. For this grace was designed to be delivered to the Gentiles not by Abraham, who, although he was great was nevertheless a servant, but by Christ. . . . Abraham was eager that what was said to him be fulfilled through and in himself, that "all the nations shall be blessed in you."[25] Nevertheless the promise to him is established in Isaac, that is, in Christ, as the apostle says: "He did not say, And to his seeds, as of many, but as of one, and to your seed, which is Christ."[26]

Nevertheless "the Lord heals Abimelech and his wife and his handmaids."[27] HOMILIES ON GENESIS 6.2.[28]

20:7 God's Injunctions to Abimelech

WHY THE LORD INFLICTED THIS PENALTY. CHRYSOSTOM: The reason why the good Lord inflicted this penalty on the king, guiltless though he was of sin, was that he might accede to the just man's prayers and thus resolve the problem, thereby rendering the just man more famous and well known. You see, all God's planning and each arrangement he makes have the purpose of rendering conspicuous those who serve him, just like lamps, and making their virtue obvious in every way. HOMILIES ON GENESIS 45.23.[29]

ABRAHAM IS A PROPHET. ANONYMOUS: Where does Abraham appear as a prophet? First, he says to Sarah, as he went down to Egypt, "You are a beautiful woman, and if the Egyptians see you, they will kill me and acquire you."[30] Then, when he was bringing Isaac to the mountain to be sacrificed, he says to the servants, "Stay here; I and the lad will go up that mountain, and after we have offered sacrifice to the Lord we will return to you."[31] Next, because either in a unique way or as one of few, he had knowledge of God. But even our Lord bears witness to him that he is a prophet, saying, "Abraham greatly desired to see my day,"[32] that is, when he saw the Lord in prophecy. CATENA ON GENESIS 3.1190.[33]

---

[24]FC 71:123. [25]Gen 22:18. [26]Gal 3:16. [27]Gen 20:17. [28]FC 71: 123-24. [29]FC 82:481. [30]Gen 12:11-12. [31]Gen 22:5. [32]Jn 8:56; Cf. Mt 13:17. [33]TEG 3:182-83.

20:8-18 ABIMELECH RESTORES
SARAH TO ABRAHAM

⁸So Abimelech rose early in the morning, and called all his servants, and told them all these things; and the men were very much afraid. ⁹Then Abimelech called Abraham, and said to him, "What have you done to us? And how have I sinned against you, that you have brought on me and my kingdom a great sin? You have done to me things that ought not to be done." ¹⁰And Abimelech said to Abraham, "What were you thinking of, that you did this thing?" ¹¹Abraham said, "I did it because I thought, There is no fear of God at all in this place, and they will kill me because of my wife. ¹²Besides she is indeed my sister, the daughter of my father but not the daughter of my mother; and she became my wife. ¹³And when God caused me to wander from my father's house, I said to her, 'This is the kindness you must do me: at every place to which we come, say of me, He is my brother.'" ¹⁴Then Abimelech took sheep and oxen, and male and female slaves, and gave them to Abraham, and restored Sarah his wife to him. ¹⁵And Abimelech said, "Behold, my land is before you; dwell where it pleases you." ¹⁶To Sarah he said, "Behold, I have given your brother a thousand pieces of silver; it is your vindication in the eyes of all who are with you; and before every one you are righted." ¹⁷Then Abraham prayed to God; and God healed Abimelech, and also healed his wife and female slaves so that they bore children. ¹⁸For the LORD had closed all the wombs of the house of Abimelech because of Sarah, Abraham's wife.

OVERVIEW: The fear of the people and the indignation of Abimelech provide an opportunity for emphasizing the importance of Abraham, who supposedly had been treated as of no account. The threats against Abimelech also serve to underline the importance of keeping God uppermost in mind and having regard for justice. Abraham's misrepresentation of Sarah is defended as pretense, due to the fear of death, rather than a deceit. The benefits that Abraham receives from Abimelech are interpreted as the rewards for boldly striving (CHRYSOSTOM). In the spiritual interpretation, Abraham's gesture is seen as his desire to share virtue (Sarah) with the Gentiles, and Abimelech represents those who live purely and philosophically, but it was not yet time for the grace of God to pass over from the former people to the Gentiles (ORIGEN).

20:8 Abimelech's Servants Fear

ALL THE PEOPLE WERE FRIGHTENED. CHRYSOSTOM: Do you see how it was not idly or to no purpose that the good man had shifted place? I mean, had he remained at his former encampment, how would all the people of Gerar have been able to realize the degree of favor he enjoyed from God? "But all the people were very frightened." A great fear fell on them; they worried about everything. Then "Abimelech summoned Abraham," the text goes on. Consider, I ask you, the degree of notoriety with which the just man is now brought into the presence of the king after being treated a little before as beneath contempt, in the manner of a vagabond and stranger. When everyone is assembled in haste, the patriarch is summoned, for the time being ignorant of all this, and he then learns from the king in person what has happened to him on his account at God's hands. HOMILIES ON GENESIS 45.16.[1]

20:9 Abimelech Complains to Abraham

WHAT DID YOU HAVE IN MIND? CHRYSOSTOM: What was the reason, he asked, that you wanted to embroil me in such a terrible sin? What on earth did you have in mind in doing it? See how Abimelech shows by his own words the threat delivered against him by God. You see, since God had said to him, "If you do not restore her, death will come upon you and all that is yours," Abimelech interprets this very thing in saying, "What offense did I give you to cause you to bring such a great sin on me and my kingdom?" I mean, surely the extent of the punishment did not stop at me? My whole kingdom was set to be utterly destroyed through the deception you contrived. "So what did you have in mind in doing it?" HOMILIES ON GENESIS 45.17.[2]

20:11 Abraham Feared for His Life

THE JUST MAN'S NOBLE PURPOSE. CHRYSOSTOM: Notice at this point, dearly beloved, the just man's noble purpose in presenting them with a lesson in the knowledge of God under the guise of an explanation. "I said to myself, 'Surely there is no respect for God in this place, and they will kill me on account of my wife.'" I was concerned, he is saying, that as a result of being still held in ignorance you would have no regard for justice, and so I made allowance for the fact that when you discovered she was my wife you would, out of lust, have wanted to kill me—that was the reason I did it. See how in a few words he takes them to task and at the same time teaches them that the person who has God uppermost in mind ought commit no crime but rather fear that unsleeping eye and in view of the heavy judgment impending from that source have regard for justice. HOMILIES ON GENESIS 45.18.[3]

20:12 Sarah Is My Sister

ABRAHAM HAD NOT LIED. CHRYSOSTOM: Then, from a wish to make excuses for himself, he said, "Don't think I lied to you in that way; 'She is my sister on my father's side, though not my mothers, and she became my wife all the same.' She claims the same father as I . . . and hence I called her my sister. So don't condemn me. Even if the fear of death brought me to this sorry pass and the dread of your killing me but sparing her, still what was said by me was not a lie in the way you imply." See what great pains the good man takes to show that he had not told a lie even in this matter. For you to learn everything precisely from me (he is saying), listen also to the plan we formed between us "when God led me out from my father's home." Observe in this case, I ask you, the good man's wisdom. He teaches them by way of story that from the very beginning he had a special relationship with God and that God had personally moved him from home and led him there so that the king might learn that he was one of those people who had great confidence in God. HOMILIES ON GENESIS 45.19.[4]

GOD LEADS US FORTH. ANONYMOUS: Whenever we leave behind customs and laws in which we were registered by our fathers, we believe it is God who is leading us forth from the house of our fathers. But you will understand that the same is true, in light of the saying "Any one who commits sin is born of the devil,"[5] of one who has in every way abandoned sin. For such a one has been led out by God from the house of his father. CATENA ON GENESIS 3.1194.[6]

20:15 Reconciliation of Abimelech

GOD DELIVERS THOSE WHO STRIVE BOLDLY. CHRYSOSTOM: Do you see, dearly beloved, God's inventive wisdom? I mean, the man who was fear-

---

[1]FC 82:477. [2]FC 82:478. [3]FC 82:478. [4]FC 82:478-79*. [5]1 Jn 3:8. [6]TEG 3:184-85.

ful of death and took every means to be able to avoid it, not only did avoid it but was granted as well great confidence and became immediately famous. This, you see, is the way things are with God. Not only does he deliver from distress those who make every effort to strive boldly against the onset of temptation, but also he guarantees them such serenity in this very distress that we have complete tranquillity and achieve great material prosperity. See now the attention of the king to the just man. Not only does he show his regard with so many gifts, but also he grants him the right to occupy the land. "'Behold,' he said, 'my land is before you; settle wherever you please.'" You see, once he had learned that it was on his account and through his prayers that his life had been spared, he was anxious now to shower attention in this way on him, as a benefactor and champion, the man who was a stranger, a vagabond, one completely unknown. HOMILIES ON GENESIS 45.21.[7]

20:17 Abraham Prays for Abimelech

ABRAHAM DESIRES TO SHARE DIVINE VIRTUE. ORIGEN: But it does not seem to me superfluous that mention is made not only of Abimelech's wife but also of his handmaids, especially in that place that says, "God healed them, and they bore children. For he had closed [their wombs] that they might not bear."[8] So far as we can perceive in such difficult passages, we think natural philosophy can be called Abimelech's wife, but his handmaids represent the contrivances of dialectic which are diverse and various by virtue of the nature of the schools.

Abraham, meanwhile, desires to share the gift of divine virtue also with the Gentiles, but it is not yet time for the grace of God to pass over from the former people to the Gentiles. For the apostle also, although under another viewpoint and figure, says nevertheless, "A woman is bound to the law so long as her husband lives; but if her husband is dead, she is loosed from the law so that she is no longer an adulteress if she is with

another man."[9] First, therefore, the law of the letter must die so that, thus free at last, the soul may now marry the spirit and receive the marriage of the New Testament. Now this present time is the time of the calling of the Gentiles and of the death of the law, in which time free souls, at last loosed from the law of the husband, can marry a new husband, Christ.

But if you wish to be taught how the law is dead, look and see. Where now are the sacrifices? Where now is the altar? Where is the temple? Where are the purifications? Where is the celebration of the Passover? Is not the law dead in all these things? Or let those friends and defenders of the letter keep the letter of the law if they can.

According to this spiritual interpretation, therefore, Pharaoh, that is, an impure man and a destroyer, could not at all receive Sarah, that is, virtue. Later Abimelech, that is, he who was living purely and philosophically, could indeed receive her, because he was seeking "with a pure heart," but "the time had not yet come."[10] Virtue therefore remains with Abraham; it remains with circumcision, until the time should come that in Christ Jesus our Lord, in whom "dwells all the fullness of deity corporeally,"[11] complete and perfect virtue might pass over to the church of the Gentiles.

At that time, therefore, the house of Abimelech and his handmaids, whom the Lord healed, will bear sons of the church. For this is the time in which "the barren" will bear and in which "many are the children of the desolate, more than of her who has a husband."[12] For the Lord opened the womb of the barren and made it fruitful, so that she bears a nation "all at once."[13] But also the saints cry out and say, "Lord, from fear of you we have conceived in the womb and given birth; we have produced the spirits of your salvation on the earth."[14] Whence also Paul likewise says, "My little children, of whom I am in labor again, until Christ be formed in you."[15]

---

[7]FC 82:479-80. [8]Gen 20:17-18. [9]Rom 7:2-3. [10]Cf. Gen 20:5; Jn 7:6. [11]Col 2:9. [12]Cf. Gal 4:27; Is 54:1. [13]Is 66:8. [14]Is 26:18. [15]Gal 4:19.

Such sons, therefore, the whole church of God produces, and such it brings forth. For "he who sows in the flesh, of the flesh also shall reap corruption."[16] Now the sons of the Spirit are those about whom also the apostle says, "The woman shall be saved through childbearing, if they continue in faith and purity."[17]

Let the church of God therefore in this way understand the births, in this way receive the procreations, in this way uphold the deeds of the fathers with a fitting and honorable interpretation, in this way not disgrace the words of the Holy Spirit with foolish and Jewish fables[18] but reckon them to be full of honor, full of virtue and usefulness. Otherwise, what edification will we receive when we read that Abraham, such a great patriarch, not only lied to king Abimelech but also surrendered his wife's chastity to him? In what way does the wife of so great a patriarch edify us if she is supposed to have been exposed to defilements through marital indulgence? These things are what the Jews suppose, along with those who are friends of the letter, not of the spirit.

But we, "comparing spiritual things with spiritual,"[19] are made spiritual in deed and understanding in Christ Jesus our Lord, "to whom belongs glory and sovereignty forever and ever. Amen."[20] HOMILIES ON GENESIS 6.3.[21]

SARAH RECEIVED RENEWED YOUTH. EPHREM THE SYRIAN: Unless Sarah received renewed youth in the seed that she had received, Abimelech would not have desired a woman ninety years old. Then Abraham prayed and God healed Abimelech, his wife and his female slaves so that they bore children, because from the time [Abimelech] had decided to marry Sarah until he returned her, pangs of childbirth struck all the women in his household; they would kneel down, but they could not give birth. COMMENTARY ON GENESIS 17.3.[22]

---

[16]Gal 6:8. [17]1 Tim 2:15. [18]1 Tim 4:7; Tit 1:14. [19]1 Cor 2:13. [20]1 Pet 4:11. [21]FC 71:124-26. [22]FC 91:166.

21:1-7 THE BIRTH OF ISAAC

[1]*The* LORD *visited Sarah as he had said, and the* LORD *did to Sarah as he had promised.* [2]*And Sarah conceived, and bore Abraham a son in his old age at the time of which God had spoken to him.* [3]*Abraham called the name of his son who was born to him, whom Sarah bore him, Isaac.* [4]*And Abraham circumcised his son Isaac when he was eight days old, as God had commanded him.* [5]*Abraham was a hundred years old when his son Isaac was born to him.* [6]*And Sarah said, "God has made laughter for me; every one who hears will laugh over me."* [7]*And she said, "Who would have said to Abraham that Sarah would suckle children? Yet I have borne him a son in his old age."*

OVERVIEW: Sarah's giving birth in her old age can be interpreted as a figure of the church, which has given birth in this final stage of history (CHRYSOSTOM). The etymology of the name Isaac ("laughter" or "joy") provides a connection to Paul, who begot spiritually through the gospel (ORIGEN). The example of the patriarch's remarkable obedience and gratitude along with God's ineffable care and considerateness provide material for moral reflection (CHRYSOSTOM).

21:2 Sarah Bears a Son

SARAH BECAME A TYPE OF THE CHURCH. CHRYSOSTOM: Do you wish to learn the symbolic meaning of Sarah's sterility? The church was to bring forth the multitude of believers. In order, therefore, that you may not find incredible how one who was childless, fruitless and barren could have given birth, she who by nature was barren went ahead, paving the way for chosen sterility, and Sarah became a type of the church. For just as she gave birth in her old age when she was barren, so too the church, though barren, has given birth for these, the final times.[1] DO NOT DESPAIR.[2]

21:4 The Circumcision of Isaac

THE HOLY SPIRIT TEACHES US SOMETHING DIVINE AND WORTHY. ORIGEN: Let us ask the Lord lest, in accordance with the apostle's word, even with us, "when Moses is read the veil be upon" our "heart."[3] For it has been read that Abraham begot a son, Isaac, when he was a hundred years old.[4] "And Sarah said, 'Who will announce to Abraham that Sarah nurses a child?' "[5] "And then," the text says, "Abraham circumcised the child on the eighth day." Abraham does not celebrate his son's birthday, but he celebrates the day of this weaning "and makes a great feast."[6]

Why? Do we think that it is the Holy Spirit's intention to write stories and to narrate how a child was weaned and a feast was made, how he played and did other childish things? Or should we understand by these things that he wishes to teach us something divine and worthy that the human race might learn from the words of God? HOMILIES ON GENESIS 7.1.[7]

21:6 God Has Made Laughter for Me

A FEAST AND GREAT JOY. ORIGEN: Isaac means "laughter" or "joy." Who is it, then, who begets such a son? It is doubtless he who said of these whom he begot through the gospel: "For you are my joy and crown of glory."[8] For sons of this kind, there is a feast and great joy when they are weaned, for these who "no longer need milk, but strong meat, who by taking up their power have their senses exercised to the discerning of good or evil."[9] There is a great feast for such as these, when they are weaned. But a feast cannot be offered nor joy possessed for those of whom the apostle says, "I gave you milk to drink, not meat; for you were not able as yet, but neither indeed are you able still. And I could not speak to you as to spiritual, but as to carnal, as to little ones in Christ."[10] Let those who wish the divine Scripture to be understood straightforwardly tell us what it means: "I could not speak to you as to spiritual, but as to carnal, as to little ones in Christ; I gave you milk to drink, not meat."[11] Can these words be taken straightforwardly? HOMILIES ON GENESIS 7.1.[12]

THE PATRIARCH'S REMARKABLE OBEDIENCE AND GRATITUDE. CHRYSOSTOM: Come now, today too, dearly beloved, let us take up the thread of yesterday's remarks and thus set before you this spiritual meal so that we may once more come to learn, as you heard yesterday, the good God's ineffable care and considerateness and the patriarch's remarkable obedience and gratitude. Do you see how the birth of Isaac made Sarah joyful? "She said, 'The Lord brought laughter to me: whoever hears of it will rejoice with me.' " Everyone who hears of it, she is saying, I will convince to be a sharer of my joy. After all, the gift given me by God is wonderful, surpassing human

---

[1]That is, in an eschatological sense. [2]TEG 3:187; PG 51:368. [3]Cf. 1 Cor 3:15. [4]Gen 21:5. [5]Gen 21:7. [6]Gen 21:8. [7]FC 71:127*. [8]1 Thess 2:19-20. [9]Heb 5:12, 14; cf. Philo *De Somniis* 2.10. [10]1 Cor 3:2. [11]1 Cor 3:1. [12]FC 71:127-28*.

limitations. I mean, who would not be struck, she is saying, to see me feeding and nursing a child in old age after being childless up to this stage of my life? As though surprised and amazed at the event, she added, "Who will let Abraham know that Sarah is nursing a child, that I have borne a son in my old age?" Since what happened was beyond the bounds of nature, she naturally demands, "Who will let him know?" as if to say, Who will imagine it? Who would entertain such an idea? What mind could grasp it? Is there any reasoning that could invent this happening in every detail? Not so remarkable was the incident of the flood of water gushing from the rock in the desert when Moses struck it with his rod[13] as was this instance of a child being born of a womb already deprived of vitality and a ready flow of milk. You see, for the birth to be known to everyone and bring everyone to acceptance of the marvel, for those who heard of it both then and later, she feeds the child and insists on nursing it. She said, "Who will let Abraham know that Sarah is nursing a child, that I have borne a son in my old age," this strange, surprising favor done me in my old age? What is the meaning of "I have borne a son in my old age"? That even without sterility my time of life was sufficient to make me despair of bearing children. But all these obstacles the Lord caused to disappear and has granted me the birth of the child and the flow of milk. HOMILIES ON GENESIS 46.1.[14]

YOUR ONLY SON. AMBROSE: I have described sufficiently the origin of holy Isaac and the grace he received in my discussion of his father. He abounds in glory, in that he was born as a reward to Abraham, his incomparably great father. And no wonder, since there were prefigured in him the birth and the passion of the Lord. An aged woman who was sterile brought him to birth according to God's promise,[15] so that we might believe that God has power to bring it about that even a virgin may give birth. He was offered for sacrifice in a singular fashion, that he might not be lost to his father and yet might fulfill the sacrifice.[16] Likewise by his very name he prefigures grace. For Isaac means "laughter," and laughter is the sign of joy. Now everybody knows that he is the joy of all who checked the dread of fearsome death, took away its terror and became for all people the forgiveness of their sins. The one is named and the other demoted; the one portrayed and the other foretold. ISAAC, OR THE SOUL 1.1.[17]

---

[13]Ex 17; Num 20. [14]FC 87:3-4. [15]Gen 18:11-15; 21:1-2. [16]Gen 22:1-19. [17]FC 65:10.

21:8-14 HAGAR AND ISHMAEL ARE SENT AWAY

[8]*And the child grew, and was weaned; and Abraham made a great feast on the day that Isaac was weaned.* [9]*But Sarah saw the son of Hagar the Egyptian, whom she had borne to Abraham, playing with her son Isaac.[b]* [10]*So she said to Abraham, "Cast out this slave woman with her son; for the son of this slave woman shall not be heir with my son Isaac."* [11]*And the thing was very displeasing to Abraham on account of his son.* [12]*But God said to Abraham, "Be not displeased because of the lad and because of your slave woman; whatever Sarah says to you, do as she tells you, for through Isaac shall your descendants be named.* [13]*And I will make a nation of the son of the slave woman also, because he is your offspring."* [14]*So Abraham rose early in the morning, and took bread*

---

and a skin of water, and gave it to Hagar, putting it on her shoulder, along with the child, and sent her away. And she departed, and wandered in the wilderness of Beer-sheba.

h Gk Vg: Heb lacks *with her son Isaac*

OVERVIEW: Isaac is interpreted as a figure of Christ, and his "growth" suggests a growth in hope in Christ and therefore of joy. Sarah's request, however, that Ishmael and Hagar be sent away, posed a problem for interpreters, because on its face, it was not edifying and indeed appeared cruel. Taking a cue from Paul, the whole story can be interpreted allegorically to represent the opposition between the flesh and the spirit. Sarah, representing virtue, is offended that the flesh, represented by Ishmael, should attract the spirit, represented by Isaac. The two sons can also be interpreted to symbolize those who cling to God on the basis of love as opposed to fear of future judgment (ORIGEN). Following a different line of interpretation, it can be inferred that Ishmael shared the characteristics of his mother, who had despised Sarah and thus gave offense (EPHREM). Another interpretation concluded that Ishmael had struck Isaac (ANONYMOUS). Similarly, the inference that Ishmael was "brash" serves to justify Sarah's attitude. God's instruction to accede to Sarah's request shows God's loving kindness and Abraham's correct attitude, thus providing material for moral edification (CHRYSOSTOM). The "skin of water" provides the opportunity for an allegorical contrast with the church that drinks from "wells" (ORIGEN).

21:8 Isaac's Weaning

THE CHILD GREW AND WAS WEANED. ANONYMOUS: You can search all of Scripture and you will never find it said about any unjust person that "he grew." For the command "increase and multiply" is a blessing that reaches only those who are worthy of a blessing. But notice too that the weaning of Ishmael is nowhere mentioned in Scripture; this is why when he is already twenty years old, he is still called a "child." CATENA ON GENESIS 3.1205.[1]

THE HOPE THAT IS IN CHRIST. ORIGEN: Isaac, Scripture says, "grew" and became strong; that is, Abraham's joy grew as he looked not at those things "which are seen but at the things which are not seen."[2] For Abraham did not rejoice about present things or about the riches of the world and the activities of the age. But do you wish to hear why Abraham rejoiced? Hear the Lord saying to the Jews: "Abraham your father desired to see my day, and he saw it and was glad."[3] In this way, therefore, "Isaac grew." That vision of Abraham, in which he saw the day of Christ and the hope which is in Christ, were increasing his joys. And would that you too might be made Isaac and be a joy to your mother the church! HOMILIES ON GENESIS 10.1.[4]

21:9 Hagar's Son Played with Isaac

SARAH IS ANGRY. ORIGEN: Sarah is angry because the son of the bondwoman plays with the son of the free woman, and she considers that play to be a disaster. She counsels Abraham and says, "Cast out the bondwoman and her son. For the son of the bondwoman shall not be heir with my son, Isaac."[5]

I shall not now consider how these words ought to be understood. The apostle discussed them in this way, saying, "Tell me, you who have read the law, have you not heard the law? For it is written that Abraham had two sons, the one by a bondwoman and the other by a free woman. But he indeed who was of the bondwoman was born according to the flesh, but he of the free woman was by promise. Which things are allegorical."[6] What then? Is Isaac not "born according to the flesh"? Did Sarah not bear him? Is he not circum-

---

[1]TEG 3:190. [2]2 Cor 4:18. [3]Jn 8:56; cf. Mt 13:17 and the same conflation in the catena. [4]FC 71:157. [5]Gen 21:10. [6]Gal 4:21-24.

cised? In regard to this very incident, that he played with Ishmael, did he not play in the flesh? This indeed is what is astonishing in the apostle's understanding, that he called things "allegorical" that are quite obviously done in the flesh. His purpose is that we might learn how to treat other passages, and especially these in which the historical narrative appears to reveal nothing worthy of the divine law.

Ishmael, therefore, is born "according to the flesh," the son of the bondwoman. But Isaac, who was "the son of the free woman," is not born "according to the flesh" but "according to promise." And the apostle says of these words that "Hagar engendered" a carnal people "unto bondage."[7] But Sarah, who was free, engendered a people which is not "according to the flesh" but has been called to freedom, by which "freedom Christ has made him free."[8] For Christ himself said, "If the Son shall make you free, you shall be free indeed."[9]

But let us see what the apostle adds to these words as he expounds them: "But as then he," Scripture says, "who was according to the flesh, persecuted him who was according to the spirit, so also it is now."[10] Notice how the apostle teaches us that in all things the flesh is opposed to the spirit, whether that carnal people is opposed to this spiritual people, or even among ourselves, if someone is still carnal, he is opposed to the spiritual. For even you, if you live "according to the flesh" and direct your life "according to the flesh," are a son of Hagar and for this reason are opposed to these who live "according to the spirit." Or even if we inquire in ourselves, we find that "the flesh lusts against the spirit and the spirit against the flesh and these are contrary to one another,"[11] and we find "a law in our members flighting against the law of our mind and leading us captive in the law of sin."[12] Do you see how great the battles of the flesh against the spirit are?

There is yet also another battle more violent perhaps than all these. These who understand the law "according to the flesh" are opposed to and persecute these who perceive it "according to the

spirit." Why? Because "the sensual man does not perceive the things that are of the spirit of God. For it is foolishness to him, and he cannot understand because it is spiritually discerned."[13] HOMILIES ON GENESIS 7.2.[14]

WHAT IS REPRESENTED? ORIGEN: And nevertheless according to those things which are written I do not see what moved Sarah to order the son of the bondwoman to be expelled. He played with her son, Isaac. How did he injure or harm him if he was playing? As if this ought not to be pleasing even at that age, that the son of the bondwoman played with the son of the free woman. Next, I marvel also at the apostle who called this play a persecution, saying, "But as then he, who was according to the flesh, persecuted him who was after the spirit, so also it is now,"[15] when certainly no persecution of Ishmael against Isaac is related to have been undertaken, except this play of the infant alone.

But let us see what Paul understood in this play and what angered Sarah. Already above in our spiritual exposition we set Sarah in the place of virtue. If therefore the flesh, which Ishmael, who was born according to the flesh, represents, attracts the spirit, which is Isaac, and deals with him with enticing deceitfulness, if it allures him with delights, if it mitigates him with pleasures, this kind of play of the flesh with the spirit especially offends Sarah, who represents virtue, and Paul judges allurements of this kind to be the most bitter persecution.

And you, therefore, O hearer of these words, do not suppose that alone is persecution whenever you are compelled by the madness of the pagans to sacrifice to idols. But if perhaps the pleasure of the flesh allures you, if the allurement of lust sports with you, flee these things as the greatest persecution if you are a child of virtue. Indeed, for this reason the apostle also says, "Flee fornication."[16] But also if injustice should attract

---

[7]Gen 4:24. [8]Gal 5:1, 13. [9]Jn 8:36. [10]Gal 4:29. [11]Gal 5:17. [12]Rom 7:23. [13]1 Cor 2:14. [14]FC 71:128-30. [15]Gal 4:29. [16]1 Cor 6:18.

you, so that, accepting "the countenance of the mighty,"[17] and because of his artful twisting you render an unjust judgment, you ought to understand that under the guise of play you suffer a seductive persecution by injustice. But you shall also consider it a persecution of the spirit by individual guises of evil, even if they are pleasant and delightful and similar to play, because in all these virtue is offended. HOMILIES ON GENESIS 7.3.[18]

LOVE AS OPPOSED TO FEAR OF FUTURE JUDGMENT. ORIGEN: Spiritually, therefore, all indeed who come to the recognition of God through faith can be called sons of Abraham; but among these some cling to God on the basis of love, others on the basis of dread and fear of future judgment. Whence also the apostle John says, "He who fears is not perfected in love, but perfect love casts out fear."[19] He therefore who "is perfected in love" is born of Abraham and is "a son of the free woman." But he who keeps the commandments, not in perfect love but in dread of future torment and in fear of punishments is, indeed, also himself a son of Abraham. He too receives gifts, that is, the reward of his work (because even "he who shall give a cup of cold water only in the name of a disciple, shall not lose his reward").[20] Nevertheless he is inferior to that person who is perfected, not in slavish fear but in the freedom of love.

The apostle also shows something similar when he says, "As long indeed as the heir is a child, he differs nothing from a servant, though he be lord of all; but he is under tutors and governors until the time appointed by the father."[21] He is "a child," therefore, who is nourished "with milk" and "is unskillful in the word of justice"; nor is he able to receive the "solid food" of the divine wisdom and knowledge of the law.[22] He cannot "compare spiritual things with spiritual."[23] He cannot yet say, "But when I became a man, I put away the things of a child."[24] He "differs," therefore, "nothing from a servant."[25]

But if "leaving the word of the first principles of Christ,"[26] he be borne to perfection and "seek the things that are above, where Christ is sitting at the right hand of God, not the things that are on the earth"[27] and "look not at the things which are seen but at the things which are not seen,"[28] nor in the divine Scriptures follow "the letter which kills" but "the spirit which quickens,"[29] from those things he will doubtless be one who does not receive "the spirit of bondage again in fear, but the spirit of adoption, whereby they cry, Abba, Father."[30] HOMILIES ON GENESIS 7.4.[31]

SARAH NOTICED ISHMAEL MOCKING. EPHREM THE SYRIAN: Then the time came for Isaac to be born, and milk flowed in the breasts of the old woman. On the day of the great feast that Abraham prepared when he circumcised and weaned Isaac, Sarah noticed Ishmael playing.[32] But Sarah also saw how much Ishmael shared the characteristics of his mother, for just as Sarah was despised in the eyes of Hagar, so too did Ishmael mock her son, and she thought, "If he acts thus to my son while I am still alive, perhaps [Abraham] will make him coheir with my son when I die and even give him two parts according to [the laws of] the firstborn." COMMENTARY ON GENESIS 18.1.[33]

ISHMAEL STRUCK ISAAC. ANONYMOUS: When Scripture speaks of "playing" here, it does so by way of covert allusion. Actually, while they were playing Ishmael struck Isaac. But Sarah got angry when she saw it, and this is why she says to Abraham, "Cast out the slave girl." CATENA ON GENESIS 3.1206.[34]

SARAH WANTED TO CHECK ISHMAEL'S BRASHNESS. CHRYSOSTOM: See, I ask you, dearly beloved, in this instance once again Sarah not tolerating the brashness of Ishmael and unable to put up equably with the maidservant's son being reared with Isaac. So just as she previously wished to check Hagar's arrogance and in her ex-

[17]Lev 19:15. [18]FC 71:130-31. [19]1 Jn 4:18. [20]Mt 10:42. [21]Gal 4:1-2. [22]Heb 5:13-14. [23]1 Cor 2:13. [24]1 Cor 13:11. [25]Gal 4:1. [26]Heb 6:1. [27]Col 3:1-2. [28]2 Cor 4:18. [29]2 Cor 3:6. [30]Rom 8:15. [31]FC 71:131-33*. [32]Gen 21:4-9. [33]FC 91:166. [34]TEG 3:190-191.

treme irritation had her sent packing, so in this case too she wanted to nip Ishmael's forwardness in the bud. Not bearing to see the son born of grace and of the very gift of God being reared along with that of the Egyptian maidservant, she said to Abraham, "Send away the maidservant and her son: surely the son of the maidservant will not share the inheritance with my son?" Since she realized that she herself was in fact in extreme old age, and she saw the patriarch was well on (after all, they were both advanced in years), she was afraid that in the event of their sudden passing Ishmael would, on the score of his being born of an association of the patriarch, endeavor to thrust himself into his father's inheritance and become a sharer of it with Isaac. Hence she said, "Send away from here the maidservant and her son." Let her learn at this stage, she is saying, that the son of the maidservant has nothing in common with my son, Isaac. It is, in fact, not fair that the slave's son should be reared with that of the mistress, my son. HOMILIES ON GENESIS 46.2.[35]

21:10 The Son of This Slave Woman

NO INHERITANCE. EPHREM THE SYRIAN: Then Sarah, who showed no envy in any matter that concerned herself, became envious in this matter concerning her son. She was not envious of Hagar whom she had given to her husband. Since it was a matter of God's promise, and the son of the concubine thought that he would be coheir with the son of the freewoman, Sarah said, "Cast out the slave woman and her son, because it is not just that a son of a handmaid should have any inheritance together with that son of the promise, to whom it was promised by God. It is not right that you be opposed to God and make an heir him whom God has not made an heir." COMMENTARY ON GENESIS 18.2.[36]

21:11 Abraham's Displeasure

THE EXTRAORDINARY CONSIDERATENESS OF

THE LOVING GOD. CHRYSOSTOM: For her part, however, Sarah was not guilty of acting unreasonably; she acted even quite logically, so logically that even God agreed with the words she spoke. The patriarch, being affectionate and well disposed toward Ishmael, did not take kindly to her remarks. "This remark about his son . . . struck Abraham as severe." It was not, you see, that he took much interest in Hagar; rather, he was well disposed toward his son for the reason that he was then still in his youth. Consider in this case, however . . . the extraordinary considerateness of the loving God: when he saw Sarah apparently having a human problem in being distressed by the parity of esteem of the children and Abraham not taking kindly to the expulsion of Ishmael and the maidservant. (After all, even if in his great restraint he did not take issue with Sarah, it still struck him as severe, that is, harsh, repugnant, and oppressive.) At that point, in fidelity to his characteristic loving kindness and wishing to strengthen the bonds of harmony between them, the Lord said to Abraham, "Don't let the remark about the child and the maidservant strike you as severe. Whatever Sarah says to you, heed her."[37] HOMILIES ON GENESIS 46.3.[38]

21:12 Descendants Named Through Isaac

ABRAHAM'S CORRECT ATTITUDE. CHRYSOSTOM: Don't object, he says, to what is said to you by her; instead, "whatever Sarah says to you, heed her." Accept everything she now says to you about Ishmael and Hagar, and pay close attention. Don't be ready to distress the woman who in all this period has given evidence of such great affection for you on more than one occasion so as to save you from death by surrendering herself for your welfare and proving the occasion of your wonderful prosperity. On the first occasion she caused you to leave Egypt with all that wealth, and later she was responsible for your being accorded remarkable esteem by Abimelech. So

---

[35]FC 87:4. [36]FC 91:166-67. [37]Gen 21:12. [38]FC 87:5.

don't allow yourself to follow a course of action contrary to what is advised by her; nor in fact will things turn out otherwise. You see, your descendants will be called after Isaac, the child born of her, and he will be your successor. "But this son of the maidservant I shall cause to become numerous; I shall make him grow into a mighty nation since he is your offspring." So do what is said to you by her, and pay attention to her words.

Consider now, I ask you, how great was the peace and harmony that all at once began to reign over their life together, God's goodness strengthening their relationship. "He arose early next morning," the text goes on, remember, "took bread and a bag of water, and gave them to Hagar; he then set the child on her shoulders and sent her off."[39] Notice once again, I ask you, the good man's utterly correct attitude in giving evidence in every way of his godly purpose. I mean, when he heard Sarah's words, "Send away the maidservant and her son," it struck him as severe, since he was kindly disposed toward Ishmael. But when the Lord gave him orders, he immediately carried them out and gave no further thought to his natural affections. In other words, he said to himself, When it is he that commands, let all feelings take no further part; after all, the one who commands is the Lord of nature. "So the maidservant took the bread and the bag of water," the text says,[40] "and went off with her son." HOMILIES ON GENESIS 46.4-5.[41]

21:14 Abraham Sent Away Hagar and Ishmael

THE CHURCH DRINKS FROM EVANGELIC AND APOSTOLIC FOUNTAINS. ORIGEN: Let us see what Abraham does meanwhile after Sarah is displeased. He casts out the bondwoman and her son, but nevertheless he gives him a bottle of water. For his mother does not have a well of living water, nor could the boy draw water from a well. Isaac has wells for which he also suffers strife against the Philistines,[42] but Ishmael drinks water from a bottle. This bottle, as it is a bottle, fails, and therefore he is thirsty and does not find a well.

But you, who are a son "of promise as Isaac,"[43] "drink water from your own fountains, and let not the waters flow forth from your wells, but let your waters run in your streets."[44] But one "who is born according to the flesh"[45] drinks water from a bottle, and the water itself fails him, and he lacks in many things. The bottle of the law is the letter, from which carnal people drink and thence receives understanding. This letter frequently fails them. It cannot extricate itself, for the historical understanding is defective in many things. But the church drinks from the evangelic and apostolic fountains that never fail but "run in its streets,"[46] because they always abound and flow in the breadth of spiritual interpretation. The church drinks also "from wells" when it draws and examines certain deeper things from the law.

On account of this mystery also, I think, our Lord and Savior said to the Samaritan woman, when, as if he were speaking with Hagar herself he said, "Whoever shall drink of this water shall thirst again; but he who shall drink of the water which I give him shall not thirst forever."[47] But she says to the Savior, "Sir, give me this water, that I may not thirst, nor come here to draw."[48] After this the Lord says to her, "There shall come to be in him who believes in me a fountain of water springing up into life everlasting."[49] HOMILIES ON GENESIS 7.5.[50]

THE THING APPEARED HARSH TO ABRAHAM. EUSEBIUS OF EMESA: But was the just Abraham inhumane in that he did not even supply Hagar and the boy with a donkey, with all the cattle he possessed? Some say it was a gesture of kindness, so that she would not have to look after the donkey; others say that he did this believing that God would protect the boy. But why does he

---

[39]Gen 21:14. [40]The Hebrew and the LXX do not say this; it is added by Chrysostom. [41]FC 87:5-6. [42]Gen 26:14-17. [43]Gal 4:28. [44]Prov 5:15-16. [45]Gal 4:29. [46]Prov 5:16. [47]Jn 4:13-14. [48]Jn 4:15. [49]Jn 6:47; 4:14. [50]FC 71:133-34.

throw her out in the first place? Was it not that he wished to have peace with his wife? And indeed he really did not want to send her away at all, for it is written that the thing appeared extremely harsh to Abraham. So he would not have done what he did except for the fact that God said to him, let not this matter trouble you, etc. CATENA ON GENESIS 3.1216.[51]

[51]TEG 3:197.

21:15-21 GOD INTERVENES TO SAVE HAGAR AND ISHMAEL

[15]*When the water in the skin was gone, she cast the child under one of the bushes.* [16]*Then she went, and sat down over against him a good way off, about the distance of a bowshot; for she said, "Let me not look upon the death of the child." And as she sat over against him, the child lifted up his voice[i] and wept.* [17]*And God heard the voice of the lad; and the angel of God called to Hagar from heaven, and said to her, "What troubles you, Hagar? Fear not; for God has heard the voice of the lad where he is.* [18]*Arise, lift up the lad, and hold him fast with your hand; for I will make him a great nation." * [19]*Then God opened her eyes, and she saw a well of water; and she went, and filled the skin with water, and gave the lad a drink.* [20]*And God was with the lad, and he grew up; he lived in the wilderness, and became an expert with the bow.* [21]*He lived in the wilderness of Paran; and his mother took a wife for him from the land of Egypt.*

i Gk: Heb *she lifted up her voice*

OVERVIEW: God's intervention to save Hagar and her son naturally demonstrates his loving kindness (CHRYSOSTOM). The "well of water" provides material for a spiritual interpretation (ORIGEN). The story also provides the opportunity to reflect that God's grace is all that is necessary, and the narrative is the starting point for a digression on the dangers of envy, implicitly attributed to Sarah (CHRYSOSTOM). Finally, Hagar, understood allegorically (following Paul) as the "mother of the Jews," continues to have the opportunity to draw from the fountain of living water (Christ) if she begins to weep (CYRIL OF ALEXANDRIA).

21:18 Ishmael Will Be a Great Nation

WHAT LOVING KINDNESS. CHRYSOSTOM: What loving kindness on the Lord's part! Far from ignoring [Hagar] as a menial servant, he deigned to show her such wonderful concern for the reason that he had made the promise to the patriarch and the child was his. Hence the words "What is it, Hagar? Don't worry: God heard the cry of the child. Get up, pick him up, and take him by the hand; after all, I am to make him grow into a mighty nation." Don't lose heart, he is saying, at being driven from home. He will enjoy such providence at my hands as to become a mighty nation, even he. HOMILIES ON GENESIS 46.7.[1]

[1]FC 87:7.

21:19 *God Opens Hagar's Eyes*

HAGAR SEES A WELL OF LIVING WATER. ORIGEN: After this, when already he had been abandoned as dead and had wept, the angel of the Lord is present with him "and opened Hagar's eyes, and she saw a well of living water."

How can these words be related to history? For when do we find that Hagar has closed eyes and they are later opened? Is not the spiritual and mystical meaning in these words clearer than light, that that people which is "according to the flesh" is abandoned and lies in hunger and thirst, suffering "not a famine of bread nor a thirst for water, but a thirst for the word of God,"[2] until the eyes of the synagogue are opened? This is what the apostle says is a "mystery": that "blindness in part has happened in Israel until the fullness of the Gentiles should come in, and then all Israel should be saved."[3] That therefore is the blindness in Hagar, who gave birth "according to the flesh," who remains blind until "the veil of the letter be removed" by the angel of God and she sees the "living water." For now the Jews lie around the well, but their eyes are closed, and they cannot drink from the well of the law and the prophets.

But let us also beware, for frequently we also lie around the well "of living water," that is, around the divine Scriptures, and err in them. We hold the books and we read them, but we do not touch upon the spiritual sense. And therefore there is need for tears and incessant prayer that the Lord may open our eyes, because even the eyes of those blind men who were sitting in Jericho would not have been opened unless they had cried out to the Lord.[4] And what am I saying? That our eyes, which are already opened, might be opened? For Jesus came to open the eyes of the blind.[5] Our eyes therefore are opened, and the veil of the letter of the law is removed. But I fear that we ourselves may close them again in a deeper sleep while we are not watchful in the spiritual meaning. Nor are we disturbed so that we dispel sleep from our eyes and contemplate things which are spiritual, that we might not err with

the carnal people set around the water itself. HOMILIES ON GENESIS 7.6.[6]

GOD'S GRACE IS ALL WE REQUIRE. CHRYSOSTOM: "He opened her eyes," the text goes on, not because she couldn't see before this but because even with her eyes open nothing was of any help to her before the visitation from on high. Hence, since his intention was to give evidence of care on his part, it says, "He opened her eyes," that is, he made clear to her in her ignorance, he activated her mind, he showed her the way to find the place flowing with springs of water. "She saw a well of running water," the text goes on, "and she went and filled the bag, and gave the boy to drink." In her neediness the Lord granted her means, and when she found herself so much at a loss and lacking all hope of survival, he gave evidence in her case of his characteristic generosity by consoling her and at the same time exercising care for the child.

In like manner, whenever God wishes, even if we are utterly alone, even if we are in desperate trouble, even if we have no hope of survival, we need no other assistance, since God's grace is all we require. You see, if we win favor from him, no one will get the better of us, but rather we will prevail against anyone. "God was with the boy," the text goes on; "he grew up and lived in the desert."[7] In similar fashion, whenever we have God on our side, even if we are utterly alone, we will live more securely than those who dwell in the cities. After all, the grace of God is the greatest security and the most impregnable fortification. HOMILIES ON GENESIS 46.7-8.[8]

THE PASSION OF ENVY. CHRYSOSTOM: Mindful of this, let us, I beseech you, shun the harm of this passion and with all our might exterminate it from our own souls. This, after all, is more deadly than all other passions and undermines our very salvation, being in fact the invention of the

---

[2]Amos 8:11. [3]Rom 11:5. [4]Mt 20:30. [5]Is 42:7. [6]FC 71:134-35. [7]Gen 21:20. [8]FC 87:7-8.

wicked demon. Hence a certain sage also said, "Through the devil's envy death entered the world."[9] What is meant by "through the devil's envy death entered the world"?

You see, since this wicked beast saw that the first-formed human being was created immortal, by his characteristic wickedness he led him on to disobedience of the command and in that way caused him to bring on himself the penalty of death. So envy caused deception, deception caused disobedience, and disobedience caused death. Hence the text says, "Through the devil's envy death entered the world."

Do you see the extent of the harm caused by this passion? It made the one given the privilege of immortality undergo death. The enemy of our salvation, however, introduced the envy characteristic of himself and caused the first-formed human being, immortal though he was, to come under sentence of death, whereas the caring and loving Lord by his own death once again bestowed upon us immortality, and so we found greater benefits than we had lost. The former took us out of paradise; the latter led us into heaven. The former caused us to be condemned to death; the latter bestowed upon us immortality. The former deprived us of the delights of paradise; the latter prepared for us the kingdom of heaven. Do you see the inventiveness of your Lord in that he directed against the devil's head his own weapons of malice against our salvation? In fact, not only did he regale us with greater benefits, but also he made him subject to us in the words "Behold, I have given you power to walk over snakes and scorpions."[10]

Accordingly, keeping all this in mind, let us banish envy from our own souls and win favor from God. This, after all, is our invincible weapon; this, our greatest resource. Hence Ishmael too, young though he was and in utter isolation and neediness, suddenly grew in strength and developed into a great nation since, the text says,

"God was with the child." . . . Let us therefore, I beseech you, despise this present life, long for the future life, esteem favor from God above all other things, and, through an excellent way of living, lay up for ourselves great confidence, so that we may be able to pass this present life without distress and attain those future blessings, thanks to the grace and loving kindness of our Lord Jesus Christ, to whom with the Father and the Holy Spirit be glory, power and honor, now and forever, for ages of ages. Amen. HOMILIES ON GENESIS 46.15-17.[11]

IF SHE SHOULD BEGIN TO WEEP. CYRIL OF ALEXANDRIA: Abraham took it very hard when Hagar fled from him, though he had sent her off at God's command. Similarly it was a great cause of sorrow to the holy apostles and evangelists when Israel fell. However, they were separated from them, not at all willingly but because of God's will and out of love for Christ. For this reason the divine Paul writes, "My sorrow is great, and I have continuous pain in my heart, for I would wish that I myself could be separated from Christ for the sake of my brothers, who are from the same race as I according to the flesh; they are Israelites."[12] So, when the mother of the Jews was sent away, she wandered for a long time in the wilderness, and there was some danger of her being wholly destroyed. But if she should begin to weep (like Hagar) in time and cry out to God, she will be shown mercy abundantly. For God will open the eyes of their understanding, and they too will see the fountain of living water, that is, Christ. And believing they too will rejoice, and having been washed they will be made clean, according to the saying of the prophet.[13] GLAPHYRA ON GENESIS 3.10.[14]

---

[9]Wis 2:24. [10]Lk 10:19. [11]FC 87:11-13. [12]Rom 9:2-3. [13]Is 1:16. [14]PG 69:136.

21:22-34 ABRAHAM'S DISPUTE WITH ABIMELECH

[22]At that time Abimelech and Phicol the commander of his army said to Abraham, "God is with you in all that you do; [23]now therefore swear to me here by God that you will not deal falsely with me or with my offspring or with my posterity,* but as I have dealt loyally with you, you will deal with me and with the land where you have sojourned." [24]And Abraham said, "I will swear."

[25]When Abraham complained to Abimelech about a well of water which Abimelech's servants had seized, [26]Abimelech said, "I do not know who has done this thing; you did not tell me, and I have not heard of it until today." [27]So Abraham took sheep and oxen and gave them to Abimelech, and the two men made a covenant. [28]Abraham set seven ewe lambs of the flock apart. [29]And Abimelech said to Abraham, "What is the meaning of these seven ewe lambs which you have set apart?" [30]He said, "These seven ewe lambs you will take from my hand, that you may be a witness for me that I dug this well." [31]Therefore that place was called Beer-sheba;[j] because there both of them swore an oath. [32]So they made a covenant at Beer-sheba. Then Abimelech and Phicol the commander of his army rose up and returned to the land of the Philistines. [33]Abraham planted a tamarisk tree in Beer-sheba, and called there on the name of the LORD, the Everlasting God. [34]And Abraham sojourned many days in the land of the Philistines.

j That is *Well of seven* or *Well of the oath*   *LXX, "that you will not wrong me or my seed or my name."

OVERVIEW: The last part of the chapter received very little comment in the patristic period. Abimelech is seen to make a covenant with Abraham because he saw that God was with Abraham (EPHREM). Abimelech's insistence that Abraham not "wrong his name" provides occasion for the observation that spreading slanderous rumors is a way of wronging someone's name (ANONYMOUS).

21:23 Abimelech's Covenant with Abraham

THEY MADE A COVENANT. EPHREM THE SYRIAN: After these things, Abimelech and Phicol, the commander of his army, spoke to Abraham, for they saw that God was with him and had helped him in the wars of the kings and had also promised him the land of the Canaanites. They also feared that after Abraham destroyed the Canaanites he would also destroy their own land, so they hastened to make a covenant with him, and the two of them made a covenant with Abraham.[1] COMMENTARY ON GENESIS 19.1.[2]

ONE WRONGS SOMEONE'S NAME. ANONYMOUS: The just man wrongs no one. But not having been persuaded regarding Abraham, Abimelech says, "Swear to me by God that you will not wrong me." But Abraham would wrong not even his "seed," or Abimelech's "name"; now one wrongs someone's name when one spreads slanderous rumours about him. CATENA ON GENESIS 3.1225.[3]

[1]Gen 21:22-24. [2]FC 91:167. [3]TEG 3:202.

22:1-8 THE TESTING OF ABRAHAM

¹*After these things God tested Abraham, and said to him, "Abraham!" And he said, "Here am I." ²He said, "Take your son, your only* son Isaac, whom you love, and go to the land of Moriah,† and offer him there as a burnt offering upon one of the mountains of which I shall tell you." ³So Abraham rose early in the morning, saddled his ass, and took two of his young men with him, and his son Isaac; and he cut the wood for the burnt offering, and arose and went to the place of which God had told him. ⁴On the third day Abraham lifted up his eyes and saw the place afar off. ⁵Then Abraham said to his young men, "Stay here with the ass; I and the lad will go yonder and worship, and come again to you." ⁶And Abraham took the wood of the burnt offering, and laid it on Isaac his son; and he took in his hand the fire and the knife. So they went both of them together. ⁷And Isaac said to his father Abraham, "My father!" And he said, "Here am I, my son." He said, "Behold, the fire and the wood; but where is the lamb for a burnt offering?" ⁸Abraham said, "God will provide himself the lamb for a burnt offering, my son." So they went both of them together.*

*LXX: "beloved" or "dearest."   †LXX: "Go into the high land."

OVERVIEW: Even the smallest detail of the text could provide inspiration for comment. Thus the fact that God never calls Abraham "Abram" shows that he did not wish to call him by a name that was to be abolished. Abraham also knew that his story was a prefiguration of future truth. The command to sacrifice Isaac was a way of testing Abraham (ORIGEN). In the same line of prefiguring future truth, Abraham could be seen as a type of God the Father and Isaac as a type of Jesus (CAESARIUS OF ARLES). The mention of the "third day" can be seen to prefigure and symbolize other mysteries (ORIGEN, CAESARIUS OF ARLES). Abraham was able to accept God's command because he believed in the resurrection (ORIGEN). The various elements of the story: the servants, the ram, the wood, all receive symbolic (allegorical) interpretations (CAESARIUS OF ARLES). Above all Isaac is a figure of Christ (ORIGEN).

22:1 God Tests Abraham

A TREASURE IN THE DETAILS. ORIGEN: Give your attention, you who have approached God—

who believe yourselves to be faithful. Consider diligently how the faith of the faithful is proved from these words that have been read to us. "And it came to pass," the text says, "after these words, God tested Abraham and said to him: 'Abraham, Abraham.' And he said, 'Here I am.'" Observe each detail that has been written. For, if one knows how to dig into the depth, he will find a treasure in the details, and perhaps also the precious jewels of the mysteries lie hidden where they are not esteemed. This man was previously called Abram. Nowhere do we read that God called him by this name or said to him, "Abram, Abram." For God could not call him by a name that was to be abolished, but he calls him by this name which he himself gave. And not only does he call him by this name, but also he repeats it. HOMILIES ON GENESIS 8.1.[1]

22:2 Isaac to Be a Burnt Offering

ABRAHAM PREFIGURED THE IMAGE OF

[1]FC 71:136.

FUTURE TRUTH. ORIGEN: What do you say to these things, Abraham? What kind of thoughts are stirring in your heart? A word has been uttered by God that is such as to shatter and try your faith. What do you say to these things? What are you thinking? What are you reconsidering? Are you thinking, are you turning over in your heart that if the promise has been given to me in Isaac but I offer him for a burnt offering, it remains that that promise holds no hope? Or rather do you think of those well-known words and say that it is impossible for him who promised to lie;[2] be that as it may, the promise shall remain?

But I, because "I am the least,"[3] am not able to examine the thoughts of such a great patriarch, nor can I know what thoughts the voice of God which had proceeded to test him stirred in him, what feeling it caused, when he was ordered to slay his only son. But since "the spirit of prophets is subject to the prophets,"[4] the apostle Paul, who, I believe, was teaching by the Spirit what feeling, what plan Abraham considered, has revealed it. He says, "By faith Abraham did not hesitate, when he offered his only son, in whom he had received the promises, thinking that God is able to raise him up even from the dead."[5]

The apostle therefore has reported to us the thoughts of the faithful man, that the faith in the resurrection began to be held already at that time in Isaac. Abraham therefore hoped for the resurrection of Isaac and believed in a future that had not yet happened. How then are they "sons of Abraham"[6] who do not believe what has happened in Christ, which Abraham believed was to be in Isaac? No rather, that I may speak more clearly, Abraham knew himself to prefigure the image of future truth. He knew the Christ was to be born from his seed, who also was to be offered as a truer victim for the whole world and was to be raised from the dead. HOMILIES ON GENESIS 8.1.[7]

GOD WAS TESTING ABRAHAM. ORIGEN: But now meanwhile the text says, "God was testing Abraham and says to him: 'Take your dearest son whom you love.'"[8] For to have said "son" would

not have been enough, but "dearest" also is added. Let this too be considered. Why is there still added also, "whom you love"? But behold the importance of the test. The affections of a father are roused by the dear and sweet appellations repeated frequently, that by awaking memories of love the paternal right hand might be slowed in slaying his son and the total warfare of the flesh might fight against the faith of the soul.

"Take," therefore, the text says, "your dearest son Isaac, whom you love."[9] Let it be, Lord, that you are reminding the father of the son; you add also "dearest," whom you are commanding to be slain. Let this be sufficient for the father's torment. You add again also, "whom you love." Let the triple torment of the father be in this. Why is there need yet that you bring to mind also "Isaac"? Did Abraham not know that that dearest son of his, that one whom he loved, was called Isaac? But why is it added at this time? That Abraham might recall that you had said to him, "In Isaac shall your seed be called, and that in Isaac the promises shall be yours."[10] The reminder of the name also produces hopelessness in the promises that were made under this name. But all these things happened because God was testing Abraham. HOMILIES ON GENESIS 8.2.[11]

ABRAHAM A TYPE OF THE FATHER. CAESARIUS OF ARLES: When Abraham offered his son Isaac, he was a type of God the Father, while Isaac prefigured our Lord and Savior. SERMON 84.2.[12]

22:2 The High Land

GO INTO THE HIGH LAND. ORIGEN: What happens after this? "Go," the text says, "into the high land, to one of the mountains which I shall show you, and there you shall offer him as a burnt offering."

Notice, in the details, how the test is aug-

---

[2]Heb 6:18. [3]1 Cor 15:9. [4]1 Cor 14:32. [5]Heb 11:17, 19. [6]Jn 8:37. [7]FC 71:137-38*. [8]Gen 22:1-2. [9]Gen 22:2. [10]Cf. Gen 21:12; Rom 9:7-8; Heb 11:18; Gal 3:16, 18; 4:23. [11]FC 71:138. [12]FC 47:16.

mented. "Go into the high land." Could not Abraham with the child first be led to that high land, and first be placed on the mountain which the Lord had chosen, and there it be said to him that he should offer his son? But first it is said to him that he ought to offer his son, and then he is ordered to go "into the high land" and ascend the mountain. For what reason? That while he is walking, while he is making the journey, throughout the whole trip he might be torn to pieces with his thoughts, that hence he might be tormented by the oppressing command, hence he might be tormented by the struggle of true affection for his only son. For this reason, therefore, likewise the journey and furthermore the ascent of the mountain is enjoined, that in all these things there might be a period of struggle between affection and faith, love of God and love of the flesh, the charm of things present and the expectation of things future.

He is sent therefore "into the high land," and the high land is not sufficient for a patriarch about to accomplish so great a work for the Lord. But he is also ordered to ascend a mountain, of course that, exalted by faith, he might abandon earthly things and ascend to things above. HOMILIES ON GENESIS 8.3.[13]

22:3 Abraham Takes Isaac to Moriah

THE PARENT'S HEART IS TORMENTED. ORIGEN: Abraham arose in the morning (because the text adds "in the morning," perhaps it wished to show that the beginning of light shone in his heart), saddled his ass, prepared wood, took along his son. He does not deliberate, he does not reconsider, he does not take counsel with any man, but immediately he sets out on the journey.

"And he came," the text says, "to the place which the Lord had said to him, on the third day."[14] I omit now what mystery the "third day" contains. I consider the wisdom and intention of the one who tests him. Since everything was done in the mountains, was there thus no mountain nearby. But a journey is prolonged for three days,

and during the whole three days the parent's heart is tormented with recurring anxieties, so that the father might consider the son in this whole lengthy period, that he might partake of food with him, that the child might weigh in his father's embraces for so many nights, might cling to his breast, might lie in his bosom? Behold to what an extent the test is heaped up. HOMILIES ON GENESIS 8.4.[15]

22:4 On the Third Day

THE MYSTERY OF THE THIRD DAY. ORIGEN: The third day, however, is always applied to mysteries. For also when the people had departed from Egypt, they offer sacrifice to God on the third day and are purified on the third day.[16] And the third day is the day of the Lord's resurrection.[17] Many other mysteries also are included within this day. HOMILIES ON GENESIS 8.4.[18]

THE MYSTERY OF THE TRINITY. CAESARIUS OF ARLES: The fact that he arrived at the place of sacrifice on the third day is shown to represent the mystery of the Trinity. That the third day should be accepted in the sense of a promise or mystery of the Trinity is found frequently in the sacred Books. In Exodus we read, "We will go a three days' journey into the wilderness."[19] Again, upon arriving at Mount Sinai it is said to the people, "Be sanctified, and be ready for the third day."[20] When Joshua was about to cross the Jordan, he admonished the people to be ready on the third day. Moreover, our Lord arose on the third day. We have mentioned all this because blessed Abraham on the third day came to the place that the Lord had showed him. SERMON 84.2.[21]

22:5 We Will Go and Worship

---

[13]FC 71:138-39*. [14]Origen is reading the phrase "the third day" as part of Genesis 22:3 rather than the beginning of Genesis 22:4. This is a possible reading of the Greek text. [15]FC 71:139-40. [16]Ex 19:11, 15-16; 24:5. [17]Mt 27:63; Mk 8:31. [18]FC 71:140. [19]Ex 8:27. [20]Ex 19:15. [21]FC 47:16-17.

ABRAHAM BELIEVED IN THE RESURRECTION.
ORIGEN: He leaves the servants. For the servants were not able to ascend with Abraham to the place of the burnt offering that God had shown him. "You," therefore, the text says, "stay here, but I and the child will go and when we have worshiped, we will return to you." Tell me, Abraham, are you saying to the servants in truth that you will worship and return with the child, or are you deceiving them? If you are telling the truth, then you will not make him a burnt offering. If you are deceiving, it is not fitting for so great a patriarch to deceive. What disposition therefore does this statement indicate in you? I am speaking the truth, he says, and I offer the child as a burnt offering. For this reason I carry wood with me, and I return to you with him. For I believe, and this is my faith, that "God is able to raise him up even from the dead."[22] HOMILIES ON GENESIS 8.5.[23]

SYMBOLIC MEANINGS. CAESARIUS OF ARLES: The two servants whom he ordered to stay with the ass typified the Jewish people, who could not ascend or reach the place of sacrifice because they would not believe in Christ. That ass signified the synagogue. The ram that was stuck among the briars with its horns also seems to represent the Lord, for Christ as it were stuck among thorns with horns when he hung on the beam of the cross, fastened with nails. When Isaac carried the wood for the sacrifice of himself, in this too he prefigured Christ our Lord, who carried his own cross to the place of his passion. Of this mystery much had already been foretold by the prophets: "And his government shall be upon his shoulders."[24] Christ then had the government upon his shoulders when he carried his cross with wonderful humility. Not unfittingly does Christ's cross signify government: by it the devil is conquered and the whole world recalled to the knowledge and grace of Christ. Finally, the apostle also said this when he spoke of the Lord's passion: "He became obedient to death, even to death on a cross. Therefore God also has exalted him

and has bestowed upon him the name that is above every name."[25] We have said this, brothers, so that your charity may know that the government of Christ of which we read, "And the government shall be upon his shoulders," is none other than his cross. For this reason this lesson is read at Easter when the true Isaac, whose type the son of Abraham illustrated, is fastened to the gibbet of the cross for the human race. SERMON 84.3.[26]

ABRAHAM'S GREAT FAITH. CAESARIUS OF ARLES: Why is it said to the servants who prefigured the Jews, "Sit here with the ass"? Could that ass sit down, dearly beloved? It is said, "Sit with the ass," because the Jewish people who would not believe in Christ could not stand but, like the weak and languid sinner who had despised the staff of the cross, were about to fall to the ground. For this reason blessed Abraham said, "Sit here with the ass while the boy and I go on; and when we have worshiped, we shall come back to you." What is it that you are saying, blessed Abraham? You are going to sacrifice your son and you say you will return with him? If you offer him as a burnt offering, surely he will not be able to return with you. Blessed Abraham could reply: I speak the truth. I am offering my son, and I will return to you with him. So great is my faith that I believe that he who deigned to give him to me of a sterile mother could raise him from the dead. For this reason I say with truth, "When we have worshiped, we shall come back to you." SERMON 84.4.[27]

22:6 Abraham Prepares a Sacrifice

ISAAC A FIGURE OF CHRIST. ORIGEN: That Isaac carries on himself "the wood for the burnt offering" is a figure, because Christ also "himself carried his own cross,"[28] and yet to carry "the wood for the burnt offering" is the duty of a

---

[22]Heb 11:19. [23]FC 71:140*. [24]Is 9:5-6. [25]Phil 2:8-9. [26]FC 47:17*. [27]FC 47:18*. [28]Jn 19:17.

priest. He therefore becomes victim and priest. But what is added also is related to this: "And they both went off together." For when Abraham carries the fire and knife as if to sacrifice, Isaac does not go behind him but with him, that he might be shown to contribute equally with the priesthood itself. HOMILIES ON GENESIS 8.6.[29]

ISAAC'S SACRIFICE PREFIGURED JESUS. CLEMENT OF ALEXANDRIA: Isaac is another type too (he can easily be taken in this other sense), this time of the Lord. He was a son, just as is the Son (he is the son of Abraham; Christ, of God). He was a victim, as was the Lord, but his sacrifice was not consummated, while the Lord's was. All he did was to carry the wood of his sacrifice, just as the Lord bore the wood of the cross. Isaac rejoiced for a mystical reason, to prefigure the joy with which the Lord has filled us, in saving us from destruction through his blood. CHRIST THE EDUCATOR 1.5.23.[30]

22:7 Where Is the Lamb?

THE WORD OF TESTING. ORIGEN: What happens after this? "Isaac," the text says, "said to Abraham, his father, 'Father.'" And in this moment the word of testing is uttered by the son. For how do you suppose the son to be killed struck the father's heart with this word? And although Abraham was very rigid by virtue of his faith, nevertheless he also returned an expression of affection and responded, "What is it, son?" And Isaac says, "Behold the fire and the wood. Where is the sheep for the burnt offering?" HOMILIES ON GENESIS 8.6.[31]

ABRAHAM BELIEVED ISAAC WOULD BE RAISED. EPHREM THE SYRIAN: In two things then was Abraham victorious: that he killed his son although he did not kill him and that he believed that after Isaac died he would be raised up again and would go back down with him. For Abraham was firmly convinced that he who said to him, "through Isaac shall your descendants be named,"[32] was not lying. COMMENTARY ON GENESIS 20.2.[33]

MY FATHER. AMBROSE: Therefore he brought his beloved son to be sacrificed, and him whom he had begotten so late he offered without delay. Nor was he held back by being addressed as father, when his son called him "father" and he answered "my son." ON HIS BROTHER, SATYRUS 2.97.[34]

22:8 God Will Provide the Lamb

ABRAHAM SPEAKS ABOUT THE FUTURE. ORIGEN: Abraham's response, sufficiently accurate and cautious, moves me. I do not know what he saw in his spirit, for he does not speak about the present but about the future: "God himself will provide himself a sheep." He responded to his son's inquiry about present things with future things. For "the Lord himself will provide himself a sheep" in Christ, because also, "Wisdom herself has built herself a house,"[35] and "He himself humbled himself unto death."[36] HOMILIES ON GENESIS 8.6.[37]

---

[29]FC 71:140-41*. [30]FC 23:23. [31]FC 71:141*. [32]Gen 21:12. [33]FC 91:168-69. [34]FC 22:240. [35]Prov 9:1. [36]Phil 2:8. [37]FC 71:141*.

22:9-14 THE ANGEL OF THE LORD INTERVENES

⁹When they came to the place of which God had told him, Abraham built an altar there, and laid the wood in order, and bound Isaac his son, and laid him on the altar, upon the wood. ¹⁰Then Abraham put forth his hand, and took the knife to slay his son. ¹¹But the angel of the LORD called to him from heaven, and said, "Abraham, Abraham!" And he said, "Here am I." ¹²He said, "Do not lay your hand on the lad or do anything to him; for now I know that you fear God, seeing you have not withheld your son, your only son, from me." ¹³And Abraham lifted up his eyes and looked, and behold, behind him was a ram, caught in a thicket by his horns; and Abraham went and took the ram, and offered it up as a burnt offering instead of his son. ¹⁴So Abraham called the name of that place The LORD will provide;ᵏ as it is said to this day, "On the mount of the LORD it shall be provided."ˡ*

k Or see l Or he will be seen *LXX, "the Lord saw."

OVERVIEW: The account is interpreted as the drama of faith as opposed to the natural affections, a drama that applies to the reader (ORIGEN). Not only is Isaac a figure of Christ in the Spirit, but also the ram symbolizes Christ in the flesh (ORIGEN, AMBROSE). Even Chrysostom abandons his customary moralizing and employs a typological interpretation. That Isaac was a type and not the reality is seen in the fact that he was not killed (CAESARIUS OF ARLES). Readers are also invited to interpret the story spiritually and apply it to themselves, so as to beget a son such as Isaac in themselves (ORIGEN).

22:9 Abraham Binds Isaac

FAITH IN GOD IS STRONGER THAN HUMAN AFFECTIONS. ORIGEN: Many of you who hear these words are fathers in the church of God. Do you think any one of you from the mere relating of the story acquires so much steadfastness, so much strength of soul, that when a son perhaps is lost by a death that is common and due to all, even if he be an only son, even if he be a beloved son, might bring in Abraham as an example for himself and set his magnanimity before his eyes? And indeed this greatness of soul is not required

of you, that you yourself should bind your son, you yourself tie him, you yourself prepare the sword, you yourself slay your only son. All these services are not asked of you. Be constant in purpose, at least, and mind. Offer your son to God with a joyful, immovable faith. Be the priest for your son's life. It is not fitting that the priest weeps who offers to God.

Do you wish to see that this is required of you? In the Gospel the Lord says, "If you were the children of Abraham, you would do the works surely of Abraham."[1] Behold, this is a work of Abraham. Do the works that Abraham did, but not with sadness, "for God loves a cheerful giver."[2] But also if you should be so inclined to God, it will be said also to you, "Ascend into the high land and into the mountain which I shall show you, and there offer your son to me."[3] "Offer your son" not in the depths of the earth or "in the vale of tears"[4] but in the high and lofty mountains. Show that faith in God is stronger than the affections of the flesh. For Abraham loved Isaac his son, the text says, but he placed the love of God before love of the flesh, and he is found not with the affection of the flesh but "with the affection of Christ,"[5] that is,

---

[1]Jn 8:39. [2]2 Cor 9:7. [3]Gen 22:2. [4]Ps 84:6 (83:7 LXX). [5]Phil 1:8.

with the affection of the Word of God and of the truth and wisdom. Homilies on Genesis 8.7.[6]

22:10 Abraham Takes the Knife

Portraying Abraham. Cyril of Alexandria: If someone of us desired to see the story of Abraham portrayed in a picture, how would the painter represent him? Would he do it in a single painting showing him doing all the things mentioned, or in successive pictures and distinctively, or in different images, but most often Abraham himself, for example, in one picture sitting on his donkey taking his son along and followed by his servants? In another one, again, with the donkey staying behind down below along with the servants, and Isaac being burdened with the wood while Abraham holds in his hands the knife and the fire? And, indeed, in a different painting, Abraham again in a different pose after he has bound the youth upon the wood and his right hand is armed with a sword in order that he might start the sacrifice? But this would not be a different Abraham each time, although he is seen most of the time in a different pose. It would be the same man in every instance with the skill of the artist continually disposing him according to the needs of the subject matter. For it would not be likely or at any rate probable that one would see him doing all the actions mentioned in a single painting. Letter 41.22.[7]

Abraham Did Not Shrink. Ambrose: The hand of a father lifted the knife over his own son, and, lest the sentence fail of execution, in his paternal love he was in the act of striking the blow. He was afraid the stroke would miss, that his right hand would weaken. He felt as a father would, but he did not shrink from his duty to God. On His Brother, Satyrus 2.97.[8]

22:12 Abraham Fears God

You Have Not Withheld Your Only Son. Ambrose: In place of the body, God showed the

ram in the bush,[9] that he might restore the son to his father and yet that a victim should not be lacking to the priest. Consequently neither was Abraham stained with the blood of his own son, nor was God deprived of a victim. When the prophet saw the ram, he did not assume a boastful attitude; he did not persist obstinately in his resolve but took the ram in place of the boy. His conduct shows all the more how piously he offered the son whom he received back so gladly. On His Brother, Satyrus 2.98.[10]

Written on Account of You. Origen: In this statement it is usually thrown out against us that God says that "now" he had learned that Abraham fears God, as though he were such as not to have known previously. God knew, and it was not hidden from him, since it is he "who has known all things before they come to pass."[11] But these things are written on account of you, because you too indeed have believed in God. But unless you fulfill "the works of faith,"[12] unless you are obedient to all the commands, even the more difficult ones, unless you offer sacrifice and show that you place neither father nor mother nor sons before God,[13] you will not know that you fear God. Nor will it be said of you, "Now I know that you fear God."

And yet it must be considered that an angel is related to have spoken these words to Abraham, and subsequently this angel is clearly shown to be the Lord. Whence I think that, just as among us "he was found in appearance as a man,"[14] so also among angels he was found in appearance as an angel. And following his example the angels in heaven rejoice "over one sinner repenting"[15] and glory in the progress people make in their relationship with God. For they, as it were, have charge over our souls, to whom, "while we are still children we are committed," as it were, "to tutors and governors until the time appointed by the

[6]FC 71:142-43*. [7]FC 76:181. [8]FC 22:240-41. [9]Gen 22:13. [10]FC 22:241. [11]Sus 42 (Dan 13:42). [12]2 Thess 1:11. [13]Mt 10:37. [14]Phil 2:7. [15]Lk 15:10.

father."[16] And they therefore now say about the progress of each of us, "Now I know that you fear God." For example, I intend to be a martyr. An angel could not say to me on this basis, "Now I know that you fear God," for an intention of the mind is known to God alone. But if I shall undertake the struggles, if I shall utter a "good confession,"[17] if I shall bear calmly all things which are inflicted, then an angel can say, as if confirming and strengthening me, "Now I know that you fear God." HOMILIES ON GENESIS 8.8.[18]

GOD CONTENDS WITH PEOPLE IN MAGNIFICENT GENEROSITY. ORIGEN: But grant that these words are spoken to Abraham, and he is said to fear God. Why? Because he did not spare his son. But let us compare these words with those of the apostle, where he says of God: "who spared not his own Son but delivered him up for us all."[19] Behold God contending with people in magnificent generosity: Abraham offered God a mortal son who was not put to death; God delivered to death an immortal Son for humanity.

What shall we say to these things? "What shall we render to the Lord for all the things that he has rendered to us?"[20] God the Father, on account of us, "spared not his own son."[21] Who of you, do you suppose, will sometime hear the voice of an angel saying, "Now I know that you fear God, because you spared not your son," or your daughter or wife? Or, you spared not your money or the honors of the world or the ambitions of the world, but you have despised all things and "have counted all things dung that you may gain Christ"[22]? Or, "you have sold all things and have given to the poor and have followed the Word of God?"[23] Who of you, do you think, will hear a word of this kind from the angels? Meanwhile Abraham hears this voice, and it is said to him, "You spared not your beloved son because of me." HOMILIES ON GENESIS 8.8.[24]

ABRAHAM'S DEVOTION. AMBROSE: Through motives of high devotion and in obedience to the word of God, Abraham offered his son as a holo-

caust, and like a man devoid of natural feeling he drew his sword that no delay might dim the brightness of his offering. Yet, when he was ordered to spare his son, he gladly sheathed his sword, and he who with the intention of faith has hastened to sacrifice his only-begotten son hurried with greater zeal for piety to put a ram in place of the sacrifice. LETTER TO LAYMEN 89.[25]

GOD'S KNOWLEDGE DIVULGED. HILARY OF POITIERS: Hence we are not permitted to doubt that the knowledge of God is adapted to the time rather than to the result of a change, since in connection with that which God knew it is a question of the opportune moment to divulge what is known rather than to acquire it. [This] we are also taught by the words that were spoken to Abraham: "Do not lay your hand on the boy, and do nothing to him, for I know now that you fear your God, and have not spared your beloved son for my sake." Accordingly, God knows now, but to know something now is an admission of previous ignorance. Since it is a contradiction for God not to know that Abraham had been previously faithful to him and of whom it had been said, "Abraham believed God, and it was credited to him as justice,"[26] that which he knew at this moment is the time when Abraham received this testimony, and not the time when God also began to acquire this knowledge. By bringing his son as a holocaust, Abraham manifested the love that he had for God. God was aware of it then when he speaks. And, since we are not to believe that he had been ignorant of it up to that moment, we must understand that he knew of it then because he speaks of it. Of the many passages in the Old Testament that contain references to the knowledge of God, we have cited only this one as an example that we may realize that God's ignorance of anything does not arise from a lack of knowledge but from the occasion. ON THE TRINITY 9.64.[27]

---

[16]Gal 4:2. [17]1 Tim 6:12. [18]FC 71:143-44*. [19]Rom 8:32. [20]Ps 116:12 (115:3 LXX). [21]Rom 8:32. [22]Phil 3:8. [23]Mt 19:21. [24]FC 71:144-45. [25]FC 26:490. [26]Cf. Gen 15:6; Gal 3:6. [27]FC 25:386.

GOD KNOWS THE JUST. JEROME: We have heard enough on how God does not know the sinner, so we ought to consider now how the just man is known by him. God said to Abraham, "Leave your country, your kinsfolk."[28] Abraham accordingly came into Palestine; he was in Abramiri;[29] he sojourned a long time in Gerar. When his son Isaac was born, he had received the promise: "In your descendants all the nations of the earth shall be blessed."[30] He took Isaac and offered him to God, and a voice from heaven was heard to say, Spare him. Straightway, at the very moment that he offered his son, what does God say to Abraham? "I know now that you fear the Lord, your God." Have you just now known Abraham, Lord, with whom you have communicated for such a long time? Because Abraham had such great faith in sacrificing his own son, on that account God first began to know him. Why have we said all this? Because it is written, "For the Lord knows the way of the just." Let us put it another way: The way, the life, and the truth is Christ;[31] let us walk therefore in Christ, and then God the Father will know our way. HOMILIES ON THE PSALMS 1.[32]

GOD'S CERTAINTY. BEDE: In the same way he said to Abraham, "Now I know that you fear God," wherein he was saying, "Now I have made people (who up to now did not know) recognize what I, in my own mind, always held to be certain, [namely], that you fear God." HOMILIES ON THE GOSPELS 2.13.[33]

22:13 A Ram Substituted

THIS RAM IS A TYPE OF CHRIST IN THE FLESH. ORIGEN: We said above, I think, that Isaac represented Christ. But this ram no less also seems to represent Christ. Now it is worthwhile to know how both are appropriate to Christ, both Isaac, who is not slain, and the ram, which is slain.

Christ is "the Word of God," but "the Word was made flesh."[34] One aspect of Christ therefore is from above; the other is received from human na-

ture and the womb of the Virgin. Christ suffered, therefore, but in the flesh; and he endured death, but it was the flesh, of which this ram is a type, as also John said: "Behold the Lamb of God, behold him who takes away the sin of the world."[35] But the Word continued "in incorruption,"[36] which is Christ according to the spirit, of which Isaac is the image. For this reason he is victim and priest. For truly according to the spirit he offers the victim to the Father, but according to the flesh he himself is offered on the altar of the cross. As it is said of him, "Behold the Lamb of God, behold him who takes away the sin of the world,"[37] so it is said of him, "You are a priest forever according to the order of Melchizedek."[38] HOMILIES ON GENESIS 8.9.[39]

BEHIND ABRAHAM WAS A LAMB. AMBROSE: Many persons say that our sacred writers did not write in accordance with the rules of rhetoric. We do not take issue with them: the sacred writers wrote not in accord with rules but in accord with grace, which is above all rules of rhetoric. They wrote what the Holy Spirit gave them to speak.[40] Yet writers on rhetoric have found rhetoric in their writings and have made use of their writings to compose commentaries and rules.

In rhetoric, these qualities in particular are demanded: a cause (*aition*), a subject (*hulē*) and an end or purpose (*apotelesma*). Now, when we read that blessed Isaac said to his father, "Behold, you have the fire and the wood, but where is the victim," are these qualities lacking? The one asking the question is in doubt; the one who answers the question gives the answer and removes the doubt. The fire is the cause; the wood is the subject, called *materia* in Latin; the third item, the purpose, is that which the child sought and which the father showed him when he asked, "Where is the victim?" "God himself," he said, "will provide the sacrifice, my son."[41]

---

[28]Gen 12:1. [29]Latin *abramio*, probably Mamre. [30]Gen 22:18. [31]Jn 14:6. [32]FC 48:13. [33]CS 111:122. [34]Jn 1:14. [35]Jn 1:29. [36]1 Cor 15:42. [37]Jn 1:29. [38]Ps 110:4 (109:4 LXX). [39]FC 71:145. [40]Cf. Acts 2:4. [41]Gen 22:7-8.

Let us discuss the meaning of the mystery for a little while. God showed a ram sticking fast with its horns; the ram is the Word, full of tranquillity and restraint and patience. By this is shown that wisdom is a good sacrifice and belongs to one who is duly wise and making atonement to understand the purpose of an action. The prophet David therefore says, "Offer up the sacrifice of justice."[42] Sacrifice belongs to justice as it does to wisdom. LETTERS TO BISHOPS 21.[43]

THE SACRIFICE. ATHANASIUS: Thus the sacrifice was not for the sake of Isaac but for that of Abraham, who was tested by being called upon to make this offering. And of course, God accepted his intentions, but he prevented him from slaying Isaac. The death of Isaac would not buy freedom for the world. No, that could be accomplished only by the death of our Savior, by whose stripes we are all healed.[44] FESTAL LETTERS 6.[45]

ABRAHAM SAW A LAMB. EPHREM THE SYRIAN: The mountain spit out the tree and the tree the ram. In the ram that hung in the tree and had become the sacrifice in the place of Abraham's son, there might be depicted the day of him who was to hang upon the wood like a ram and was to taste death for the sake of the whole world. COMMENTARY ON GENESIS 20.3.[46]

ALL THIS HAPPENED AS A TYPE OF THE CROSS. CHRYSOSTOM: All this, however, happened as a type of the cross. Hence Christ too said to the Jews, "Your father Abraham rejoiced in anticipation of seeing my day; he saw it and was delighted."[47] How did he see it if he lived so long before? In type, in shadow. Just as in our text the sheep was offered in place of Isaac, so here the rational Lamb was offered for the world. You see, it was necessary that the truth be sketched out ahead of time in shadow. Notice, I ask you, dearly beloved, how everything was prefigured in shadow: an only-begotten son in that case, an only-begotten in this; dearly loved in that case, dearly loved in this. "This is my beloved Son,"

Scripture says, in fact, "in whom I have found satisfaction."[48] The former was offered as a burnt offering by his father, and the latter his Father surrendered. Paul too shouts aloud in the words "He who in fact did not spare his own Son but handed him over for the sake of us all—how will he not also grant us every gift along with him?"[49] Up to this point there is shadow, but now the truth of things is shown to be more excellent. This rational Lamb, you see, was offered for the whole world; he purified the whole world; he freed human beings from error and led them forward to the truth; he made earth into heaven, not by altering the nature of the elements but by transferring life in heaven to human beings on earth. Through him all worship of demons is made pointless; through him people no longer worship stone and wood. Nor do those endowed with reason bend the knee to material things—instead, all error has been abolished, and the light of truth has shone brightly on the world. Do you see the superiority of the truth? Do you see what shadow is, on the one hand, and truth, on the other? HOMILIES ON GENESIS 47.14.[50]

THE LOCATION OF THE SACRIFICES OF ISAAC AND CHRIST. CAESARIUS OF ARLES: But when the ram was killed and Isaac was not killed, it happened thus because Isaac was a figure and not the reality; for in him was designated what was later fulfilled in Christ. Behold, God is contending with people in great devotion. Abraham offered God his mortal son who was not to die, while God surrendered in death his immortal Son for the sake of humankind. Concerning blessed Isaac and that ram it can be further understood that in Isaac was signified the divinity of Christ, in the ram his humanity. Just as in his passion not the divinity but the humanity is believed to have been crucified, so the ram but not Isaac was immolated: the only-begotten Son of God is offered, the firstborn of the Virgin is sacri-

---

[42]Ps 4:5 (4:6 LXX). [43]FC 26:115-16. [44]Is 53:5. [45]ARL 106*. [46]FC 91:169. [47]Jn 8:56. [48]Mt 3:17. [49]Rom 8:32. [50]FC 87:21-22.

ficed. Listen to another mystery. Blessed Jerome, a priest, wrote that he knew most certainly from the ancient Jews and elders that Christ our Lord was afterward crucified in the place where Isaac was offered. Last, from the place whence blessed Abraham was commanded to depart, he arrived on the third day at the place where Christ our Lord was crucified. This too is mentioned in the account of the ancients, that in the very place where the cross was fastened the first Adam once was buried.[51] Moreover, it was called the place of Calvary for the very reason that the first head of the human race is said to have been buried there. Truly, brothers, not unfittingly is it believed that the physician was raised up where the sick man lay. It was right that divine mercy should bend down in the place where human pride had fallen. The precious blood may be believed to have corporally redeemed the ashes of the sinner of old by deigning to touch it with its drops. We have gathered these facts as well as we could, dearly beloved, from the different books of Scripture for the progress of your soul, and we suggest them to the consideration of your charity. If, with the Lord's help, you will read over the sacred Scriptures rather frequently and heed them carefully, I believe that you can find an even better explanation. SERMON 84.5.[52]

22:14 The Lord Provides

A WAY OF SPIRITUAL UNDERSTANDING OPENS. ORIGEN: A clear way of spiritual understanding is opened for those who know how to hear these words.[53] For everything that has been done reaches to the vision, for it is said that "the Lord saw." But the vision that "the Lord saw" is in the spirit so that you too might see these things in the spirit which are written. And, just as there is nothing corporeal in God, so also you might perceive nothing corporeal in all these things. Rather, you too might beget a son Isaac in the spirit when you begin to have "the fruit of the Spirit, joy, peace."[54] . . . Now you beget joy if "you count it all joy when you fall into various temptations"[55] and you offer that joy in sacrifice to God.

For when you have approached God joyfully, he again gives back to you what you have offered and says to you, "You will see me again, and your heart shall rejoice, and no man shall take your joy from you."[56] So, therefore, what you have offered to God you shall receive back multiplied. Something like this, although in another figure, is related in the Gospels when in a parable someone is said to have received a pound that he might engage in business, and the master of the house demanded the money. But if you have caused five to be multiplied to ten, they themselves are given to you, they are granted to you. For hear what Scripture says: "Take his pound, and give it to him who has ten pounds."[57]

So, therefore, we appear at least to engage in business for the Lord, but the profits of the business go to us. And we appear to offer victims to the Lord, but the things we offer are given back to us. For God needs nothing, but he wishes us to be rich; he desires our progress through each individual thing. HOMILIES ON GENESIS 8.10.[58]

---

[51]2 Esdr 3:21. [52]FC 47:18-19*. [53]To understand this comment, it is necessary to keep in mind that Isaac is interpreted etymologically to mean "joy." Origen relies heavily on the principle of interpreting the Scriptures by means of the Scriptures (see the introduction, p. xxxiv) in order to find related passages. [54]Gal 5:22. [55]Jas 1:2. [56]Jn 16:22. [57]Lk 19:24. [58]FC 71:146-47.

22:15-19 ABRAHAM RECEIVES A SECOND BLESSING

> [15]And the angel of the LORD called to Abraham a second time from heaven, [16]and said, "By myself I have sworn, says the LORD, because you have done this, and have not withheld your son, your only son, [17]I will indeed bless you, and I will multiply your descendants as the stars of heaven and as the sand which is on the seashore. And your descendants shall possess the gate of their enemies, [18]and by your descendants shall all the nations of the earth bless themselves, because you have obeyed my voice." [19]So Abraham returned to his young men, and they arose and went together to Beer-sheba; and Abraham dwelt at Beer-sheba.

OVERVIEW: The repetition of the promise to Abraham can be seen to apply to the promise of descendants "in faith," whereas the first promise referred to those of the flesh. The promise is steadfast because of the passion of Christ. The promise of descendants is fulfilled in the church and in the individual soul (ORIGEN). Abraham's obedience shows that God seeks self-dedication, not blood (PETER CHRYSOLOGUS). The true seed of Abraham is Christ (AUGUSTINE).

22:15 The Angel Calls to Abraham

THE MYSTERY OF THE SECOND PROMISE. ORIGEN: These words require a concerned and attentive hearer. For this part of the statement is new: "And the angel of the Lord called to Abraham a second time from heaven." But what the text adds is not new. For "I shall certainly bless you" has already been said earlier, and "I shall certainly multiply you" has been promised earlier, and "your seed shall be as the stars of heaven and as the sand of the sea" also had been announced previously.[1] What therefore is there now in addition which is declared a second time from heaven? What new word is added to the old promises? What additional reward is given in that which the text says, "Because you have done this thing," that is because you have offered your son, because you have not spared your only son? I see nothing additional. The same things are repeated which

were previously promised. Will it, therefore, seem superfluous to go over the same things again and again? On the contrary, it is necessary. For all things that happen occur in mysteries.

One promise would have sufficed if Abraham had lived only "according to the flesh" and had been the father of one people whom he begot "according to the flesh."[2] But now, to show in the first place that he is to be the father of those who are circumcised "according to the flesh," the promise that should affect the people of circumcision is given to him at the time of his circumcision. In the second place, because he was to be the father also of those who "are of faith"[3] and who come to the inheritance through the passion of Christ, the promise that should apply to that people which is saved by the passion and resurrection of Christ is renewed at the time, no less, of the passion of Isaac.

The same things indeed appear to be repeated, but they are widely different. For those things that are said first and apply to the previous people are said on the earth. For thus the Scripture says: "And he brought him forth"—from the tent, of course—"and said to him, 'Look at the stars of heaven. Can they be numbered in their multitude?'" And he adds, "So shall your seed be."[4] But when the promise is repeated the second time, the text designates that it is said to him "from

---

[1]Gen 22:17; cf. 12:2; 13:16. [2]Gal 4:29. [3]Gal 3:9. [4]Gen 15:5.

heaven." The first promise is given from the earth, the second "from heaven." Does not this clearly seem to represent that which the apostle says: "The first man was of the earth, earthly; the second man from heaven, heavenly."[5] This latter promise, therefore, which applies to the faithful people is "from heaven," the former from the earth. HOMILIES ON GENESIS 9.1.[6]

22:17 Promises to Abraham's Descendants

THE PROMISE REMAINS STEADFAST. ORIGEN: In the former promise there was only the statement; here an oath is interposed, which the holy apostle writing to the Hebrews interprets in this way, saying, "God, meaning to show the heirs of the promise the immutability of his counsel, interposed an oath."[7] And again, Scripture says, "Men swear by one greater than themselves."[8] "But God, because he had no one greater by whom he might swear,"[9] " 'I swear by myself,' said the Lord."[10] It was not that necessity forced God to swear (for who would exact the oath from him?), but as the apostle Paul has interpreted it, that by this he might point out to his worshipers "the immutability of his counsel."[11] So also elsewhere it is said by the prophet, "The Lord has sworn nor will he repent: You are a priest forever according to the order of Melchizedek."[12]

At that time in the first promise there is no reason stated why the promise is given, only that he brought him forth and "showed him," Scripture says, "the stars of heaven, and said, 'So shall your seed be.' "[13] But now he adds the reason on account of which he confirms with an oath the promise which will be steadfast. For he says, "Because you have done this thing and have not spared your son." He shows therefore that because of the offering or passion of the son the promise is steadfast. This clearly points out that the promise remains steadfast because of the passion of Christ for the people of the Gentiles "who are of the faith of Abraham."[14] HOMILIES ON GENESIS 9.1.[15]

GOD RENEWS HIS PROMISES. ORIGEN: Let us return now to ourselves and treat the moral subject in every detail.

The apostle says, as we have already related above, "The first man was of the earth, earthly; the second man from heaven, heavenly. Such as is the earthly, such also are the earthly; and such as is the heavenly, such also are they that are heavenly. As we have borne the image of the earthly, let us bear also the image of the heavenly."[16] You see what he is showing, that if you remain in that which is first, which is of the earth, you will be rejected, unless you change yourself, unless you have been converted, unless, having been made "heavenly," you have received "the image of the heavenly."[17] This is the same thing he also says elsewhere: "Stripping yourselves of the old man with his deeds and putting on the new, who has been created according to God."[18] He writes that very thing also in another place: "Behold, the old things are passed away, all things are made new."[19]

For this reason therefore God renews his promises to show you that you also ought to be renewed. He does not continue in the old, lest you also continue as "the old man";[20] this is said "from heaven," that you also might receive "the image of the heavenly."[21] For what will it profit you if God should renew the promises and you should not be renewed? If he should speak from heaven and you should hear from earth? What does it profit you if God binds himself with an oath and you should pass over these things as if hearing a common story? HOMILIES ON GENESIS 9.2.[22]

HOW THE SEED OF CHRIST IS MULTIPLIED. ORIGEN: Nevertheless the apostle interprets this passage also, saying, "To Abraham God promised and to his seed. He did not say, 'And to his seeds' as of many; but as of one, 'And to your seed,' which is Christ."[23] It is said therefore of Christ: "I

---

[5]1 Cor 15:47. [6]FC 71:148-50. [7]Heb 6:17. [8]Heb 6:16. [9]Heb 6:13. [10]Gen 22:16. [11]Heb 6:17. [12]Ps 110:4 (109:4 LXX). [13]Gen 15:15. [14]Rom 4:16. [15]FC 71:150-51. [16]1 Cor 15:47-49. [17]1Cor 15:49. [18]Col 3:9-10. [19]2 Cor 5:17. [20]Rom 6:6. [21]1 Cor 15:49. [22]FC 71:151-52. [23]Gal 3:16.

shall certainly multiply your seed, and they shall be as the stars of heaven in multitude and as the sand which is by the seashore." What person now needs an explanation to know how the seed of Christ is multiplied, who sees the preaching of the gospel extended from the ends of the earth "to the ends of the earth"[24] and who sees that there is now almost no place which has not received the seed of the word? For indeed this also was prefigured in the beginnings of the world when God said to Adam, "Increase and multiply."[25] This same thing also the apostle says "is said in Christ and in the church."[26] HOMILIES ON GENESIS 9.2.[27]

THAT CHRIST MAY POSSESS THE CITY OF HIS SOUL. ORIGEN: But what does it profit me, if the seed of Abraham, "which is Christ,"[28] should possess "the cities of his enemies for an inheritance" and should not possess my city? If in my city, that is, in my soul, which is "the city of the great king,"[29] neither his laws nor his ordinances should be observed? What does it profit me that he has subjected the whole world and possesses the cities of his enemies if he should not also conquer his enemies in me, if he should not destroy "the law which is in my members fighting against the law of my mind and which leads me captive in the law of sin"?[30]

So therefore let each one of us do what is necessary that Christ may also conquer the enemies in his soul and in his body and, subjecting and triumphing over them, may possess the city even of his soul. For in this way we are made to belong to his portion, the better portion, which is "as the stars of heaven in glory,"[31] that also we might be able to receive the blessing of Abraham through Christ our Lord, "to whom belongs glory and sovereignty forever and ever. Amen."[32] HOMILIES ON GENESIS 9.3.[33]

22:17 God's Blessings for Abraham

THE WAY OF BLESSEDNESS. CLEMENT OF ROME: Let us then cling to his blessing, and let us see what are the ways of blessedness. Let us recall the events of old.[34] Why was our father Abraham blessed? Was it not because he performed justice and truth through faith? Isaac, knowing the future in confidence, was willingly led forth as a sacrifice. 1 CLEMENT 31.1-3.[35]

BLESSED FOR FAITHFULNESS. TERTULLIAN: Rightly then is he blessed because he was faithful; and rightly was he faithful because he was patient. ON PATIENCE 6.2.[36]

CHRIST WAS ISAAC IN TYPE. ORIGEN: It is written in the prophet speaking in the person of the Lord, "I have used similitudes by the ministries of the prophets."[37] What this statement means is this: Although our Lord Jesus Christ is one in his substance and is nothing other than the Son of God, nevertheless he is represented as various and diverse in the figures and images of the Scripture.

For example, as I recall we have explained in what precedes that Christ himself was Isaac, in type, when he was offered as a holocaust. Nevertheless the ram also represented him. I say furthermore that he is exhibited also in the angel who spoke to Abraham and says to him, "Lay not your hand on the boy."[38] For he says to him, "Because you have done this thing, I will certainly bless you."

He is said to be the sheep or the lamb that is sacrificed in the Passover,[39] and he is designated as the shepherd of the sheep.[40] He is also described, no less, as the high priest who offers the sacrifice.[41] HOMILIES ON GENESIS 14.1.[42]

MULTIPLYING THE SEED. ORIGEN: What person now needs an explanation to know how the seed of Christ is multiplied who sees the preaching of the gospel extended from the ends of the earth "to the ends of the earth"?[43] And who sees

---

[24]Rom 10:18. [25]Gen 1:28. [26]Eph 5:32. [27]FC 71:152. [28]Gal 3:16. [29]Ps 48:2 (47:3 LXX); Mt 5:35. [30]Rom 7:23. [31]1 Cor 15:41. [32]1 Pet 4:11; Rev 1:6. [33]FC 71:156. [34]See Gen 12:2-3; 18:18; 22:7-19; 28:1-4. [35]FC 1:34. [36]FC 40:204. [37]Hos 12:10. [38]Gen 22:12. [39]1 Cor 5:7. [40]Jn 10:11, 14; Heb 13:20. [41]Heb 5:1-10. [42]FC 71:196. [43]Rom 10:18.

that there is now almost no place which has not received the seed of the Word? For indeed this also was prefigured in the beginnings of the world when God said to Adam, "Increase and multiply."[44] HOMILIES ON GENESIS 9.2.[45]

BREAKING THE BONDS. ORIGEN: The bonds indeed with which they bind us are our passions and vices with which we are bound until "we crucify our flesh with the vices and concupiscences"[46] and so at last "break their bonds asunder and cast away their yoke from us."[47]

The seed of Abraham, therefore, that is, the seed of the Word, which is the preaching of the gospel and faith in Christ, has occupied "the cities of their enemies." HOMILIES ON GENESIS 9.2.[48]

POSSESSING THE ENEMIES' GATE. ORIGEN: To be able to find [these treasures], we need the help of God who alone can "break in pieces the doors of bronze" by which they are shut up and hidden and who "cuts asunder the bars of iron"[49] and the bolts by which access was prohibited for attaining all the truths that were written and hidden in Genesis. [These truths are] concerning the different kinds of souls, concerning the seeds and generations that either pertain directly to Israel or are separated much further from his offspring. ON FIRST PRINCIPLES 3.11.[50]

MAY GOD POSSESS HIS ENEMIES IN ME. ORIGEN: But what does it profit me, if the seed of Abraham, "which is Christ,"[51] should possess "the cities of his enemies for an inheritance" and should not possess my city? If in my city, that is in my soul, which is "the city of the great king,"[52] neither his laws nor his ordinances should be observed? What does it profit me that he has subjected the whole world and possesses the cities of his enemies if he should not also conquer his enemies in me, if he should not destroy "the law which is in my members fighting against the law of my mind and which leads me captive in the law of sin"?[53]

So therefore let each one of us do what is necessary that Christ may also conquer the enemies

in his soul and in his body, and, subjecting and triumphing over them, may possess the city even of his soul. For in this way we are made to belong to his portion, the better portion, which is "as the stars of heaven in glory,"[54] that also we might be able to receive the blessing of Abraham through Christ our Lord, "to whom belongs glory and sovereignty forever and ever. Amen."[55] HOMILIES ON GENESIS 9.3.[56]

22:18 All Nations Blessed

GOD SEEKS FAITH, NOT DEATH. PETER CHRYSOLOGUS: God seeks belief from you not death. He thirsts for self-dedication, not blood. He is placated by good will, not by slaughter. God gave proof of this when he asked holy Abraham for his son as a victim. For what else than his own body was Abraham immolating in his son? What else than faith was God requiring in the father, since he ordered the son to be offered but did not allow him to be killed? SERMON 108.[57]

HIS SEED IS CHRIST. AUGUSTINE: And to Abraham's seed he promised—what? In your seed shall all the nations of the earth be blessed. His seed is Christ; because from Abraham came Isaac, from Isaac Jacob, from Jacob twelve sons, from these twelve the people of the Jews, from the people of the Jews the Virgin Mary, from the Virgin Mary our Lord Jesus Christ. And what was promised to Abraham we find fulfilled among ourselves. In your seed, it says, shall all the nations of the earth be blessed. He believed this before he had seen anything; he believed, and he never saw what was promised. SERMON 113A.10.[58]

THE MEANING OF HISTORY FOR US. BEDE: In the third age of the world, God, testing Abra-

---

[44]Gen 1:28. [45]FC 71:152. [46]Gal 5:24. [47]Ps 2:3. [48]FC 71:154-55. [49]Is 45:2. [50]OSW 199. [51]Gal 3:16. [52]Ps 47:3 (46:4 LXX); Mt 5:35. [53]Rom 7:23. [54]1 Cor 15:41. [55]1 Pet 4:11; Rev 1:6. [56]FC 71:156. [57]FC 17:170. [58]WSA 3 4:178*.

ham's obedience, commanded him to offer to him as a holocaust his one and only son, whom he loved. Abraham did not delay in doing what he was ordered, but a ram was immolated in place of his son. Nevertheless for his virtue of extraordinary obedience he was granted the inheritance of an everlasting blessing. Behold, [here] you have the third hydria, for when you hear that a greater obedience is repaid by a greater prize, you yourself [will] attempt to learn and to possess obedience. If in the immolation of his one and only son, whom he loved, you understand the passion of the one concerning whom the Father says, "This is my beloved Son in whom I am well-pleased"[59] (in him, since his divinity remaining impassible, only his humanity suffered death and sorrow, it is as though a son was offered but a ram was slain); if you understand the blessing which was promised to Abraham about the nation's coming to belief as a gift fulfilled in you—then he has truly

made wine out of water for you, since he has opened to you the spiritual sense, by whose new fragrance you are intoxicated. HOMILIES ON THE GOSPELS 1.14.[60]

WE ARE HIS SEED. BEDE: For, in all humility, we too belong among those descendants of whom it was said that it shall be an everlasting law for him and for his descendants throughout their generations. We are not born of the lineage of Aaron, but we have believed in him in whom Aaron also, with the saints of that age, believed. Concerning him, it was promised to Abraham that in "in your descendants all the families of the earth shall be blessed."[61] ON THE TABERNACLE 3.14.139.[62]

---

[59]Mt 3:17. [60]CS 110:140-41. [61]Acts 3:25; cf. Gen 22:18. [62]TTH 18:162-63.

[22:20-24 DESCENDANTS OF NAHOR]

23:1-16 ABRAHAM'S PURCHASE OF A BURIAL PLACE

[1]*Sarah lived a hundred and twenty-seven years; these were the years of the life of Sarah.* [2]*And Sarah died at Kiriath-arba (that is, Hebron) in the land of Canaan; and Abraham went in to mourn for Sarah and to weep for her.* [3]*And Abraham rose up from before his dead, and said to the Hittites,* [4]*"I am a stranger and a sojourner among you; give me property among you for a burying place, that I may bury my dead out of my sight."* [5]*The Hittites answered Abraham,* [6]*"Hear us, my lord; you are a mighty prince among us. Bury your dead in the choicest of our sepulchres; none of us will withhold from you his sepulchre, or hinder you from burying your dead."* [7]*Abraham rose and bowed to the Hittites, the people of the land.* [8]*And he said to them, "If you are willing that I should bury my dead out of my sight, hear me, and entreat for me Ephron the son of Zohar,* [9]*that he may give me the cave of Mach-pelah, which he owns; it is at the end of his field. For the full price let him give it to me in your presence as a possession for a burying place."* [10]*Now Ephron was sitting*

among the Hittites; and Ephron the Hittite answered Abraham in the hearing of the Hittites, of all who went in at the gate of his city, [11]"No, my lord, hear me; I give you the field, and I give you the cave that is in it; in the presence of the sons of my people I give it to you; bury your dead." [12]Then Abraham bowed down before the people of the land. [13]And he said to Ephron in the hearing of the people of the land, "But if you will, hear me; I will give the price of the field; accept it from me, that I may bury my dead there." [14]Ephron answered Abraham, [15]"My lord, listen to me; a piece of land worth four hundred shekels of silver, what is that between you and me? Bury your dead." [16]Abraham agreed with Ephron; and Abraham weighed out for Ephron the silver which he had named in the hearing of the Hittites, four hundred shekels of silver, according to the weights current among the merchants.

OVERVIEW: This passage was the subject of very little comment in the patristic period. For Chrysostom it provides the opportunity to comment on riches.

23:2 Sarah's Death

ABRAHAM MOURNED FOR SARAH. MARTIN OF BRAGA: A brother asked an old man, "What shall I do for my sins?" He replied, "He who desires to be free from his sins shall be freed from them by weeping, and he who wishes to build virtues in himself will build them by weeping. Even the Scriptures are composed of mourning, for our fathers said to their disciples, 'Wail.'[1] There is no other way to life except this."

A brother asked an old man, "What shall I do, father?" He replied, "When Abraham entered the Promised Land, he first bought a tomb for himself, and near the tomb he made sure of land for a possession." The brother said to him, "What is a tomb?" He answered, "A place of mourning and weeping." SAYINGS OF THE EGYPTIAN FATHERS 33-34.[2]

23:6 Buying a Tomb

ABRAHAM HAD SUFFICIENT RICHES IN HIS ATTITUDE. CHRYSOSTOM: Sarah's death was the occasion for the patriarch's first instance of acquiring land. Sacred Scripture in fact shows us in every case the patriarch's virtue, in that he passed all his time as an alien and a nomad. And it mentions this latest item for us to learn that the man who enjoyed so much assistance from on high, who had become so famous and had increased in number to such a vast multitude, could not call a place his own, unlike many people today, who give all their attention to acquiring land, whole towns and great wealth beyond telling. You see, he had sufficient riches in his attitude, and he put no store by these other things. Let those heed this who in the twinkling of an eye take to themselves every conceivable thing and, so to say, stretch out in all directions their passion for avarice. Let them also imitate the patriarch, who had not even a place to inter Sarah's remains until, under pressure of very necessity, he bought the field and cave from the Hittites. For proof that he was in fact respected by the inhabitants of Canaan, listen to the words addressed to him by the Hittites: "You are king among us by God's appointment; bury your dead in our best tombs. None of us, after all, will keep this tomb from you." HOMILIES ON GENESIS 48.2.[3]

THE HITTITES OFFERED THEIR BEST SEPULCHER. CLEMENT OF ALEXANDRIA: The subjects by a free decision obey the good man in their enthusiasm for virtue. The philosopher Plato puts forward happiness as the goal of life and says it consists in "the greatest possible likeness to

---

[1]Jer 4:8 and elsewhere. [2]FC 62:24. [3]FC 87:25-26*.

God."[4] This may come from his going along with the general principles of the law (Philo the Pythagorean says in expounding the text of Moses, "Great natures free from passion aim fairly successfully in the direction of truth").[5] STROMATEIS 2.19.100.2-3.[6]

23:13 Purchasing the Field

ABRAHAM'S CHARACTERISTIC COMMON SENSE. CHRYSOSTOM: Notice, however, how the good man instructs even those people with his characteristic common sense, through his very actions, by forbearing to take possession of it before paying a just price. "Even if you for your part . . . have proved so kindly disposed toward me, I still cannot bring myself to take the tomb from you unless first I pay the proper price." He gave them money, the text says, took possession of the tomb "and buried his wife Sarah in the double cave of the field overlooking Mamre."[7] The man who was so famous and respected, who enjoyed such confidence with God and was the object of such attention from everyone, so to say, in that place that even the Hittites called him king—he owned not even one foot of land. Hence blessed Paul also celebrated this good man's virtue in writing these words: "By faith Abraham dwelt in the land of promise, like a foreigner living in tents with Isaac and Jacob, coheirs of the same promise."[8] Then to teach us how it was through faith that he dwelt there, he added, "He looked forward, you see, to the city built on foundations of which the builder and creator was God."[9] In the hope of things to come, he is saying, he overlooked present realities, and, in the expectation of greater things, he set less store by those of this life—and this before the law and the age of grace.

So what excuse will we have, tell me, who despite such wonderful promises and guarantees of ineffable blessings hanker for present realities, buying up property, ever concerned for our image, amassing all these possessions out of greed and avarice and fulfilling in practice what the blessed prophet said in his lament, "Woe to those who pile house on house and add property to property for the purpose of robbing their neighbor of something."[10] Do we not see this happening each day—widows being robbed, orphans despoiled and the weak oppressed by the strong? This good man, on the contrary, did not behave in that fashion; instead, he insisted on buying the tomb, and, when he saw those from whom he sought it ready and willing to hand it over, he could not bring himself to accept it before he paid the right price. HOMILIES ON GENESIS 48.3-4.[11]

---

[4]Plato *Theaetetus* 176b. [5]Philo *Life of Moses* 1.22. Clement refers to his fellow Alexandrian as "the Pythagorean" because of his use of symbolic numbers. [6]FC 85:223. [7]Gen 23:19. [8]Heb 11:9. [9]Heb 11:10. [10]Is 5:8. [11]FC 87:26-27.

23:17-20 ABRAHAM BURIES SARAH

[17]So the field of Ephron in Mach-pelah, which was to the east of Mamre, the field with the cave which was in it and all the trees that were in the field, throughout its whole area, was made over [18]to Abraham as a possession in the presence of the Hittites, before all who went in at the gate of his city. [19]After this, Abraham buried Sarah his wife in the cave of the field of Mach-pelah east of Mamre (that is, Hebron) in the land of Canaan. [20]The field and the cave that is in it were made over to Abraham as a possession for a burying place by the Hittites.

OVERVIEW: Abraham's detachment from material possessions provides occasion for additional moral exhortation (CHRYSOSTOM).

23:19 Abraham Buries Sarah

THE BURIAL OF SARAH. PRUDENTIUS:

This is the lodging place of the Lord, where an
   oak branch at Mamre[1]
Covered the pastoral roof of the ancient seer;
   in this hospice
Sarah laughed at the joy of bearing a child in
   her old age
And at the faith her venerable husband could
   have in the marvel.
Abraham purchased a field wherein he might
   bury his wife's bones,[2]
Inasmuch as justice and faith on the earth
   dwell as strangers:
This is the cave for which he expended a great
   sum of money,
To prepare a fit resting place for his wife's holy
   ashes.
SCENES FROM SACRED HISTORY 4-5.[3]

23:20 Abraham Purchased the Burial Site

IMITATE THE MAN WHO LIVED BEFORE THE LAW. CHRYSOSTOM: With this in mind, dearly beloved, let us who live in the age of grace imitate the man who lived before the law, not burn with desire for more and heap up for ourselves to a greater and more intense degree the fire that cannot be extinguished and the flame that is intolerable. We will hear, in fact, if we persist in such awful deeds of injustice and avarice, the words spoken to that notorious rich man, "Fool, this night they are looking for your soul from you; but as for what you have put aside, whom will it belong to?"[4] I mean, what is the reason, dearly beloved, that you are anxious to amass so many things that you will shortly leave here, due as you are to be snatched away from the scene, not only powerless to gain any advantage from them but even saddled with the burden of sins on your own shoulders, at this stage too late for worthwhile repentance? While the goods you have amassed with avarice oftentimes finish even in the hands of enemies, you yourself will be required to give an account of them. So what folly would it be to labor for others' benefit and pay the price for them yourself? HOMILIES ON GENESIS 48.5.[5]

PAY ATTENTION TO DOING GOOD. CHRYSOSTOM: Even if in the past, however, we have to this degree managed our affairs with indifference, now at least let us plan for what is needful and not simply be anxious to bedeck ourselves with the trappings of wealth, but rather pay much attention to doing good. After all, our being will not come to an end with this present life, nor shall we be always in exile; instead, before long we shall reach our true homeland. So let us do everything in the hope of not being found wanting there. I mean, what good is it to leave behind great wealth in foreign parts while wanting for bare necessities in our true country? Consequently let us strive, dearly beloved, while there is still time, to transfer there what we own in this foreign country. Although in fact the distance may be great, nevertheless the transfer is quite easy. You see, there are those ready to make the transfer, to travel there safely and deposit in a secure treasury whatever we are able to send ahead by means of them. I mean, the hands of the poor lay up in the treasuries of heaven what is given them by us. Since then the ease and security are so great, why do we delay and not rather with all haste act on this so that we will have those things at our disposal in the place where we most have need of them? HOMILIES ON GENESIS 48.6.[6]

---

[1]Gen 18:1. [2]Gen 23:16-19. [3]FC 52:180. [4]Lk 12:20. [5]FC 87:27. [6]FC 87:28.

24:1-9 SEARCHING FOR A WIFE FOR ISAAC

[1]Now Abraham was old, well advanced in years; and the LORD had blessed Abraham in all things. [2]And Abraham said to his servant, the oldest of his house, who had charge of all that he had, "Put your hand under my thigh, [3]and I will make you swear by the LORD, the God of heaven and of the earth, that you will not take a wife for my son from the daughters of the Canaanites, among whom I dwell, [4]but will go to my country and to my kindred, and take a wife for my son Isaac." [5]The servant said to him, "Perhaps the woman may not be willing to follow me to this land; must I then take your son back to the land from which you came?" [6]Abraham said to him, "See to it that you do not take my son back there. [7]The LORD, the God of heaven, who took me from my father's house and from the land of my birth, and who spoke to me and swore to me, 'To your descendants I will give this land,' he will send his angel before you, and you shall take a wife for my son from there [8]But if the woman is not willing to follow you, then you will be free from this oath of mine; only you must not take my son back there." [9]So the servant put his hand under the thigh of Abraham his master, and swore to him concerning this matter.

OVERVIEW: Abraham remains a moral exemplar in providing for Isaac (CHRYSOSTOM). The phrase "under my thigh" gave rise to various explanations, including "by the covenant of circumcision" (EPHREM) and an allegorical explanation equating it with the altar or the temple (CAESARIUS OF ARLES). The account also provides the occasion for a polemic against riches and a teaching about God's great kindness and personal care (CHRYSOSTOM).

24:1 Abraham Was Old and Blessed

ABRAHAM WAS OLD. CHRYSOSTOM: So let us listen to sacred Scripture's account to us: "Abraham was old, advanced in years. The Lord had blessed Abraham in every respect." Why did it mention this to us? Since he was about to give good care and attention to Isaac, to the point of bringing him a bride, accordingly it mentioned to us the patriarch's age. HOMILIES ON GENESIS 48.7.[1]

THE DESCENDANTS OF KETURAH. ORIGEN: But indeed, we should not fail to notice from these things that are reported by the literal meaning, what generations and of what sort they are, which are propagated from Keturah.

For if we remember these things, we will be able to recognize more easily those things that are said about the diverse nations in the Scriptures. For example, as when it is said that Moses took as his wife the daughter of Jethro, priest of Midian, this Midian is found to be a son of Keturah and Abraham.[2] We know therefore that Moses' wife is from the seed of Abraham and was not a foreigner. But also when it is written, "the queen of Kedar,"[3] it should be known no less that also Kedar descends from the very stock of Kedar and Abraham.[4] HOMILIES ON GENESIS 11.2.[5]

---

[1]FC 87:28. [2]Gen 25:2. [3]Jer 49:28. [4]Cf. Gen 25:13. According to Genesis 25:12-13, Kedar is a descendant of Abraham and Hagar. [5]FC 71:172.

24:2 Abraham's Servant Makes a Promise

ABRAHAM INSTRUCTS HIS SERVANT. CHRYSOSTOM: You see, since he had reached extreme old age, the text says, he wished to preserve Isaac from association with the Canaanites, lest he take a wife from among them. So he summoned the more prudent of his servants, the text says, and gave him the following instructions: "Place your hand under my thigh." In Greek the verse is written this way: "under my thigh"; whereas in Hebrew it says "under my loins." Why did he speak in this fashion? It was an idiom of people in the past. But on other grounds it was also because the birth of Isaac takes its origin from there.

For you to learn that the action was done according to a certain custom, notice that when he was ordering him to put his hand there, he immediately added, "and I will make you swear by the Lord, the God of heaven and the God of earth." See how he teaches the servant to recognize the Creator of all things. By saying, "the God of heaven and the God of earth," he encompassed all creation. HOMILIES ON GENESIS 48.7-8.[6]

BY THE COVENANT OF CIRCUMCISION.
EPHREM THE SYRIAN: Abraham made him swear by the covenant of circumcision. Because God saw that the two heads of the world had dishonored this member, he set the sign of the covenant on it so that this member, which was the most despised of all the limbs, would now be the most honored of all the limbs. The sign of the covenant that was set on it bestowed such great honor that those who take oaths now swear by it and all those who administer oaths make them swear by it. COMMENTARY ON GENESIS 21.2.[7]

THESE THINGS WERE FULFILLED FOR US.
CAESARIUS OF ARLES: When the sacred lesson was read a little while ago, we heard that blessed Abraham called his servant and said to him, "Put your hand under my thigh that I may adjure you by the God of heaven and of earth, not to obtain a wife for my son from the daughters of this region."[8] And [the servant] obediently placed his hand under his thigh and swore to him. Indeed, brothers, all these things that are read in the Old Testament, if we are willing to accept them only according to the letter, will bring us little or no profit of soul. For of what benefit is it to us who assemble in church with devotion to hear the Word of God, if it is mentioned that Abraham sent his servant to bring his son a wife from a distant country, when we see this happen frequently also in this land? However, brothers, following the blessed apostle Paul, we should believe that all things which were written for the Jews "happened to them as a type"[9] but in reality were fulfilled for us. Therefore Abraham said to his servant, "Put your hand under my thigh and swear by the God of heaven and of earth." Thus blessed Abraham said, "Put your hand under my thigh," as if he were saying, put your hand upon the altar, or put your hand upon the ark of the testament, or stretch forth your hand to God's temple, and swear to me. He touched his thigh and swore by the God of heaven and earth. For blessed Abraham did not err when he commanded that this be done but because he was filled with the spirit of prophecy and knew that from his own seed Christ the Lord of heaven and earth would be born. Therefore, when his servant touched his thigh, he did not utter an oath by any carnal member but by the living and true God, because "Abraham begot Isaac, Isaac begot Jacob, and Jacob begot Judah,"[10] of whose seed Christ the Lord was born. SERMON 85.1.[11]

THE BLESSING OF PROGENY. AUGUSTINE: For an important thing was being done when a spouse was being sought for the seed of Abraham. But that the servant might learn this which Abraham knew, that he did not desire grandchildren carnally and that he did not have any carnal conception about his progeny, he said to his slave

---

[6]FC 87:28-29. [7]FC 91:169-70. [8]Gen. 24:2-3. [9]1 Cor 10:11. [10]Mt 1:2. [11]FC 47:20-21.

whom he was sending, "Put your hand under my thigh and swear by the God of heaven." What does the God of heaven want to signify in respect to the thigh of Abraham? Already you understand the hidden meaning: by the thigh, his progeny. Therefore what was that swearing but a signifying that the God of heaven would come in the flesh from the progeny of Abraham? TRACTATE ON THE GOSPEL OF JOHN 43.6.3.[12]

THE BLESSING OF MARRIAGE. AUGUSTINE: For, putting the hand under the thigh of a man and swearing by the God of heaven, what else did that signify except that in that flesh, which took its origin from that thigh, the God of heaven would come?

Marriage therefore is a good in which the married are better in proportion as they fear God more chastely and more faithfully, especially if they also nourish spiritually the children whom they desire carnally. ON THE GOOD OF MARRIAGE 19.[13]

THE INCARNATE LORD. AUGUSTINE: This surely was prophetic of the fact that the Lord God of heaven and the Lord of the earth would one day come in flesh fashioned from that thigh. CITY OF GOD 16.33.[14]

24:4 Find a Wife for Isaac

MY COUNTRY AND MY RELATIVES. CHRYSOSTOM: Do you note the patriarch's command given to the servant? I mean, don't pass idly by these words; instead, consider the good man's purpose, and study how in ancient times their concern was not to look for abundance of possessions, not for great wealth, slaves, so many acres of land, not charm of external beauty—rather, they looked for beauty of soul and nobility of manners.

You see, since he saw the wickedness of the inhabitants of Canaan and realized how great a good it is to have a partner of similar manners, he directed his servant and put him under oath to procure a wife for Isaac from his relatives. Nei-

ther the distance between the places nor the other difficulties caused him to delay the task. Rather, in the realization of the necessity of the business, he showed all haste in dispatching the servant. For his part, the patriarch acted in this from concern for the soul's virtue and abhorrence of the wickedness of the [land's] inhabitants. HOMILIES ON GENESIS 48.8-9.[15]

24:6 Do Not Take Isaac to Mesopotamia

ISAAC SHALL NOT GO BACK THERE. CHRYSOSTOM: The patriarch, on the other hand, delivered an adequate direction to his servant and put him under oath. But let us now see the servant's sense of duty in imitating his master's godliness; when he saw the good man directing him with great earnestness, he said to him, "If the woman does not want to accompany me, do you want me to take your son back to the country you came from?" In case some problem arises, he is saying, and I seem to overstep your commands, I would consequently like to know what rules I should observe and whether it is your will that Isaac should go there, take his wife and then return here if she does not agree to accompany me, as you commanded? So what did the good man reply? He rejected this alternative, saying, "Be sure not to take my son back there." There is no need for you to do it, he says. The One who made the promise to me and guaranteed that his descendants would be increased to such an extent will also bring this to a happy end. HOMILIES ON GENESIS 48.10.[16]

24:7 The Lord's Angel

GOD WILL SEND HIS ANGEL. CHRYSOSTOM: Notice how previously, in placing the servant under oath, he instructed him about the Creator of all. Now, as Abraham was about to pray, he used the same words, by every means teaching the servant to have confidence in him and, in this spirit,

---

[12]FC 88:173. [13]FC 27:38. [14]FC 14:548. [15]FC 87:29-30*. [16]FC 87:30*.

set out on the journey, as also to trust in its outcome. You see, Abraham teaches him how much favor from the God of all Abraham had enjoyed from the outset and the fact that this same benefactor, who had plucked him from his own country, had managed his fortunes so well to this point. At the height of old age, God had granted him the birth of Isaac and would personally also take care of what lay ahead. "The Lord, the God of heaven and earth, who took me from my father's house and from the land where I was born," the same who spoke to me in the words, "I will give this land to you and your descendants," who has demonstrated such extraordinary care for me, "he will personally send his angel before you, and you will take a wife for my son from there." HOMILIES ON GENESIS 48.11.[17]

HE WILL PREPARE THE WAY. CHRYSOSTOM: Have confidence, Abraham is saying, and depart. I am convinced that the One who has demonstrated such great kindness in my regard will add this to his former blessings and send his angel before you. He will personally prepare the way before you; he will also personally make the woman known to you; you will take her and return. But should it happen—perish the thought—that she refuses to accompany you, you will be discharged from the obligation of the oath. "Nevertheless don't take my son there." You see, I have no doubt that the Lord will take care of you. Showing how he trusted in God's power, Abraham forbade the servant to conduct Isaac there. Then, after he had given detailed instructions to the servant and relieved him of concern (the servant, after all, was afraid he would be convicted of perjury if he failed to discharge his command), "he placed his hand under his thigh," the text goes on, "and gave him his oath on this matter," that he would not take Isaac there. HOMILIES ON GENESIS 48.12.[18]

---

[17]FC 87:31*. [18]FC 87:31*.

24:10-14 THE SERVANT WAITS AT THE WELL

[10]Then the servant took ten of his master's camels and departed, taking all sorts of choice gifts from his master; and he arose, and went to Mesopotamia, to the city of Nahor. [11]And he made the camels kneel down outside the city by the well of water at the time of evening, the time when women go out to draw water. [12]And he said, "O LORD, God of my master Abraham, grant me success today, I pray thee, and show steadfast love to my master Abraham. [13]Behold, I am standing by the spring of water, and the daughters of the men of the city are coming out to draw water. [14]Let the maiden to whom I shall say, 'Pray let down your jar that I may drink,' and who shall say, 'Drink, and I will water your camels'—let her be the one whom thou hast appointed for thy servant Isaac. By this I shall know that thou hast shown steadfast love to my master."

OVERVIEW: These verses provide the opportunity to underscore the servant's dutifulness and sagacity and Rebekah's noble soul (CHRYSOSTOM). On an allegorical level, Rebekah represents patience, which is adorned by the jewels from the house of the wise man, Abraham (ORIGEN).

24:10 *The Servant Left on His Mission*

See the Servant's Dutifulness. Chrysostom: Do you see how from the outset the servant showed his regard for his master? See him now showing the benefit of the patriarch's instruction by imitating the good man's godliness. "The servant took ten camels," the text relates, "and a selection of all his master's goods; he set out and traveled into Mesopotamia to the city of Nahor, where he rested the camels outside the city at the well toward evening when the women come out to draw water. He said, 'Lord, the God of my master Abraham.'"[1] See the servant's dutifulness: he names the Lord of the world after the patriarch, saying, "Lord, the God of my master Abraham," who has given evidence of so many kindnesses to him. Why are you surprised if the servant calls him the God of Abraham in this way? The God of all shows how he sets great store by the virtue of good people and says, "I am the God of Jacob, the God of Isaac and the God of Abraham."[2] Homilies on Genesis 48.13.[3]

24:11 *Arriving at the Right Time*

Patience Adorned from the Wise Man's House. Origen: "In the evening," therefore, she came to the waters. We have already spoken above about evening. But behold the prudence of the servant. He does not wish to take a bride for his master, Isaac, unless he finds a virgin becoming and beautiful in appearance, and not only a virgin, but one whom a man has not touched. She must be one whom he should discover drawing water. He does not wish to betroth another to his master.

He does not give her jewelry unless she is such a person. He does not give "earrings"; he does not give "bracelets."[4] She remains simple, unlearned, unadorned. Do we suppose that Rebekah's father, a rich man, did not have bracelets and earrings that he might place on his daughter? Was he so negligent or greedy that he would not give jewelry to his daughter? But Rebekah does not wish to be adorned with Bethuel's gold. The jewelry of a barbarous and ignorant man is not worthy of her. She needs jewels of the house of Abraham because patience is adorned from the house of the wise man.

Rebekah's ears, therefore, could not receive their beauty, unless Abraham's servant come and himself adorn them; nor could her hands receive jewelry except that which Isaac sent. For she wishes to receive golden words in her ears and to have golden deeds in her hands. But she could not previously receive or deserve these things unless she had come to the wells to draw water. How will you, who do not wish to come to the waters, who do not wish to receive the golden words of the prophets in your ears, be able to be adorned with instruction, adorned with deeds, adorned with character? Homilies on Genesis 10.4.[5]

24:12 *The Servant Prays for Success*

The Servant's Sagacity. Chrysostom: "Lord," he says, "the God of my master Abraham, be my guide today, and have compassion on my master Abraham," as if to say, "Bring his wishes to effect, and conduct everything according to his intention." "Have compassion on my master Abraham": what does "have compassion" mean? Fulfill his desire. Then he said, "Lo, I am standing at the spring, and the daughters of the inhabitants of the city are coming out to draw water. Whichever maiden to whom I say, 'Lower your water jar that I may drink,' and she says, 'Drink and I shall water your camels till they all stop drinking'—let her be the one you have prepared for your servant Isaac, and in this I shall know that you have had compassion on my master Abraham."[6] Note the servant's sagacity. He was aware of the patriarch's hospitality and the fact that the maiden destined to be brought there should have similar qualities to those of the good man. So, far from looking for any other indication, he was anxious to distinguish the maiden's

---

[1]Gen 24:10-12. [2]Ex 3:6. [3]FC 87:32. [4]Cf. Gen 24:22. [5]FC 71:164-65*. [6]Gen 24:13-14.

hospitality from her attitude. He said, "If, in response to my request to her for water, she lowers her water jar and not only heeds my request but also gives evidence of the generosity of her own attitude by saying, 'I will water your camels as well,' she will have given me sufficient demonstration of the mildness of her manners by the offer of water." HOMILIES ON GENESIS 48.14.[7]

REBEKAH'S NOBILITY OF SOUL. CHRYSOSTOM: Consider, in fact, I ask you, dearly beloved, how important it was that a tender maiden while drawing water not only did not decline the request but also took down the water jar from her shoulders and gave the petitioner his fill, stranger though he was and quite unknown to her. She gave water not only to him but also to all the camels, thus betraying by her behavior indications of her nobility of soul. Did she not realize that many, men included, often decline such requests? Why do I refer to the gift of water? Sometimes, when people holding torches are asked by those approaching them to wait a while so as to allow a lamp to be lit, they refuse even to do this, despite the fire's suffering no diminution even should those intending to light their torch be beyond count. In this case, on the contrary, a woman, a maiden, carrying a water jar on her shoulders, not only did not object to the request but even was more generous than the request in supplying the drink, hurrying of her own volition to water the camels as well. HOMILIES ON GENESIS 48.15.[8]

24:13 The Spring Outside the City

STANDING BY THE WATER. ORIGEN: Observe how many things take place at waters, so that you too may be invited to come daily to the waters of the Word of God and stand by its wells, as also Rebekah used to do, of whom the Scripture says, "The virgin was very beautiful; a virgin, a man had not known her."[9] HOMILIES ON GENESIS 10.[10]

24:14 Let Her Be the One for Isaac

LET HER BE THE ONE APPOINTED. CAESARIUS OF ARLES: Now, dearly beloved, let us briefly see, as far as we can, what these facts mean. When blessed Abraham directed his servant to take a wife for his son, he portrayed an image of God the Father. Just as when he offered the boy as a holocaust, he then presented an image of God the Father, so also his servant signified the words of prophecy. For this reason Abraham sent his servant into a distant land to take a wife for his son, because God the Father intended to send his prophetic word throughout the world to search for the Catholic church as a spouse for his only-begotten Son. SERMON 85.3.[11]

A WOMAN PROCLAIMS CHRIST. ORIGEN: Here, then, a woman proclaims Christ to the Samaritans,[12] and at the end of the Gospels also the woman who saw him before all the others tells the apostles of the resurrection of the Savior.[13] COMMENTARY ON THE GOSPEL OF JOHN 13.179.[14]

---

[7]FC 87:32-33*. [8]FC 87:33*. [9]Gen 24:16. [10]FC 71:163. [11]FC 47:21-22. [12]Jn 4:28-30. [13]Jn 20:18. [14]FC 89:106.

24:15-21 THE SERVANT ENCOUNTERS REBEKAH

---

[15]*Before he had done speaking, behold, Rebekah, who was born to Bethuel the son of Milcah, the wife of Nahor, Abraham's brother, came out with her water jar upon her shoulder.* [16]*The maiden was very fair to look upon, a virgin, whom no man had known. She went down to the*

---

spring, and filled her jar, and came up. [17]Then the servant ran to meet her, and said, "Pray give me a little water to drink from your jar." [18]She said, "Drink, my lord"; and she quickly let down her jar upon her hand, and gave him a drink. [19]When she had finished giving him a drink, she said, "I will draw for your camels also, until they have done drinking." [20]So she quickly emptied her jar into the trough and ran again to the well to draw, and she drew for all his camels. [21]The man gazed at her in silence to learn whether the LORD had prospered his journey or not.

OVERVIEW: In general these verses indicate mysteries; that is, they prefigure the mystery of Christ and the soul or the church. The servant represents the prophetic word (ORIGEN). In the same line of interpretation, the story foreshadows the church finding Christ in the sacrament of baptism (CAESARIUS OF ARLES). Rebekah symbolizes the church or the soul going down to the font of wisdom (AMBROSE). The text also provides the occasion for moral teaching about modesty, humility and hospitality (CHRYSOSTOM).

24:15 Rebekah with Her Water Jar

REBEKAH'S ACTIONS REPRESENT GREAT MYSTERIES. ORIGEN: Rebekah came to the wells daily; she drew water daily. And because she spent time at the wells daily, therefore, she could be found by Abraham's servant and be united in marriage with Isaac.

Do you think these are tales and that the Holy Spirit tells stories in the Scripture? This is instruction for souls and spiritual teaching which instructs and teaches you to come daily to the wells of the Scripture, to the waters of the Holy Spirit, and always to draw water and carry home a full vessel just as also holy Rebekah used to do. Otherwise he could not have been joined to so great a patriarch as Isaac, who "was born by promise."[1] It is only by drawing water and by drawing so much that she could give a drink not only to those who are at home but also to Abraham's servant, and not only to the servant. She also had such an abundance of water that she drew from the wells that she could also water the camels "until," the text says, "they stopped drinking."[2]

All these things that are written are mysteries.

Christ wishes to espouse you also to himself, for he speaks to you through the prophets, saying, "I will espouse you to me forever, and I will espouse you to me in faith and in mercy, and you shall know the Lord."[3] Because therefore he wishes to espouse you to himself, he dispatches that servant to you in advance. That servant is the prophetic word. Unless you have received it first, you cannot be married to Christ.

Know, however, that no one untrained and inexperienced receives the prophetic word, but he who knows how to draw water from the depth of the well, who knows how to draw in such quantity that it may be sufficient also for these who appear irrational and perverse, whom the camels represent. [So that person] may be able to say, "I am a debtor to the wise and to the unwise."[4] ... So therefore Rebekah, which means "patience," when she saw the servant and contemplated the prophetic word, "puts the water jar down" from her shoulder.[5] For she puts down the exalted arrogance of Greek eloquence and, stooping down to the lowly and simple prophetic word, says, "Drink, and I will water your camels."[6] HOMILIES ON GENESIS 10.2.[7]

THE SACRAMENT OF BAPTISM. CAESARIUS OF ARLES: Now, dearly beloved, let us briefly see, as far as we can, what these facts mean. When blessed Abraham directed his servant to take a wife for his son, he portrayed an image of God the Father. Just as when he offered the boy as a burnt offering, he then presented an image of God the Father, so also his servant signified the

---

[1]Gal 4:23. [2]Gen 24:22. [3]Hos 2:19-20. [4]Rom 1:14. [5]Gen 24:18. [6]Gen 24:14. [7]FC 71:159-61*.

words of prophecy. For this reason Abraham sent his servant into a distant land to take a wife for his son, because God the Father intended to send his prophetic word throughout the world to search for the Catholic church as a spouse for his only-begotten Son. Just as through Abraham's servant a bride is brought for blessed Isaac, so by his prophetic word the church of the Gentiles is invited to Christ the true bridegroom from distant lands. But where is found that spouse who was to be joined to Christ? Where, unless near the water? It is true, dearly beloved: If the church had not come to the waters of baptism, it would not have been joined to Christ. For this reason Rebekah found Abraham's servant at the well, and the church finds Christ at the sacrament of baptism. SERMON 85.3.[8]

THE SERVANT REPRESENTS THE PROPHETIC WORD. ORIGEN: But you say perhaps, if the servant represents the prophetic word, how is he given a drink by Rebekah, to whom he rather ought to give a drink?

Consider therefore whether it may be as follows. Although, on the one hand, the Lord Jesus is "the bread of life,"[9] and he himself feeds the hungry souls, on the other hand, he admits that he hungers when he says, "I was hungry, and you gave me to eat."[10] Again, on the one hand, although he is "the living water"[11] and gives drink to all who thirst, on the other hand, he says to the Samaritan woman, "Give me to drink."[12] So also, although the prophetic word gives drink to the thirsting, it is nevertheless said to be given a drink by these when it receives the exercises and vigilances of the zealous. A soul such as this, then, which does all things patiently, which is so eager and is undergirded with so much learning, which has been accustomed to draw streams of knowledge from the depths, can be united in marriage with Christ.

Unless therefore you come daily to the wells, unless you daily draw water, not only will you not be able to give a drink to others, but also you yourself also will suffer "a thirst for the Word of God."[13] Hear also the Lord saying in the Gospels,

"Let him who thirsts come and drink."[14] But, as I see it, "you neither hunger nor thirst after justice,"[15] and how will you be able to say, "As the deer pants after the fountains of water, so my soul pants after you, O God. My soul has thirsted after the living God; when shall I come and appear before his presence"?[16] HOMILIES ON GENESIS 10.3.[17]

24:16 Rebekah Was Beautiful

A VIRGIN. ORIGEN: This is not written of her in vain. Nevertheless the meaning of the statement disturbs me: "She was a virgin, whom no man had known." It is indeed as if a virgin were something other than one whom a man has not touched. And what does the addition seem to mean in reference to a virgin that it should be said, "A man had not known her"? Is there indeed another virgin whom a man has touched?

I have often said already that in these stories history is not being narrated but mysteries are interwoven. I think therefore that something such as this is indicated in this story.

Just as Christ is said to be the husband of the soul, to whom the soul is married when it comes to faith, so also, contrary to this, he who also is called "an enemy" when "he sows tares among the wheat"[18] is called the husband to whom the soul is married when it turns away to faithlessness. It is not sufficient, therefore, for the soul to be pure in body; it is necessary also that this most wicked man "has not known it." For it can happen that someone may possess virginity in body, and knowing that most wicked man, the devil, and receiving darts of concupiscence from him in the heart destroy the purity of the soul. Because, therefore, Rebekah was a virgin "holy in body and spirit,"[19] for this reason the Scripture doubles her praise and says, "She was a virgin; a man had not known her." HOMILIES ON GENESIS 10.4.[20]

---

[8]FC 47:21-22*. [9]Jn 6:35, 48. [10]Mt 25:35. [11]Jn 7:38. [12]Jn 4:7. [13]Amos 8:11. [14]Jn 7:37. [15]Mt 5:6. [16]Ps 42:1-2 (41:2-3 LXX). [17]FC 71:161-62. [18]Mt 13:25. [19]1 Cor 7:34. [20]FC 71:163-64.

**THE SOUL WENT TO THE FOUNTAIN OF WIS-
DOM.** AMBROSE: And so Isaac is good and true,
for he is full of grace and a fountain of joy. To that
fountain came Rebekah to fill her water jar. For
Scripture says that "going down to the fountain
she filled her water jar and came up." And so the
church or the soul went down to the fountain of
wisdom to fill its own vessel and draw up the
teachings of pure wisdom, which the Jews did not
wish to draw from the flowing fountain. Listen to
him as he says who that fountain is. "They have
abandoned me, the fountain of living water."[21]
The soul of the prophets ran thirsting to this
fountain, even as David says, "My soul has thirsted after the living God,"[22] that he might fill his
thirst with the richness of the knowledge of God
and might wash away the blood of foolishness
with watering of spiritual streams. ISAAC, OR THE
SOUL 1.2.[23]

24:20 Rebekah Served

**REBEKAH'S MODESTY, HUMILITY AND HOSPI-
TALITY.** CHRYSOSTOM: The loving God, you see,
granted the patriarch's prayers, sent his angel on
ahead and saw to the outcome of all these events;
everything turned out as the servant requested.
Then when he saw the power of the patriarch's
prayers in the event and chanced upon the maid-
en as he desired, he also saw her surpassing hospitality. "She hastened" the text goes on,
remember, "to empty the water jar into the
trough, and ran to draw more at the well, and watered all the camels." See her heightened enthusiasm. The verse "She hastened to empty the water
jar into the trough and ran to the well" shows the
maiden's indescribable enthusiasm in neither
snubbing him as a stranger nor declining his request on the pretext of prudence but rather saying with great restraint, "Drink, sir."[24] I ask you to
consider how very proper, despite her tender
years, was her modesty, her surpassing humility

and the extremity of her hospitality. What riches,
at any rate, do these qualities not far surpass? Are
there treasures you would value more highly than
these qualities? This is the greatest gift; this constitutes countless blessings, a treasure never expended. HOMILIES ON GENESIS 48.16.[25]

AGAIN TO THE WELL. ORIGEN: Rebekah is
found "at a well." Rebekah in turn finds Isaac "at a
well." There she gazed upon his countenance for
the first time. There "she dismounted from the
camels."[26] There she sees Isaac, who was pointed
out to her by the servant. Do you think these are
the only words related about wells? HOMILIES ON
GENESIS 10.5.[27]

24:21 God Blessed the Servant's Journey

THE MAIDEN'S GREAT VIRTUE. CHRYSOSTOM:
The dutiful servant therefore now saw God's
providence distinctly. "He kept observing her
closely," the text goes on, "and remained silent so
as to know if the Lord had made his journey successful or not."[28] What is the meaning of "kept observing her closely"? He kept studying the
maiden's very words, her gaze, her walk, her appearance, everything else about her, and waited to
see "if the Lord had successfully conducted his
journey or not." You see, what had happened so
far, the text is saying, showed the maiden's great
virtue that exceeded ordinary limits. Hence, to
reward her for her response and the offer of water, the text goes on, he pressed upon her "golden
earrings and two bracelets."[29] He carefully made
enquiries about her, asking, "Whose daughter are
you?" and "Is there room in your father's house for
us to rest?"[30] HOMILIES ON GENESIS 48.17.[31]

---

[21]Jer 2:13. [22]Ps 42:3 (41:3 LXX). [23]FC 65:11. [24]Gen 24:18. [25]FC
87:33-34**. [26]Gen 24:64. [27]FC 71:165. [28]Gen 24:21. [29]Gen 24:22.
[30]Gen 24:23. [31]FC 87:34*.

24:22-27 THE SERVANT ASKS FOR LODGING

²²*When the camels had done drinking, the man took a gold ring weighing a half shekel, and two bracelets for her arms weighing ten gold shekels,* ²³*and said, "Tell me whose daughter you are. Is there room in your father's house for us to lodge in?"* ²⁴*She said to him, "I am the daughter of Bethuel the son of Milcah, whom she bore to Nahor."* ²⁵*She added, "We have both straw and provender enough, and room to lodge in."* ²⁶*The man bowed his head and worshiped the LORD,* ²⁷*and said, "Blessed be the LORD, the God of my master Abraham, who has not forsaken his steadfast love and his faithfulness toward my master. As for me, the LORD has led me in the way to the house of my master's kinsmen."*

OVERVIEW: Allegorically interpreted, the gold earrings signify divine words, and the gold bracelets good works (CAESARIUS OF ARLES, AMBROSE). Following a moral interpretation, Rebekah gives an example of lavish hospitality (CHRYSOSTOM).

24:22 The First Encounter

THE EARRINGS SIGNIFY DIVINE WORDS.
CAESARIUS OF ARLES: The servant brought gold earrings and gold bracelets and gave them to Rebekah. Those gold earrings signify the divine words; the gold bracelets signify good works, because works are designated by the hands. Let us observe, brothers, how Christ also gave these gifts to the church. For this reason the servant brought gold earrings for adorning Rebekah's face, while Christ put into the church's ears divine words that are of greater value than all pearls. The servant put bracelets on Rebekah's wrists, while Christ put good works into the church's hands. Consider, dearly beloved, and rejoice, giving thanks to God because what was prefigured in them has been fulfilled in us by Christ's gift. Moreover, just as Rebekah could not have had the earrings or bracelets if Isaac had not sent them through his servant, so also the church could not have had divine words in her ears or good works in her hands if Christ by his grace

and through his apostles had not conferred them. Furthermore, the fact that the girl, when asked by her parents whether she wished to go with the servant, replied, "I am going"—this we see clearly fulfilled in the church. There Rebekah's will is asked; here the church's will is sought. To Rebekah it is said, "Are you willing to go with this man?" And she replied, "I am going." To the church it is said, "Do you believe in Christ?" And it replies, "I do believe." Rebekah would not be led to Isaac if she did not say, "I am going"; neither would the church be joined to Christ if it did not say, "I believe." SERMON 85.3.[1]

A GOLD RING AND TWO BRACELETS.
AMBROSE: For this also is evidence of familiar association with the virtues, that each person walks about in the innocence of . . . heart, in no wise involves himself in earthly vices, and with the mind's unhindered step takes the path that is without reproach and does not open up any place in himself to corruption.

Such was Isaac as he awaited Rebekah's coming and made ready for a spiritual union.[2] For she came already endowed with heavenly mysteries. She came bearing mighty adornments in her ears and on her arms, because in her hearing and in the works of her hands there is clearly revealed the

---

[1]FC 47:22**. [2]See Gen 24:62.

beauty of the church, and we note that it was rightly said to her, "May you become thousands of myriads, and may your seed possess the cities of their enemies."[3] Therefore the church is beautiful, for it has acquired sons from hostile nations. But this passage can be interpreted in reference to the soul, which subdues the bodily passions, turns them to the service of the virtues and makes resistant feelings subject to itself. And so the soul of the patriarch Isaac, seeing the mystery of Christ, seeing Rebekah coming with vessels of gold and silver,[4] as if she were the church with the people of the nations, and marveling at the beauty of the Word and of his sacraments, says, "Let him kiss me with the kisses of his mouth."[5] And Rebekah, seeing the true Isaac, that true joy and true source of mirth, desires to kiss him. ISAAC, OR THE SOUL 3.6-7.[6]

24:25 Rebekah's Hospitality

THE SERVANT WAS AMAZED. CHRYSOSTOM: Consider here too the maiden's response. As with the water, she not only provided what was asked but also watered the camels after giving him something to drink, so here too, when the servant inquired if there was merely room and whose daughter she was, the maiden replied, "I am daughter of Bethuel, son of Milcah, whom she bore to Nahor himself." She mentioned her father and grandfather so that this knowledge would further arouse the servant's interest. Observe the child's candor: asked about her father, she not only tells the truth about him but also about her father's father. And to the inquiry as to whether there was simply a place to rest she replied, "not only a place" but "also much straw and feed at our place." On hearing this, the servant was amazed at the girl for her lavish hospitality and learned as well that he had come not to some strangers but to the house of Nahor, who was the patriarch's brother; so, the text tells us, "the man bowed low in gratitude to the Lord." Overjoyed at what he had learned, at the words spoken by the girl, "he bowed low to the Lord," offering thanks to the Lord for giving evidence of such favor to the patriarch and care for him and for bringing all his endeavors to a successful conclusion with ease. He said, "Blessed be the Lord, the God of my master Abraham, who has not withheld his steadfast goodness from my master."[7] HOMILIES ON GENESIS 48.18.[8]

---

[3]Gen 24:60 LXX. [4]See Gen 24:53, 63. [5]Song 1:2. [6]FC 65:14-15. [7]Gen 24:27. [8]FC 87:34-35**.

24:28-33 LABAN WELCOMES ABRAHAM'S SERVANT

[28]*Then the maiden ran and told her mother's household about these things.* [29]*Rebekah had a brother whose name was Laban; and Laban ran out to the man, to the spring.* [30]*When he saw the ring, and the bracelets on his sister's arms, and when he heard the words of Rebekah his sister, "Thus the man spoke to me," he went to the man; and behold, he was standing by the camels at the spring.* [31]*He said, "Come in, O blessed of the LORD; why do you stand outside? For I have prepared the house and a place for the camels."* [32]*So the man came into the house; and Laban ungirded the camels,* and gave him straw and provender for the camels, and water to wash his feet and the feet of the men who were with him.* [33]*Then food was set before him to eat; but he said, "I will not eat until I have told my errand." He said, "Speak on."*

---

*LXX, "he unloaded the camels."

OVERVIEW: The detail of "running" in the text provides the opportunity to emphasize Rebekah's enthusiasm for hospitality (CHRYSOSTOM).

24:28 Rebekah Told Her Family

SHE SHOWS HER ENTHUSIASM. CHRYSOSTOM: When he saw the child's candor and learned everything from her clearly, then he in turn made known to her who he was. Through his thanksgiving to God, he made clear to her the fact that he had not come from some alien house but that the man who had sent him was brother to Nahor. On learning this "the girl ran off," the text says, with great joy. See how in everything done by her she shows her enthusiasm for hospitality—by running, by her words, by her restraint. Note that the text says, "She ran and reported these words in her mother's house." She made known to her parents everything she had heard from the servant. "Laban ran to the one outside at the spring,"[1] the text continues. Notice also this man showing his interest by running; seeing the person standing at the spring with the camels, "he said to him, 'Come inside—blessed by the Lord—why stay outside? I have made ready the house and a place for the camels.'"[2] Observe this man also blessing the Lord at the arrival of the stranger and making earnest supplication before putting hospitality into practice. "Come inside," he says; "I have taken the precaution of 'making ready the house and a place for the camels.'" HOMILIES ON GENESIS 48.19.[3]

[1]Gen 24:29. [2]Gen 24:31. [3]FC 87:35*.

24:34-41 THE SERVANT EXPLAINS HIS MISSION

[34]So he said, "I am Abraham's servant. [35]The LORD has greatly blessed my master, and he has become great; he has given him flocks and herds, silver and gold, menservants and maidservants, camels and asses. [36]And Sarah my master's wife bore a son to my master when she was old; and to him he has given all that he has. [37]My master made me swear, saying, 'You shall not take a wife for my son from the daughters of the Canaanites, in whose land I dwell; [38]but you shall go to my father's house and to my kindred, and take a wife for my son.' [39]I said to my master, 'Perhaps the woman will not follow me.' [40]But he said to me, 'The LORD, before whom I walk, will send his angel with you and prosper your way; and you shall take a wife for my son from my kindred and from my father's house; [41]then you will be free from my oath, when you come to my kindred; and if they will not give her to you, you will be free from my oath.'

OVERVIEW: The text offers the opportunity to stress the great prudence of the servant and to warn against riches (CHRYSOSTOM).

24:34-38 The Servant Relates His Mission

THE SERVANT'S GREAT PRUDENCE. CHRYSOSTOM: Consider . . . in this instance, I ask you, the servant's great prudence. What in fact did he say? "I will not eat until I have said my piece."

"Whereas you have made a show of your resources," he says, "I, for my part, will not attach any importance to resting until I inform you of the reason why I was sent on this mission, why I arrived here from Canaan, and how I was guided to your house. Thus, by learning everything, you will give evidence of your own good dispositions toward my master." HOMILIES ON GENESIS 48.20.[1]

NO EMPTY DISPLAY OF LUXURY. CHRYSOSTOM: See how the servant narrates everything to them with precision: "I am servant of that man Abraham," he says, "whom you know; so, learn that he enjoyed such blessing from the Lord of all as to arrive at great wealth." Then, to teach them the abundance of his wealth, he said, "Sheep and cattle, silver and gold, male and female servants, camels and asses" came his way. Take heed, you people of wealth, you who acquire such and such acres of land day in and day out, building baths and walkways and splendid buildings—see in what lay the good man's riches: no property, no buildings, no empty display of luxury, but rather sheep and cattle, camels and asses, servants male and female. The text added in another place that they were all born in the household, so that you

could learn how Abraham gained so many servants.[2] "So this master of mine came into such great wealth and enjoyed great favor from on high; when he had reached old age Sarah bore him a son, and, having this only child, he has already made him heir of everything. He has given him everything he owned." HOMILIES ON GENESIS 48.21.[3]

24:39 The Woman's Willingness

PERHAPS SHE WILL NOT FOLLOW. EPHREM THE SYRIAN: Then they called the young woman to learn from her [whether she would return with him or not]. Because she heard about the oath that Abraham had made him swear, and about the prayer that the servant had prayed at the well and about the sign for which he had asked and which had been granted to him, she feared to say "I will not go," because she knew that it was the will of the Lord that she go. So she went and became Isaac's [wife]. COMMENTARY ON GENESIS 21.4.[4]

---

[1]FC 87:36. [2]Gen 17:23. [3]FC 87:36**. [4]FC 91:170.

24:42-49 THE SERVANT RECOUNTS HIS EXPERIENCE

[42]"I came today to the spring, and said, 'O LORD, the God of my master Abraham, if now thou wilt prosper the way which I go, [43]behold, I am standing by the spring of water; let the young woman who comes out to draw, to whom I shall say, "Pray give me a little water from your jar to drink," [44]and who will say to me, "Drink, and I will draw for your camels also," let her be the woman whom the LORD has appointed for my master's son.'

[45]"Before I had done speaking in my heart, behold, Rebekah came out with her water jar on her shoulder; and she went down to the spring, and drew. I said to her, 'Pray let me drink.' [46]She quickly let down her jar from her shoulder, and said, 'Drink, and I will give your camels drink

also.' So I drank, and she gave the camels drink also. [47]*Then I asked her, 'Whose daughter are you?' She said, 'The daughter of Bethuel, Nahor's son, whom Milcah bore to him.' So I put the ring on her nose, and the bracelets on her arms.* [48]*Then I bowed my head and worshiped the LORD, and blessed the LORD, the God of my master Abraham, who had led me by the right way to take the daughter of my master's kinsman for his son.* [49]*Now then, if you will deal loyally and truly with my master, tell me; and if not, tell me; that I may turn to the right hand or to the left."*

OVERVIEW: These verses offered the opportunity to stress signs of God's providence (EPHREM, CHRYSOSTOM).

24:47 The Daughter of Bethuel

WHOSE DAUGHTER ARE YOU? EPHREM THE SYRIAN: The servant swore the oath to his master and went off with many choice gifts. He sat beside a well, prayed and asked for a sign. Even though he rejoiced in the sign that came to him, he still waited to see whether she was from [Abraham's] tribe. When he learned that she was the daughter of Bethuel, the son of Nahor, he praised God and went and stayed in their house. COMMENTARY ON GENESIS 21.3.[1]

24:48 The Servant Worshiped God

GOD'S HAND MANIFESTLY ACTIVE. CHRYSOSTOM: "Seeing now God's providence so manifestly in action, I asked whose daughter she was. Learning from what she said that she belonged not to alien people but to the household of Nahor, my master's brother, I was bold enough to 'put earrings and bracelets on her. In my satisfaction I prayed to the Lord and praised the God of my master Abraham for bringing my journey to a successful conclusion so as to take the daughter of my master's brother.'[2] God's hand in this has been so manifestly active; as you can see, the prayers offered by my master have been granted. Now you, for your part, if you are to give evidence of your dispositions, 'show steadfast kindness toward my master; if not, let me know it.'[3] Tell me the truth now, I ask you, so that I may be in a position to know what I must do. But if the answer is no, tell me so that I may travel in another direction, 'going left or right.'"[4] HOMILIES ON GENESIS 48.24.[5]

[1]FC 91:170. [2]Gen 24:47-48. [3]Gen 24:49. [4]Gen 24:49. [5]FC 87:38.

24:50-51 LABAN GIVES HIS CONSENT

[50]*Then Laban and Bethuel answered, "The thing comes from the LORD; we cannot speak to you bad or good.* [51]*Behold, Rebekah is before you, take her and go, and let her be the wife of your master's son, as the LORD has spoken."*

OVERVIEW: These verses offered the opportunity to stress again God's providential conduct of the affair in response to the prayers of the pa-triarch (CHRYSOSTOM).

24:50 The Lord's Arrangement

GOD WAS CONDUCTING EVERYTHING. CHRYSOSTOM: Then, since God was conducting everything in the wake of the patriarch's prayers, the maiden's father and brother said to him, "This thing has come from the Lord; we cannot deny you, for good or ill." Your account shows the whole thing has happened by God's arrangement. So don't think we oppose the decisions of God;

after all, it is beyond our powers to do it. Here, the maid is in your hands; "take her, and be on your way, and she will be wife to your master's son, as the Lord has said."[1] HOMILIES ON GENESIS 48.25.[2]

---

[1]Gen 24:51. [2]FC 87:38.

24:52-61 REBEKAH CONSENTS TO RETURN WITH ABRAHAM'S SERVANT

[52]*When Abraham's servant heard their words, he bowed himself to the earth before the LORD.* [53]*And the servant brought forth jewelry of silver and of gold, and raiment, and gave them to Rebekah; he also gave to her brother and to her mother costly ornaments.* [54]*And he and the men who were with him ate and drank, and they spent the night there. When they arose in the morning, he said, "Send me back to my master."* [55]*Her brother and her mother said, "Let the maiden remain with us a while, at least ten days; after that she may go."* [56]*But he said to them, "Do not delay me, since the LORD has prospered my way; let me go that I may go to my master."* [57]*They said, "We will call the maiden, and ask her."* [58]*And they called Rebekah, and said to her, "Will you go with this man?" She said, "I will go."* [59]*So they sent away Rebekah their sister and her nurse, and Abraham's servant and his men.* [60]*And they blessed Rebekah, and said to her, "Our sister, be the mother of thousands of ten thousands; and may your descendants possess the gate of those who hate them!"* [61]*Then Rebekah and her maids arose, and rode upon the camels and followed the man; thus the servant took Rebekah, and went his way.*

OVERVIEW: The passage offers the occasion to emphasize the quest for nobility of soul as opposed to riches in a spouse. The servant shows his confidence in Rebekah. God's providence emerges clearly in every situation (CHRYSOSTOM).

24:52 Abraham's Servant Was Delighted

THEY LOOKED FOR NOBILITY. CHRYSOSTOM: Do you see how much care they took in ancient times to obtain wives for their sons? How they

looked for nobility ahead of money? None of the agreements, none of the contracts or the other ridiculous things that happen these days, nor those terms committed to writing: If someone dies childless, one says, if this or that happens. Instead, among people of those times things were not like this. Rather, the maid's behavior alone was the most secure contract—no pomp and circumstance. You will realize this when you see the maid led to her nuptials. "Hearing this from the father and the brother ... the servant prostrated himself in worship to God."[1] Note how in everything that happened he gave thanks to the Lord of all. You see, it was God who prepared everything in advance and in response to the patriarch's prayer sent his angel ahead of him—he it was who conducted the whole business for him. HOMILIES ON GENESIS 48.26.[2]

24:53 Jewelry and Clothing for Rebekah

THE SERVANT WAITED WITH CONFIDENCE.
CHRYSOSTOM: Learning now that he had the desired end in view, "he brought out presents of silver and gold and clothing and gave them to Rebekah." Then he waited on her with confidence, as though she were already betrothed in word to Isaac. He presented her brother and mother with gifts, and, when he saw the matter had worked out in accord with his master's command, only then was his own refreshment seen to. "They ate and drank," the text says, remember, "he and the men who were with him, and he slept there the night. Rising the next morning he said, 'Allow me to go that I may return to my master.'"[3]

Since everything has worked out well in this way from my point of view, he is saying, and, instead of anything being now left undone, since it also appeared satisfactory to you, "allow me to go that I may return to my master." HOMILIES ON GENESIS 48.27.[4]

THE LORD ARRANGES FOR THE FUTURE.
CHRYSOSTOM: Why do you hesitate and delay, he is saying, if God makes everything so easy for me? . . . Observe how even these men in their ignorance suggest to the maid what is going to happen, with God directing their minds to it. You see, they foretell to her both facts, that she would become countless thousands and that her offspring would take possession of the cities of their enemies. Do you see God's providence emerging clearly in every situation, and how the Lord of all arranges for the future to be foretold even by nonbelievers? HOMILIES ON GENESIS 48.28.[5]

---

[1]Gen 24:52 in Chrysostom's version. [2]FC 87:38-39**. [3]Gen 24:54. [4]FC 87:39*. [5]FC 87:39-40.

24:62-67 ISAAC MEETS REBEKAH IN THE FIELD

[62]Now Isaac had come from[n] Beer-lahai-roi, and was dwelling in the Negeb. [63]And Isaac went out to meditate in the field in the evening; and he lifted up his eyes and looked, and behold, there were camels coming. [64]And Rebekah lifted up her eyes, and when she saw Isaac, she alighted from the camel, [65]and said to the servant, "Who is the man yonder, walking in the field to meet us?" The servant said, "It is my master." So she took her veil and covered herself. [66]And the servant told Isaac all the things that he had done. [67]Then Isaac brought her into the tent,[o] and took Rebekah, and she became his wife; and he loved her. So Isaac was comforted after his mother's death.

n Syr Tg: Heb from coming to   o Heb adds Sarah his mother

OVERVIEW: The encounter of Isaac and Rebekah in the field gave rise to a variety of allegorical interpretations: it represents the union of the soul with the Word of God (ORIGEN); Isaac's going out to meditate in the field symbolizes his withdrawal from the vices of this world (AMBROSE).

The field also represents the world. Isaac's comfort (Ephrem) in taking Rebekah as his veiled and modest wife (Tertullian, Ambrose) can be seen as Christ establishing the church in place of the synagogue (Caesarius of Arles).

24:62 Isaac in the Negeb

The Meeting at the Well. Caesarius of Arles: Therefore the servant took Rebekah and showed her to Isaac. However, let us see where she found him. "She found him at the well of the oath."[1] Look, brothers: Isaac's servant found Rebekah at the well, and Rebekah in turn found Isaac at the well. It is true: Christ does not find the church, or the church Christ, except at the sacrament of baptism. Sermon 85.4.[2]

24:63 Isaac Meditated in the Field

He Withdrew from Worldly Vices. Ambrose: He withdrew and lifted himself away from the vices of this world, he lifted up his soul, even as Isaac meditated—or, as others have it, walked about—in the field. Isaac, or the Soul 3.6-7.[3]

The Figure in the Field. Caesarius of Arles: That field contained a figure of the world. Isaac went out into the field, because Christ was to come into the world; Isaac toward the evening of the day, Christ at the end of the world. "He went out," it says, "to meditate." For this reason Isaac went to meditate in the field, because Christ came into the world to fight against the devil, that he might justly conquer him while being unjustly killed by him, so that by dying he might destroy death, and by rising again bring life to all who believe. Moreover, just as Rebekah was corporally joined to Isaac, so the church was spiritually joined to Christ, receiving at present the blood of her spouse as a precious dowry and later to receive the dowry of his kingdom. The blessed apostle Peter clearly proclaims this when he says, "You were redeemed, not with gold or silver but with the precious blood of Christ, as of a lamb

without blemish."[4] Sermon 85.4.[5]

The Well Is a Spiritual Symbol of Scripture. Origen: Are you not yet moved to understand that these words are spoken spiritually? Or do you think that it always happens by chance that the patriarchs go to wells and obtain their marriages at waters? He who thinks in this way is "a sensual man" and "does not perceive these things which are of the Spirit of God."[6] But let him who wishes remain in these understandings, let him remain "a sensual man." I, following Paul the apostle, say that these things are "allegories,"[7] and I say that the marriages of the saints are the union of the soul with the Word of God: "For he who joins himself to the Lord is one spirit."[8]

But it is certain that this union of the soul with the Word cannot come about otherwise than through instruction in the divine books, which are figuratively called wells. If anyone should come to these and draw from these waters, that is, by meditating on these words should perceive the deeper sense and meaning, that one will find a marriage worthy of God; for [that person's] soul is united with God. Homilies on Genesis 10.5.[9]

24:64 When Rebekah Saw Isaac

The Union of the Soul with the Word of God. Origen: Rebekah followed the servant and comes to Isaac. The church followed the prophetic word, to be sure, and comes to Christ. Where does she find him? "Walking," the text says, "at the well of the oath."[10] On no occasion is one withdrawn from wells; on no occasion does one stand apart from waters. Rebekah is found "at a well."[11] Rebekah in turn finds Isaac "at a well."[12] There she gazed upon his countenance for the first time. There "she dismounted from the camels." There she sees Isaac, who was pointed out to her by the servant.

---

[1]Cf. Gen 21:32; 24:62 LXX. [2]FC 47:23. [3]FC 65:14. [4]1 Pet 1:18-19. [5]FC 47:23. [6]1 Cor 2:14. [7]Gal 4:24. [8]1 Cor 6:17. [9]FC 71:166. [10]Cf. Gen 24:62. [11]Gen 24:16. [12]Gen 24:62.

Do you think these are the only words related about wells? Jacob also goes to a well and finds Rachel there. . . . But also Moses finds Zipporah, the daughter of Reuel, at a well.[13] . . .

She also "dismounts from the camels," that is, she departs from vices; she casts off the irrational senses and is united with Isaac. For it is worthy that Isaac pass "from virtue to virtue."[14] He who is the son of virtue, that is, of Sarah, is now united and joined with patience, which is Rebekah. And this is to pass "from virtue to virtue"[15] and "from faith to faith."[16] But let us come also to the Gospels. Let us see where the Lord seeks rest when he was "wearied from the journey." "He came," Scripture says, "to the well and sat upon it."[17]

You see that everywhere the mysteries are in agreement. You see the patterns of the New and Old Testament to be harmonious. There one comes to the wells and the waters that brides may be found; and the church is united to Christ in the bath of water.[18]

You see how great a heap of mysteries presses upon us. We cannot treat all the things that present themselves. These things at least ought to stimulate you to listen, to assemble. Even if we hurry over some things for the sake of brevity, you yourself even, when you read the text again and inquire into it, may dispel the mystery and discover . . . that the Word of God, finding you also at the waters, may take you up and unite you with himself, that you may be made "one spirit"[19] with him in Christ Jesus our Lord. "To him belongs glory and sovereignty forever and ever. Amen."[20] HOMILIES ON GENESIS 10.5.[21]

24:65 The Servant Identifies Isaac

THE MODESTY OF THE BETROTHED. TERTULLIAN: However, in regard to those who are betrothed, I can declare and avow this with more than my usual firmness: their heads should be covered from the day when they first trembled at the kiss and handclasp of their future husband. For in these symbols they have pledged every bit of themselves—their life throughout its full development, their flesh throughout their lifetime, their spirit through their understanding [of the contract], their modesty through the exchange of a kiss, their hope through their expectation and their mind through their willingness. For us, Rebekah stands as sufficient example; when her future husband had been pointed out to her, she covered her head with her veil merely because she knew she was to marry him. ON PRAYER 22.10.[22]

SHE TOOK A VEIL. AMBROSE: Rebekah, when she knew that Isaac was coming to meet her, dismounted from her camel and covered herself with a mantle. Just so this soul anticipated the mark of the wedding garment, so that she might not be cast out as one not having a wedding garment.[23] ISAAC, OR THE SOUL 6.55.[24]

24:67 Isaac Loved Rebekah

CHRIST ESTABLISHED THE CHURCH. CAESARIUS OF ARLES: Therefore Isaac took Rebekah "and led her into the tent of his mother." Christ also took the church and established it in place of the synagogue. . . . As the apostle says, by pride "the branches" of the olive tree "have been broken off,"[25] in order that the lowly wild olive may be engrafted. For this reason Isaac took Rebekah, "and because he loved her he was consoled for the loss of his mother." Christ took the church and loved it so much that by this very love he tempered the grief that was occasioned by the death of his mother, the synagogue. Indeed, just as the synagogue's lack of faith caused Christ sorrow, so the church's faith produced joy in him. . . . Moreover, dearly beloved, because from us Christ the Lord prepared for himself a spiritual spouse that, as I said, he even redeemed with his precious blood. Therefore, with his help, each one of us should not only guard the benefits conferred . . .

---

[13]Ex 2:15-16. [14]Ps 84:7 (83:8 LXX). [15]Ps 84:7 (83:8 LXX). [16]Rom 1:17. [17]Jn 4:6. [18]Origin is referring to baptism. [19]1 Cor 6:17. [20]1 Pet 4:11; Rev 1:6. [21]FC 71:165-67. [22]FC 40:181. [23]See Mt 22:12-13. [24]FC 65:45. [25]Rom 11:17.

by divine gift but also should strive to increase them. Thus there will appear to [that one] nothing sordid because of luxury, nothing puffed up with pride or consumed with anger, nothing blind with avarice or struck with the snakelike poison of envy. Truly it is right that our spouse, "fairer in beauty than the sons of men,"[26] should find in us none of the above-mentioned sins to offend the eyes of his majesty. To him, together with the Father and the Holy Spirit, is honor and might forever. Amen. SERMON 85.5.[27]

ISAAC'S MOURNING COMFORTED. EPHREM THE SYRIAN: By the joy [which he received] from Rebekah, who came three years later, Isaac was comforted from the mourning of his mother with which he had been shrouded for three years. COMMENTARY ON GENESIS 21.4.[28]

---

[26]Ps 45:2 (44:3 LXX). [27]FC 47:23-24. [28]FC 91:170.

25:1-6 ABRAHAM'S SONS BY KETURAH

¹Abraham took another wife, whose name was Keturah. ²She bore him Zimran, Jokshan, Medan, Midian, Ishbak, and Shuah. ³Jokshan was the father of Sheba and Dedan. The sons of Dedan were Asshurim, Letushim, and Le-ummim. ⁴The sons of Midian were Ephah, Epher, Hanoch, Abida, and Eldaah. All these were the children of Keturah. ⁵Abraham gave all he had to Isaac. ⁶But to the sons of his concubines Abraham gave gifts, and while he was still living he sent them away from his son Isaac, eastward to the east country.

OVERVIEW: This passage offered rich material for allegorical interpretation. Since Abraham represents learning and wisdom, his taking of another wife at age one hundred signifies that there is no end to the vitality of wisdom. The spiritual progress of the saints is figuratively portrayed in their marriages (ORIGEN). In another line of interpretation, however, Abraham's marriage to Keturah was intended to spread the knowledge and worship of the one true God (EPHREM), and to bless a valid second marriage (AUGUSTINE).

25:1 Abraham's Wife Keturah

ABRAHAM KNEW THERE IS NO END OF WISDOM. ORIGEN: The holy apostle always offers us opportunities for spiritual understanding and shows the zealous signs by which one may recognize in all things that "the law is spiritual."[1]

Though few, these signs are nevertheless necessary.

Paul says, discussing Abraham and Sarah in a certain passage, "not weakened in faith." Scripture says, "He considered his own body dead, since he was almost a hundred years old, and Sarah's womb dead."[2] This man, therefore, whom Paul says to have been dead in his body at the age of 100 and to have begotten Isaac more by the power of his faith than by the fertility of his body, Scripture now relates has taken a wife named Keturah and has begotten more sons from her when he seems to have been about 137 years old.[3] For Sarah his wife is recorded to have been ten years younger than he. Since Sarah died in her 127th year, it shows that Abraham was more than 137 years old when he took Keturah as his wife.

What then? Are we to suppose that induce-

---

[1]Rom 7:14. [2]Rom 4:19. [3]Gen 25:1-2.

ments of the flesh have flourished in so great a partriarch at that time? And shall he who is said to have been dead long ago in his natural impulses now be supposed to have been revived for passion? Or, as we have already often said, do the marriages of the patriarchs indicate something mystical and sacred, as also he suggests who said of wisdom:"I decided to take her as my wife"?[4]

Perhaps, therefore, already at that time Abraham also thought something like this. And, although he was wise, for this very reason nevertheless he knew that there is no end of wisdom, nor does old age impose a limit on learning. For when can that man who has been accustomed to share a marriage in that manner in which we indicated above, that is, who is accustomed to have virtue in marriage, cease from such a union? For indeed the death of Sarah is to be understood as the consummation of virtue. But a man of consummate and perfect virtue ought always to be engaged in some learning. The divine language calls this learning his wife. HOMILIES ON GENESIS 11.1.[5]

ABRAHAM TOOK ANOTHER WIFE. ORIGEN: [One] who wishes to show himself to be a child of Abraham by doing the works of Abraham in accordance with the Savior's explanation need not literally have sexual intercourse with a handmaid[6] or take another wife in old age after the death of his wife. We also learn from this quite clearly that we must interpret the whole story of Abraham allegorically and make each thing he did spiritual, beginning with the command,"Go forth from your land, your kindred, and your father's house, into the land that I will show you."[7] This statement is made not only to Abraham but also to everyone who will be his child. COMMENTARY ON THE GOSPEL OF JOHN 20.67.[8]

KETURAH. ORIGEN: Indeed, Keturah, whom Abraham, now an old man, obtains in marriage means *thymiama*,[9] which is incense or a pleasing

fragrance. He also in fact was saying, just as Paul said,"We are the pleasing fragrance of Christ."[10] But let us see how someone becomes "Christ's pleasing fragrance." Sin is a foul affair. In fact, sinners are compared with pigs that wallow in sins as in foul dung.[11] And David, as a repentant sinner, says,"My sores have putrified and are abscessed."[12]

If there is therefore any one of you in whom there is now no odor of sin but an odor of justice, the sweetness of mercy, if anyone, by praying "without ceasing"[13] always offers incense to the Lord and says,"Let my prayer be directed as incense in your sight, the lifting up of my hands as the evening sacrifice,"[14] this man has married Keturah. In this way, therefore, I think the marriages of the elders are interpreted more fittingly; in this way the unions entered by the patriarchs in their now final and weakened age are understood nobly; in this way I hold the necessary begetting of children should be reckoned. For young men are not so well fitted as old men for such marriages and for offspring of this kind. For to the extent that someone is feeble in the flesh, to such an extent will he be stronger in virtue of the soul and more fit for the embraces of wisdom. HOMILIES ON GENESIS 11.1-2.[15]

SCRIPTURE DESIGNATES THE PROGRESS OF THE SAINTS FIGURATIVELY. ORIGEN: In this way also you can, if you wish, be a husband of marriages of this kind. For example, if you freely practice hospitality, you will appear to have taken her as your wife. If you shall add to this care of the poor, you will appear to have obtained a second wife. But if you should also join patience to yourself and gentleness and the other virtues, you will appear to have taken as many wives as the virtues you enjoy.

Thus it is, therefore, that Scripture recounts

---

[4]Wis 8:9. [5]FC 71:168-69*. [6]Gen 16:1-4. [7]Gen 12:1. [8]FC 89:220. [9]Rufinus preserves the Greek term in his Latin translation. [10]2 Cor 2:15. [11]Mt 8:30. [12]Ps 38:5 (37:6 LXX). [13]1 Thess 5:17. [14]Ps 141:2 (140:2 LXX). [15]FC 71:169-70*.

that some of the patriarchs had many wives at the same time, that others took other wives when previous wives had died.[16] The purpose of this is to indicate figuratively that some can exercise many virtues at the same time; others cannot begin those that follow before they have brought the former virtues to perfection. Accordingly Solomon is reported to have had many wives at the same time,[17] to whom the Lord had said, "There was no wise man like you before you and there will not be after you."[18] Because therefore the Lord had given him an abundance of prudence, "like the sand of the sea,"[19] that he might judge his people "in wisdom,"[20] for this reason he could exercise many virtues at the same time. HOMILIES ON GENESIS 11.2.[21]

TO MARRY FOREIGN WIVES. ORIGEN: However, beyond this which we are taught from the law of God, if we also are in touch with some of these instructions that appear to be on the outside in the world—for example, as the knowledge of literature or the theory of grammar, as geometry or mathematics or even the discipline of dialectic—and we bring over to our purposes all these things which have been sought from without and we approve them in the declaration of our law, then we will appear to have taken in marriage either foreign wives or even "concubines."[22] And if, from marriages of this kind, by disputing, by discussing, by refuting those who contradict, we shall be able to convert some to the faith, and if, overcoming them with their own reasonings and skills, we shall persuade them to receive the true philosophy of Christ and the true piety of God, then we shall appear to have begotten sons from dialectic or rhetoric as if from some foreign wife or concubine. HOMILIES ON GENESIS 11.2.[23]

SPREADING KNOWLEDGE AND WORSHIP OF

GOD. EPHREM THE SYRIAN: Because no law concerning virginity or chastity had been set down, lest desire ever make a stain in the mind of that just man. . . . Abraham took for himself a concubine after the death of Sarah, so that through the uprightness of his many sons who were to be scattered throughout the entire earth, knowledge and worship of the one God would be spread. Abraham then had sons from Keturah, and he sent them eastward with gifts. Abraham died 175 years old and was buried next to Sarah, his wife. COMMENTARY ON GENESIS 22.1.[24]

THE PERMISSION OF SECOND MARRIAGE. AUGUSTINE: As for those who prefer to read no symbolic meanings into such facts, they still have no ground of complaint against Abraham. For, in the literal sense, there may be meant to be here an argument against those heretics who are opposed to second marriages, since the example of the very father of many nations proves that there is no sin in a second marriage that is made after one's wife is dead. CITY OF GOD 16.34.[25]

25:6 The Sons of Abraham's Concubines

ABRAHAM GAVE GIFTS. AUGUSTINE: If then we are the sons of the free Jerusalem, let us realize that some gifts belong to those who are disinherited; others, to the heirs. For they are heirs to whom it is said, "You have not received a spirit of bondage so as to be again in fear, but you have received a spirit of adoption as sons, by virtue of which we cry: 'Abba! Father!' "[26] ON PATIENCE 28.[27]

---

[16]Cf. Gen 16:3; 25:1. [17]See Song 6:7. [18]2 Chron 1:2; 1 Kings 3:13. [19]Gen 22:17. [20]2 Chron 1:11. [21]FC 71:170-71. [22]Song 6:7. [23]FC 71:171. [24]FC 91:170-71. [25]FC 14:549. [26]Rom 8:15. [27]FC 16:263.

25:7-11 THE DEATH OF ABRAHAM

[7]*These are the days of the years of Abraham's life, a hundred and seventy-five years.* [8]*Abraham breathed his last and died in a good old age, an old man and full of years, and was gathered to his people.* [9]*Isaac and Ishmael his sons buried him in the cave of Mach-pelah, in the field of Ephron the son of Zohar the Hittite, east of Mamre,* [10]*the field which Abraham purchased from the Hittites. There Abraham was buried, with Sarah his wife.* [11]*After the death of Abraham God blessed Isaac his son. And Isaac dwelt at Beer-lahai-roi.**

*LXX, "the well of vision."

OVERVIEW: The "death of Abraham" must be interpreted in the light of the New Testament affirmations about him. Isaac's dwelling at Beer-lahai-roi, interpreted as "the well of vision," represents spiritual illumination in general, which should be the goal of all (ORIGEN). All who are made children of Abraham through faith live as sojourners in hope of a heavenly inheritance (BEDE). All of the faithful will be gathered to Abraham's bosom (ORIGEN). No one was called "old" before Abraham even when they lived to great ages (JEROME). Since the body pertains to the very nature of humanity, the funerals of the just men of old were cared for with dutiful devotion (AUGUSTINE). Isaac remained at the well of vision, which the faithful may again pass by (ORIGEN).

25:7 Abraham's Life

THE YEARS OF ABRAHAM'S LIFE. BEDE: Isaac, the son of the promise, was born in Abraham's hundredth [year],[1] because the blessing of the inheritance that is promised to all the families of the earth through his seed will doubtless be conferred in the heavenly homeland that is to come. [Abraham] sojourned a hundred years in the land of promise,[2] because all of us who are made children of Abraham through faith ought to live as sojourners in the present church in hope of a heavenly inheritance. In this manner, "Isaac sowed in Gerar (which is interpreted as "resi-

dence [as an alien]"), and "in that same year he acquired a hundredfold,"[3] because as soon as we go forth from the body into the heavenly life, we receive back whatever good works we have done while sojourning in this life as children of the promise. ON THE TABERNACLE 2.13.85.[4]

25:8 An Aged Man

HE DIED AT A GOOD OLD AGE. JEROME: I am reviewing carefully the places in Scripture where I might find old age mentioned for the first time. Adam lived for 930 years, yet he is not called an old man. Methuselah's life was 969 years, and he is not called an old man. I am coming down all the way to the flood, and after the flood for almost three thousand years, and I find no one who has been called old. Abraham is the first one, and certainly he was much younger than Methuselah, but he is called an old man because his old age had been anointed with rich oil. In fine, it is written there in the Scripture, "Abraham died at a good old age; full of days." His was a good old age because it was full of days, for the whole of his life was day and not night. HOMILIES ON THE PSALMS 21.[5]

25:10 Abraham Was Buried with Sarah

---

[1]Gen 21:5. [2]Cf. Gen 12:4. Abraham was 75 years old when he left Haran for the land of Canaan and 175 when he died. [3]Gen 26:6, 12. [4]TTH 18:96-97. [5]FC 48:172.

THE SOLEMNITY OF BURIAL. AUGUSTINE: Yet the bodies of the dead, especially of the just and faithful, are not to be despised or cast aside. The soul has used them as organs and vessels for all good work in a holy manner. If a paternal garment or a ring or anything else of this kind is as dear to children as is their love for their parents, in no way are their very bodies to be spurned, since they are much more familiar and intimate than any garment we put on. Bodies are not for ornament or for aid, as something that is applied externally, but pertain to the very nature of the man. Hence the funerals of the just men of old were cared for with dutiful devotion, the processions solemnized and a fitting burial provided. Oftentimes they themselves, while they were yet alive, gave directions to their sons concerning everything pertaining to their burial.[6] THE CARE TO BE TAKEN FOR THE DEAD 3.5.[7]

25:11 God Blessed Isaac

GATHERED TO ABRAHAM'S BOSOM. ORIGEN: What more can we say about the death of Abraham than what the Word of the Lord in the Gospels contains, saying, "Concerning the resurrection of the dead, have you not read how he says in the bush: 'the God of Abraham, and the God of Isaac and the God of Jacob'? Now he is not God of the dead but of the living. For all those are living."[8] Let us also therefore choose this kind of death, as also the apostle says, that "we may die to sin but live to God."[9] For indeed the death of Abraham should be understood to be such, which death has amplified his bosom so much that all the saints who come from the four parts of the earth "may be borne by the angels into the bosom of Abraham."[10] HOMILIES ON GENESIS 11.3.[11]

ISAAC LIVED AT THE WELL OF VISION. ORIGEN: "The Lord blessed Isaac," the text says, "and he dwelt at the well of vision." This is the whole blessing with which the Lord blessed Isaac: that he might dwell "at the well of vision." That is a great blessing for those who understand it.

Would that the Lord might give this blessing to me too, that I might deserve to dwell "at the well of vision."

What kind of person can know and understand what the vision is "which Isaiah the son of Amos saw"?[12] What kind of person can know what Nahum's vision is?[13] What kind of person can understand what that vision contains which Jacob saw in Bethel when he was departing into Mesopotamia, when he said, "This is the house of the Lord and the gate of heaven"?[14] And if anyone can know and understand each individual vision or the things that are in the law or in the prophets, that one dwells "at the well of vision."

But also consider this more carefully, that Isaac deserved to receive such a great blessing from the Lord that he might dwell "at the well of vision." But when shall we sufficiently deserve to pass by, perhaps, "the well of vision"? He deserved to remain and dwell in the vision; we, what little we have been illuminated by the mercy of God, can scarcely perceive or surmise of a single vision. HOMILIES ON GENESIS 11.3.[15]

THE NEGLIGENT WILL NOT DWELL BY THIS WELL. ORIGEN: If, however, I shall have been able to perceive some one meaning of the visions of God, I shall appear to have spent one day "at the well of vision." But if I shall have been able to touch something not only according to the letter but also according to the spirit, I shall appear to have spent two days "at the well of vision." But if also I shall have touched the moral point, I shall have spent three days. Or certainly even if I shall not have been able to understand everything, if I am nevertheless busily engaged in the divine Scriptures and "I meditate on the law of God day and night"[16] and at no time at all do I desist inquiring, discussing, investigating and certainly, what is greatest, praying God and asking for understanding from him who "teaches human-

---

[6]Cf. Gen 23:1-20; 47:30. [7]FC 27:356. [8]Mk 12:26-27. [9]Rom 6:10. [10]Lk 16:22. [11]FC 71:172-73. [12]Is 1:1. [13]Nahum 1:1-2. [14]Gen 28:17. [15]FC 71:173. [16]Ps 1:2.

kind knowledge,"[17] I shall appear to dwell "at the well of vision."

But if I should be negligent and be neither occupied at home in the Word of God nor frequently enter the church to hear the Word, as I see some among you who only come to the church on festive days, those who are of this sort do not dwell "by the well of vision." But I fear that perhaps those who are negligent, even when they come to the church, may neither drink from the well of water nor be refreshed, but they may devote themselves to the occupations and thoughts of their heart which they bring with them and may depart thirsty no less from the wells of the Scriptures.

You, therefore, hasten and act sufficiently that that blessing of the Lord may come to you, that you may be able to dwell "at the well of vision," that the Lord may open your eyes and you may see "the well of vision" and may receive from it "living water,"[18] which may become in you "a fountain of water springing up into eternal life."[19] But if anyone rarely comes to church, rarely draws from the fountains of the Scriptures and dismisses what he hears at once when he departs and is occupied with other affairs, this one does not dwell "at the well of vision." HOMILIES ON GENESIS 11.3.[20]

---

[17]Ps 94:10 (93:10 LXX). [18]Gen 26:19. [19]Jn 4:14. [20]FC 71:173-74.

25:12-26 THE DESCENDANTS OF ISHMAEL AND THE BIRTH OF ESAU AND JACOB

[12]*These are the descendants of Ishmael, Abraham's son, whom Hagar the Egyptian, Sarah's maid, bore to Abraham.* [13]*These are the names of the sons of Ishmael, named in the order of their birth: Nebaioth, the first-born of Ishmael; and Kedar, Adbeel, Mibsam,* [14]*Mishma, Dumah, Massa,* [15]*Hadad, Tema, Jetur, Naphish, and Kedemah.* [16]*These are the sons of Ishmael and these are their names, by their villages and by their encampments, twelve princes according to their tribes.* [17] *(These are the years of the life of Ishmael, a hundred and thirty-seven years; he breathed his last and died, and was gathered to his kindred.)* [18]*They dwelt from Havilah to Shur, which is opposite Egypt in the direction of Assyria; he settled[p] over against all his people.*

[19]*These are the descendants of Isaac, Abraham's son: Abraham was the father of Isaac,* [20]*and Isaac was forty years old when he took to wife Rebekah, the daughter of Bethuel the Aramean of Paddan-aram, the sister of Laban the Aramean.* [21]*And Isaac prayed to the LORD for his wife, because she was barren; and the LORD granted his prayer, and Rebekah his wife conceived.* [22]*The children struggled together within her; and she said, "If it is thus, why do I live?"[q] So she went to inquire of the LORD.* [23]*And the LORD said to her,*

"Two nations are in your womb,
    and two peoples, born of you, shall be divided;
the one shall be stronger than the other,
    the elder shall serve the younger."

[24]When her days to be delivered were fulfilled, behold, there were twins in her womb. [25]The first came forth red, all his body like a hairy mantle; so they called his name Esau. [26]Afterward his brother came forth, and his hand had taken hold of Esau's heel; so his name was called Jacob.[r] Isaac was sixty years old when she bore them.

p Heb *fell*   q Syr: Heb obscure   r That is *He takes by the heel* or *He supplants*

OVERVIEW: While the descendants of Ishmael received little attention from the Fathers, much attention was given to the descendants of Isaac. The word *barren* is used of women in Scripture to indicate that after sterility they gave birth to a holy person (ORIGEN). Isaac's prayer (APHRAHAT, BEDE) and Rebekah's patience undid the knot of sterility (AMBROSE). Sterility is not the result of sin; in fact the barren woman prepares the way for the Virgin Mary (CHRYSOSTOM). Rebekah's departure to inquire of the Lord signifies her spiritual progress, an example for all to follow (ORIGEN). In a different and curious interpretation she goes to inquire of Melchizedek (EPHREM). The two nations within her womb (TERTULLIAN, AUGUSTINE) represent the opposing virtues and vices within the human soul (ORIGEN). They also represent the opposing people within the womb of the church as well as the Jewish people and the church (CAESARIUS OF ARLES).

25:21 Rebekah Conceived Because of Isaac's Prayer

BARRENNESS OFTEN PRECEDES HOLY BIRTH. ORIGEN: First of all consider why it is that many holy women in the Scriptures are related to have been barren, as Sarah herself, and now Rebekah.[1] But also Rachel, Israel's beloved, was barren.[2] Hanna also, the mother of Samuel, is recorded to have been barren.[3] But also in the Gospels Elizabeth is related to have been barren.[4] Yet in all these instances this term is used because after sterility they all gave birth to a holy person. HOMILIES ON GENESIS 12.1.[5]

BY HER PATIENCE. AMBROSE: Now Rebekah conceived and by her patience untied the knot of

sterility. Let us consider what her prophetic and apostolic soul brought to birth, and how. "She went to consult the Lord,"[6] because the children leapt up in her womb, and she received the reply, "Two nations are in your womb." For of herself she presumes nothing but invokes God as supreme protector of her counsels; filled with peace and piety, she joins two nations together by her faith and by prophecy and encloses them in her womb, so to speak. Not without reason is she called sister[7] rather than wife, because her gentle and peaceable soul enjoys a reputation for affection common to all rather than for union with one individual and because she thought that she was bound to all rather than to one. ISAAC, OR THE SOUL 4.18-19.[8]

BARRENNESS NOT THE RESULT OF SIN. CHRYSOSTOM: One question is worth raising initially: If she and her husband were conspicuous for their good life and both concerned for chaste living, why was she barren? We cannot find fault with their life or say barrenness was the result of sin. To grasp the full extent of this remarkable circumstance, remember that it was not only herself who was barren but also the good man's mother, Sarah; and not only his mother but also his daughter-in-law—I mean Jacob's wife Rachel.

What is the meaning of this gallery of sterile people? All were good people, all virtuous, all given testimony by God; of them he said, "I am the God of Abraham, the God of Isaac and the God of Jacob."[9] And blessed Paul says, "Hence God is not ashamed to be called their God."[10] There is great commendation of them in the New Testament; great praise of them in the Old.

---

[1]Gen 11:30. [2]Gen 29:31. [3]1 Sam 1:2. [4]Lk 1:7. [5]FC 71:176. [6]Gen 25:22. [7]Gen 26:7. [8]FC 65:23*. [9]Ex 3:6. [10]Heb 11:16.

In each case they were distinguished and remarkable men, yet all had barren wives. They spent a long period in a childless condition. So whenever you see a man and wife of virtuous life experiencing childlessness, whenever you see pious people devoted to religion yet childless, don't think it is the result of sin. After all, many reasons for God's designs are beyond our understanding, and we ought to thank God for everything and brand as wicked only those living in sin, not those without children. It frequently happens, in fact, that God works things for our good without our realizing the reason for what happens. Hence in every case we should marvel at his wisdom and praise his ineffable love. HOMILIES ON GENESIS 49.5-6.[11]

PREPARING THE WAY FOR THE VIRGIN. CHRYSOSTOM: These things are told for our benefit so that we may give evidence of much goodwill and not pry into God's plans. Yet we need to explain the reason why these women were barren. What, then, is the reason? So that when you see the Virgin giving birth to our common Lord you may not be incredulous. Exercise your mind, it is saying, on the womb of these sterile women, so that when you see an infertile and sealed womb opened for childbearing by God's grace, you may not be surprised to hear that a maiden gave birth. Or rather, feel surprise and amazement but don't refuse faith in the marvel. So when the Jew says, "How did the Virgin give birth?" say to him, "How did the sterile old woman give birth?" In that case, you see, there were two impediments, her advanced age and the imperfect condition of nature, whereas with the Virgin there was one impediment, her not having experienced marriage. Consequently the barren woman prepares the way for the virgin. HOMILIES ON GENESIS 49.7.[12]

THE POWER OF PRAYER. APHRAHAT: Isaac too demonstrated the power of prayer when he prayed over Rebekah, and she gave birth. ON PRAYER 4.[13]

ISAAC PRAYED FOR REBEKAH. BEDE: Thus Isaac, the son of the promise,[14] who as a figure of our Redeemer became obedient to his father even unto death,[15] was born of parents who were old. He had a mother who had long been barren.[16] Thus Jacob, the patriarch Joseph,[17] Samson, [who was] the bravest of the chieftains,[18] and Samuel, [who was] the most distinguished of the prophets,[19] [all] had as their progenitors [mothers who were] for a long time barren in body but always fruitful in virtues. In this way their dignity would be known from the miraculous nativity of those who were born, and it might be proven that they would be famous in their lives, since at the very outset of their lives they transcended the norms of the human condition. HOMILIES ON THE GOSPELS 2.19.[20]

25:22 Rebekah Asked the Lord

WHERE DID REBEKAH GO? ORIGEN: Now, meanwhile, let us see what the statement means: "Rebekah departed to inquire of the Lord." "She departed." Where did she go? Did she depart from that place where the Lord was not to that place where he was? This indeed appears to be indicated when it is said, "She departed to inquire of the Lord." Is not the Lord everywhere? Did he not say, "I fill heaven and earth, says the Lord"?[21] Where then did Rebekah go?

I think that she did not depart from one place to another, but she passed over from one life to another, from one deed to another, from good things to better. She proceeded from profitable things to more profitable. She hastened from holy things to holier. For it is absurd if we suppose Rebekah, who had been educated in the house of wise Abraham by her most learned husband Isaac, to have been so ignorant and uninstructed that she thought the Lord was enclosed within some place and she might go there to inquire

---

[11]FC 87:44-45*. [12]FC 87:45-46. [13]CS 101:8. [14]Gen 18:10. [15]Gen 22:9; Phil 2:8. [16]Gen 18:11. [17]Gen 30:22-24. [18]Judg 13:2, 24. [19]1 Sam 1:2, 20. [20]CS 111:192. [21]Jer 23:24.

what the leaping of the children in her womb might mean.

But do you wish to see that this kind of speech has become customary among the faithful, so that when they have seen that God shows anything to them, they say that they either depart or pass over?

When Moses had seen the bush burning but not being consumed, he was astonished at the sight and said, "I will cross over and see this sight."[22] He certainly also did not mean that he was about to cross over some earthly space, or to ascend mountains or to descend the steep sides of valleys. The vision was near him, in his countenance and in his eyes. But he says, "I will cross over,"[23] that he might show that he, reminded forcefully by the heavenly vision, ought to ascend to a higher life and cross over to better things than those in which he was. HOMILIES ON GENESIS 12.2.[24]

THE TWINS STRUGGLED BEFORE BIRTH. TERTULLIAN: The very vitals of Rebekah are stirred, though the child is a long way from birth and there is no breath of air. Behold, the twin offspring struggles in the womb of their mother, though there yet is no sign of the two nations. We might regard as prophetic this struggle of the two infants, who are at enmity even before they are born, who show animosity before animation, for their restlessness disturbed their mother. When, however, the womb is opened, their number known and the symbolic implications of their condition made manifest, we see clearly not only the separate souls of those children but even then the beginning of their rivalry. ON THE SOUL 26.2.[25]

THE STRUGGLE WITHIN REBEKAH. CAESARIUS OF ARLES: Almost everyone accepts the fact that blessed Isaac represented a type of the Lord our Savior. Therefore Isaac prefigured Christ and blessed Rebekah the church, because although like the church she remained sterile for a long time, she conceived through the prayer of blessed Isaac and the Lord's gift. Now the children struggled in her womb, and not tolerating this annoyance, she said, "If this be so, why am I pregnant?" Then the Lord replied to her, "Two nations are in your womb; two peoples shall stem from your body. One people shall be stronger than the other, and the elder shall serve the younger." Indeed, as the apostle says, dearly beloved, "All these things happened to them as a type, and they were written for us."[26] Therefore Rebekah corporally conceived of blessed Isaac, because the church was going to conceive spiritually of Christ. Moreover, just as the two children struggled in Rebekah's womb, so two peoples continually oppose each other in the church's womb. If there were only wicked or only good persons, there would be just one people. In the church, so much the worse, good and bad people are found, two peoples struggling as in the womb of the spiritual Rebekah—the humble, indeed, and the proud, chaste and adulterous, meek and irascible, kind and envious, merciful and avaricious. SERMON 86.2.[27]

TWO PEOPLES WRESTLING. AUGUSTINE: They were wrestling in the womb of their mother, and it was said to Rebekah, when they were wrestling there, "Two peoples are in your womb." Two men, two peoples, a good people, an evil people; but still they are wrestling in one womb.

How many evil people there are in the church! And one womb carries them until they are separated in the end. And the good shout against the evil, and the evil shout back against the good, and both are wrestling in the bowels of the one. TRACTATE ON THE GOSPEL OF JOHN 11.10.2-3.[28]

YOU ALSO WILL HAVE DEPARTED. ORIGEN: So therefore also now it is related of Rebekah: "She departed to inquire of the Lord." As we have said, she should be considered to have departed not by the steps of her feet but by the advances of her mind.

[22]Ex 3:3. [23]Ex 3:3. [24]FC 71:177-78*. [25]FC 10:241. [26]1 Cor 10:11. [27]FC 47:25*. [28]FC 88:20*.

You also therefore will be said to have departed "to inquire of the Lord" if you have begun to contemplate not those things "which are seen but those which are not seen,"[29] that is, not carnal but spiritual things, not present but future things.

Tear yourself away from your old manner of life and from the fellowship of those with whom you have lived shamefully and notoriously. Associate yourself with honorable and religious actions, when you shall have been searched for among companions of shamefulness and shall never have been found in crowds of the guilty. If so, then it will be said also of you: "He departed to inquire of the Lord."

So therefore the saints depart not from one place to another but from one life to another, from beginning instructions to more advanced instructions. Homilies on Genesis 12.2.[30]

Rebekah Inquired of Melchizedek.
Ephrem the Syrian: "God blessed Isaac,"[31] and Isaac prayed for Rebekah, who was barren. After twenty years God heard him, and she conceived. Her sons struggled together within her womb. She went to inquire of the Lord, and it was told her, "Two nations are in your womb," that is, the Edomite and Hebrew nations. To whom did she go to inquire? It was to Melchizedek that she went to inquire, as we mentioned above in the genealogy of Melchizedek.[32] She returned quickly because of the pangs that were striking her, and she gave birth to Esau and Jacob. Commentary on Genesis 23.1.[33]

25:23 Two Nations, Divided

Two Nations Within You. Origen: I think that this can be said also of each of us as individuals that "two nations and two peoples are within you." For there is a people of virtue within us, and there is no less a people of vice within us. "For from our heart proceed evil thoughts, adulteries, thefts, false testimonies"[34] but also "deceits, contentions, heresies, jealousies, revelings and such

like."[35] Do you see how great a people of evil is within us? But if we should deserve to utter that word of the saints, "From fear of you, Lord, we have conceived in the womb and have brought forth. We have wrought the spirit of your salvation on the earth."[36] Thus another people, begotten in the Spirit, is found within us. For "the fruit of the spirit is love, joy, peace, patience, goodness, gentleness, temperance, purity" and so forth.[37] You see another people that is also itself within us. But this one is less; that one greater. For there are always more evil than good people, and vices are more numerous than virtues. But if we should be such as Rebekah and should deserve to conceive from Isaac, that is, from the Word of God, "one people shall overcome the other, and the elder shall serve the younger,"[38] even in us, for the flesh shall serve the Spirit, and vices shall yield to virtues. Homilies on Genesis 12.3.[39]

Two People Oppose Each Other in the Church's Womb. Caesarius of Arles: Good souls want to win over the evil, but the wicked long to destroy the just. It is the desire of the good that those who are bad be corrected, while the destruction of the good is the pursuit of the wicked. There is one class of the pious, another of the impious. The class of the good are raised up to heaven through humility, while the class of the wicked are plunged into hell through pride. For all those members of the Catholic church belong to Esau who are inclined toward earthly possessions, love the earth, desire the earth and place all their hopes in the earth. Whoever wishes to serve God in order to increase in honors or receive material profits is known to belong to Esau, that is, to earthly happiness. For in Esau carnal souls are understood, while spiritual ones are truly in Jacob. These are the two people whom the apostle

[29]2 Cor 4:18. [30]FC 71:178. [31]Gen 25:11. [32]Ephrem thinks that it is Melchizedek that Rebekah inquires about her pregnancy because she believes Melchizedek is greater than Abraham and the length of his life extends to that of Jacob and Esau. [33]FC 91:171. [34]Mt 15:19. [35]Gal 5:20-21. [36]Is 26:18 LXX. [37]Gal 5:22-23. [38]Gen 25:23. [39]FC 71:179*.

clearly mentions when he distinguishes the carnal and the spiritual. As he says, "Now the works of the flesh are manifest, which are immorality, uncleanness, licentiousness, idolatry, witchcrafts, enmities, contentions, jealousies, anger, quarrels, factions, parties, envies, drunkenness, carousing and suchlike."[40] Behold the fruits of the people who belong to Esau. In the following passage the same apostle adds the fruits of those who belong to Jacob, saying, "But the fruit of the Spirit is: charity, joy, peace, patience, goodness, kindness, faith, modesty, continence."[41] Behold the spiritual works belonging to blessed Jacob, that is, to people who are pious. SERMON 86.2.[42]

THE OLDER TO SERVE THE YOUNGER. AUGUSTINE: We must now take a look at the history of the city of God, as it takes its course from this point on among the descendants of Abraham. In the period from Isaac's birth to his seventieth year, when his first children were born, there is one memorable fact: He asked God that his wife, who was barren, might bear him a child. God heard the prayer, and she conceived twins who leaped while still in her womb. She was troubled by the disturbance, and, asking the Lord, she received this answer: "Two nations are in your womb; two people shall stem from your body. One people shall be stronger than the other, and the elder shall serve the younger."

This is interpreted by the apostle Paul as an obvious proof of the working of grace: "For before the children had yet been born or had done anything of good or evil,"[43] the younger was chosen, through no merits of his own, and the older rejected. So far as original sin goes, both were equal. As for personal sins, neither had any. CITY OF GOD 16.35.[44]

THE SERVICE OF THE JEWS. CAESARIUS OF ARLES: The fact that we read "One people shall be stronger than the other, and the elder shall serve the younger"[45] we do not see fulfilled according to the letter in Esau and Jacob. For Scripture does not mention that Esau served blessed Jacob bodi-

ly. Therefore we ought to inquire how this is to be understood spiritually, or how the elder shall serve the younger, for if this were not to happen holy Scripture would not mention it. Therefore if one pays careful attention, one will know how the elder people shall serve the younger in the case of Christians and Jews. The greater and older people of the Jews are proved to serve the younger, that is, the Christian people, for like servants of the Christians they are known to carry the books of the divine law throughout the world for the instruction of all nations. Therefore the Jews were scattered in every land, so that when we want to invite some pagan to faith in Christ by testifying that Christ was announced by all the prophets, and he resists and says that the holy books of the divine law were written by us rather than the Holy Spirit, we may thus have a means of refuting him with positive arguments. To such a person we may say, "If a doubt arises in you concerning my books, behold the books of the Jews, apparently our enemies, which I certainly could neither have written nor changed. Read them over, and when you have found in them the same thing as in my books, 'Be not unbelieving but believing.' "[46] In this way the elder people is known to serve the younger, for through their books the people of the Gentiles are invited to belief in Christ. SERMON 86.3.[47]

HOW DID THE WICKED SERVE THE GOOD? CAESARIUS OF ARLES: How then do the wicked serve the good? As persecutors serve the martyrs; as a file or hammer, gold; as a mill, wheat; as ovens, the baking of bread: those are consumed, so that these may be baked. How, I say, do the wicked serve the good? As chaff in the furnace of the goldsmith serves gold. . . . Therefore the wicked should not boast or extol themselves when they send tribulations to the good. For while they are persecuting the good in their bodies, they are killing themselves in their hearts. If the misfortune

---

[40]Gal 5:19-21. [41]Gal 5:22-23. [42]FC 47:25-26*. [43]Rom 9:11. [44]FC 14:550*. [45]Gen 25:23. [46]Jn 20:27. [47]FC 47:26-27.

of an evil person affects a good person, the iniquity has already caused his own soul to decay. Therefore if in an evil spirit someone who is inflamed with the fury of wrath tries to stir up a good man, it is still doubtful whether the good man can be consumed with rage, but there is no doubt that the evil man is already glowing with anger. Perhaps that good man who is full of spiritual vigor and the refreshment of the Holy Spirit will not get excited, even if the fire of persecution is inflicted; but without any doubt the one who tried to arouse him cannot fail to burn with passion. Esau and Jacob were born of the one seed of Isaac, just as Christian people are begotten of our Lord and Savior's one baptism and one womb of the church. However, just like Esau and Jacob, these people are divided into two parts because of their moral differences. For from the fruits of their works one part is known to be carnal, the other spiritual. For this reason, then, Scripture says, "The elder shall serve the younger,"[48] because the number of the wicked is always greater than that of the good. So just like those two children in the womb of Rebekah, so these people will struggle in the womb of the church until judgment day, as we said above, while the proud resist the humble, while adulterers persecute the chaste, while drunkards whose number is infinite rail at the sober, while the envious rival the good, while robbers desire to destroy those who give alms like the irascible do the peaceable, and while the dissolute attempt to drag down to earth those who have a taste for heavenly things. SERMON 86.4.[49]

25:24 Rebekah Bears Twins

THE FULFILLMENT OF HER DAYS. ORIGEN: "And her days were fulfilled," the text says, "that she should give birth, and there were twins in her womb."[50] This statement, that is, "her days were fulfilled that she should give birth," is almost never written except of holy women. For this is said of this Rebekah and of Elizabeth the mother of John[51] and of Mary the mother of our Lord Jesus Christ.[52] Whence a birth of this kind seems to me to show something extraordinary and beyond other human beings. The fulfillment of the days seems to indicate the birth of perfect offspring. HOMILIES ON GENESIS 12.3.[53]

25:25 Esau Was Red and Hairy

HOW DIFFERENT THE TWINS. AUGUSTINE: Two twins were born at so short an interval of time that the second had a hold on the foot of the first. Yet they were so unlike in their lives, character, conduct and the love their parents bore them that this unlikeness made them enemies one of the other. When I say unlike, I do not mean that one would sit while the other walked, or that one slept while the other was awake or that one talked while the other kept quiet.

One of our twins led a life of servile toil, while the other served no one. One was loved by his mother; the other was not. One lost the title to primogeniture, which was then so highly esteemed, and the other obtained it. Further, there were immense differences between them in regard to their wives, children and possessions. If such differences are to be explained by those split seconds between the births of twins which are considered negligible in their horoscopes, why are such matters mentioned when other people's horoscopes are in question? CITY OF GOD 5.4.[54]

ESAU, RED AND HAIRY. ORIGEN: This Esau proceeded from his mother's womb "hairy all over like a skin," but Jacob was smooth and simple. Thus Jacob received his name from wrestling or supplanting, but Esau—as those who interpret Hebrew names say—received his name either from redness or from earth, that is, "red" or "earthly," or, as it seemed to others, his name appears to mean "something made."

Certainly, as the apostle says, both sons were

---

[48]Gen 25:23. [49]FC 47:27-28. [50]Gen 25:24. [51]Lk 1:57. [52]Lk 2:16. [53]FC 71:179-80. [54]FC 8:246-47.

conceived "from our one father Isaac."[55] But why these prerogatives are given is not mine to know. Neither do I know why one "supplanted his brother" and was born smooth and simple, nor why the other was born "hairy all over" and shaggy and, so to speak, enwrapped in the squalor of sin and vileness. This is not mine to discuss. HOMILIES ON GENESIS 12.4.[56]

25:26 Jacob Held Esau's Heel

JACOB SUPPLANTED. ORIGEN: In addition, because [Christ] supplanted[57] the activity of the adversary and because he alone sees the Father, he is "Jacob" and "Israel"[58] when he has become man. As we become light because he is the light of the world, so we become Jacob because he is called "Jacob" and Israel because he is named "Is-

rael." COMMENTARY ON THE GOSPEL OF JOHN 1.260.[59]

ISAAC FAILED OF HIS SIGHT. GREGORY OF NYSSA: There was the example of the patriarch Isaac, who did not marry at the peak of his youth, in order that marriage should not be a deed of passion; because of the blessing of God upon his seed.[60] He continued in the marriage until the birth of his twin sons, and later, closing his eyes, he entered again fully the realm of the unseen. This is what the story of the patriarch seems to mean, in my opinion, when it refers to the failing of his sight.[61] ON VIRGINITY 7.[62]

---

[55]Rom 9:10. [56]FC 71:180*. [57]Cf. Gen 25:25. [58]Cf. Is 49:5-6. [59]FC 80:86-87. [60]See Gen 25:20. [61]See Gen. 27:1. [62]FC 58:33.

25:27-34 ESAU SELLS HIS BIRTHRIGHT

[27]When the boys grew up, Esau was a skilful hunter, a man of the field, while Jacob was a quiet man, dwelling in tents. [28]Isaac loved Esau, because he ate of his game; but Rebekah loved Jacob.
    [29]Once when Jacob was boiling pottage, Esau came in from the field, and he was famished. [30]And Esau said to Jacob, "Let me eat some of that red pottage, for I am famished!" (Therefore his name was called Edom.[s]) [31]Jacob said, "First sell me your birthright." [32]Esau said, "I am about to die; of what use is a birthright to me?" [33]Jacob said, "Swear to me first."[t] So he swore to him, and sold his birthright to Jacob. [34]Then Jacob gave Esau bread and pottage of lentils, and he ate and drank, and rose and went his way. Thus Esau despised his birthright.

s That is Red t Heb today

OVERVIEW: This passage could be interpreted as a teaching about the contrast between the temporary satisfactions provided by material things as opposed to the permanent honor of virtue. This can be applied to those within the church as well as to the contrast between the Jewish people and

those of the church (AUGUSTINE). The passage also provided material for preaching against the desire for wealth (CHRYSOSTOM). Gluttony deprived Esau of his birthright (BASIL). Wealth does not match the free gifts from God (CHRYSOSTOM). The birthright meant nothing to Esau (EPHREM, AMBROSE).

25:28 The Parents' Favoritism

ISAAC LOVED ESAU; REBEKAH LOVED JACOB.
AMBROSE: But we ought not to leave his parents
without excuse for having preferred their younger
son to the elder. At the same time we must take
care so that no one, in turning to their example,
would make an unfair judgment between his sons
or suppose that he should love the one and esteem the other less. From this line of conduct fraternal hatreds are aroused, and the crime of
fratricide is contrived to gain a worthless sum of
money. Let children be nurtured with a like measure of devotion. Granted that one's love may fasten more upon some trait in a child who is more
agreeable or similar to oneself, the exercise of justice ought to be the same in regard to all. The
more that is given to the child that is loved and
who seeks his brothers' love, the more is taken
away from the one who is burdened with jealousy
at the unfair preference. Esau threatened that he
would kill his brother.[1] Neither the fact of brotherhood nor respect for their parents kept him
from his fratricidal madness. He grieved that the
blessing had been snatched away from him,
whereas he should have proved himself worthy of
it by forbearance rather than by crime. JACOB
AND THE HAPPY LIFE 2.2.5.[2]

25:30 Esau's Hunger

COVETING CENSURED. AUGUSTINE: Let frugality be joined to fasting. Just as overeating is to be
censured, so stimulants of the appetite must be
eliminated. It is not that certain kinds of food are
to be detested but that bodily pleasure is to be
checked. Esau was censured not for having desired a fat calf or plump birds but for having cov-
eted a dish of lentils. SERMONS ON THE LITURGI-
CAL SEASONS 207.2.[3]

25:31-32 Esau Sells His Birthright

TEMPORARY PLEASURES. AUGUSTINE: I have
already put it to your holinesses yesterday that

the reason why the elder son is called Esau is that
no one becomes spiritual without first having
been "of the flesh" or materialistic. But if they
persist in "the mind of the flesh,"[4] they will always
be Esau. If, however, they become spiritual, they
will then be the younger son. But then the junior
will be the senior; the other takes precedence in
time, this one in virtue. Before it ever came to
this blessing, Esau had longed to have the lentils
Jacob had cooked. And Jacob said to him, "Give
me your birthright, and I will give you the lentils
I have cooked."[5] He sold his right as firstborn to
his younger brother. He went off with a temporary satisfaction; the other went off with a permanent honor. So those in the church who are slaves
to temporary pleasures and satisfactions eat lentils—lentils that Jacob certainly cooked but that
Jacob did not eat. Idols, you see, flourished more
than anywhere else in Egypt; lentils are the food
of Egypt; so lentils represent all the errors of the
Gentiles. So because the more obvious and manifest church which was going to come from the
Gentiles was signified in the younger son, Jacob is
said to have cooked the lentils and Esau to have
eaten them. . . .

Now apply this. You have a Christian people.
But among this Christian people it is the ones
who belong to Jacob that have the birthright or
right of the firstborn. Those, however, who are
materialistic in life, materialistic in faith, materialistic in hope, materialistic in love, still belong to
the old covenant, not yet to the new. They still
share the lot of Esau, not yet in the blessing of Jacob. SERMON 4.12.[6]

OF WHAT USE IS A BIRTHRIGHT? AMBROSE:
Reason would then curtail the attractions of gluttony and the other excessive desires and would
check the passions and emotions of the body.
Therefore temperance comes before correction
and is the mistress of learning.

---

[1]Gen 27:41. [2]FC 65:149. [3]FC 38:91**. [4]Rom 8:6. [5]Gen 25:31.
[6]WSA 3 1:191-92*.

Proceeding from it, holy Jacob received from his brother the primacy that he had not possessed; by his agreement to that preference, Esau taught for the future that those who do not govern their own selves are worthless in judgment. JACOB AND THE HAPPY LIFE 1.2.5-6.[7]

THE VICE OF GLUTTONY. BASIL THE GREAT: This vice of gluttony delivered Adam up to death; by the pleasure of the appetite consummate evil was brought into the world. Through it Noah was mocked,[8] Canaan was cursed,[9] Esau was deprived of his birthright and married into a Canaanite family.[10] Lot became his own son-in-law and father-in-law, by marrying his own daughter.[11] ON RENUNCIATION OF THE WORLD.[12]

25:34 Esau Forfeits His Birthright

RECOGNIZE THE DANGERS OF WEALTH. CHRYSOSTOM: Listening to this, however, let us learn the lesson never to neglect the gifts from God or forfeit important things for worthless trifles. I mean, why, tell me, should we be obsessed with a desire for money when the kingdom of heaven and those ineffable blessings are within our grasp, and why prefer blessings that endure forever and ever to those that are passing and scarcely last until evening? What could be worse than the folly of being deprived of the former through lust after the latter and never being able to enjoy them in a pure fashion? What good, after all, tell me, is such wealth? Are you not aware that acquisition of great wealth brings us nothing else than an increase in worry, anxiety and sleeplessness? Do you not see that these people (in particular those possessing great wealth) are, so to say, everyone's slaves, and day in and day out are in fear even of shadows? This, you see, is the source of plotting, envy, deep hatred and countless other evils. Often you would see the person with ten thousand talents of gold hidden away calling blessed the one behind the shop counter who prepares his own meals by hand. HOMILIES ON GENESIS 50.7.[13]

AS IF IT WERE NOTHING. EPHREM THE SYRIAN: Jacob saw that the right of the firstborn was despised by Esau, and he contrived to take it from him, trusting in God who had said, "The elder shall serve the younger."[14] Jacob boiled some lentils, and "Esau came home famished after hunting and said to Jacob, 'Let me eat some of that red pottage,'" that is, "Let me eat some of your lentils." "Jacob said to him, 'Give me your birthright and you may take all of them.' After Esau swore to him and sold him his birthright, Jacob then gave Esau [the lentils]." To show that it was not by reason of his hunger that Esau sold his birthright, Scripture says, "After he had eaten he arose and went away, and Esau despised his birthright." Therefore Esau did not sell it because he was hungry, but rather, since it had no value to him, he sold it for nothing as if it were nothing. COMMENTARY ON GENESIS 23.2.[15]

---

[7]FC 65:123. [8]Gen 9:21. [9]Gen 9:25. [10]Gen 25:33; 36:2. [11]Gen 19:35. [12]FC 9:25. [13]FC 87:53**. [14]Gen 25:23. [15]FC 91:171.

26:1-11 ISAAC AT GERAR

[1]*Now there was a famine in the land, besides the former famine that was in the days of Abraham. And Isaac went to Gerar, to Abimelech king of the Philistines.* [2]*And the LORD appeared to him, and said, "Do not go down to Egypt; dwell in the land of which I shall tell you.* [3]*Sojourn in*

this land, and I will be with you, and will bless you; for to you and to your descendants I will give all these lands, and I will fulfil the oath which I swore to Abraham your father. [4]*I will multiply your descendants as the stars of heaven, and will give to your descendants all these lands; and by your descendants all the nations of the earth shall bless themselves:* [5]*because Abraham obeyed my voice and kept my charge, my commandments, my statutes, and my laws."*

[6]*So Isaac dwelt in Gerar.* [7]*When the men of the place asked him about his wife, he said, "She is my sister"; for he feared to say, "My wife," thinking, "lest the men of the place should kill me for the sake of Rebekah"; because she was fair to look upon.* [8]*When he had been there a long time, Abimelech king of the Philistines looked out of a window and saw Isaac fondling Rebekah his wife.* [9]*So Abimelech called Isaac, and said, "Behold, she is your wife; how then could you say, 'She is my sister'?" Isaac said to him, "Because I thought, 'Lest I die because of her.'"* [10]*Abimelech said, "What is this you have done to us? One of the people might easily have lain with your wife, and you would have brought guilt upon us."* [11]*So Abimelech warned all the people, saying, "Whoever touches this man or his wife shall be put to death."*

OVERVIEW: Following a moral interpretation, the words of God to Isaac reflect his considerateness and loving kindness and are uttered out of consideration for our limitations. God shows his wisdom in stirring up the patriarch's thinking and strengthening his resolve through the memory of his father's virtue. God causes his servants to be celebrated by their enemies (CHRYSOSTOM). Abimelech represents symbolically wisdom above this world (CLEMENT OF ALEXANDRIA). For the father's faith God was good to the son (AUGUSTINE, JUSTIN MARTYR).

26:1 Isaac Goes to Gerar

ANOTHER FAMINE. CHRYSOSTOM: In case you might think he was talking about that previous famine, accordingly he added, "besides the famine in the patriarch's time," that is to say, another similar famine beset the land in Isaac's time as in his father's time. The scarcity of the necessities of life threw everyone into great apprehension, compelled them to leave their own home and travel to those places where it was possible to find an abundance of resources.

Hence this good man too, on seeing the famine, "took the journey," the text says, "to visit

Abimelech in Gerar." This was where Abraham came too, you remember, after his return from Egypt.[1] HOMILIES ON GENESIS 51.5-6.[2]

26:2 Living in Gerar

A SOJOURNER. CHRYSOSTOM: Now it is likely that Isaac also made for there on account of his intention to continue on from there into Egypt; for proof of this, listen to what Scripture says: "God appeared to him and said, 'Don't go down into Egypt.'" I do not want you to make that long journey, he is saying, but to stay here. Instead of allowing you to experience that hardship, I am going to put into effect the promise made to your father; the promises to him will be fulfilled in you, and you will experience the pledges to him. "Don't go down into Egypt but dwell in the land that I show you, and be a sojourner in that land." HOMILIES ON GENESIS 51.6.[3]

26:3 God's Presence and Blessing

GOD UNDERSTANDS OUR LIMITATIONS. CHRY-

---

[1]Gen 20:1-2. [2]FC 87:58-59. [3]FC 87:59.

sostom: Lest the good man think it was out of a wish for him to experience the hardship of famine that God gave this direction not allowing him to go into Egypt, God said, Don't be distressed; don't be concerned—stay here: "I will be with you." You have the supplier of all good things, so entertain no concern. After all, I the Lord of all will be with you—and not only that, but "I will bless you." That is to say, I will make you prosperous and provide you with blessing from myself. What could be more blessed than this good man in receiving such a wonderful promise from God, "I will be with you and bless you?" . . . But how will I bless you? "To you and your descendants I will give this land." You think you are visiting these parts as a stranger and nomad; know that to you and your descendants all this land will be given. That you may have confidence, realize that "the oath I swore to your father Abraham" I will fulfill in you.

Observe God's considerateness; he did not simply say, "The covenant I made with your father, nor the promises I made"; instead, what? "The oath I swore." "I assured him with an oath," he is saying, "and I must put my oath into effect and bring it to fulfillment." Do you see God's loving kindness? His words are uttered not with a view to his own dignity but out of considerateness of our limitations. Homilies on Genesis 51.7-8.[4]

26:4 Multiplying Isaac's Descendants

God's Wisdom Stirs Isaac's Thought. Chrysostom: Then he teaches Isaac what it was he promised and the things about which God had given him confirmation. "I will make your descendants as numerous as the stars of heaven." This, you remember, he had said to the patriarch as well, that his descendants would be so numerous as to be compared with the stars and the sand: "I will give all this land to your descendants," he said, "and in your descendants will all the nations of the earth be blessed."[5] Hence the promises made to him I will fulfill in you, "for

the reason that your father Abraham obeyed my voice and kept my commands, my judgments and my laws."[6] See God's wisdom in stirring up the good man's thinking, making him more enthusiastic and having the effect of rendering him an imitator of his father. After all, God is saying, if Abraham was judged worthy of such a wonderful promise for obeying my voice, on account of his virtue I am about to fulfill it in you, the child born to him. And if you yourself become an imitator of him and tread in his path, consider the degree of favor you will enjoy from me and the care you will be accorded. I mean, the man destined to prosper for someone else's virtue will be accorded much greater favor if he himself proves virtuous. Homilies on Genesis 51.9.[7]

The Same Promise to Isaac. Justin Martyr: By our similar faith we have become children of Abraham. For, just as he believed the voice of God and was justified thereby, so have we believed the voice of God (which was spoken again to us by the prophets and the apostles of Christ) and have renounced even to death all worldly things. Thus God promised Abraham a religious and righteous nation of similar faith and a delight to the Father; but it is not you, "in whom there is no faith."[8]

Notice how he makes the same promises to Isaac and Jacob. Here are God's words to Isaac: "In your seed shall all the nations be blessed." And to Jacob: "In you and in your seed all the tribes of the earth shall be blessed."[9] But God does not address this blessing to Esau, or to Reuben or to any other but only to them from whom Christ was to come through the Virgin Mary in accordance with the divine plan of our redemption. If you were to think over the blessing of Judah, you would see what I mean. For the seed is divided after Jacob and comes down through

---

[4]FC 87:59-60**. [5]A composite text: cf. Gen 12:7; 13:15; 15:18; 22:18. [6]Gen 26:5. [7]FC 87:60-61. [8]Deut 32:20. [9]Gen 28:14.

Judah and Perez and Jesse and David. Now this was a sign that some of you Jews would be certainly children of Abraham and at the same time would share in the lot of Christ. DIALOGUE WITH TRYPHO 119-20.[10]

26:5 Abraham's Obedience Recalled

THE MEMORY OF ABRAHAM'S VIRTUE. CHRYSOSTOM: But what is the meaning of "for the reason that he obeyed my voice and kept my commands, my orders, and my judgments"? I said to Abraham, "Go forth from your country and your kindred, onward to a land that I will show you."[11] He left what he had and set off for an uncertain goal. He did not dally or delay; instead, with complete enthusiasm, Abraham obeyed my call and carried out my commands. In turn I promised him things beyond nature and, despite his despair on the score of age and the unsuitability for childbearing on the part of himself and your mother, he heard from me that his descendants would develop into such a great number as to fill the whole land. Yet he did not become deranged in mind or lose faith. Hence it was reckoned as righteousness in Abraham[12] to trust in my power and have confidence in my promises. . . .

After your birth your mother was ill disposed toward her maidservant's child Ishmael and wanted to drive him out of the house with Hagar so that he should have nothing in common with you. The patriarch had some natural inclination toward him out of his fatherly affection; but when he heard from me, "Do what Sarah wants," he ignored his natural affection and drove out Ishmael along with the maidservant, obeying my call and keeping my commands in every detail. I mean, when he received the ultimate command from me to offer up as a sacrifice the son he so much desired, the gift of his old age, Abraham did not pry into the reasons. Neither was he disturbed in his thinking; nor did he betray the news to your mother or reveal to you what was about to be done by him. Instead, with steadfast resolve and heightened zeal, he pressed ahead to put my command into effect. So I rewarded his intention by preventing the execution of the deed. Since, then, he had in everything given evidence of complete obedience and observance of my commands, consequently I am making you, his child, the inheritor of the promises made to him. So imitate his obedience, and believe my words so as to be found worthy of a manifold reward for your father's virtue and also for your own obedience. Don't go down into Egypt; rather, stay here. Do you see God's loving kindness in strengthening Isaac's resolve through the memory of his father's virtue? HOMILIES ON GENESIS 51.10-11.[13]

ABRAHAM'S MERIT. AUGUSTINE: Isaac is a patriarch who had no second wife, nor any concubine, but was content with the twins who were the fruit of a single intercourse. He too had the same fears as his father of the perilous beauty of his wife when he lived among strangers, and he too called her sister without a word about her being his wife, since in fact she was nearly related on the paternal and the maternal side. And Rebekah too was safe, once it was known that she was his wife. Not, however, that we should esteem him higher than his father for knowing no woman other than his single wife; undoubtedly the merits of his father's faith and obedience were so much greater that it was because of the father that God was so good to the son. CITY OF GOD 16.36.[14]

26:7 Questions About Rebekah

WHETHER ISAAC LIED. AUGUSTINE: Those who assert that sometimes we must lie make inappropriate mention of Abraham as having lied about Sarah whom he called his sister. For he did not say "She is not my wife" but "She is my sister," because Sarah was in fact of a family so closely related that without lying she could be called his

---

[10]FC 6:332-33*. [11]Gen 12:1. [12]Gen 15:6. [13]FC 87:61-62*. [14]FC 14:551-52.

sister. This fact Abraham confirmed afterward when Sarah was returned by him who had led her away. Abraham replied to him, saying, "Also she is truly my sister, the daughter of my father, and not the daughter of my mother,"[15] that is to say, belonging to his father's family but not to his mother's. Thus he concealed something of the truth but did not say anything false in concealing the fact that she was his wife and in saying that she was his sister. His son Isaac also did this, for we know that he too chose a relative of his as wife. Hence it is not a lie when truth is passed over in silence but when falsehood is brought forth in speech. AGAINST LYING 10.23.[16]

26:8 Abimelech Learns the Truth

THE KING SAW ISAAC FONDLING REBEKAH. CLEMENT OF ALEXANDRIA: Isaac means "rejoicing." The inquisitive king saw him playing with his wife and helpmate, Rebekah. The king (his name was Abimelech) represents, I believe, a wisdom above this world, looking down upon the mystery signified by such childlike playing. Rebekah means "submission." Oh, what prudent playing! Rejoicing joined to submission, with the king as audience. The Spirit exults in such merrymaking in Christ, attended with submissiveness. This is in truth godly childlikeness....

It is possible to interpret the meaning of the inspired Word in still another sense: that it refers to our rejoicing and making merry because of our salvation, like Isaac's. He rejoiced because he had been saved from death; that is why he played and rejoiced with his spouse, as we with our helpmate in salvation, the church. The church too has been given the reassuring name "submissive endurance," either because its enduring continues for all eternity in unending joy or because it is formed of the submission of those who believe: of us who are the members of Christ. The testimony given by those who have submissively endured until the end, and their gratitude as well, is a mystical playing; the helpmate of this holy gladness of heart is salvation. The king is Christ,

looking down from above on our rejoicing and "peering through the door," as Scripture says, on our gratitude and benediction that works in us joy and cheerfulness with submission. CHRIST THE EDUCATOR 1.5.21-22.[17]

ISAAC FOLLOWED THE SAME PATH. CHRYSOSTOM: Now Isaac was there a long time. Abimelech looked out of the window and saw him fondling his wife, Rebekah; he summoned him and said to him, "So she is your wife? Why did you say, 'She is my sister?'"[18] Since the good man was unmasked by this evidence, instead of dissembling any further, he admitted it and gave a clear explanation of why he brought himself to call her his sister. He said, "I was afraid I might be killed on her account; the fear of death drove me to this extreme."

Perhaps, however, he had been forewarned, since Isaac's father too had saved his own life by devising such a stratagem, and, for this reason, Isaac followed the same path. The king, however, had a lively memory of what he had suffered in the case of the patriarch for abducting Sarah, and at once he admitted his liability to punishment from on high by saying to him, "Why did you do it? Some one of my people could easily have slept with your wife, whereas you would have had us be in ignorance."[19] This deception, he is saying, we have already undergone at the hands of your father, and in the present case had we not quickly come upon the truth, we were on the verge of undergoing the same. "You would have let us be in ignorance." You see, that time too they were on the verge of sinning through ignorance, and this time you were within a hairsbreadth of causing us to fall into sin out of ignorance. HOMILIES ON GENESIS 51.12-13.[20]

26:11 Abimelech Warned

[15]Gen 20:2, 12. [16]FC 16:152. [17]FC 23:22-23. [18]Gen 26:8-9. [19]Gen 26:10. [20]FC 87:62-63*.

**GOD'S SERVANTS CELEBRATED BY THEIR ENE-
MIES.** CHRYSOSTOM: See God's providence; see
his ineffable care. The One who had said, "Don't
go down into Egypt; stay in this land, and I will
be with you," was the one arranging all this and
putting the good man in such a safe position. I
mean, notice the king going to such trouble to
ensure that he could live in peace and be free from
all concern. After all, Abimelech threatened them
all with death, the text says, "if anyone laid a hand
on him or his wife." You see, since it was the
fear—of death, I mean—that shook Isaac's
resolve, consequently the loving Lord caused him
to be rid of it and from then on to live in complete
security. See the strange and remarkable thing in
the way God, who is creative and wise and transforms everything according to his own wish and
finds means where there are none, brings about in
every way the security of his servants.

Whence was it, after all . . . that this king
showed such care for the good man, as if proclaiming his merits to all the inhabitants of the
city and presenting him as a famous person and
much admired by himself? In this way too Neb-
uchadnezzar, after casting the three children in
the furnace and learning by experience the invincible power of the young men's virtue, began then
to sing their praises and in every way to render
them famous by his own tongue.[21] This, after all,
is a particular index of the abundance of God's
power, when he causes his servants to be celebrated by their enemies. The man who with relish
had the furnace lit and then saw that, on account
of help from on high, the children's virtue survived even the fire's heat, was all at once changed,
and he cried out, "Servants of God the most
high."[22] HOMILIES ON GENESIS 51.14-15.[23]

---

[21]Dan 3. [22]Dan 3:93 in the Greek version of Theodotion. [23]FC 87:63-
64**.

26:12-25 THE WELLS BETWEEN
GERAR AND BEERSHEBA

[12]*And Isaac sowed in that land, and reaped in the same year* a hundredfold. The LORD blessed
him,* [13]*and the man became rich, and gained more and more until he became very wealthy.* [14]*He
had possessions of flocks and herds, and a great household, so that the Philistines envied him.* [15] *(Now
the Philistines had stopped and filled with earth all the wells which his father's servants had dug in
the days of Abraham his father.)* [16]*And Abimelech said to Isaac, "Go away from us; for you are
much mightier than we."*

[17]*So Isaac departed from there, and encamped in the valley of Gerar and dwelt there.* [18]*And
Isaac dug again the wells of water which had been dug in the days of Abraham his father; for the
Philistines had stopped them after the death of Abraham; and he gave them the names which his
father had given them.* [19]*But when Isaac's servants dug in the valley and found there a well of
springing water,* [20]*the herdsmen of Gerar quarreled with Isaac's herdsmen, saying, "The water is
ours." So he called the name of the well Esek,ᵘ because they contended with him.* [21]*Then they dug
another well, and they quarreled over that also; so he called its name Sitnah.ᵛ* [22]*And he moved*

from there and dug another well, and over that they did not quarrel; so he called its name Reho-
both,[w†] *saying, "For now the LORD has made room for us, and we shall be fruitful in the land."*

[23]*From there he went up to Beer-sheba.*[‡] [24]*And the LORD appeared to him the same night and*
said, "I am the God of Abraham your father; fear not, for I am with you and will bless you and
multiply your descendants for my servant Abraham's sake." [25]*So he built an altar there and called*
upon the name of the LORD, and pitched his tent there. And there Isaac's servants dug a well.

u That is *Contention*   v That is *Enmity*   w That is *Broad places* or *Room*   *LXX adds "barley." This allows Origen to make the connection with the use of the word in the
NT.   †LXX, "breadth" or "room enough."   ‡LXX, "the well of the oath."

OVERVIEW: A variant mentioning "barley" in the
Septuagint provides the basis for a spiritual interpretation of the hundredfold. Isaac's greatness
and wealth are applied to the spiritual interpretation of the Scriptures, whose meaning increases.
Likewise the mention of the "wells" can be explained in terms of the spiritual interpretation of
Scripture, while the Philistines, who filled in the
wells, are those who insist on an earthly interpretation. The wells that Abraham dug are the Scriptures of the Old Testament. The new wells are
the wells of the New Testament. All who serve
the word of God are engaged in digging wells.
These wellsprings are already flowing within our
rational selves (ORIGEN). Abimelech's request
that Isaac depart is interpreted as motivated by
envy (CHRYSOSTOM). Isaac undertook to open
wells out of a depth of vision to strengthen the
reasoning faculty of his soul (AMBROSE).

26:12 Isaac Reaps Bountifully

ISAAC REAPED A HUNDREDFOLD. ORIGEN:
And after these things the text says, "Isaac sowed
barley and found a hundredfold. And the Lord
blessed him, and the man was magnified, and by
his progress he became greater until he became
very great."
    Why is it that Isaac "sowed barley" and not
wheat, and [why] is [he] blessed because he sows
"barley," and [why] is [he] magnified "until he
becomes great"? It appears, therefore, that he was
not yet great until after "he sowed barley" and
gathered "a hundredfold." Then he became "very
great."

Barley is the food especially of beasts or of
peasants. For it is a harsher species and would
seem to prick one who touches it as if with some
kind of barbs. Isaac is likened to the Word of
God. This Word sows barley in the law but wheat
in the Gospels. He provides the one food for the
perfect and spiritual, the other for the inexperienced and natural, because it is written, "Men and
beasts you will preserve, O Lord."[1] Isaac, therefore, the Word of the law, sows barley, and yet in
that very barley he finds "fruit a hundredfold."[2]
For even in the law you find martyrs, whose
"fruit" is "a hundredfold."
    But also our Lord, the Isaac of the Gospels,
said certain things that were more perfect to the
apostles, but to the crowds he said things which
were plain and common.[3] But do you wish to see
that even he presents barley to beginners? It is
written in the Gospels that he fed the crowds a
second time.[4] But those whom he feeds the first
time, that is, the beginners, he feeds "with barley
loaves."[5] But later, when they had progressed by
this time in the word and teaching, he presents
them loaves of wheat. HOMILIES ON GENESIS
12.5.[6]

26:13 Isaac's Wealth Grows

ISAAC BECOMES GREAT. ORIGEN: Isaac was
insignificant in the law, but with the passing of
time he becomes great. He becomes great, with

---

[1]Ps 36:6 (35:7 LXX). [2]Mt 13:8. [3]Mt 13:34-35. [4]Mt 15:32-37. [5]Jn
6:9; Mt 14:19. [6]FC 71:181-82.

the passing of time, in the prophets. For while he is in the law alone he is not yet great, since indeed it too is covered with a veil. He grows, therefore, now in the prophets; but when he has arrived at this point that also he may cast aside the veil, then he will be "very great." When the letter of the law has begun to be separated like the chaff of its barley and it has appeared that "the law is spiritual,"[7] then Isaac will be magnified and will become "very great."

For notice that also the Lord in the Gospels breaks a few loaves, and notice how many thousand people he refreshes "and how many baskets" of leftovers remain.[8] While the loaves are whole, no one is filled, no one is refreshed, nor do the loaves themselves appear to be increased. Now consider, therefore, how we break a few loaves: we take up a few words from the divine Scriptures and how many thousand men are filled. But unless those loaves have been broken, unless they have been crumbled into pieces by the disciples, that is, unless the letter has been discussed and broken in little pieces, its meaning cannot reach everyone. But when we have begun to investigate and discuss each single matter, then the crowds indeed will assimilate as much as they shall be able. But what they haven't been able to digest should be gathered and preserved, "lest anything be lost."[9]

We also, therefore, preserve whatever the "crowds" cannot receive and gather it into baskets and hampers. . . . Let us see what fragments we have diligently collected lest they be lost, and what we are preserving in baskets until the Lord command what also should become of them. HOMILIES ON GENESIS 12.5.[10]

LIVING WATER WITHIN YOU. ORIGEN: But now, as much as possible, let us either eat of the bread or draw water from the wells. Let us attempt to do also that which wisdom admonishes, saying, "Drink the waters of your own springs and wells, and let your spring be your own."[11]

Therefore you also attempt, O hearer, to have your own well and your own spring, so that you too, when you take up a book of the Scriptures, may begin even from your own understanding to bring forth some meaning, and in accordance with those things which you have learned in the church, you too attempt to drink from the fountain of your own abilities. You have the nature of "living water" within you.[12] There are within you perennial veins and streams flowing with rational understanding, if only they have not been filled with earth and rubbish. But get busy to dig out your earth and to clean out the filth, that is, to remove the idleness of your natural ability and to cast out the inactivity of your heart. For hear what the Scripture says: "Prick the eye, and it will bring forth a tear; prick the heart, and it brings forth understanding."[13] HOMILIES ON GENESIS 12.5.[14]

ISAAC CULTIVATED VIRTUES. ORIGEN: Do you want to know how "grow" should be understood? Listen to what Isaac did. Scripture says of him, "Isaac progressed and became greater, until he became great, and very much so." His will always tended toward the better and kept making progress. His mind kept contemplating something more divine, and he kept exercising his memory, to store up more in his treasure house and retain it more securely. So this is the way it came about. Isaac cultivated all his virtues in the field of his soul, and thus he fulfilled the command that ordered him to "grow." HOMILIES ON LUKE 11.2.[15]

26:15 Abraham's Wells

THE MYSTERY OF DIGGING THE WELLS OF SCRIPTURE. ORIGEN: And Isaac began, the text says, to dig wells, "wells that his servants had dug in the time of his father Abraham, but the Philistines had stopped them up and filled them with earth." First, therefore, "he dwelt at the well of

---

[7]Rom 7:14. [8]Mt 14:20; 15:37; 16:9. [9]Jn 6:12. [10]FC 71:182-83*. [11]Prov 5:15, 18. [12]Gen 26:19. [13]Sir 22:19. [14]FC 71:183. [15]FC 94:45.

vision,"[16] and having been illuminated by the well of vision, he undertakes to open other wells, and not first new wells but those that his father Abraham had dug.

And when he had dug the first well, "the Philistines," the text says, "were envious of him."[17] But he was not deterred by their envy, nor did he yield to their jealousy. But the text says, "he again dug the wells which the servants of his father Abraham had dug and the Philistines had stopped up after the death of his father Abraham; and he gave them names in accordance with the names which his father had given them."[18] He dug therefore those wells that his father had dug and that had been filled with earth by the malice of the Philistines. He dug also other new wells "in the valley of Gerar," not indeed himself, but his servants, "and he found there," the text says, "a well of living water. But the shepherds of Gerar quarreled with Isaac's shepherds saying the water was theirs. And he called the name of the well 'Injustice.' For they dealt unjustly with him."[19] But Isaac withdraws from their malice and "again dug another well, and for it no less," the text says, "they quarreled, and he called its name 'Enmity.' And he withdrew from there and dug again another well, and they did not quarrel about it; and he called its name 'Breadth,' saying that now God has given us room and has increased us on the earth."[20]

Well does the holy apostle say in a certain passage when considering the magnitude of mysteries: "And for these things who is sufficient?"[21] In a similar way—nay, rather dissimilar by far, to the extent that we are by far inferior to him—we also seeing such great depth in the mysteries of the wells, say, "And for these things who is sufficient?" For who is able worthily to explain either the mysteries of such great wells or of those things that are related to have been done for the wells? Who is able unless we invoke the Father of the living Word and he should deign to put the word in our mouth so that we may be able to draw a little "living water"[22] for you who thirst from those wells which are so copious and numerous? HOMILIES ON GENESIS 13.1.[23]

AN EARTHLY INTERPRETATION OF THE LAW.
ORIGEN: This Isaac, therefore, our Savior, when he has come into that valley of Gerar, first of all wishes to dig those wells that the servants of his father had dug; he wishes to renew the wells of the law, of course, and the prophets, which Philistines had filled with earth.

Who are those who fill the wells with earth? Those, doubtless, who put an earthly and fleshly interpretation on the law and close up the spiritual and mystical interpretation so that neither do they themselves drink nor do they permit others to drink.

Hear our Isaac, the Lord Jesus, saying in the Gospels: "Woe to you, scribes and Pharisees, since you have taken away the key of knowledge, and you yourselves have not entered, nor have you permitted those who wish to enter."[24] Those therefore are the ones who have filled with earth the wells "which the servants of Abraham had dug;" those who teach the law carnally and defile the waters of the Holy Spirit; who hold the wells for this purpose, not that they might bring forth water but that they might put earth in them. Isaac therefore undertakes to dig these wells. And let us see how he digs them.

When the servants of Isaac, who are the apostles of our Lord, were passing through grain fields on the sabbath, Scripture says, "they plucked the ears and ate, rubbing them in their hands."[25] At that time, therefore, those who had filled his father's wells with earth said to him, "Behold, your disciples are doing that which is not lawful on the sabbath day."[26] In order to dig out their earthly understanding, Jesus says to them, "Have you not read what David did when he was hungry, and those who were with him, how he went in to Abiathar the priest and ate the consecrated bread, he and his servants, which it was not lawful to eat but for the priests only?"[27] And he adds these words: "If you knew what this means: 'I desire

---

[16]Gen 26:11. [17]Gen 26:14. [18]Gen 26:18. [19]Gen 26:19-20. [20]Gen 26:21-22. [21]2 Cor 2:16. [22]Cf. Gen 26:19. [23]FC 71:185-86. [24]Mt 23:13; cf. Lk 11:52. [25]Lk 6:1. [26]Mt 12:2. [27]Mt 12:3-4.

mercy and not sacrifice,' you would certainly never have condemned the innocent."[28] But what do those men reply to these words? They quarrel with his servants and say, "This man is not of God who does not keep the sabbath."[29] In this way, therefore, Isaac dug the wells "which the servants of his father had dug." HOMILIES ON GENESIS 13.2.[30]

ISAAC DUG NEW WELLS AND OLD. ORIGEN: Isaac therefore digs also new wells; no, rather, Isaac's servants dig them. Isaac's servants are Matthew, Mark, Luke, John; his servants are Peter, James, Jude; the apostle Paul is Isaac's servant. These all dig the wells of the New Testament. But those who "mind earthly things"[31] nor permit new things to be established nor old things to be cleansed also quarrel for these wells. They oppose the gospel wells; they resist the apostolic wells. And since they oppose in all things, since they quarrel in all things, it is said to them, "Since you have made yourselves unworthy of God's grace, henceforth now we go to the Gentiles."[32] HOMILIES ON GENESIS 13.2.[33]

26:16 Isaac Sent Away

ENVY CANNOT ACCEPT ANOTHER'S SUCCESS. CHRYSOSTOM: Consider the degree of evil of those inhabitants such as even to begrudge the good man water. Not even the king, despite his having so much wealth, could withstand the impulse of envy but said, "Depart from us, because you have become far too powerful for us." What terrible malice; why, in fact, are you driving the good man off? Surely Isaac caused your subjects no harm? Surely he did no wrong? But that is what envy is like: It does nothing out of calm reason. I mean, on seeing the good man enjoying such favor from the God of all, Abimelech should rather have respected him, should rather have shown him honor so as himself to win favor from on high because of the honor shown him. But instead of doing that, he even tried to drive him off, saying, "Depart from us, because you have

become far too powerful for us."

That is what envy is like, after all: It cannot simply accept others' success but instead regards the neighbor's prosperity as a disaster for itself and is devastated by the neighbor's good fortune. That is precisely what happened here: having authority over the whole city and holding everyone in his thrall, the king said to this nomad, this vagrant, wandering hither and yon, "Depart from us, because you have become far too powerful for us." Isaac really was more powerful, with help from above in every circumstance and protected by God's right hand. HOMILIES ON GENESIS 52.6-7.[34]

26:19 A Well in a Valley

THE PHILISTINES FILL THE WELLS WITH EARTH. ORIGEN: For who is able worthily to explain either the mysteries of such great wells or of those things that are related to have been done for the wells, unless we invoke the Father of the living Word and he should deign to put the word in our mouth so that we may be able to draw a little "living water" for you who thirst from those wells which are so copious and numerous?

There are, therefore, wells that the servants of Abraham dug, but the Philistines had filled these with earth. Isaac therefore undertakes first to clear these wells. The Philistines hate water; they love earth. Isaac loves water; he is always seeking wells; he cleans old wells, he opens new ones.

Consider our Isaac, who "has been offered as a sacrifice for us,"[35] coming into the valley of Gerar, which means "wall" or "hedge." [He is] coming, I say, that "he might destroy the middle wall of hedge, the enmities, in his flesh."[36] [He is] coming to remove the wall that is between us and the heavenly virtues, that he might make "both one"[37] and carry back to the mountains[38] "on his shoulder" the lamb which had strayed and restore it to

---

[28]Mt 12:7; Hos 6:6. [29]Jn 9:16. [30]FC 71:187-88*. [31]Phil 3:19. [32]Acts 13:46; 18:6. [33]FC 71:188. [34]FC 87:68-69*. [35]Eph 5:2. [36]Eph 2:14. [37]Eph 2:14. [38]Mt 18:12.

the other "ninety-nine which had not strayed."[39] HOMILIES ON GENESIS 13.1-2.[40]

FOUNTAINS OF FAITH. AMBROSE: For Abraham dug wells and Isaac too—that is, the mighty patriarchs—and Jacob also, as we find in the Gospel,[41] as if they were fountains of the human race, and specifically fountains of faith and devotion. For what is a well of living water but a depth of profound instruction? On this account Hagar saw the angel by a well[42] and Jacob found his wife Rachel by a well;[43] Moses too earned the first rewards of his future marriage beside a well.[44] Therefore Isaac undertook to open wells out of a depth of vision and in good order, so that the water of his well might first wash and strengthen the reasoning faculty of the soul and its eye, to make its sight clearer. ISAAC, OR THE SOUL 4.21-22.[45]

26:22 Isaac's New Well, Rehoboth

THE SERVANTS OF ISAAC DUG WELLS. ORIGEN: After these things, then, Isaac dug a third well and "called the name of that place 'Room-Enough,' saying, 'Now the Lord has given us room and has increased us on the earth.' "[46] For truly now Isaac is given room and his name is increased on all the earth since he has fulfilled for us the knowledge of the Trinity. For then "God was known" only "in Judea"[47] and his name was named in Israel, but now "their sound has gone forth into all the earth and their words into the ends of the world."[48] For the servants of Isaac going throughout the whole world have dug wells and have shown "the living water"[49] to all, "baptizing all the nations in the name of the Father and of the Son and of the Holy Spirit."[50] For "the earth is the Lord's and the fullness thereof."[51] HOMILIES ON GENESIS 13.3.[52]

THE SERVANT OF THE WORD SEEKS LIVING WATER. ORIGEN: But also each of us who serves the Word of God digs wells and seeks "living water," from which he may renew his hearers. If,

therefore, I too shall begin to discuss the words of the ancients and to seek in them a spiritual meaning, if I shall have attempted to remove the veil of the law and to show that the things which have been written are "allegorical,"[53] I am indeed digging wells. But immediately the friends of the letter will stir up malicious charges against me and will lie in ambush for me. They will contrive immediately hostilities and persecutions, denying that the truth can stand except upon earth.

But if we are servants of Isaac, let us love "wells of living water" and springs. Let us withdraw from those who are contentious and contrive malicious charges and leave them in the earth, which they love. But let us never cease digging "wells of living water." And by discussing now indeed things that are old and again things that are new, let us become like that scribe in the Gospel, of whom the Lord said, "He brings forth from his treasures new things and old."[54] HOMILIES ON GENESIS 13.3.[55]

THE WELLS ABRAHAM DUG. ORIGEN: So therefore the wells that Abraham dug, that is, the Scriptures of the Old Testament, have been filled with earth by the Philistines, or evil teachers, scribes and Pharisees, or even hostile powers; and their veins have been stopped up lest they provide a drink for these who are of Abraham. For that people cannot drink from the Scriptures but suffer a "thirst for the word of God"[56] until Isaac should come and open them that his servants may drink. Thanks therefore to Christ, the son of Abraham—of whom it is written, "The book of the generation of Jesus Christ, the son of David, the son of Abraham"[57]—who has come and opened the wells for us. For he opened them for those men who said, "Was not our heart burning in us when he opened to us the Scriptures?"[58] He

---

[39]Lk 15:5-6. [40]FC 71:186-87*. [41]Jn 4:6, 12. [42]Gen 21:14. [43]Gen 29:2, 9-10. [44]Ex 2:15-22. [45]FC 65:24. [46]Gen 26:22. [47]Ps 76:1 (75:2 LXX). [48]Ps 19:4 (18:5 LXX). [49]Gen 26:19. [50]Mt 28:19. [51]Ps 24:1 (23:1 LXX). [52]FC 71:188-89. [53]Gal 4:24. [54]Mt 13:52. [55]FC 71:189. [56]Amos 8:11. [57]Mt 1:1. [58]Lk 24:32.

opened therefore these wells and "called them," the text says, "as his father Abraham had called them."[59] For he did not change the names of the wells.

And it is astonishing that Moses is called Moses even among us, and each of the prophets is addressed by his own name. For Christ did not change the names in the Scriptures but the understanding. And he changes it there that now later we might not pay attention "to Jewish fables"[60] and "endless genealogies,"[61] because "they turn their hearing away from the truth indeed but are turned to fables."[62]

Christ opened therefore the wells and taught us, that we might not seek God in some one place but might know that "sacrifice is offered to his name in every land."[63] For it is now that time "when the true worshipers worship the Father" neither in Jerusalem nor on Mt. Gerazim "but in spirit and truth."[64] God therefore dwells neither in a place nor in a land, but he dwells in the heart. And if you are seeking the place of God, a pure heart is his place. For he says that he will dwell in this place when he says through the prophet, "I will dwell in them and walk in them; and they shall be my people, and I will be their God," says the Lord.[65] HOMILIES ON GENESIS 13.3.[66]

EACH SOUL CONTAINS A WELL. ORIGEN: Consider therefore that perhaps even in the soul of each of us there is "a well of living water," there is a kind of heavenly perception and latent image of God, and the Philistines, that is, hostile powers, have filled this well with earth. With what kind of earth? With carnal perceptions and earthly thoughts, and for that reason "we have borne the image of the earthly."[67] At that time, therefore, when we were bearing "the image of the earthly," the Philistines filled our wells. But now, since our Isaac has come, let us receive his advent and dig our wells. Let us cast the earth from them. Let us purge them from all filth and from all muddy and earthly thoughts, and let us discover in them that "living water" that the Lord mentions: "He who believes in me, from within him shall flow rivers

of living water."[68] Behold how great the Lord's liberality is: the Philistines filled our wells and hindered our small and trifling veins of water, and in place of these, springs and rivers are restored to us.

If therefore you also hearing these words today should faithfully perceive what is said, Isaac would work also in you; he would cleanse your hearts from earthly perceptions. And seeing these mysteries that are so great to be lying hidden in the divine Scriptures, you progress in understanding, you progress in spiritual perceptions. You yourselves will also begin to be teachers, and "rivers of living water" will proceed from you.[69] For the Word of God is present, and this now is his work, that he might remove the earth from the soul of each of you and open your spring. For he is within you and does not come from without, just as "also the kingdom of God is within you."[70] HOMILIES ON GENESIS 13.3-4.[71]

A DEPTH OF VISION. AMBROSE: Now Isaac reopened many wells that his father had dug, but strangers had filled them after the death of his father Abraham. Beyond the others he dug the following wells: one in the valley of Gerar, and he found there a well of living water; and the shepherds of Gerar disputed with Isaac's shepherds, because they claimed the water of this well as their own, and he called its name "Injustice." And he dug another well over which a quarrel arose, and he called it "Enmity." And he dug a third well, over which no dispute began among the shepherds, and he called it "Room Enough." He also dug a well and did not find water in it and called that well "Well of the Oath." Would anyone reading of these things consider that those works were earthly rather than spiritual? ISAAC, OR THE SOUL 4.20-21.[72]

26:24 The God of Abraham

[59]Gen 26:18. [60]Tit 1:14. [61]1 Tim 1:4. [62]2 Tim 4:4. [63]Mal 1:11. [64]Jn 4:20-23. [65]2 Cor 6:16; Lev 26:12. [66]FC 71:190-91*. [67]1 Cor 15:49. [68]Jn 7:38. [69]Jn 7:38. [70]Lk 17:21. [71]FC 71:191-92. [72]FC 65:23-24.

THE WORD IN THE LAW OR THE PROPHETS.
ORIGEN: As therefore the Lord himself accommodates his form in correspondence to the place and time and certain individual conditions, so also the saints, who prefigured him, should be believed to have represented types of mysteries in correspondence to places and times and conditions. [This] also we see now to be the case in Isaac, of whom we have heard it read, "He went up," the text says, "from there to the well of the oath, and the Lord appeared to him that night and said, I am the God of Abraham your father; fear not. For I am with you, and I will bless you and multiply your seed because of Abraham your father."[73]

The apostle Paul set forth two figures of this Isaac to us. One, about which he said that Ishmael indeed, the son of Hagar, represented the people according to the flesh, but Isaac the people who are of faith.[74] The other, about which he said, "He did not say, and to his seeds, as of many, but to his seed, as of one, which is Christ."[75] Isaac therefore represents the people and Christ. Now it is certain that Christ is spoken of as the Word of God not only in the Gospels but also in the law and prophets. But in the law he teaches beginners; in the Gospels he teaches the perfect. And Isaac therefore represents now the Word that is in the law or the prophets. HOMILIES ON GENESIS 14.1.[76]

THE INCREASE OF THE PROPHETS. ORIGEN: We have also already said previously that the embellishment of the temple and of those divine services which were performed therein was an ascent of the law. The increase of the prophets also can be called an ascent of the law. And for this reason perhaps Isaac is said to have gone up to the well of the oath and there the Lord is said to have appeared to him. For through the prophets "the Lord has sworn and he will not repent, that he is a priest forever according to the order of Melchizedek."[77] God appeared to him, therefore, "at the well of the oath" confirming the fulfillment of the promises made to him. HOMILIES ON GENESIS 14.2.[78]

26:25 Isaac Builds an Altar

ISAAC'S TENT WILL BE FOLDED. ORIGEN: Isaac builds indeed an altar even now in the law and pitches his tent, but in the Gospels he does not pitch a tent but builds a house and establishes a foundation. For hear Wisdom saying of the church: "Wisdom," Scripture says, "has built herself a house and has set up seven columns."[79] Hear Paul also saying about this: "For no man can lay a foundation but that which is laid, which is Christ Jesus."[80]

Where, therefore, there is a tent, even if it should be pitched, it is doubtless to be folded up. But where there are foundations and a house is built "upon a rock," that house is never destroyed, "for it has been founded on a rock."[81] Nevertheless Isaac digs a well there too, nor does he ever cease digging wells until "the fountain of living water"[82] arises and "the stream of the river makes the city of God joyful."[83] HOMILIES ON GENESIS 14.2.[84]

---

[73]Gen 26:23-24. [74]Gal 4:22. [75]Gal 3:16. [76]FC 71:197. [77]Ps 110:4 (109:4 LXX). [78]FC 71:197-98. [79]Prov 9:1. [80]1 Cor 3:11. [81]Mt 7:24-25. [82]Gen 26:19. [83]Ps 46:4 (45:5 LXX). [84]FC 71:198.

26:26-35 THE ALLIANCE WITH ABIMELECH

[26]Then Abimelech went to him from Gerar with Ahuzzath his adviser and Phicol the commander of his army. [27]Isaac said to them, "Why have you come to me, seeing that you hate me and have sent me away from you?" [28]They said, "We see plainly that the LORD is with you; so we say, let there be an oath between you and us, and let us make a covenant with you, [29]that you will do us no harm, just as we have not touched you and have done to you nothing but good and have sent you away in peace. You are now the blessed of the LORD." [30]So he made them a feast, and they ate and drank. [31]In the morning they rose early and took oath with one another; and Isaac set them on their way, and they departed from him in peace. [32]That same day Isaac's servants came and told him about the well which they had dug, and said to him, "We have found water." [33]He called it Shibah; therefore the name of the city is Beer-sheba to this day.

[34]When Esau was forty years old, he took to wife Judith the daughter of Be-eri the Hittite, and Basemath the daughter of Elon the Hittite; [35]and they made life bitter for Isaac and Rebekah.

OVERVIEW: Abimelech represents the learned and wise of this world, philosophy that is neither opposed to everything in the law of God nor in harmony with everything. The three figures of Abimelech, Ahuzzath and Phicol represent all of philosophy. The great feast of understanding awaits those who search the Scriptures (ORIGEN). Isaac yielded to those who drove him out and received them again when they were sorry (AMBROSE). Esau reveals his indiscretion and lack of discipline (CHRYSOSTOM).

26:26 Abimelech Went to Isaac

PHILOSOPHY AND THE WORD. ORIGEN: This Abimelech, as I see it, does not always have peace with Isaac, but sometimes he disagrees, at other times he seeks peace. If you remember how, in what precedes, we said of Abimelech that he represents the learned and wise of the world who have comprehended many things even of the truth through the learning of philosophy, you can understand how he can be neither always in dissension nor always at peace with Isaac, who represents the Word of God in the law. For philosophy is neither opposed to everything in the law of God nor in harmony with everything.

For many of the philosophers write that there is one God who has created all things. In this they agree with the law of God. Some also have added this, that God made and rules all things by his Word and it is the Word of God by which all things are directed. In this they write in harmony not only with the law but also with the Gospels. Indeed, almost the total philosophy that is called moral and natural holds the same views we do. But it disagrees with us when it says matter is co-eternal with God. It disagrees when it denies that God is concerned about mortal things but that his providence is confined beyond the spaces of the lunar sphere. They disagree with us when they appraise the lives of those being born by the courses of the stars. They disagree when they say this world is permanent and is to have no end. But there are also many other things in which they either disagree with us or are in harmony. And therefore in accordance with this figure, Abimelech is sometimes described as being at peace with Isaac and sometimes as disagreeing. HOMILIES ON GENESIS 14.3.[1]

THESE THREE REPRESENT ALL PHILOSOPHY. ORIGEN: But also I do not think that this was of idle concern to the Holy Spirit, who writes these things, to relate that two others "came with Abimelech, that is, "Ahuzzath his kinsman and Phicol the leader of his army."

Now Ahuzzath means "containing" and Phicol "the mouth of all," but Abimelech himself means "my father is king." These three, in my opinion, figuratively represent all philosophy, which is divided into three parts among them: logic, physics, ethics, that is, rational, natural, moral. The rational is that which acknowledges God to be Father of all, that is, Abimelech. The natural is that which is fixed and contains all things, as depending on the forces of nature itself, which Ahuzzath, which means "containing," professes to be. The moral is that which is in the mouth of all and pertains to all and is situated in the mouth of all because of the likeness of the common precepts. Phicol, which means "the mouth of all," signifies this.

All these therefore come to the law of God in the learning of instructions of this kind and say, "We certainly saw that the Lord is with you, and we said, 'Let there be an oath between us and you and let us establish a covenant with you, lest you do evil with us, but as we have not cursed you, so also you are blessed by the Lord.' "[2]

Those three, who seek peace from the Word of God and desire to anticipate his fellowship with a covenant, can indeed represent the magi who come from parts of the East learned in the books of their fathers and in the instruction of their ancestors and say, "We certainly saw"[3] "the one born king,"[4] "and we have seen that God is with him,"[5] "and we have come to worship him."[6]

But also if there is anyone who has been instructed in learning of this kind, seeing that "God was in Christ reconciling the world to himself"[7] and who has admired the majesty of his works, let him say, "We certainly saw that the Lord is

with you, and we said, 'Let there be an oath between us.' "[8] For approaching the law of God he says necessarily, "I have sworn and am determined that I shall keep your commandments."[9] HOMILIES ON GENESIS 14.3.[10]

26:30 Isaac Provides a Feast

A GREAT FEAST OF UNDERSTANDING. ORIGEN: For it is certain that he who serves the Word "is debtor to the wise and the unwise."[11] Because, therefore, he is producing a feast for the wise, for this reason it is said that "he made" not a small but "a great feast."

And you, if you should not still be "a little child" and in need of "milk" but should bring your "senses exercised"[12] and should come more capable to an understanding of the Word of God after very much instruction has been set before you, there will also be "a great feast" for you. The "vegetables" of the weak[13] will not be prepared for you as food, nor will you be nourished with milk with which "little children" are nourished, but the servant of the Word will make a "great feast" for you. He will speak to you the "wisdom" that is offered "among the perfect." He will offer you the "wisdom of God hidden in a mystery, which none of the princes of this world knew."[14] He will reveal Christ to you in this respect, that in him "all the treasures of wisdom are hidden."[15]

He makes you therefore "a great feast," and he himself eats with you if he should not find you to be such that he should say to you, "I could not speak to you as to spiritual, but as to carnal, as to little ones in Christ."[16]

He says this to the Corinthians, to which he also adds, "For when there are contentions and dissensions among you, are you not carnal and walk in a human way?"[17] Paul did not "make a great feast" for these, insofar that when he was

---

[1]FC 71:198-99. [2]Gen 26:28-29. [3]Gen 26:28. [4]Mt 2:2. [5]Gen 26:28. [6]Mt 2:2. [7]2 Cor 5:19. [8]Gen 26:28. [9]Ps 119:106 (118:106 LXX). [10]FC 71:199-201*. [11]Rom 1:14. [12]Heb 5:12-14. [13]Rom 14:2. [14]1 Cor 2:6-8. [15]Col 2:3. [16]1 Cor 3:1-2. [17]1 Cor 3:3.

with them and was in need, he was a burden to no one. Nor did he eat bread he did not pay for from anyone, but laboring night and day, his own hands served himself and all who were with him.[18] The Corinthians therefore were so far from having a "great feast" that the preacher of the Word of God could have not even the least or a little feast with them.

But there is a great feast for those who know how to hear more perfectly, who bring their "senses" instructed and "exercised"[19] for hearing the Word of God. HOMILIES ON GENESIS 14.4.[20]

READY FORGIVENESS. AMBROSE: Let us imitate Isaac's goodness; let us imitate his purity. Isaac was certainly a good and virtuous man, devoted to God and faithful to his wife. He did not return evil for evil. He yielded to those who drove him out, but he received them again when they were sorry, being neither harsh to insolence nor obdurate to kindness. When he went away from others, he fled to avoid strife. When he received them again, he readily forgave them, and he was exceptionally kind when he pardoned. Men sought to associate with him, and he added a delightful feast. ON HIS BROTHER, SATYRUS 2.99.[21]

26:35 Esau's Wives

ESAU'S UNDISCIPLINED CHARACTER. CHRYSOSTOM: See how much can be learned from these few words. I mean, why did it indicate to us Esau's age? Not idly, but for us to learn from it Isaac's advanced years and the fact that he was now well beyond his prime. You see, if we recall what was said before, that at the time he married Rebekah he was in fact forty years old, whereas when the children were born he was sixty, we will realize that now at a hundred he had reached the height of old age. Since, in fact, it is next about to recount to us that because of his age he had poor eyesight, accordingly it indicates his age to us so that we might be in a position to know precisely Isaac's time of life. So it said, "Now, Esau was forty."

Then for us to learn the boy's indiscretion in taking brides from races he should not have, it revealed to us that one was from the race of the Hittites, the other from the Hivites.[22] Yet knowing as Esau did the pains taken by the patriarch in giving express orders to his servant to select a bride for Isaac from his own tribe and the fact that their mother Rebekah came from Haran, he should not have set his mind on any such thing. In order, however, to show from the outset the undisciplined character of Esau's behavior, he took those wives before seeking advice. And for us to learn their intractable nature Scripture says, "They were at odds with Isaac and Rebekah." What could be more galling than this antipathy when they were due to show complete respect and not only did not do this but were even prepared for hostility? HOMILIES ON GENESIS 53.1-2.[23]

---

[18]1 Cor 4:12; 2 Thess 3:8. [19]Heb 5:14. [20]FC 71:201-2*. [21]FC 22:241-42. [22]LXX reads "the Evaios" (Hivite) for the second wife. Hebrew reads "Hittite" for both. [23]FC 87:79-80*.

27:1-17 JACOB'S DECEPTION

[1]*When Isaac was old and his eyes were dim so that he could not see, he called Esau his older son, and said to him, "My son"; and he answered, "Here I am."* [2]*He said, "Behold, I am old; I do not know the day of my death.* [3]*Now then, take your weapons, your quiver and your bow, and go*

out to the field, and hunt game for me, ⁴and prepare for me savory food, such as I love, and bring it to me that I may eat; that I may bless you before I die."

⁵Now Rebekah was listening when Isaac spoke to his son Esau. So when Esau went to the field to hunt for game and bring it, ⁶Rebekah said to her son Jacob, "I heard your father speak to your brother Esau, ⁷'Bring me game, and prepare for me savory food, that I may eat it, and bless you before the LORD before I die.' ⁸Now therefore, my son, obey my word as I command you. ⁹Go to the flock, and fetch me two good kids, that I may prepare from them savory food for your father, such as he loves; ¹⁰and you shall bring it to your father to eat, so that he may bless you before he dies." ¹¹But Jacob said to Rebekah his mother, "Behold, my brother Esau is a hairy man, and I am a smooth man. ¹²Perhaps my father will feel me, and I shall seem to be mocking him, and bring a curse upon myself and not a blessing." ¹³His mother said to him, "Upon me be your curse, my son; only obey my word, and go, fetch them to me." ¹⁴So he went and took them and brought them to his mother; and his mother prepared savory food, such as his father loved. ¹⁵Then Rebekah took the best garments of Esau her older son, which were with her in the house, and put them on Jacob her younger son; ¹⁶and the skins of the kids she put upon his hands and upon the smooth part of his neck; ¹⁷and she gave the savory food and the bread, which she had prepared, into the hand of her son Jacob.

OVERVIEW: The deception practiced by Rebekah and Jacob posed a considerable problem for interpreters, since it could hardly be accepted at face value in the light of New Testament teaching. One solution was to interpret it allegorically or prophetically. For example, Isaac's request to Esau that he prepare him a meal signifies the call of the Word to the first people (HIPPOLYTUS). The story could also be read as an edifying moral tale in which virtue triumphs and a mother's affection is demonstrated (CHRYSOSTOM). Another possibility was to interpret the story as a prophetical allegory in which Esau's garments symbolize the "the likeness of sinful flesh" taken on by Christ, while Jacob's smooth skin represents the sinless character of Christ's flesh (HIPPOLYTUS, QUODVULTDEUS). Rebekah's order to Jacob to fetch two small goats prefigures the future activity of the church, as does her acceptance of the curse that would fall on Jacob (HIPPOLYTUS). In a different allegorical interpretation Esau's garments are interpreted as the clothing of the Old Testament put on by the Christian people represented by Jacob (AMBROSE).

27:3 Isaac's Request of Esau

THE CALL OF THE WORD. HIPPOLYTUS: The fact that the prophet asks Esau for food by giving him an order signifies the call that the Word addresses to the first people when he asks them for the fruit of the works of justice, that justice which was considered to be a nourishment for the Father.[1] In fact, the words "go out to the field, and hunt game for me" signify worldly life. On the other hand, the fact that he says, "Take your quiver and your bow" shows that the people, inflated with their personal glory, would not be justified by their faith but by being proud of their wars would ask for a tyrant as their king,[2] just as Moses had said to them: "And the sword is your boast."[3] ON THE BLESSINGS OF ISAAC AND JACOB 3.[4]

GOD'S INEFFABLE WISDOM. CHRYSOSTOM: Notice in this, dearly beloved, God's ineffable wisdom: Whereas the father gave evidence of natural

---

[1]See Jn 4:32-34. [2]See 1 Sam 8:9-20. [3]Deut 33:29 LXX. [4]PO 27:12.

affection by giving these directions to Esau, the wise and resourceful Lord caused his own prediction to be brought to pass by means of Rebekah, thus teaching us the power of virtue and mildness of manner. I mean, one son considered himself to hold pride of place by birthright and by his father's preference for him, and yet he was suddenly found to be bereft of all this. The other son, on the contrary, being endowed with homely virtues and enjoying the help of favor from above, won his father's blessing against his will. Nothing is more powerful than the person helped by that mighty right hand.

In any case, look carefully at all this so as to learn the extraordinary nature of God's designs: One man enjoyed favor from that source and was accorded great cooperation in everything so that the father's blessing was transferred to him. The other lost everything, forfeiting what was his because of the evil of his ways. HOMILIES ON GENESIS 53.3-4.[5]

27:8 Isaac's Command

A MYSTICAL PLOT MADE WITH PROPHETICAL ART. QUODVULTDEUS: I will try to explain briefly how wonderful, great and full of mysteries according to the promises of God are the events that occurred in these two twins. Isaac, their father, who had become blind in his physical eyes while his interior light continued to shine, promised Esau, his firstborn son, to give him the blessing, if he would prepare a tasteful dish of game for him.[6] And Esau immediately hurried to carry out what had been ordered. The mother, who had heard the promise of the blessing for the elder brother, since she was divinely inspired, prepared a mystical plot made with prophetical art in order to direct the blessing to Jacob, the younger son. She took the garments of the firstborn son that she had at home, and dressed the younger brother with them, and put skins of young goats on his arms and his naked neck and dressed him in such a way that who he was would not be recognized.[7] And this symbolical action in a sense shows us the Christ: he did not take the sinful flesh but "the likeness of sinful flesh"[8] by receiving also the law of the Old Testament as the garments of the firstborn, since the Lord said that he had come not in order to abolish the law, but in order to accomplish it.[9] In this attire Jacob, the younger son, who had already taken away from his brother the right of primogeniture, also gets hold of the blessing. BOOK OF PROMISES AND PREDICTIONS OF GOD 1.21.28.[10]

THIS IS A MOTHER'S LOVE. CHRYSOSTOM: See a mother's affection, or rather God's designs: He it was who prompted her to make plans and also made sure all turned out well. Do you see the mother's excellent planning? See also Jacob's circumspection in showing his mildness of manner in his reply. "He replied to his mother, 'My brother Esau is hairy, whereas my skin is smooth. Perhaps my father may touch me, and I will appear ridiculous to him and bring on myself a curse, and not blessing' "[11] Remarkable the child's dutifulness and his respect for his father: "I am afraid," he says. "My efforts may have the contrary effect. I may seem out of step with my father's wishes and win a curse instead of a blessing." So what does Rebekah do, this extraordinary woman of great affection? Since she was not concocting this only out of her own thinking but was also implementing the prediction from on high, she took every care to banish fear from the child and instill courage so as to bring off the plan. Instead of promising him that he would be able to deceive his father and elude detection, what did she say? "Let the curse on you fall on me, child; just heed my word, and go and fetch it for me."[12] "Even if anything like this should happen," she is saying, "you personally will suffer no harm. So don't be afraid: Take heart, 'heed my word,' and do what I advise you." This really is a mother's love, readily accepting everything for her child's sake. HOMILIES ON GENESIS 53.5.[13]

---

[5]FC 87:80-81. [6]Gen 27:1-4. [7]Gen 27:5-16. [8]Rom 8:3. [9]See Mt 5:17. [10]SC 101:214-16. [11]Gen 27:11-12. [12]Gen 27:13. [13]FC 87:81-82.

27:9 Food Prepared for Isaac

TENDER AND BEAUTIFUL. HIPPOLYTUS: On the one hand, Rebekah, who bears the image of the church, already prefigures the future events that would be accomplished through her younger son. She says to him, "Go to the pasture of the sheep, and fetch me from there two small, tender and beautiful young goats." Esau is sent to the plain as if he lived abroad in the world; but Jacob is sent [to the pasture] of the sheep, in order that the words of the Lord, "I have been sent only to the lost sheep of Israel,"[14] might come true.

On the other hand, by saying, "Fetch me from there two small, tender and beautiful young goats," she signified the two calls that appear to have been addressed by the Gospel. In fact, even though we are originally goats, because we are all sinners, through obedience we become tender and beautiful, justified by faith in Christ. No more [are we] like condemned goats[15] but like sheep in pure sacrifice, in "sweet savor,"[16] offered to God and made nourishment for the Word, who gives similes their full accomplishment by saying to his disciples, "I have food to eat that you do not know."[17] ON THE BLESSINGS OF ISAAC AND JACOB 4.[18]

27:11 A Smooth Man

THE SINLESS CHARACTER OF THE LORD. HIPPOLYTUS: How clearly Jacob has shown here his piety! . . . In other respects it was also true what was said by Jacob, that is: "My brother Esau is a hairy man," that is, a sinner, "but I am a man of smooth skin." In fact, through these words the faultless and sinless character of the flesh of the Lord is revealed. ON THE BLESSINGS OF ISAAC AND JACOB 5.[19]

27:13 Rebekah's Command

FULFILLED IN THE CHURCH. HIPPOLYTUS: We can see that the words spoken by Rebekah a long time ago have now been fulfilled in the church.

The words "Let your curse be on me, my son" show that now certain people offend the church by their blasphemies, because she worships the Crucified, and for that reason they throw curses and contempt at us. In fact, the passion of the Lord is held to be a curse for the unbelievers, whereas his life is peace for those who believe.[20] The apostle says, "Christ redeemed us from the curse of the law by becoming a curse for us."[21] That is what the Savior has now accomplished by receiving in himself, through his body, death on the cross. By his obedience he has erased the curse of Adam, which was received in the law: "You are dust, and to dust you shall return."[22] ON THE BLESSINGS OF ISAAC AND JACOB 5.[23]

27:15 Rebekah Disguised Jacob

CHRIST HAS BORNE OUR SINS. HIPPOLYTUS: The fact that Jacob wears the robe signifies that the Word has been clothed by the flesh, while the skins of the kids wrapped around his arms show that he has received in himself all our sins by stretching his hands and arms on the cross, as Isaiah himself has said: "He has borne our sins and carried our diseases."[24] ON THE BLESSINGS OF ISAAC AND JACOB 6.[25]

THE BEST GARMENTS OF ESAU. AMBROSE: Accordingly Jacob received his brother's clothing, because he excelled the elder in wisdom. Thus the younger brother took the clothing of the elder because he was conspicuous in the merit of his faith. Rebekah presented this clothing as a symbol of the church; she gave to the younger son the clothing of the Old Testament, the prophetic and priestly clothing, the royal Davidic clothing, the clothing of the kings Solomon and Hezekiah and Josiah. She gave it too to the Christian people, who would know how to use the garment they had received, since the Jewish people kept it with-

---

[14]Mt 15:24. [15]Mt 25:32. [16]Gen 8:21. [17]Jn 4:32. [18]PO 27:14. [19]PO 27:16. [20]Rom 8:6. [21]Gal 3:13. [22]Gen 3:19. [23]PO 27:18. [24]Is 53:4-5. [25]PO 27:20.

out using it and did not know its proper adornments. This clothing was lying in shadow, cast off and forgotten; it was tarnished by a dark haze of impiety and could not be unfolded further in their confined hearts. The Christian people put it on, and it shone brightly. They made it bright with the splendor of their faith and the light of their holy works. Isaac recognized the familiar fragrance that attached to his people.[26] He recognized the clothing of the Old Testament, but the voice of the people of old he did not recognize; therefore he knew that it had been changed. For even today the same clothing remains, but the confession of a people of greater devotion begins to sound harmonious; Isaac was right to say, "The voice indeed is the voice of Jacob, but the hands are the hands of Esau."[27] And Isaac "smelled the fragrance of his garments."[28] And perhaps that means that we are not justified by works but by faith, because the weakness of the flesh is a hindrance to works, but the brightness of faith puts the error that is in humanity's deeds in the shadow and merits for us the forgiveness of our sins. JACOB AND THE HAPPY LIFE 2.2.9.[29]

IT WAS ALL DUE TO GRACE FROM ABOVE.
CHRYSOSTOM: Notice here, I ask you, along with Rebekah's affection, her great wisdom as well.

Since it was mentioned previously that one was hairy and the other smooth-skinned, she clad him in Esau's clothing, the text says, and covered his skin, disguising him all over so as to bring off the deception. And after putting the food and bread into Jacob's hands she had him take it to his father.

Consider here again, I ask you, how it was all due to grace from above. I mean, whereas we contribute our utmost, we enjoy in generous measure as well cooperation from God. You see, in case we show indifference and prove recalcitrant, he wants us also to make an effort so that in this way our contribution may be demonstrated. It is neither the case that everything is due to help from on high (rather we, too, must contribute something), nor on the other hand does he require everything of us, knowing as he does the extraordinary degree of our limitations. On the contrary, out of fidelity to his characteristic love and wishing to find some occasion for demonstrating his own generosity, he awaits the contribution of what we have to offer. HOMILIES ON GENESIS 53.6-7.[30]

---

[26]Gen 27:27. [27]Gen 27:22. [28]Gen 27:27. [29]FC 65:150-51*. [30]FC 87:82-83*.

27:18-29 JACOB RECEIVES THE BLESSING FROM ISAAC

[18]*So he went in to his father, and said, "My father"; and he said, "Here I am; who are you, my son?"* [19]*Jacob said to his father, "I am Esau your first-born. I have done as you told me; now sit up and eat of my game, that you may bless me."* [20]*But Isaac said to his son, "How is it that you have found it so quickly, my son?" He answered, "Because the LORD your God granted me success."* [21]*Then Isaac said to Jacob, "Come near, that I may feel you, my son, to know whether you are really my son Esau or not."* [22]*So Jacob went near to Isaac his father, who felt him and said, "The*

voice is Jacob's voice, but the hands are the hands of Esau." [23]*And he did not recognize him, because his hands were hairy like his brother Esau's hands; so he blessed him.* [24]*He said, "Are you really my son Esau?" He answered, "I am."* [25]*Then he said, "Bring it to me, that I may eat of my son's game and bless you." So he brought it to him, and he ate; and he brought him wine, and he drank.* [26]*Then his father Isaac said to him, "Come near and kiss me, my son."* [27]*So he came near and kissed him; and he smelled the smell of his garments, and blessed him, and said,*

> *"See, the smell of my son*
> > *is as the smell of a field* which the Lord has blessed!*
> [28]*May God give you of the dew of heaven,*
> > *and of the fatness of the earth,*
> > *and plenty of grain and wine.*
> [29]*Let peoples serve you,*
> > *and nations bow down to you.*
> *Be lord over your brothers,*
> > *and may your mother's sons bow down to you.*
> *Cursed be every one who curses you,*
> *and blessed be every one who blesses you!"*

---

*LXX, "plentiful" or "fruitful."

Overview: Jacob's answer to his father reflects the obedience of the Word to his Father, for Jacob represents Christ prophetically (Hippolytus). Scripture compares Christ with an abundant field blessed by God, because he is the perfume of the knowledge of God the Father (Cyril of Alexandria). The "plentiful [LXX] field" represents Christ from whom have come cleansing, rest, grace and peace. On the moral level, Jacob's "fragrance" represents his many virtues (Ambrose). In another allegorical interpretation the field represents the church (Augustine). Through his mother's love Jacob was given the preference over his elder brother, and through the gift of his father's blessing he was set apart (Ambrose). Isaac's blindness stands for the blindness of the unfaithful, but in his heart he knew that a mystery was being enacted (Augustine). Isaac's words of blessing were fulfilled completely not in Jacob but in Christ, the dew of heaven (Hippolytus, Cyril of Alexandria).

27:19 Jacob Goes to Isaac

The Word Always Obeys His Father. Hippolytus: The words of Jacob to his father, "I have done as you told me," demonstrate that the Word is always obedient to his Father, as is confirmed by what he says in Ezekiel: "I did just as I was commanded."[1] On the Blessings of Issac and Jacob 6.[2]

27:22 Isaac Doubts

Jacob Prefigured the Mysteries. Hippolytus: This signifies that the Word, who in Jacob prefigured the mysteries, has also become the voice of the prophets, since he is the one who predicts in them what will happen. On the contrary, his hands have become hands of Esau. In fact he [the Word] was executed because of the sins of the people. On the Blessings of Issac and Jacob 6.[3]

27:27 A Smell Like That of a Field

---

[1]Ezek 12:7. [2]PO 27:20. [3]PO 27:22.

THE FIELD THAT THE LORD HAS BLESSED.

AMBROSE: For of him it is written, "Behold, the smell of my son is as the smell of a plentiful field." He had been made perfect in virtue's every flower and was fragrant with the grace of the holy blessing and of the happiness of heaven. He is indeed the field that the Lord has blessed. [This field is] not the earthly field with its rugged woods and crashing torrents, its swampy, sluggish waters, unproductive grain lands, and barren vineyards, filled with sterile rock and gravel, pockmarked and arid with drought or wet with blood, and choked over with brambles and thorns, but the field of which the church speaks in the Canticle, "I have adjured you, O daughters of Jerusalem, by the powers and virtues of the field."[4] This is the field of which the Lord also says, "With me is the beauty of the field."[5] In this field the grape is found that was pressed and poured out blood and washed the world clean. In this field is the fig tree, and beneath it the saints will find rest and be renewed by a good and spiritual grace.[6] In this field is the olive tree fruitful in the overflowing ointment of the Lord's peace. In this field flourish the pomegranate trees[7] that shelter many fruits with the one bulwark of faith and, so to speak, nurture them with the warm embrace of love. JACOB AND THE HAPPY LIFE 2.1.3.[8]

JACOB WAS FRAGRANT.

AMBROSE: And so Jacob was fragrant with the fragrance of such fruits; he followed God amid dangers and believed that he was safe everywhere, led by the Lord. Although the fragrance of the field is pleasant and sweet because it is a natural fragrance, still there breathed in the holy patriarch the fragrance of grace and virtue. How moderate and restrained he was! He did not claim the food that had been prepared for him but yielded without delay to his brother's request for it and received from him the birthright of the firstborn.[9] How respectful he was toward his parents! Through his mother's love he earned the preference over his elder brother,[10] and through the gift of his father's blessing he was made holy.[11] How respectful of God's commands he was! He refused to do wrong to his brother. How honorable! He resisted practicing deceit upon his father.[12] How respectful! He could not refuse his mother what she ordered.[13] JACOB AND THE HAPPY LIFE 2.1.4.[14]

THIS FIELD IS THE CHURCH.

AUGUSTINE: "He smelled his clothes and said, 'Behold, the smell of my son is as the smell of an abundant field, which the Lord has blessed.'"[15] This field is the church. Let's prove that the church is a field. Listen to the apostle telling the faithful: "You are God's tilled field; you are God's building."[16] Not only is the church a field, but also God is the tiller of the field. Listen to the Lord himself: "I am the vine, you the branches, and my Father is the vinedresser."[17] Toiling in this field as a laborer and hoping for an eternal reward, the apostle claims no credit for himself, except a laborer's due. "I planted," he says, "Apollo watered, but God gave the increase. And so neither the one who plants is anything, nor the one who waters, but God who gives the increase."[18] Notice how Paul safeguards humility to make sure of belonging to Jacob, to that field which is the church, and of not losing the robe whose scent was as the smell of an abundant field. He does not pass over to the pride of Esau, materialistic in thought and abounding in arrogance. So the smell of the field comes from the garment of the son. But this field is nothing in itself. That's why he added, "which the Lord has blessed. And the Lord will give you from the dew of heaven above and from the fruitfulness of the earth, and quantities of corn and wine. And nations will serve you, and you shall be lord of your brother, and the sons of your father shall pay you homage. Whoever curses you shall be cursed, and whoever blesses you shall be blessed."[19] That is the blessing of Jacob. If Esau had not been blessed too, there would be no problem. But he is blessed

---

[4]Song 2:7 LXX. [5]Ps 49:11 (50:11 LXX). [6]See Mic 4:4. [7]See Song 8:2. [8]FC 65:147-48*. [9]Gen 25:29-34. [10]Gen 27:1-17. [11]Gen 27:18-29. [12]Gen 27:12. [13]Gen 27:13-14. [14]FC 65:148. [15]Gen 27:27. [16]1 Cor 3:9. [17]Jn 15:1—5. [18]1 Cor 3:6-7. [19]Gen 27:27-29.

too, not with this blessing, and yet one not altogether different from this one. SERMON 4.28.[20]

HE KNEW THE MYSTERY BEING ENACTED.
AUGUSTINE: What advice does Rebekah give? That Jacob should take the skins of the kids and go to his father. The father is expecting the elder and blesses the younger. The Old Testament has the Jews in mind according to its literal meaning, and by the spiritual understanding of it, it is a blessing to Christians. Would your holinesses please concentrate on this great mystery, this great sacrament.

Isaac says, "Your brother came with guile" about a man without guile. Isaac undoubtedly knew what was happening since he had the spirit of prophecy, and he himself was acting symbolically. He stakes everything on the sublime truths being symbolically, sacramentally enacted. For if he hadn't known what he was doing, he would surely have been angry with his son for deceiving him. The elder comes and says, "Here, father, eat; I have done just as you ordered me." He says, "Who are you?" He replies, "I am your elder son, Esau." "And who is the one," Isaac says, "at whose hands I have already eaten, and I blessed him, and blessed he shall be?"[21] He seemed to be angry; Esau was expecting from his lips some sort of curse upon his brother. While he is expecting a curse, Isaac confirms the blessing. What splendid anger, what marvelous indignation! But he knew the mystery being enacted. The blindness of his bodily eyes stood for the mental blindness of the Jews. But the eyes of his heart were able to see the sublimity of the mysteries being unfolded. SERMON 4.21.[22]

CHRIST IS A SWEET PERFUME. CYRIL OF ALEXANDRIA: In fact, these things were not completely fulfilled in Jacob but in Christ and in those who were justified through faith, who were also made sons according to the promise in Isaac.[23] Therefore the meaning of the prophecy will also suit the new people and Christ himself, who is beginning and leading. He is also considered to be a second Adam[24] and was born as a second root of humanity. For that which is in Christ is a new creation,[25] and we are renewed in him to sanctification, incorruption and life.[26] The words of the blessing, I believe, signify the sweetness of the spiritual perfume in Christ, like that of a garden or a plentiful field spreading a sweet and beautiful perfume from its spring flowers. And so Christ described himself to us in the Song of Songs: "I am the flower of the field, the lily of the valleys."[27] He was actually a lily and a rose born of the earth for the sake of humanity. Since he did not know sin, he was the most divine of all those who inhabited the whole world and produced a perfume though his works. For this reason [Scripture] compares Christ with a field blessed by God, and with very good reason, because he is the perfume of the knowledge of God the Father. So again the divine Paul says, "But thanks be to God, who in Christ always leads us in triumphal procession, and through us spreads in every place the fragrance that comes from knowing him."[28] Our Lord Jesus Christ is revealed through the holy apostles like the perfume of the knowledge of God the Father. "If someone knows the Son, he also fully knows the Father,"[29] because of the sameness of nature, as in everything he possesses the same things in the same degree. GLAPHYRA ON GENESIS, 3.5.[30]

27:28 Isaac Blesses Jacob

THE PROPHET SIGNIFIES THE SAINTS. HIPPOLYTUS: If one believes that this blessing was accomplished in Jacob, he is mistaken. Nothing of this ever happened to Jacob. First we find him in Mesopotamia at the service of Laban for twenty years;[31] then he prostrates himself before his brother Esau and tries to make himself pleasing to him by offering presents;[32] after this he goes down to Egypt to avoid starvation with his chil-

---

[20]*WSA* 3 1:200*. [21]Gen 27:32-33. [22]*WSA* 3 1:196-97. [23]Gal 4:28. [24]1 Cor 15:45. [25]2 Cor 5:17; Gal 6:15. [26]2 Tim 1:10. [27]Song 2:1. [28]2 Cor 2:14. [29]Jn 14:9. [30]PG 69:172. [31]Gen 31:38. [32]Gen 33:3, 8, 10.

dren.[33] In whom then have the words "Ah, the smell of the clothes of my son is like the smell of a fruitful field that the Lord has blessed" been accomplished? In nobody else but Christ, Son of God. In fact, the field is the world, and the smell of his clothes are all those who believe in him, according to what the apostle says: "We are the aroma of Christ to God among those who are being saved and among those who are perishing; to the one a fragrance from death to death, to the other a fragrance from life to life."[34]

The words "May God give you of the dew of heaven, and of the fatness of the earth, and plenty of grain and wine" signify clearly the Word, who came down from heaven like dew. The earth is the flesh that he has assumed from the Virgin. Through the words "plenty of grain and wine," the prophet signifies the saints, who are gathered together like the grain in a barn[35] and are justified by the Spirit as by wine.[36] On the Blessings of Isaac and Jacob 7.[37]

The Dew of Heaven Is the Word. Cyril of Alexandria: These things therefore fit with Christ and also fit quite reasonably with the new people: "May God give you of the dew of heaven and of the fatness of the earth and plenty of grain and wine." The dew of heaven and the fatness of the earth, that is, the Word, was given to us by the Father, together with the participation through the Spirit, and therefore we were made participants in the divine nature through him.[38] And we also received plenty of grain and wine, that is, strength and happiness. In fact, it is said truly, "Bread strengthens the heart of man, and wine makes glad his heart."[39] Bread is the symbol of spiritual strength, wine of the physical. They are given to those who are in Christ through him. In which other way were we made stable and firm in piety and immovable and aware to think the right things? Certainly the power "to trample serpents and scorpions underfoot and the whole power of the enemy"[40] was given to us. This, I believe, is the meaning of the abundance of grain. But we have also received wine. "We rejoice in

hope,"[41] and "we have become glad,"[42] according to Scripture. We expect heavenly dwellings, an eternal life in incorruption, and to reign together with Christ. Therefore these things may be said about us. Glaphyra on Genesis, 3.5.[43]

27:29 Blessings on Those Who Bless Jacob

The Blessings Accomplished in the Savior. Hippolytus: And also the words "Let peoples serve you, and princes bow down to you" have been accomplished now. Whom else do the faithful peoples serve and the princes of the church worship but Christ, in whose name they also receive their salvation? The Word has predicted all this through Isaiah by saying, "My servants shall be called by a new name, which will be blessed on the earth; for they shall bless the true God, and those who swear upon the earth shall swear in the name of the true God."[44] And he adds, "Behold, my servants shall eat, but you shall hunger; behold, my servants shall drink, but you shall thirst; behold, my servants shall exult with joy, but you shall be ashamed and shall cry for the vexation of your spirit."[45]

Then he continues by saying, "Be lord of your brother, and the sons of your father shall bow to you." But nobody adored Jacob, nor did he become lord of his brother Esau; on the contrary, he ran away from him in a fright and was the first to adore him, for seven times.[46] Therefore the words of Isaac have been accomplished in the Savior: He has become lord and master of those who are considered to be his brothers by the flesh, in order to be adored by them as their king. That is why Isaac says, "Cursed be everyone who curses you, and blessed be everyone who blesses you." The Blessings of the Patriarchs 7.[47]

The Blessing Is Transferred to the Im-

[33]Gen 42:2; 46:3. [34]2 Cor 2:15-16. [35]Mt 13:30. [36]1 Tim 3:16. [37]PO 27:24-26. [38]2 Pet 1:4. [39]Ps 104:15 (103:15 LXX). [40]Lk 10:19. [41]Rom 12:12. [42]Ps 126:3 (125:3 LXX). [43]PG 69:172-73. [44]Is 65:15-16. [45]Is 65:13-14. [46]Gen 32:7-8; 33:3. [47]PO 27:28-30.

MANUEL. CYRIL OF ALEXANDRIA: Afterward the power of blessing is transferred again to the Immanuel himself. "And let nations serve you, and princes bow down to you, and be lord of your brother." The Immanuel was called "the firstborn" when he became so with reference to us, "among many brothers."[48] But for this reason we must not forget that he is God and the Lord of the universe. We worship him as God, and he has reigned as God over those who are called from the brothers through grace. "Who in the heavens shall be compared to the Lord, and who shall be likened to the Lord among the sons of God?"[49] Therefore the Immanuel has reigned as God over those who were received into the brotherhood, and to him "every knee should bow in heaven and on earth, and under the earth, and every tongue should confess that Jesus Christ is Lord, to the glory of God the father."[50] And cursed is he who curses, "and blessed is he that blesses." These words are quite clear. Those who curse are detestable and hateful to God; those who bless, that is, who announce his divine glory, are filled with heavenly and divine goods. This is the blessing of Jacob, whose strength refers to the Immanuel himself and to those who are justified in the faith. GLAPHYRA ON GENESIS, 3.173B-C.[51]

---

[48]Rom 8:29. [49]Ps 89:6 (88:7 LXX). [50]Phil 2:10-11. [51]PG 69:173.

27:30-38 ESAU DISCOVERS THE DECEPTION

[30]*As soon as Isaac had finished blessing Jacob, when Jacob had scarcely gone out from the presence of Isaac his father, Esau his brother came in from his hunting.* [31]*He also prepared savory food, and brought it to his father. And he said to his father, "Let my father arise, and eat of his son's game, that you may bless me."* [32]*His father Isaac said to him, "Who are you?" He answered, "I am your son, your first-born, Esau."* [33]*Then Isaac trembled violently,* and said, "Who was it then that hunted game and brought it to me, and I ate it all[x] before you came, and I have blessed him?—yes, and he shall be blessed."* [34]*When Esau heard the words of his father, he cried out with an exceedingly great and bitter cry, and said to his father, "Bless me, even me also, O my father!"* [35]*But he said, "Your brother came with guile, and he has taken away your blessing."* [36]*Esau said, "Is he not rightly named Jacob? For he has supplanted me these two times. He took away my birthright; and behold, now he has taken away my blessing." Then he said, "Have you not reserved a blessing for me?"* [37]*Isaac answered Esau, "Behold, I have made him your lord, and all his brothers I have given to him for servants, and with grain and wine I have sustained him. What then can I do for you, my son?"* [38]*Esau said to his father, "Have you but one blessing, my father? Bless me, even me also, O my father." And Esau lifted up his voice and wept.*

x Cn: Heb *of all*   *LXX, "was seized with a great ecstasy or astonishment."

OVERVIEW: The bestowal of the blessing on Jacob rather than Esau revealed that the kingdom was to be bestowed on the church rather than the synagogue (AMBROSE). The two men, Jacob and

Esau, represent two peoples, but the one blessing signifies the unity of the church (AUGUSTINE). The dishes prepared by Esau symbolize the cult of the people under the law. Isaac's ecstatic reaction[1] to Esau's arrival shows his comprehension of the divine plan (HIPPOLYTUS). Esau's disappointment is attributed to his materialistic expectations (EPHREM). Since Jacob is understood to prefigure Christ, Isaac's statement that he came with "guile" must be interpreted figuratively as a reference to Christ's human nature "in the form of a slave" or the fact that he bears the sins of others (HIPPOLYTUS, AUGUSTINE). Esau's reference to the etymology of the name Jacob (Gen 27:36) as the "tripper-up" can be explained allegorically as a reference to the role of the spiritually minded in tripping up the materialistically minded (AUGUSTINE).

27:30 Esau Returns from Hunting

THE KINGDOM TO BE BESTOWED ON THE CHURCH. AMBROSE: Afterward, when the blessing had been pronounced, the elder brother arrived. By this it is revealed that the kingdom was predestined to be bestowed on the church rather than on the synagogue but had secretly entered the synagogue so that sin might abound, and, when sin had abounded, that grace might also abound.[2] At the same time, it would be clear that the candidate for the kingdom of heaven must be quick to carry off the blessing and to appropriate the prerogative for which he has been recommended. On this account the younger son was not blamed by his father but praised, for Isaac says, "Your brother came deceitfully and received your blessing."[3] For deceit is good when the plunder is without reproach. Now the plunder of piety is without reproach, because "from the days of John the kingdom of heaven suffers violence, and the violent bear it away."[4] Our fathers celebrated the Passover in haste and ate the lamb in haste,[5] not making delay, and the holy Joseph summoned his brother Benjamin by a holy fabrication and deceit.[6] JACOB AND THE HAPPY LIFE 2.3.10.[7]

TWO MEN, TWO PEOPLES. AUGUSTINE: The other one, you see, comes along in the evening, and brings what his father ordered, and finds his brother has been blessed instead of himself and is not blessed with a second blessing. Because those two men were two peoples.[8] One blessing signifies the unity of the church. But they are two peoples. . . . But the two peoples who belong to Jacob are represented in other ways. You see, our Lord Jesus Christ, who had come to Jews and Gentiles, was repudiated by the Jews, who belonged to the elder son. However, he chose some of them who belonged to the younger son, who had begun to desire and understand the Lord's promises, not taking that land they desired materialistically but spiritually desiring that city where no one is materially born, because in it no one either materially or spiritually dies. SERMON 4.17.[9]

27:31 Savory Food

THE DISHES OF ESAU. HIPPOLYTUS: The dishes of Esau signify the cult of the people under the law. Since they are inflated with pride and are certain of being justified by circumcision, they offer the pagan converts as nourishment, whereas they themselves need nourishment because they cannot touch the heavenly bread. ON THE BLESSINGS OF ISAAC AND JACOB 8.[10]

27:33 Isaac Learns the Truth

A MYSTERY OF THE DIVINE ECONOMY. HIPPOLYTUS: What had actually occurred from the action of Jacob was a mystery of the [divine] economy in view of the Christ prefigured [by Jacob], [of the Christ] who, blessed by the Father, has been blessed forever after his [temporal] birth.

The words of Scripture, "Besides himself, Isaac was seized with great amazement," have

---

[1]Cf. Gen 27:33 LXX. [2]Rom 5.20. [3]Gen 27:35. [4]Mt 11:12. [5]Ex 12:11. [6]Gen 42:20. [7]FC 65:151-52. [8]Gen 25:23. [9]WSA 3 1:194. [10]PO 27:30.

the same meaning as "Isaac was filled with admiration" for what had happened, because he foresaw that the Gentiles, according to the will of God, had to be blessed and take part in the covenant of the promise made to the fathers through the younger son. That is why Jacob, when he was brought forth and emerged the last from his mother's womb, took hold on Esau's heel.[11] This means that by closely following the footsteps of the prophets the last peoples had to take hold of the right of primogeniture, since they are the first ones to be found in the New Testament. ON THE BLESSINGS OF THE ISAAC AND JACOB 8.[12]

27:34 Esau Pleads for the Blessing

ESAU'S BITTERNESS. EPHREM THE SYRIAN: And Esau cried out and wailed bitterly, not because he lost his spiritual blessings but because he was now deprived of the bountiful produce of the blessed earth. [Esau wept] not because he was no longer able to be righteous but because he would not be able to make his brother his servant; not because he would not inherit eternal life but because the land of the Canaanites would not be his portion. Since Esau had such spite for his brother that he wished to kill him, Rebekah persuaded Jacob to go to the house of Laban lest they kill each other in their strife, and she became bereft of both of them at the same time. COMMENTARY ON GENESIS 25.3.[13]

27:35 Jacob Has Taken the Blessing

THE FORM OF A SLAVE. HIPPOLYTUS: The fact that he says to him, "Your brother came by trickery and took away your blessing" means, in a way that implies a mystery, that the Word of God, after his incarnation, had to take the form of a slave. [Thus] thanks to him who was unknown in his generation, he might receive the blessing of the Father and transmit it to us, who believe in him. ON THE BLESSINGS OF ISAAC AND JACOB 8.[14]

BEARING THE SINS OF OTHERS. AUGUSTINE: So what can it mean when it says, "Your brother came with guile and stole the blessing"? . . . So what can it mean when it says, "He came along with guile and stole the blessing"?

First of all, let us note what guile means, and so see what Jacob ought to do. He is bearing the sins of others, and he is bearing them patiently although they are other people's. That is what it means to have the skins of the kids on him; he is bearing the sins of others, not clinging to his own. In this way all those who put up with the sins of others for the sake of unity in the church are imitating Jacob. Because Jacob too is in Christ, inasmuch as Christ is in the seed of Abraham; as it was said, "In your seed shall all the nations be blessed."[15] So our Lord Jesus Christ, who committed no sin, bore the sins of others. And will those whose sins have been forgiven disdain to bear the sins of others? So if Jacob turns into Christ, he bears the sins of others—that, is the skins of the kids. And where is the guile in that? SERMON 4.15-16.[16]

HE KNEW THE SYMBOLIC MYSTERY. AUGUSTINE: What then is guile? Guile is when one thing is done and another pretended. When there is one thing in intention and another in deeds, it is called guile. So guile in the proper sense is reprehensible, just like rock in the proper sense. If you said Christ was a rock in the proper sense, it would be a blasphemy, just as if you said Christ was a calf in the proper sense it would be blasphemy. In the proper sense a calf is a beast; in the figurative sense it is a victim in a sacrifice. In the proper sense a stone is compacted earth; in the figurative sense it is firmness. Guile in the proper sense is deceit; in the figurative sense. . . . Every figurative and allegorical text or utterance seems to mean one thing materially and to suggest another thing spiritually. So he called this figurative sense by the name of guile. At long last then,

[11]Gen 25:26. [12]PO 27:32-34. [13]FC 91:173. [14]PO 27:34-36. [15]Gen 22:18. [16]WSA 3 1:194.

what does it mean, "He came with guile and stole your blessing"? The reason it says "He came with guile" is that what was being done had a figurative sense. Isaac, after all, would not have confirmed the blessing on a guileful, deceitful man who more justly would deserve a curse. So it wasn't a case of real guile, especially since he did not in fact lie when he said, "I am your elder son Esau."[17] For that one had already made a bargain with his brother and sold him his rights as firstborn. So he told his father that he had what he had bought from his brother; what that one had lost had passed to this one. The title of firstborn had not been eliminated from Isaac's household. The title of firstborn was still here—but not with the one who had sold it. Where else was it but with the younger brother? Because he knew the symbolic mystery in all this, Isaac confirmed the blessing and said to this other son, "What am I to do for you?" He answered, "Bless me too, father; you do not only have one blessing."[18] But Isaac knew only of one. SERMON 4.23.[19]

27:36 Rightly Named

MATERIALISTS ARE TRIPPED UP. AUGUSTINE: "And Esau said, 'Rightly is his name called Jacob.'" Tripping up is what Jacob means. And not even tripping up is empty of meaning, because it is to be taken figuratively, like guile. Jacob, you see, was not yet so malicious as to plan to trip his brother up, when he was given his name. He was called a tripper-up when as his brother was being born he held his foot with his own hand. That is when he was called "Tripper-up." Now tripping up the materialistically minded is the very life of the spiritually minded. All the materialists are tripped up when they envy the spiritual people in the church, and they thereby become worse. Listen to the apostle saying this very thing, especially because he there mentions the smell that Isaac talked about here, saying, "Behold, the smell of my son is as the smell of an abundant field, which the Lord has blessed." So the apostle says, "We are the sweet smell of Christ in every place," and he says, "For some indeed the smell of life, for life; for the others the smell of death, for death. And for this who is sufficient?"[20] Sufficient, that is, to understand how we can be the smell of death for the death of other people, without any fault of ours. Spiritual people walk their ways, knowing nothing except how to live a good life. And those who are spiteful about their innocent lives commit grave sins, which is why God will punish them. And thus a person who is a sweet smell for life to others becomes to them a smell for death. For the Lord himself was the first to become a sweet smell for life to believers and a bad smell for death to persecutors. Because so many people had believed him, the Jews were full of spite and committed that enormous crime of killing the innocent one, the saint of saints. If they had not done this, the sweet smell of Christ would not have meant death for them. So Esau was tripped up in his father's blessing. SERMON 4.28.[21]

---

[17]Gen 27:24. [18]Gen 27:37-39. [19]*WSA* 3 1:198. [20]2 Cor 2:14-16. [21]*WSA* 3 1:200.

27:39-40 ISAAC'S BLESSING TO ESAU

[39]*Then Isaac his father answered him:*
"Behold, away from[y] *the fatness of the earth shall your dwelling be,*
and away from[y] *the dew of heaven on high.*

⁴⁰*By your sword you shall live,*
  and you shall serve your brother;
but when you break loose
  you shall break his yoke from your neck."

y Or *of*

OVERVIEW: Since the descendants of Esau, the Edomites, did settle on the edges of the land of Canaan, the prophecy about "the dew of heaven above" is best interpreted allegorically as a reference to the oracles of the prophets (HIPPOLYTUS). The Lord was the first to become a sweet smell for life to believers and a bad smell for death to persecutors. The blessing that Isaac gives to Esau foreshadows the tolerance that must be given to bad and quarrelsome people in the church (AUGUSTINE). The "yoke" (Gen 27:40) can by reference to another passage of Scripture be interpreted as the yoke of the law (HIPPOLYTUS, AMBROSE). Esau's blessing is in accordance with his foolish and immoderate behavior, for he is a slave to passions and sin, and therefore he is to serve his moderate and wise brother. Isaac had two sons, one without moderation and the other moderate and wise. In order to take care for both like a good father, he placed the moderate son over the immoderate one. The person who masters the will, judges over his or her counsels and restrains the longing of the bodily passions is assuredly free (AMBROSE).

27:39 Isaac Answers Esau

THE DEW OF HEAVEN. HIPPOLYTUS: Are the words spoken there by the blessed Isaac meant either as a blessing or as a prophecy? It is necessary to understand the previous statement. This is what he says: "By the fatness of the earth shall your dwelling be, and by the dew of heaven above."[1] In fact, it happens that the people settled down in the land of the Canaanites, which they shared with Joshua, son of Nun. And the words of Isaac "and by the dew of heaven above" signify that the prophets, like a cloud, left them soaked

in dew after revealing to them the oracles of God. ON THE BLESSINGS OF ISAAC AND JACOB 10.[2]

TOLERATED FOR THE SAKE OF PEACE. AUGUSTINE: But why was it after being "roughly handled"[3] that Isaac gave his blessing? For in the last resort what Isaac said to Esau was spoken under constraint and force: "Behold, your dwelling will be by the fruitfulness of the earth and by the dew of heaven." And in case you should imagine yourself for that reason to be good—"You shall live by your sword and be servant to your brother." But in order that you shouldn't despair of yourself, since you can after all correct yourself—"But the time will come when you will put off and undo the yoke from your neck." There you are, he will receive of the fruitfulness of the earth and of the dew of heaven. But when Isaac is roughly handled, he throws this blessing at him. He does not give it to him. Doesn't it happen now in the church with evil people who want to cause trouble in the church that they are tolerated for the sake of peace, that they are admitted to share in the common sacraments? And sometimes it is public knowledge that they are evil, but for some reason or other they cannot be convicted of it. No proof or conviction can be obtained so that they may be corrected and removed from office, excluded, excommunicated.

---

[1]Although the LXX can be understood to correspond to the Hebrew text "away from," Hippolytus seems to have understood it to mean "by" or "among," as did also the Vulgate (see the following comment by Augustine) and, curiously, the *Targum Jonathan.* [2]PO 27:40-42. [3]The phrase used by Augustine does not correspond either to the LXX or to the Vulgate. The latter does contain the word *motus* at the beginning of Genesis 27:39, which taken together with Genesis 27:33 may account for Augustine's interpretation. The word *motus* could also be taken to mean "shaken," but Augustine interprets the passage to mean that Isaac acted under constraint.

If someone presses charges, it sometimes comes to the disruption of the church. The church leader is forced in effect to say, "Here you are with the fruitfulness of the earth and the dew of heaven; make use of the sacraments; you are eating judgment to yourself, you are drinking judgment to yourself." Whoever eats and drinks unworthily eats and drinks judgment to himself."[4] "You know that you are being admitted to the sacraments for the sake of the peace of the church; all you have at heart is stirring up trouble and causing divisions. That is why you will live by the sword. For as to what you receive from the dew of heaven and the fruitfulness of the earth, you won't live by that. That gives you no delight; you do not see that the Lord is sweet. If this did give you delight, if you did find the Lord sweet, you would imitate the Lord's humility instead of the devil's pride." So although he receives the mystery of the Lord's humility from the dew of heaven and the fruitfulness of the earth, he does not set aside the pride of the devil (may I have nothing to do with him!) who always takes pleasure in quarrels and dissension. "Yes, you may have this communion in the dew of heaven and the fruitfulness of the earth, but all the same you are living by your sword, and either rejoicing in the quarrels and dissension, or being scared out of your wits by them. So change yourself, and take the yoke from your neck." SERMON 4.35.[5]

27:40 Esau to Serve Jacob

THE AGE THAT CONTINUES. HIPPOLYTUS: And the words: "You shall live by your sword" mean that the people never stop being in defensive or aggressive war with the nations living around them, as Scripture itself shows. And the sentence "You shall be the servant of your brother" indicates the age that still continues, the age in which the Savior was present and came to visit his own brothers according to the flesh, and the Savior the prophet here suggests to serve after humanity has become obedient. That is why he said: "There

will come a time when you shall shake and break the yoke from your neck." Which yoke, but the yoke that lies in the law? Provided that they do not live any more as slaves under the yoke of the law but believe in the gospel as free men, they can still be saved. ON THE BLESSINGS OF ISAAC AND JACOB 10.[6]

THE FOOLISH CANNOT BE DISCIPLES OF VIRTUE. AMBROSE: Nevertheless Esau brought it about by his demands and entreaties that he did receive a blessing but such a blessing as was in agreement and correspondence with the earlier one, namely, that he should serve his brother.[7] Indeed, the one who could not command and rule the other ought to have served him, in order to be ruled by the one who was wiser. It was not the role of the holy patriarch to deliver his own son to the ignoble state of slavery. But since he had two sons, one without moderation and the other moderate and wise, in order to take care for both like a good father, he placed the moderate son over the immediate one, and he ordered the foolish one to obey the one who was wise. For the foolish man cannot of his own accord be a disciple of virtue or persevere in his intent, because the fool changes like the moon.[8] Isaac was right to deny Esau freedom to make his own choices; else he might drift like a ship in the waves without a helmsman. But Isaac made him subject to his brother according to that which is written, "The unwise man is the slave of the wise man."[9] Therefore the patriarch was right to make him subject, so that he might amend his dispositions under rule and guidance. And so Isaac says, "By your sword shall you live; you shall serve your brother," for holiness has mastery over cruelty and kindness excels over emotions that are harsh. JACOB AND THE HAPPY LIFE 2.3.11.[10]

SOLD TO MANY MASTERS. AMBROSE: Everyone who does not possess the authority conferred by a

---

[4]1 Cor 11:29. [5]*WSA* 3 1:204-5. [6]PO 27:42. [7]Gen 27:38-40. [8]Sir 27:11-12. [9]Prov 11:29. [10]FC 65:152-53*.

clear conscience is a slave; whoever is crushed by fear or ensnared by pleasure or seduced by desires or provoked by wrath or felled by grief is a slave. In fact, every passion is servile, because "everyone who commits sin is a slave of sin,"[11] and, what is worse, he is the slave of many sins. The person who is subject to vices has sold himself to many masters, so that he is scarcely permitted to go out of servitude. But take the one who is the master over his own will, judge over his counsels, agent of his judgment, the man who restrains the longing of his bodily passions and does well what he does. (Note that by acting well he acts rightly, and one who acts rightly acts without blame or reproach because he has power over his actions.) Such a person is assuredly free. For the one who does all things wisely and in complete accord with his will is the only free man. It is not accidental status that makes the slave but shameful and foolish conduct. Indeed, the wise servant rules the foolish master, and "their own servants will lend to the masters."[12] What will they lend? Not money, surely, but wisdom, just as the law also says, "You will lend to many nations and will not borrow."[13] For the Jew lent to the proselyte the prophecies of God's law. JACOB AND THE HAPPY LIFE 2.3.12.[14]

PEOPLE WHO FOCUS ON THE LETTER.
AMBROSE: This then is what the patriarch Isaac says, "You shall serve your brother. But the time will be, when you shall shake off and loose his yoke from your neck." He means that there will be two peoples, one the son of the slave girl, the other of the free woman[15]—for the letter is a slave, whereas grace is free[16]—and that the people that attends to the letter is going to be a slave as long as it needs to follow the expounder of learning in the spirit. Then that will also come to pass which the apostle says, "that the remnant may be saved by reason of the election made by grace."[17] "You shall serve your brother," but then you will perceive your advancement in servitude only when you begin to obey your brother voluntarily and not under compulsion. JACOB AND THE HAPPY LIFE 2.3.13.[18]

---

[11]Jn 8:34. [12]Prov 22:7 LXX. [13]Deut 15:6. [14]FC 65:153*. [15]Gal 4:22-31. [16]2 Cor 3:6. [17]Rom 9:27; cf. Is 10:22. [18]FC 65:154*.

27:41-45 ESAU RESOLVES TO REVENGE HIMSELF ON JACOB

[41]*Now Esau hated Jacob because of the blessing with which his father had blessed him, and Esau said to himself, "The days of mourning for my father are approaching; then I will kill my brother Jacob."* [42]*But the words of Esau her older son were told to Rebekah; so she sent and called Jacob her younger son, and said to him, "Behold, your brother Esau comforts himself by planning to kill you.* [43]*Now therefore, my son, obey my voice; arise, flee to Laban my brother in Haran,* [44]*and stay with him a while, until your brother's fury turns away;* [45]*until your brother's anger turns away, and he forgets what you have done to him; then I will send, and fetch you from there. Why should I be bereft of you both in one day?"*

OVERVIEW: Rebekah's behavior is excused or justified because she did not arbitrarily prefer one son to the other but preferred the just son to the unjust. She is a model of patience, the guardian of blamelessness, in the face of wrath and intemperateness (AMBROSE).

27:41 Esau Hated Jacob

REBEKAH PREFERRED A JUST SON TO AN UNJUST ONE. AMBROSE: But we shouldn't leave his parents without excuse for having preferred their younger son to the elder. At the same time we must take care so that no one, in turning to their example, would make an unfair judgment between his sons or suppose that he should love the one and esteem the other less. From this line of conduct fraternal hatreds are aroused and the crime of fratricide is contrived to gain a worthless sum of money. Let children be nurtured with an equal measure of devotion. Granted that one's love may fasten more upon some trait in a child who is more agreeable or similar to oneself, the exercise of justice ought to be the same in regard to all. The more that is given to the child that is loved and who seeks his brother's love, the more is taken away from the one who is burdened with jealousy at the unfair preferment. Esau threatened that he would kill his brother. Neither the fact of brotherhood nor respect for their parents kept him from his fratricidal madness, and he grieved that the blessing had been snatched away from him, whereas he should have proved himself worthy of it by forbearance rather than by crime.

However, Rebekah did not prefer one son to another son but a just son to an unjust one. And indeed, with that pious mother, God's mysterious plan was more important than her offspring. She did not so much prefer Jacob to his brother; rather, she offered him to the Lord, for she knew that he could protect the gift that the Lord had bestowed. In the Lord she took counsel also for her other son; she withdrew him from God's disfavor, lest he incur graver culpability if he lost the grace

of the blessing he did receive. JACOB AND THE HAPPY LIFE 2.2.5-6.[1]

27:43 Rebekah Urges Jacob to Flee

LET US NOT GIVE IN TO ANGER. AMBROSE: But if needs be, let us learn from Rebekah how to make provision so that enmity does not provoke wrath and wrath rush headlong into fratricide. Let Rebekah come—that is, let us put on patience, the good guardian of blamelessness—and let her persuade us not to give in to our anger.[2] Let us withdraw somewhat further, until our anger is softened by time and we are taken by surprise at having forgotten the wrong done us. Therefore patience is not much afraid of exile but readily enters upon it, not so much to avoid the danger to salvation as to escape giving incitement to wrongdoing. The loving mother too endures the absence of her dearly beloved son and purposes to give more to the one whom she has harmed, while still consulting the interests of both, to render the one safe against fratricide and the other blameless of crime. JACOB AND THE HAPPY LIFE 2.4.14.[3]

DEEDS OF TRUE VIRTUE. AMBROSE: We have heard the words of an intemperance that is drunk with bodily desires; let us consider the deeds of true virtue. Virtue needs nothing but the grace of God. It pursues the only and supreme good, and it is content with that only good from which we receive all things but on which we bestow nothing because it has no need of anything, just as David says, "I have said to the Lord, 'You are my Lord, for you have no need of my goods.'"[4] And what does the Lord need, when he abounds in all things and imparts everything to us, while providing all things without deficiency? JACOB AND THE HAPPY LIFE 2.4.15.[5]

---

[1]FC 65:149*. [2]Rom 12:19. [3]FC 65:154-55**. [4]Ps 16:2 (15:2 LXX). [5]FC 65:155.

27:46 ISAAC SENDS JACOB TO LABAN

[46]*Then Rebekah said to Isaac, "I am weary of my life because of the Hittite women. If Jacob marries one of the Hittite women such as these, one of the women of the land, what good will my life be to me?"*

OVERVIEW: Rebekah's stratagem for saving Jacob from Esau's wrath by diverting Isaac's attention to the danger of the Hittite women could be interpreted as a divine inspiration and seen as part of her zeal for the fulfillment of the divine plan (CHRYSOSTOM).

27:46 Rebekah Complains About Esau's Wives

HELP FROM ON HIGH. CHRYSOSTOM: Notice how she found a plausible excuse. You see, whenever help from on high comes to support us, problems become simple and difficulties easy. So, since she too had the Lord of all seconding her intention, he put into her mind everything capable of bringing to realization the plan in process for her son's survival. "I am disgusted with life on account of the daughters of the Hittites. If Jacob takes a wife from the daughters of this land, what meaning would life have for me?"[1] Here there seems to be a reference to the immorality of Es-au's wives and the fact that they proved a source of great disgust to Isaac and Rebekah. Sacred Scripture narrated to us previously, you remember, that Esau took wives from the Hittites and Hivites: "They were at odds with Isaac and Rebekah."[2] So, wishing to remind him of this, she more or less says to him, "You know how Esau's wives made life unpleasant for me, and how, on account of their hostility, I am now alienated from all the daughters of the Hittites and hate the lot of them on their account. So if it happens that Jacob takes a wife from among them, what hope of survival would then be left for me? What meaning would life have for me?" I mean, "if we can't put up with them, if even Jacob goes so far as to marry one of the daughters of this land, life is over for us." HOMILIES ON GENESIS 54.13.[3]

---

[1]LXX. [2]Gen 26:34-35. [3]FC 87:98.*

28:1-9 JACOB TO FIND A WIFE; ESAU TAKES A NON-CANAANITE WIFE

[1]*Then Isaac called Jacob and blessed him, and charged him, "You shall not marry one of the Canaanite women. [2]Arise, go to Paddan-aram to the house of Bethuel your mother's father; and take as wife from there one of the daughters of Laban your mother's brother. [3]God Almighty[z] bless you and make you fruitful and multiply you, that you may become a company of peoples. [4]May he*

give the blessing of Abraham to you and to your descendants with you, that you may take posses-sion of the land of your sojournings which God gave to Abraham!" [5]Thus Isaac sent Jacob away; and he went to Paddan-aram to Laban, the son of Bethuel the Aramean, the brother of Rebekah, Jacob's and Esau's mother.

[6]Now Esau saw that Isaac had blessed Jacob and sent him away to Paddan-aram to take a wife from there, and that as he blessed him he charged him, "You shall not marry one of the Canaanite women," [7]and that Jacob had obeyed his father and his mother and gone to Paddan-aram. [8]So when Esau saw that the Canaanite women did not please Isaac his father, [9]Esau went to Ishmael and took to wife, besides the wives he had, Mahalath the daughter of Ishmael Abraham's son, the sister of Nebaioth.

z Heb El Shaddai

OVERVIEW: In blessing Jacob and directing him to go to a distant country to take a wife, Isaac foreshadows God the Father, while Jacob repre-sents Christ. The women of the region are a sym-bol of the synagogue, which is to be rejected in favor of the Gentiles, who are represented by the distant country (CAESARIUS OF ARLES). Rebekah is seen as a prudent and loving mother who found a way to remove her son from danger by urging Isaac (Gen 27:46) to find a non-Hittite wife for Jacob (CHRYSOSTOM).

28:2 A Wife Among Laban's Daughters

TYPES OF THE FATHER AND THE SON. CAE-SARIUS OF ARLES: When the lesson was read just now, dearly beloved, we heard that in reply to holy Rebekah's plea Isaac called his son Jacob and told him to proceed to Mesopotamia of Syria and take a wife from there. Jacob departed in humble obedience to his father and on the way came to a certain place where he put a stone under his head and went to sleep. In his slumber he saw a ladder extending to heaven with angels of God ascend-ing and descending on it, while the Lord leaned on the ladder and said to him, "Jacob, Jacob, do not be afraid, I am with you, and I will be the companion of your journey." Now when blessed Isaac directed his son to Mesopotamia, dearly be-loved, Isaac represented a type of God the Father, while Jacob signified Christ the Lord. Disregard-

ing the women of the region in which he lived, blessed Isaac sent his son into a distant country to take a wife, because God the Father would re-ject the synagogue of Jews and send his only-be-gotten Son to form a church out of the Gentiles. This was fulfilled in truth when the apostles said to the Jews, "It was necessary that the Word of God should be spoken to you first, but since you judge yourselves unworthy of eternal life, behold, we now turn to the Gentiles."[1] SERMON 87.1.[2]

28:4 The Blessings of Abraham

MANY NATIONS FROM HIS DESCENDANTS. CHRYSOSTOM: See how this good man foretells everything to him and gives Jacob sufficient sup-port for his comfort by forecasting to him his re-turn and possession of the land and the fact that not only will he grow into a multitude but also that a league of nations will come from his de-scendants. On hearing this the young man car-ried out his father's wishes and traveled to Meso-potamia to his mother's brother, Laban. . . . Do you see, dearly beloved, how much perspicacity this loving mother showed in rescuing Jacob from danger by supplying a plausible excuse for his journey, neither highlighting Esau's wickedness nor revealing the reason to the father but giving

---

[1]Acts 13:46. [2]FC 47:29-30*.

appropriate advice to her son so that he might be persuaded through fear to accept what was said by her and propose a convincing plan to his father? Hence the good man went along with what she said and sent Jacob on his way after plying him with his blessings. HOMILIES ON GENESIS 54.14-15.[3]

---

[3]FC 87:99-100.

28:10-17 JACOB DREAMS OF A LADDER REACHING TO HEAVEN

[10]*Jacob left Beer-sheba, and went toward Haran.* [11]*And he came to a certain place, and stayed there that night, because the sun had set. Taking one of the stones of the place, he put it under his head and lay down in that place to sleep.* [12]*And he dreamed that there was a ladder set up on the earth, and the top of it reached to heaven; and behold, the angels of God were ascending and descending on it!* [13]*And behold, the LORD stood above it[a] and said, "I am the LORD, the God of Abraham your father and the God of Isaac; the land on which you lie I will give to you and to your descendants;* [14]*and your descendants shall be like the dust of the earth, and you shall spread abroad to the west and to the east and to the north and to the south; and by you and your descendants shall all the families of the earth bless themselves.[b]* [15]*Behold, I am with you and will keep you wherever you go, and will bring you back to this land; for I will not leave you until I have done that of which I have spoken to you."* [16]*Then Jacob awoke from his sleep and said, "Surely the LORD is in this place; and I did not know it."* [17]*And he was afraid, and said, "How awesome is this place! This is none other than the house of God, and this is the gate of heaven."*

a Or *beside him*   b Or *be blessed*

OVERVIEW: The Christian interpretation of Jacob's ladder begins already in the New Testament (Jn 1:51). The stone upon which Jacob rested his head is interpreted as Christ (JEROME, CAESARIUS OF ARLES). On a moral level it manifests Jacob's hardy spirit and common sense (CHRYSOSTOM). The ladder of Jacob's dream symbolizes the cross of Christ (APHRAHAT, CHROMATIUS). It also means that Jacob foresaw Christ on earth (AMBROSE), but in another interpretation Christ is at the top of the ladder (CYRIL OF ALEXANDRIA). The angels ascending and descending represent good preachers (AUGUSTINE). Christ is also seen to be represented simultaneously by Jacob sleeping on the ground and by the top of the ladder (CAESARIUS OF ARLES). In yet another interpretation the ladder is understood to be the church (BEDE). The promise of the Lord standing above the ladder (Gen 28:13) manifests the extraordinary care and love of God (CHRYSOSTOM). The higher one's ascent, the greater one's fall (JEROME).

28:11 Jacob Escapes

THOSE WHO SUFFER PERSECUTION. JEROME: Consider our ascetic [Jacob]: he was running away from a very cruel man; he was fleeing his brother, and he found help in stone. That stone is Christ. That stone is the support of all those who suffer persecution, but to the unbelieving Jew, it is "a stone of stumbling, and a rock of scandal."[1] "Jacob saw there a ladder set up on the ground with its top reaching to heaven, and in heaven the Lord leaning upon it. And he saw angels ascending and descending."[2] Note: he saw angels ascending; he saw Paul ascending; he saw angels descending; Judas, the betrayer, was falling headlong. He saw angels ascending—holy men going from earth to heaven; he saw angels descending—the devil and his whole army cast down from heaven. It is very difficult indeed to ascend from earth into heaven. We fall more easily than we rise. We fall easily; it requires great labor, a great deal of sweat to climb upwards. If I am on the lowest step, how many more are there before I reach heaven? If I am on the second, the third, the fourth, the tenth, what benefit to me unless I reach the top? Grant with me that this ladder has fifteen rungs. I climb as high as the fourteenth, but unless I reach and hold the fifteenth, what profit to me to have mounted the fourteenth? If I should arrive at the fifteenth and then fall, the higher my ascent, the greater my fall. HOMILIES ON THE PSALMS 41.[3]

THE STONE WAS CHRIST. JEROME: When Jacob was in flight from his brother, in Mesopotamia he came to Luza, and there to rest, Scripture says, he placed a stone under his head. The stone under his head was Christ. Never before had he put a stone under his head; only at the time when he was escaping from his persecutor. When he was in his father's house, and as long as he was in his father's house and enjoyed the comforts of the flesh, he had no stone at his head. He departed from his home, poor and alone; he left with only a staff, and immediately that very night he found a stone and placed it at his head. Because he had a pillow of that kind upon which to rest his head, think of the vision he saw. "He dreamed that a ladder was set up on the ground with its top

reaching to heaven; angels were ascending and descending on it."[4] He saw angels descend from heaven to earth and others ascend from earth to heaven. Would you know that the stone at Jacob's head was Christ, the cornerstone? "The stone which the builders rejected has become the cornerstone."[5] That is the stone that is called Ebenezer in the Book of Samuel. That stone is Christ. The name Ebenezer, moreover, means "the Stone of Help."[6] "Jacob woke from his sleep,"[7] Scripture says, and what did he say? "This is the house of God." What did he do? "He poured oil over the stone." Unless we penetrate the spiritual mystery of holy Scripture, what reason is there that he should anoint the stone? HOMILIES ON THE PSALMS 46.[8]

IMBUED WITH COMMON SENSE. CHRYSOSTOM: When the sun was setting, the text tells us, he slept where the night came upon him: "He took a stone and put it under his head." See the young fellow's hardy spirit: He used the stone as a pillow and slept on the ground. Consequently, since he was imbued with common sense and a hardy attitude and was free of all human pretence, he was found worthy of that remarkable vision. Our Lord is like that, you see: When he sees a dutiful soul that makes no account of present realities, he demonstrates his own great care for him. HOMILIES ON GENESIS 54.17.[9]

YOU WILL RECOGNIZE CHRIST. CAESARIUS OF ARLES: We do not read of blessed Jacob that he departed with horses or asses or camels, but we read only that he carried a staff in his hand. Thus, indeed, when entreating the Lord he said, "Lord, I am not worthy of all your kindnesses. With only my staff I crossed this Jordan; behold, now I have grown into two camps."[10] Jacob displayed his staff to take a wife, but Christ bore the wood of the cross to redeem the church. In his sleep Jacob put

---

[1]Rom 9:33; 1 Pet 2:8; Is 8:14; 28:16. [2]Gen 28:12-13. [3]FC 48:302-3. [4]Gen 28:12. [5]Ps 118:22 (117:22 LXX). [6]1 Sam 4:1; 7:12. [7]Gen 28:16-22. [8]FC 48:351-52*. [9]FC 87:100*. [10]Gen 32:10.

a stone under his head and saw a ladder extending to heaven, while the Lord leaned upon the ladder. Consider, brothers, how many mysteries there are in this place. Jacob represented a type of the Lord our Savior; the stone that he put under his head no less prefigured Christ the Lord. Listen to the apostle telling why the stone at the head signifies Christ: "The head of man is Christ."[11] Finally, notice that blessed Jacob anointed the stone. Pay attention to the anointing, and you will recognize Christ: Christ is explained from an anointing, that is, from the grace of anointing. SERMON 87.2.[12]

28:12 Jacob Dreams of a Ladder

A LADDER SET ON THE EARTH. APHRAHAT: Our father Jacob too prayed at Bethel and saw the gate of heaven opened, with a ladder going up on high. This is a symbol of our Savior that Jacob saw; the gate of heaven is Christ, in accordance with what he said, "I am the gate of life; every one who enters by me shall live for ever."[13] David too said, "This is the gate of the Lord, by which the righteous enter."[14] Again, the ladder that Jacob saw is a symbol of our Savior, in that by means of him the just ascend from the lower to the upper realm. The ladder is also a symbol of our Savior's cross, which was raised up like a ladder, with the Lord standing above it. ON PRAYER 5.[15]

HE FORESAW CHRIST ON EARTH. AMBROSE: Jacob set out and slept—evidence of tranquility of spirit—and saw angels of God ascending and descending. This means he foresaw Christ on earth; the band of angels was descending to Christ and ascending to him,[16] so as to render service to their rightful master in loving servitude. JACOB AND THE HAPPY LIFE 2.4.16.[17]

THE LADDER IS THE CROSS OF CHRIST. CHROMATIUS: Through the resurrection of Christ the way was opened. Therefore with good reason the patriarch Jacob relates that he had seen in that place a ladder whose end reached heaven and that

the Lord leaned on it. The ladder fixed to the ground and reaching heaven is the cross of Christ, through which the access to heaven is granted to us, because it actually leads us to heaven. On this ladder different steps of virtue are set, through which we rise toward heaven: faith, justice, chastity, holiness, patience, piety and all the other virtues are the steps of this ladder. If we faithfully climb them, we will undoubtedly reach heaven. And therefore we know well that the ladder is the symbol of the cross of Christ. As, in fact, the steps are set between two uprights, so the cross of Christ is placed between the two Testaments and keeps in itself the steps of the heavenly precepts, through which we climb to heaven. SERMON 1.6.[18]

GOOD PREACHERS ASCEND AND DESCEND. AUGUSTINE: But what did he see that time on the ladder? Angels ascending and descending. So also is the church, brothers; the angels of God, good preachers, preaching Christ; that is, they ascend and descend upon the Son of man. How do they ascend, and how do they descend? From one we have an example. Hear the apostle Paul; what we find in him, let us believe also about the rest of the preachers of truth. See Paul ascending: "I know a man in Christ who fourteen years ago (whether in the body or out of the body I do not know, God knows) was caught up to the third heaven, and heard unutterable words which it is not granted to man to speak."[19] You heard him ascending; hear him descending: "I could not speak to you as spiritual men but only as carnal, as to little ones in Christ. I gave you milk to drink, not solid food."[20] Look, he who had ascended descended. Seek where he had ascended: "Up to the third heaven." Seek where he had descended: "I became a little one," he says, "in your midst, as if a nurse were fondling her own children."[21] TRACTATE ON THE GOSPEL OF JOHN 7.23.3-4.[22]

---

[11]1 Cor 11:3. [12]FC 47:30. [13]Jn 10:7. [14]Ps 117:20 LXX. [15]CS 101:8-9. [16]Cf. Jn 1:51. [17]FC 65:155-56. [18]SC 154:132. [19]2 Cor 12:2-4. [20]1Cor 3:1-2. [21]1 Thess 2:7. [22]FC 78:176-77.

CHRIST IS ON TOP OF THE STAIRWAY. CYRIL OF ALEXANDRIA: This is, I believe, the stairway, the running to and fro of the holy spirits, who "are sent forth to minister for those who shall be the heirs of salvation."[23] Christ is firmly placed on top of the stairway for those holy spirits who can reach him, who have him as their overseer, not as someone who exists among them but as God and Lord. In another passage David says to all people who want to live in the protection of the Most High:"He shall give his angels charge concerning you to keep you in all your ways. They shall bear you up on their hands, lest at any time you dash your foot against a stone. You shall tread on the asp and the basilisk, and shall trample on the lion and the dragon."[24] We trod on serpents and scorpions and on every power of the enemy,[25] thanks to the power given to us by Christ. Those who are in Christ are also worthy of the divine look, so that he may promise them that he will be by them and help them, and will save them everywhere and will declare them fruitful."I am with you always, even to the end of the world."[26] The fact that the blessed disciples were enriched and made the fathers of innumerable nations by their faith in Christ, and as by a spiritual generation, is manifest to everybody. Paul himself said clearly to those who believed through him:"Though you have one thousand teachers in Christ, yet you have not many fathers: For in Christ Jesus I have begotten you through the gospel."[27] Therefore their seed was made as numerous as the grains of sand and was spread to the east and the west, to the left and the right, to the south and the north. GLAPHYRA ON GENESIS, 3.4.[28]

THE LORD IS IN HEAVEN AND ON EARTH. CAESARIUS OF ARLES: Now if Jacob sleeping on the ground prefigured the Lord, why is it that the Lord in heaven rested and leaned upon the ladder? How was Christ the Lord seen on top of the ladder in heaven and in blessed Jacob on the ground? Listen to Christ himself say that he is in heaven and on earth:"No one has ascended into heaven except him who has descended from heav-

en: the Son of Man who is in heaven."[29] Notice that the Lord himself said he is both in heaven and on earth. We confess, dearly beloved, that Christ the Lord is head of the church; if this is true, he is in heaven with regard to the head but on earth as far as the body is concerned. Moreover, when the blessed apostle Paul was persecuting the church, Christ exclaimed from heaven: "Saul, Saul, why do you persecute me?"[30] He did not say,"Why do you persecute my servants?" Nor did he say,"Why do you persecute my members?" But he said,"Why do you persecute me?" Now the tongue cries out if the foot is stepped on, You stepped on me, even though the tongue cannot be stepped on at all; through the harmony of charity the head cries out for all the members. Therefore Jacob was sleeping and saw the Lord leaning on the top of the ladder. What does it mean to lean on the ladder, except to hang on the cross? Consider, brothers, that while hanging upon the wood of the cross he prayed for the Jews, and you will realize who shouted from heaven while leaning on the ladder of Jacob. But why did this happen on the road, before Jacob obtained a wife? Because our Lord, the true Jacob, first leaned on the ladder, that is, the cross, and afterward formed a church for himself. At the time he gave it the wages of his blood, intending to give it later the dowry of his kingdom. SERMON 87.3.[31]

JACOB AND THE LORD PREFIGURED CHRIST. CAESARIUS OF ARLES: Listen and see the sublimity of the fact that Jacob asleep and the Lord leaning on the ladder prefigured Christ. Indeed, when our Savior in speaking of Nathanael had named blessed Jacob, he said,"Behold, an Israelite in whom there is no guile."[32] Continuing, he said, "Presently you shall see heaven opened, and the angels of God ascending and descending upon the Son of man."[33] In the Gospels our Lord preached

---

[23]Heb 1:14. [24]Ps 91:11-13 (90:11-13 LXX). [25]Lk 10:19. [26]Mt 28:20. [27]1 Cor 4:15. [28]PG 69:189. [29]Jn 3:13. [30]Acts 9:4. [31]FC 47:30-31. [32]Jn 1:47. [33]Jn 1:51.

concerning himself what Jacob had seen prefigured in his sleep: "You shall see heaven opened, and the angels of God ascending and descending upon the Son of man." If the angels of God were descending to the Son because he was on earth, how is it that those same angels were ascending to the Son of man except because he is in heaven? Therefore he himself was sleeping in Jacob, and from heaven he likewise called to Jacob. SERMON 87.4.[34]

GOD'S PREACHERS ASCEND AND DESCEND.
CAESARIUS OF ARLES: "All these things," as the apostle proclaims, brothers, "happened to them as a type, and they were written for us upon whom the final age of the world has come."[35] Carefully notice, brothers, how the angels of God ascend to the Son of man in heaven and descend to the same Son on earth. When God's preachers announce deep and profound truths from sacred Scripture, which are understood only by devout men, they ascend to the Son of man; when they preach matters pertaining to the correction of morals, which all the people can understand, they descend to the son of man. Thus the apostle says, "Wisdom we speak among those who are mature, yet not a wisdom of this world nor of the rulers of this world, but a secret, hidden wisdom which God foreordained before the world to our glory."[36] When the apostle said these words doubtless he was ascending to the Son of man. However, when he said, "Flee immorality";[37] when he said, "do not be drunk with wine, for in that is debauchery";[38] when he declared, "covetousness is the root of all evils,"[39] in these words he descended like the angel of God to the Son of man. When he further said, "Mind the things that are above, not the things that are on earth,"[40] he was ascending. However, when he taught, "Be sober, and do not sin,"[41] and preached the other truths that pertain to the correction of morals, he was descending; ministering the milk of doctrine like a nurse to children, he spoke words that even the ignorant could grasp. In this manner, then, there is ascending and descending to the Son of man, since solid food is offered to the perfect while the milk of doctrine is not denied even to the young. Blessed John also was ascending when he said, "In the beginning was the Word, and the Word was with God; and the Word was God;"[42] by these words he ascended on high sufficiently. However, since God's angels not only ascend but also descend, bending down he says to the little ones, "The Word was made flesh, and dwelt among us."[43] SERMON 87.5.[44]

THE LADDER IS THE CHURCH. BEDE: Now when Jacob, wishing to rest in a certain place, put a stone under his head, he saw in his sleep a ladder standing upon the earth with its top touching heaven. [He saw] also angels of God ascending and descending on it and the Lord resting on the ladder saying to him, "I am the God of Abraham your father, and the God of Isaac."[45] And rising in the morning and rendering praise to the Lord with due trepidation, he took the stone and set it up as a mark, pouring oil on it.[46]

The Lord made mention of this place and most clearly bore witness in a figurative way concerning himself and his faithful ones. The ladder which he saw is the church, which has its birth from the earth but its "way of life in heaven,"[47] And by it angels ascend and descend, when evangelists announce at one time to perfect hearers the preeminent hidden mysteries of [Christ's] divinity and at another time announce to those still untaught the weaknesses of his humanity. Or they ascend when [in their teaching] they pass to heavenly things to be contemplated by the mind, and they descend when they educate their listeners as to how they ought to live on earth. HOMILIES ON THE GOSPELS 1.17.[48]

28:13 Land for Jacob's Descendants

[34]FC 47:31-32. [35]1 Cor 10:11. [36]1 Cor 2:6-7. [37]1 Cor 6:18. [38]Eph 5:18. [39]1 Tim 6:10. [40]Col 3:2. [41]1 Cor 15:34. [42]Jn 1:1. [43]Jn 1:14. [44]FC 47:32-33. [45]Gen 28:11-13. [46]Gen 28:18. [47]Phil 3:20. [48]CS 110:175-76.

EXTRAORDINARY CARE. CHRYSOSTOM: Notice here, I ask you, the extraordinary care of the loving God. When he saw [Jacob] consenting to the journey in accordance with his mother's advice, which came out of fear of his brother, and taking to the road like some athlete, with no support from any source, leaving everything instead to help from on high, Christ wanted at the very beginning of the journey to strengthen Jacob's resolve. And so he appeared to him with the words "I am the God of Abraham and the God of your father Isaac."[49] I have caused the patriarch and your father to experience a great increase in prosperity; so, far from being afraid, believe that I am he who fulfilled my promises and will shower on you my care. HOMILIES ON GENESIS 54.18.[50]

---

[49]Chrysostom transfers "your father" from Abraham to Isaac. [50]FC 87:101*.

28:18-22 JACOB ANOINTS THE STONE

[18]*So Jacob rose early in the morning, and he took the stone which he had put under his head and set it up for a pillar and poured oil on the top of it.* [19]*He called the name of that place Bethel;[c] but the name of the city was Luz at the first.* [20]*Then Jacob made a vow, saying, "If God will be with me, and will keep me in this way that I go, and will give me bread to eat and clothing to wear,* [21]*so that I come again to my father's house in peace, then the LORD shall be my God,* [22]*and this stone, which I have set up for a pillar, shall be God's house; and of all that thou givest me I will give the tenth to thee."*

c That is *The house of God*

OVERVIEW: The anointing of the pillar of stone also signifies the mystery of Christ as the "anointed one" (EPHREM, AUGUSTINE, CYRIL OF ALEXANDRIA, CAESARIUS OF ARLES, BEDE), but it points as well to the calling of the Gentiles (APHRAHAT). Jacob's action in setting up the pillar and promising a tithe to God shows his godly attitude (CHRYSOSTOM).

28:18 Jacob Sets Up a Pillar

THE MYSTERY OF CHRIST. EPHREM THE SYRIAN: As for the oil that Jacob poured upon the pillar, he either had it with him or he had brought it out of the village. In the oil that he poured upon the stone, he was depicting the mystery of Christ who was hidden inside it. COMMEN-TARY ON GENESIS 26.2.[1]

JACOB ACTED SYMBOLICALLY. APHRAHAT: Now Jacob called that place Bethel; and Jacob raised up there a pillar of stone as a testimony, and he poured oil over it. Our father Jacob did this too in symbol, anticipating that stones would receive anointing, for the peoples who have believed in Christ are the stones that are anointed, just as John says of them: "From these stones God is able to raise up children for Abraham."[2] For in Jacob's prayer the calling of the nations was symbolized. ON PRAYER 5.[3]

HE MADE THE PLACE MEMORABLE. CHRYSOS-

---

[1]FC 91:174. [2]Lk 3:8. [3]CS 101:9.

tom: Since he had been granted wonderful favors by way of the vision, [Jacob] wished to make the place memorable by a name and to keep the memory fresh for future ages. He set up the stone as a monument, poured oil on it (this, after all, was probably all he had with him, traveling as he was like this), and to the loving God he offered a prayer characterized by complete good sense. Homilies on Genesis 54.23.[4]

Christ Was Represented. Augustine: In a dream Jacob saw a ladder, and on this ladder he saw angels ascending and descending; and he anointed the stone that he had placed at his head. You have heard that the Messiah is the Christ; you have heard that the Christ is the Anointed. For he did not place the anointed stone so that he might come and adore it; otherwise it would be idolatry and not a representation of Christ. Therefore a representation was made, so far as a representation needed to be made, and Christ was represented. The stone was anointed. Why a stone? "Behold, I lay in Zion a chosen stone, precious; and he who believes in it shall not be confounded."[5] Why anointed? Because [the name] "Christ" [is derived] from [the word] *chrisma*.[6] Tractate on the Gospel of John 7.23.2.[7]

A Symbol of Christ. Cyril of Alexandria: On the other hand the stone also had been erected and honored as a symbol of Christ and had been sprinkled with oil. The Immanuel was anointed by God the Father "with the oil of gladness above his fellows."[8] Then he was raised from the dead, even though he had descended to death voluntarily. And that is, I believe, the meaning of erecting the stone. Glaphyra on Genesis, 4.4.[9]

Prefiguration and Fulfillment. Caesarius of Arles: In order that what we have mentioned above may adhere more firmly to your pious hearts, we will briefly repeat what was said. Blessed Isaac, as we said, sending his son away was a type of God the Father; Jacob who was sent signified Christ our Lord. The stone that he had

at his head and anointed with oil also represented the Lord our Savior. The ladder touching heaven prefigured the cross; the Lord leaning on the ladder is shown to be Christ fastened to the cross. The angels ascending and descending on it are understood to be the apostles, apostolic men and all doctors of the church. They ascend by preaching perfect truths to the just; they descend by telling the young and ignorant what they can understand. For our part, brothers, we who see fulfilled in the New Testament all the truths which were prefigured in the Old should thank God as well as we can because he has deigned to give us such great gifts without any preceding merits on our part. With his help let us labor with all our strength so that these great benefits may not bring us judgment but progress. Rather, let us be zealous to live spiritually and always to engage in good works in such a way that when the day of judgment finds us chaste, sober, merciful and pious, we may not be punished with wicked sinners. But with the just and all who fear God we will merit to arrive at eternal bliss: with the help of our Lord who together with the Father and the Holy Spirit lives and reigns world without end. Amen. Sermon 87.6.[10]

The Stone Is the Lord. Bede: The stone under Jacob's head is the Lord, upon whom we ought to support ourselves with all our concentration, the more so insofar as it is surely clear to us that without him we can do nothing.[11]

Jacob anointed the stone and set it up as a mark, because a true Israelite understands that our Redeemer was anointed by the Father with the oil of gladness above his fellows.[12] From this ointment (that is, chrism) Christ received his name, and the mystery of his incarnation is the mark of our redemption. It is good that when the stone was anointed on the earth and raised up as a mark, the Lord was revealed in heaven, for un-

---

[4]FC 87:103. [5]1 Pet 2:6; Is 28:16. [6]"Which means "anointing." [7]FC 78:176. [8]Ps 45:7 (44:8 LXX); Heb 1:9. [9]PG 69:189. [10]FC 47:33-34. [11]Jn 15:5. [12]Ps 45:7 (44:8 LXX).

doubtedly he appeared in time as a man among men while he remained eternal with God the Father. When death was overcome "he ascended over the heaven of heavens to the east,"[13] remaining with us as a mark of our salvation "for all days, up to the consummation of the world."[14] He who transferred the body he had assumed from earth to heaven was the One who filled earth, and heaven as well, with the presence of deity. Homilies on the Gospels 1.17.[15]

28:22 God's House

His Godly Attitude. Chrysostom: See the good man's gratitude: In making his request Jacob did not bring himself to ask for anything lavish—just bread and clothing. On the other hand, he promised to the Lord what lay within his power, realizing God's generosity in giving and the fact that he surpasses our expectations in rewarding us. And so he said, "I will consider the monument God's house, and of all the things provided me by you I will set aside a tenth." Do you see his godly attitude? He still had not received anything, and yet he promised to devote to God a tenth of what was due to be given him.

Let us not pass idly by these words, dearly beloved. Instead, may we all imitate this good man, we in the age of grace imitating this man who lived before the law, and let us ask the Lord for nothing of this world. After all, he does not wait for a reminder from us. Even if we don't ask, he grants us what we need. "He makes the sun rise on evil people and good, and rains on just and unjust."[16] Let us believe him as he advises us in these words, "Seek first the kingdom of God, and all these things will come to you in addition."[17] Do you see that he personally has made the former things ready for us and promises to give the latter as a bonus? Accordingly, don't request as an initial favor what you are likely to receive as a bonus, thus reversing the due order. Instead, let us seek the former things, as he directed, so that we may come to enjoy the former and the latter. Homilies on Genesis 54.25-26.[18]

---

[13]Ps 67:34 LXX. [14]Mt 28:20. [15]CS 110:176. [16]Mt 5:45. [17]Mt 6:33. [18]FC 87:104-5.

29:1-14 JACOB ARRIVES IN HARAN

[1]Then Jacob went on his journey, and came to the land of the people of the east. [2]As he looked, he saw a well in the field, and lo, three flocks of sheep lying beside it; for out of that well the flocks were watered. The stone on the well's mouth was large, [3]and when all the flocks were gathered there, the shepherds would roll the stone from the mouth of the well, and water the sheep, and put the stone back in its place upon the mouth of the well.

[4]Jacob said to them, "My brothers, where do you come from?" They said, "We are from Haran." [5]He said to them, "Do you know Laban the son of Nahor?" They said, "We know him." [6]He said to them, "Is it well with him?" They said, "It is well; and see, Rachel his daughter is coming with the sheep!" [7]He said, "Behold, it is still high day, it is not time for the animals to be gathered together; water the sheep, and go, pasture them." [8]But they said, "We cannot until all the flocks are gathered together, and the stone is rolled from the mouth of the well; then we water the sheep."

⁹*While he was still speaking with them, Rachel came with her father's sheep; for she kept them.*
¹⁰*Now when Jacob saw Rachel the daughter of Laban his mother's brother, and the sheep of Laban his mother's brother, Jacob went up and rolled the stone from the well's mouth, and watered the flock of Laban his mother's brother.* ¹¹*Then Jacob kissed Rachel, and wept aloud.* ¹²*And Jacob told Rachel that he was her father's kinsman, and that he was Rebekah's son; and she ran and told her father.*

¹³*When Laban heard the tidings of Jacob his sister's son, he ran to meet him, and embraced him and kissed him, and brought him to his house. Jacob told Laban all these things,* ¹⁴*and Laban said to him, "Surely you are my bone and my flesh!" And he stayed with him a month.*

OVERVIEW: Jacob's removal of the stone from the well signified his betrothal to Rachel, and his kiss was the marriage (EPHREM). Rachel is interpreted as a symbol of the church among the nations (CYRIL OF ALEXANDRIA). Just as Jacob found his wife Rachel at the well, so Christ found his bride the church at the waters of baptism (CAESARIUS OF ARLES).

29:11 Jacob Kisses Rachel

JACOB MARRIED HER WITH A KISS. EPHREM THE SYRIAN: Jacob continued on and turned aside to a well where he saw Rachel the shepherd girl, who, with her bare feet, her shabby clothing and her face burned from the sun, could not be distinguished from the charred brands that come out of the fire. Jacob knew at once that he who had provided the beautiful Rebekah at the spring now provided Rachel in her shabby clothing at the well. Then he performed a heroic deed in her presence, for, through the Son who was hidden in it, he rolled away the stone that even many could raise only with great difficulty. When he betrothed her to God through this marvelous deed, Jacob then returned and married himself to her with a kiss. COMMENTARY ON GENESIS 27.1.[1]

RACHEL SYMBOLIZES THE CHURCH AMONG THE NATIONS. CYRIL OF ALEXANDRIA: In addition Rachel is interpreted as a "sheep of God." And some consider her to be with good reason a symbol of the church among the nations. She is also the sheep of Christ, mixed in the ancient folds, and finally received in the fold of the Savior. Therefore he said, "And other sheep I have, which are not of this fold, them also I must bring, and they shall hear my voice; and there shall be one fold, and one shepherd."[2] And the holy disciples acted as shepherds of the church of Christ, when they supported her as reasonable creatures and when they were her lovers and bridegrooms and presented her to God as a pure virgin[3] without spots or wrinkles, or as something similar, "holy and immaculate."[4] GLAPHYRA ON GENESIS, 4.4.[5]

MYSTERIES AT THE WELLS. CAESARIUS OF ARLES: We have frequently mentioned to your charity, dearly beloved, that blessed Jacob was a type and figure of our Lord and Savior. Moreover, how Christ was to come into the world to be joined to the church was prefigured also in blessed Jacob when he traveled into a distant country to choose a wife. Therefore blessed Jacob, as you have heard, went into Mesopotamia to take a wife. When he had come to a certain well, he saw Rachel coming with her father's sheep—after he recognized her as his cousin, he kissed her as soon as the flock was supplied with water. If you notice carefully, brothers, you can recognize that it was not without reason that the holy patriarchs found their wives at wells or fountains. If this had happened only once, someone might

---

[1]FC 91:174-75*. [2]Jn 10:16. [3]2 Cor 11:2. [4]Eph 5:27. [5]PG 69:201.

say it was accidental and not for some definite reason. Blessed Rebekah who was to be united to blessed Isaac was found at the well; Rachel whom blessed Jacob was to marry was recognized at the well; and Zipporah who was joined to Moses was found at the well. Doubtless then we ought to understand some mysteries in these facts. Since all three of those patriarchs typified our Lord and Savior, for this reason they found their wives at fountains or wells, because Christ was to find his church at the waters of baptism. Moreover, when Jacob came to the well, Rachel first watered the flock, and then he kissed her. It is true, dearly be-

loved, unless the Christian people are first washed from all evil by the waters of baptism, they do not deserve to possess the peace of Christ. Could not blessed Jacob have kissed his cousin upon seeing her, before the flock was watered? Doubtless he could have, but a mystery was involved: for it was necessary for the church to be freed from all iniquity and dissension by the grace of baptism and thus to merit peace with God. SERMON 88.1.[6]

---

[6]FC 47:34-35.

29:15-30 JACOB MARRIES LEAH AND RACHEL

[15]Then Laban said to Jacob, "Because you are my kinsman, should you therefore serve me for nothing? Tell me, what shall your wages be?" [16]Now Laban had two daughters; the name of the older was Leah, and the name of the younger was Rachel. [17]Leah's eyes were weak, but Rachel was beautiful and lovely. [18]Jacob loved Rachel; and he said, "I will serve you seven years for your younger daughter Rachel." [19]Laban said, "It is better that I give her to you than that I should give her to any other man; stay with me." [20]So Jacob served seven years for Rachel, and they seemed to him but a few days because of the love he had for her.

[21]Then Jacob said to Laban, "Give me my wife that I may go in to her, for my time is completed." [22]So Laban gathered together all the men of the place, and made a feast. [23]But in the evening he took his daughter Leah and brought her to Jacob; and he went in to her. [24] (Laban gave his maid Zilpah to his daughter Leah to be her maid.) [25]And in the morning, behold, it was Leah; and Jacob said to Laban, "What is this you have done to me? Did I not serve with you for Rachel? Why then have you deceived me?" [26]Laban said, "It is not so done in our country, to give the younger before the first-born. [27]Complete the week of this one, and we will give you the other also in return for serving me another seven years." [28]Jacob did so, and completed her week; then Laban gave him his daughter Rachel to wife. [29] (Laban gave his maid Bilhah to his daughter Rachel to be her maid.) [30]So Jacob went in to Rachel also, and he loved Rachel more than Leah, and served Laban for another seven years.

OVERVIEW: Jacob demonstrates right attitude and a lack of desire for gain as well as great love in

his willingness to serve seven years in return for Rachel. The fact that Jacob took two wives can be explained by the necessity of increasing the race in those former times, but now this practice has been changed through Christ's teaching (CHRYSOSTOM). On an allegorical level, Jacob's two wives prefigured the two people of the Jews and the Gentiles (CAESARIUS OF ARLES).

29:15 Jacob's Wages Set

GREAT HUMILITY. CHRYSOSTOM: Notice, I ask you, how when someone is helped by the hand from on high, everything goes favorably for him. "You shall not serve me for nothing," Laban says. "Tell me what your wages should be." In fact, this blessed man was acting out of love and was content simply to receive board and lodging and return him sincere thanks for it. But, since Jacob demonstrated great humility, Laban took the initiative in promising to pay him whatever wage he named. HOMILIES ON GENESIS 55.6.[1]

29:18 Seven Years' Service

LOVE REDUCES WORK AND TIME. CHRYSOSTOM: See in this case too, I ask you, his keen discernment and how he had no desire for accumulating money. Far from haggling with Laban in the manner of a hireling and demanding something more, Jacob remembered his mother and his father's directions and showed his extraordinary meekness in saying, "I will serve you seven years for your younger daughter Rachel." You see, on seeing her from the outset at the well, he fell in love with her. See the man's right attitude: He sets a time for himself and by means of this period of years he provides himself with an adequate incentive for his own continence. Why are you surprised, dearly beloved, that he promised to serve seven years for the maiden he loved? To show, in fact, how his great love reduced the labor and the period of time, sacred Scripture says, "Jacob served seven years for Rachel, and in his eyes they were but a few days when measured against his love for her."[2] The period of seven years, it is saying, was counted but a few days because of his

surpassing love for the maiden. You see, when someone is smitten with love's desire, far from seeing any problem, he easily puts up with everything, albeit fraught with danger and much difficulty besides, having in view one thing only—obtaining the object of his desire. HOMILIES ON GENESIS 55.7.[3]

29:23 Leah Brought to Jacob

SOLEMN WEDDINGS. CHRYSOSTOM: Do you see with how much solemnity they conducted weddings in ancient times? Take heed, you who are swept up in the excitement of satanic rituals and besmirch the solemnity of marriage at its very beginnings. Surely there's no place for flutes? Surely there's no place for cymbals? Surely there's no place for satanic dances? Why is it, tell me, that you introduce such a nuisance into the house and call in people from the stage and the theater so as to undermine the girl's chastity with this regrettable expenditure and make the young person shameless? HOMILIES ON GENESIS 56.2.[4]

LABAN'S DECEPTION. CHRYSOSTOM: Don't idly pass by this sentence, either. Much can be understood from it. [First], there is Jacob's simplicity in being deceived through his own ignorance of any wickedness; second, the fact that everything was conducted with such extreme decorum, no unnecessary display of lamps and dancers and torches, that Laban's deception took effect. It is possible, however, to learn from this incident Laban's affection for Jacob. You see, his purpose in devising this scheme was to keep the good man with him longer. I mean, he realized that Jacob was madly in love with one daughter and that, had he attained the object of his desire, he would then not have chosen to undergo servitude for the sake of Leah or reside with Laban. Hence, seeing Jacob's virtue and realizing that he would not otherwise get the better of him or persuade him, he

---

[1]FC 87:110*. [2]Gen 29:20. [3]FC 87:110-11*. [4]FC 87:119*.

had recourse to this deception and gave him Leah with her maidservant Zilpah. Homilies on Genesis 56.10.[5]

29:28 Rachel Given to Jacob

Conditions Change. Chrysostom: You observe once again that the nuptials were conducted with all seemliness. Don't be disturbed, however, to hear that he married the elder girl and then the younger or judge happenings in those times by present conditions. In those times, you see, since it was the very beginning, people were allowed to live with two or three wives or more so as to increase the race; now, on the contrary, because through God's grace the human race has expanded into a vast number, the practice of virtue has also increased. I mean, Christ by his coming has sown the seeds of virtue among human beings and turned them into angels, so to say, thus rooting out all that former practice. Do you see how we should not be proposing that practice but rather seek out everywhere what is useful? Take note. Since the practice itself was evil, see how it has been rooted out, and no one is free now to propose it. Consequently I beseech you, far from seeking to adopt it in any way, search rather for what is useful, not what is spiritually harmful. If something good comes our way, even if it is not general practice, let us adopt it; but if it is harmful, even if general practice, let us avoid and turn away from it. Homilies on Genesis 56.12.[6]

29:30 Jacob's Love for Rachel

The Peace of Jews and the Gentiles Prefigured. Caesarius of Arles: In that journey Jacob took two wives, and those two wives prefigured the two people of the Jews and the Gentiles. For at Christ's coming not a small number even of the Jewish people are read to have believed in him, and again in the Acts of the Apostles there is recorded the fact that on one day three thousand people believed, on another day five thousand and afterward many thousands more.[7] The Lord himself in the Gospel confirms the fact that Jews and Gentiles believed in Christ when he said, "And other sheep I have that are not of this fold. I must also bring them, so that there may be one fold and one shepherd."[8] Therefore those two women who were married to blessed Jacob, that is, Leah and Rachel, prefigured those two people: Leah the Jews and Rachel the Gentiles. Like a cornerstone Christ is joined to those two people, like two walls coming from different directions. In him they have kissed, and in him they have merited to find eternal peace, as the apostle says, "For he himself is our peace, he it is who has made both one."[9] How did he make both one? By uniting the two flocks and connecting the two walls to himself. Sermon 88.2.[10]

---

[5]FC 87:123*. [6]FC 87:124. [7]Acts 2:41; 4:4; 21:20. [8]Jn 10:16. [9]Eph 2:14. [10]FC 47:35*.

29:31-35 JACOB'S CHILDREN

[31]*When the Lord saw that Leah was hated, he opened her womb; but Rachel was barren.* [32]*And Leah conceived and bore a son, and she called his name Reuben;[d] for she said, "Because the Lord has looked upon my affliction; surely now my husband will love me."* [33]*She conceived again and bore a son, and said, "Because the Lord has heard[e] that I am hated, he has given me this son also"; and she called his name Simeon.* [34]*Again she conceived and bore a son, and said, "Now this*

time my husband will be joined[f] to me, because I have borne him three sons"; therefore his name was called Levi. [35]And she conceived again and bore a son, and said, "This time I will praise[g] the LORD"; therefore she called his name Judah; then she ceased bearing.

d That is *See, a son* **e** Heb *shama* **f** Heb *lawah* **g** Heb *hodah*

OVERVIEW: God's creative wisdom is shown by his giving sons to Leah before Rachel (CHRYSOSTOM). Just as those born after the firstborn Reuben resembled him, so those reborn through water and the Spirit should resemble the firstborn of many brothers, Christ (GREGORY OF NYSSA).

29:31 God Opens Leah's Womb

GOD'S CREATIVE WISDOM. CHRYSOSTOM: See God's creative wisdom. Whereas one woman by her beauty attracted her husband's favor, the other seemed to be rejected because she lacked it. But it was the latter God awoke to childbirth while leaving the other's womb inactive. He thus dealt with each in his characteristic love so that one might have some comfort from what was born of her and the other might not triumph over her sister on the score of charm and beauty. HOMILIES ON GENESIS 56.14.[1]

29:32 The Lord Sees Leah's Affliction

FAMILY RESEMBLANCE KNOWN BY CHARACTER OF LIFE. GREGORY OF NYSSA: Reuben was the firstborn of those born after him, and their resemblance to him bore witness to their relationship to him, so that their brotherhood was not unrecognized, being testified to by the similarity of appearance. Therefore, if through the same rebirth "by water and the spirit," we also have become brothers of the Lord, he having become for us "the firstborn among the many brothers,"[2] it follows that our nearness to him will show in the character of our life, because "the firstborn of every creature"[3] has informed our life. But what have we learned from the Scripture about the character of his life? What we have said many times: that "he committed no sin, nor was deceit found in his mouth."[4] Therefore, if we are going to act as brothers of the One who gave us birth, the sinlessness of our life will be a pledge of our relationship to him, and no filth will nullify our union with his purity. But the firstborn is also justice and holiness and love and redemption and such things. So if our life is characterized by such qualities, we furnish clear tokens of our noble birth, and anyone, seeing these qualities in our life, will bear witness to our brotherhood with Christ. ON PERFECTION.[5]

[1]FC 87:125*. [2]Rom 8:29. [3]Col 1:15. [4]1 Pet 2:22. [5]FC 58:115*.

30:1-8 JACOB'S CHILDREN BY BILHAH

[1]When Rachel saw that she bore Jacob no children, she envied her sister; and she said to Jacob, "Give me children, or I shall die!" [2]Jacob's anger was kindled against Rachel, and he said, "Am I in the place of God, who has withheld from you the fruit of the womb?" [3]Then she said, "Here is my maid Bilhah; go in to her, that she may bear upon my knees, and even I may have children through

her." ⁴*So she gave him her maid Bilhah as a wife; and Jacob went in to her.* ⁵*And Bilhah conceived and bore Jacob a son.* ⁶*Then Rachel said, "God has judged me, and has also heard my voice and given me a son"; therefore she called his name Dan.*^b ⁷*Rachel's maid Bilhah conceived again and bore Jacob a second son.* ⁸*Then Rachel said, "With mighty wrestlings I have wrestled*ⁱ *with my sister, and have prevailed"; so she called his name Naphtali.*

h That is *He judged*   **i** Heb *niphtal*

OVERVIEW: Rachel's demand for children from Jacob is explained by attributing to her the thought that Jacob had not prayed for her as the cause of her barrenness (EPHREM). Jacob's response to Rachel is evidence of great wisdom, insisting as he does on the agency of God (CHRYSOSTOM). Jacob's consent to Rachel's offer of her maid was practical, to avoid her nagging, and prophetic in that it foreshadowed the sons of the maidservants becoming joint heirs with the sons of the free women (EPHREM).

30:1 Give Me Children, or I Shall Die!

RACHEL THOUGHT JACOB HAD NOT PRAYED FOR HER. EPHREM THE SYRIAN: Leah bore Reuben, Simeon, Levi and Judah and then ceased giving birth, whereas Rachel was barren. Because she heard Jacob say that Abraham had prayed over the barren Sarah and was heard and that Isaac had also prayed for Rebekah and was answered, she thought that it was because Jacob had not prayed for her that her closed womb had not been opened. For this reason, she said in anger and in tears, "Give me children, or I shall die!" COMMENTARY ON GENESIS 28.1.1.[1]

30:2 Jacob's Anger with Rachel

JACOB REPLIED WITH GREAT WISDOM. CHRYSOSTOM: Why, Jacob says, do you ignore the Lord of nature and fix the blame on me? He it is who has deprived you of the fruit of the womb. Why not make your request to him, who can open nature's workplace and quicken the womb

to childbirth? So understand that God is the one who has deprived you of the fruit of the womb and granted your sister such fertility. So don't look to me for what I am powerless to provide and over which I have no lordship. I mean, if it lay in my power, I would certainly give you pride of place ahead of your sister by securing greater respect for you. But since, no matter to what degree I am kindly disposed to you, I can do nothing to solve your problem, address your request to him who inflicted the sterility and has the power to remedy it. See the good man's common sense in that, though provoked to anger by her words, he replied to her with great wisdom, instructing her precisely in everything and making the responsibility clear to her, lest by ignoring the Lord she might seek from another what God alone was able to provide. HOMILIES ON GENESIS 56.19.[2]

30:4 Rachel's Maid Bilhah

JOINT HEIRS. EPHREM THE SYRIAN: So, lest she nag him, asking him every day for children, Jacob, who was sent from his parents to take a daughter of Laban, agreed to take the foreign woman. But it was also so that the sons of the maidservants might become joint heirs with sons of the freewomen that Jacob took maidservants and freewomen. So he took Bilhah, and she conceived and bore Dan and Naphtali. COMMENTARY ON GENESIS 28.1.2.[3]

---

[1]FC 91:176. [2]FC 87:128*. [3]FC 91:176.

30:9-24 JACOB'S SONS BY ZILPAH, LEAH AND RACHEL

⁹When Leah saw that she had ceased bearing children, she took her maid Zilpah and gave her to Jacob as a wife. ¹⁰Then Leah's maid Zilpah bore Jacob a son. ¹¹And Leah said, "Good fortune!" so she called his name Gad.ʲ ¹²Leah's maid Zilpah bore Jacob a second son. ¹³And Leah said, "Happy am I! For the women will call me happy"; so she called his name Asher.ᵏ

¹⁴In the days of wheat harvest Reuben went and found mandrakes in the field, and brought them to his mother Leah. Then Rachel said to Leah, "Give me, I pray, some of your son's mandrakes." ¹⁵But she said to her, "Is it a small matter that you have taken away my husband? Would you take away my son's mandrakes also?" Rachel said, "Then he may lie with you tonight for your son's mandrakes." ¹⁶When Jacob came from the field in the evening, Leah went out to meet him, and said, "You must come in to me; for I have hired you with my son's mandrakes." So he lay with her that night. ¹⁷And God hearkened to Leah, and she conceived and bore Jacob a fifth son. ¹⁸Leah said, "God has given me my hireˡ because I gave my maid to my husband"; so she called his name Issachar. ¹⁹And Leah conceived again, and she bore Jacob a sixth son. ²⁰Then Leah said, "God has endowed me with a good dowry; now my husband will honorᵐ me, because I have borne him six sons"; so she called his name Zebulun. ²¹Afterwards she bore a daughter, and called her name Dinah. ²²Then God remembered Rachel, and God hearkened to her and opened her womb. ²³She conceived and bore a son, and said, "God has taken away my reproach"; ²⁴and she called his name Joseph,ⁿ saying, "May the LORD add to me another son!"

j That is Fortune   k That is Happy   l Heb sakar   m Heb zabal   n That is He adds

---

OVERVIEW: Most of this passage attracted almost no comment. The mandrakes used by Leah seem to symbolize cheerfulness and faith (EPHREM).

30:14 Mandrakes

CHEERFULNESS SEASONED WITH FAITH.
EPHREM THE SYRIAN: Some say that the man-drake is a plant whose fruit resembles apples, which have a scent and are edible. So by means of these mandrakes, with cheerfulness seasoned with faith, Leah made Jacob take her that night. COMMENTARY ON GENESIS 28.3.1.[1]

[1]FC 91:177.

30:25-43 HOW JACOB GREW RICH

²⁵When Rachel had borne Joseph, Jacob said to Laban, "Send me away, that I may go to my own home and country. ²⁶Give me my wives and my children for whom I have served you, and let me go; for you know the service which I have given you." ²⁷But Laban said to him, "If you will allow me to say so, I have learned by divination that the LORD has blessed me because of you; ²⁸name your wages, and I will give it." ²⁹Jacob said to him, "You yourself know how I have served you, and how your cattle have fared with me. ³⁰For you had little before I came, and it has increased abundantly; and the LORD has blessed you wherever I turned. But now when shall I provide for my own household also?" ³¹He said, "What shall I give you?" Jacob said, "You shall not give me anything; if you will do this for me, I will again feed your flock and keep it: ³²let me pass through all your flock today, removing from it every speckled and spotted sheep and every black lamb, and the spotted and speckled among the goats; and such shall be my wages. ³³So my honesty will answer for me later, when you come to look into my wages with you. Every one that is not speckled and spotted among the goats and black among the lambs, if found with me, shall be counted stolen." ³⁴Laban said, "Good! Let it be as you have said." ³⁵But that day Laban removed the he-goats that were striped and spotted, and all the she-goats that were speckled and spotted, every one that had white on it, and every lamb that was black, and put them in charge of his sons; ³⁶and he set a distance of three days' journey between himself and Jacob; and Jacob fed the rest of Laban's flock.

³⁷Then Jacob took fresh rods of poplar and almond and plane, and peeled white streaks in them, exposing the white of the rods. ³⁸He set the rods which he had peeled in front of the flocks in the runnels, that is, the watering troughs, where the flocks came to drink. And since they bred when they came to drink, ³⁹the flocks bred in front of the rods and so the flocks brought forth striped, speckled, and spotted. ⁴⁰And Jacob separated the lambs, and set the faces of the flocks toward the striped and all the black in the flock of Laban; and he put his own droves apart, and did not put them with Laban's flock. ⁴¹Whenever the stronger of the flock were breeding Jacob laid the rods in the runnels before the eyes of the flock, that they might breed among the rods, ⁴²but for the feebler of the flock he did not lay them there; so the feebler were Laban's, and the stronger Jacob's. ⁴³Thus the man grew exceedingly rich, and had large flocks, maidservants and menservants, and camels and asses.

OVERVIEW: Jacob's appeal to Laban to let him leave shows him to be a model of meekness. His desire is to live in freedom (CHRYSOSTOM). The seemingly mysterious account of Jacob's placing rods of three different trees before his flocks produced elaborate allegorical explanations: the three trees signified the mysteries of the blessed Trinity (AMBROSE). In another interpretation they symbolized the Spirit, the Virgin and Christ (PAULINUS); in still another the three trees indicate different aspects of the mystery of Christ. The watering troughs in which Jacob inserted the

rods symbolize the writings of Moses and the prophets from which Christ removed the shadow and the veil respectively (CYRIL OF ALEXANDRIA). Jacob's separation of the flocks was inspired by grace from on high (CHRYSOSTOM). It also foreshadows the separation of Christians from the pagans (CYRIL OF ALEXANDRIA). The effect of the rods on the cattle is explained through the unchanging and invisible wisdom of God (AUGUSTINE).

30:26 Jacob Speaks with Laban

WHAT A GREAT THING MEEKNESS IS. CHRYSOSTOM: Nothing is really more efficacious than meekness and nothing more powerful than it. See at any rate how, by a disarming use of meekness, Jacob also brought Laban to reply to him with great deference. "Laban replied to him," the text goes on, remember, "If I have found favor in your sight, and the omens do not deceive me, God has blessed me in your coming. Name your wage to me, and I will pay."[1] "I am not unaware," he is saying, that in the wake of your coming I enjoyed favor from God more richly. So, since I recognize the kindness done me in your coming, "name any wage you care to mention, and I will readily pay it."

Consider what a great thing meekness is, and don't pass idly by these words. Instead, keep in mind that the good man had made no mention of this nor looked for any payment for his trouble. [He] had said only this: "Let me have my wives and children, for whom I was in your service, so that I may depart." And yet the other man, out of respect for the good man's great meekness, replied, "Tell me what wage you want to be paid by me, and I will cheerfully pay it." After all, were not "Jacob's wives and children in his company"? So why did he say, "Let me have my wives and children"? Jacob was giving him due respect and displaying in every circumstance his typical behavior, and wishing as well to take his leave without hindrance. Notice, at any rate, from these words how he won Laban over to the extent of promising to pay a wage and to leave the decision

to him. HOMILIES ON GENESIS 57.2-3.[2]

30:30 The Lord Has Blessed You

TO LIVE NOW IN FREEDOM. CHRYSOSTOM: "I call you to witness my labors," he is saying. "I mean, you know how I did my best with good grace and how, after taking charge of your poor creatures, I made them grow into a vast herd through my attention and vigilance." Then, to show his godly attitude, he added, "The Lord, you see, has blessed you in my coming. So isn't it high time for me to build a house of my own?" You yourself know that after my arrival grace from on high increased your prosperity. So now, since I too have made every effort on my part with good grace in discharge of my service and the grace of God has become manifest, it is only fair that I too should build a house for myself." Now, what is the meaning of "build a house for myself"? It means, to live now in freedom and to pay attention to a house of one's own. HOMILIES ON GENESIS 57.4.[3]

30:37 Jacob's Device

A FLOCK RESPLENDENT. AMBROSE: The just man Jacob comes in like a hired hand and yet is the master who, in his ministry of preaching the gospel, gathered together a flock that is resplendent in the brilliance of its many signal virtues.[4] Thus, when the flock came to drink, he would set before them in the troughs the bough of storax and walnut and that from the plane tree; those who felt desire for the mysteries of the most blessed Trinity that were prefigured there could engender offspring that were not at all discolored, by conceiving them in a devout mind.[5] Good were the sheep that produced the offspring that were good works and that were not degenerate in holy faith. By the storax is meant the incense and the evening sacrifice that is offered to God the Father in the psalm;[6] by the walnut bough, the priestly

---

[1]Gen 30:27-28. [2]FC 87:134*. [3]FC 87:135*. [4]Gen 30:31-35. [5]Gen 30:37-43. [6]Ps 141:2 (140:2 LXX).

gift that is offered by Christ. For this is Aaron's bough, that blossomed when it was set down, and through it the grace of priestly holiness was manifested.[7] By the plane tree is meant an abundance of spiritual fruit, because a vine attaches itself to this tree so that the tree may be fertile through the symbiosis and pour itself out into rich offspring. Even so, the addition of the grace of the Spirit has generally nurtured the gifts of the Lord's passion as well as the forgiveness of all sins. JACOB AND THE HAPPY LIFE 2.4.19.[8]

THE SYMBOLISM OF THE KINGDOM IMPLICIT. PAULINUS OF NOLA: Because the three rods have been mentioned, we can examine further, if you are agreeable, the symbolism of the kingdom implicit in them. The patriarch chose for himself three rods from three trees. The first was perfumed from the storax tree, the second smooth from the plane tree, the third unbending from the almond tree.[9] The plane contains the Spirit, the storax the Virgin, and the almond Christ. For the plane extends its spreading branches to provide shade; so the Holy Spirit fashioned Christ by casting his shadow over the Virgin. I believe that the rod from the storax, the tree of David, is the Virgin who in childbirth brought forth a sweet-smelling Blossom. The rod of the almond tree is Christ, for there is food within that tree, which has an outer casing consisting of bitter bark over its green skin. Here you must recognize the divine Christ clothed in our human body. In that flesh he can be broken; the food lies in the Word, the bitterness in the cross. His hard covering consists of the tidings of the cross and the food of that cross, and it encloses within the divine remedy in the flesh of Christ. POEM 27.273.[10]

THE ROD SYMBOLIZES IMMANUEL. CYRIL OF ALEXANDRIA: The rod also enigmatically symbolizes for us the Immanuel, for he is actually called by this name in the divinely inspired Scriptures. "And there shall sprout a rod," the divine Isaiah says, "out of the root of Jesse, and a blossom shall come up from his root."[11] David ... proclaimed to the heavenly Father and God: "Your rod and your staff have comforted me."[12] We received consolation in Christ and made him our pillar. In fact, it was written, "The Lord shall support the righteous."[13] And Christ in a sense displays a sort of rod to us as to reasonable goats and herds spread all over the earth and in the whole world. But it is not a rod of any kind, but it is made out of storax wood and walnut and plane tree. The storax tree is placed as a witness of righteousness. This tree is the symbol of death. The body of the dead is treated with perfumes, and a very sweet perfume is the oil of the storax tree. Christ died for us and was buried, according to Scripture. The rod made of walnut wood is a symbol of watchfulness. GLAPHYRA ON GENESIS, 5.3-4.[14]

30:38 The Flocks Breed

JESUS REMOVES THE SHADOW FROM THE LAW. CYRIL OF ALEXANDRIA: But where did Jacob place his rods? In the troughs of water. And these troughs, in which the reasonable herd, that is we, go to water, must be interpreted as the writings of Moses and the prophetical predictions that nearly burst forth for us like a heavenly sermon from God. In fact, it was written, "You draw water with joy out of the wells of salvation."[15] And there we will find the Immanuel, the rod of power. And in his death for us he is also the firstborn from the dead,[16] and is exalted in glory and increases the number of the believers, as I have just said. Every word of the holy prophets, including Moses, hints at the mystery of Christ. Therefore also the wise Paul says, "Christ is the end of the prophets and the law."[17] Jacob peeled in the rods white stripes alternated with green ones, and the sheep that were by them conceived a spotted and speckled progeny. Jesus somehow removed the shadow from the law and the veil from the prophetical writings. And he showed the pure and

---

[7]Num 17:6-8. [8]FC 65:156. [9]In the Hebrew text the first tree is the poplar, but the LXX has storax, the incense-bearing shrub, as here. [10]ACW 40:280. [11]Is 11:1. [12]Ps 23:4 (22:4 LXX). [13]Ps 37:17 (36:17 LXX). [14]PG 69:237-41. [15]Is 12:3. [16]Col 1:18. [17]Rom 10:4.

beautiful doctrine which was in them, and he transferred it to the spiritual song, in order that he might lead people to virtue since they wanted to be speckled, that is, they wanted to exercise a double virtue in words and actions. And therefore the divine prophets of those who were justified in the faith, by bringing the image before them, openly proclaim, "Because of the fear of you, we conceived, O Lord, and were in pain and brought forth the spirit of your salvation."[18] And the same blessed Isaiah, in another passage, says properly: "Strengthen your relaxed hands and palsied knees; comfort one another, you faint-hearted; be strong, fear not. Behold, our God renders judgment, and will render it." And again: "Behold the Lord! The Lord is coming with strength, and his arm is with power. He shall tend his flock as a shepherd, and shall gather the lambs with his arm and shall soothe them who are with young."[19] That is, he will be a spiritual consolation for those who have already brought forth the divine sermon, for those who will be fruitful and for those who are about to bring forth the glories of evangelical life. This is the fruit of the holy and uncorrupted soul. GLAPHYRA ON GENESIS, 5.4.[20]

30:40 Jacob Separates the Flock

WITH GRACE FROM ON HIGH. CHRYSOSTOM: The good man did this, not of his own devising but with grace from on high inspiring his mind. You see, it was not done according to human reasoning but was quite unusual and beyond natural logic. HOMILIES ON GENESIS 57.7.[21]

THOSE WHO BELONG TO CHRIST. CYRIL OF ALEXANDRIA: There is no association between the holy and the profane, between the pure and the impure. Those who belong to Christ are separated and refuse to mix with those who are in the world; they are free from carnal desires. They are marked by their way of life or rather are distinguished by their virtue. "The unmarked ones

were Laban's, and the marked ones were Jacob's." GLAPHYRA ON GENESIS, 5.4.[22]

30:41 The Strong Animals

UNCHANGEABLE AND INVISIBLE WISDOM OF GOD. AUGUSTINE: Again, Jacob was in no sense the creator of the piebald colors of the flocks he managed, just because he put the peeled and particolored rods in the drinking troughs for the ewes to gaze at as they conceived. Nor for that matter were the ewes creators of the piebald effects in their young, just because the vivid impressions of piebaldness they received from look-ing at the particolored rods remained embedded in their souls. And so [these impressions] could not help having a sympathetic effect on their bodies, which were animated by these souls thus affected, so that the impression was passed on to color the progeny in their sensitive and impressionable beginnings. That soul and body should thus psychosomatically react upon each other is due to those archetypal harmonies of reason which live immutably in the very wisdom of God, something that is not localized within the limits of space. While this wisdom is unchanging in itself, it does not hold itself aloof from anything that is, even in a changing mode of existence, because there is nothing that was not created by it. That the ewes gave birth to lambs and not to rods is due to the unchangeable and invisible disposition of God's wisdom by which all things were created. And that the lambs conceived were colored as an effect of the particolored rods was due to the souls of their pregnant mothers being affected from the outside through their eyes and having inside them their own proper "program" of embryo formation which they received from their Creator, whose power was active at the inner roots of their being. ON THE TRINITY 3.2.15.[23]

---

[18]Is 26:18. [19]Is 40:10-11. [20]PG 69:241. [21]FC 87:136. [22]PG 69:241-44. [23]WSA 1 5:136.

31:1-21 JACOB FLEES FROM LABAN

¹*Now Jacob heard that the sons of Laban were saying, "Jacob has taken all that was our father's; and from what was our father's he has gained all this wealth." ²And Jacob saw that Laban did not regard him with favor as before. ³Then the LORD said to Jacob, "Return to the land of your fathers and to your kindred, and I will be with you." ⁴So Jacob sent and called Rachel and Leah into the field where his flock was, ⁵and said to them, "I see that your father does not regard me with favor as he did before. But the God of my father has been with me. ⁶You know that I have served your father with all my strength; ⁷yet your father has cheated me and changed my wages ten times, but God did not permit him to harm me. ⁸If he said, 'The spotted shall be your wages,' then all the flock bore spotted; and if he said, 'The striped shall be your wages,' then all the flock bore striped. ⁹Thus God has taken away the cattle of your father, and given them to me. ¹⁰In the mating season of the flock I lifted up my eyes, and saw in a dream that the he-goats which leaped upon the flock were striped, spotted, and mottled. ¹¹Then the angel of God said to me in the dream, 'Jacob,' and I said, 'Here I am!' ¹²And he said, 'Lift up your eyes and see, all the goats that leap upon the flock are striped, spotted, and mottled; for I have seen all that Laban is doing to you. ¹³I am the God of Bethel, where you anointed a pillar and made a vow to me. Now arise, go forth from this land, and return to the land of your birth.'" ¹⁴Then Rachel and Leah answered him, "Is there any portion or inheritance left to us in our father's house? ¹⁵Are we not regarded by him as foreigners? For he has sold us, and he has been using up the money given for us. ¹⁶All the property which God has taken away from our father belongs to us and to our children; now then, whatever God has said to you, do."*

¹⁷*So Jacob arose, and set his sons and his wives on camels; ¹⁸and he drove away all his cattle, all his livestock which he had gained, the cattle in his possession which he had acquired in Paddan-aram, to go to the land of Canaan to his father Isaac. ¹⁹Laban had gone to shear his sheep, and Rachel stole her father's household gods. ²⁰And Jacob outwitted Laban the Aramean, in that he did not tell him that he intended to flee. ²¹He fled with all that he had, and arose and crossed the Euphrates, and set his face toward the hill country of Gilead.*

OVERVIEW: The story of Jacob's fall from favor with Laban and his flight to the land of Canaan provide the occasion for reflections on the effects of envy as well as on the great care and considerateness of God, who helps those who bear wrongdoing meekly and mildly (CHRYSOSTOM). On an allegorical level of interpretation, Jacob's departure with his wives prefigures the departure of

Christ with his brides, the churches (CYRIL OF ALEXANDRIA).

31:1 *Laban's Sons Complain*

ENVY DROVE THEM TO INGRATITUDE. CHRYSOSTOM: See how envy drove them to ingratitude, and not only them but also Laban himself. "Jacob

saw Laban's attitude to him," the text goes on, remember, "and, lo, it was not as it had previously been."[1] You see, his sons' words deranged his mind and made him forget what he had said some time before in conversation with Jacob, "God has blessed me in your coming." After thanking the Lord for making his wealth increase through the arrival of the good man, he was now disturbed in mind under the influence of his sons and inflamed with envy, perhaps because he saw the good man's fortunate circumstances, and so he was not prepared to behave toward him in the same way. HOMILIES ON GENESIS 57.9.[2]

31:3 God to Be with Jacob

TAKE TO THE ROAD WITH CONFIDENCE. CHRYSOSTOM: Do you see the good man's great meekness, on the one hand, and their ingratitude, on the other, and how they could not bear to hold their envy in check but even affected their father's attitude? See now God's ineffable care and the degree of considerateness he employs when he sees us doing our best. I mean, when he saw the good man the object of their envy, he said to Jacob, "Return to the land of your father and to your birthplace, and I will be with you."[3] You have had enough of living in a foreign land, he is saying. What I promised you previously in the words "I will return you to your country,"[4] this I now intend to bring to pass. So go back without fear; after all, "I will be with you." You see, to prevent the good man becoming lethargic in departing instead of taking to the road with confidence, he says, "I will be with you." The One who has managed your affairs until now and caused your descendants to increase, "I will be with you" in future as well. HOMILIES ON GENESIS 57.10.[5]

31:12 Look and See

VENGEANCE IS GOD'S, NOT OURS. CHRYSOSTOM: We learn from this that whenever we bear people's wrongdoing meekly and mildly, we enjoy help from on high in a richer and more abundant

measure. Accordingly, far from resisting those bent on abusing us, let us bear it nobly in the knowledge that the Lord of all will not forget us, provided we ourselves give evidence of our good will. "Vengeance is mine," Scripture says, remember, "I will repay, says the Lord."[6] Hence Jacob also said, "God did not allow him to do me harm." I mean, since he actually intended to deprive me of payment for my work, he is saying, the Lord gave evidence of his care for us in such marvelous abundance as to transfer all his substance to us. He has shown such care for us, aware that I performed his service with good grace, whereas Laban was not kindly disposed to me. For proof that I do not idly say this or with any intention of accusing him without rhyme or reason, I even have God as my witness to what has been done to me by your father. "I have observed all that Laban has been doing to you," God says, remember—not only that he has deprived you of your wage but as well, instead of being disposed toward you as he was previously, he has a completely distorted attitude. HOMILIES ON GENESIS 57.13.[7]

31:17 Jacob Gathers His Family

THE GOOD MAN'S NOBLE RESOLVE. CHRYSOSTOM: Consider, I ask you, the good man's noble resolve in quelling every sentiment of fear or reluctance when responding to the command of the Lord. I mean, when he saw Laban's attitude was not promising, he refrained from confronting him as before; instead, he discharged the direction from the Lord by taking his wives and children and making tracks. HOMILIES ON GENESIS 57.16.[8]

31:19 Household Gods

THEY CLUNG TO THEIR ANCESTRAL HABITS. CHRYSOSTOM: This was included not by chance but for us to know how they still clung to their ancestral habits and showed great devotion to the

---

[1]Gen 31:2. [2]FC 87:137. [3]Gen 31:3. [4]Gen 28:15. [5]FC 87:137-38. [6]Rom 12:19; cf. Deut 32:35. [7]FC 87:139. [8]FC 87:141.

household gods. I mean, consider how [Rachel] went to so much trouble as to steal nothing else of her father's than the household gods alone and did it without her husband noticing; Jacob would not have allowed it to happen, you see. HOMILIES ON GENESIS 57.17.[9]

31:21 Jacob Flees

LABAN REPRESENTS THE WORLD'S ANGER.
CYRIL OF ALEXANDRIA: The fact that the world should have been offended because of Christ, after the increase in the flocks of believers, and that it, excited by its anger, would have reacted, does not need to be confirmed with a long speech. Just see how Laban, together with his sons, pursued Jacob, who was running away, and recalled him. Christ himself, in a sense, departed from the world with his brides, that is, the churches, and moved out with the entire household by spiritually addressing his companions with these words: "Arise, let us go from here."[10] The action of departing and moving away certainly is not material; there is no concrete move from one place to another. In fact, it would be incongruous to think or say these things in a material sense. But the fullness of life is in the moving from worldly

thoughts to the accomplishment of the things that God approves. This is confirmed by the blessed Paul, who writes, "Here we have no lasting city, but we seek one to come,"[11] whose "maker and creator is God."[12] And another of the holy apostles writes thus: "I beseech you as pilgrims and strangers: abstain from sinful desires which war against the soul."[13] While we walk on earth, our way of life is in heaven,[14] and certainly we do not want to live carnally anymore but rather in a holy and spiritual way. Paul encourages us to do that by writing, "Be not conformed to this world, but be transformed by the renewing of your mind, so that you may prove what is that good and acceptable and perfect will of God."[15] When we are not conformed anymore to the world and out of the worldly errors, we will be imitators of Christ. And perfectly understanding that this is the right way to think the Savior himself said, "If you were of the world, the world would love his own: but because you are not of the world, therefore the world hates you."[16] GLAPHYRA ON GENESIS, 5.5.[17]

---

[9]FC 87:141. [10]Jn 14:31. [11]Heb 13:14. [12]Heb 11:10. [13]1 Pet 2:11. [14]See Phil 3:20. [15]Rom 12:2. [16]Jn 15:19. [17]PG 69:249.

31:22-42 LABAN PURSUES JACOB

[22]*When it was told Laban on the third day that Jacob had fled,* [23]*he took his kinsmen with him and pursued him for seven days and followed close after him into the hill country of Gilead.* [24]*But God came to Laban the Aramean in a dream by night, and said to him, "Take heed that you say not a word to Jacob, either good or bad."*

[25]*And Laban overtook Jacob. Now Jacob had pitched his tent in the hill country, and Laban with his kinsmen encamped in the hill country of Gilead.* [26]*And Laban said to Jacob, "What have you done, that you have cheated me, and carried away my daughters like captives of the sword?* [27]*Why did you flee secretly, and cheat me, and did not tell me, so that I might have sent you away with mirth and songs, with tambourine and lyre?* [28]*And why did you not permit me to kiss my sons*

and my daughters farewell? Now you have done foolishly. ^{29}It is in my power to do you harm; but the God of your father spoke to me last night, saying, 'Take heed that you speak to Jacob neither good nor bad.' ^{30}And now you have gone away because you longed greatly for your father's house, but why did you steal my gods?" ^{31}Jacob answered Laban, "Because I was afraid, for I thought that you would take your daughters from me by force. ^{32}Any one with whom you find your gods shall not live. In the presence of our kinsmen point out what I have that is yours, and take it." Now Jacob did not know that Rachel had stolen them.

^{33}So Laban went into Jacob's tent, and into Leah's tent, and into the tent of the two maidservants, but he did not find them. And he went out of Leah's tent, and entered Rachel's. ^{34}Now Rachel had taken the household gods and put them in the camel's saddle, and sat upon them. Laban felt all about the tent, but did not find them. ^{35}And she said to her father, "Let not my lord be angry that I cannot rise before you, for the way of women is upon me." So he searched, but did not find the household gods.

^{36}Then Jacob became angry, and upbraided Laban; Jacob said to Laban, "What is my offense? What is my sin, that you have hotly pursued me? ^{37}Although you have felt through all my goods, what have you found of all your household goods? Set it here before my kinsmen and your kinsmen, that they may decide between us two. ^{38}These twenty years I have been with you; your ewes and your she-goats have not miscarried, and I have not eaten the rams of your flocks. ^{39}That which was torn by wild beasts I did not bring to you; I bore the loss of it myself; of my hand you required it, whether stolen by day or stolen by night. ^{40}Thus I was; by day the heat consumed me, and the cold by night, and my sleep fled from my eyes. ^{41}These twenty years I have been in your house; I served you fourteen years for your two daughters, and six years for your flock, and you have changed my wages ten times. ^{42}If the God of my father, the God of Abraham and the Fear of Isaac, had not been on my side, surely now you would have sent me away empty-handed. God saw my affliction and the labor of my hands, and rebuked you last night."

OVERVIEW: God's admonition to Laban is a sign of his creative wisdom in that he turns the enemies of truth into witnesses to truth. God's command restrained Laban's anger. Laban's accusation about the stealing of his household gods provides the occasion for reflection about the impotence of such gods (CHRYSOSTOM). Jacob's response to Laban offers the opportunity for reflections about the nature of true wisdom and the wealth of the soul as opposed to material possessions (AMBROSE). On a mystical (allegorical) level of interpretation, Jacob represents the person in whom the devil, represented by Laban, is not able to find anything of his own, as was the case also

with Christ. Rachel, hiding the gods, represents the Gentile church's prudence in putting away idolatry (AMBROSE, CAESARIUS OF ARLES).

31:24 God Speaks to Laban

A SIGN OF GOD'S CREATIVE WISDOM. CHRYSOSTOM: Wonderful is the Lord's goodness. When God saw Laban bent on fighting and intent on conflict with the good man, he said as if to check his intention by word, "Watch yourself, lest you be guilty of evil words to Jacob." Don't try even in word to harass Jacob, he is saying, but watch yourself; check this wicked assault of

yours, repress your anger, rein in your seething thoughts and forbear harassing him even in word. Notice, I ask you, God's loving kindness. Instead of bidding Laban return to his own place, he only directed him to deliver no harsh or severe words to the good man. What on earth was the reason for that? For the good man to learn in fact and by experience the degree of care he was accorded by God.

You see, had Laban turned back, how would the good man or his wives have known this? Hence God allowed Laban to come and from his own lips to confess the words spoken to him by God. He did so that the good man might also gain greater enthusiasm for his journey and embrace it in confidence and that his wives might come to know how much care Jacob was accorded by the God of all and so reject their father's deception and imitate the good man. They thus gained from the incident considerable instruction in knowing God. I mean, what came from Jacob was not so convincing as the words spoken by Laban, who was still a devotee of idols. After all, the testimony of infidels and opponents of religion always carries with it great power to convince. This in fact is a sign of God's creative wisdom, when he turns the enemies of truth into the very witnesses to truth, who then by their own mouth fight on its side. HOMILIES ON GENESIS 57.19-20.[1]

31:26 Laban Argues with Jacob

GOD'S COMMAND REPRESSED LABAN'S RAGE. CHRYSOSTOM: See how the command from God repressed [Laban's] great rage and restrained his anger. Hence Laban directs his words to [Jacob] with extreme mildness, almost apologetically, and shows signs of fatherly affection for him. In fact, whenever we enjoy providence from on high, we not only succeed in avoiding the schemes of wicked people, but should we even encounter untamed beasts, we would suffer no harm. You see, the Lord of all gives evidence of the abundance of his characteristic power by transforming the nature of the beasts and turning it into the gentle-

ness of sheep, not by removing their animal characteristics but, while leaving these in their nature, causing the beasts to appear as sheep. You could observe this not only in wild beasts but also in the elements themselves; at his will the very elements forget their power, and not even fire shows the characteristics of fire. HOMILIES ON GENESIS 57.21.[2]

31:30 Laban Accuses Jacob

WHAT KIND OF GODS ARE THESE? CHRYSOSTOM: What extraordinary folly—what kind of gods are these of yours that can be stolen? Aren't you ashamed to say, "Why did you steal my household gods?" See the extraordinary extent of Laban's self-deception such that people endowed with reason should worship wood and stone. These gods of yours, Laban, could not prevent their being stolen. How could they, after all, being made out of stone? The God of this good man, on the contrary, even if the good man was unaware of it, checked your aggression. Are you ignorant of your own error while still charging the good man with theft? After all, why on earth would the good man bring himself to steal them when he despised them, or rather realized they were made of stone and had no feeling? HOMILIES ON GENESIS 57.26.[3]

31:32 Jacob Responds

JUSTICE BROUGHT GAIN WITHOUT INFLICTING LOSS. AMBROSE: Now let us consider how the just person ought to behave if enmity arises. First, let him avoid it; it is better to go away without strife than to settle down with contention. Next, let him possess a property that he can carry off with him so that he cannot be held under any obligation by the adversary but may say, "Identify whatever of yours I may have."[4] And Laban searched and found nothing of his with Jacob.[5]

---

[1]FC 87:142-43*. [2]FC 87:143*. [3]FC 87:145-46*. [4]Gen 31:32. [5]Gen 31:33.

He was a great man and truly happy who could lose nothing of his and possess nothing of another's, that is, possess nothing too little and nothing to excess. Therefore the person who has no lack of anything has been perfected; the person who has nothing to excess is just—this is to observe the proper mean of justice. How powerful virtue is! Alliance with it brought gain but did not inflict loss. This is what perfection is; it gives the greatest advantage to those who hold to it but brings them no disadvantage whatsoever.

Accordingly the man who desired to do harm to Jacob was not able to send him away empty. For the wise person is never empty but always has the garment of prudence on himself and is able to say, "I was clad with justice, and I clothed myself with judgment,"[6] as Job said. Surely these are the inner veils of the spirit, and no one can take them away except when someone strips them off by his own guilty action. In fact, Adam was found stripped so, and naked,[7] whereas Joseph was not naked even though he had thrown off his external clothing, as he possessed the safe covering of virtue. Therefore the wise person is never empty. How could he be empty? He has taken from the fullness of Christ and keeps what he has received. How could he be empty? His soul is filled, for it guards the garments of grace it has received. We must be afraid that someone may lose the veil of blamelessness and that ungodly people may transgress the bonds of justice with onslaughts of sacrilege and persecution and snatch away the garment of the soul and of the spirit. This does not readily happen unless a person has first been stripped of his clothing by the voice of his iniquity. On this account David also says, "If there is iniquity in my hands, let me deservedly fall empty before my enemies. Let the enemy pursue my soul and take it."[8] JACOB AND THE HAPPY LIFE 5.21-22.[9]

THE FRUIT OF JUSTICE. AMBROSE: Therefore none of the enemies can take your soul unless it has first been made empty. Do not be afraid of those who can plunder treasures of gold and silver; such people take nothing from you. They take away what you do not have, they take away what you are not able to possess, they take away not an ornament to your soul but a burden on it. They take away what does not enrich your heart but weighs it down; "for where your treasure is, there also will your heart be,"[10] as you have heard in today's reading. Many people shut in their gold with bars upon their gates, but they have no confidence in either their bolts or their barricades. Many people employ guards, but they too are generally more afraid of the guards. Many go to bed upon buried gold; their gold is beneath the ground, and so is their heart. Watch out, then, that you do not entrench your heart in the ground while you are still living. We have no need to be afraid of thieves who steal such gold; but you must watch out for the usurer who examines the wealth of your soul, if you have bargained for any coin of more serious sin. He confines your heart in the earth and buries your soul in the ground, where you have hidden your gold. He crushes your spirit with interest compounded a hundredfold and buries it in a heavy tomb, from which no one rises again. Follow the example of holy Jacob; he had no part in the vices of others, nor was he empty and devoid of his own virtues, but he was filled with the fruit of justice. JACOB AND THE HAPPY LIFE 5.23.[11]

31:33 A Fruitless Search

THE DEVIL HAS NO LASTING POSSESSION. AMBROSE: But this pertains to the moral sense, whereas the mystical sense is that Laban, whose name means "lie that has been purified"—and even Satan transfigures himself into an angel of light[12]—came to Jacob and began to demand his possessions from him.[13] Jacob answered him, "Identify whatever of yours I may have,"[14] that is, "I have nothing of yours. See if you recognize any of your vices and crimes. I have not carried off

---

[6]Job 29:14. [7]Gen 3:10-11. [8]Ps 7:4-6. [9]FC 65:157-59. [10]Mt 6:21. [11]FC 65:159. [12]2 Cor 11:14. [13]Gen 31:25-30. [14]Gen 31:32.

with me any of your deceits, and I have no share in your guile; all that is yours I have shunned as a contagion." Laban searched and found nothing that was his.[15] How happy is the one in whom the enemy has found nothing that he could call his own, and in whom the devil has come upon nothing that he could call his own, and in whom the devil has come upon nothing that he would recognize as his own. That appeared to be impossible in the case of humanity, but Christ supplied the model of it when he said in the Gospel, "The prince of this world will come, and in me he will find nothing."[16] Now whatever belongs to the devil is nothing, because he can have no lasting possession. JACOB AND THE HAPPY LIFE 5.24.[17]

31:34 Rachel Hid the Household Gods

PRUDENCE HID THE IDOLS. AMBROSE: Moreover, holy Rachel—that is, the church, or prudence—hid the idols, because the church does not know representations and figures of idols that are totally devoid of reality, but it knows the real existence of the Trinity. Indeed, it has destroyed darkness and revealed the splendor of glory. FLIGHT FROM THE WORLD 5.27.[18]

31:35 Rachel's Excuse

THE FOOLISHNESS OF MUTE IDOLS. CHRYSOSTOM: Wonderful is the shrewdness of Rachel, by which she succeeded in outwitting Laban. Let those heed it who are victims of deceit and give great importance to the worship of idols. "She put them under the camel saddles," the text says, "and sat on them." What could be more ridiculous than these people? Although endowed with reason and accorded such wonderful preeminence in God's loving kindness, they bring themselves to worship lifeless stone, and, far from being ashamed or having any sense of such absurdity, they even make a habit of it like dumb animals. Hence Paul also wrote in these words, "You know that when you were pagans, it was to mute idols you went off in your frenzy."[19] Rightly did he say

"mute"; people with the faculty of speech, enjoying reason and hearing, betake themselves to things of no such faculties like irrational animals. What excuse would such people in fact deserve? HOMILIES ON GENESIS 57.28.[20]

LET THE DEVIL FIND NOTHING OF HIS OWN IN YOU. CAESARIUS OF ARLES: As Jacob was returning to his own country, Laban and his companions pursued them. Upon examination of Jacob's possessions Laban found nothing of his, and therefore he could not hold him. Laban here is not unfittingly said to represent a type of the devil, because he served idols and was opposed to blessed Jacob, who prefigured the Lord. For this reason he pursued Jacob but was unable to find anything of his own with him. Listen to the true Jacob declaring this fact in the Gospel: "Behold, the prince of the world is coming, and in me he will find nothing."[21] May the divine mercy grant that our adversary may find nothing of his works in us, for if he finds nothing of his own he will not be able to keep us or recall us from eternal life. Therefore, dearly beloved, let us look at the treasury of our conscience, let us examine the secret places of our heart, and if we find nothing there which belongs to the devil let us rejoice and thank God. With his help let us strive as well as we can that the doors of our heart may always be open for Christ but closed forever to the devil. However, if we recognize something of the devil's works or cunning in our souls, let us hasten to cast it out and get rid of it as deadly poison. Then when the devil wants to ensnare us and can find nothing that belongs to him, he will depart in confusion while we can thank God with the prophet and shout to the Lord: "You freed us from our foes, and those who hated us you put to shame."[22] Therefore Leah, as we said above, signified the people of the Jews who were joined to Christ; Rachel typified the church, that is, the nation of the Gentiles. For this reason Rachel, not

---

[15]Gen 31:33-35. [16]Jn 14:30. [17]FC 65:159-60. [18]FC 65:302. [19]1 Cor 12:2. [20]FC 87:147. [21]Jn 14:30. [22]Ps 44:7 (43:8 LXX).

Leah, stole the idols of her father, because after Christ's advent the synagogue of the Jews is not known to have served idols everywhere, as is clearly proved concerning the church of the Gentiles. Besides, not with Leah, that is, the synagogue, do we read that Laban's idols were hidden, but with Rachel, who typified the Gentiles. SERMON 88.4.[23]

---

[23]FC 47:36-37.

31:43-55 THE COVENANT BETWEEN JACOB AND LABAN

[43]*Then Laban answered and said to Jacob, "The daughters are my daughters, the children are my children, the flocks are my flocks, and all that you see is mine. But what can I do this day to these my daughters, or to their children whom they have borne?* [44]*Come now, let us make a covenant, you and I; and let it be a witness between you and me."** [45]*So Jacob took a stone, and set it up as a pillar.* [46]*And Jacob said to his kinsmen, "Gather stones," and they took stones, and made a heap; and they ate there by the heap.* [47]*Laban called it Jegar-sahadutha:*[o] *but Jacob called it Galeed.*[p] [48]*Laban said, "This heap is a witness between you and me today." Therefore he named it Galeed,* [49]*and the pillar*[q] *Mizpah,*[r] *for he said, "The LORD watch between you and me, when we are absent one from the other.* [50]*If you ill-treat my daughters, or if you take wives besides my daughters, although no man is with us, remember, God is witness between you and me."*

[51]*Then Laban said to Jacob, "See this heap and the pillar, which I have set between you and me.* [52]*This heap is a witness, and the pillar is a witness, that I will not pass over this heap to you, and you will not pass over this heap and this pillar to me, for harm.* [53]*The God of Abraham and the God of Nahor, the God of their father, judge between us." So Jacob swore by the Fear of his father Isaac,* [54]*and Jacob offered a sacrifice on the mountain and called his kinsmen to eat bread; and they ate bread and tarried all night on the mountain.*

[55s]*Early in the morning Laban arose, and kissed his grandchildren and his daughters and blessed them; then he departed and returned home.*

o In Aramaic *The heap of witness*   p In Hebrew *The heap of witness*   q Compare Sam: Heb lacks *the pillar*   r That is *Watchpost*   s Ch 32.1 in Heb   *LXX adds, "See, there is no one with us. Behold, God is witness between you and me."

OVERVIEW: The story of the covenant between Jacob and Laban provides the opportunity for observations about God's omnipresence and great wisdom (CHRYSOSTOM).

31:44 *Making a Covenant*

THE ONE WHO SEES EVERYTHING. CHRYSOSTOM: Consider how Laban is gradually introduced to knowledge of God. The man who previously brought the charge of theft of his household gods against the good man and conducted such a close search now says, "Since there

is no one capable of acting between us, in case anything happens later, let God act as witness between us to witness what is now being done by us. He is present, the one who sees everything, whose attention nothing can escape, who reads each person's mind." HOMILIES ON GENESIS 57.37.[1]

31:55 Laban Blesses His Grandchildren and Daughters

OBSERVE GOD'S GREAT WISDOM. CHRYSOSTOM: Do you see, dearly beloved, God's great wisdom in demonstrating his care for the good man, as well as at the same time deterring the other from his injustice and, by forbidding him from speaking evil against Jacob, conducting him gradually to the path of knowledge of God? Though Laban had been pacing about like a wild beast intent on snaring and destroying him, he made his excuses, kissed his daughters and their sons good-bye and returned home. HOMILIES ON GENESIS 57.39.[2]

---

[1]FC 87:151. [2]FC 87:152.

32:1-5 JACOB SENDS MESSENGERS TO ESAU

[1]*Jacob went on his way and the angels of God met him;* [2]*and when Jacob saw them he said, "This is God's army!" So he called the name of that place Mahanaim.*[t]

[3]*And Jacob sent messengers before him to Esau his brother in the land of Seir, the country of Edom,* [4]*instructing them, "Thus you shall say to my lord Esau: Thus says your servant Jacob, 'I have sojourned with Laban, and stayed until now;* [5]*and I have oxen, asses, flocks, menservants, and maidservants; and I have sent to tell my lord, in order that I may find favor in your sight.'"*

---

t Here taken to mean *Two armies*

OVERVIEW: In a midrashic style of interpretation, the angels met Jacob to show that God would protect him from Laban and Esau (EPHREM, CHRYSOSTOM). Jacob was afraid of Esau and wished to placate him, but God allayed Esau's anger (CHRYSOSTOM). Jacob's bow to Esau posed a problem in the light of the prediction in Genesis 27 that the elder would be slave of the younger. The fact that this was not fulfilled in the lives of the two men shows that it was said of the future Jacob (AUGUSTINE).

32:1 The Angels of God

MANY ANGELS WERE WITH JACOB. EPHREM THE SYRIAN: After Jacob and Laban had parted from each other, "angels of God met Jacob" to make known to him that if Laban did not obey God, who had appeared to him in the evening, he and those with him would be destroyed at dawn by the hands of those angels who protect Jacob. Just as God had shown Jacob the angels that accompanied him when he went down, he also showed him angels when he was going up to make him know that the word was true which God had spoken to him: "I will go down with you, and I will bring you up from there."[1] The army of angels that God had shown Jacob was so that he

---

[1]Gen 46:4; cf. 28:15. The verse cited had not yet been "spoken" to him. In Genesis 28:15 God promised Jacob to be with him always.

---

would not fear Esau, for there were many more [angels] with Jacob than were with Esau. COMMENTARY ON GENESIS 30.1.[2]

A CONSTANT REMINDER OF THE VISION.

CHRYSOSTOM: You see, once fear of Laban faded and was no more, then fear of his brother took hold of Jacob; so the loving Lord wanted to give the good man heart and drive out all his apprehension. Thus he caused Jacob to see the angels' camp. "God's angels accosted him," the text says, remember. "Jacob said, 'This is God's camp,' and he called that place Camps,"[3] with the result that from the name there was a constant reminder of the vision that occurred to him there. HOMILIES ON GENESIS 58.2.[4]

32:3 Jacob Sends Messengers to Esau

GOD ALLAYED ESAU'S ANGER. CHRYSOSTOM: See how great was Jacob's fear even after the vision had affected the good man. He was afraid of his brother's aggression and was concerned lest the memory of what had been done by him previously might provoke Esau into an attack on him. "Say to my lord Esau, 'Thus says your servant Jacob: I was dwelling with Laban and tarried until now; I acquired cattle and asses and sheep, servants male and female. I have sent word to my lord in the hope that your servant may find favor with you.' "[5] Notice how Jacob was afraid of his brother, and hence out of a wish to placate him he

sent word ahead alerting him to his coming, the wealth acquired by him and where he had spent all the time, so as to calm Esau's anger and succeed in making him gracious. This in fact happened, for God placated his heart, allayed his anger and rendered him gracious. After all, if by the words Jacob spoke to Laban, who had hunted him down in such awful rage, he caused him to suffer such great apprehension, much more did he cause his brother to be more affable to the good man. HOMILIES ON GENESIS 58.3.[6]

A FUTURE JACOB. AUGUSTINE: Jacob did not want to see Esau before he had appeased him with presents, and he only saw him afterward when the presents had been accepted. And when Jacob came to him, he bowed down to him from a long way off. So how shall the elder be slave to the younger,[7] when the younger manifestly bows down to the elder? But the reason why these things were not fulfilled in the actual history of the two men is to make us understand that they were said of a future Jacob. The younger son received the first place, and the elder son, the people of the Jews, lost the first place. See how Jacob has filled the whole world, has taken possession of nations and kingdoms. SERMON 5.5.[8]

---

[2]FC 91:180. [3]Chrysostom is commenting on the LXX, in which the translator had translated literally the root of the place name Mahanayim, meaning "two camps." [4]FC 87:155*. [5]Gen 32:4-5. [6]FC 87:155*. [7]Gen 27:40. [8]WSA 3 1:220-21.

32:6-8 JACOB PREPARES TO MEET ESAU

[6]And the messengers returned to Jacob, saying, "We came to your brother Esau, and he is coming to meet you, and four hundred men with him." [7]Then Jacob was greatly afraid and distressed; and he divided the people that were with him, and the flocks and herds and camels, into two companies, [8]thinking, "If Esau comes to the one company and destroys it, then the company which is left will escape."

OVERVIEW: The news about four hundred men struck Jacob with great fear and terror, but he invoked the promises made to him by God (CHRYSOSTOM).

32:6 Esau's Approach

JACOB WAS TERRIFIED. CHRYSOSTOM: See how this was sufficient to aggravate the good man's fear. Far from realizing precisely his brother's intent, Jacob was terrified to learn the number of those approaching and suspected that they were bent on hostilities and so wanted to catch up with him. Note the text says, "Jacob was in a state of fear and perplexity." Fear disturbed his thinking, and instead of knowing what to do, he was at a loss; hence Jacob was terrified of almost every-thing, and, with the prospect of death before him, "he divided all the people with him into two camps." You see, he said, "If he comes upon one camp and attacks it, the other will have the chance of being saved."[1] While it was Jacob's fear and great terror that suggested this, . . . seeing himself caught in a trap he had recourse to the invincible Lord and invoked the promises made him by the God of all, as if to say to him, "Now the time has come for a good man to enjoy your complete assistance on account of the virtue of his forebears and the promises made by you." HOMILIES ON GENESIS 58.4.[2]

---

[1]Gen 32:7-8. [2]FC 87:155-56*.

32:9-12 JACOB PRAYS FOR DELIVERANCE

[9]And Jacob said, "O God of my father Abraham and God of my father Isaac, O LORD who didst say to me, 'Return to your country and to your kindred, and I will do you good,' [10]I am not worthy of the least of all the steadfast love and all the faithfulness which thou hast shown to thy servant, for with only my staff I crossed this Jordan; and now I have become two companies. [11]Deliver me, I pray thee, from the hand of my brother, from the hand of Esau, for I fear him, lest he come and slay us all, the mothers with the children. [12]But thou didst say, 'I will do you good, and make your descendants as the sand of the sea, which cannot be numbered for multitude.'"

OVERVIEW: The staff with which Jacob crossed the Jordan was a symbol of the cross (APHRAHAT). Jacob represented a type of the Lord our Savior, and most of his actions foreshadow aspects of the mystery of Christ (CAESARIUS OF ARLES).

32:10 Jacob's Staff

A WONDROUS SYMBOL. APHRAHAT: "With only his staff he crossed the Jordan." It was a wondrous symbol Jacob held in his hand in anticipation—the sign of the cross of the great prophet.[1] He lifted up his feet on to the land of the people of the east, because it was from there that "a light shone out to the peoples."[2] He reclined by the well that had a stone on its mouth that many men had not been able to lift—for many shepherds had been unable to lift it and open up the well, until Jacob

---

[1]Cf. Gen 29:1. [2]Lk 2:32.

---

came[3] and, through the power of the Shepherd who was hidden in his limbs, lifted up the stone and watered his sheep. Many prophets too had come without being able to unveil baptism, before the great Prophet came and opened it up by himself and was baptized in it, calling out and proclaiming in a gentle voice: "Let everyone who thirsts come to me and drink."[4] ON PRAYER 6.[5]

A TYPE OF OUR SAVIOR. CAESARIUS OF ARLES: We do not read of blessed Jacob that he departed with horses or asses or camels, but we read only that he carried a staff in his hand. Thus indeed, when entreating the Lord he said, "Lord, I am not worthy of all thy kindnesses. With only my staff I crossed this Jordan; behold, now I have grown into two camps."[6] Jacob displayed his staff to take a wife, but Christ bore the wood of the cross to

redeem the church. In his sleep Jacob put a stone under his head and saw a ladder extending to heaven, while the Lord leaned upon the ladder. Consider, brothers, how many mysteries there are in this place. Jacob represented a type of the Lord our Savior; the stone that he put under his head no less prefigured Christ the Lord. Listen to the apostle telling why the stone at the head signifies Christ: "The head of man is Christ."[7] Finally, notice that blessed Jacob anointed the stone. Pay attention to the anointing, and you will recognize Christ. Christ is explained from an anointing, that is, from the grace of anointing. SERMON 87.2.[8]

---

[3]Gen 29:8. [4]Jn 4:13-14. [5]CS 101:9-10*. [6]Gen 32:10. [7]1 Cor 11:3. [8]FC 47:30.

32:13-21 JACOB SEEKS TO APPEASE ESAU

[13]So he lodged there that night, and took from what he had with him a present for his brother Esau, [14]two hundred she-goats and twenty he-goats, two hundred ewes and twenty rams, [15]thirty milch camels and their colts, forty cows and ten bulls, twenty she-asses and ten he-asses. [16]These he delivered into the hand of his servants, every drove by itself, and said to his servants, "Pass on before me, and put a space between drove and drove." [17]He instructed the foremost, "When Esau my brother meets you, and asks you, 'To whom do you belong? Where are you going? And whose are these before you?' [18]then you shall say, 'They belong to your servant Jacob; they are a present sent to my lord Esau; and moreover he is behind us.'" [19]He likewise instructed the second and the third and all who followed the droves, "You shall say the same thing to Esau when you meet him, [20]and you shall say, 'Moreover your servant Jacob is behind us.'" For he thought, "I may appease him with the present that goes before me, and afterwards I shall see his face; perhaps he will accept me." [21]So the present passed on before him; and he himself lodged that night in the camp.

OVERVIEW: Jacob's sleeping in the camp before meeting Esau manifests his tranquility and inner peace, the fruit of perfect virtue (AMBROSE). The fact that Jacob sent gifts ahead to Esau shows

that he made every effort on his part to ensure a peaceful meeting (CHRYSOSTOM).

32:13 Jacob Prepares to Meet Esau

Perfect Virtue Possesses Tranquility.

Ambrose: Then, intending to ask for peace from his brother, Jacob slept in the encampment.[1] Perfect virtue possesses tranquility and a calm steadfastness; likewise the Lord has kept his gift for those who are more perfect and has said, "My peace I leave to you, my peace I give to you."[2] It is the part of those who have been perfected not to be easily influenced by worldly things or to be troubled with fear or tormented with suspicion or stunned with dread or distressed with pain. Rather, as if on a shore of total safety, they ought to calm their spirit, immovable as it is in the anchorage of faith, against the rising waves and tempests of the world. Christ brought this support to the spirits of Christians when he brought an inner peace to the souls of those who had proved themselves, so that our hearts should not be troubled or our spirits be distressed. That this peace is beyond all understanding our apostolic teacher proclaimed when he said, "And the peace of God, which surpasses all understanding, will guard your hearts and feelings in Christ Jesus."[3] And so the fruit of peace is the absence of disturbance in the heart. In short, the life of the just person is calm, but the unjust person is filled with disquiet and disturbance. Therefore the ungodly person is struck down more by his own suspicions than people are by the blows of others, and the stripes of the wounds in his soul are greater than those in the bodies of people who are lashed by others.

It is a sublime thing that someone is tranquil within himself and in agreement with himself. Externally, peace is sought through the anxious forethought of the emperor or the hands of the soldiers. Or it results from the favorable outcome of wars or some massacre among the barbarians, if they turn their own weapons on one another in a hostile move. Such a peace comes to pass through no power of ours, but it is a stroke of good fortune. Surely the glory of that peace is assigned to the emperor, but we have in us the benefit of inward peace, which is in the spirit and is held in the heart of every one of us. The benefit of this peace is greater in that temptations coming from a spirit of wickedness,[4] rather than hostile arms, are repulsed. This peace that shuts out the enticements of the bodily passions and calms the disturbances arising from them is nobler than the peace that checks the attacks of barbarians; it is a greater thing to withstand the enemy shut up within oneself than the one that is far off. Jacob and the Happy Life 6.28-29.[5]

Jacob Made Every Effort. Chrysostom:

See the good man's godliness and proper sense of values in requesting nothing from the Lord other than fulfillment of his promises. After giving thanks for his former benefits by confessing that while naked and destitute he had been brought to such affluence, Jacob entreats God to snatch him from danger. Recall that Jacob says, "You told me, 'I will make your descendants to be like the sand of the sea, which in number will defy counting.'" Having made this appeal to the Lord, however, and having offered this supplication to the Lord, Jacob also made every effort on his own part. Selecting gifts from what he brought with him, the text says, Jacob sent them to his brother, spacing out what was sent and giving instructions with the aim of appeasing Esau by word and alerting him to his own arrival. Recall that the text says, "'Behold, your servant is right behind us,' so as first to appease him, and then we can meet face to face." "After this," remember Jacob says, "I will meet him face to face; perhaps he will be pleased to see me." The gifts went ahead of him.[6] Homilies on Genesis 58.6.[7]

---

[1]Gen 32:21. [2]Jn 14:27. [3]Phil 4:7. [4]Eph 6:12. [5]FC 65:162-63. [6]Gen 32:20-21. [7]FC 87:156-57*.

32:22-32 JACOB WRESTLES WITH A MAN

²²*The same night he arose and took his two wives, his two maids, and his eleven children, and crossed the ford of the Jabbok.* ²³*He took them and sent them across the stream, and likewise everything that he had.* ²⁴*And Jacob was left alone; and a man wrestled with him until the breaking of the day.* ²⁵*When the man saw that he did not prevail against Jacob, he touched the hollow* of his thigh; and Jacob's thigh was put out of joint as he wrestled with him.* ²⁶*Then he said, "Let me go, for the day is breaking." But Jacob said, "I will not let you go, unless you bless me."* ²⁷*And he said to him, "What is your name?" And he said, "Jacob."* ²⁸*Then he said, "Your name shall no more be called Jacob, but Israel,ᵘ for you have striven with God and with men, and have prevailed."* ²⁹*Then Jacob asked him, "Tell me, I pray, your name." But he said, "Why is it that you ask my name?" And there he blessed him.* ³⁰*So Jacob called the name of the place Peniel,ᵛ† saying, "For I have seen God face to face, and yet my life is preserved."* ³¹*The sun rose upon him as he passed Penuel, limping because of his thigh.* ³²*Therefore to this day the Israelites do not eat the sinew of the hip which is upon the hollow of the thigh, because he touched the hollow of Jacob's thigh on the sinew of the hip.*

u That is *He who strives with God* or *God strives*   v That is *The face of God*   *LXX, "flat of his thigh."   †The LXX translator has rendered the Hebrew place name Penuel as "visible form of God" or "sight of God," which enables him to establish an etymological relationship with the verb for "seeing" that follows. This meaning forms the basis of Chrysostom's extended comment.

OVERVIEW: This passage attracted considerable comment in the patristic period. The name Jacob had already been interpreted by Philo of Alexandria to signify "the ascetic" or "athlete," that is, the one who is in training and seeking to overcome vices and acquire virtue. The name Jacob he explained as "the one who sees God." The present scene represented the point in the spiritual life (the spiritual contest or struggle) where one is granted the gift of inner tranquility and is able to engage in the contemplative life or "see God." The influence of this interpretation on Christian writers was extensive and can be seen in some of the passages below (AMBROSE, CHRYSOSTOM, AUGUSTINE). The Christian interpretation of the passage perceived in Jacob and in the one with whom he struggled images of Christ. Thus the numbness in Jacob's thigh foreshadowed the cross of Christ (AMBROSE). The man overcome by Jacob represents Christ overcome by unbelieving Jews, although Ja-

cob represents believing and unbelieving Jews and his withered thigh signifies bad Christians or unbelieving Jews. Jacob's lengthy struggle (EPHREM) is to hold on to Christ, the promise (AUGUSTINE, CAESARIUS OF ARLES). The fact that the struggle ends at daybreak means that for those who live in the light, there is no struggle (CYRIL OF ALEXANDRIA). The figure with whom Jacob wrestled was God and man, foreshadowing Christ, who was God and man (NOVATIAN, HILARY OF POITIERS).

32:24 Jacob Wrestles with a Stranger

THE STRUGGLE FOR VIRTUE. AMBROSE: Therefore Jacob, who had purified his heart of all pretenses and was manifesting a peaceable disposition, first cast off all that was his, then remained behind alone and wrestled with God.[1]

[1]Gen 32:23-25.

For whoever forsakes worldly things comes nearer to the image and likeness of God. What is it to wrestle with God other than to enter upon the struggle for virtue, to contend with one who is stronger and to become a better imitator of God than the others are? Because Jacob's faith and devotion were unconquerable, the Lord revealed his hidden mysteries to him by touching the side of his thigh.[2] For it was by descent from him that the Lord Jesus was to be born of a virgin, and Jesus would be neither unlike nor unequal to God. The numbness in the side of Jacob's thigh foreshadowed the cross of Christ, who would bring salvation to all people by spreading the forgiveness of sins throughout the whole world and would give resurrection to the departed by the numbness and torpidity of his own body. On this account the sun rightly rose on holy Jacob,[3] for the saving cross of the Lord shone brightly on his lineage. And at the same time the Sun of justice rises on the person who recognizes God,[4] because he is himself the everlasting Light. JACOB AND THE HAPPY LIFE 7.30.[5]

32:25 Jacob Prevails

WHEN HE WAS OVERCOME, HE OVERCAME FOR US. AUGUSTINE: Believing Jews and unbelieving Jews. Where were they first condemned? In the first of them, in the father of all of them, Jacob himself, who was also called Israel. Jacob means "supplanter" or "heel"; Israel means "seeing God." When Jacob returned from Mesopotamia with his children, an angel wrestled with him, representing Christ; and while he wrestled, though the angel surpassed Jacob in strength, he still seemed to succumb to him, and Jacob to prevail. In the same sort of way the Lord Christ too succumbed to the Jews; they prevailed when they killed him. He was overcome by superior strength; precisely when he was overcome, he overcame for us. What's that—when he was overcome, he overcame for us? Yes, because when he suffered, he shed the blood with which he redeemed us.

So then, that is what is written: Jacob prevailed over him. And yet Jacob himself, who was wrestling, acknowledged the mystery involved. A man, wrestling with an angel, prevailed over him; and when he said, "Let me go," the one who had prevailed said, "I am not letting you go, unless you bless me." O grand and splendid mystery! Overcome, he blesses, just as having suffered, he sets free; that is when the blessing was completed. "What are you called?" he said to him. He replied, "Jacob." "You shall not be called Jacob," he said, "but you shall be called Israel."[6] The imposition of such a great name is a great blessing. "Israel," as I said, means "seeing God"; one man's name, everyone's reward. Everyone's, provided they believe and are blessed, Jews and Greeks. Greeks, you see, are what the apostle calls all nationalities, the reason being that the Greek language has such prestige among the nations. "Glory," he says, "and honor"—they are the apostle's words— "glory and honor and peace to everyone doing good, to Jew first and Greek; wrath and indignation, trouble and distress on every soul doing evil, to Jews first and Greeks."[7] Good for good Jews, bad for bad ones; good for good Gentiles, bad for bad ones. SERMON 229F.2.[8]

FOR THE TIME BEING THE CHURCH IS LAME. AUGUSTINE: Jacob's withered thigh stands for bad Christians, so that we find in him blessing and limping. He is blessed with respect to those who live good lives; he limps with respect to those who live bad lives. But each kind is still included in one man. They will be separated and set apart later. This is what the church is longing for in that psalm: "Judge me, O God, and distinguish my case from an unholy people."[9] Yes, of course, because the Gospel says, "If your foot is a scandal to you, cut it off and throw it away. It is better for you to enter the kingdom of God having one foot, than with two feet to go to the ever-

---

[2]Gen 32:26. [3]Gen 32:32. [4]See Mal 4:2 (3:20 LXX). [5]FC 65:163-64*. [6]Gen 32:25-29. [7]Rom 2:10, 9. Note that Augustine has cited the verses in reverse order. [8]WSA 3 6:286*. [9]Ps 43:1 (42:1 LXX).

lasting fire."[10] So these bad people have to be cut off in the end. For the time being the church is lame. It puts one foot down firmly; the other one, being crippled, it drags. Look at the pagans, brothers. Sometimes they find good Christians serving God, and they admire them and are attracted and believe. Sometimes they notice those who are living bad lives, and they say, "Look at these Christians!" But those who live evil lives belong to the hollow of Jacob's thigh that was touched, and they have withered. Yet the touch of the Lord is the hand of the Lord, chastising and giving life. SERMON 5.8.[11]

WITHERED AND LIMPING, JACOB IS BLESSED.
AUGUSTINE: So what does it mean, Jacob's wrestling and refusing to let go? The Lord says in the Gospel, "The kingdom of heaven suffers violence, and those who act violently plunder it."[12] This is what we were saying earlier on: struggle, wrestle, to hold on to Christ, to love your enemy. You hold Christ here and now if you have loved your enemy. And what does the Lord himself say, that is, the angel in the person of the Lord, when he had got the upper hand and was holding him fast? He has touched the hollow of his thigh, and it has withered, and so Jacob was limping. He says to Jacob, "Let me go, it is already morning." He answered, "I will not let you go unless you bless me."[13] And he blessed Jacob. How? By changing his name: "You shall not be called Jacob but Israel; since you have got the upper hand with God, you shall also get the upper hand with men."[14] That is the blessing. Look, it's a single man; in one respect he is touched and withers and in another he is blessed. This one single person in one respect has withered up and limps; in another he is blessed to give him vigor. SERMON 5.6.[15]

32:26 Jacob Demands a Blessing

THE STRUGGLE CEASES AT DAYBREAK. CYRIL OF ALEXANDRIA: You see how he does not continue fighting at daybreak. In fact, there is no fight for those who already live in the light. It is fitting for those who have been brought to such magnificence to say, "God, my God, I watch you from the light."[16] And in addition, "In the morning you shall hear my voice, in the morning I shall wait on you, and you shall see me."[17] When the light of justice, that is, Christ, rises in our mind and introduces his brilliance into our hearts, then we also will be waited on as noble souls and will be made worthy of the divine attention. "The eyes of the Lord are over the righteous."[18] At daybreak the fight ceases. GLAPHYRA ON GENESIS, 5.3.[19]

THE ANGEL TYPIFIED OUR LORD AND SAVIOR. CAESARIUS OF ARLES: Now as to the fact that Jacob came to the Jordan and after sending over all his possessions remained alone and wrestled with a man until the break of day. In that struggle Jacob prefigured the people of the Jews; the angel with whom he wrestled typified our Lord and Savior. Jacob wrestled with the angel because the Jewish people were to wrestle with Christ even to death. However, not all the Jews were unfaithful to Christ, as we said above, but a considerable number of them are read to have believed in his name, and for this reason the angel touched Jacob's thigh, which began to be lame. That foot with which he limped typified the Jews who did not believe in Christ; the one that remained uninjured signified those who received Christ the Lord. Finally, notice carefully that in the struggle Jacob was victorious and sought a blessing. When the angel had said to him, "Let me go," Jacob replied, "I will not let you go till you bless me." In the fact that he was victorious Jacob signified the Jews who persecuted Christ; inasmuch as he asked a blessing he prefigured the people who were to believe in Christ the Lord. What then did the angel say to him? "You have contended with God and men and have triumphed." This was fulfilled at the time when the Jewish people crucified Christ the Lord. "Let me

---

[10]Mt 18:8. [11]*WSA* 3 1:223*. [12]Mt 11:12. [13]Gen 32:29. [14]Gen 32:28. [15]*WSA* 3 1:222. [16]Ps 63:1 (62:2 LXX). [17]Ps 5:3 (5:4 LXX). [18]Ps 34:15 (33:16 LXX). [19]PG 69:273.

go," said the angel, "it is dawn." This prefigured the Lord's resurrection, for the Lord, as you know very well, is read to have risen before dawn. SERMON 88.5.[20]

JACOB HELD ON BRAVELY. AUGUSTINE: "Let me go, because it is already morning." "Morning" we understand as the light of truth and wisdom, through whom all things were made.[21] You will enjoy the morning when this night has gone, that is, the iniquity of this world. That's when it will be morning, when the Lord comes, in order to be seen by us as he is already seen by the angels. Because "now we see through a mirror in a riddle, but then it will be face to face."[22] So let us hold fast to this saying, brothers, "Let me go; behold, it is already morning." But what did *he* say? "I will not let you go, unless you bless me." The Lord, you see, does bless us first through the flesh. The faithful know what they receive, that they are blessed through the flesh.[23] And they know that they would not be blessed unless that flesh had been crucified and given for the life of the world.[24] But how is Jacob blessed? In that he got the upper hand with God, in that he held on bravely and persevered and did not lose from his grasp what Adam lost. So let us, the faithful, hold on to what we receive, in order that we may deserve to be blessed. SERMON 5.7.[25]

32:28 A New Name

THIS STRUGGLE PREFIGURED ANOTHER STRUGGLE. NOVATIAN: A man, Scripture says, wrestled with Jacob. If he is a mere man, who is he? Where did he come from? Why does he struggle and wrestle with Jacob? What had come between them? What had happened? What was the cause of so great a conflict and struggle as that? Moreover, why is it that Jacob proves to be the stronger even to the holding of the man with whom he was struggling? And why still, because the morning star was rising, is it he who, on that account, asks a blessing from him whom he held? It can only mean that this struggle was prefigur-

ing that future contention between Christ and the sons of Jacob, which is said to have had its completion in the gospel. For Jacob's people struggled against this man and proved to be more powerful in the conflict, because they obtained the triumph of their own unrighteousness over Christ. Then, on account of the crime they had perpetrated, they began to limp very badly in the gait of their own faith and salvation, stumbling and slipping in their course. Though Jacob's people proved superior by their condemnation of Christ, they still need his mercy and still need his blessing. Now this man who wrestled with Jacob says to him, "Your name shall no longer be called Jacob, but Israel shall be your name."[26] And if Israel is a man who "sees God," then the Lord was showing in an elegant manner that he who wrestled with Jacob was not only man but also God. Undoubtedly Jacob saw God with whom he wrestled, though it was a man whom he held in his grip. That there might not remain any doubt, he himself gave the interpretation when he said, "For you have prevailed with God, and with men you are powerful."[27] That is why this same Jacob, understanding now the meaning of the prefiguration and realizing the authority of him with whom he had wrestled, called the name of the place where he had wrestled "Vision of God." Furthermore, Jacob added his reason for giving his interpretation of God: "I have seen God face to face, and my soul has been saved."[28] For he saw God with whom he wrestled, as though he were wrestling with a man; but while as if victor he held the man, as an inferior[29] he asked a blessing of him, as one would of God. Thus he wrestled with God and with man. Now if this struggle was then prefigured and has been actually fulfilled in the gospel between Christ and Jacob's people—a struggle in which the people proved superior yet were found to be inferior because of their guilt—who will

[20]FC 47:37. [21]See Jn 1:3; 14:6; 1 Cor 1:24. [22]1 Cor 13:12. [23]Here Augustine refers to the Eucharist and the human reality of the incarnation. [24]See Jn 6:51. [25]WSA 3 1:222-23*. [26]Gen 32:28-29. [27]Gen 32:28-29. [28]Gen 32:31. [29]See Heb 7:7.

hesitate to acknowledge that Christ in whom this figure of a struggle was fulfilled was not only human but also God, when that very figure of a struggle seems to have proved that he is both God and human? ON THE TRINITY 19.8-14.[30]

YOU BEHOLD GOD FACE TO FACE. HILARY OF POITIERS: O holy and blessed patriarch, Jacob, be with me, be with me now by the spirit of your faith against the poisonous hissing of infidelity, and, while you prevail in the struggle with the man, plead with him as the stronger to bless you.[31] What is this that you are asking from one who is weak? What do you expect from one who is feeble? This one for whose blessing you pray is the one whom you, as the more powerful, weaken by your embrace. The activity of your soul is not in harmony with the deeds of your body, for you think differently from the way you act. By your bodily motions during this struggle you keep this man helpless, but this man is for you the true God, not in name but in nature. You do not ask to be sanctified by adoptive but by true blessings. You struggle with a man, but you behold God face to face. You do not see with your bodily eyes what you perceive with the glance of your faith. In comparison with you he is a feeble man, but your soul has been saved by the vision of God.

During this struggle you are Jacob, but after your faith in the blessing for which you prayed you are Israel. The man is subject to you according to the flesh in anticipation of the sufferings in the flesh. You recognize God in the weakness of his flesh in order to foreshadow the mystery of his blessing in the spirit. His appearance does not prevent you from remaining steadfast in the fight, nor does his weakness deter you from seeking his blessing. Nor does the man bring it about that he is not God who is man, nor is he who is God not the true God, because he who is God cannot but be the true God by the blessing, the transfer and the name. ON THE TRINITY 5.19.[32]

ISRAEL MEANS "SEEING GOD." CHRYSOSTOM: Do you see how God revealed the complete expla-

nation of why he demonstrated such considerateness? At the same time God taught this good man [Jacob] through the imposition of the name [Israel] who it was that he had seen and had been allowed to hold on to. Recall the text says, "You will no longer be called Jacob but Israel." Now Israel means "seeing God." "Since you are privileged to see God, insofar as it is possible for a human being to see him, hence I also give you this name so that it may be clear to everyone in future that you were accorded a vision." And he added, "For you have fought with God and will thus be powerful in dealing with human beings." No longer have any fear or expect to suffer any harm from anyone. Having gained such might in the first place as to succeed in wrestling with God, much more will you prevail over human beings and prove superior to all. HOMILIES ON GENESIS 58.10.[33]

JACOB'S TRIUMPH SIGNIFIED CHRIST'S PASSION. AUGUSTINE: Now, as I said just a little while ago, Jacob was also called Israel, which was the name generally borne by the people descended from him. This name was given him by the angel who wrestled with him when Jacob was on his way back from Mesopotamia. This angel obviously presents a type of Christ. For the fact that Jacob "prevailed over" him (the angel, of course, being a willing loser to symbolize the hidden meaning) represents the passion of Christ, in which the Jews seemed to prevail over him. And yet Jacob obtained a blessing from the very angel whom he had defeated; thus the giving of the name was the blessing. Now "Israel" means "seeing God,"[34] and the vision of God will be the reward of all the saints at the end of the world. Moreover, the angel also touched the apparent victor on the broad part of his thigh and thus made him lame. And so the same man, Jacob, was the same time blessed and lame—blessed in those

---

[30]FC 67:74-75*.   [31]Gen 32:26-30.   [32]FC 25:149-50.   [33]FC 87:158-59.
[34]Israel probably means "God perseveres," but in Genesis 32:28 it is interpreted as "one who perseveres with God." Augustine here adopts a traditional etymology deriving the name from *ish* ("man"), *ra'ah* ("see") and *el* ("God"). See the overview above.

who among this same people of Israel have believed in Christ and crippled in respect of those who do not believe. For the broad part of the thigh represents the general mass of the race. For in fact it is to the majority of that stock that the prophetic statement applies, "They have limped away from their paths."[35] CITY OF GOD 16.39.[36]

32:29 Jacob's Request

THE STRENGTH AND WEAKNESS OF JACOB.
EPHREM THE SYRIAN: That night an angel appeared to [Jacob] and wrestled with him. He overcame the angel and was overcome by the angel so that [Jacob] learned how weak he was and how strong he was. He was weak when the angel touched the hollow of his thigh and it became dislocated, but he was strong, for the angel said to him, "Let me go." It was to show how long they had been contending with each other that [the angel] said, "Behold, the dawn is rising." Then Jacob sought to be blessed in order to make known that it was in love that they had laid hold of each other. Then the angel blessed him to show that he was not angry that an earthly being had prevailed over him. COMMENTARY ON GENESIS 30.3.[37]

32:30 Peniel

THE LORD'S CONSIDERATION FOR OUR LIMITATIONS. CHRYSOSTOM: Do you see how much confidence Jacob gained from the vision he had? That is to say, "my spirit survived," he is saying, "which had almost perished from fear. Since I was privileged to see God face to face, 'my spirit survived.'" Now the sun rose on him as he passed the sight of God.[38]

Do you see how the Lord shows considerateness for our human limitations in all he does and in arranging everything in a way that gives evidence of his characteristic love? Don't be surprised, dearly beloved, at the extent of his considerateness; rather, remember that with the patriarch as well, when Abraham was sitting by the oak tree, God came in human form as the good man's guest in the company of the angels, giving us a premonition from on high at the beginning that he would one day take human form to liberate all human nature by this means from the tyranny of the devil and lead us to salvation. At that time, however, since it was the very early stages, God appeared to each of them in the guise of an apparition, as he says himself through the inspired author, "I multiplied visions and took various likenesses in the works of the inspired authors."[39] HOMILIES ON GENESIS 58.11-12.[40]

32:32 The Hollow of Jacob's Thigh

NUMBNESS TOWARD THE GRACE OF FAITH.
AMBROSE: But Jacob limped because of his thigh. "On account of this the children of Israel do not eat the sinew even to the present day." Would that they had eaten it and had believed! But because they were not about to do the will of God, therefore they did not eat. There are those too who take the passage in the following sense, that Jacob limped from one thigh. Two peoples flowed from his lineage, and there was then being revealed the numbness that one of them would presently exhibit toward the grace of faith. And so it is the people itself that limped by reason of the numbness of its unbelief. JACOB AND THE HAPPY LIFE 7.31.[41]

JACOB'S WISH FOR FUTURE GENERATIONS.
CHRYSOSTOM: Just as the truth is quite plain in this case, however, so with the good man a kind of apparition occurred that had the effect of convincing the good man of the degree of care he enjoyed from God and the fact that Jacob would be unvanquished by all those plotting against him. Then, in order that the vision he had would not be forgotten by anyone in the future, "his thigh made him limp. For this reason the sons of Israel do not eat the nerve that stiffened on the flat of his thigh, because he lay hold of the flat of Jacob's

---

[35]Ps 18:44 (17:45 LXX). [36]CG 704*. [37]FC 91:180-81. [38]Gen 32:31. [39]Hos 12:10. [40]FC 87:159-60*. [41]FC 65:164.

thigh, and it stiffened."[42] You see, since the good man had completed his lifespan and was about to leave this life, and since the providence accorded him by God and the marvelous considerateness should be known to the whole human race, accordingly it says, "The sons of Israel do not eat the nerve that stiffened on the flat of his thigh." Aware of their ingratitude and the way, they forgot God's kindnesses; he therefore devised a constant reminder for them to have of the kindnesses done by him and arranged for these reminders to be preserved in their observances of this kind. You can find this throughout the whole of Scripture. In fact, this in particular is the explanation of the great number of observances. They represent God's wish that future generations would unfailingly meditate on God's kindnesses and, by consigning them to oblivion, not have recourse again to their own errors—a particular weakness of the Jewish people. I mean, those who give evidence of their typical ingratitude in the face of these very kindnesses would all the more readily, had this not happened, have banished from their mind all that had been done for them by God. HOMILIES ON GENESIS 58.14.[43]

---

[42]Gen 32:31-32. [43]FC 87:160-61.

33:1-20 JACOB RECONCILES WITH ESAU

[1]And Jacob lifted up his eyes and looked, and behold, Esau was coming, and four hundred men with him. So he divided the children among Leah and Rachel and the two maids. [2]And he put the maids with their children in front, then Leah with her children, and Rachel and Joseph last of all. [3]He himself went on before them, bowing himself to the ground seven times, until he came near to his brother.

[4]But Esau ran to meet him, and embraced him, and fell on his neck and kissed him, and they wept. [5]And when Esau raised his eyes and saw the women and children, he said, "Who are these with you?" Jacob said, "The children whom God has graciously given your servant." [6]Then the maids drew near, they and their children, and bowed down; [7]Leah likewise and her children drew near and bowed down; and last Joseph and Rachel drew near, and they bowed down. [8]Esau said, "What do you mean by all this company which I met?" Jacob answered, "To find favor in the sight of my lord." [9]But Esau said, "I have enough, my brother; keep what you have for yourself." [10]Jacob said, "No, I pray you, if I have found favor in your sight, then accept my present from my hand; for truly to see your face is like seeing the face of God, with such favor have you received me. [11]Accept, I pray you, my gift that is brought to you, because God has dealt graciously with me, and because I have enough." Thus he urged him, and he took it.

[12]Then Esau said, "Let us journey on our way, and I will go before you." [13]But Jacob said to him, "My lord knows that the children are frail, and that the flocks and herds giving suck are a care to me; and if they are overdriven for one day, all the flocks will die. [14]Let my lord pass on before his servant, and I will lead on slowly, according to the pace of the cattle which are before me

and according to the pace of the children, until I come to my lord in Seir."

[15]So Esau said, "Let me leave with you some of the men who are with me." But he said, "What need is there? Let me find favor in the sight of my lord." [16]So Esau returned that day on his way to Seir. [17]But Jacob journeyed to Succoth,[w] and built himself a house, and made booths for his cattle; therefore the name of the place is called Succoth.

[18]And Jacob came safely to the city of Shechem, which is in the land of Canaan, on his way from Paddan-aram; and he camped before the city. [19]And from the sons of Hamor, Shechem's father, he bought for a hundred pieces of money[x] the piece of land on which he had pitched his tent. [20]There he erected an altar and called it El-Elohe-Israel.[y]

w That is *Booths*   **x** Heb *a hundred qesitah*   **y** That is *God, the God of Israel*

OVERVIEW: This chapter does not seem to have inspired much comment in the patristic period. The reconciliation of Jacob with Esau could be seen to foreshadow the reconciliation of Christ with Israel (CYRIL OF ALEXANDRIA).

33:4 Esau Encounters Jacob

CHRIST WILL BE RECONCILED WITH ISRAEL. CYRIL OF ALEXANDRIA: At the end of time our Lord Jesus Christ will be reconciled with Israel, his ancient persecutor, just as Jacob kissed Esau after his return from Haran. No one who listens to the words of holy Scripture can actually doubt that with the passing of time Israel also will have to be received again into the love of Christ through faith. The Lord proclaims to everybody through the voice of one of the holy prophets: "For the children of Israel shall abide many days without a king, and without a prince, and without a sacrifice, and without an altar, and without priesthood and without manifestations. And af-terward the children of Israel shall return and shall seek the Lord, their God, and David, their king, and shall be amazed at the Lord and at his goodness in the latter days."[1] While Christ, the Savior of us all, gathers believers from the nations, Israel is deserted, since it has no law to elect its leaders, and it cannot offer to the divine altar the sacrifices prescribed by the laws. It therefore awaits Christ's return from his action of converting the nations, so that he may receive it as well and unite it with the law of his love to the others. See how Jacob, who rejoiced in the generation of his children and in his numerous herds of sheep, came back from Haran and received again Esau into his friendship. In time Israel itself will be converted after the calling of the nations and will admire these riches in Christ. GLAPHYRA ON GENESIS, 5.3.[2]

---

[1]Hos 3:4-5. [2]PG 69:261.

34:1-31 THE REVENGE OF JACOB'S SONS

[1]Now Dinah the daughter of Leah, whom she had borne to Jacob, went out to visit the women of the land; [2]and when Shechem the son of Hamor the Hivite, the prince of the land, saw her, he

seized her and lay with her and humbled her. ³And his soul was drawn to Dinah the daughter of Jacob; he loved the maiden and spoke tenderly to her. ⁴So Shechem spoke to his father Hamor, saying, "Get me this maiden for my wife." ⁵Now Jacob heard that he had defiled his daughter Dinah; but his sons were with his cattle in the field, so Jacob held his peace until they came. ⁶And Hamor the father of Shechem went out to Jacob to speak with him. ⁷The sons of Jacob came in from the field when they heard of it; and the men were indignant and very angry, because he had wrought folly in Israel by lying with Jacob's daughter, for such a thing ought not to be done.

⁸But Hamor spoke with them, saying, "The soul of my son Shechem longs for your daughter; I pray you, give her to him in marriage. ⁹Make marriages with us; give your daughters to us, and take our daughters for yourselves. ¹⁰You shall dwell with us; and the land shall be open to you; dwell and trade in it, and get property in it." ¹¹Shechem also said to her father and to her brothers, "Let me find favor in your eyes, and whatever you say to me I will give. ¹²Ask of me ever so much as marriage present and gift, and I will give according as you say to me; only give me the maiden to be my wife."

¹³The sons of Jacob answered Shechem and his father Hamor deceitfully, because he had defiled their sister Dinah. ¹⁴They said to them, "We cannot do this thing, to give our sister to one who is uncircumcised, for that would be a disgrace to us. ¹⁵Only on this condition will we consent to you: that you will become as we are and every male of you be circumcised. ¹⁶Then we will give our daughters to you, and we will take your daughters to ourselves, and we will dwell with you and become one people. ¹⁷But if you will not listen to us and be circumcised, then we will take our daughter, and we will be gone."

¹⁸Their words pleased Hamor and Hamor's son Shechem. ¹⁹And the young man did not delay to do the thing, because he had delight in Jacob's daughter. Now he was the most honored of all his family. ²⁰So Hamor and his son Shechem came to the gate of their city and spoke to the men of their city, saying, ²¹"These men are friendly with us; let them dwell in the land and trade in it, for behold, the land is large enough for them; let us take their daughters in marriage, and let us give them our daughters. ²²Only on this condition will the men agree to dwell with us, to become one people: that every male among us be circumcised as they are circumcised. ²³Will not their cattle, their property and all their beasts be ours? Only let us agree with them, and they will dwell with us." ²⁴And all who went out of the gate of his city hearkened to Hamor and his son Shechem; and every male was circumcised, all who went out of the gate of his city.

²⁵On the third day, when they were sore, two of the sons of Jacob, Simeon and Levi, Dinah's brothers, took their swords and came upon the city unawares, and killed all the males. ²⁶They slew Hamor and his son Shechem with the sword, and took Dinah out of Shechem's house, and went away. ²⁷And the sons of Jacob came upon the slain, and plundered the city, because their sister had been defiled; ²⁸they took their flocks and their herds, their asses, and whatever was in the city and in the field; ²⁹all their wealth, all their little ones and their wives, all that was in the houses, they captured and made their prey. ³⁰Then Jacob said to Simeon and Levi, "You have brought trouble on me by making me odious to the inhabitants of the land, the Canaanites and the Perizzites; my

numbers are few, and if they gather themselves against me and attack me, I shall be destroyed, both I and my household." [31]*But they said, "Should he treat our sister as a harlot?"*

OVERVIEW: The story of the revenge, deceit and violence practiced by the sons of Jacob, Simeon and Levi in particular, against Hamor and the inhabitants of Shechem was a cause of scandal rather than edification to Christian readers of these Scriptures. This probably accounts for the little attention given to it by commentators. Dinah could be interpreted on a moral allegorical level to represent the soul, but violence must be avoided, for it is in conflict with the teaching of Christ (CYRIL OF ALEXANDRIA).

34:30 Bringing Trouble to Jacob

TAKE SHELTER IN THE LORD'S TABERNACLE.
CYRIL OF ALEXANDRIA: Those who are brothers according to faith to the injured one, if they are in the priestly order, like Levi, are among the subjects (Simon, in fact, is interpreted as "obedience"). They are extremely displeased if somebody who is their intimate friend according to faith is offended. However, they should not proceed to demand blood, nor should they expect extremely severe punishments for the corruptors, so as not to listen to Christ, who said to them, "You have made me hateful, so that I am now evil in the eyes of all the inhabitants of the land."[1] It is necessary to remember what Jesus said in reproof to Peter, who was holding his sword, "Put up again your sword into its sheath: all those who take the sword shall perish with the sword."[2] In fact, it is not fitting for us, who are inclined toward piety in God, to be armed with swords but rather to be patient. Even though some people want to persecute us, we must reproach them to be good. We must be patient but never silent, as we must refer to him who judges rightly.[3] Those who want to avoid destruction must be careful not to leave the tabernacle of the father, that is, the house of God, in order not to be received into the herds of the heretics and other strangers. After moving out of the father's tabernacle, Dinah was brought to the house of Shechem. She would have never been reproached if she had stayed in the paternal houses and had lived constantly in the holy tabernacles. David declares how that thing is beautiful and very useful by singing, "One thing I have asked of the Lord, this I will earnestly seek: that I should dwell in the house of the Lord all the days of my life, that I should behold the fair beauty of the Lord and survey his temple. For in the days of my affliction he hid me in his tabernacle: he sheltered me in the secret of his tabernacle."[4] GLAPHYRA ON GENESIS, 5.4-5.[5]

---

[1]LXX. [2]Mt 26:52. [3]See 1 Pet 2:23. [4]Ps 27:4-5 (26:4-5 LXX). [5]PG 69:280-81.

35:1-15 JACOB GOES TO BETHEL

[1]*God said to Jacob, "Arise, go up to Bethel, and dwell there; and make there an altar to the God who appeared to you when you fled from your brother Esau."* [2]*So Jacob said to his household and to all who were with him, "Put away the foreign gods that are among you, and purify yourselves, and change your garments;* [3]*then let us arise and go up to Bethel, that I may make there an altar to the*

God who answered me in the day of my distress and has been with me wherever I have gone." [4]So they gave to Jacob all the foreign gods that they had, and the rings that were in their ears; and Jacob hid them under the oak which was near Shechem.

[5]And as they journeyed, a terror from God fell upon the cities that were round about them, so that they did not pursue the sons of Jacob. [6]And Jacob came to Luz (that is, Bethel), which is in the land of Canaan, he and all the people who were with him, [7]and there he built an altar, and called the place El-bethel,[z] because there God had revealed himself to him when he fled from his brother. [8]And Deborah, Rebekah's nurse, died, and she was buried under an oak below Bethel; so the name of it was called Allon-bacuth.[a]

[9]God appeared to Jacob again, when he came from Paddan-aram, and blessed him. [10]And God said to him, "Your name is Jacob; no longer shall your name be called Jacob, but Israel shall be your name." So his name was called Israel. [11]And God said to him, "I am God Almighty:[b] be fruitful and multiply; a nation and a company of nations shall come from you, and kings shall spring from you. [12]The land which I gave to Abraham and Isaac I will give to you, and I will give the land to your descendants after you." [13]Then God went up from him in the place where he had spoken with him. [14]And Jacob set up a pillar in the place where he had spoken with him, a pillar of stone; and he poured out a drink offering on it, and poured oil on it. [15]So Jacob called the name of the place where God had spoken with him, Bethel.

z That is *God of Bethel*   a That is *Oak of weeping*   b Heb *El Shaddai*

OVERVIEW: Jacob's command to his household to change their garments foreshadows the ritual of baptism. Jacob's action in setting up a stone and pouring oil on it is a symbol of the mystery of Christ (CYRIL OF ALEXANDRIA).

35:2 Purifying the Household

WE TOO MUST CHANGE OUR GARMENT. CYRIL OF ALEXANDRIA: After he was called by God, Jacob ascends to Bethel, that is, to the house of God (this is how the name Bethel is interpreted), offers sacrifices to God and is declared chief and master of the holy rites. He teaches his successors and descendants how they must enter the house of God. He orders the foreign gods to be rejected like dung and filth and to change the garments. It is fitting for us to do likewise when we are called before God, or enter the divine temple, especially in the time of the holy baptism. We, as if we drive away the foreign gods and part from such error, must assert, "I refuse you, Satan,

and all your pomp and all your worship." We also must change completely our garment by stripping off "the old self that is corrupt through deceitful lusts"[1] and by clothing ourselves with "the new self, which is being renewed in knowledge according to image of its Creator."[2] The women who were with Jacob took off their earrings. And in fact women by entering the house of God without wearing any carnal ornament and with loose hair remove from their head any accusation of pride. That is why, I believe, those women took off the precious stones they wore in their ears. GLAPHYRA ON GENESIS, 5.4.[3]

35:14 A Pillar of Stone

THE ANOINTED CORNERSTONE PREFIGURES CHRIST. CYRIL OF ALEXANDRIA: When we ascend to Bethel, that is, to the house of God, we will know the stone, I mean, the elected stone,

---

[1]Eph 4:22.   [2]Col 3:10.   [3]PG 69:284.

which was made into a cornerstone,[4] that is, Christ. We will see the one who is anointed by the Father in joy and exultation for all the creatures that live under the sky. As I said, the Son is anointed by God the Father: "Joy of us all, universal exultation" according to the words of the psalmist.[5] And you see how this is prefigured in the words that were just said to us: "And Jacob set

up a stone and poured oil upon it." That action is a symbol of the mystery of Christ, through whom and with whom be glory to God the Father and the Holy Spirit, world without end. Amen. GLAPHYRA ON GENESIS, 5.5.[6]

---

[4]1 Pet 2:6. [5]Ps 45:7 (44:8 LXX). [6]PG 69:284.

[35:16-29 THE SONS OF JACOB]

[36:1-43 THE DESCENDANTS OF ESAU]

37:1-4 JOSEPH AND HIS BROTHERS

[1]*Jacob dwelt in the land of his father's sojournings, in the land of Canaan.* [2]*This is the history of the family of Jacob.*

Joseph, being seventeen years old, was shepherding the flock with his brothers; he was a lad with the sons of Bilhah and Zilpah, his father's wives; and Joseph brought an ill report of them to their father. [3]*Now Israel loved Joseph more than any other of his children, because he was the son of his old age; and he made him a long robe with sleeves.** [4]*But when his brothers saw that their father loved him more than all his brothers, they hated him, and could not speak peaceably to him.*

*LXX, "many-colored" or "variegated" instead of "long sleeves."

OVERVIEW: The Joseph cycle of stories (Gen 37—50) with its vivid and dramatic scenes attracted much comment in the patristic period, since it could easily be used as a vehicle for moral teaching and could also be interpreted allegorically. Even a small detail such as Joseph's age was seen to contain the teaching that youth is no obstacle to virtue and that his virtue caused envy (CHRYSOSTOM). The brothers' hatred for Joseph was caused by the father's special love and favor for his younger son (CHRYSOSTOM, AMBROSE). Jacob's predilection for Joseph and his gift of the

robe offer the opportunity to warn against stirring up envy unnecessarily and to insist that virtue is a just cause for greater love, although in the case of Joseph this was also prophetic (AMBROSE). On an allegorical level, Joseph prefigured Christ, and his tunic of many colors represents the variety of gifts in the church (CAESARIUS OF ARLES). It was grace and the virtue of his soul that made Joseph more loved (CHRYSOSTOM, AMBROSE). The true spiritual sense of the passage is to be found by interpreting Jacob as a figure of God the Father and Joseph as Christ and by connecting it

with the New Testament declaration "this is my beloved Son" (CAESARIUS OF ARLES). The multicolored tunic also represents the multiform glory of Christ that caused the envy of the Jews (CYRIL OF ALEXANDRIA). In addition, the passage gave rise to simple meditations on the effects of envy (CHRYSOSTOM, CAESARIUS OF ARLES).

37:2 Joseph Was Seventeen

YOUTH NO OBSTACLE TO VIRTUE. CHRYSOSTOM: Why does he also indicate to us Joseph's age? For you to learn that his youth constituted no obstacle to virtue and for you to have a complete awareness of the young man's obedience to his father and his sympathy for his brothers despite their savagery. Despite his being so well disposed to them, Joseph was unable to win them over to concord with him on the grounds of his youth so as to be willing to maintain the bond of love. Instead, they saw from the outset the youth's inclination to virtue and the father's favor for him and were prompted to envy him. You see, "they brought false reports about Joseph to their father Israel."[1] HOMILIES ON GENESIS 61.2.[2]

37:3 Israel Favored Joseph

JOSEPH LOST THE LOVE OF HIS BROTHERS. AMBROSE: And so we are taught the proper nature of parental love and filial gratitude. It is pleasant to love one's children and very pleasant to love them exceedingly, but often even parental love does harm to the children unless it is practiced with restraint; for it may give the beloved child free rein out of excessive indulgence or, by preference shown to one child, may alienate the others from the spirit of brotherly love. That son gains more who gains the love of his brothers. This is a more splendid manifestation of generosity on the part of the parents and a richer inheritance for the sons. Let the children be joined in a like favor, who have been joined in a like nature. . . .

What wonder if quarrels arise among brothers over an estate or a house, when enmity blazed up among the sons of holy Jacob over a tunic?[3] What then? Should we find fault with Jacob because he preferred the one son to the others? But we cannot take from parents their freedom to love the more those children whom they believe to be the more deserving, nor ought we to cut off the sons from their eager desire to be the more pleasing. To be sure, Jacob loved the more that son in whom he foresaw the greater marks of virtue; thus he would not appear to have shown preference so much as father to son but rather as prophet to a sacred sign. And Jacob was right to make for his son a tunic of many colors, to indicate by it that Joseph was to be preferred to his brothers with his clothing of manifold virtues. ON JOSEPH 2.5-6.[4]

GRACE ENABLED HIS VIRTUE. CHRYSOSTOM: What is meant by "he loved Joseph more than all his other sons, as he was a son of his old age"? Since he was born in Jacob's old age, it is saying, toward the end of his life, on this account he loved Joseph more than all the others. You see, somehow the children born to one in old age seem particularly dear and manage to attract their father's favor in greater measure. For us to learn, however, that this was not the only factor in winning his father and causing him to prefer him to his brothers, sacred Scripture teaches us that even after him another son was born. If the manifestation of love had proceeded according to natural inclination, that last son would have been loved more for being truly a son of his old age and born at the time the good man reached the end of his life. So what can we say it means? That it was a kind of grace from on high that made the young man amiable and rendered him preferable to all the others on account of the virtue of his soul. . . . In Scripture the reason is given as his being a son of his old age and on that account he loved him more, in case the real reason might increase the brothers' envy. HOMILIES ON GENESIS 61.3.[5]

---

[1]In the Hebrew, it is Joseph who reports on his brothers; the LXX is divided on the point. [2]FC 87:186-87*. [3]Gen 37:3-4. [4]FC 65:190-91. [5]FC 87:187-88*.

A SON OF HIS OLD AGE. CYRIL OF ALEXANDRIA: Therefore, in order that our words do not wander from the right way, we say that the Immanuel was born to the Father as a Son of his old age, because he appeared in the latter times of the world, that is, in these times, and after him there will be no other. We expect to be saved in no one else. He alone is sufficient, because we say that the salvation and life of the world is placed in no one else.[6] He shepherds us forever, according to the words of the psalmist,[7] and we will be the subjects of him who is beloved, who appeared in the latter times of the world, as I just said, after he had assumed the flesh and who preexisted as God. In fact, we say that he is coeternal with the Father. GLAPHYRA ON GENESIS, 6.4.[8]

JACOB PREFIGURED GOD THE FATHER. CAESARIUS OF ARLES: When the Christian people devoutly come to church, of what benefit is it that they hear how the holy patriarchs took their wives or begot their children, unless they perceive in a spiritual sense why these things happened or what the facts prefigured? Behold, we have heard that blessed Jacob begot a son and called his name Joseph and that he loved him more than the rest of his sons. In this place blessed Jacob prefigured God the Father; holy Joseph typified our Lord and Savior. Therefore Jacob loved his son because God the Father loved his only-begotten Son, as he himself said, "This is my beloved Son."[9] SERMON 89.1.[10]

A VARIETY OF GRACES. CAESARIUS OF ARLES: According to a mystical or allegorical interpretation Joseph prefigured a type of our Lord. Now if we consider the actions of Joseph, at least in part, we clearly recognize in him an obvious figure of the Lord. Joseph had a multicolored tunic; our Lord and Savior is known to have had one also, since he took the church, which was composed of various nations, like the covering of a garment. The variety of this tunic, that is, of the church that Christ took, is of a different sort; the church has different, varied graces—the martyrs, confessors, priests, ministers, virgins, widows and those who perform works of justice. This variety of the church is not one of colors but of graces; for in this variety of his church our Lord and Savior shines with a multicolored, precious garment. Joseph was sold by his brothers and procured by the Ishmaelites; our Lord and Savior was sold by the Jews and acquired by the Gentiles. Moreover, the Ishmaelites who bought Joseph carried different kinds of perfumes with them; this was to show that the Gentiles who came to believe would be fragrant throughout the world with the different odors of justice. SERMON 93.3.[11]

37:4 Joseph's Brothers Hate Him

ENVY DAMAGES THE SOUL. CHRYSOSTOM: Envy is a terrible passion, you see, and when it affects the soul, it does not leave it before bringing it to an extremely sorry state. [It damages] the soul that gives it birth and affect[s] the object of its envy in the opposite way to that intended, rendering him more conspicuous, more esteemed, more famous—which in turn proves another severe blow to the envious person. Notice at any rate in this instance how this remarkable man is depicted as ignorant of what was going on and conversing cheerfully in great simplicity with them as his brothers who had caused the same birth pangs as he. . . . They for their part were in the grip of the passion of envy and were thus brought to hate him. HOMILIES ON GENESIS 61.4.[12]

CLOTHED BY GOD THE FATHER WITH A MULTIFORM GLORY. CYRIL OF ALEXANDRIA: And Joseph was loved by his father a great deal. And he gave him a multicolored garment as an excellent gift and a proof of the love with which he accompanied him. And this was an incentive to envy for his brothers and a cause of hatred, as the following events will demonstrate. In fact, the Pharisees

---

[6]See Acts 4:12. [7]Ps 48:14 (47:15 LXX). [8]PG 69:301. [9]Mt 3:17. [10]FC 47:38-39. [11]FC 47:59**. [12]FC 87:188.

were inflamed with anger against the beloved, that is, Christ, because he had been clothed by God the Father with a multiform glory. He was admirable in different forms, partly as a vivifying God, partly as a light that was able to illuminate those who were in the darkness, and to purify the lepers, and to raise from the dead those who were already decomposing,[13] and to reprove the seas and to be carried on the waves through his power.[14] And the Jews being in difficulty and burning with the flames of envy, said to each other, "What are we to do? This man is performing many signs."[15] The multicolored garment is the symbol of the multiform glory with which God the Father clothed the Son made similar to us through his human nature. However, with regard to his own nature, he himself is the Lord of glory, even though, because of the likeness he has with us, he says, "Father, glorify your Son."[16] Therefore for the reasons that I have examined, the sons of the concubines were induced to anger and envy and became suspicious after the dream was related. Since they knew in advance that in time they would have become subjects to their brother and would have adored him, and he would have been superior to them by far and would have been brought to such a glory to be adored by their own parents, they gnashed their teeth and planned to kill him. And so the Jews were angered too, and

not less afflicted, since they understood that the Immanuel would have been superior to the holy patriarchs themselves[17] and would have been necessarily adored by all the people and indeed by the whole world. And being aware of this, they said, "This is the heir; come, let us kill him, and the inheritance will be ours."[18] GLAPHYRA ON GENESIS, 6. 4.[19]

THE DISEASE OF ENVY. CAESARIUS OF ARLES: It is written concerning blessed Joseph, dearly beloved, that his brothers envied him and therefore "could not even greet him." It is true, beloved brothers, that so dangerous is the disease of envy that it cannot even spare brothers, not to mention strangers. Indeed, at the very beginning of the world Cain, a wicked brother, killed the just Abel through envy. Holy and faithful Joseph then was shown to be a more just servant of the Lord because of his tribulations. Through envy he was first sold by his brothers to the Ishmaelites as a slave, and after having been sold by the very people by whom he had seen himself worshiped, he was later handed over to an Egyptian master. SERMON 90.1.[20]

---

[13]See Jn 11:39. [14]See Mt 8:24-27. [15]Jn 11:47. [16]Jn 17:1. [17]See Jn 8:58. [18]Mt 21:38. [19]PG 69:301-4. [20]FC 47:43.

37:5-11 JOSEPH HAS A DREAM

[5]*Now Joseph had a dream, and when he told it to his brothers they only hated him the more.* [6]*He said to them, "Hear this dream which I have dreamed:* [7]*behold, we were binding sheaves in the field, and lo, my sheaf arose and stood upright; and behold, your sheaves gathered round it, and bowed down to my sheaf." * [8]*His brothers said to him, "Are you indeed to reign over us? Or are you indeed to have dominion over us?" So they hated him yet more for his dreams and for his words.* [9]*Then he dreamed another dream, and told it to his brothers, and said, "Behold, I have dreamed another dream; and behold, the sun, the moon, and eleven stars were bowing down to me." * [10]*But*

when he told it to his father and to his brothers, his father rebuked him, and said to him, "What is this dream that you have dreamed? Shall I and your mother and your brothers indeed come to bow ourselves to the ground before you?" [11]And his brothers were jealous of him, but his father kept the saying in mind.

OVERVIEW: The brothers' increased hatred of Joseph provides the occasion for a meditation on the self-destructive effects of envy (CHRYSOSTOM). Joseph's dream was not fulfilled in his lifetime but was a prophetic vision of the final age and the coming of Christ (HIPPOLYTUS). More specifically the dream could be interpreted as a figure of the resurrection of Jesus with the eleven stars representing the eleven disciples (AMBROSE, CAESARIUS OF ARLES). Jacob's reproach foreshadows the hardness of the people of Israel (AMBROSE).

37:5 Joseph's Dream

OBSTACLES PERMITTED TO DEVELOP. CHRYSOSTOM: See the extraordinary degree of their blindness: they themselves interpreted the dream. In fact, it is not possible to claim that it was in ignorance of the future that they bore him ill will; rather, it was learning the future from the dreams that added to their hatred. O excess of stupidity! They should have shown Joseph greater favor after learning the facts, set aside any grounds for hatred, banished the passion of envy. But they were dulled in their thinking and could not see at a glance that everything they were doing rebounded on themselves, and so they aggravated their hatred of him. O why, poor tormented creatures, do you display such envy, denying your condition as brothers and the fact that the revelation of dreams makes obvious God's favor for him? After all, surely you do not now believe that the events foretold by God can be thwarted? You see, just as you made an interpretation of the dream, so will it shortly come to pass, no matter how many ruses you intend to devise. I mean, the Lord of all, creative and wise as he is, revealing the abundance of his characteristic power, often allows many obstacles to develop before fulfillment so that he may put into effect his previous decisions and thus demonstrate the extraordinary degree of his power. HOMILIES ON GENESIS 61.7.[1]

37:8 Joseph's Brothers Hate Him More

A VISION OF THE COMING AGE. HIPPOLYTUS: Why do you envy and hate the righteous, if God revealed to him his own mysteries and made clear through visions what would have happened at the end of time? Why do you grieve at the sight of his embroidered tunic, if the just Father honored him by loving him more than everybody else, and sent him to visit you as a Shepherd among the shepherds, and presented to the world a trustworthy witness and a sheaf for his old age, and raised from the dead a holy firstborn as first fruits? Why do you get angry if the sun and the moon and the eleven stars worship him? They are there from the ancient times to prefigure him. And neither Jacob was called "sun," nor Rachel was called "moon," and the events did not happened in this manner. ON THE BLESSINGS OF ISAAC AND JACOB 2.[2]

THE VISION REVEALS JESUS' RESURRECTION. AMBROSE: Indeed, God's grace shone on Joseph even in his boyhood. For he had a dream that when he was binding sheaves with his brothers—so it appeared to him in the vision—this sheaf rose up and stood straight, while the sheaves of his brothers turned and bowed down to his sheaf.[3] Now in this the resurrection of the Lord Jesus that was to come was revealed. When they saw him at Jerusalem, the eleven disciples and all the saints bowed down; when they rise, they will

---

[1]FC 87:189-90*. [2]PO 27:4. [3]Gen 37:5-8.

bow down bearing the fruits of their good works, just as it is written, "Coming they shall come with joyfulness, carrying their sheaves."[4] Although his brothers disparaged the reliability of the dream out of their envy, still they expressed his interpretation of it in their own words when they replied, "Are you to be our king? Are you to rule over us?" For that vision indicated the King who was to come, and before him all human flesh would bow down with bended knee.[5] On Joseph 2.7.[6]

37:10 Jacob Rebukes Joseph

All Will Bow Down to Christ. Ambrose: Moreover, Joseph saw another dream and told it to his father and brothers, that the sun and moon and eleven stars were bowing down to him.[7] On this account his father reproved him and said, "What will be the meaning of this vision that you have dreamed? Can it be that I and your mother and your brothers will come and bow to the ground before you?"[8] Who is he before whom parents and brothers bowed down to the ground but Jesus Christ? Joseph and his mother with the disciples bowed down before him and confessed the true God in that body, of whom alone it was said, "Praise him, sun and moon; praise him, all you stars and light."[9] Further, what is the meaning of the father's reproach but the hardness of the people of Israel? Christ comes from them according to the flesh, but today they do not believe that he is God and are not willing to bow down to him as their Lord, because they know that he was born from among themselves. Accordingly they hear his replies, but they do not understand them. They themselves read that the sun and moon praise Christ, but they are unwilling to believe this was said with reference to Christ. Therefore Jacob is mistaken in regard to the symbol, which refers to another, but is not mistaken in the love, which is his own. In him paternal love did not go astray, but rather there is depicted an affection for a people that was going to go astray. On Joseph 2.8.[10]

Our True Joseph. Caesarius of Arles: Moreover, Joseph had another dream in which the sun, the moon and eleven stars worshiped him. His father replied to him, "Can it be that I and your mother and your brothers will come to bow to the ground before you?" This could not be fulfilled in that Joseph; but in our true Joseph, that is, our Lord Jesus Christ, the mysteries of that dream were fulfilled. The sun, the moon and eleven stars worshiped him when after the resurrection holy Mary as the moon, blessed Joseph as the sun and eleven stars, that is, the blessed apostles, bent down and prostrated before him. Then was fulfilled the prophecy that said, "Praise him, sun and moon; praise him, all you shining stars."[11] The interpretation of this dream was not accomplished in that Joseph for the important reason that we read his mother had died many years before he saw the aforementioned dreams. Truly, how could it happen to his brothers that they should adore him like the stars, since the night of envy had made them obscure and gloomy? They had lost the brightness of the stars, because they had extinguished in themselves the light of charity. We truly believe that this was deservedly fulfilled in our Lord and Savior, for, as I already said, we read that blessed Joseph, blessed Mary and the eleven apostles worshiped him quite frequently. That the apostles possessed the light of the stars our Lord himself tells us in the Gospel: "You are the light of the world."[12] Again, he says concerning the same men and those who are similar: "When the just will shine forth like the sun in the kingdom of their Father."[13] Sermon 89.4.[14]

---

[4]Ps 126:5 (125:6 LXX). [5]See Phil 2:10. [6]FC 65:191*. [7]Gen 37:9. [8]Gen 37:10. [9]Ps 148:3. [10]FC 65:191-92*. [11]Ps 148:3. [12]Mt 5:14. [13]Mt 13:43. [14]FC 47:40-41.

37:12-24 JOSEPH'S BROTHERS CONSPIRE AGAINST HIM

^{12}Now his brothers went to pasture their father's flock near Shechem. ^{13}And Israel said to Joseph, "Are not your brothers pasturing the flock at Shechem? Come, I will send you to them." And he said to him, "Here I am." ^{14}So he said to him, "Go now, see if it is well with your brothers, and with the flock; and bring me word again." So he sent him from the valley of Hebron, and he came to Shechem. ^{15}And a man found him wandering in the fields; and the man asked him, "What are you seeking?" ^{16}"I am seeking my brothers," he said, "tell me, I pray you, where they are pasturing the flock." ^{17}And the man said, "They have gone away, for I heard them say, 'Let us go to Dothan.'" So Joseph went after his brothers, and found them at Dothan. ^{18}They saw him afar off, and before he came near to them they conspired against him to kill him. ^{19}They said to one another, "Here comes this dreamer. ^{20}Come now, let us kill him and throw him into one of the pits; then we shall say that a wild beast has devoured him, and we shall see what will become of his dreams." ^{21}But when Reuben heard it, he delivered him out of their hands, saying, "Let us not take his life." ^{22}And Reuben said to them, "Shed no blood; cast him into this pit here in the wilderness, but lay no hand upon him"—that he might rescue him out of their hand, to restore him to his father. ^{23}So when Joseph came to his brothers, they stripped him of his robe, the long robe with sleeves that he wore; ^{24}and they took him and cast him into a pit. The pit was empty, there was no water in it.

OVERVIEW: Jacob, in sending Joseph to see if all was well with the sheep, foreshadowed the mysteries of the incarnation (AMBROSE, CHRYSOSTOM). Joseph "wandering about" represents Christ not finding the people of God whom he was seeking (AMBROSE, CAESARIUS OF ARLES). The etymology of the name Dothan ("desertion") indicates the moral state of the brothers and by implication that of those who rejected Christ. The words "we shall see what will become of his dreams" foreshadow the taunts offered to Christ on the cross. Joseph's tunic represents Christ's tunic and his flesh, of which he was stripped (AMBROSE).

37:14 Jacob Sends Joseph to His Brothers

JACOB FORESAW THE MYSTERIES OF FATHER'S SENDING OF THE SON. AMBROSE: Therefore the patriarch did not refuse to believe in a dream so mighty, for in a twofold prophecy he prophesied both together; that is, he represented and personified the just man and the people, because the Son of God was going to come to earth to be loved by just men and denied by unbelievers. And so Jacob, in sending his son to his brothers to see if it was well with the sheep,[1] foresaw the mysteries of the incarnation that was to come. What sheep was God searching for in the concern manifested even at that time by the patriarch? The very ones of whom the Lord Jesus himself said in the Gospel, "I did not come except to the lost sheep of the house of Israel."[2] "And he sent him to Shechem,"[3] which name is interpreted as "shoulder" or "back." That is, to those who did not turn to the Lord but fled from

---

[1]Gen 37:11-14. [2]Mt 15:24. [3]Gen 37:14.

his face and turned away, an expression properly applied to the sinner, for "Cain went out from the face of the Lord,"[4] and the psalmist says, "You will make them turn their back."[5] Now the just person does not turn away from the Lord but runs to meet him and says, "My eyes are ever toward the Lord."[6] And when the Lord said, "Whom shall I send?" Isaiah offered himself of his own accord and said, "Behold, here I am."[7] Simeon also waited to see Christ the Lord; after he saw him, because he had seen the Pardoner of sins and Redeemer of the whole world, he asked to be freed from the use of this flesh, just as he had been relieved of his sin, and said, "Now dismiss your servant, Lord, because my eyes have seen your salvation."[8] Zacchaeus too first gained the special privilege of having the Lord's commendation bestowed on him for this, that he climbed a tree to see Christ.[9] Therefore Joseph was sent by his father to his brothers, or rather by that Father "who has not spared his own Son but has delivered him for us all,"[10] by that Father of whom it is written, "God, sending his Son in the likeness of sinful flesh."[11] ON JOSEPH 3.9.[12]

TYPES OF THINGS TO COME. CHRYSOSTOM: Now all this happened so that Joseph's regard for his brothers might be demonstrated and their murderous intent might come to light. On the other hand it happened also as a type of things to come, the outlines of truth being sketched out ahead of time in shadow. As Joseph went off to his brothers to visit them, to those who had no respect for brotherhood or for the reason of his coming and who first intended to do away with him and then sold him to foreigners, so too our Lord in fidelity to his characteristic love came to visit the human race. Taking flesh of the same source as ours and deigning to become our brother, he thus arrived among us. Paul too cries out in these words, "It is not the condition of angels he takes to himself but descent from Abraham. Hence the need for him to become like his brothers in everything."[13] HOMILIES ON GENESIS 61.10.[14]

37:15 Wandering the Fields

HE COULD NOT FIND HIS BROTHERS. AMBROSE: "And Joseph was wandering about,"[15] because he could not find his brothers. And it was right that he wandered about, for he was seeking those that were going astray. Yes, "the Lord knows who are his."[16] Indeed, Jesus also, when he was wearied from his journey, sat at the well.[17] He was wearied, for he was not finding the people of God whom he was seeking; they had gone out from the face of the Lord.[18] The person who follows sin goes out from Christ. The sinner goes out; the just person enters in. Indeed, Adam hid himself as a sinner,[19] but the just person says, "Let my prayer enter in before you."[20] ON JOSEPH 3.10.[21]

CHRIST ALSO SOUGHT THE HUMAN RACE. CAESARIUS OF ARLES: Jacob sent his son to manifest solicitude for his brothers, and God the Father sent his only-begotten Son to visit the human race, which was weak from sin and like lost sheep. When Joseph was looking for his brothers he wandered in the desert. Christ also sought the human race, which was wandering in the world; he too as it were, wandered in the world because he was seeking the erring. Joseph searched for his brothers in Shechem. Shechem is interpreted as a shoulder, for sinners always turn their backs in the face of the just, and shoulders are behind. Just as Joseph's brothers, struck with envy, offered their back rather than their face to fraternal love, so also the unhappy Jews preferred to envy rather than to love the Author of salvation who came to them. Of such people it is said in the psalms: "Let their eyes grow dim so that they cannot see, and keep their backs always feeble."[22] SERMON 89.1.[23]

---

[4]Gen 4:16. [5]Ps 21:12 (20:13 LXX). [6]Ps 25:15 (24:15 LXX). [7]Is 6:8. [8]Lk 2:29-31; cf. 2:21-40. [9]Lk 19:4; cf. 19:1-10. [10]Rom 8:32. [11]Rom 8:3. [12]FC 65:192-93*. [13]Heb 2:16-17. [14]FC 87:191*. [15]Gen 37:15. [16]2 Tim 2:19; cf. Jn 10:14. [17]See Jn 4:6. [18]See Gen 4:16. [19]Gen 3:8. [20]Ps 88:2 (87:3 LXX). [21]FC 65:194*. [22]Ps 69:23 (68:24 LXX). [23]FC 47:39*.

37:17 *Joseph Finds His Brothers at Dothan*

Dothan Means "Desertion." Ambrose: Now Joseph found his brothers in Dothan, which means "desertion." And where is the person who deserts God but in desertion? No wonder if they deserted who did not hear him saying, "Come to me, all you who labor and are burdened, and I will give you rest."[24] Therefore Joseph came to Dothan, "and they saw him coming from afar, before he drew near to them, and they raged that they might kill him."[25] It is right that they were far off who were in desertion, and so they were raging, because Christ had not drawn near to them. For if the model of Christ had drawn near to them, they would surely have loved their brother. But they could not be near, for they were plotting fratricide. "Behold, that dreamer is coming. Now therefore come, let us kill him."[26] Were not the men who were saying such words plotting a sacrilegious fratricide, as Solomon says of them, "Let us remove the just one, because he is profitless to us"?[27] On Joseph 3.11.[28]

37:20 *The Brothers' Scheme*

Fulfilled in Regard to Christ. Ambrose: And in Genesis they also said, "And we shall see what will become of his dreams."[29] This is written in regard to Joseph, but it is fulfilled in regard to Christ, when the Jews said in the course of his passion, "If he is the King of Israel, let him come down now from the cross, and we will believe him. He trusts in God; let him deliver him now, if he wants him."[30] But were those brothers so unholy as to kill their brother? And from what source do the merits of the mighty patriarchs derive, so that the law designates the tribes of the entire people by their names? How are names of holiness in accord with marks of crime? In this also they served as a model of the people; their own souls were not toiling under a burden of crime. This gave rise to all the enmity and the plotting of fratricide; the enmity is by way of figure, the holiness by way of love. On Joseph 3.12.[31]

37:21 *Reuben Spares Joseph*

The Holy Bonds of Brotherhood. Ambrose: Indeed, Reuben and Judah observed the holy bonds of brotherhood and desired to free Joseph from their hands.[32] Judah receives the preference by his father's blessing, and rightly so, when it is said to him, "The sons of your father shall bow down to you. A lion's whelp is Judah, and he is the expectation of nations."[33] Surely this is appropriate to Christ alone, for whom it was in store that he should be worshiped by his brothers and awaited by the nations and that he should wash his tunic in wine by the passion of his own body, because he did not stain his flesh with any spot of sin. . . .

Conferring together against that counsel, the brothers abused him in whom "the blessing prevailed over the blessings of the enduring mountains and was stronger than the desires of the everlasting hills."[34] Who did Joseph understand was being prefigured in himself? Only he who surpasses the merits of all people and possesses the summit of limitless power beyond the desires of all the saints, he whom no one matches in prayer. And so, in the case of the patriarchs, enmity is repaid through grace, for they are excused from their guilt and made holy by the gift of revelation. For it is not so much a matter of blame in having said what refers to the people as it is a matter of happiness in having seen what refers to Christ. The people assumed the character of a sinner to receive the grace of their Lord and Redeemer. Assuredly grace destroyed guilt; guilt did not diminish grace. On Joseph 3.13.[35]

37:23 *Joseph Stripped of His Robe*

The Prefigurement of the Cross. Ambrose: Accordingly, even at that time, the cross that was to come was prefigured in sign;

---

[24]Mt 11:28. [25]Gen 37:18. [26]Gen 37:19-20 LXX. [27]Wis 2:12. [28]FC 65:194-95*. [29]Gen 37:20. [30]Mt 27:42-43. [31]FC 65:195. [32]Gen 37:21-22, 26-27. [33]Gen 49:8-10. [34]Gen 49:26. [35]FC 65:195-96**.

and at the same time that he was stripped of his tunic,[36] that is, of the flesh he took on, he was stripped of the handsome diversity of colors that represented the virtues. Therefore his tunic, that is, his flesh, was stained with blood, but not his

divinity; and his enemies were able to take from him his covering of flesh but not his immortal life. ON JOSEPH 3.15.[37]

---

[36]See Jn 19:23-24. [37]FC 65:198.

37:25-28 JOSEPH IS SOLD INTO SLAVERY

[25]*Then they sat down to eat; and looking up they saw a caravan of Ishmaelites coming from Gilead, with their camels bearing gum, balm, and myrrh, on their way to carry it down to Egypt.* [26]*Then Judah said to his brothers, "What profit is it if we slay our brother and conceal his blood?* [27]*Come, let us sell him to the Ishmaelites, and let not our hand be upon him, for he is our brother, our own flesh." And his brothers heeded him.* [28]*Then Midianite traders passed by; and they drew Joseph up and lifted him out of the pit, and sold him to the Ishmaelites for twenty shekels of silver;* and they took Joseph to Egypt.*

*LXX, "twenty pieces of gold."

OVERVIEW: The perfumes carried by the Ishmaelites prefigure the spreading of the perfumes of justice all over the world by the pagans represented by the Ishmaelites (CHROMATIUS, CAESARIUS OF ARLES). The different prices at which Joseph was sold mentioned in different translations represent the different value placed on Christ by different people (AMBROSE, CAESARIUS OF ARLES). Although Joseph appears to have been sold at a higher price than Christ, the One who ransomed us through his passion is in fact invaluable (CHROMATIUS, CAESARIUS OF ARLES). In a rather different interpretation, the sale of Joseph offers the occasion for a meditation on the corrupting effects of envy (CHRYSOSTOM). The various episodes of Joseph's life, being sold, going down to Egypt, saving Egypt from famine, all symbolize aspects of the mystery of the true Joseph, Christ (CAESARIUS OF ARLES).

37:25 Ishmaelites on Their Way to Egypt

THE FRAGRANCE OF JUSTICE. CHROMATIUS: Joseph was rejected by his brothers and was received by the Ishmaelites;[1] in the same manner our Lord and Savior was rejected by the Jews and received by the pagans. The Ishmaelites who received Joseph carried along with them all kinds of perfumes, and this fact showed that the pagans by embracing the faith would spread the different perfumes of justice all over the world. SERMON 24.3.[2]

37:27 Joseph Sold to the Ishmaelites

THE MYSTERY OF THE PRICE. AMBROSE: And so that we may recognize that all this is a mystery in reference to the people and to the Lord Jesus, "Come, let us sell Joseph to the Ishmaelites." What is the interpretation of the name Joseph? Only that it means "God's grace" and "expression

---

[1]Gen 37:25-27. [2]SC 164:74.

of God the highest." And so who is being sold? Only that man who "since he was in the form of God, thought it not robbery to be equal with God but emptied himself, taking the form of a servant."[3] . . . They sold him to traders; the latter bought a good fragrance from traitors. Judah sold him, the Ishmaelites bought him,[4] and in our tongue their name means "holding their own God in hatred." Therefore we find that Joseph was bought for twenty gold pieces by one account, for twenty-five by another and thirty by another, because Christ is not valued at the same price by all people.[5] To some he is worth less, to others more. The faith of the buyer determines the increase in the price. To one who is more pious, God is more valuable; to a sinner a Redeemer is more valuable. He is also more valuable to the people who have more grace. But he is more valuable as well to the one to whom many things have been given, because he loves more to whom more has been forgiven. The Lord himself said just this in the Gospel in reference to the woman who poured ointment over his feet, bathed them with her tears, wiped them with her hair and dried them with her kisses. Of her Christ says to Simon, "Wherefore I say to you, her sins, many as they are, have been forgiven her, because she has loved much. But he to whom less is forgiven, loves less."[6] ON JOSEPH 3.14.[7]

SYMBOLIC REPRESENTATION. AMBROSE: Here too, so that you may note the symbolic representation of the Lord's passion, the patriarch Judah says, "Let us sell Joseph to the Ishmaelites and let not our hands be laid upon him." And earlier he had done well to say, "Do not lay hands upon him,"[8] which is what the Jews said in the Lord's passion, "It is not lawful for us to put anyone to death."[9] Thus the word of Jesus could be fulfilled, signifying by what death he was going to die.[10] ON JOSEPH 3.14.[11]

37:28 *Twenty Shekels of Silver*

ESTIMATING THE PASSION CHEAPLY. CHROMA-

TIUS: Let us observe a great mystery: for Joseph twenty pieces of gold were given, for the Lord thirty pieces of silver.[12] The servant was sold at a higher price than the Master. To be sure people are wrong in fixing the price of the Lord, because the One who is sold is beyond human evaluation. Let us consider this mystery with more attention. For the Lord the Jews offered thirty pieces of silver; for Joseph the Ishmaelites offered twenty pieces of gold. The Ishmaelites bought the servant at a higher price than that paid by the Jews for the Master. The first worshiped in Joseph the image of Christ; the latter only had contempt for the reality itself that was in Christ. Therefore the Jews offered a lower price for Christ, because they estimated the passion of the Lord to be cheap. But how is it possible to estimate the passion of the Lord to be cheap, when it is the price for the redemption of the entire world? Listen to the apostle, who demonstrates that to us by saying, "You were bought at a high price."[13] And listen to the apostle Peter, who says in a similar manner, "You were ransomed from your futile ways not with perishable things like silver and gold but with the precious blood of the immaculate Son of God."[14] If we were bought back from death with gold or silver, our ransom would have been cheap, because humanity is more precious than gold and silver; but in truth we are ransomed at an invaluable price, because the one who ransomed us through his passion is invaluable. SERMON 24.4.[15]

THEY WERE UNCONCERNED THAT HE WAS THEIR BROTHER. CHRYSOSTOM: What an unlawful contract! What baleful profit! What illicit sale! The one who caused the same birth pangs as yourselves, the one so dear to your father, the one who came to see you, who never did you the slightest wrong, you endeavored to sell—and sell to savage people traveling down to Egypt.

[3]Phil 2:6-7. [4]Cf. Gen 37:25-28; Mt 26:14-15; 27:5-6. [5]Cf. Gen 37:28, where LXX and Vulgate agree on twenty pieces of silver as the price. [6]Lk 7:47. [7]FC 65:196-97*. [8]Gen 37:22. [9]Jn 18:31. [10]Jn 18:32. [11]FC 65:197-98. [12]See Mt 26:15. [13]1 Cor 6:20. [14]1 Pet 1:18-19. [15]SC 164:74-76.

What unlawful frenzy! What dreadful malice! I mean, even if you did this out of fear of the dreams, convinced that they would certainly come to pass in every detail, why did you attempt the impossible and give evidence by what you did of your hostility toward God, who had foretold this to Joseph? If, on the contrary, you give no credence to the dreams but consider them nonsense, why did you do what brought you everlasting defilement and caused your father irreparable grief? But what excess of passion—or rather, of a bloodthirsty intention! You see, when someone is obsessed with some improper exploit and becomes intoxicated with improper designs, he does not keep before him the unsleeping eye; he has no respect even for nature or anything else that could bring him to compassion. That was the situation with these men too. They were not concerned that he was their brother, that he was only a youth, that he was so dear to their father, that he had no experience of life in foreign parts or living in exile and yet was on the point of departing for such a land and living among savages. Instead, they abandoned every sane consideration and had one thing on their minds, allowing their envy to have (as they thought) an immediate effect. HOMILIES ON GENESIS 61.15-16.[16]

CHRIST IS THE TRUE JOSEPH. CAESARIUS OF ARLES: Upon seeing Joseph, his brothers dis-

cussed his death; just as when the Jews saw the true Joseph, Christ the Lord, they all resolved with one plan to crucify him. His brothers robbed Joseph of his outside coat that was of divers colors; the Jews stripped Christ of his bodily tunic at his death on the cross. When Joseph was deprived of his tunic he was thrown into a cistern, that is, into a pit; after Christ was despoiled of human flesh, he descended into hell. Afterward Joseph is lifted up out of the cistern and is sold to the Ishmaelites, that is, to the Gentiles; when Christ returns from hell, he is bought by all nations at the price of faith. Upon the advice of Judah, Joseph is sold for thirty pieces of silver; Christ is sold for the same amount upon the counsel of Judas Iscariot. Now in different translations Joseph is not written as sold at the same price, for some say it was twenty pieces of silver and others thirty. This spiritually signifies that Christ was not to be believed and loved equally by all people. In fact, even in the church some love him more, others less, for Christ means more to the soul that loves him with greater charity. Joseph went down to Egypt; Christ went into the world. Joseph saves Egypt from want of grain; Christ frees the world from a famine of the Word of God. SERMON 89.2.[17]

[16]FC 87:194-95*. [17]FC 47:39-40*.

37:29-36 JACOB IS INFORMED OF JOSEPH'S DEATH

[29]When Reuben returned to the pit and saw that Joseph was not in the pit, he rent his clothes [30]and returned to his brothers, and said, "The lad is gone; and I, where shall I go?" [31]Then they took Joseph's robe, and killed a goat, and dipped the robe in the blood; [32]and they sent the long robe with sleeves and brought it to their father, and said, "This we have found; see now whether it is your son's robe or not." [33]And he recognized it, and said, "It is my son's robe; a wild beast has devoured him; Joseph is without doubt torn to pieces." [34]Then Jacob rent his garments, and put

sackcloth upon his loins, and mourned for his son many days. [35]*All his sons and all his daughters rose up to comfort him; but he refused to be comforted, and said, "No, I shall go down to Sheol to my son, mourning." Thus his father wept for him.* [36]*Meanwhile the Midianites had sold him in Egypt to Poti-phar, an officer of Pharaoh, the captain of the guard.*

OVERVIEW: The sprinkling of the tunic with the blood of a goat foreshadows the false testimony brought against Christ (AMBROSE). The same action reveals the hypocrisy of the brothers (EPHREM). Joseph's deliverance into slavery offers the opportunity for a moral interpretation. True slavery or freedom are determined by vice or virtue (AMBROSE). Similarly Joseph's status as slave allows his virtue to emerge even more conspicuously (CHRYSOSTOM).

37:31 The Robe Dipped in Goat's Blood

THE BLOOD OF A GOAT. AMBROSE: Now the fact that they sprinkled his tunic with the blood of a goat seems to have this meaning, that they attacked with false testimony[1] and brought into enmity for sin him who forgives the sins of all people. For us there is a lamb, for them a goat.[2] For us the Lamb of God has been killed, who took from us the sins of the world, whereas for them a goat piled up sins and amassed offenses. Therefore "fill up the measure of your fathers."[3] And Jacob rightly lamented the losses to his posterity; as a father he wept for his lost son,[4] and as a prophet he mourned the destruction of the Jews. Indeed, Jacob also tore his clothing; similarly, at the time of the Lord Jesus' passion, the chief priest tore his robe. He exercised not a private role but an office with a public function.[5] The curtain of the temple was also torn,[6] so that it might be made clear by such signs that the mysteries had been profaned, the people stripped of the garments of salvation, and that the kingdom had been divided and was to be destroyed, because every divided kingdom will easily be destroyed.[7] ON JOSEPH 3.18.[8]

37:36 Joseph Sold to Potiphar

ENVY AND FALSE SORROW MINGLE. EPHREM THE SYRIAN: Then Jacob sent Joseph to the flock that he might bring back to him a report on his brothers. But the brothers, by means of the cloak that was bespattered with blood, sent Jacob a report on Joseph. With no mercy they cast him into a pit in the desert, but they wept over Joseph with tears in the house. They sold him naked to the Arabs but wept over him and wailed in the presence of the Canaanites. They put irons on his hands and feet and sent him on his way but composed lamentations over him in the village. Joseph went down to Egypt and was sold; within a few days he had changed owners twice. COMMENTARY ON GENESIS 33.2.[9]

JOSEPH'S STORY CALLS ALL TO DEEP SELF-KNOWLEDGE. AMBROSE: But as for what pertains to the moral interpretation, because our God wishes all people to be saved,[10] through Joseph he also gave consolation to those who are in slavery, and he gave them instruction. Even in the lowliest status, people should learn that their character can be superior and that no state of life is devoid of virtue if the soul of the individual knows itself. The flesh is subject to slavery, not the spirit, and many humble servants are more free than their masters, if in their condition of slavery they consider that they should abstain from the works of a slave. Every sin is slavish, while blamelessness is free. On this account the Lord also says, "Everyone who commits sin is a slave of sin."[11] Indeed, how is each greedy person not a slave, seeing that he auctions himself off for a very tiny sum of money? The person who has

---

[1]See Mt 26:59-61. [2]Cf. Jn 1:19; Ex 12:4-5. [3]Mt 23:32. [4]See Gen 37:34. [5]Cf. Gen 37:34; Mt 26:65. [6]See Mt 27:51. [7]See Mt 12:25. [8]FC 65:200**. [9]FC 91:182. [10]1 Tim 2:4. [11]Jn 8:34.

piled up what he is not going to use is afraid that he may lose all that he has piled up; the more numerous his acquisitions, the greater the risk he will run in keeping them....

Moreover, how is that person who is subject to lust not also a slave? First, he blazes with his own fires, and he is burned up by the torches within his own breast. To such people the prophet rightly says, "Walk in the light of your own fire and in the flame that you have kindled."[12] Fear takes hold of them all and lies in wait for each one when he is asleep; so that he may gain control over one object of desire, a person becomes the slave of them all. The one who makes his own masters is the slave to a wretched slavery indeed, for he wishes to have masters that he may fear; indeed, nothing is so characteristic of slavery as the constant fear. But that one, whatever his servile status, will always be free who is not seduced by love or held by the chains of greed or bound by fear of reproach, who looks to the present with tranquility and is not afraid of the future. Doesn't it seem to you that a person of the latter kind is the master even in slavery, while one of the former kind is a slave even in liberty? Joseph was a slave, Pharaoh a ruler; the slavery of the one was happier than the sovereignty of the other. Indeed, all Egypt would have collapsed from famine unless Pharaoh had made his sovereignty subject to the counsel of a mere servant.[13] ON JOSEPH 4.20.[14]

VIRTUE UNDER ATTACK. CHRYSOSTOM: I think this was a further blow to those men: they saw that Jacob gave evidence of such ardent love for the one who was not present, nay rather was considered taken by wild beasts, and they were even more racked with envy. But whereas they would merit no excuse for being so cruel to their brother and their father, even the Midianites . . . serve the divine plan further by handing Joseph over to Potiphar, Pharaoh's chief steward.[15] Do you see how things proceed gradually and systematically, and how in every circumstance Joseph shows his characteristic virtue and endurance so that, just as an athlete who has nobly contended will be crowned with the kingdom's garland, likewise the fulfillment of the dreams would . . . teach those who sold him that no advantage accrued to them from their awful ruse? Virtue, you see, has such power that even when under attack it emerges even more conspicuous. Nothing, after all, is stronger than virtue, nothing more powerful . . . not because it has such power of itself but because the one who acquires it also enjoys grace from on high. By enjoying grace from on high and being accorded assistance from there, virtue would be more powerful than anything, invincible and proof against not only the wiles of human beings but also the snares of the demons. HOMILIES ON GENESIS 61.20.[16]

---

[12]Is 50:11. [13]Gen 41:55-56. [14]FC 65:201-2*. [15]Gen 37:36. [16]FC 87:197*.

[38:1-11 THE SONS OF JUDAH]

38:12-19 TAMAR'S STRATAGEM

[12]*In course of time the wife of Judah, Shua's daughter, died; and when Judah was comforted, he went up to Timnah to his sheepshearers, he and his friend Hirah the Adullamite. *[13]*And when*

Tamar was told, "Your father-in-law is going up to Timnah to shear his sheep," [14]she put off her widow's garments, and put on a veil, wrapping herself up, and sat at the entrance to Enaim, which is on the road to Timnah; for she saw that Shelah was grown up, and she had not been given to him in marriage. [15]When Judah saw her, he thought her to be a harlot, for she had covered her face. [16]He went over to her at the road side, and said, "Come, let me come in to you," for he did not know that she was his daughter-in-law. She said, "What will you give me, that you may come in to me?" [17]He answered, "I will send you a kid from the flock." And she said, "Will you give me a pledge, till you send it?" [18]He said, "What pledge shall I give you?" She replied, "Your signet and your cord, and your staff that is in your hand." So he gave them to her, and went in to her, and she conceived by him. [19]Then she arose and went away, and taking off her veil she put on the garments of her widowhood.

OVERVIEW: The story of Tamar was puzzling and scandalous for societies unfamiliar with the traditions of Mosaic law and thus required explanation. Tamar did not desire a second marriage but only the blessing, that is, an offspring of her first marriage. Although she was not an Israelite, she desired to receive the treasure hidden in the circumcised and prayed to God to move Judah to cooperate. Thus Judah's otherwise scandalous behavior was divinely inspired (EPHREM). Tamar's stratagem was by divine design, and her motives were good. The two children born to Tamar and Judah were a type of the two peoples, prefiguring the Jewish life and the spiritual life (CHRYSOSTOM). Although the text of the story does not seem very suitable, in Judah and Tamar the mystery of the incarnation of our Savior is described, which is the purpose of all the Scriptures (CYRIL OF ALEXANDRIA).

38:14 Shelah Not Given to Tamar in Marriage

I YEARN FOR THE BLESSING. EPHREM THE SYRIAN: When Shelah had become a young man and Judah did not wish to bring her back to his house, Tamar thought, "How can I make the Hebrews realize that it is not marriage for which I am hungering, but rather that I am yearning for the blessing that is hidden in them? Although I am able to have relations with Shelah, I would not be able to make my faith victorious through Shelah.

I ought then to have relations with Judah so that by the treasure I receive, I might enrich my poverty, and in the widowhood I preserve, I might make it clear that I did not desire marriage." COMMENTARY ON GENESIS 34.2.[1]

WHAT HAPPENED WAS BY DIVINE DESIGN. CHRYSOSTOM: So, buoyed up with these promises Tamar sat in her father's house, the text says, waiting for her father-in-law's promise to take effect. When she saw that Judah was not prepared to honor his promise, for a while she accepted it mildly, forbearing to have relations with another man, being content with her widowhood and waiting for a suitable opportunity. She was anxious, you see, to have children by her father-in-law. When she saw her mother-in-law die and Judah make for Timnah to shear the flocks, she wished to obtain by stealth intercourse with her father-in-law and desired to have children by him, not out of incontinence—perish the thought—but to avoid appearing to be some nameless person. As a matter of fact, what happened was by divine design, and the result was that her scheme took effect.[2] HOMILIES ON GENESIS 62.3.[3]

SHE ASKED FOR A SIGN. EPHREM THE SYRIAN: Because Tamar was afraid lest Judah find out and kill her in vengeance for his two sons of whose

---

[1]FC 91:183. [2]Gen 38:12-13. [3]FC 87:199.

deaths she was accused, she, like Eliezer, asked for a sign saying, "Let your knowledge not condemn me for this act of desire, for you know that it is for what is hidden in the Hebrews that I thirst. I do not know whether this thing is pleasing to you or not. Grant that I may appear to him in another guise lest he kill me. [Grant] also that an invitation to lie with him might be found in his mouth, so that I may know that it is acceptable to you that the treasure, which is hidden in the circumcised, might be transmitted even through a daughter of the uncircumcised. May it be that, when he sees me, he will say to me, 'Come, let me come into you.'" COMMENTARY ON GENESIS 34.3.[4]

38:15 Judah Mistakes Tamar for a Harlot

SHE KNEW GOD WAS PLEASED. EPHREM THE SYRIAN: While Tamar was making supplication to God for these things, behold, Judah came out and saw her. The prayer of Tamar inclined him, contrary to his usual habit, [to go] to a harlot. When she saw him, she was veiled, for she was afraid. After the word of the sign for which she had asked had been spoken, she knew that God was pleased with what she was doing. Afterward she revealed her face without fear and even demanded remuneration from the lord of the treasure. COMMENTARY ON GENESIS 34.4.[5]

38:18 Tamar Conceives

CARRYING OUT THE DIVINE PLAN. CHRYSOSTOM: Let no one who hears this, however, condemn Tamar. As I said before, she was carrying out the divine plan, and hence neither did she incur any blame, nor did Judah lay himself open to any charge. I mean, as you proceed along from this point, you will find Christ tracing his lineage from the two children born to him.[6] In particular, the two children born to him were a type of the two people, prefiguring Jewish life and the spiritual life. For the time being, however, let us see how after Judah's departure a short time elapsed and then the affair came to light; Judah admitted his own involvement and acquitted her of any guilt. So, after Tamar had achieved what she wanted, she once more changed her dress, the text says, left the spot and returned to her home. Judah, of course, was aware of none of this; he kept his promise by sending a kid so as to recover the pledge given by him, but the woman was nowhere to be found, and the servant returned informing Judah that no word of the woman could be had anywhere. Learning this, Judah said, the text goes on, "Let's hope we are never condemned for being thought ungrateful." He was unaware of what had happened, you see. HOMILIES ON GENESIS 62.5.[7]

THE INCARNATION IS DESCRIBED. CYRIL OF ALEXANDRIA: The purpose and intention of the divinely inspired Scripture is to describe to us the mystery of Christ through countless facts. And with good reason some have compared it with a magnificent and illustrious city that does not have a single statue of its king or imperator but many statues placed in a most frequented spot, where everybody can admire them. See how Scripture does not omit any fact that refers to such mystery but rather describes at length any and all of them. Even though sometimes the text of the story does not seem to be very suitable, this does not prevent Scripture at all from rightly constructing and accomplishing its proposed demonstration. Its purpose is not to relate the lives of saints (this is not the case at all) but rather to instruct us in the knowledge of the mystery of Christ through facts, which can make our speech about him true and manifest. Therefore it cannot be criticized as if it were wandering from the truth. And in Judah and Tamar the mystery of the incarnation of our Savior is again described to us. GLAPHYRA ON GENESIS, 6.1.[8]

---

[4]FC 91:183. [5]FC 91:184. [6]Perez and Zerah; see Mt 1:3. [7]FC 87:200*. [8]PG 69:308.

38:20-26 TAMAR DISAPPEARS AND THEN IS VINDICATED

²⁰*When Judah sent the kid by his friend the Adullamite, to receive the pledge from the woman's hand, he could not find her.* ²¹*And he asked the men of the place, "Where is the harlot*ᵇ *who was at Enaim by the wayside?" And they said, "No harlot*ᵇ *has been here."* ²²*So he returned to Judah, and said, "I have not found her; and also the men of the place said, 'No harlot*ᵇ *has been here.'"* ²³*And Judah replied, "Let her keep the things as her own, lest we be laughed at; you see, I sent this kid, and you could not find her."*

²⁴*About three months later Judah was told, "Tamar your daughter-in-law has played the harlot; and moreover she is with child by harlotry." And Judah said, "Bring her out, and let her be burned."* ²⁵*As she was being brought out, she sent word to her father-in-law, "By the man to whom these belong, I am with child." And she said, "Mark, I pray you, whose these are, the signet and the cord and the staff."* ²⁶*Then Judah acknowledged them and said, "She is more righteous than I, inasmuch as I did not give her to my son Shelah." And he did not lie with her again.*

h Or *cult prostitute*

OVERVIEW: Tamar is vindicated and declared innocent by Judah (EPHREM). To fulfill the divine plan, Tamar needed the seed of procreation, which her husband lacked (CYRIL OF ALEXANDRIA). She is acknowledged to be guiltless by Judah, who now no longer blames her for his sons' deaths but accepts that they were punished for their wickedness (CHRYSOSTOM). Just as the prophet Hosea took a prostitute as his wife and this was a metaphor of God, so the adultery of Tamar and Judah was a type of spiritual union (CYRIL OF ALEXANDRIA).

38:26 Judah Admits Tamar's Innocence

SHE IS INNOCENT. EPHREM THE SYRIAN: He then said, "She is more innocent than I," that is, "She is more righteous than I. What great sinners my sons were. 'Because of this, I did not give her to my son Shelah.' She is innocent of that evil suspicion that I held against her and [for which] I withheld my son Shelah from her." She who had been cheated out of marriage was justified in her

fornication, and he who sent her out on account of his first two sons brought her back for the sake of his last two sons. "He did not lie with her again" because she had been the wife of his first two sons; nor did he take another wife, for she was the mother of his last two sons. COMMENTARY ON GENESIS 34.6.[1]

JUDAH ADMITTED HIS SIN. CHRYSOSTOM: What is the meaning of "She has more right on her side than I"? In other words, she is guiltless, whereas I condemn myself and without anyone to accuse me I confess—or rather, I have sufficient accuser in the pledge given by me. Then Judah goes on to supply a defense for Tamar by saying, "because I did not give her to my son Shelah." Perhaps, however, this happened for the reason that I am about to give. I mean, Judah thought that it was through her fault that death fell on Er and Onan. For fear of this he did not give Shelah to her despite promising to do so. Accordingly, so

[1]FC 91:184-85.

as to prove in fact that she was not responsible for their death but rather that they were punished for their own wickedness ("God took his life" the text says, remember, and again, "he put him to death," in reference to the second one), Judah himself had intercourse with his own daughter-in-law all unawares. He learned by later developments that, far from it being her fault, those men's wickedness made them liable to suffer punishment. So Judah admitted his own sin, delivered her from punishment and, the text says, "had no further relations with her," showing that he would not previously have had intercourse with her if he had not done so in ignorance. HOMILIES ON GENESIS 62.7.[2]

TYPES OF SPIRITUAL UNION. CYRIL OF ALEXANDRIA: In the first place it must be said that, even though there are some famous characters who are discovered to be guilty of acting in a not entirely honest way, however, since God in the holy Scriptures produces through them something useful for our salvation, let us drive away from us what may offend. If we take good care of our wisdom and intelligence, we are not unaware of what regards our profit. Let us consider how the blessed prophet Hosea took a prostitute as his wife, nor [did he refuse] a notorious marriage and was called the father of hateful sons, whose names were "Not my people" and "Unpitied."[3] I will not hesitate to declare what this means. In fact, after those who were the nobles and the princes in Israel opposed the preaching of the prophets and the divine word was unpleasing to them, in the meantime God acted through his saints so that they might see the future from what was happening as if it was magnificently and expressly depicted in a picture. God did this so they might rededicate their minds to understanding their hope and might look with the strongest application for what would have been salutary to them and might also persuade others to do the same. And they learned that they would not have been the elected people anymore but would have been received among those who show no mercy, if they behaved with hardness and immoderation. Were not they afflicted by evils and overwhelmed by them everywhere? . . . Since we now understand the criterion and direction of the divine plan in those times, we will not condemn anymore the adultery of Tamar and Judah, but rather we will say that their union occurred in the divine plan. In fact, the former was in need of the seed of procreation as her legitimate husband was lacking it. The latter was guilty of a slight fault since he was free after his first wife had already died. So this union and generation teach us about our spiritual union and the rebirth of our mind. The human mind cannot be drawn to truth in a more appropriate way. GLAPHYRA ON GENESIS, 6.2.[4]

---

[2]FC 87:201*. [3]Hos 1:2, 6, 9. [4]PG 69:312-13.

38:27-30 TAMAR HAS TWINS

[27]*When the time of her delivery came, there were twins in her womb.* [28]*And when she was in labor, one put out a hand; and the midwife took and bound on his hand a scarlet thread, saying, "This came out first."* [29]*But as he drew back his hand, behold, his brother came out; and she said, "What a breach you have made for yourself!" Therefore his name was called Perez.*[i] [30]*Afterward*

his brother came out with the scarlet thread upon his hand; and his name was called Zerah.

i That is *A breach*

OVERVIEW: The twins are interpreted to represent the two peoples, the Jews or the legal observance, and the church (CHRYSOSTOM, JEROME). The scarlet thread symbolizes the conscience of the Jews, speckled with the passion of Christ (JEROME).

38:27 *Twins in Tamar's Womb*

ZERAH A TYPE OF THE CHURCH. CHRYSOSTOM: Observe in this, I ask you, a mystery and a prediction of what is to come. You see, after the midwife bound the scarlet thread around his hand to make Zerah recognizable, then "he drew his hand back, and his brother came out."[1] He yielded precedence to his brother, it is saying, and the one thought last came out first, and the one thought first emerged after him. "The midwife said, 'What a breach you have made for yourself!' He was called Perez." The name, in fact, means "breach" or "division," as you might say. "After him came his brother with the mark on his right hand; he was given the name Zerah,"[2] which means "sunrise."

It was not idly or to no purpose that these things happened; rather, it was a type of things to come, revealing the events themselves. You see, what happened was not according to natural processes. I mean, how would it have been possible, after his hand was bound with crimson, for him to draw back again and give way to the one after him, unless there were some divine power arranging this in advance? It was also prefiguring, as if in a kind of shadow, the fact that right from the outset Zerah, which means sunrise (he is, after all, a type of the church), began to peer ahead; as he moved gradually forward and then retired, the legal observance denoted by Perez made its entrance. After that had held precedence for a long time, the former one—I mean Zerah, who had retired—came forward, and the whole Judaic way of life in turn yielded place to the church. HOMILIES ON GENESIS 62.8-9.[3]

A WALL THAT DIVIDES TWO PEOPLES. JEROME: What is one to say of Tamar, who brought to birth the twins Zerah and Perez? Their separation at the moment of birth was like a wall that divides the two peoples, and the hand tied with the scarlet ribbon already then speckled the conscience of the Jews with the passion of Christ. LETTER 123.12.[4]

---

[1]Gen 38:29. [2]Gen 38:30. [3]FC 87:201-2*. [4]CSEL 56:87.

39:1-6 JOSEPH'S SUCCESS

[1]*Now Joseph was taken down to Egypt, and Poti-phar, an officer of Pharaoh, the captain of the guard, an Egyptian, bought him from the Ishmaelites who had brought him down there.* [2]*The LORD was with Joseph, and he became a successful man; and he was in the house of his master the Egyptian,* [3]*and his master saw that the LORD was with him, and that the LORD caused all that he did to prosper in his hands.* [4]*So Joseph found favor in his sight and attended him, and he made him overseer of his house and put him in charge of all that he had.* [5]*From the time that he made him*

overseer in his house and over all that he had the LORD blessed the Egyptian's house for Joseph's sake; the blessing of the LORD was upon all that he had, in house and field. [6]*So he left all that he had in Joseph's charge; and having him he had no concern for anything but the food which he ate.*

OVERVIEW: Joseph's prosperity, although he was a slave, provides the opportunity for a meditation on true spiritual freedom (AMBROSE). The same text offers the occasion for seeing the grace of God at work in human affairs and the practical effects of virtue (CHRYSOSTOM).

39:2 The Lord Is with Joseph

GENUINE FREEDOM. AMBROSE: Lowly servants have grounds on which they may glory; Joseph also was a servant. Those who have passed from freedom into slavery through some exigency have a source of consolation. They have something to imitate, so that they may learn that their status can change but not their character; that among household servants there is liberty; and that in servitude there is constancy. Masters have something to hope for through good and humble servants. Abraham found a wife for his son through a servant of his household.[1] The Lord blessed the Egyptian's house on account of Joseph, and the blessing of the Lord was granted to all his property in house and in fields.[2] "And he entrusted all things whatsoever were his into the hands of Joseph."[3] We note that what the masters could not govern, mere servants governed. ON JOSEPH 4.20-21.[4]

GRACE FROM ON HIGH. CHRYSOSTOM: What is the meaning of "the Lord was with Joseph"? Grace from on high stood by him, it is saying, and smoothed over all his difficulties. It arranged all his affairs; it made those traders well disposed to him and led them to sell him to the chief steward so that he should advance gradually and, by proceeding through those trials, manage to reach the throne of the kingdom. But you, dearly beloved, hearing that Joseph endured slavery at the hands of the traders and then experienced the slavery of the chief steward, consider how he was

not alarmed and did not give up hope or debate within himself in these terms: "How deceitful were those dreams that foretold such prosperity for me! I mean, look, I have gone from slavery to harsh slavery and a range of masters, from one to another, forced to associate with savage races. Surely we haven't been abandoned? Surely we haven't been passed over by grace from on high?" He said nothing of the sort; he gave it not a thought; on the contrary, he bore everything meekly and nobly. "The Lord was with Joseph" after all, "and he became a man of means." HOMILIES ON GENESIS 62.13.[5]

A MAN OF MEANS. CHRYSOSTOM: What is the meaning of "a man of means"? Everything went well for him, grace from on high preceded him everywhere, and the grace that flourished with regard to Joseph was so obvious as to become plain even to his master, the chief steward. Recall the text says, "His master realized that the Lord was with him, and whatever he did the Lord conducted successfully in his person. Joseph found favor with his master, who set him over his household and entrusted to him all his possessions."[6] Do you see what it means to be helped by the right hand from above? I mean, behold, a young man, a stranger, a captive slave, yet entrusted by his master with his whole household: "he entrusted everything to him," the text says. Why? Because along with power from on high Joseph also contributed his own way of doing things. Recall the text states, "He gave him satisfaction"; that is to say, he did everything to his complete satisfaction. HOMILIES ON GENESIS 62.14.[7]

39:4 Joseph Oversees Potiphar's House

---

[1]Gen 24. [2]Gen 39:5. [3]Gen 39:6. [4]FC 65:202-3. [5]FC 87:204. [6]Gen 39:3-4. [7]FC 87:204-5*.

VIRTUE PREVAILS OVER ALL THINGS. CHRYSOSTOM: Then the loving God, though wanting to make Joseph feel completely secure, did not release him from slavery or set him at liberty. This, after all, is ever God's way, not to free virtuous people from dangers or preserve them from trials but, in the midst of such trials, to give evidence of his characteristic grace to such an extent that the very trials prove an occasion of festivity for them. Hence blessed David also said, "In my distress you gave me room to move";[8] "you did not take away the distress," he is saying, "or free me from it and make me be completely at ease, but, what is quite remarkable, you brought me peace though I was in fact still in distress." This is exactly what the loving Lord does in this case: "He blessed the house of the Egyptian in Joseph."[9] Even the bar-

barian now learned that the man thought to be a slave was particularly close to God. "He turned over all his possessions into Joseph's keeping," the text says, "and had no care for anything except the food he ate."[10] It was as if he had appointed him master of his whole household. The slave, the captive, held in his care all his master's possessions. This is what virtue is like: wherever it appears, it prevails over all things and controls them. You see, just as darkness is driven out with the rising sun, so too in this case every evil is absent with the approach of virtue. HOMILIES ON GENESIS 62.15.[11]

---

[8]Ps 4:1. [9]Gen 39:5. [10]Gen 39:6. [11]FC 87:205*.

39:6-18 JOSEPH'S TEMPTATION

Now Joseph was handsome and good-looking. [7]And after a time his master's wife cast her eyes upon Joseph, and said, "Lie with me." [8]But he refused and said to his master's wife, "Lo, having me my master has no concern about anything in the house, and he has put everything that he has in my hand; [9]he is not greater in this house than I am; nor has he kept back anything from me except yourself, because you are his wife; how then can I do this great wickedness, and sin against God?" [10]And although she spoke to Joseph day after day, he would not listen to her, to lie with her or to be with her. [11]But one day, when he went into the house to do his work and none of the men of the house was there in the house, [12]she caught him by his garment, saying, "Lie with me." But he left his garment in her hand, and fled and got out of the house. [13]And when she saw that he had left his garment in her hand, and had fled out of the house, [14]she called to the men of her household and said to them, "See, he has brought among us a Hebrew to insult us; he came in to me to lie with me, and I cried out with a loud voice; [15]and when he heard that I lifted up my voice and cried, he left his garment with me, and fled and got out of the house." [16]Then she laid up his garment by her until his master came home, [17]and she told him the same story, saying, "The Hebrew servant, whom you have brought among us, came in to me to insult me; [18]but as soon as I lifted up my voice and cried, he left his garment with me, and fled out of the house."

OVERVIEW: The observation that Joseph was handsome and good-looking leads to the reflection that his character was even more beautiful than his body (CHROMATIUS). Joseph's physical attractiveness is emphasized as well as his spiritual charm in order to explain the behavior of the Egyptian woman, who perceived only the former (CHRYSOSTOM). The same text provides the occasion for a meditation on how bodily splendor should be governed by splendor of soul (CAESARIUS OF ARLES). Joseph's refusal of the woman's advances shows that, more important than ruling an empire, he was ruler of himself. True beauty does not seduce the eyes of others, and Joseph was more handsome for his cultivation of modesty (AMBROSE). Joseph was concerned not with himself but with delivering this woman from her folly, and so he offered advice calculated to arouse her sense of shame. We should be alert and vigilant and imitate this young man's self-control (CHRYSOSTOM). The continued provocation of the mistress showed that she burned with lust and not with the flame of chastity. Joseph's continued refusal to give into temptation revealed the interior and spiritual beauty of chastity (CAESARIUS OF ARLES). Although Joseph left behind his garments when he fled, he was not naked but covered by modesty (AMBROSE). The same text leads to a comparison with Adam, who was naked because he was exposed by guilt; Joseph instead preserved the garments of virtue incorrupt and was blessed in prison (CAESARIUS OF ARLES, QUODVULTDEUS). The false accusation against Joseph by the woman revealed that she had lost all the coverings of chastity (AMBROSE). The same text shows that wickedness tries to attribute its faults to virtue (CHRYSOSTOM). The false accusation against Joseph can also be compared with the false accusations brought against the apostles (CYRIL OF ALEXANDRIA).

39:6 Joseph Was Handsome

THE SOUL MASTERS THE FLESH. CHROMATIUS: This holy Joseph, about whom your charity[1] has heard in this reading, was beautiful in his body but even more beautiful in his soul, because he was chaste in his body and had a chaste soul. The beauty of his body shone in him, but that of his character even more so. Therefore, even though for many people the beauty of the body is usually an obstacle to salvation, it could do no harm to our saint, because the beauty of his character ruled that of his body. So the soul must subdue the flesh, and not the flesh the soul, because the soul is the master of the flesh, and the flesh is the servant of the soul. Woe to the soul that is dominated by flesh and is changed from master to servant by neglecting the faith in the Lord and by submitting to the slavery of sin. But the soul of the patriarch Joseph securely preserved its power, and the flesh could not dominate it at all. SERMON 24.2.[2]

WHY THE TEXT DESCRIBES JOSEPH'S PHYSICAL CHARM. CHRYSOSTOM: That wicked beast the devil, however, seeing the good man's standing and the fact that he emerged even more conspicuous from those very things thought to be adversities, gnashed his teeth and fell into a rage. He could not bear to see the good man becoming so much more commendable as each day passed. He dug a deep pit for him and prepared what he thought was a mighty precipice that would bring him to his ruin and a terrible storm capable of causing him shipwreck. But the devil discovered before long that he was wasting his time and only heaping coals on his own head. "Joseph cut a fine figure and was good-looking," the text says. Why does it describe to us his physical charm? For us to learn that he was striking not only for charm of soul but also for his person. After all, Joseph was in the bloom of youth, "cut a fine figure and was good-looking." Sacred Scripture tells us this about him in advance so as to teach us that the Egyptian woman was under the spell of the young man's beauty in inviting him to that illicit association. HOMILIES ON GENESIS 62.16.[3]

HANDSOME IN BODY, MORE SPLENDID IN

---

[1]Chromatius's listeners. [2]SC 164:70. [3]FC 87:206.

MIND. CAESARIUS OF ARLES: However, let us now come to holy Joseph, so that we may be fed with the example of his chastity and purity as with a sort of heavenly food. This holy Joseph, then, of whom your charity[4] heard in the present lesson, was handsome in body but more splendid in mind, because he was chaste in body and virtuous in mind. Bodily beauty shone in him, but even more so shone the beauty of his soul. Now although physical beauty is apt to be a hindrance to salvation for many men, it could not harm this holy man because the beauty of his soul governed the splendor of his body. Thus the soul should rule the body, not the body the soul, for the soul is the mistress of the body while the body is the handmaid of the soul. Therefore unhappy is the soul that is dominated by the body and makes a mistress out of a servant. Truly the soul that is subject to vices of the flesh becomes the servant of the body, because it loses the faith of its Lord and endures the slavery of sin. The soul of the patriarch Joseph, however, faithfully kept its power, for the flesh could in no way dominate it. Indeed, when asked by his mistress, an unchaste woman, to lie with her, he refused consent because even in his position as a slave he had not lost the dominion of his soul. As a result of this, he was attacked by false accusations and thrown into prison, but the holy man considered that prison a palace, or rather he himself was a palace within the prison. For where there is faith, chastity, and purity, there is the palace of Christ, the temple of God, the dwelling of the Holy Spirit. Therefore if any man flatters himself because of the splendor of his body, or if any woman boasts about the beauty of hers, they should follow the example of Joseph and that of Susanna.[5] Let them be chaste in body and pure in mind. Then they will be beautiful not only to people but also to God. SERMON 93.2.[6]

39:8 Joseph Resists Illicit Love

TRUE BEAUTY REFUSES TO HARM ANOTHER. AMBROSE: But why should I enlarge on arrangements that pertained to a private house in the case of that slave who ruled an empire? It counts for still more that Joseph earlier ruled himself; although he was good-looking and very handsome in appearance, he did not direct the charm of his countenance toward another's wrongdoing but kept it to win grace for himself.[7] He thought that he would be even more attractive if he were proved more handsome not by the loss of his chastity but by the cultivation of modesty. That is the true beauty that does not seduce the eyes of others or wound their fragile hearts but gains the approval of all. It will do harm to none but win praise for itself. Now if any woman gazes with wanton eyes, the sin is attributable only to her who cast the wicked glance, not to him who did not wish to be looked upon with wicked intent, and there is no guilt in the fact that he was looked upon. It was not within the power of a mere servant not to be looked upon. The husband should have been on his guard against the roving eyes of his wife. If the husband had no fear in regard to his spouse, Joseph thought it to be evidence of her chastity, not the permissiveness of neglect. Still, let men also learn to guard against the roving eyes of women; even those men who do not wish to be loved are very much loved. Indeed, Joseph was very much loved, although he rejected the lover. And Scripture did well to absolve him, for it said, "The wife of his master cast eyes on Joseph";[8] that is, he did not show himself or take her unawares, but she cast her nets and was captured in her encircling of him. She spread her snares and stuck fast in her own bonds. ON JOSEPH 5.22.[9]

THE SERVANT COUNSELS THE MISTRESS. CHRYSOSTOM: "Afterwards," it says. What is

---

[4]An address to the audience. [5]A Jewish woman in Babylonian exile whose beauty attracts her husband's colleagues—two elders—so much that they try to force her to have sexual relations with them by threatening to accuse her of adultery with a young man. The story of Susanna has been transmitted in Greek in two forms (LXX and Theodotion) as an appendix to the book of Daniel. [6]FC 47:58-59. [7]Gen 39:6-7. [8]Gen 39:7. [9]FC 65:203-4*.

meant by "afterwards"? After Joseph had been entrusted with control of the whole household and after his being shown such esteem by his master, "his master's wife set her eye on Joseph."[10] See the shamelessness of this wanton woman. It was not because she considered herself to be mistress of the house that she took this into her head; it was not because he was a servant. Instead, under the spell of Joseph's charm and aflame with satanic desire, she endeavored at this point to assail the young man. With this evil intent fixed in her mind, she looked for a suitable moment of privacy for putting into effect this illicit endeavor. "But he refused," the text says. He did not submit, nor did he accept the invitation. Joseph realized, you see, the great ruin it would bring him. Instead of thinking of himself, he was greatly concerned as well to deliver her from this folly and improper desire, as far as was possible. He offered her advice calculated to awaken her to a sense of shame and make her realize what was for her good. HOMILIES ON GENESIS 62.17.[11]

39:9 Sin Against God

WE WILL NOT ESCAPE NOTICE. CHRYSOSTOM: What a grateful man! See how Joseph counts the blessings from his master so as to demonstrate the ingratitude she shows to her partner. "After all, I the servant," he is saying, "the stranger, the captive, enjoyed such security at his hands that everything came under my control, and there is nothing that he has kept from my control except you; whereas I am personally in charge of everything, to you alone am I subordinate, and you in fact are beyond my authority." Then, to deal her an opportune blow by reminding her of her husband's favor and persuade her not to prove ungrateful to her partner, he said, "You in fact are beyond my authority 'for the reason that you are his wife.'[12] So if you are really his wife, 'how then could I do this wicked deed and commit sin in God's eyes?'" You see, since she was looking for privacy and waiting for an opportunity in her anxiety to escape the notice of her husband and

all the servants of the household, he said, "How could I manage to do this wicked thing and commit sin in God's eyes?" I mean, what are you thinking of? Even if we succeed in escaping the notice of everyone, we will not be able to escape the notice of the unsleeping eye. That is the only one you need to fear, to be concerned and tremble about so as not to commit anything unlawful under his scrutiny. HOMILIES ON GENESIS 62.18.[13]

REMAIN VIGILANT AND ALERT. CHRYSOSTOM: Let us therefore make this our concern too, to have the Lord with us always so that what is done by us will be concluded successfully by him. You see, the person accorded this grace, even should he happen to find himself in the midst of troubles, will think nothing of them since the Lord of all, who creates and transforms everything, makes everything prosper for him and renders all difficulties easy. But how will we succeed in having the Lord with us and enjoying his guidance in everything? If we are vigilant and alert and imitate this young man's self-control, his other virtues and noble attitude, and if we see that it is so necessary for us to perform all our duties precisely so as never to be condemned by the Lord. We perform our duties to acknowledge that it is impossible to escape the notice of that unsleeping eye and that instead the sinner cannot but become liable to his punishments. Let us not place greater weight on respect for human beings than on God's anger but rather recall in every circumstance those words of Joseph, "How could I do this wicked deed and commit sin in God's eyes?" So when some temptation disturbs us, let us turn these words over in our mind, and every unholy desire will immediately be put to flight. HOMILIES ON GENESIS 62.24.[14]

39:10 Joseph Refuses the Advance

JOSEPH'S SURPASSING VIRTUE. CHRYSOSTOM: For us to learn the surpassing virtue of the good

---

[10]Gen 39:7. [11]FC 87:206-7*. [12]Gen 39:9. [13]FC 87:207*. [14]FC 87:210-11*.

man and the fact that not once or twice but many times he endured this pressure and resisted the invitation by ceaselessly counseling her, Scripture says, "Although she kept inviting him day after day, he did not yield to her."[15] When she observed him performing his duties in the house, she fell upon the young man like a wild animal grinding its teeth and grabbed his clothing to lay hold of him.[16] Let us not pass this passage idly by. Instead, let us consider how much pressure the good man endured. I mean, in my view at any rate, it was not so remarkable that the three children survived unharmed in the middle of the Babylonian furnace and sustained no harm from the fire[17] as it was remarkable and unprecedented that this remarkable young man had his clothes torn from him by this frenzied and intemperate woman without yielding to her. Instead, Joseph left the clothes in her hands and fled the scene in that condition.[18] You see, just as those three children on account of their virtue enjoyed grace from on high and were seen to prove superior to the fire,[19] so this man too, after making whatever effort he could and giving evidence of his struggle for continence with great intensity, enjoyed abundant help from on high. He all at once prevailed, thanks to such cooperation from God's right hand, and slipped from the clutches of that lustful woman. Then one could see this remarkable man emerging, divested of his clothes but garbed in the vesture of chastity, as though escaping unharmed from some fiery furnace, not only not scorched by the flames but even more conspicuous and resplendent. HOMILIES ON GENESIS 62.19.[20]

THE INTERIOR AND SPIRITUAL BEAUTY OF CHASTITY. CAESARIUS OF ARLES: The young man is desired by his mistress but is not provoked to lust. He is asked and runs away. She who commanded in other matters, in this one thing coaxes and pleads. She loved him, or was it rather herself? I think that it was neither him nor herself. If she loved him, why did she want to ruin him? If she loved herself, why did she want to perish? Behold, I have proved that she did not love: she burned with the poison of lust but did not shine with the flame of charity. He, however, knew how to see what she did not know. Joseph was more beautiful within than without, fairer in the light of his heart than in the beauty of his body. Where the eye of that woman could not penetrate, there he enjoyed his own beauty. Therefore, as he beheld the interior beauty of chastity in the mirror of his conscience, when would he allow it to be stained or violated by the temptation of that woman? For this reason what he saw you too can see if you will—namely, the interior and spiritual beauty of chastity—provided that you have eyes for it. I will tell you something by way of an example. You love it in your wife; therefore do not hate in the wife of another what you love in your own. What do you love in your own wife? Chastity, of course. You hate it in another's wife, when you are willing to destroy chastity by intimacy with her. What you love in your own wife you want to kill in the wife of another. How can you have a prayer of devotion, O murderer of chastity? Therefore preserve in the wife of another what you want to protect in your own, for in your wife you love her chastity rather than her body. SERMON 90.2.[21]

39:12 Joseph Flees from Potiphar's Wife

JOSEPH VALUED HIS SOUL. AMBROSE: Further, she said to him, "Lie with me." The first weapons of the adulteress are those of the eyes, the second those of words, but one who is not seduced by the eyes can resist the word. A defense is at hand when the passions are still free. And so it is written that "he refused."[22] Therefore Joseph first overcame her attack through a struggle in his heart and drove her back with the shield of his soul, so to speak; then he launched his word like a spear to force her retreat. "And he spoke to the wife of his master."[23] She is correctly called the

---

[15]Gen 39:10. [16]Gen 39:11-12. [17]Dan 3:19-27. [18]Gen 39:12. [19]Dan 3. [20]FC 87:207-8. [21]FC 47:43-44. [22]Gen 39:8. [23]Gen 39:8.

wife of the master, and not the mistress of the house, for she could not extort what she wanted to obtain. For how was she the mistress? She did not have the power of one who rules; she did not observe the discipline of a mistress; she provided mere servants with enticements to lust. But Joseph was a master who did not take up the torches of that lover, did not feel the bonds of that seducer, was not terrified by any fear of death and preferred to die free of sin rather than to choose participation in guilty power. He was free who believed it shameful not to make recompense for favor. Indeed, Joseph does not make his excuses as a frightened man, nor is he on his guard as one fearful of danger. Rather, he flees the charge of ingratitude and the stain of sin as one who owes a debt to his master's kindness and his own blamelessness, and, as a just man, he is terrified of the contagion of guilt. The adulteress threw her third dart by the persistency of her invitation, but Joseph did not listen to her.[24] After the first words, one has something to guard against. Lust is not only impure but insolent, demanding and wanton as well, and the adulteress has respect for nothing. She who felt no sorrow at her first loss of modesty lies in wait to perform her seduction.

Finally, when Joseph went in by reason of his duty and the office entrusted to him and the witnesses and household servants were far off,[25] she seized him and said, "Lie with me." He is absolved by the testimony of Scripture, because he was unable to abandon the service entrusted to him by his master. Indeed, it is not enough that Joseph entered the inside of his house without concern as one who could not be seduced; the just man had an obligation to take care not to give opportunity to a woman in a state of frenzy, else she might be undone by his sin. But while he perceived that the wife of his master was his adversary, still he had to guard against giving offense to his master by neglecting his duty. At the same time, he supposed her forwardness still consisted in speech, not in laying hands on him. Joseph is absolved for having entered in and praised for

having slipped away; he did not value the clothing of his body higher than the chastity of his soul. He left the clothing, which the adulteress held back in her hands, as if it were not his, and considered foreign to him the garments that the impure woman had been able to touch and seize. Joseph was, after all, a great man. Although sold, he did not know the nature of a slave. Although much loved, he did not love in return. Although asked, he did not acquiesce. Although seized, he fled away. When he was approached by his master's wife, he could be held by his garment but not seduced in his soul. He did not endure even her words for long, either, because he judged it to be a contagion if he should delay very long; else the incentives to lust might pass over to him through the hands of the adulteress. Therefore Joseph stripped off his garment and cast off the sin. He left behind the clothing by which he was held and fled away, stripped to be sure, but not naked, because he was covered better by the covering of modesty. Yes, a man is not naked unless guilt has made him naked. ON JOSEPH 5.23-25.[26]

THE ONE WHOM GUILT HAS EXPOSED. CAESARIUS OF ARLES: When Joseph was accused by his master's wife, he could be held by his clothing but was unable to be captivated in soul. He did not even tolerate her words for a long time, considering it a dangerous influence if he delayed any longer, lest through the hands of the adulteress the attractions of lust penetrate his soul. Therefore by removing his garments he shook off all accusation; leaving the clothes with which he was held he fled, robbed indeed but not naked, for he was covered still more with the clothing of purity. No one is naked except the man whom guilt has exposed. In earlier times too we have the fact that after Adam had disregarded God's command by his transgression and contracted the debt of serious sin, he was naked; for this reason he himself said, "I heard you in the garden, and I was afraid because I was naked; and I hid."[27] Adam asserts

---

[24]Gen 39:10. [25]Gen 39:11-12. [26]FC 65:204-6. [27]Gen 3:10.

he is naked because he has lost the adornment of divine protection; and he hid himself because he did not have the garment of faith, which he had laid aside by his transgression. You see an important fact: Adam was naked, although he did not lose his tunic; Joseph, who was stripped of his clothing, which he left in the hands of the adulteress, was not naked. The same Scripture asserts that the former was naked and the latter was not. Therefore Joseph despoiled himself rather than become naked when he preserved the garments of virtue incorrupt. He stripped himself of the old man with its actions, in order to put on the new man who is renewed unto knowledge according to the image of the Creator. Adam, however, remained naked because he could not clothe himself again after he was stripped of his singularly privileged virtue. For this reason he took a tunic made of skins, since as a sinner he could not have a spiritual one.[28] SERMON 92.3.[29]

39:14 Potiphar's Wife Falsely Accuses Joseph

SHE REVEALED WHAT SHE SHOULD HAVE CONCEALED. AMBROSE: Indeed, Joseph went out of doors while she spread the news of the temptation that arose from her own adultery; she said in a loud voice that the Hebrew had fled and left his garment behind.[30] Thus she revealed what she should have concealed, so as to do harm to an innocent man by inventing a crime. But the just man Joseph did not know how to make accusation, and so the impure woman accomplished this with impunity. Therefore I might say that she was the one who had really been stripped, although she was keeping the clothing of another. She had lost all the coverings of chastity, whereas he was sufficiently provided for and protected; his voice was not heard, and yet his blamelessness spoke for itself. ON JOSEPH 5.26.[31]

WICKEDNESS ATTRIBUTES ITS FAULTS TO VIRTUE. CHRYSOSTOM: But despite such a victory, despite such wonderful fortitude for which Joseph ought to have been rewarded, for which he

ought to have been extolled, once more he endures countless troubles as though a guilty party. You see, the Egyptian woman did not take kindly at that stage to her shame and insult brought on herself by attempting the impossible. First she summoned those in the household and accused the young man and tried to mislead them all by claiming that the commands given by her in her frenzy had been uttered by him. This, in fact, is the way with wickedness, that it endeavors to attribute its own faults to the virtue that is under attack. That is exactly what she did in this case, portraying the young man as incontinent and giving herself the guise of chastity, saying that was the reason he had abandoned his clothes and she was left with them. HOMILIES ON GENESIS 62.20.[32]

THE APOSTLES WERE HATED. CYRIL OF ALEXANDRIA: When Joseph was still young and at the end of his adolescence, he overcame the impudence of the Egyptian woman, even though he was dragged with great force to commit what was not lawful. In fact, this woman arguing with him impudently took the clothes off him and urged him to sin against his will. Actually he escaped from the furious lust of the woman after abandoning his cloak and could not be defeated by her strong will. Therefore he was accused of that action, since the woman turned the fault to him. In that dishonorable accusation, however, Joseph demonstrated great modesty and nobility. And he was thrown into the prison. Christ also was among the pagans, especially in the person of the holy apostles, who declared that they carried around on their own body his scars.[33] They did not want to adjust themselves to those things that belong to the world but kept away from any desire of the flesh. And such is always the life of the saints. Therefore, for this reason, they were the object of many plots and were oppressed by the slander of those who were accustomed to re-

---

[28]See 1 Cor 15:42-49. [29]FC 47:54-55. [30]Gen 39:12-18. [31]FC 65:207. [32]FC 87:208. [33]Gal 6:17.

gard those who wanted to live in Christ as unbearable, so that they fell into tremendous temptations and were imprisoned. However, they always bore in mind Christ's saying: "If you belonged to the world, the world would love you as its own. Because you do not belong to the world,

therefore the world hates you,"[34] exactly as the lustful woman hated Joseph. GLAPHYRA ON GENESIS, 6.[35]

---

[34]Jn 15:19. [35]PG 69:321.

39:19-23 JOSEPH'S IMPRISONMENT

[19]*When his master heard the words which his wife spoke to him, "This is the way your servant treated me," his anger was kindled.* [20]*And Joseph's master took him and put him into the prison, the place where the king's prisoners were confined, and he was there in prison.* [21]*But the LORD was with Joseph and showed him steadfast love, and gave him favor in the sight of the keeper of the prison.* [22]*And the keeper of the prison committed to Joseph's care all the prisoners who were in the prison; and whatever was done there, he was the doer of it;* [23]*the keeper of the prison paid no heed to anything that was in Joseph's care, because the LORD was with him; and whatever he did, the LORD made it prosper.*

OVERVIEW: The unsatisfied cravings of the Egyptian woman led to cruelty and injustice (AMBROSE). Although he was thrown into prison, Joseph was not guilty in God's sight, nor did God abandon him (AMBROSE, CAESARIUS OF ARLES). Joseph was in prison, but he was the palace of Christ and the temple of God (CHROMATIUS). These actions were accomplished under the veil of allegory: the imprisonment of Joseph foreshadows that of Christ (QUODVULTDEUS). Joseph was more blessed when he was cast into prison, for he endured martyrdom for the sake of chastity (CAESARIUS OF ARLES). Christ visits those who are imprisoned, and so Joseph found such favor that he became the guardian of the prison (AMBROSE, CAESARIUS OF ARLES). The creative wisdom of God preserved Joseph from all distress in prison (CHRYSOSTOM).

39:19 Potiphar's Fury

SHE JOINED DECEIT TO DECEIT. AMBROSE: When she could not protect her own vices, she accused the innocent; she joined deceit to deceit, held on to the possessions of others, herself condemned others and set no limit to her fury. Whatever was the reason for her cruelty? Only that she saw that her cravings were meeting with resistance and her forbidden desires were being frustrated of receiving consent. See the reason why the prison opens—to admit the innocent. Why criminals are freed of their chains—that these may be put on the faithful! Why falsifiers of the truth are let go—that one who refused to falsify his trust may be locked in! ON JOSEPH 6.28.[1]

THE LORD WAS WITH HOLY JOSEPH. CAESARIUS OF ARLES: That woman, however, did what she threatened, lied to her husband and was

---

[1]FC 65:208*.

believed; and still God was patient. Holy Joseph was thrown into prison. He was held captive like a guilty man, although God was not offended by him. Nor did God fail him there, since Jacob was not guilty in his sight. The Lord was with holy Joseph; because he loved what was holy, he was not overcome by the love of a woman. Her age did not arouse the chaste mind of the youth, nor did the authority of the one who loved him move him to associate with his despised mistress. With her own lips she plotted against the young man. Secretly and without witnesses the shameless woman seized him with her own hand, urging him by her insolent words to sin. Indeed, he is not overcome there, but as words followed words, so one thing followed another; although he had refused when asked repeatedly, still he was seized at the time he fled. SERMON 90.3.[2]

39:20 Joseph Is Imprisoned

THE LORD NEVER ABANDONED JOSEPH.
AMBROSE: Therefore I might say Joseph was happier when he was put into prison, because he was giving witness on behalf of chastity. For modesty is a good gift but one of lesser merit when it involves no risk. Where, however, it is maintained at the risk of one's safety, there it wins a more abundant crown. With his case unheard, his truthfulness unexamined, Joseph is sent into prison as if guilty of a crime.[3] But the Lord did not abandon him even in prison. The innocent should not be troubled when they are attacked on false charges, when justice is overcome and they are shoved into prison. God visits his own even in prison, and so there is more help for them there, where there is more danger. ON JOSEPH 5.26.[4]

HE WAS A PALACE IN HIS PRISON. CHROMA-
TIUS: But the holy man considered that prison to be a palace; and Joseph himself was a palace in his prison, because where faith, chastity and modesty are, there the palace of Christ is, the temple of God, the dwelling of the Holy Spirit.... In the church there are three models of chastity that ev-

erybody must imitate: Joseph, Susanna[5] and Mary. May men imitate Joseph, women Susanna and the virgin Mary. SERMON 24.2.[6]

UNDER THE VEIL OF ALLEGORY. QUODVULT-
DEUS: Joseph was imprisoned. Our Joseph, that is, Christ, as Isaiah says, "was numbered with the transgressors."[7] The innocent man is led among the guilty by the wisdom of God, who "went down with him"—as was written—"into the pit, and did not leave him in bonds."[8] This Joseph of ours, Christ, claims, "I became as a man without help, free among the dead."[9] What followed had to happen, that is, the fact that Joseph found in the commander of the prison the grace of which he was full and that all the keys and the entire surveillance were given to him.[10] This occurred in order that to the one before whom heaven prostrated in the figure of the sun, the moon and the stars, and the earth in that of its crops, also the subterranean creatures of the prison might submit. And therefore before our Joseph, that is, Christ, "every knee should bend, in heaven and on earth and under the earth."[11] I also think that the fact that two eunuchs of Pharaoh were imprisoned together with him[12] is not incompatible with the mystery of the passion. In fact, it was completed in this manner by the number of the three crucified, of whom our Joseph, that is, Christ, by unveiling the mysteries, had to punish one with a deserved chastisement and had to save the other with a free grace.[13] These holy actions were accomplished then under the veil of allegory, so that their full revelation might be reserved to us. BOOK OF PROMISES AND PREDICTIONS OF GOD 1.28.40.[14]

JOSEPH BLESSED IN PRISON. CAESARIUS OF
ARLES: Now when Joseph was accused by his mistress, he refused to say that she was guilty, be-

[2]FC 47:45. [3]Gen 39:19-20. [4]FC 65:207. [5]Sus (Dan 13). [6]SC 164:70-72. [7]Is 53:12. [8]Wis 10:13-14. [9]Ps 88:4-5 (87:5-6 LXX). [10]Gen 39:21-23. [11]Phil 2:10. [12]Gen 40:2-3. [13]Cf. Gen 40:21-22; Lk 23:33, 39-43. [14]SC 101:238-40.

cause as a just man he did not know how to accuse anyone; for this reason the unchaste woman acted with impunity. Therefore I might say that she was truly stripped even though she held the skirt of his garment in her hand, for she had lost all the adornments of purity and the covering of chastity. I might say further that he was sufficiently adorned and clothed even though his voice was not heard, for his innocence spoke. In this way, Susanna later spoke better than the prophet even though she was silent at her trial; since she did not seek the help of her own voice she thus merited the defense of the prophet. I might have said Joseph was more blessed when he was cast into prison, for he endured martyrdom in defense of chastity. The gift of purity is a great thing, even when it is preserved without danger, but when it is defended, although at the risk of personal safety, then it is crowned still more fully. SERMON 92.4.[15]

39:21 The Lord Steadfastly Loves Joseph

CHRIST VISITS THOSE IN PRISON. AMBROSE: But what wonder if Christ visits those who lie in prison? He reminds us that he himself was shut up in prison in his followers, as you find it written, "I was in prison, and you did not come to me."[16] Where does God's mercy not enter in? Joseph found favor of this sort; he who had been shut up in the prison kept the locks of the prison, while the jailer withdrew from his post and entrusted all the prisoners to his power.[17] Consequently Joseph did not suffer from prison but even gave relief to others as well from the calamity of imprisonment. ON JOSEPH 5.27.[18]

THE CREATIVE WISDOM OF GOD. CHRYSOSTOM: You notice how even when Joseph encountered troubles he had no sense of distress; instead, the creative wisdom of God transformed all his distress. Just as a pearl reveals its peculiar beauty even if someone buries it in the mire, so too virtue, wherever you cast it, reveals its characteristic power, be it in servitude, in prison, in distress or in prosperity. So since, even when cast into prison, he won over the chief jailer and received from him control of everything there, let us see in this case as well how Joseph reveals the force of grace coming his way. HOMILIES ON GENESIS 63.2.[19]

THE LORD VISITS HIS OWN EVEN IN PRISON. CAESARIUS OF ARLES: While his case was unheard, Joseph was thrown into prison as if guilty of a crime, but the Lord did not desert him there. It is not a source of shame for the innocent when they are attacked by false charges and cast into prison because justice is crushed; the Lord visits his own even in prison, and therefore there is more help where the danger is greater. What wonder is it that Christ visits his own who are in prison, when he recalls that he has been locked up in prison in the person of his people? As you have it written: "I was in prison, and you did not come to me."[20] Where does the divine mercy not penetrate? Joseph found such favor that he who had been shut up in prison rather guarded the bars of the prison. SERMON 92.4.[21]

---

[15]FC 47:55-56. [16]Mt 25:43. [17]Gen 39:21-23. [18]FC 65:207-8. [19]FC 87:212. [20]Mt 25:43. [21]FC 47:56.

40:1-8 JOSEPH, AN INTERPRETER OF DREAMS

[1]*Some time after this, the butler of the king of Egypt and his baker offended their lord the king of Egypt.* [2]*And Pharaoh was angry with his two officers, the chief butler and the chief baker,* [3]*and he put them in custody in the house of the captain of the guard, in the prison where Joseph was confined.* [4]*The captain of the guard charged Joseph with them, and he waited on them; and they continued for some time in custody.* [5]*And one night they both dreamed—the butler and the baker of the king of Egypt, who were confined in the prison—each his own dream, and each dream with its own meaning.* [6]*When Joseph came to them in the morning and saw them, they were troubled.* [7]*So he asked Pharaoh's officers who were with him in custody in his master's house, "Why are your faces downcast today?"* [8]*They said to him, "We have had dreams, and there is no one to interpret them." And Joseph said to them, "Do not interpretations belong to God? Tell them to me, I pray you."*

OVERVIEW: Although the text offers no explanation of the offenses of the butler and the baker, it is assumed that they boasted of their high positions and thus gave offense (AMBROSE). Joseph, even in prison, gave evidence of his virtue and showed concern to relieve the sadness of others (CHRYSOSTOM).

40:4 Joseph Remains in Prison

IN THE WILL OF THE KING. AMBROSE: What can I say in regard to those eunuchs? They ought to serve as an example to other eunuchs that their standing is fragile and weak and all their hope lies in the will of the king; for them a slight offense is a very great danger, while prosperity is a paltry condition of service. One boasted because he was the chief butler, the other because he was the chief baker. Both committed offenses, were put into prison and were entrusted to the holy Joseph by the jailer of the prison.[1] ON JOSEPH 6.29.[2]

40:7 Pharaoh's Officers

EVIDENCE OF JOSEPH'S CHARACTERISTIC VIRTUE. CHRYSOSTOM: This remarkable man, however, concerned for their comfort, noticed that they were dismayed by the experience of the dreams and confused in mind; so he asked, "Why so downcast today?" The dejection on their faces, you see, betrayed the apprehension within them. Hence a sage too has said, "When the heart is free from care, the face beams, but when it is in mourning the face falls."[3] So, when he saw them lost in dejection from the experience of their dreams, he questioned them to discover the cause. See how, even when he found himself in prison, he gave evidence of his characteristic virtue and was concerned to relieve the sadness of others. HOMILIES ON GENESIS 63.4.[4]

---

[1]Gen 40:1-4. [2]FC 65:208. [3]Prov 15:13. [4]FC 87:213*.

40:9-15 THE CHIEF BUTLER'S DREAM

⁹So the chief butler told his dream to Joseph, and said to him, "In my dream there was a vine before me, ¹⁰and on the vine there were three branches; as soon as it budded, its blossoms shot forth, and the clusters ripened into grapes. ¹¹Pharaoh's cup was in my hand; and I took the grapes and pressed them into Pharaoh's cup, and placed the cup in Pharaoh's hand." ¹²Then Joseph said to him, "This is its interpretation: the three branches are three days; ¹³within three days Pharaoh will lift up your head and restore you to your office; and you shall place Pharaoh's cup in his hand as formerly, when you were his butler. ¹⁴But remember me, when it is well with you, and do me the kindness, I pray you, to make mention of me to Pharaoh, and so get me out of this house. ¹⁵For I was indeed stolen out of the land of the Hebrews; and here also I have done nothing that they should put me into the dungeon."

OVERVIEW: Joseph's interpretation of the butler's dream serves as the basis for a meditation on the triviality of worldly power compared with the mysteries of God. Joseph prefigures the true Hebrew, Christ, who was the interpreter of reality and who was tempted yet without sin (AMBROSE). Joseph's appeal to the butler to remember him and intercede with Pharaoh for him can be interpreted as a sign of his philosophical attitude and his great humility (CHRYSOSTOM).

40:13 The Butler to Be Restored

DREAM AND REALITY. AMBROSE: I do not choose to speak of the dream of the other man. You surely remember my words, that even then I avoided its interpretation in the case of one from whose end I shy away, at whose death I shudder.[1] Rather, let us speak of him who thought he was happy since he was chief butler and believed that this was the summit and crown of all power, that he would give the cup to the king. This was his glory, this was his grandeur in this world. When he was deprived of this he felt sorrow, and when he was restored to it he rejoiced. But this is a dream, and all worldly power is a dream, not a reality. To be sure, he saw by way of a dream that his preeminent position was restored to him. Isa-iah also says that people of this kind are such as take delight in prosperity in this world.[2] One who eats and drinks in his sleep thinks he is filled with food and drink, but when he awakens, he begins to be more hungry. Then he understands how insubstantial were that dreamer's food and drink. Just so, one who is asleep in this world and does not open his eyes to the mysteries of God, as long as he is in a deep corporeal sleep, supposes that such worldly power is of some importance, seeing it, as it were, in his dreams. But when he has awakened, he discovers how insubstantial the pleasure of this world is.

Look now upon that true Hebrew, the interpreter not of a dream but of reality and of a signal vision. He came from the fullness of divinity and the liberty of heavenly grace into this prison of the body.[3] The allurement of this world could work no change in him, no corrupt and worldly pleasure could subvert him, and although tempted he did not fall. Although attacked, he did not

---

[1]The allusion here is to the eunuch Calligonus, the Syrian grand chamberlain to the emperor Valentinian II. Calligonus had threatened Ambrose with death in 385 or 386 in the course of the dispute over the Arian attempt to gain possession of Ambrose's basilica in Milan, but after two years he had fallen into disfavor and was executed. Calligonus is mentioned by Ambrose in his *Letter* 76.28 to his sister Marcellina and by Augustine *Against Julian* 6.845. [2]Is 29:8. [3]See Col 2:9.

attack; at the last, when he was grasped by his bodily garment by the adulterous hand of the synagogue, as it were, he stripped off the flesh and ascended free of death. The harlot made false accusation when she could not hold him; but the prison did not frighten him, and hell did not hold him. Yes, he delivered others even from that place where he had descended as if for punishment. Where the bonds of death were drawn tight for him, even there he loosened the bonds of the dead. ON JOSEPH 6.30-31.[4]

40:14 Remember Me

THE BUTLER DID NOT REMEMBER. AMBROSE: Look therefore on that Hebrew as he says to the chief of the eunuchs, who had incurred the displeasure of the king but had been restored to his post, "Remember me by your own case, when it shall be well with you, and you will do me a kindness and remember me."[5] He made his request a second time for this reason, because he knew that the other would not remember what harm he had escaped, when he had regained power. And so Joseph reminded him a second time, because he freed him a second time. Thus, if the recollection of the earlier kindness did not have a hold on him, at least the remembrance of the later one would present itself, and that man would not scorn the author of his deliverance or do violence to him out of treacherous deceit. But what is worse, forgetfulness of the kindness swiftly stole in during time of prosperity. The butler, once restored to his post, did not remember the interpreter of his dream but forgot about him.[6] But even though he forgot, Christ did not forget but spoke to the butler, yes, spoke to him through a mere servant and said, "Remember me by your own case," that is, "Remember what you have heard in regard to your office. But even though you have forgotten now, you will remember me to get out of a danger, while you forgot a kindness." Nevertheless when he was raised up in power, he did not remember. Yet how important was this power, the charge of the wine? See the basis of all his boasting—that he was chief of the eunuchs who supplied the wine for the cups of the king! ON JOSEPH 6.32.[7]

CONSIDER JOSEPH'S PHILOSOPHICAL ATTITUDE. CHRYSOSTOM: When you hear this, dearly beloved, far from despising the good man's pusillanimity, be amazed rather at the fact that despite the onset of such awful difficulties, he put up with his internment there nobly and thankfully. I mean, even though he had often been given authority by the chief jailer, still he found it harsh to be locked up and live with squalid and filthy people. Notice, in fact, his philosophical attitude even from his bearing it in courageous fashion and giving evidence of great humility in every circumstance. "Have compassion on me, remind Pharaoh of me, and get me out of this dungeon." Consider in this, I ask you, how Joseph says nothing against that disgusting adulteress, does not blame his master or recount his brothers' inhumanity to him. Instead, he suppresses all that in saying, "Remember me, and have me taken out of this dungeon, for I was really abducted from the land of the Hebrews and have done nothing here and yet have been cast into this prison."

Instead of passing this idly by, let us consider his philosophical frame of mind in finding such a suitable opportunity and in not maligning the Egyptian woman (I make the same point, note) or drawing attention to his master or his brothers, aware as he was that the chief cupbearer was in the ideal position to acquaint the king of his situation once he had come into his own. Joseph assigned no blame for his being sentenced to a term in prison and was in no hurry to demonstrate the injustice committed against him. Rather, his one concern was not for them to be roundly condemned but only for someone to speak on his behalf. On the one hand, he obscured the role of his brothers when he said, "I was abducted from the land of the Hebrews," and, on the other hand, he drew attention neither

---

[4]FC 65:209-10. [5]Gen 40:14. [6]Gen 40:23. [7]FC 65:210-11.

to the doings of the wanton Egyptian woman nor to his master's unjust rage against him. Instead, what did he say? "I have done nothing here, and yet have been cast into this prison."

Hearing this let us learn, when we fall foul of such people, not to be bent on railing against them and sharpening our tongue in accusing them. [Instead, let us] . . . demonstrate our innocence meekly and mildly and imitate this remarkable man in that, though being in difficulties, he did not bring himself to parade the Egyptian woman's incontinence even by word of mouth. You are aware, of course, that often enough many people who are liable to accusation have recourse to vile abuse in endeavoring to fix their own

crimes on others. This man, on the contrary, though in fact more spotless than the sun and in a position to tell the complete truth in exposing her frenzy and putting himself in the clear, did not draw attention to them. You see, far from hankering for the esteem of mortals, Joseph was content with favor from on high and wanted for an admirer of his conduct only that unsleeping eye. Hence, as he kept silence and endeavored to conceal everything, the loving Lord brought him to wonderful prominence when he saw with approbation the athlete under pressure. HOMILIES ON GENESIS 63.7-9.[8]

---

[8]FC 87:214-15*.

40:16-23 THE CHIEF BAKER'S DREAM AND THE FULFILLMENT OF THE DREAMS

[16]*When the chief baker saw that the interpretation was favorable, he said to Joseph, "I also had a dream: there were three cake baskets on my head,* [17]*and in the uppermost basket there were all sorts of baked food for Pharaoh, but the birds were eating it out of the basket on my head."* [18]*And Joseph answered, "This is its interpretation: the three baskets are three days;* [19]*within three days Pharaoh will lift up your head—from you!—and hang you on a tree; and the birds will eat the flesh from you."*

[20]*On the third day, which was Pharaoh's birthday, he made a feast for all his servants, and lifted up the head of the chief butler and the head of the chief baker among his servants.* [21]*He restored the chief butler to his butlership, and he placed the cup in Pharaoh's hand;* [22]*but he hanged the chief baker, as Joseph had interpreted to them.* [23]*Yet the chief butler did not remember Joseph, but forgot him.*

OVERVIEW: The fact that the butler forgot Joseph after his restoration allows for a further demonstration of Joseph's virtue in not showing signs of alarm, panic or disappointment. In fact the forgetfulness of the butler was part of the plan of the wise and creative Lord to allow Joseph

to play an even greater role (CHRYSOSTOM).

40:23 The Butler Forgot Joseph

JOSEPH REALIZED THE RACE WAS LONGER FOR HIM. CHRYSOSTOM: See once again the good man, as though competing in some gymnasium or wrestling ring, giving a demonstration of his characteristic virtue by not showing signs of alarm, panic or disappointment. I mean, had it been somebody else, any one of a thousand, he might have said, What's this? The chief cupbearer was all too ready to regain his former prosperity by my interpreting what he saw in his dream but now has no thought for me despite my predicting it. He is enjoying great relief, whereas I, who committed no crime, am locked up here with murderers, grave robbers, thieves and perpetrators of countless crimes. Joseph said nothing of the sort; he entertained no such thoughts. He realized that the race was longer for him, so that by striving consistently he might win a glorious crown. . . .

Joseph, you see, had to await the right moment for release from there to come his way along with renown. After all, if before Pharaoh's dreams the chief cupbearer had by his own intervention freed him from prison, perhaps his virtue would not have become known to many people. As it was, however, the wise and creative Lord, who like a fine craftsman knew how long the gold should be kept in the fire and when it ought be taken out, allowed forgetfulness to affect the chief cupbearer for a period of two years so that the moment of Pharaoh's dreams should arrive and that by force of circumstances the good man should become known to the whole of Pharaoh's kingdom. HOMILIES ON GENESIS 63.11-12.[1]

---

[1]FC 87:216-17*.

41:1-13 THE BUTLER RECOMMENDS JOSEPH TO PHARAOH

[1]*After two whole years, Pharaoh dreamed that he was standing by the Nile,* [2]*and behold, there came up out of the Nile seven cows sleek and fat, and they fed in the reed grass.* [3]*And behold, seven other cows, gaunt and thin, came up out of the Nile after them, and stood by the other cows on the bank of the Nile.* [4]*And the gaunt and thin cows ate up the seven sleek and fat cows. And Pharaoh awoke.* [5]*And he fell asleep and dreamed a second time; and behold, seven ears of grain, plump and good, were growing on one stalk.* [6]*And behold, after them sprouted seven ears, thin and blighted by the east wind.* [7]*And the thin ears swallowed up the seven plump and full ears. And Pharaoh awoke, and behold, it was a dream.* [8]*So in the morning his spirit was troubled; and he sent and called for all the magicians of Egypt and all its wise men; and Pharaoh told them his dream, but there was none who could interpret it[j] to Pharaoh.*

[9]*Then the chief butler said to Pharaoh, "I remember my faults today.* [10]*When Pharaoh was angry with his servants, and put me and the chief baker in custody in the house of the captain of the guard,* [11]*we dreamed on the same night, he and I, each having a dream with its own meaning.* [12]*A young Hebrew was there with us, a servant of the captain of the guard; and when we told him, he interpreted our dreams to us, giving an interpretation to each man according to his dream.*

[13]And as he interpreted to us, so it came to pass; I was restored to my office, and the baker was hanged."

j Gk: Heb *them*

OVERVIEW: The forgetfulness of the chief butler can be attributed to the arrogance of power (AMBROSE). In an alternative view it was part of God's wonderful design to show the inability of the Egyptian wise men to unravel the mystery (CHRYSOSTOM).

41:9 The Butler Recalls Joseph

EARS BLUNTED BY THE ARROGANCE OF POWER. AMBROSE: Now then, the butler was reminded of his own dream through the dream of the king and said, "I remember my sin."[1] That confession was late indeed, but would it were true. After committing sin, you confess what you should have avoided before you committed sin. How swiftly you had forgotten, "Remember me."[2] Of course you know that this word was spoken at that time, but you had ears blunted by the arrogance of power, and being drunk with wine, you did not hear the words of sobriety. Even now, "remember me," you that confess your sin late. You that inquire of the mere servant, why do you deny the Master? Now be drunk, not with wine but with the Holy Spirit. Remember what the baker suffered, with whom you slept your sleep and dreamed your dream.[3] He too was a chief, and chief over the royal banquets, which were part of the work of the bakers.[4] He believed that he was exalted because he had in his power the king's bread; he did not know that such power took many turns. He threatened others, although he was shortly to be given over to the extreme penalty himself, and he did not listen to Joseph, who spoke prophecy even though he was only a humble servant of the Lord. The prophecy was that he was going to lose his head at the command of that king in whose regard he flattered himself so very much, and he was to be left as food for the birds.[5] At least this example should restrain you from giving credence to unbelief. ON JOSEPH 6.34.[6]

GOD'S WONDERFUL DESIGN. CHRYSOSTOM: See God's wonderful design. First he let him have recourse to all those considered wise in those parts so that, when their ignorance was demonstrated, then this prisoner, this captive, this slave, this Hebrew, might be brought forward and unravel what was a mystery to so many, and thus Joseph might make clear to everyone the grace that had descended on him from above. So when all the wise men arrived and were unable to say anything or even open their mouths, then the chief cupbearer's memory returned, and he informed Pharaoh of what had happened to him, saying, "Today I'm going to bring to light my fault." HOMILIES ON GENESIS 63.13.[7]

---

[1]Gen 41:9. [2]Gen 40:14. [3]Ps 76:5 (75:6 LXX). [4]Gen 40:16. [5]Gen 40:16-19. [6]FC 65:212*. [7]FC 87:217.

41:14-24 PHARAOH RECOUNTS
HIS DREAM TO JOSEPH

[14]Then Pharaoh sent and called Joseph, and they brought him hastily out of the dungeon; and when he had shaved himself and changed his clothes, he came in before Pharaoh. [15]And Pharaoh said to Joseph, "I have had a dream, and there is no one who can interpret it; and I have heard it said of you that when you hear a dream you can interpret it." [16]Joseph answered Pharaoh, "It is not in me; God will give Pharaoh a favorable answer." [17]Then Pharaoh said to Joseph, "Behold, in my dream I was standing on the banks of the Nile; [18]and seven cows, fat and sleek, came up out of the Nile and fed in the reed grass; [19]and seven other cows came up after them, poor and very gaunt and thin, such as I had never seen in all the land of Egypt. [20]And the thin and gaunt cows ate up the first seven fat cows, [21]but when they had eaten them no one would have known that they had eaten them, for they were still as gaunt as at the beginning. Then I awoke. [22]I also saw in my dream seven ears growing on one stalk, full and good; [23]and seven ears, withered, thin, and blighted by the east wind, sprouted after them, [24]and the thin ears swallowed up the seven good ears. And I told it to the magicians, but there was no one who could explain it to me."

OVERVIEW: The misfortunes of Joseph appear in the end to have been arranged by divine providence so that at the opportune moment his wisdom might shine forth. Yet Joseph's wisdom is not human wisdom like that of Pharaoh's sages but comes from the Lord of all, who reveals the truth (CHRYSOSTOM).

41:14 Joseph Brought from Prison

PURIFIED BY ENDURANCE. CHRYSOSTOM: Notice immediately how much esteem Joseph enjoys from the outset. After being completely purified by endurance and emerging from prison like some piece of glittering gold, he was brought into Pharaoh's presence.

Do you see how wonderful a thing it is to be helped by grace from on high? See how many things divine providence had arranged so that the events affecting Joseph should come to pass. After surviving that greatest challenge and avoiding the clutches of that wanton Egyptian, he was thrown into prison. It was arranged that Pharaoh's chief cupbearer and chief baker should be imprisoned there at the same time and should come to know the man's wisdom through his interpretation of dreams, so that now at the opportune moment the cupbearer should remember and bring him forward. HOMILIES ON GENESIS 63.13-14.[1]

41:15 Joseph Can Interpret Dreams

JOSEPH'S GOOD SENSE AND DISCRETION. CHRYSOSTOM: Notice how Pharaoh was ashamed to say openly, "None of my sages can interpret the dream." Instead, what? "I had a dream, and there is no one to interpret it; but I have heard them say of you that once you hear of a dream you interpret it." Consider in this case too, I ask you, Joseph's good sense and discretion in the way he replies to Pharaoh: "Don't suspect," he says, "that I utter anything of myself or interpret them by human wisdom. There is, in fact, no way of coming to knowledge of them without revelation

---

[1]FC 87:217-18*.

from on high. So be aware that without God it is not possible for me to give you a reply." Without God, the text says, Pharaoh will not be given the right solution. So, now that you know that the Lord of all is the one who gives this revelation, don't look for something from human beings (he is saying) that God alone has it in his power to bring to light.

See how through his reply Joseph brings Pha-

raoh to the realization of the limitations of the sages attending him and the power of the Lord. "Since, then, you have learned from me that these utterances of mine spring not from human wisdom or from my own reasoning, tell me what God has communicated to you." HOMILIES ON GENESIS 63.14-15.[2]

---

[2]FC 87:218*.

41:25-36 JOSEPH INTERPRETS PHARAOH'S DREAM

[25]Then Joseph said to Pharaoh, "The dream of Pharaoh is one; God has revealed to Pharaoh what he is about to do. [26]The seven good cows are seven years, and the seven good ears are seven years; the dream is one. [27]The seven lean and gaunt cows that came up after them are seven years, and the seven empty ears blighted by the east wind are also seven years of famine. [28]It is as I told Pharaoh, God has shown to Pharaoh what he is about to do. [29]There will come seven years of great plenty throughout all the land of Egypt, [30]but after them there will arise seven years of famine, and all the plenty will be forgotten in the land of Egypt; the famine will consume the land, [31]and the plenty will be unknown in the land by reason of that famine which will follow, for it will be very grievous. [32]And the doubling of Pharaoh's dream means that the thing is fixed by God, and God will shortly bring it to pass. [33]Now therefore let Pharaoh select a man discreet and wise, and set him over the land of Egypt. [34]Let Pharaoh proceed to appoint overseers over the land, and take the fifth part of the produce of the land of Egypt during the seven plenteous years. [35]And let them gather all the food of these good years that are coming, and lay up grain under the authority of Pharaoh for food in the cities, and let them keep it. [36]That food shall be a reserve for the land against the seven years of famine which are to befall the land of Egypt, so that the land may not perish through the famine."

OVERVIEW: The dream of plenty leads to the reflection that the seven years of plenty are as nothing compared with everlasting repose and that affliction tests character (AMBROSE). The fact that Joseph did not mention his name in the counsel he gave to Pharaoh shows his modesty (EPHREM).

41:26 The Dream Interpreted

EVERLASTING REST IN THE AGES TO COME.
AMBROSE: And yet I judge that this dream was not revealed only to one or two but was set out before all men for this reason: because the seven years of this world that are fat and sleek with worldly plenty are swallowed up by those ages to come in which there will be everlasting rest and the observance of the spiritual law. Among the fathers, that tribe of Ephraim, rich in God, keeps

such observance like a good heifer, not taut in the udder of the body but abundant in spiritual milk and grace. God says that he sits upon her beautiful neck, as is written, "Ephraim is a heifer taught to love victory, but I passed over upon her beautiful neck."[1] Accordingly let not the oil of the sinner anoint our head,[2] and false fruits ought not to delight us; else it may be said also of us, "You have planted wickedness and gathered in its iniquities. You have eaten false fruit because you have trusted in your chariots."[3] And it does not trouble me that such a one has lean ears and ears destroyed by the wind, because David also was a better man at the time when he was wasting away like a spider,[4] and a sacrifice to God is an afflicted spirit.[5] Those people turn out better whom the wicked spirit has tried in this world with severe wrongs. ON JOSEPH 7.39.[6]

41:33 An Overseer for Egypt

JOSEPH'S MODESTY. EPHREM THE SYRIAN: When Joseph said, "Let Pharaoh select a man," he spoke about himself. Joseph, out of modesty, did not say it openly in his own name, but he would not give it to another, for he knew that no one else would be able to make suitable provision for the great scourge that was coming upon them. Joseph became great in the eyes of Pharaoh through his interpretation of Pharaoh's dreams but even more through the beneficial counsel that his mind had devised. COMMENTARY ON GENESIS 35.5.[7]

---

[1]Hos 10:11. [2]Ps 141:5 (140:5 LXX); 23:5 (22:5 LXX). [3]Hos 10:13. [4]Ps 39:12 (38:13 LXX). [5]Ps 51:17 (50:19 LXX). [6]FC 65:215*. [7]FC 91:186.

41:37-45 JOSEPH SET OVER THE LAND OF EGYPT

[37]This proposal seemed good to Pharaoh and to all his servants. [38]And Pharaoh said to his servants, "Can we find such a man as this, in whom is the Spirit of God?" [39]So Pharaoh said to Joseph, "Since God has shown you all this, there is none so discreet and wise as you are; [40]you shall be over my house, and all my people shall order themselves as you command; only as regards the throne will I be greater than you." [41]And Pharaoh said to Joseph, "Behold, I have set you over all the land of Egypt." [42]Then Pharaoh took his signet ring from his hand and put it on Joseph's hand, and arrayed him in garments of fine linen, and put a gold chain about his neck; [43]and he made him to ride in his second chariot; and they cried before him, "Bow the knee!"[k] Thus he set him over all the land of Egypt. [44]Moreover Pharaoh said to Joseph, "I am Pharaoh, and without your consent no man shall lift up hand or foot in all the land of Egypt." [45]And Pharaoh called Joseph's name Zaphenath-paneah; and he gave him in marriage Asenath, the daughter of Potiphera priest of On. So Joseph went out over the land of Egypt.

k *Abrek,* probably an Egyptian word similar in sound to the Hebrew word meaning *to kneel*

OVERVIEW: Pharaoh's decision to appoint Joseph over all his house offers renewed opportunity for meditation on how nothing can stand in the way of the design of God. Joseph is the personification of the hope described by the apostle Paul (CHRYSOSTOM). On an allegorical level, Pharaoh's gifts to Joseph represent a wide range of divine re-wards (AMBROSE). In an engaging elaboration of the text, Ephrem describes the reaction of Potiphar and his wife to Joseph's elevation. Their fears of retaliation turn out to be unfounded be-cause of Joseph's awareness of the divine plan (EPHREM).

41:39 Wisdom and Discretion

GOD'S RESOURCEFUL PROVIDENCE. CHRYSOSTOM: Do you see how even Pharaoh realized that these things became clear to Joseph through a revelation from on high? I mean, whom would we find, he is saying, so imbued with grace as to have the spirit of God in him? "He said to Joseph, 'Since God has revealed all this to you, there is no person more discerning than you.'" Consider in this instance how, when the resourceful God wishes to put his decisions into effect, no difficulty can arise from events that occur in the meantime. Witness, for example, the slaughter that nearly occurred, so to say, at the hands of his brothers, the selling, the accusation that led him into the utmost peril, imprisonment for such a long period of time, and how after all this happened to him he was raised, you might almost say, to the royal throne. HOMILIES ON GENESIS 63.16.[1]

41:40 Only Pharaoh Greater Than Joseph

ENDURANCE GAVE JOSEPH CHARACTER. CHRYSOSTOM: See how all of a sudden the prisoner is made king of the whole of Egypt; the one sent to prison by the chief steward was raised by the king to the highest rank; his former master suddenly saw that the man whom he had cast into prison as an adulterer was awarded authority over the whole of Egypt. Do you see how important it is to bear trials thankfully? Hence Paul also said, "Distress promotes endurance, endurance promotes character, character promotes hope, and hope does not disappoint."[2] So take note: Joseph bore distress

with endurance, endurance gave him character, having such character he acted in hope, and hope did not disappoint him. HOMILIES ON GENESIS 63.17.[3]

41:42 Pharaoh's Signet

JOSEPH SPOKE CONCERNING MYSTICAL THINGS. AMBROSE: On this account I think that Joseph merited rewards that were more mystical, because he spoke concerning mystical things. For what is the meaning of the ring that was put upon his finger? Only this, that we may understand that the pontificate of faith was bestowed on him so that he could himself seal others. What of the robe, which is the garment of wisdom? Only this, that preeminence in wisdom was granted to him by the King of heaven. The chain of gold appears to represent good understanding; the chariot[4] too signifies the exalted height of merit. ON JOSEPH 7.40.[5]

41:44 Pharaoh Grants Joseph More Power

JOSEPH HAS BECOME OUR MASTER. EPHREM THE SYRIAN: Joseph's [former] master was there when the dreams of Pharaoh were being interpreted. When [Potiphar] saw that only in respect to the throne was [Joseph] less than Pharaoh, he returned quickly to his house. In his haste to go to tell his wife of [Joseph's] greatness, he closely resembled his wife when she had come out to meet him to accuse Joseph. Potiphar said to his wife, "Joseph, our servant, has become our master. He whom we sent to prison without clothing, Pharaoh has now clothed with a garment of fine white linen. He whom we cast prostrate into prison now sits upon the chariot of Pharaoh. He whom we had bound in irons now has a gold necklace set on his neck. . . . How then can I look again upon him whom my eyes are unable to look upon?"

---

[1]FC 87:219-20*. [2]Rom 5:3-5. [3]FC 87:220*. [4]Gen 41:43. [5]FC 65:215-16.

Then she said to him, "Do not fear Joseph to whom you did no evil, for he knows that the disgrace that came upon him in our home, whether justly or not, came upon him from my hands. Go, then, without fear with the princes and army commanders who follow behind his chariot, lest he think that the royal dignity that he has received is an affliction to us. To show you that he is not evil, I will now speak the truth, which is contrary to my previous lie. I was enamored of Joseph when I falsely accused him. I made assault upon his clothing because I was overcome by his beauty. If he is just, it is I whom he will bring to grief and not you. And if he is [truly] upright, he will not bring me to grief, either, because if he had not been wronged he would not have been imprisoned. If he had not been imprisoned, he would not have interpreted the dreams of Pharaoh and he would not have come to this royal dignity of which you just informed me. Although we did not exalt him, it is as if we did exalt him, for it was due to our afflicting him that he has been accorded such honor and become second to the king."

Then Joseph's [former] master went and, with those who were higher in rank than he, followed Joseph's chariot through the streets of Egypt. But Joseph did him no evil because he knew that it was God who had permitted his brothers to throw him into the pit in the desert, and [who had delivered him] from the pit, in order to send him in irons to Egypt, and who had permitted his master to send him to prison so that from that humble seat he might set him upon the chariot of Pharaoh. COMMENTARY ON GENESIS 35.7-9.[6]

---

[6]FC 91:187-88.

41:46-49 THE SEVEN YEARS OF PLENTY

[46]*Joseph was thirty years old when he entered the service of Pharaoh king of Egypt. And Joseph went out from the presence of Pharaoh, and went through all the land of Egypt.* [47]*During the seven plenteous years the earth brought forth abundantly,* [48]*and he gathered up all the food of the seven years when there was plenty[l] in the land of Egypt, and stored up food in the cities; he stored up in every city the food from the fields around it.* [49]*And Joseph stored up grain in great abundance, like the sand of the sea, until he ceased to measure it, for it could not be measured.*

l Sam Gk: Heb *which were*

OVERVIEW: The mention of Joseph's age gives rise to an extended meditation on the fact that youth is no hindrance to virtue, on the benefits of endurance and on the virtues of hope and faith. We must keep our minds on the wealth and spiritual riches that can be acquired through suffering and endurance (CHRYSOSTOM).

41:46 Joseph Went Throughout Egypt

NO EXCUSE FOR ANYONE TO NEGLECT VIRTUE. CHRYSOSTOM: Far from idly considering that there is merely reference here to his age, let us learn that there is no excuse for anyone to neglect virtue or any grounds for claiming the pretext of youth when virtue needs to be demonstrated. See, after all, this man: he was not only young but also charming in appearance and handsome to behold. It is possible, you see, for a young man not to be blessed with bodily charm. But in addition to his youth this man was also charming in appearance and good looking. Joseph was near the bloom of youth when he was captured and became a slave. He was in fact, the text says, seventeen when he was carried off into Egypt. Then he was in the burning heat of youth when the wanton Egyptian, who happened to be his employer, set upon him without overcoming the good man's resistance. Then came prison and his hardship there for such a long period of time; he remained firm as iron, not only not becoming less resistant but even gaining greater strength. Joseph had grace from on high, you see, to strengthen him. Since he had previously given evidence of every virtue from his own resources, accordingly he was summoned from prison to take charge of all of Egypt.

After hearing this, let us never despair in the midst of distress or become frustrated by following our own reasoning. Rather, let us give evidence of sound endurance and be buoyed up by hope, secure in the knowledge of our Lord's resourcefulness and the fact that instead of ignoring us and abandoning us to the experience of troubles, he wants to crown us with a resplendent garland for our struggles. It is for this that all holy people have been distinguished. Hence the apostles also said, " It is through great distress that we must enter the kingdom of God."[1] Christ himself said to the disciples, "In the world you will have distress."[2] So let us not be upset at the thought of distress but rather listen to Paul's statement that "those who wish to live religiously in Christ Jesus will suffer persecution."[3] Far from being surprised or troubled, let us endure developments with complete fortitude and endurance, having regard not to the distress but to the gain accruing to us from it. This transaction, you see, is spiritual. And just as people intent on making money and being involved in a transaction of this

life would succeed in increasing their wealth in no other way than by being exposed to great danger on land and at sea (they must, after all, put up with the onset of brigands and wiles of pirates), and yet they are ready to accept every thing with great enthusiasm, having no sense of hardship through the expectation of gain, in just the same way must we keep our mind on the wealth and spiritual riches accruing to us from this. We must rejoice and be glad, considering not what can be seen but what cannot be seen, as Paul's exhortation goes, "not considering what can be seen."[4]

This in fact is what faith is, when we do not rely on our bodily eyes alone but imagine with the eyes of the mind things that are not visible. In particular, you see, we ought to consider the things that are not visible as more reliable than the things seen with bodily eyes. In this way the patriarch Abraham won his good name, by believing God's promise and proving superior to nature and human reasoning. Hence "it was reckoned as righteousness in him."[5] Call to mind that righteousness consists in believing what is said by God. I mean, whenever he promises something, don't look for things according to human logic, I ask you, but prove superior to such reasoning and trust in the power of the one making the promise. This was the way each of the good people won their name. This too was the way the remarkable man Joseph, despite the great number of difficulties confronting him after his dream, resisted panic and trepidation and instead nobly bore everything with resolute determination, secure in the knowledge that what God had decided could not fail. Hence, despite enslavement, despite imprisonment and such terrible calumny, he was granted control over the whole of Egypt. HOMILIES ON GENESIS 63.19-21.[6]

---

[1]Acts 14:22. [2]Jn 16:33. [3]2 Tim 3:12. [4]2 Cor 4:18. [5]Gen 15:6; cf. Rom 4:3. [6]FC 87:221-23*.

41:50-52 JOSEPH'S SONS

⁵⁰*Before the year of famine came, Joseph had two sons, whom Asenath, the daughter of Potiphera priest of On, bore to him.* ⁵¹*Joseph called the name of the first-born Manasseh,ᵐ "For," he said, "God has made me forget all my hardship and all my father's house."* ⁵²*The name of the second he called Ephraim,ⁿ "For God has made me fruitful in the land of my affliction."*

m That is *Making to forget*   n From a Hebrew word meaning *to be fruitful*

OVERVIEW: The name given by Joseph to his son Manasseh recalls his past sufferings and expresses his constant thankfulness. The name given to his second son also expresses his forgetfulness of past distress and gratitude for his prosperity (CHRYSOSTOM).

41:51 Manasseh

HARDSHIPS FORGOTTEN UNDER THE POWER OF GRACE. CHRYSOSTOM: Consider the man's God-fearing attitude. By recording the memory of everything by the name of his son, Joseph purposely expressed his constant thankfulness. He did so that the one born to him might be in a position to know from his own name the trials and endurance that characterized the good man and so brought Joseph to such prominence. "Because he made me forget all my hardships and all those of my father." What is the meaning of "all those of my father"? Here I think there is reference to the former enslavement and the latter, as well as the deprivation in prison. "All those of my father" means the separation he endured in being away from his father's embrace and the fact that, being raised with such care, at a tender age he exchanged freedom for slavery. HOMILIES ON GENESIS 64.2.[1]

41:52 Ephraim

THE NAME SUGGESTS GRATITUDE. CHRYSOSTOM: Notice that this child's name too is suggestive of gratitude. "Not only did he grant me forgetfulness of my distress," he is saying, "but he also made me prosper in the land where I suffered such awful humiliation as to be reduced to the limit and run a risk to life itself." HOMILIES ON GENESIS 64.2.[2]

[1]FC 87:224-25*.   [2]FC 87:225*.

41:53-57 THE SEVEN YEARS OF FAMINE

⁵³*The seven years of plenty that prevailed in the land of Egypt came to an end;* ⁵⁴*and the seven years of famine began to come, as Joseph had said. There was famine in all lands; but in all the land of Egypt there was bread.* ⁵⁵*When all the land of Egypt was famished, the people cried to Pharaoh for bread; and Pharaoh said to all the Egyptians, "Go to Joseph; what he says to you, do."*

[56] *So when the famine had spread over all the land, Joseph opened all the storehouses,[o] and sold to the Egyptians, for the famine was severe in the land of Egypt.* [57] *Moreover, all the earth came to Egypt to Joseph to buy grain, because the famine was severe over all the earth.*

o Gk Vg Compare Syr: Heb *all that was in them*

OVERVIEW: During the seven years of famine Joseph provided for the orphans, widows and needy persons so that there was no anxiety in Egypt. Grain became expensive even in Egypt because the whole world hungered (EPHREM). Joseph, in providing for those suffering from famine, is a figure of Christ, who provides for all those suffering from spiritual famine. We should seek to buy the spiritual nourishment that can avert famine (AMBROSE).

41:55 Do As Joseph Says

ORPHANS AND WIDOWS. EPHREM THE SYRIAN: Joseph went out to gather in the grain, and he stored it in every city.... Then at the end of the good years, when those of famine came, Joseph took special care of the orphans, widows and every needy person in Egypt so that there was no anxiety in Egypt. COMMENTARY ON GENESIS 36.1.[1]

JOSEPH PREFIGURES CHRIST'S MERCY.
AMBROSE: Indeed, anyone who was suffering from famine was sent to Joseph. Who are these people? Those of whom it is said, "They shall return at evening and shall suffer hunger like dogs."[2] Now there was famine, not in one locality alone but over the whole land, because there was no one to do good. Therefore the Lord Jesus, taking pity on the hungers of the world, opened his granaries[3] and disclosed the hidden treasures of the heavenly mysteries, of wisdom and of knowledge, so that none would lack for nourishment. For Wisdom said, "Come, eat my bread,"[4] and only the one who is filled with Christ can say, "The Lord feeds me, and I shall want nothing."[5] Therefore Christ opened his granaries and sold, while asking not monetary payments but the price of faith and the recompense of devotion. He sold, moreover, not to

a few people in Judea but to all, so that he might be believed by all peoples. ON JOSEPH 7.41.[6]

41:57 All Nations Came for Grain

GRAIN BECAME EXPENSIVE. EPHREM THE SYRIAN: If this famine had been only in Egypt, Egypt would have had no fear, because of the grain Joseph [had stored up]. However, there was famine throughout the entire world, and because the entire earth stood in need of [the grain in] Egypt, the grain supply quickly dwindled and became expensive even for the Egyptians. The Egyptians would have consumed the grain at little expense, because of its abundance, if the entire earth had not come down to buy grain there. To make known that the entire earth hungered, [Moses] said, "The entire world came to Egypt to buy grain from Joseph." COMMENTARY ON GENESIS 36.2.[7]

AVERTING SPIRITUAL FAMINE. AMBROSE: Yes, the famine had taken hold of them. For all people that have not been fed by Christ are hungry. And so let us buy the nourishment with which we can avert famine. Let no one hold back out of consideration of his poverty; let no one who does not have money be afraid. Christ does not ask money but faith, which is more valuable than money. Indeed Peter, who did not have money, bought him. "Silver and gold I do not have," he said, "but what I have I give you. In the name of Jesus Christ arise and walk."[8] And the prophet Isaiah says, "All you who are thirsty, come to the water, and you that have no money come, buy, and drink and eat without money and without the price of the wine."[9] For he who paid the price of his blood for

[1]FC 91:188. [2]Ps 59:6 (58:7 LXX). [3]See Gen 41:56. [4]Prov 9:5. [5]Ps 23:1 (22:1 LXX). [6]FC 65:216*. [7]FC 91:188. [8]Acts 3:6. [9]Is 55:1.

us did not ask a price from us, because he redeemed us not with gold or silver but with his precious blood.[10] Therefore you owe that price with which you have been bought. Even though he does not always demand it, you still owe it. Buy Christ for yourself, then, not with what few people possess, but with what all people possess by nature but few offer on account of fear. What Christ claims from you is his own. He gave his life for everyone; he offered his death for everyone. Pay on behalf of your Creator what you are going to pay by law. He is not bargained for at a slight price, and not all persons see him readily.

Indeed, those virgins in the Gospel whom the bridegroom kept out upon his coming were left out of doors exactly because they did not buy the oil that was for sale.[11] On this account it is said to them, "Go rather to those who sell it, and buy some for yourselves."[12] Likewise that merchant deserves praise who sold all his goods and bought the pearl.[13] ON JOSEPH 7.42.[14]

---

[10]1 Pet 1:18-19. For references to humanity as purchased by Christ see 1 Cor 6:19-20; 7:23; Acts 20:28. [11]Mt 25:1-13. [12]Mt 25:9. [13]Mt 13:45-46. [14]FC 65:216-17*.

42:1-5 JACOB'S SONS GO TO BUY GRAIN IN EGYPT

[1]*When Jacob learned that there was grain in Egypt, he said to his sons, "Why do you look at one another?"** [2]And he said, "Behold, I have heard that there is grain in Egypt; go down and buy grain for us there, that we may live, and not die." [3]So ten of Joseph's brothers went down to buy grain in Egypt. [4]But Jacob did not send Benjamin, Joseph's brother, with his brothers, for he feared that harm might befall him. [5]Thus the sons of Israel came to buy among the others who came, for the famine was in the land of Canaan.*

*LXX, "remain idle."

OVERVIEW: Jacob's question to his sons is also addressed to those who come to Christ's grace too late. In Benjamin Christians see Paul, who was of the tribe of Benjamin (AMBROSE).

42:1 Grain in Egypt

AN OLD MAN WORTHY OF RESPECT.
AMBROSE: And Jacob said to his sons, "Why are you idle? Behold, I have heard that there is grain in Egypt. Go down there and buy food for us."[1] This is not something Jacob said one time; he says it daily to his sons who come to Christ's grace too late, "Why are you idle? Behold, I have heard that there is grain in Egypt." From this

grain there comes the grain that rises again.[2] And so whoever suffers famine ought to attribute it to his own laziness. "Behold, I have heard that there is grain in Egypt." Generally, indeed, younger men hear of something more quickly than their elders, for many of the former travel about and are engaged out of doors. But an old man is the first to hear of this business matter, yet an old man who has lived to a great age in faith, an old man whose old age is worthy of respect, and the time of his old age is a spotless life.[3] ON JOSEPH 8.43.[4]

---

[1]Gen 42:1-2. [2]Cf. Jn 12:24-25. [3]Cf. Wis 4:8-9. [4]FC 65:217-18.

42:4 Benjamin Remains at Home

BENJAMIN PREFIGURES PAUL. AMBROSE: Nor does everyone undertake this business matter, but only the sons of Jacob and only those sons of more mature age. Thus ten sons go, whereas the youngest son does not go.[5] The father did not send him; else "infirmity may befall him." Benjamin, the youngest, was still subject to infirmity. Granted, [in] the name Benjamin the patriarch is read, but Paul, who was of the tribe of Benjamin,[6] was being prefigured. Jacob was right to hesitate over his infirmity. Indeed, he was made infirm so that he could be healed. Paul suffered blindness, but this was an infirmity unto salvation.[7]

Yes, that blindness brought Paul light. We have received the story; let us come to know the mystery. The patriarchs had gone at first without Benjamin, as the apostles first went without Paul. Each came, not as the first, but was summoned by those who were the first, and by his arrival he made the goods of those who were first more plenteous. ON JOSEPH 8.44-45.[8]

---

[5]Gen 42:3. [6]Rom 11:1. [7]Acts 9:8-9. [8]FC 65:218*.

42:6-17 JOSEPH IMPRISONS HIS BROTHERS

> [6]*Now Joseph was governor over the land; he it was who sold to all the people of the land. And Joseph's brothers came, and bowed themselves before him with their faces to the ground. [7]Joseph saw his brothers, and knew them, but he treated them like strangers and spoke roughly to them. "Where do you come from?" he said. They said, "From the land of Canaan, to buy food." [8]Thus Joseph knew his brothers, but they did not know him. [9]And Joseph remembered the dreams which he had dreamed of them; and he said to them, "You are spies, you have come to see the weakness of the land." [10]They said to him, "No, my lord, but to buy food have your servants come. [11]We are all sons of one man, we are honest men, your servants are not spies." [12]He said to them, "No, it is the weakness of the land that you have come to see." [13]And they said, "We, your servants, are twelve brothers, the sons of one man in the land of Canaan; and behold, the youngest is this day with our father, and one is no more." [14]But Joseph said to them, "It is as I said to you, you are spies. [15]By this you shall be tested: by the life of Pharaoh, you shall not go from this place unless your youngest brother comes here. [16]Send one of you, and let him bring your brother, while you remain in prison, that your words may be tested, whether there is truth in you; or else, by the life of Pharaoh, surely you are spies." [17]And he put them all together in prison for three days.*

OVERVIEW: Although the brothers may not have recognized Joseph because of his now mature age and their belief that he had been sold into servitude, still it all happened as a result of the dispensation of God. The brothers' response ("one is no more") to Joseph's accusation shows their duplicity and unwillingness to admit their guilt (CHRYSOSTOM). An ingenious defense against Joseph's accusation of spying can be attributed to the brothers on the grounds of their ignorance of the

Egyptian language and their different style of dress (EPHREM).

42:6 Joseph's Brothers Bow Before Him

GOD'S DISPENSATION. CHRYSOSTOM: They did all this out of ignorance for the time being. You see, it was a long time since they had last seen Joseph, and so they no longer recognized their brother's appearance. After all, it was likely that some change had occurred in him now that he had reached maturity. Still, I'm inclined to think that it all happened as a result of the dispensation of the God of all so that they would fail to recognize their brother either from conversing with him or by sight. After all, how on earth would they have formed such an idea? I mean, they were under the impression that he had become a slave of the Ishmaelites and by now was enduring slavery under the barbarians. Whereas they were in no position to conceive any other idea and so recognize Joseph, he recognized them as soon as he saw them and took every care to conceal his identity, wishing to deal with them as with foreigners. HOMILIES ON GENESIS 64.5.[1]

42:9 The Brothers Accused of Spying

IGNORANT OF THE EGYPTIAN LANGUAGE. EPHREM THE SYRIAN: They answered and said, "We do not even know the Egyptian language so that, by speaking Egyptian, we might escape notice and deceive the Egyptians. That we dwell in the land of Canaan you can learn from our offering. Moreover, there are twelve of us, and it is impossible that we should all have the same evil purpose of spying. We have come of our own will to stand before you. That we are completely ignorant of the Egyptian language and do not wear

the clothing of Egyptians also testifies to our truthfulness. It is clear that we are not spies, for we are twelve. We are recognized everywhere because of our race and our number. "Behold, one of our brothers is with our father and another is no more." COMMENTARY ON GENESIS 36.4.[2]

42:13 Twelve Brothers

THEY DID NOT ADMIT THEIR GUILT. CHRYSOSTOM: O what duplicity! They included in the number even the one sold to merchants and said not "We were twelve" but "We are twelve; see, the youngest is with our father." This in fact was what Joseph was anxious to learn, whether or not they had treated their brother in the same way. "See, the youngest is with our father, while the other one is no longer alive." They did not admit their guilt openly but said simply, "He is no longer alive." From this he arrived at the suspicion that they had done the same thing to Benjamin as well, and so he replied, "That is what I said to you—you are spies. In fact, you are not to leave here until your youngest brother comes here."[3] I want to see him, I desire to set my eyes on the one who caused the same birth pangs as I. Actually, I suspect the same hatred for your brother as you displayed toward me. So if you are prepared to, "send one of your number and bring him here to me";[4] as for yourselves, stay in prison until he arrives. You see, when he arrives he will clear you of all suspicion. If in fact this doesn't happen, it will be clear that you are spies and have come here for that purpose. With these words "he put them in jail."[5] HOMILIES ON GENESIS 64.7.[6]

---

[1]FC 87:226*. [2]FC 91:189. [3]Gen 42:14-15. [4]Gen 42:16. [5]Gen 42:17. [6]FC 87:227-28.

42:18-25 JOSEPH GIVES GRAIN TO HIS BROTHERS

[18]*On the third day Joseph said to them, "Do this and you will live, for I fear God:* [19]*if you are honest men, let one of your brothers remain confined in your prison, and let the rest go and carry grain for the famine of your households,* [20]*and bring your youngest brother to me; so your words will be verified, and you shall not die." And they did so.* [21]*Then they said to one another, "In truth we are guilty concerning our brother, in that we saw the distress of his soul, when he besought us and we would not listen; therefore is this distress come upon us."* [22]*And Reuben answered them, "Did I not tell you not to sin against the lad? But you would not listen. So now there comes a reckoning for his blood."* [23]*They did not know that Joseph understood them, for there was an interpreter between them.* [24]*Then he turned away from them and wept; and he returned to them and spoke to them. And he took Simeon from them and bound him before their eyes.* [25]*And Joseph gave orders to fill their bags with grain, and to replace every man's money in his sack, and to give them provisions for the journey. This was done for them.**

OVERVIEW: The danger in which the brothers find themselves helps them to clear their minds of the dense fog caused by sin and to admit their guilt. Joseph's order to bind Simeon is for the purpose of testing his brothers, to see whether they show any sign of affection (CHRYSOSTOM). Joseph's seemingly hard conduct toward his brothers can be defended on the grounds that he wanted to arouse them to a confession of sin and the healing of repentance (CAESARIUS OF ARLES). In a typological interpretation Joseph prefigures Christ, Benjamin the apostle Paul, and Simeon the apostle Peter bound by the threefold chain of denial (QUODVULTDEUS).

42:21 Guilty Indeed

SIN BLINDS THE INTELLECT. CHRYSOSTOM: This, you see, is what sin is like: when it is done and takes effect, then it shows the excess of its own impropriety. Just as an inebriate imbibes great quantities of drink without feeling any harmful effects of the wine but later comes to know the extent of the damage from his exploits, so too with sin. When it is committed, it clouds the mind, and like a dense fog it blinds the intellect, but later conscience is stirred and flays the mind unmercifully with every kind of accusation, highlighting the impropriety of what was done. Notice, after all, in this case too, these men coming to their senses, and, when they saw danger pressing upon them from all sides, they then admitted what had been done by them and said, "True, we are being punished for our brother since we ignored his distress of spirit." It is not idly or to no purpose, they are saying, that we suffer this, but rightly so, and quite rightly: we are paying the penalty for the inhumanity and savagery we displayed toward our brother. "We ignored his distress of spirit when he pleaded with us without our heeding him." Since we proved lacking in compassion, they say, and displayed great savagery, hence we too now experience the same: "So for this reason this distress has come upon us." HOMILIES ON GENESIS 64.9.[1]

JOSEPH'S PURPOSE WAS TO CORRECT THEM. CAESARIUS OF ARLES: If we notice carefully, dear-

---

[1]FC 87:228-29.

ly beloved, we will realize that Joseph did to his brothers what we believe God did to blessed Jacob. Truly he was so holy that he could not have hated them. Therefore we must believe that he wearied them with so many tribulations, in order to arouse them to a confession of their sin and the healing of repentance. Finally, with great grief, they said they suffered those ills deservedly, because they had sinned against their brother, "whose anguish of heart they witnessed." Since blessed Joseph knew that his brothers could not be forgiven their sin of murder without much penance, once, twice and a third time he worried them with salutary trials as with a spiritual fire. His purpose was not to vindicate himself but to correct them and free them from so grave a sin. Furthermore, before they confessed their sin and consumed the crime that they had committed by mutual reproaches, he did not cause himself to be recognized or give them the kiss of peace. However, when Joseph saw them humbly afflicted for the sin they had committed, he kissed them one by one and wept over each one, moistening their necks as they trembled in fear with the dew of his tears and washing away the hatred of his brothers with the tears of charity. SERMON 91.6.[2]

42:24 Simeon Bound

PETER AND PAUL. QUODVULTDEUS: Hearing people talk about his brother, Joseph longed for him and said, "I will prove in this manner that you are not spies, if your younger brother comes along with you."[3] And taking Simeon from them he had him bound before him and sent him to prison.[4] If you want to know who is Benjamin, our younger brother, desired by our Joseph, that is, Christ, he is Paul, formerly Saul, from the tribe of Benjamin according to his testimony,[5] who asserts to be the least among the apostles.[6] In Simeon we can recognize Peter bound by the threefold chain of denial, that Peter whom fear has bound and love has untied. BOOK OF PROMISES AND PREDICTIONS OF GOD 1.30.42.[7]

SIGNS OF AFFECTION. CHRYSOSTOM: See how Joseph takes every means of putting fear into them so that, on seeing Simeon's bonds, they may reveal whether they manifested any sympathy for their brother. You see, everything he does is to test their attitude out of his wish to discover if they had been like that in dealing with Benjamin. Hence Joseph also had Simeon bound in front of them to test them carefully and see if they showed any signs of affection for him. That is to say, concern for Simeon led them to hasten Benjamin's arrival, which he was anxious for, so as to gain assurance from his brother's arrival. HOMILIES ON GENESIS 64.11.[8]

---

[2]FC 47:52. [3]Gen 42:14-15. [4]Gen 42:24. [5]Phil 3:5. [6]1 Cor 15:9. [7]SC 101:244-46. [8]FC 87:230*.

42:26-28 THE BROTHERS FIND THEIR MONEY

[26]*Then they loaded their asses with their grain, and departed.* [27]*And as one of them opened his sack to give his ass provender at the lodging place, he saw his money in the mouth of his sack;* [28]*and he said to his brothers, "My money has been put back; here it is in the mouth of my sack!" At this their hearts failed them, and they turned trembling to one another, saying, "What is this that God has done to us?"*

OVERVIEW: The grain given the brothers symbolizes God's mysteries that cannot be bought with money but can only be obtained by grace, and so their money is returned to them (AMBROSE).

42:28 What Has God Done?

ABUNDANCE GREATER THAN FAMINE.

AMBROSE: "There is grain in Egypt"; that is, where the famine is greater, the abundance is greater. There is much grain in Egypt. Surely, and God the Father says, "Out of Egypt I called my son!"[1] Such is the fecundity of that grain, for there could not have been a harvest unless the Egyptians had sown the grain earlier. There is then grain that no one earlier believed to exist. The patriarchs engaged in negotiations in regard to this grain. And they indeed brought money, but the good Joseph gave them the grain and gave them back the money.[2] For Christ is not bought with money but with grace. Your payment is faith, and with it are bought God's mysteries. Moreover, this grain is carried by the ass,[3] which before was unclean according to the law but now is clean in grace.[4] ON JOSEPH 8.45.[5]

---

[1]Cf. Hos 11:1; Mt 2:15. [2]Gen 42:25-28. [3]Gen 44:3. [4]Cf. Jn 12:14-15; Zech 9:9. [5]FC 65:219*.

42:29-38 THE BROTHERS RETURN AND JACOB REFUSES TO LET BENJAMIN GO

[29]When they came to Jacob their father in the land of Canaan, they told him all that had befallen them, saying, [30]"The man, the lord of the land, spoke roughly to us, and took us to be spies of the land. [31]But we said to him, 'We are honest men, we are not spies; [32]we are twelve brothers, sons of our father; one is no more, and the youngest is this day with our father in the land of Canaan.' [33]Then the man, the lord of the land, said to us, 'By this I shall know that you are honest men: leave one of your brothers with me, and take grain for the famine of your households, and go your way. [34]Bring your youngest brother to me; then I shall know that you are not spies but honest men, and I will deliver to you your brother, and you shall trade in the land.'"

[35]As they emptied their sacks, behold, every man's bundle of money was in his sack; and when they and their father saw their bundles of money, they were dismayed. [36]And Jacob their father said to them, "You have bereaved me of my children: Joseph is no more, and Simeon is no more, and now you would take Benjamin; all this has come upon me." [37]Then Reuben said to his father, "Slay my two sons if I do not bring him back to you; put him in my hands, and I will bring him back to you." [38]But he said, "My son shall not go down with you, for his brother is dead, and he only is left. If harm should befall him on the journey that you are to make, you would bring down my gray hairs with sorrow to Sheol."

OVERVIEW: Joseph's apparently harsh behavior that causes such distress to his father, Jacob, can be justified on the grounds that it was part of the divine dispensation and was aimed at cleansing

Jacob of even his slight offenses, an interpretation that perhaps owes something to the heritage of the Pelagian controversy (CAESARIUS OF ARLES). Joseph's brothers plead with Jacob to send Benjamin, trying to soften his refusal by urging him to think of Simeon's sons and his wife (EPHREM).

42:36 Bereaved of My Children

GOD ACTED WITH GREAT MERCY. CAESARIUS OF ARLES: Now notice a still greater wonder and see how blessed Joseph, who knew that his father suffered intolerable sorrow on his account, as if what he had endured before were not enough, now causes Benjamin to be taken from him. Surely by this act he knew that his father would suffer increased grief. I do not believe that all these things happened without the dispensation of the Holy Spirit. God, whose judgments are often hidden but never unjust and who refused to notify blessed Jacob that his son was living, likewise did not allow holy Joseph to declare his glory to his father. Rather, as was said, by keeping Simeon in bonds and taking away Benjamin, he increased the distress of his father. If we heed these facts devoutly and carefully, dearly beloved, we realize that God acted with great mercy. Since the beginning of the world he has done to his saints what he fulfilled in blessed Jacob with great kindness. However, notice carefully why this happened.

Although servants and friends of God have avoided capital sins and perform many good works, still we do not believe that they have been without slight offenses, because God does not lie when he says, "Not even an infant one day old upon the earth is without sin."[1] Moreover, blessed John the Evangelist, who surely was not inferior to holy Jacob in merits, proclaims, "If we say that we have no sin, we deceive ourselves, and the truth is not in us."[2] Furthermore, we read elsewhere: "The just man falls seven times and rises again."[3] Therefore, since blessed Jacob could not be without those slight sins, as was already said, God wanted to consume those small offenses in

this world by the fire of tribulation. Thus was fulfilled in him what God said through the Holy Spirit: "As the test of what the potter molds is in the furnace, so in his conversation is the test of a man."[4] Moreover, "God scourges every son whom he received,"[5] and "through many tribulations we must enter the kingdom of God."[6] Therefore, in order that our God might present holy Jacob as purified gold at the future judgment, he first removed all the stains of sin from him, so that the other fiery witness might be able to find in him nothing to burn. SERMON 91.3-4.[7]

42:38 Benjamin Shall Not Go

THE BROTHERS PLEAD WITH JACOB. EPHREM THE SYRIAN: After they had loaded their supplies, the [brothers] went up and related to their father the evils that they had endured on this trip and how they had become objects of ridicule in Egypt, having been falsely accused of spying in Egypt, and that they would not have escaped this suffering had it not been for Benjamin. While some of them were recounting these things to their father, the others were emptying their sacks, and behold, each one found his money in the opening of his sack.

Jacob was full of grief because of all that had happened to them, but even more because of Simeon who was imprisoned. Although the brothers implored him daily to send Benjamin with them, Jacob would not assent because of his fear due to [what had happened to] Joseph. Then, when their grain had run out and all the children of his household were languishing from hunger, all his sons drew near and said to Jacob, "Spare Simeon for the sake of his children and be without your youngest son for a few days, lest Simeon's wife be widowed of Simeon." COMMENTARY ON GENESIS 37.1-2.[8]

---

[1]Job 14:4. [2]1 Jn 1:8. [3]Prov 24:16. [4]Sir 27:6. [5]Heb 12:6. [6]Acts 14:21. [7]FC 47:50-51. [8]FC 91:191.

43:1-15 THE SONS OF JACOB
DEPART AGAIN WITH BENJAMIN

[1]Now the famine was severe in the land. [2]And when they had eaten the grain which they had brought from Egypt, their father said to them, "Go again, buy us a little food." [3]But Judah said to him, "The man solemnly warned us, saying, 'You shall not see my face, unless your brother is with you.' [4]If you will send our brother with us, we will go down and buy you food; [5]but if you will not send him, we will not go down, for the man said to us, 'You shall not see my face, unless your brother is with you.'" [6]Israel said, "Why did you treat me so ill as to tell the man that you had another brother?" [7]They replied, "The man questioned us carefully about ourselves and our kindred, saying, 'Is your father still alive? Have you another brother?' What we told him was in answer to these questions; could we in any way know that he would say, 'Bring your brother down'?" [8]And Judah said to Israel his father, "Send the lad with me, and we will arise and go, that we may live and not die, both we and you and also our little ones. [9]I will be surety for him; of my hand you shall require him. If I do not bring him back to you and set him before you, then let me bear the blame for ever; [10]for if we had not delayed, we would now have returned twice."

[11]Then their father Israel said to them, "If it must be so, then do this: take some of the choice fruits of the land in your bags, and carry down to the man a present, a little balm and a little honey, gum, myrrh, pistachio nuts, and almonds. [12]Take double the money with you; carry back with you the money that was returned in the mouth of your sacks; perhaps it was an oversight. [13]Take also your brother, and arise, go again to the man; [14]may God Almighty[p] grant you mercy before the man, that he may send back your other brother and Benjamin. If I am bereaved of my children, I am bereaved." [15]So the men took the present, and they took double the money with them, and Benjamin; and they arose and went down to Egypt, and stood before Joseph.

p Heb El Shaddai

OVERVIEW: In an allegorical reading of the text, Reuben and Judah, representing humility and confession as well as the law and the gospel, lead Benjamin, who prefigures the apostle Paul, to Egypt (AMBROSE). Jacob, constrained by the famine, reluctantly consents to send Benjamin, and they depart with the choice fruits of the land (EPHREM).

43:11 Choice Fruits as a Present

THE LAW AND THE GOSPEL. AMBROSE: Never-

theless Benjamin, the youngest, was kept back and still stayed close to his loving father. The bonds of the law held him back, and ancestral custom. The famine was increasing because he was coming late.[1] Two brothers, Reuben and Judah—that is, humility and confession—make intercession on his behalf. He has them as guarantees with his father; to them Benjamin is entrusted. One of them is the firstborn, the other restored to life. The firstborn represents the law;

[1]Gen 43:1-14.

the one restored to life, the gospel. The young Benjamin is led down by them and arrives, accompanied by good fragrances and carrying with him the cement with which stones of marble are fastened together; thus by his own preaching as by a spiritual cement he might fasten together living stones. He also carries honey, which destroys the harmful effects of an internal wound, without the bitter pain of any cutting. Such indeed was the preaching of Paul that it destroyed the festering infection and drained off the tainted fluid with the sting of its argument, for it sought rather to cauterize the sick vitals of the heart than to cut them. That the incense is a sign of prayer[2] and the cassia and aloes are signs of burial, David the psalmist taught us when he said, "myrrh and aloes and cassia from your garments."[3] For Paul came to preach the cross of the Lord, an oak that is always verdant. And almonds appear, which are rather hard in the shell but more tender in the meat—it was right that Aaron's priestly rod was of the almond tree,[4] and Jeremiah's staff as well[5]—double money too.[6] Who would doubt that these gifts were useful? For the life of the patriarch and the preaching of the apostle are always verdant in the heart of each person, and the speech of the saints shines brightly with the splendor of the precept of salvation, like silver tried by the fire.[7] And it is with reason that they carry double money, for in them there is prefigured the coming of Paul, who presented presbyters who labor in the word and in the teaching with a double honor.[8] ON JOSEPH 9.46.[9]

43:13 Take Benjamin with You

JACOB WAS CONSTRAINED BY THE FAMINE.
EPHREM THE SYRIAN: Then Jacob was constrained by the famine, whether he was willing or not, to send Benjamin with them. So he gave them supplies and sent them off with blessings and said, "Just as I was bereaved of Rachel, so am I now bereaved of Rachel's children."[10] Judah comforted his father and said, "If I do not bring back Benjamin and set him before you, then let me bear the blame forever."[11] Then they took some of the choice fruits of the land: gum, pistachio nuts, which are berries, and so forth. They then went down and stood before Joseph. Joseph commanded his steward to give them lodging in his house.[12] COMMENTARY ON GENESIS 37.3.[13]

---

[2]Ps 141:2 (140:2 LXX). [3]Ps 45:8 (44:9 LXX). [4]Num 17:8. [5]Jer 1:11-12. [6]Gen 43:12, 15. [7]Ps 12:6 (11:7 LXX). [8]1 Tim 5:17. [9]FC 65:219-20. [10]Gen 43:14. [11]Gen 43:9. [12]Gen 43:15-16. [13]FC 91:191.

43:16-25 THE BROTHERS PREPARE TO MEET JOSEPH

[16]*When Joseph saw Benjamin with them, he said to the steward of his house, "Bring the men into the house, and slaughter an animal and make ready, for the men are to dine with me at noon."* [17]*The man did as Joseph bade him, and brought the men to Joseph's house.* [18]*And the men were afraid because they were brought to Joseph's house, and they said, "It is because of the money, which was replaced in our sacks the first time, that we are brought in, so that he may seek occasion against us and fall upon us, to make slaves of us and seize our asses."* [19]*So they went up to the steward of Joseph's house, and spoke with him at the door of the house,* [20]*and said, "Oh, my lord, we*

came down the first time to buy food; ^{21}*and when we came to the lodging place we opened our sacks, and there was every man's money in the mouth of his sack, our money in full weight; so we have brought it again with us,* ^{22}*and we have brought other money down in our hand to buy food. We do not know who put our money in our sacks."* ^{23}*He replied, "Rest assured, do not be afraid; your God and the God of your father must have put treasure in your sacks for you; I received your money." Then he brought Simeon out to them.* ^{24}*And when the man had brought the men into Joseph's house, and given them water, and they had washed their feet, and when he had given their asses provender,* ^{25}*they made ready the present for Joseph's coming at noon, for they heard that they should eat bread there.*

OVERVIEW: The brothers are seized with fear when they are brought into Joseph's house because of the money that had been placed in their sacks, and they suspect treachery. Joseph's steward puts them at ease, assuring them that his master is just (EPHREM). In an allegorical interpretation the steward's answer is to be interpreted mystically: Christ is the master and Moses, Peter and Paul are stewards. The money in their sacks represents the true spiritual gift given by Christ (AMBROSE).

43:18 He May Make Us Slaves

IT IS BECAUSE OF THE MONEY. EPHREM THE SYRIAN: But when the [brothers] saw Joseph's servants hurrying to unburden their beasts and to bring in their baggage, they said to themselves, grieving, "We have bereaved our father of Benjamin, and we shall never again see the face of our father. It was with treachery that our money was put into the openings of our packs, so that if we escape [the charge of] spying they might seize us and make us slaves [on the charge] of theft. Let us confess to the steward about the money before he begins to accuse us so that our brother Benjamin might free us from [the charge of] spying and the confession of our lips from [the charge of] theft." COMMENTARY ON GENESIS 37.4.[1]

43:19 Joseph's Steward

THE TRUTH THAT IS FOUND. EPHREM THE SYRIAN: Then the [brothers] approached Joseph's steward and said to him, "When we returned the first time we opened our sacks, and behold, there was each one's money in the opening of his sack. We are now returning it to you because it is not right that we take the money for the grain together with the grain."[2] But when the steward saw how terrified they were, he consoled them and said, "Rest assured, do not be afraid. It is not because of the money, which I received, that we are bringing you into this house.[3] We have eagerly awaited you because of the truth that is found among you. You are not going to be condemned for something that you did not take. You have been summoned to recline and be seated before our master, for he is just, and by the honor that he has reserved for you this second time, he wishes to make you forget the disgrace that you endured the first time." COMMENTARY ON GENESIS 37.5.[4]

THEY PREFERRED TO BE JUSTIFIED BY THEIR WORKS. AMBROSE: And they began to desire to plead their case to the man who was steward of the house at the door of the house.[5] They still hesitate to enter in and prefer to be justified from their works,[6] for they desire to prove a case rather than to receive grace, and so they are refuted at the gates. But the one who awaits the fruit of the Virgin's womb and the inheritance of the Lord is

---

[1]FC 91:191-92. [2]Gen 43:20-22. [3]Gen 43:23. [4]FC 91:192. [5]Gen 43:19-24. [6]See Gal 2:16.

dealing in the goods of the Son and is not ashamed at the gate. Rather, at the end of this life he drives back the enemy so that the latter, who is aware of his quite serious guilt, may not hinder him as he hastens to higher things. On this account, the steward answered them in a mystical sense. And know who this is, when you read that Moses was faithful in all his house. For Moses and Peter and Paul and the other saints are the stewards, but Christ alone is the master. It is written, "Moses was faithful in all his house as a servant for a testimony of those things which had been said, but Christ as the Son in his own house, which house we are, if we hold fast liberty and the glory of the hope."[7] ON JOSEPH 9.48-49.[8]

43:23 Your God and Your Father's God

CHRIST IS THE GIFT OF GLADNESS. AMBROSE: They indeed had said to him, "We found the money of each one of us in our sacks. We have brought back our money in full weight."[9] O mighty mysteries, and mysteries clearly portrayed! This is to say: Why are you puffed up? Do you assume too often that the money you have in your sacks is your own? What indeed do you have which you have not received? But if you have received it, why do you boast as if you have not received it? Now you have been satisfied, you have become rich;[10] you believe that you possess the money, but the God of your fathers has given the money to you. He is your God, he is the God of your ancestors, and you have denied him. But he grants pardon and forgiveness and receives you back if you should return. He is the one who does not ask your money but gives his own. He has given you money in your sacks. Now your sacks hold mon-

ey that used to hold mire; and therefore he is your companion who says, "You have cut off my sackcloth and have clothed me with gladness."[11] The gift of gladness is Christ. He is your money; he is your price. The Lord Jesus does not demand from you the price of his grain, does not ask the weight of your money. Your money is unsound; the money in your purse is not good. "I have received your good money";[12] that is, it is not your material money but your spiritual money that is good. You have brought it down out of faith and devotion like the sons of Jacob; it is expended without loss and is counted out without any deficit, seeing that for such a price the loss that is death is avoided and the profit that is life is gained. ON JOSEPH 9.50-51.[13]

43:25 The Present for Joseph

NOON SYMBOLIZES THE OPTIMAL LIGHT OF JUSTICE. AMBROSE: "And they made ready the presents, until Joseph came at noon." Paul's faith hastened the coming of noon. Before, Paul was blind; afterward he began to see the light of justice, because if anyone opens his way to the Lord and hopes in him, the Lord will also bring forth his justice as the light and his judgment as the noon.[14] And when God appeared to Abraham by the oak of Mamre, it was noon, and the everlasting light from the Lord's presence shone on him.[15] It is noon when the real Joseph enters into his house to dine. The day shines more at that time, when we celebrate the sacred mysteries. ON JOSEPH 10.52.[16]

---

[7]Heb 3:5-6. [8]FC 65:221. [9]Gen 43:21. [10]See 1 Cor 4:7-8. [11]Ps 30:11 (29:12 LXX). [12]Gen 43:23. [13]FC 65:222. [14]Ps 37:5-6 (36:5-6 LXX); Wis 5:6. [15]Gen 18:1. The LXX text speaks of an oak. [16]FC 65:223.

43:26-34 THE BROTHERS MEET JOSEPH

²⁶*When Joseph came home, they brought into the house to him the present which they had with them, and bowed down to him to the ground.* ²⁷*And he inquired about their welfare, and said, "Is your father well, the old man of whom you spoke? Is he still alive?"* ²⁸*They said, "Your servant our father is well, he is still alive." And they bowed their heads and made obeisance.* ²⁹*And he lifted up his eyes, and saw his brother Benjamin, his mother's son, and said, "Is this your youngest brother, of whom you spoke to me? God be gracious to you, my son!"* ³⁰*Then Joseph made haste, for his heart yearned for his brother, and he sought a place to weep. And he entered his chamber and wept there.* ³¹*Then he washed his face and came out; and controlling himself he said, "Let food be served."* ³²*They served him by himself, and them by themselves, and the Egyptians who ate with him by themselves, because the Egyptians might not eat bread with the Hebrews, for that is an abomination to the Egyptians.* ³³*And they sat before him, the first-born according to his birthright and the youngest according to his youth; and the men looked at one another in amazement.* ³⁴*Portions were taken to them from Joseph's table, but Benjamin's portion was five times as much as any of theirs. So they drank and were merry with him.*

Overview: Joseph gives a moral lesson by his practice of consideration and courtesy. Allegorically Joseph represents Christ and Benjamin the apostle Paul. Joseph's affection for his younger brother, Benjamin, brought him to tears (Ambrose). Joseph's behavior toward his brothers causes them to take heart and puts them at ease. It was because of the Lord that the brothers still did not recognize Joseph until his dreams should be fulfilled in them (Ephrem). The mention that they drank and were merry with Joseph echoes Noah's inebriation and suggests a mystical anticipation of the apostles at Pentecost filled with the Spirit (Jerome).

43:26 The Brothers Bowed to Joseph

Joseph's Consideration and Courtesy.
Ambrose: "And they brought him the presents." We bring the presents; he renews the banquet.[1] He says, "Serve the bread,"[2] which the Hebrews take by themselves, but the Egyptians cannot eat it.[3] But how generous was his kindness before the banquet! What a moral lesson in his practice of consideration and courtesy! The brothers were still suspicious concerning the false accusation that they thought was being prepared against them by Joseph. He invited them to dinner. Their inclination wavered; his kindness persevered. He is the first to speak, the first to ask, "How are you?" And again he says, "Is the old man your father well?"[4] It is the part of a superior to invite the inferior to conversation, to inspire confidence in his discourse, to ask not only after them but also after their parents. They answer him, "Your servant, our father, is well."[5] Joseph said "the old man" so as to do him honor; they called him "servant" so as to offer the service of their humility. "Old age" suggests honor and dignity, whereas "servitude" appears submissive and more closely related to modesty than to pride. On Joseph 10.53-55.[6]

---

[1]There is probably intended here a reference to the eucharistic meal. [2]Gen 43:31. [3]Gen 43:32-34. [4]Gen 43:27. [5]Gen 43:28. [6]FC 65:223-24.

43:27 Joseph Inquires About Jacob

THEY TOOK HEART. EPHREM THE SYRIAN:
When Joseph entered the house, his brothers
brought him an offering and bowed down to him
trembling. He inquired about their welfare, and
they took heart. He asked if their father was alive,
and they were put at ease. He asked whether that
one was their brother, and he blessed him and said,
"God be gracious to you my son," and all fear was
taken from their mind.[7] It was in the Egyptian language that Joseph blessed Benjamin, and it was
through an interpreter that they heard these initial
[exchanges]. COMMENTARY ON GENESIS 37.6.[8]

43:29 Joseph Sees Benjamin

BENJAMIN PREFIGURES PAUL. AMBROSE: Moreover, "Joseph saw them and Benjamin his brother
by the same mother." The Hebrews are seen now,
and they are seen by Christ, who is the true Joseph, when they come with the figure who symbolizes Paul. And Joseph speaks to them gently and
mildly, inviting them to take food together. Earlier,
however, when they came without Benjamin, he
did not even recognize them but turned away from
them, as it is written, "and he spoke harshly to
them."[9] For they did not recognize him by whom
they were recognized. They advance, then, by the
merit of Paul, whom the Lord Jesus loved more
than the other brothers, as being a younger brother
begotten from the same mother. Let the Jews turn
to him whom they have denied to be their Lord.
Even though he was crucified from their synagogue, yet he loves them more as born of the same
parent, if only they come to know, even late, the
Author of their salvation. But being aware of their
own offenses, they do not believe that Christ is so
very merciful as to forgive their sin and pardon
their wrongdoing. And thus their future line of
conduct was prefigured in the patriarchs. They
were invited to grace, were summoned to the banquet of the table of salvation and suspected that a
false accusation was being readied against them
and an ambush was being laid. ON JOSEPH 9.47.[10]

WE SEE THOSE WE LOVE BEFORE OTHERS.
AMBROSE: Now "raising his eyes he saw Benjamin, his brother by the same mother." The moral sense is that we see those we love before others,
and the gaze of our eyes lights first on those
whom we consider first in our mind's eye. And
for the most part, when we are busy all around
with another mental employment, we do not see
those whom we find before our eyes. Thus our
sight is directed by the guidance of our mind.
And so, holy Joseph saw Benjamin his brother; he
remembered him, he looked for him, he almost
had not seen his brothers in Benjamin's absence
because the sight of them was of no help whatsoever. Neither was he satisfied only to have seen
him; as if not knowing him, Joseph asked, "Is this
your youngest brother?" It is the way and the favor of love that we should possess those we love
not only with our eyes but also by our conversation. Joseph had recognized his beloved brother,
but he asked for this reason, that he might speak
the name of him that he had in his heart. Indeed,
Joseph did not wait for a reply but at once blessed
him and was troubled at the attainment of his
wish. Now "his heart was tormented,"[11] because
his freedom to embrace the brother he longed for
was postponed. Thereupon, "entering into his
chamber he wept and washed his face and restrained himself."[12] The stings of a great love
swiftly prick the heart, unless the reins of desire
are relaxed. Joseph was being overcome by feeling
but put off by deliberation; reason was in contest
with love. He wept, so that he could moderate
the surges of his holy love. ON JOSEPH 10.56-57.[13]

**IN THE MYSTICAL SENSE THE LORD JESUS
SAW PAUL.** AMBROSE: The foregoing is in the
moral sense. In the mystical sense, however, the
Lord Jesus saw Paul—for "the eyes of the Lord
are upon the just"[14]—and said, "Is this your
youngest brother?" He is still called the youngest,
for he did not yet exhibit a venerable faith of ma-

---

[7]Gen 43:26-29. [8]FC 91:192. [9]Gen 42:7. [10]FC 65:220-21. [11]Gen
43:30. [12]Gen 43:30-31. [13]FC 65: 224. [14]Ps 34:15 (33:16 LXX).

ture age, and he had not yet grown into mature manhood, "into that measure of the age of the fullness of Christ,"[15] as Paul himself says. Indeed, he is called a young man only in that passage where he kept the garments of those who were stoning Stephen.[16] And on that account he desired that Philemon imitate not his youth but his old age, as he wrote, "I rather beseech, since you are such a one as Paul, an old man."[17] On that account he preaches that younger widows are to be refused, not by reason of their age but on account of a kind of wantonness in offenses that are reaching full growth and an immaturity in virtue.[18] But chastity merits greater praise in a young man than in one who is old. Moreover, I think it is not far from the truth if we adopt the following interpretation. Although Paul was struck and taken up and was terrified because blindness had befallen him, still he began to come near when he said, "Lord, what will you have me do?"[19] For that reason he is called the youngest by Christ, so that he who was called to grace could be excused from the guilt of his hazardous years. Yes, Christ saw him when the light shone round him;[20] because young men are recalled from sin more by fear than by reason, Christ applied the goad and mercifully admonished him not to kick against it.[21] ON JOSEPH 10.58.[22]

43:33 The Seating Amazes the Brothers

WHY JOSEPH REMAINED HIDDEN. EPHREM THE SYRIAN: Joseph began to make his brothers sit down as if around his [divining] cup; the elder according to his status as elder and the youngest according to his youth.[23] It is amazing that his brothers did not recognize him: not by the money in their provisions when they went home the first time, not when Joseph had Simeon bound, not when he asked about his old father when they brought Benjamin back, not when they were accused of cheating, not from the fact that he made them stay in his house and blessed Benjamin, not even from the fact that he knew the names of all of them. This was all the more [amazing] since

even his appearance was so similar. Even if his majesty had deluded them, his dreams should have jarred their memory. Although they did not recognize Joseph because of his majesty, his rank and his angry tongue, it was nevertheless because of the Lord that he remained hidden from them until his dreams should be fulfilled in them who had sold him in order to render them false. COMMENTARY ON GENESIS 37.7.[24]

43:34 Benjamin Receives More Portions Than Others

EXAMINE THE MYSTERY. JEROME: Joseph, as I was saying, was a holy man who conquered cruelty with true piety; who was sold into Egypt not by chance but that he might supply Egypt with food and his own brothers too, who had sold him. That Joseph invited his brothers to dine. But just listen to what happened: "And he drank, and became merry at noon."[25] Is that true, and is it literally possible that a holy man became drunk? Noah also was inebriated but had been really inebriated. Joseph had been intoxicated; Noah also was intoxicated in his own house. See, there is a mystery. First, let us review the mystery itself, and when we have done that, let us fathom its meaning. After the deluge, Noah drank and became drunk in his own house, and his thighs were uncovered, and he was exposed in his nakedness. The elder brother came along and laughed; the younger, however, covered him up.[26] All this is said in type of the Savior, for on the cross he had drunk of the passion: "Father, if it is possible, let this cup pass away from me."[27] He drank and was inebriated, and his thighs were laid bare—the dishonor of the cross. The older brothers, the Jews, came along and laughed; the younger, the Gentiles, covered up his disagreement. Hence the imprecation: "Cursed be Canaan; he shall be the lowest of slaves to his brothers."[28]

---

[15]Eph 4:13. [16]Acts 7:58. [17]Philem 9. [18]See 1 Tim 5:11. [19]Acts 9:6. [20]Acts 9:3. [21]Acts 9:5. [22]FC 65:224-25. [23]Gen 43:30-34. [24]FC 91:193*. [25]Gen 43:25, 34. [26]Gen 9:20-24. [27]Mt 26:39. [28]Gen 9:25.

Behold, that condemnation continues down to this day. We, the younger people, give orders to the older people, the Jews. As the Lord is inebriated in his passion, his saints are inebriated every day in the ardor of their faith, inebriated in the Holy Spirit. You, who yesterday were heaping together gold, today, you are throwing it away. Are you not a madman to those who do not know what it is all about? Finally, when the Holy Spirit descended upon the apostles and filled them, and they spoke many different languages; they were accused of being full of new wine.[29] HOMILIES ON THE PSALMS 13.[30]

---

[29]Acts 2:13. [30]FC 48:94-95*.

44:1-17 THE CUP IS FOUND IN BENJAMIN'S SACK

[1]*Then he commanded the steward of his house, "Fill the men's sacks with food, as much as they can carry, and put each man's money in the mouth of his sack,* [2]*and put my cup, the silver cup, in the mouth of the sack of the youngest, with his money for the grain." And he did as Joseph told him.* [3]*As soon as the morning was light, the men were sent away with their asses.* [4]*When they had gone but a short distance from the city, Joseph said to his steward, "Up, follow after the men; and when you overtake them, say to them, 'Why have you returned evil for good? Why have you stolen my silver cup?[q]* [5]*Is it not from this that my lord drinks, and by this that he divines? You have done wrong in so doing.'"*

[6]*When he overtook them, he spoke to them these words.* [7]*They said to him, "Why does my lord speak such words as these? Far be it from your servants that they should do such a thing!* [8]*Behold, the money which we found in the mouth of our sacks, we brought back to you from the land of Canaan; how then should we steal silver or gold from your lord's house?* [9]*With whomever of your servants it be found, let him die, and we also will be my lord's slaves."* [10]*He said, "Let it be as you say: he with whom it is found shall be my slave, and the rest of you shall be blameless."* [11]*Then every man quickly lowered his sack to the ground, and every man opened his sack.* [12]*And he searched, beginning with the eldest and ending with the youngest; and the cup was found in Benjamin's sack.* [13]*Then they rent their clothes, and every man loaded his ass, and they returned to the city.*

[14]*When Judah and his brothers came to Joseph's house, he was still there; and they fell before him to the ground.* [15]*Joseph said to them, "What deed is this that you have done? Do you not know that such a man as I can indeed divine?"* [16]*And Judah said, "What shall we say to my lord? What shall we speak? Or how can we clear ourselves? God has found out the guilt of your servants; behold, we are my lord's slaves, both we and he also in whose hand the cup has been found."* [17]*But*

he said, "Far be it from me that I should do so! Only the man in whose hand the cup was found shall be my slave; but as for you, go up in peace to your father."

q Gk Compare Vg: Heb lacks *Why have you stolen my silver cup?*

OVERVIEW: Because Paul was from the tribe of Benjamin, it is possible to see a parallel between the situation of Benjamin and that of Paul before his conversion (AMBROSE). Joseph's insistence that only Benjamin remain and be a slave is interpreted to be for his own good (EPHREM). The whole story of the finding of the cup reflects the light of God's mysterious plans, in particular his choice of Paul. The money in the sacks symbolizes Christ's gift of grace that he finds in us (AMBROSE).

44:2 The Silver Cup

THE DAY OF FAITH WAS NEAR. AMBROSE: And the silver cup is put in his sack alone.[1] Benjamin did not know this. So Paul was in error, but he was called. They sent after him in the morning; indeed, the night of his blindness had advanced, and the day of faith was near at hand.[2] ON JOSEPH 11.61.[3]

44:12 The Cup in Benjamin's Sack

THEY WERE CONFOUNDED. EPHREM THE SYRIAN: The brothers did not know what to say; they found it impossible not to put the blame on Benjamin because the cup had come out from his sack, but the money that had twice come out from their own sacks did not permit them to put the blame on him. Then the brothers, confounded by the things that had befallen them, rent their garments and went back weeping to that house from which they had just departed rejoicing.[4] COMMENTARY ON GENESIS 38.3.[5]

GOD'S MYSTERIOUS PLANS. AMBROSE: The sacks of the brothers are first examined according to the order of age of each brother. God's Scripture is teaching you a moral lesson. Previously they sat at the banquet in Joseph's presence in or-der of age from the firstborn.[6] You see that the place of honor is to be given to the eldest. On the other hand, the sacks of each are searched in order of age[7] so that you may know that Paul has been chosen by the judgment of heaven. The rest were examined, but this man was given the preference. The silver cup was not found in the sack of anyone else, only in his sack. What is the meaning of its being put in his humble sack? Joseph . . . sent the cup so that he might by a holy trick recall the brother whom he loved; yet the light of God's mysterious plans is clearly reflected. ON JOSEPH 11.62.[8]

CHRIST FINDS THIS MONEY IN US. AMBROSE: Christ finds this money in us which he has himself given us. We possess the money of nature; we also possess the money of grace. Nature is the work of the Creator, grace the gift of the Redeemer. Even though we are unable to see Christ's gifts, nevertheless he is giving them. He is working in a hidden way and is giving them to all people, but there are few who are able to keep them and not lose them. Yet he does not give all things to all people. Wheat is given to many, but the cup to one, who is presented with the prophetic and priestly function. For it is not everyone but only the prophet who says, "The cup of salvation I will take up, and I will call upon the name of the Lord."[9] Therefore the word of heavenly teaching already shone in Paul's body, since he was instructed in the law. But because he was still not subject to the justice of God, the cup was within the sack, the teaching within the law, the lamp within the bushel.[10] Nevertheless Ananias was sent to give a blessing and to lay on his hand and

---

[1]Gen 44:2. [2]See Rom 13:12. [3]FC 65:226*. [4]Gen 44:13. [5]FC 91:194. [6]Gen 43:33. [7]Gen 44:11-12. [8]FC 65:226-27. [9]Ps 116:13 (115:4 LXX). [10]Cf. Rom 6:20; Mt 5:15; Mk 4:21; Lk 11:33.

open the sack.[11] When the sack was opened, the money shone forth, and when the scales fell, in a way like fastenings on the sack, Paul saw straightway.[12] His fetter was unbelief; the loosening of it became faith. And for that reason, when the veil that is set over the heart of the Jews was set aside[13]—like the opening of the sack—he turned to the Lord. Free of the bond, he obtained the grace of liberty and said, "But we all, beholding the glory of God with faces unveiled, are transformed into the same image."[14] ON JOSEPH 11.63-64.[15]

44:16 God Has Found Our Guilt

BETTER FOR BENJAMIN. EPHREM THE SYRIAN: Then Judah said, "Before God the sins of your servants have been discovered"—not this one [of the cup] but the one for which we have been requited with these things." Therefore not only he in whose sack the cup was found but we also will become slaves to our master." And Joseph said, "Far be it from" the just Egyptian "to do this!"[16] These men, because of their great virtue, do not even eat bread with Hebrews lest they become unclean by them. How then can we do what is foreign to our conduct? The justice that hinders us from sinning against one who has not sinned against us compels us to be avenged on that one who has caused us offence. "The one in whose hand the cup was found shall remain and be a slave." This will be better for him than freedom, for this later servitude, which will free him from theft, will be better for him than that first freedom that enslaved him to theft.[17] COMMENTARY ON GENESIS 38.4.[18]

---

[11]See Acts 9:12, 17. [12]See Acts 9:18. [13]2 Cor 3:13-18. [14]2 Cor 3:18. [15]FC 65:227-28*. [16]Gen 44:17. [17]Gen 44:17. [18]FC 91:195.

[44:18-34 JUDAH PLEADS ON BEHALF OF HIS FATHER]

45:1-15 JOSEPH MAKES HIMSELF KNOWN TO HIS BROTHERS

[1]Then Joseph could not control himself before all those who stood by him; and he cried, "Make every one go out from me." So no one stayed with him when Joseph made himself known to his brothers. 2And he wept aloud, so that the Egyptians heard it, and the household of Pharaoh heard it. 3And Joseph said to his brothers, "I am Joseph; is my father still alive?" But his brothers could not answer him, for they were dismayed at his presence.

[4]So Joseph said to his brothers, "Come near to me, I pray you." And they came near. And he said, "I am your brother, Joseph, whom you sold into Egypt. [5]And now do not be distressed, or angry with yourselves, because you sold me here; for God sent me before you to preserve life. [6]For the famine has been in the land these two years; and there are yet five years in which there will be neither plowing nor harvest. [7]And God sent me before you to preserve for you a remnant on earth,

and to keep alive for you many survivors. [8]So it was not you who sent me here, but God; and he has made me a father to Pharaoh, and lord of all his house and ruler over all the land of Egypt. [9]Make haste and go up to my father and say to him, 'Thus says your son Joseph, God has made me lord of all Egypt; come down to me, do not tarry; [10]you shall dwell in the land of Goshen, and you shall be near me, you and your children and your children's children, and your flocks, your herds, and all that you have; [11]and there I will provide for you, for there are yet five years of famine to come; lest you and your household, and all that you have, come to poverty.' [12]And now your eyes see, and the eyes of my brother Benjamin see, that it is my mouth that speaks to you. [13]You must tell my father of all my splendor in Egypt, and of all that you have seen. Make haste and bring my father down here." [14]Then he fell upon his brother Benjamin's neck and wept; and Benjamin wept upon his neck. [15]And he kissed all his brothers and wept upon them; and after that his brothers talked with him.

OVERVIEW: Joseph's dramatic self-disclosure foreshadows the self-disclosure of Jesus, of whom Joseph is a type. Joseph's forgiveness of his brothers prefigures Christ's forgiveness on the cross. A series of parallels may be drawn between Joseph's behavior and that of Christ (AMBROSE). On a more literal level, Joseph's ability to conceal his identity up to this point shows his remarkable fortitude and equanimity, which are related to his ability to see all that takes place as part of God's providence (CHRYSOSTOM). Joseph appears now as a model not only of chastity but of generosity and true charity as well (CAESARIUS OF ARLES).

45:3 I Am Joseph

SIMILARLY JESUS STRETCHED OUT HIS HANDS. AMBROSE: And Joseph ordered all to withdraw so that he could be recognized by his brothers. For, even as Jesus said, he had not come except to the lost sheep that were the lost of the house of Israel.[1] And lifting up his voice with weeping he said, "I am Joseph. Is my father still alive?" This means, Jesus stretched out his hands to an unbelieving and contradicting people, for he did not seek an envoy or messenger but, as their very Lord, desired to save his own people.[2] "I myself who spoke, I am here,"[3] and "I was made manifest to those who sought me not; I appear to

those who asked me not."[4] What else did he cry out at that time but "I am Jesus"?[5] When the leaders of the Jews tempted him and asked, "Are you the Son of God?" he answered, "You say that I am," and to Pilate he said, "You say that I am a king; in this I was born."[6] And when the chief priest said, "I adjure you by the living God, that you tell us whether you are Christ, the Son of God,"[7] Jesus responded, "You have said it. Nevertheless I say to you, hereafter you shall see the Son of man sitting at the right hand of the power and coming upon the clouds of heaven."[8] This is what Joseph means when he says, "I am Joseph." ON JOSEPH 12.67.[9]

THEY WERE DUMBFOUNDED. CHRYSOSTOM: I cannot but be amazed here at this blessed man's remarkable fortitude in putting up with the strain of concealing his identity to this point and not letting on. And [I] am particularly surprised at the way they could stand there and gape without their soul parting company with their body, without their going out of their mind or hiding themselves in the ground. "His brothers were unable to say anything to him in reply. They were dumbfounded." No wonder! Aware of the way they had

---

[1]Mt 15:24. [2]Is 65:2; Ps 28:9 (27:9 LXX). [3]Is 52:6. [4]Is 65:1. [5]Jn 18:5, 8. [6]Jn 18:37. [7]Mt 26:63. [8]Mt 26:64. [9]FC 65:228-29.

treated Joseph, of his position in comparison with theirs and realizing the high office he had attained, they feared for their very lives, so to say. HOMILIES ON GENESIS 64.27.[10]

45:4 Your Brother, Joseph

CHRIST IS REVEALED. AMBROSE: "Come to me," because I have come near to you, yes, even so far that I made myself a sharer in your nature by taking on flesh. At least do not flee a partaker of your fellowship, if you do not know the Author of your salvation. "And they came to him, and he said, 'I am Joseph your brother, whom you sold into Egypt. Now therefore be not grieved, and let it not seem to you a hard case that you sold me here; for God sent me before you for life.'"[11] What fraternal devotion! . . . Christ would even excuse his brothers' crime and say that it was God's providence and not humanity's wickedness, since he was not offered up to death by humans but was sent by the Lord to life. What else is the meaning of that intervention made by our Lord Jesus Christ, who excelled all his brothers in holiness? When he was on the cross, Jesus said in behalf of the people, "Father, forgive them; for they do not know what they are doing."[12] . . . And when they were startled and panic-stricken and thought they saw a spirit, again Jesus said to them, "Why are you disturbed, and why do doubts arise in your hearts? See my hands and feet, that it is I myself. Feel and see, for a spirit does not have flesh and bones, as you see I have."[13] ON JOSEPH 12.68-69.[14]

GOD'S WISDOM AND INEFFABLE LOVE. CHRYSOSTOM: "Don't be hard on yourselves; don't think," Joseph says, "that you did these things to me out of your intent. It was not so much from your malice in my regard as from God's wisdom and ineffable love that I should come here and now be in a favorable position to provide nourishment to you and the whole country." HOMILIES ON GENESIS 64.28.[15]

45:9 Reassurance for Jacob

HE WHO SPOKE BEFORE IN JOSEPH AND AFTERWARD IN HIS OWN BODY. AMBROSE: Indeed they are expressed in the same words, so that we may know that Jesus is the same who spoke before in Joseph and afterward in his own body, seeing that he did not change even the words. For at that time Jesus said, "Be not grieved,"[16] and later, "Go up to my father and say to him, 'Thus says your son Joseph: God has made me master of the whole land of Egypt.'" And in the Gospel Christ says, "Do not be afraid. Go, tell my brothers to go into Galilee, and there they shall see me."[17] And later he says, "All power in heaven and on earth has been given to me,"[18] which is to say, "This was the doing of God's design in order that I might receive power, and not the work of human cruelty." He who is counting out the reward does not reproach the crime. Now as to what appears in Genesis, "for God sent me before you to life,"[19] Christ repeats this in the Gospel when he says, "Teach all nations, baptizing them in the name of the Father, and of the Son and of the Holy Spirit."[20] For this is the recompense and the life of the saints, that they have also brought about the redemption of others. And notice that the following too was not written without purpose in Genesis, "And you will be near me, you and your sons and your sons' sons."[21] For this is what Christ said in the Gospel, "Behold, I am with you all days, even unto the consummation of the world."[22] How clear also is that mystery! For when every commandment had been fulfilled, so to speak, Joseph embraced his brother Benjamin and fell upon his neck.[23] Likewise, when the gospel is brought to completion, Christ embraces Paul in the arms of his mercy, as it were, so as to lift him up into heaven. ON JOSEPH 12.70-73.[24]

---

[10]FC 87:238-39*. [11]Gen 45:4-5. [12]Lk 23:34. [13]Lk 24:38-39. [14]FC 65:229-30*. [15]FC 87:239. [16]Gen 45:5. [17]Mt 28:10. [18]Mt 28:18. [19]Gen 45:5. [20]Mt 28:19. [21]Gen 45:10. [22]Mt 28:20. [23]Gen 45:14. [24]FC 65:230-31.

Let Us Comfort Those Badly Disposed to Us. Chrysostom: That servitude, Joseph is saying, procured for me this position. That sale brought me to this prominence. That distress proved the occasion of this honor for me. That envy produced this glory for me. Let us not simply hear this but also emulate it. In the same way let us comfort those badly disposed to us, relieving them of responsibility for what has been done to us and putting up with everything with great equanimity, like this remarkable man. Homilies on Genesis 64.29.[25]

45:15 Joseph Reconciles with His Brothers

Tears of Charity Wash Away Former Enmity. Caesarius of Arles: You have admired the chastity of Joseph; now behold his generosity. He repays hatred with charity. When he saw his brothers, or rather enemies in his broth-ers, he gave evidence of the affection of his love by his pious grief when he wanted to be recognized by them. He tenderly kissed each one of them and wept over them individually. As Joseph moistened the necks of his frightened brothers with his refreshing tears, he washed away their hatred with the tears of his charity. He loved them always as with the love of their living father and dead brother. He did not recall that pit into which he had been thrown to be murdered; he did not think of himself, a brother, sold for a price. Instead, by returning good for evil, even then he fulfilled the precepts of the apostles that were not yet given. Therefore, by considering the sweetness of true charity, blessed Joseph, with God's help, was eager to repel from his heart the poison of envy with which he knew his brothers had been struck. Sermon 90.4.[26]

---

[25]FC 87:239-40. [26]FC 47:45-46.

45:16-20 PHARAOH'S INVITATION

[16]*When the report was heard in Pharaoh's house, "Joseph's brothers have come," it pleased Pharaoh and his servants well. [17]And Pharaoh said to Joseph, "Say to your brothers, 'Do this: load your beasts and go back to the land of Canaan; [18]and take your father and your households, and come to me, and I will give you the best of the land of Egypt, and you shall eat the fat of the land.' [19]Command them[r] also, 'Do this: take wagons from the land of Egypt for your little ones and for your wives, and bring your father, and come. [20]Give no thought to your goods, for the best of all the land of Egypt is yours.'"*

r Compare Gk Vg: Heb *you are commanded*

Overview: Pharaoh and his servants are pleased at the news of the arrival of Joseph's brothers, for they had believed that such a person could only be the son of a freeman (Ephrem). The rejoicing in Pharaoh's house and his invitation to Joseph's brothers and father foreshadow the rejoicing of the Christian people at the redemption of the Jews (Ambrose).

45:16 Joseph's Brothers Have Arrived

The Princes Entered Rejoicing. Ephrem the Syrian: When the things that needed to be said between them were finished, the doors of that judgment room were opened. The princes entered rejoicing and the army commanders full of gladness. This news was pleasing in the eyes of Pharaoh and his servants, for they had believed that he who had become like a father to Pharaoh and ruler over the freemen and princes of Egypt was no slave but was a son of a freeman from the blessed race of the house of Abraham. COMMENTARY ON GENESIS 40.1.[1]

A GREAT MYSTERY WAS BEING REVEALED.
AMBROSE: And Pharaoh rejoiced because Joseph had known his brothers. From there the news spread in Pharaoh's house, and he urged the holy

Joseph to invite his brothers to come with their father. He also gives orders that their packs be filled with grain and loaded onto wagons.[2] What can account for such consideration shown to a stranger? Only that a great mystery was being revealed, a mystery the church today does not deny. The Jews will be redeemed; the Christian people will rejoice at this union, give aid to the limit of their resources and send people to preach the good news of the kingdom of God,[3] so that their call may come sooner. ON JOSEPH 13.74.[4]

---

[1]FC 91:196. [2]Gen 45:16-20. [3]See Lk 8:1. [4]FC 65:231-32.

45:21-28 THE RETURN TO CANAAN

[21]The sons of Israel did so; and Joseph gave them wagons, according to the command of Pharaoh, and gave them provisions for the journey. [22]To each and all of them he gave festal garments;* but to Benjamin he gave three hundred shekels of silver and five festal garments. [23]To his father he sent as follows: ten asses loaded with the good things of Egypt, and ten she-asses loaded with grain, bread, and provision for his father on the journey. [24]Then he sent his brothers away, and as they departed, he said to them, "Do not quarrel on the way." [25]So they went up out of Egypt, and came to the land of Canaan to their father Jacob. [26]And they told him, "Joseph is still alive, and he is ruler over all the land of Egypt." And his heart fainted, for he did not believe them. [27]But when they told him all the words of Joseph, which he had said to them, and when he saw the wagons which Joseph had sent to carry him, the spirit of their father Jacob revived; [28]and Israel said, "It is enough;† Joseph my son is still alive; I will go and see him before I die."

*LXX, "double garments." †LXX, "It is a great thing."

OVERVIEW: The festal garments given by Pharaoh point to the diversity of gifts of the Spirit. The gift to Benjamin represents the gift received by Paul to preach the cross of Christ. The presents sent to Joseph's father are in a figurative way the presents of Christ (AMBROSE). Joseph's command not to "quarrel on the way" was to forbid his brothers to engage in recrimination about

who was responsible for his fate (EPHREM). It can also be interpreted more generally to mean that we must guard against anger on the way of life (AMBROSE). And it can be identified with Christ's command to "love your enemies" (CHRYSOSTOM). That they went "up out of Egypt" is to be interpreted mystically as going to a holy place (ORIGEN), in this case the land of Canaan looking toward the time of the apostles (AMBROSE). The words "Joseph is still alive" are to be understood above all in the moral sense: Joseph did not fall into sin but remained alive spiritually. That Joseph had "dominion over all Egypt" means that he dominated all the passions, for, in a tradition that goes back to Philo of Alexandria, Egypt represents the human body as the seat of the passions (ORIGEN). The words "he is alive" may be understood of the risen Christ, of whom Joseph is a figure (AMBROSE). On a more literal level, the joy experienced by Jacob on hearing that Joseph was alive was all the greater because it was unexpected. And so, without delay, Jacob took to the road to see the object of his desire (CHRYSOSTOM). Jacob's spirit is rekindled like a lamp by the light of truth after being darkened by the deceit of a lie. In an interpretation based on the etymology of the name Israel as "he who sees God," Jacob, now called Israel, sees the life in the spiritual Joseph, that is, Christ, the true God (ORIGEN). In an interpolated scene, Joseph's brothers explain their crime to Jacob and receive his forgiveness (EPHREM).

45:22 Presents for the Brothers

ONE IS MYSTICAL, THE OTHER MORAL. AMBROSE: They each receive two garments. What are these garments? You should have no hesitancy about identifying them, because you have read what was said of Wisdom, "She made for her husband double garments."[1] One is mystical, the other moral. But not all the apostles or prophets or pastors or powers have the grace of healing, nor do all speak in tongues. Where there are diverse rewards, there are diverse merits. ON JOSEPH 13.76.[2]

CHRIST GIVES PAUL THREE HUNDRED PIECES OF GOLD. AMBROSE: To each of the brothers two garments are given. And it is Paul who is dispatched when his words are published. To him Christ gives three hundred pieces of gold and five garments of various colors. A man who preaches the cross of Christ already has three hundred

pieces of gold, and so he says, "For I determined not to know anything among you, except Jesus Christ and him crucified."[3] And it is appropriate that he receives the gold pieces, because he preached not in the persuasive words of wisdom but in the demonstration of the Spirit.[4] Moreover, Paul receives five robes, either as the manifold teachings of wisdom or because he was not seduced by any enticements of the bodily passions. Where there was danger for others, he maintained the victory. He overcame all the pleasures of the flesh by a signal self-control and exercise of virtue; no bodily infirmity blunted his character or his zeal. When Paul was in the body, he did not know that he had a body. Indeed, when he was caught up into paradise, whether in the body or out of the body he did not know, he heard secret words that a man may not repeat.[5] At the last, Paul had no earthly fragrance at all on earth, as he teaches when he says, "For we are the fragrance of Christ for God as regards those who are saved."[6] ON JOSEPH 13.75.[7]

45:23 Presents for Jacob

THE PRESENTS OF CHRIST. AMBROSE: And presents are also sent on ahead to the father. The son does honor to the father; so Christ invites his people with promises and invites them with presents. The presents are carried on asses that before were profitless and fit only for toil but now are profitable.[8] They carry in a figurative way the presents of Christ, and in the gospel the donkeys are going to carry the giver of the presents.[9] ON JOSEPH 13.77.[10]

45:24 Quarrels Forbidden

FORGIVE EACH OTHER. EPHREM THE SYRIAN: Joseph commanded them not to quarrel on the way. The quarrel which he forbade them was that

---

[1]Prov 31:22 LXX. [2]FC 65:232-33. [3]1 Cor 2:2. [4]See 1 Cor 2:4. [5]2 Cor 12:2-4. [6]2 Cor 2:15. [7]FC 65:232*. [8]See Philem 11. [9]See Mt 21:7. [10]FC 65:233.

one say to another, "It was you who counseled us to throw him into the pit," while another would contend with his brother, saying, "It was you who urged us to sell him naked and in chains to the Arabs." "As I have forgiven all of you, you forgive each other."[11] COMMENTARY ON GENESIS 40.2.[12]

GUARD AGAINST DISCORD ON THE WAY.
AMBROSE: Now "he sent away his brothers, and they departed. And Joseph said to them, 'Be not angry on the way.'" How well he teaches us to guard against anger, for that can separate even brothers who love one another. . . . Is this not what our Lord Jesus said when he was about to depart from this body, when he was sending away his disciples, that they should not be angry on the way? For he says, "Peace I leave with you, my peace I give to you."[13] For where there is peace, wrath does not have place, discord is removed, dissension routed. And so this is what he is saying, "My peace I give to you," that is, "Be not angry on the way." . . . On this account also, when the Lord Jesus sent away his disciples to preach the gospel, he sent them without gold, without silver, without money, without a staff,[14] and he did it so that he might remove incentives to quarreling and the tools of vengeance. ON JOSEPH 13.78.[15]

GOD'S CARE PERMITTED THIS ALL TO HAPPEN.
CHRYSOSTOM: Hence to allay their ill feeling and hostility to one another, Joseph said, "Don't squabble on the way," but rather remember that I hold no grudge against you for what was done to me, and be kindly disposed to one another. Who could adequately admire the virtue of this good man who fulfilled in generous measure the moral values of the New Testament? What Christ recommends to the apostles in these words, "Love your enemies; pray for those who abuse you,"[16] this man even surpassed. I mean, not only did he give evidence of such wonderful love for those who did away with him as far as they could, but he did everything to convince them that they had not sinned against him. O

what extraordinary good sense! O what marvelous degree of sound values and generosity of love for God! "Surely it was not you who did this against me," he is saying, you see. "It was God's care for me that permitted this to happen so as to guarantee the realization of my dreams and so that I might prove an adequate occasion of survival for you." HOMILIES ON GENESIS 64.32.[17]

45:25 The Brothers Came Back to Canaan

SCRIPTURE IS DEVOTED TO MYSTICAL THINGS AND IDEAS.
ORIGEN: We should observe in reading the holy Scriptures how "to go up" and "to go down" are employed in each individual passage. For if we were to give diligent consideration, we would discover that almost never is anyone said to have gone down to a holy place, nor is anyone related to have gone up to a blameworthy place. These observations show that the divine Scripture was not composed, as it seems to most, in illiterate and uncultivated language but was adapted in accordance with the discipline of divine instruction. Nor is Scripture devoted so much to historical narratives as to things and ideas that are mystical.

You will find it written, therefore, that those who are born of the seed of Abraham have gone down into Egypt and again that the sons of Israel have gone up out of Egypt. Indeed Scripture speaks thus also of Abraham himself: "But Abraham went up out of Egypt into the desert, he and his wife and all that was his, and Lot with him."[18] HOMILIES ON GENESIS 15.1.[19]

LABAN FORESHADOWS THE TIME OF THE APOSTLES.
AMBROSE: What is the land of Canaan? A land that was faltering. Is it not clear that the time of the apostles is being described? They entered the faltering synagogues of the Jews and preached the power of the Lord Jesus, as we

---

[11]See Col 3:13. [12]FC 91:196*. [13]Jn 14:27. [14]Mt 10:9-10; Mk 6:8; Lk 9:3; 22:35. [15]FC 65:233-34. [16]Mt 5:44. [17]FC 87:241. [18]Gen 13:1. [19]FC 71:203.

find in the Acts of the Apostles, when Peter says, "This Jesus God has raised up, and we are all witnesses of it. Therefore, exalted by the right hand of God and receiving from the Father the promise of the Holy Spirit, he has poured forth this gift which you see."[20] ON JOSEPH 13.79.[21]

45:26 Jacob Disbelieves His Sons' Account

THESE WORDS HAVE NOT BEEN SAID IN THE USUAL SENSE. ORIGEN: I do not understand these words to have been said in the usual sense. For if, for example, we should assume that he could have been overcome with lust and sinned with his master's wife,[22] I do not think that this would have been announced about him by the patriarchs to his father Jacob: "Your son Joseph is living." For if he had done this, without doubt he would not be living. For "the soul that sins, the same shall die."[23]

But Susanna also teaches the same things when she says, "I am straitened on every side. For if I do this thing—that is, if I sin—it is death to me; and if I do not do it, I shall not escape your hands."[24] Notice, therefore, that she too understood that there is death in sin.

But also the judgment revealed by God to the first man contains the same things when he says, "But on the day that you shall eat of it you shall die the death."[25] For as soon as he has transgressed the commandment, he is dead. For the soul that has sinned is dead, and the serpent, which said, "You shall not die the death,"[26] is shown to have deceived him.

And these words have been about that which was said by the sons of Israel to Jacob: "Your son Joseph is living." HOMILIES ON GENESIS 15.2.[27]

JOSEPH HAD DOMINION OVER TEMPTATION. ORIGEN: But Jacob is excited not only about the fact that he has heard that "Joseph his son is living," but also especially about that which has been announced to him that it is Joseph who holds "dominion over all Egypt."

For the fact that he has reduced Egypt to his rule is truly great to him. For to tread on lust, to flee luxury and to suppress and curb all the pleasures of the body, this is what it means to have "dominion over all Egypt." And this is what is considered great and held in admiration by Israel.

But if there is someone who should subject at least some vices of the body but yield to others and be subject to them, it is not said correctly of him that he holds "dominion over the whole land of Egypt," but, for example, he will appear to hold dominion over one, perhaps, or two or three cities. But Joseph, whom no bodily lust ruled, was prince and lord "of all Egypt." HOMILIES ON GENESIS 15.3.[28]

HE IS ALIVE AND RULER OF THE WHOLE LAND. AMBROSE: We surely notice how the Scripture says that he is alive and ruler of the whole land, for he opened his storehouses of spiritual grace and gave the abundance to all people.[29] But when the apostles spoke this way, the Jews did not believe them; rather, they laid hands on them and thrust the preachers of salvation into prison.[30] On this account also it is written of Jacob, "He was greatly frightened in heart," for he did not believe his sons. He was greatly frightened from love of an unbelieving people, but afterward he came to recognize Christ's deeds. Won over by the mighty benefactions and mighty works, he revived and said, "It is a great thing for me, if my son Joseph is still alive. I will go and see him, before I die."[31] The first and greatest foundation of faith is belief in the resurrection of Christ.[32] For whosoever believes Christ has been restored to life, quickly searches for him, comes to him with devotion and worships God with his inmost heart. Indeed, he believes that he himself will not die if he has faith in the source of his resurrection. ON JOSEPH 13.79-80.[33]

---

[20]Acts 2:32-33. [21]FC 65:234. [22]Gen 39:7-9. [23]Ezek 18:4. [24]Dan 13:22 (Sus 22 LXX). [25]Gen 2:17. [26]Gen 3:4. [27]FC 71:204-5. [28]FC 71:206-7. [29]Gen 41:56. [30]Acts 5:17-18. [31]Gen 45:28. [32]See 1 Cor 15:12-19. [33]FC 65:234-35*.

UNEXPECTED BLESSINGS. CHRYSOSTOM: Who could describe the joy he experienced then on learning that Joseph was alive and in fact enjoyed such wonderful fame? You know, of course, that it is unexpected blessings that give rise to the keenest surge of enjoyment. Well, in this case the person he thought for so many years had become the prey of wild beasts he now learned had attained complete authority over Egypt; so how could he fail to be dumbfounded by the greatness of his joy? After all, what is caused by excessive despair is often the effect also of extreme rejoicing. We can see many people shedding tears from exceeding joy, whereas others are frequently rendered speechless when they see things they did not expect to happen, and suddenly behold alive those they thought to be dead. HOMILIES ON GENESIS 65.1.[34]

45:27 Jacob Revived by Joseph

JACOB'S SPIRIT REKINDLED. ORIGEN: What Latin expresses by saying: "his spirit was revived," is written in Greek *anezōpyrēsen*.[35] This means not so much to revive as to rekindle, so to speak, and reignite. This expression is usually used when, perhaps in some material, the fire fails to the point that it appears to be extinguished; and if perhaps it is renewed when kindling has been added, it is said to have been rekindled. Or if the light of a lamp should reach the point that it is thought to have gone out, if perhaps it be revived when oil has been poured in; although the expression is less refined, the lamp is said to have been rekindled. One will speak similarly also of a torch or other lights of this kind.

This expression seems to indicate something like this also in Jacob. As long as he was far from Joseph and received no information about his life, his spirit had failed in him, as it were, and the light which was in him had been darkened, as the kindling already failed. But when those who reported to him about Joseph's life came, that is, those who said that "the life was the light of all people,"[36] he rekindles his spirit in himself, and

the brightness of the true light is renewed in him. HOMILIES ON GENESIS 15.2.[37]

THE SPIRIT WAS REVIVED. ORIGEN: But not even this is to be neglected idly, that the text says not the soul, but the spirit as its better part, was revived or rekindled. For indeed the brightness of the light that was in him, even if it was not completely extinguished then when his sons showed him Joseph's robe stained with the blood of a kid. He could be deceived by their lie, so that "he tore his garments and put sackcloth on his loins and mourned his son, nor did he wish at all to be consoled," but said, "I go down to my son into the nether world, mourning."[38] Even if then, as we said, the light in him had not been completely extinguished, nevertheless it had been darkened in the greatest degree because he could be deceived, because he could tear his garments, because he could mourn by mistake, because he could call on death, because he desired to go down into the nether world, mourning. On account of these things, therefore, he now revives and "rekindles his spirit," because it followed logically that hearing the truth would rekindle and restore the light that the deceit of a lie had obscured in him. HOMILIES ON GENESIS 15.3.[39]

JACOB ACCEPTED HIS SONS' APOLOGY. EPHREM THE SYRIAN: When they told Jacob about the honor of Joseph, about the wisdom with which he administered his affairs and about how their last judgment was more bitter than the first, their father asked them and said, "Did you not ask Joseph how or why he went down to Egypt?" Then, when they all looked at each other and did not know what to say, Judah opened his mouth and said to his father, "We are recalling our crime today before our father." Because of the dreams of Joseph, Joseph's brothers thought, in their simplicity, that you and they would soon serve him as slaves. They also imagined, in their foolishness,

---

[34]FC 87:243*. [35]This is obviously the comment of the Latin translator Rufinus. [36]Jn 1:4. [37]FC 71:205-6. [38]Gen 37:31-35. [39]FC 71:207.

that "it was better that he alone should be the servant than that we and our father should serve him as slaves." They did this because they took pity on you and on Benjamin and not because you loved Joseph. "You also loved Benjamin, but because he did not say that we would become servants to him, all of us love him. Forgive us then for having humiliated Joseph, for it is on account of our humiliating him that he has come to this exalted state." Their father then accepted their apology and said to them, "Because of the good news about Joseph by which you have brought me joy, this offense, which caused me great suffering when I heard it, is forgiven you." COMMENTARY ON GENESIS 40.4.[40]

JACOB FINDS PEACE AT LAST. CHRYSOSTOM: Despite these words and the fact that they brought what he had sent, the carts and the gifts sent by Joseph, only with difficulty did they succeed in convincing their father that what they had told him was a lie. In fact, when Jacob saw the carts that had been sent to carry him down to Egypt, "he gained new life," the text says. This old graybeard, all stooped and bent, suddenly takes on new vigor and heart: observe the text says, "he gained new life." What is the force of "he gained new life"? Just as the light of the lamp, when the supply of oil runs out and the light is on the point of going out, suddenly emits a brighter flame . . . when someone puts in a little oil, in just the same way this old man . . . on the point of expiring from disappointment . . . next learned that Joseph was alive and was in charge of Egypt. Seeing the carts, "he gained new life," the text says. From being old, Jacob became young; he put aside the cloud of disappointment; he repelled the storm in his mind and then found himself at peace, with God disposing everything so that the good man should enjoy relief from all these awful trials and share the happiness of his son. In particular, the dream was to be fulfilled that Jacob himself had interpreted in the words, "Do you mean to say that I and your mother and your brothers will come to bow to the ground before you?"[41] HOMILIES ON GENESIS 65.3.[42]

45:28 I Will See Joseph

TRUE VISION COMES TO ISRAEL. ORIGEN: But because occasionally the divine fire can be extinguished even in the saints and faithful, hear the apostle Paul warning these who were worthy to receive gifts of the Spirit and grace, and saying, "Do not extinguish the Spirit."[43] The Scripture says of Jacob, therefore, "And Jacob rekindled his spirit, and Israel said, 'It is a great thing for me if my son Joseph is still living,'"[44] as if he has experienced something like that which Paul warned against and has renewed himself through those words that had been spoken to him about Joseph's life.

But this also should be noticed, that he who "rekindled his spirit," meaning, of course, that spirit which seemed almost extinguished, is said to be Jacob. But he who says, "It is a great thing for me if my son Joseph is living," as if he understands and sees that the life which is in the spiritual Joseph is great, is no longer called Jacob but Israel, as it were, he who sees in his mind the true life which is in Christ, the true God.[45] HOMILIES ON GENESIS 15.3.[46]

ISRAEL TOOK TO THE ROAD. CHRYSOSTOM: "So let us hasten now so that I may savor something of our meeting before I die. I mean, already the news has dumbfounded me, has banished an old man's weakness and invigorated my resolve; so once I have the good fortune to meet him and enjoy the consummation of joy, I shall then bring my life to a close." Without delay the good man took to the road, showing all haste and anxiety to see the object of his desire and gaze upon him, dead for so many years and become the prey of wild beasts, as he thought, and now made king of Egypt. HOMILIES ON GENESIS 65.4.[47]

---

[40]FC 91:197. [41]Gen 37:10. [42]FC 87:244-45*. [43]1 Thess 5:19. [44]Gen 45:27-28 [45]The explanation is based on the supposed etymology of the name Israel as "he who sees God," found already in Philo. [46]FC 71:206*. [47]FC 87:245.

46:1-7 JACOB DEPARTS FOR EGYPT

¹*So Israel took his journey with all that he had, and came to Beer-sheba, and offered sacrifices to the God of his father Isaac. ²And God spoke to Israel in visions of the night, and said, "Jacob, Jacob." And he said, "Here am I." ³Then he said, "I am God, the God of your father; do not be afraid to go down to Egypt; for I will there make of you a great nation. ⁴I will go down with you to Egypt, and I will also bring you up again;* and Joseph's hand shall close your eyes." ⁵Then Jacob set out from Beer-sheba; and the sons of Israel carried Jacob their father, their little ones, and their wives, in the wagons which Pharaoh had sent to carry him. ⁶They also took their cattle and their goods, which they had gained in the land of Canaan, and came into Egypt, Jacob and all his offspring with him, ⁷his sons, and his sons' sons with him, his daughters, and his sons' daughters; all his offspring he brought with him into Egypt.*

*The LXX adds "in the end," a phrase important for Origen's interpretation.

OVERVIEW: God's promise to Israel is confirmed (AMBROSE). Jacob's piety in offering sacrifices to the God of his father, Isaac, remains a model for us all when we are undertaking a new project or beginning a journey (CHRYSOSTOM). Encouraged by his vision, Jacob was not afraid to approach the struggles of this world. In the same way, Paul, encouraged by the Lord, struggled for the word and preaching of the Lord. On the mystical level, the "great nation" promised to Jacob represents the church of the Gentiles. On an individual level the promise can be fulfilled in each one of us through the righteousness that leads to eternal life (ORIGEN). The prediction that Joseph would close the eyes of his father can be interpreted mystically of the true Joseph, Christ, who placed his hands on the eyes of the blind man that he might see and on the eyes of the law that the spiritual vision and understanding might appear in the law (ORIGEN, AMBROSE). On a more literal level of interpretation, the promises, seen as an expression of God's fidelity to his characteristic love, allow Jacob to make the journey happy and free from all concern (CHRYSOSTOM).

46:1 Israel Sacrifices to God

THE JOURNEY BEGINS WITH SACRIFICE.
AMBROSE: It is appropriate, for that person rises up who is hastening to Christ. Faith precedes devotion. First Jacob rose up; later he sacrificed. The man who has searched out the knowledge of God offers a good sacrifice. Now "at night in a vision God spoke to Israel, saying, 'Jacob, Jacob.' He said, 'What is it?' God said, 'I am the God of your fathers, do not fear, go down into Egypt; for there I will make you into a great people, and I will lead you forever.'"[1] ON JOSEPH 14.81-82.[2]

IMITATE THESE GOOD PEOPLE'S GODLINESS.
CHRYSOSTOM: On hearing this, let us learn in whatever we do, whether embarking on some project or beginning a journey, first of all to offer a sacrifice to the Lord in prayer and, by calling on his help to address the matter in hand, thus also imitate these good people's godliness. "He offered a sacrifice to the God of his father, Isaac," the text says, for you to learn that Jacob followed in his father's footsteps and thus demonstrated the reverence for divine things that Isaac had. Because he took the initiative in showing his own right atti-

[1]Gen 46:2-4. [2]FC 65:235*.

tude in thanksgiving, at once he felt the influence of grace from on high. I mean, because he had in view the length of the journey and kept in mind his advanced age, Jacob was afraid that death might come upon him before the meeting and rob him of the sight of his son; so he offered prayers to God to grant him life enough to enable him to enjoy this final satisfaction. HOMILIES ON GENESIS 65.5.[3]

46:3 God Speaks to Israel in Visions

THE FAITHFUL APPROACH THE STRUGGLES OF THIS WORLD. ORIGEN: It appears fitting indeed after these things, to contemplate and look into what God says to Israel himself through the vision and how he sends him to Egypt strengthening and encouraging him as if he were setting out to some struggles. For he says, "Fear not to descend into Egypt." This is to say, you shall contend "against principalities and powers and against the rulers of this world of this darkness"[4]—which is figuratively called Egypt—fear not, be not afraid. But if also you wish to know the reason that you ought not fear, hear my promise: "For I will make a great nation of you there, and I will go down with you into Egypt, and I will recall you from there in the end."[5] He therefore with whom God shall go down into the struggles is not afraid "to go down into Egypt." He is not afraid to approach the struggles of this world and the battles with resisting demons. For hear the apostle Paul saying, "I have labored more," he says, "than all those, yet not I, but the grace of God with me."[6] But also when dissension had been stirred up against him in Jerusalem, and he performed a most brilliant struggle for the word and preaching of the Lord, the Lord stood by him and said the same things that now are said to Israel. "Fear not, Paul," Scripture says, "for as you have testified of me in Jerusalem, so must you bear witness also at Rome."[7] HOMILIES ON GENESIS 15.5.[8]

46:4 God Will Accompany Him to Egypt

FOR THE SALVATION OF THE WORLD. ORIGEN: But I think a still greater mystery lies hidden in this passage. For this statement disturbs me: "I will make a great nation of you, and I will go down with you into Egypt, and I will recall you from there in the end."[9] Who is it who is made "into a great nation" in Egypt and is recalled "in the end"? To the extent that it pertains to that Jacob of whom one supposes it to be said, it will not appear true. For he was not recalled from Egypt "in the end," since he died in Egypt. But it will be absurd if someone says Jacob was recalled by God in that his body was carried back. But if it is accepted, it will not be true that "God is not the God of the dead but of the living."[10] It is not proper, therefore, that these words be understood of a dead body but that they apply to the living and vigorous.

Let us consider therefore whether there may be depicted in this statement a figure of the Lord who descends into this world and is made "into a great nation," that is, the church of the Gentiles, and after all things were completed, returned to the Father. Or, whether it is a figure of "the first-formed man"[11] who descends to the struggles of this world after he was cast out of the delights of paradise. The struggle with the serpent was set before him when it is said, "You shall watch for his head, and he shall watch for your heel,"[12] and again, when it is said to the woman, "I will put enmity between you and him, and between your seed and his seed."[13]

Nevertheless God does not desert those placed in this struggle but is always with them. He is pleased with Abel; he reproaches Cain;[14] he is present with Enoch, when he is invoked.[15] He commands Noah to construct an ark of salvation in the flood;[16] he leads Abraham "from the house of his father" and "from his kinsmen";[17] he blesses

---

[3]FC 87:245-46*. [4]Eph 6:12. [5]Gen 46:3-4. [6]1 Cor 15:10. [7]Acts 23:11. [8]FC 71:210. [9]Gen 46:3-4. [10]Mt 22:32. [11]Wis 7:1. [12]Gen 3:15. [13]Gen 3:15. In each citation of Genesis 3:15 here Origen has changed the addressee. Both statements are addressed to the serpent in Genesis. [14]Gen 4:4, 10-12. [15]Gen 5:22. [16]Gen 6:14. [17]Gen 12:1.

Isaac and Jacob;[18] he leads the sons of Israel out of Egypt.[19] He writes the law of the letter through Moses. He completes what was lacking through the prophets. This is what it means to be with them in Egypt.

But regarding the statement "I will recall you from there in the end,"[20] I think this means, as we said above, that at the end of the ages his only-begotten Son descended even into the nether regions[21] for the salvation of the world and re-called "the first-formed man"[22] from there. For what he said to the thief, "This day you shall be with me in paradise,"[23] understand not to have been said to him alone but also to all the saints for whom he had descended into the nether regions. In this man, therefore, more truly than in Jacob the words "I will recall you from there in the end" will be fulfilled. HOMILIES ON GENESIS 15.5.[24]

EACH OF US ALSO ENTERS EGYPT. ORIGEN:
But each of us also, in the same manner and in the same way, enters Egypt and struggles and, if he is worthy that God should always remain with him, he will make him "into a great nation." For the number of virtues and the multitude of right-eousness in which all the saints are said to be multiplied and to increase is a great nation.

That which is said is also fulfilled in the saint: "I will recall you from there in the end."[25] For the end is considered to be the perfection of things and the consummation of virtues. Indeed, for this reason also another saint said, "Recall me not in the midst of my days."[26] And again the Scripture bestows testimony on the great patri-arch Abraham since "Abraham died full of days."[27] This statement, therefore, "I will recall you from there in the end," is as if he had said, Since "you have fought a good fight, you have kept the faith, you have finished the course,"[28] I will now recall you from this world to the future blessing, to the perfection of eternal life, to "the crown of justice which the Lord will give in the end of the ages to all who love him."[29] HOMILIES ON GENESIS 15.6.[30]

46:4 Joseph's Hand Shall Close Your Eyes

MANY MYSTERIES HIDDEN IN THE VEIL OF THIS SCRIPTURE. ORIGEN:
But let us see how also the statement after that should be under-stood: "And Joseph shall put his hands upon your eyes." I think many mysteries indeed of secret understanding are hidden within the veil of this statement. It belongs to another time to approach and touch upon these mysteries. Now, mean-while, it will not appear to be said without rea-son, since it has appeared also to some of our predecessors that a certain prophecy seemed to be designated in this statement. Since indeed that Jeroboam who made two golden calves that he might seduce the people to worship them[31] was from the tribe of Joseph, by this he blinded and closed the eyes of Israel, as if his hands were placed on them, lest they see their impiety, of which it is said, "Because of the impiety of Jacob are all these things, and because of the sin of the house of Israel. But what is the impiety of Jacob? Is it not Samaria?"[32]

But if someone perhaps asserts that those things that are said by God about a future form of piety ought not be turned to a censurable func-tion, we will say that just as the true Joseph, our Lord and Savior, put his physical hand on the eyes of the blind man and restored his sight that he had lost, so also he put his spiritual hands on the eyes of the law, which had been blinded by the corporeal understanding of the scribes and Phari-sees. He restored sight to them, that to these to whom the Lord has opened the Scriptures[33] spiri-tual vision and understanding might appear in the law.

And would that the Lord Jesus might put "his hands on" our "eyes" too, that we too might begin to look not at those things "which are seen but at the things which are not seen."[34] And would that

---

[18]Gen 25:11; 32:27, 29. [19]Ex 14. [20]Gen 46:4. [21]Eph 4:9. [22]Wis 7:1. [23]Lk 23:43. [24]FC 71:210-12. [25]Gen 46:4. [26]Ps 102:24 (101:25 LXX). [27]Gen 25:8. [28]2 Tim 4:7. [29]2 Tim 4:8; Jas 1:12. [30]FC 71:212. [31]1 Kings 12:28. [32]Mic 1:5. [33]Lk 24:32. [34]2 Cor 4:18.

he might open for us those eyes which contemplate not present things but future, and might reveal to us the aspect of the heart by which God is seen in spirit, through the Lord Jesus Christ himself, to whom belongs "glory and power forever and ever. Amen."[35] HOMILIES ON GENESIS 15.7.[36]

THE TRUE JOSEPH RESTORES THE VISION OF ISRAEL. AMBROSE: Our God himself also exhorts that people with his own prophecy and promises them advancement in the faith, the fruit of his gift, for he says to them, "Joseph shall put his hand on your eyes." It was not that the holy patriarch was troubled as to who should close his eyes, although in the clear understanding of it a natural love is also being expressed. For we often desire to embrace those whom we love. How much more, when we are about to depart from this body, do we take delight in the last touch of our beloved children and find consolation in such a provision for our journey. Yet in a mystical sense we may take it to mean that afterward the Jewish people are going to know their God. For this is a mystery, that the true Joseph places his hands over the eyes of another, so that he who before did not see may now see.[37] Come to the Gospel, read how the blind man was healed, when Jesus put his hand on him and took away his blindness. Indeed, Christ does not put his hand on those who are going to die but on those who are going to live or, if on those who are going to die, rightly

so, because we first die in order that we may live again.[38] For we cannot see God unless we die to sin previously. ON JOSEPH 14.83.[39]

REASSURED BY GOD'S PROMISE. CHRYSOSTOM: See how whatever the good man longed for the Lord promises him, and in fact much more. That is to say, in his generosity he exceeds our requests out of fidelity to his characteristic love. "Do not be afraid to go down to Egypt," he says. Because Jacob dreaded the length of the journey, accordingly he says, "Have no regard for the weakness of your old age—I will make you into a great nation there. I will accompany you and make everything easy for you." Notice the considerateness of the expression: "I will go down with you to Egypt." What could be more blessed than to have God as traveling companion? Then he spoke the consoling thought that the old man had particular need of: "Joseph's hands will close your eyes in death." That dearly beloved son of yours will personally prepare your body for burial, and his hands will close your eyes in death.

So, quite happy and free from all concern, Jacob took to the road. Consider at this point, I ask you, with what cheerfulness the good man makes the journey, being so reassured by God's promise. HOMILIES ON GENESIS 65.6-7.[40]

---

[35]Rev 5:13. [36]FC 71:212-13*. [37]Jn 9:6-7. [38]Rom 6:1-11. [39]FC 65:235-36*. [40]FC 87:246.

46:8-27 JACOB'S FAMILY

[8]Now these are the names of the descendants of Israel, who came into Egypt, Jacob and his sons. Reuben, Jacob's first-born, [9]and the sons of Reuben: Hanoch, Pallu, Hezron, and Carmi. [10]The sons of Simeon: Jemuel, Jamin, Ohad, Jachin, Zohar, and Shaul, the son of a Canaanitish woman. [11]The sons of Levi: Gershon, Kohath, and Merari. [12]The sons of Judah: Er, Onan, Shelah, Perez, and Zerah (but Er and Onan died in the land of Canaan); and the sons of Perez were Hezron and Hamul. [13]The sons of Issachar: Tola, Puvah, Iob, and Shimron. [14]The sons of Zebulun: Sered,

Elon, and Jahleel [15]*(these are the sons of Leah, whom she bore to Jacob in Paddan-aram, together with his daughter Dinah; altogether his sons and his daughters numbered thirty-three).* [16]*The sons of Gad: Ziphion, Haggi, Shuni, Ezbon, Eri, Arodi, and Areli.* [17]*The sons of Asher: Imnah, Ishvah, Ishvi, Beriah, with Serah their sister. And the sons of Beriah: Heber and Malchiel* [18]*(these are the sons of Zilpah, whom Laban gave to Leah his daughter; and these she bore to Jacob—sixteen persons).* [19]*The sons of Rachel, Jacob's wife: Joseph and Benjamin.* [20]*And to Joseph in the land of Egypt were born Manasseh and Ephraim, whom Asenath, the daughter of Potiphera the priest of On, bore to him.* [21]*And the sons of Benjamin: Bela, Becher, Ashbel, Gera, Naaman, Ehi, Rosh, Muppim, Huppim, and Ard* [22]*(these are the sons of Rachel, who were born to Jacob—fourteen persons in all).* [23]*The sons of Dan: Hushim.* [24]*The sons of Naphtali: Jahzeel, Guni, Jezer, and Shillem* [25]*(these are the sons of Bilhah, whom Laban gave to Rachel his daughter, and these she bore to Jacob—seven persons in all).* [26]*All the persons belonging to Jacob who came into Egypt, who were his own offspring, not including Jacob's sons' wives, were sixty-six persons in all;* [27]*and the sons of Joseph, who were born to him in Egypt, were two; all the persons of the house of Jacob, that came into Egypt, were seventy.* *

*LXX, "seventy-five."

OVERVIEW: In Christian interpretation, the deeds of the patriarchs are to be considered symbols of events to come. The "seventy-five" souls who go to Egypt represent the number of forgiveness (AMBROSE). The number can also be connected with Psalm 75 and with the etymology of the name Israel (QUODVULTDEUS). Scripture indicates the same number so that we may know that God's prediction of a "great nation" took effect, since Israel grew into six hundred thousand (CHRYSOSTOM).

46:27 Seventy Persons of Jacob's House

SYMBOLS OF EVENTS TO COME. AMBROSE: Therefore seventy-five souls go down into Egypt, just as it is written,[1] and this in the mystical sense is the number of forgiveness. For after such great hardness, after such great sins, they would be considered unworthy unless there were granted them the forgiveness of sins. Judah—that is, the confession of sin—goes to meet Joseph. The people of the Jews that is to come sends him ahead as a forerunner of itself. So also the true Joseph, that is, "the witness and interpreter of the God-

head," comes to meet those who before were in the possession of unbelief, because now their confession precedes them. For Christ is the interpreter of the Godhead, because "no one has at any time seen God, except the only-begotten Son, who is in the bosom of the Father; he has revealed him."[2] It is he who in the last times will receive the people of the Jews, by then in an advanced age and grown weary, and do so, not according to its merits but according to the election of his grace; and he will put his hand on its eyes to take away its blindness. And so he postponed its healing, so that the people who earlier did not think it should be believed might be the last to believe and might lose the prerogative of earlier election. On this account also the apostle says, "that a partial blindness has befallen Israel, until the full number of the Gentiles should enter, and thus all Israel should be saved."[3] And thus it is that the deeds of the patriarchs are symbols of events to come. Indeed, Jacob himself speaks to this effect to his sons: "Gather yourselves together, that I

---

[1]The LXX gives the number as seventy-five; the Vulgate, as seventy. [2]Jn 1:18. [3]Rom 11:25-26.

may tell you the things that shall befall you in the last days. Gather yourselves together, and hear Israel your father."[4] ON JOSEPH 14.84-85.[5]

JACOB AND SIMEON DEPART IN PEACE. QUOD-VULTDEUS: Therefore Jacob went down to Egypt together with seventy-five people,[6] and his son Joseph came to meet him. After seeing him Jacob said, "I see you, son, now I can die willingly."[7] When Simeon, that venerable old man, called a father because of his age and not because he could father children, saw Christ because of whom he was still kept in this world as in Egypt, even though he was extremely old, said, "Master, now you are dismissing your servant in peace, according to your word; for my eyes have seen your salvation."[8] David's Psalm 75, which coincides with the number of the people, proclaims, "God is known in Judea, and his name is great in Israel."[9] Since Israel means "he who sees God," it is necessary that every person enlightened by grace, Jew or Greek, is freed from the slavery of Egypt, even though Pharaoh, that is, the devil, oppresses him with a heavy yoke. BOOK OF PROMISES AND PREDICTIONS OF GOD 1.32.44.[10]

BE AMAZED AT GOD'S PROVIDENCE. CHRYSOSTOM: Why did sacred Scripture indicate the number to us precisely? So that we might be in a position to know how God's prediction took effect that said, "I will make you into a great nation there." You see, from those seventy-five persons the people of Israel grew into six hundred thousand. You notice how it was not idly or to no purpose that it taught us the number of those that went down to Egypt, but for us to know from how few that great number came and not to lose confidence in God's promises. I mean, when you consider that after the death of Jacob and Joseph the king of the Egyptians went to such lengths to reduce their numbers and prevent them from growing, be amazed and overcome at God's providence and the fact that his wishes can never fail, no matter how many people try their utmost. HOMILIES ON GENESIS 65.7.[11]

---

[4] Gen 49:1-2. [5] FC 65:236-37. [6] Gen 46:27 LXX; Acts 7:14. [7] Gen 46:30. [8] Lk 2:29-30. [9] Ps 76:1 (75:1 LXX). [10] SC 101:250. [11] FC 87:247.

46:28-34 JOSEPH RECEIVES JACOB HIS FATHER

[28]He sent Judah before him to Joseph, to appear* before him in Goshen; and they came into the land of Goshen. [29]Then Joseph made ready his chariot and went up to meet Israel his father in Goshen; and he presented himself to him, and fell on his neck, and wept on his neck a good while.* [30]Israel said to Joseph, "Now let me die, since I have seen your face and know that you are still alive." [31]Joseph said to his brothers and to his father's household, "I will go up and tell Pharaoh, and will say to him, 'My brothers and my father's household, who were in the land of Canaan, have come to me; [32]and the men are shepherds, for they have been keepers of cattle; and they have brought their flocks, and their herds, and all that they have.' [33]When Pharaoh calls you, and says, 'What is your occupation?' [34]you shall say, 'Your servants have been keepers of cattle from our youth even until now, both we and our fathers,' in order that you may dwell in the land of Goshen;

for every shepherd is an abomination to the Egyptians."

s Sam Syr Compare Gk Vg: Heb *to show the way*   *LXX, "wept with abundant weeping" or "a flood of tears."

OVERVIEW: The expression of the Septuagint—
"a flood of tears"—reveals the exceeding joy and
gratitude of Jacob, whose hopes and desires have
been fulfilled (CHRYSOSTOM). Joseph's counsel to
his brothers to say that they are keepers of cattle
is for the purpose of keeping their distance from
those who worship sheep and bulls and to allow
them to live in prosperity (EPHREM, CHRYSOS-
TOM).

46:29 Joseph Meets His Father

THANKING THE LORD. CHRYSOSTOM: This is
what I said at the outset, that in many cases an
excess of joy causes the tears to flow. "He fell on
his neck," the text says, and not simply "wept" but
"wept a flood of tears." You see, immediately there
came to his mind what he himself had suffered,
what his father had endured on his account. Joseph thought of the great length of time that had
elapsed in the meantime and the fact that, contrary to all expectation, he saw his father, and his
father set eyes on his son. So he shed a flood of
tears, revealing his exceeding joy and, at the same
time, thanking the Lord for what had happened.
HOMILIES ON GENESIS 65.8.[1]

46:34 The Land of Goshen

DWELL IN GOSHEN. EPHREM THE SYRIAN: Joseph went out to meet his father with chariots
and with many people. [Joseph] got down [from
his horse] and bowed down to his father, and
they wept on each other's neck. Then Joseph
commanded his brothers to say to Pharaoh, "We
and our fathers are keepers of cattle," so that they
might dwell in Goshen and thus keep their distance from those who worship sheep and bulls.[2]
COMMENTARY ON GENESIS 40.6.[3]

JOSEPH ADVISED THEM SHREWDLY. CHRYSOS-
TOM: Note the shrewdness with which Joseph advises them, not idly or to no purpose making
these suggestions but anxious to put them in a
more secure position and at the same time to ensure their assimilation among the Egyptians. You
see, since they loathed and despised those who
tended flocks for having no time for Egyptian
wisdom, consequently he counsels them to make
a pretense of their occupation so that he may
plausibly apportion them the most attractive land
and cause them to live in considerable prosperity.
HOMILIES ON GENESIS 65.9.[4]

---

[1]FC 87:247. [2]Gen 46:33-34. [3]FC 91:198. [4]FC 87:248.

47:1-12 JOSEPH SETTLES HIS FATHER
AND BROTHERS IN EGYPT

[1]*So Joseph went in and told Pharaoh, "My father and my brothers, with their flocks and herds
and all that they possess, have come from the land of Canaan; they are now in the land of Goshen."*
[2]*And from among his brothers he took five men and presented them to Pharaoh.* [3]*Pharaoh said to*

his brothers, "What is your occupation?" And they said to Pharaoh, "Your servants are shepherds, as our fathers were." ⁴They said to Pharaoh, "We have come to sojourn in the land; for there is no pasture for your servants' flocks, for the famine is severe in the land of Canaan; and now, we pray you, let your servants dwell in the land of Goshen." ⁵Then Pharaoh said to Joseph, "Your father and your brothers have come to you. ⁶The land of Egypt is before you; settle your father and your brothers in the best of the land; let them dwell in the land of Goshen; and if you know any able men among them, put them in charge of my cattle."

⁷Then Joseph brought in Jacob his father, and set him before Pharaoh, and Jacob blessed Pharaoh ⁸And Pharaoh said to Jacob, "How many are the days of the years of your life?" ⁹And Jacob said to Pharaoh, "The days of the years of my sojourning are a hundred and thirty years; few and evil have been the days of the years of my life, and they have not attained to the days of the years of the life of my fathers in the days of their sojourning." ¹⁰And Jacob blessed Pharaoh, and went out from the presence of Pharaoh. ¹¹Then Joseph settled his father and his brothers, and gave them a possession in the land of Egypt, in the best of the land, in the land of Rameses, as Pharaoh had commanded. ¹²And Joseph provided his father, his brothers, and all his father's household with food, according to the number of their dependents.*

---

*LXX, "to everybody." The Greek expression is less precise than that of the Hebrew text, but Chrysostom's comment depends on taking literally the Greek expression *kata sōma* ("body").

OVERVIEW: Jacob's use of the phrase "my sojourn" in his response to Pharaoh reveals his attitude toward this life as one living in a foreign land, an attitude seen in numerous other citations from Scripture. Provision for Jacob's family occurs in the midst of famine (CHRYSOSTOM). Joseph's gift of the best parts of the land to his father and brothers is a sign that Christ will receive the Israelites in the end together with the new people symbolized by Benjamin (CYRIL OF ALEXANDRIA).

47:8 Pharaoh Asks About Jacob's Age

LIFE IS A SOJOURN. CHRYSOSTOM: Since he saw the old man was in extreme old age, he asked his age. "Jacob replied, 'The years of my sojourn on earth.'"[1] See how all good people have the same attitude to this life as if living in a foreign land. I mean, hear what David also says later: "I am a sojourner upon earth, sojourning in a strange place";[2] while Jacob says, "The years of my sojourn on earth." Hence Paul too said about these good people that "they recognized they were

strangers and sojourners on earth."[3] "The years of my sojourn on earth," he says, "a hundred and thirty of them, have been few and harsh; they do not compare with the lifespan of my forebears." Here Jacob is referring to the years of servitude he endured under Laban in consequence of the flight made on account of his brother, and as well, following his return from there, the grief he suffered for so long on account of Joseph's death and all the misfortunes in the meantime. After all, how great do you think was the fear he had when in retribution for their sister the company of Simeon and Levi in one fell swoop wiped out a city and took captive everyone in Shechem? He said at that time, too, remember, to show the anguish with which he was stricken, "You have made me so hated as to be an enemy to the inhabitants of the land. I for my part am few in number, and if they assemble against me they will strike me and

---

[1]Gen 47:9. [2]Ps 39:12 (38:13 LXX), slightly amplified to strengthen Chrysostom's point. [3]Heb 11:13, quoting this psalm.

I shall be exterminated along with my house."[4] Hence Jacob says, "Few and harsh have been the days of the years of my life." HOMILIES ON GENESIS 65.10.[5]

47:11 Jacob Lives in Rameses

THE ISRAELITES WILL BE RECEIVED BY CHRIST. CYRIL OF ALEXANDRIA: And to that we also add that Joseph together with Benjamin was recognized by his brothers who had arrived, and he admitted them to his dining table, as I have just said. However, he did not give them any gift but ordered them to leave again in order that they bring to him the father, I mean, Jacob. After he came down and Joseph saw him there together with his children and family, he gave them the best parts of his land. This narrative is a clear sign that the Israelites themselves, by coming back in the latter times of the world, will be received by Christ, that is, when they will be in accord with the new people, that is symbolized, as I have said, by Benjamin. In addition, the inheritance we hope for will be given to us only by the holy fathers. As those who died in the faith, as the wise Paul says, "did not receive what was promised, since God had provided something better so that they would not, apart from us, be made perfect,"[6] so we wait for the fathers, so that we will not be made perfect apart from them. In the same manner and together with the holy fathers of the first, the second and the last people we will receive the very good inheritance of the heavenly kingdom that is not made by human hands in Christ, through whom and with whom be glory to God the Father with the Holy Spirit, world without end. Amen. GLAPHYRA ON GENESIS, 6.[7]

47:12 Joseph Provides for His Family

PROVISION IN FAMINE. CHRYSOSTOM: "He gave everybody rations individually," the text says. What is meant by "everybody individually"? Enough for everyone. You see, it is customary with Scripture to refer to every person sometimes as a soul and sometimes as a body. As it said previously, "Jacob's company traveling to Egypt numbered seventy-five souls" so as to describe seventy-five men and women, so here too "everybody individually," that is, each person. Even though the whole of Egypt and Canaan was laid waste with famine, these people were comfortable through having a supply of grain flowing as if from a spring. HOMILIES ON GENESIS 65.11.[8]

---

[4]Gen 34:30. [5]FC 87:248-49. [6]Heb 11:39-40. [7]PG 69:325. [8]FC 87:249-50.

47:13-26 THE FAMINE IN EGYPT

[13]Now there was no food in all the land; for the famine was very severe, so that the land of Egypt and the land of Canaan languished by reason of the famine. [14]And Joseph gathered up all the money that was found in the land of Egypt and in the land of Canaan, for the grain which they bought; and Joseph brought the money into Pharaoh's house. [15]And when the money was all spent in the land of Egypt and in the land of Canaan, all the Egyptians came to Joseph, and said, "Give us food; why should we die before your eyes? For our money is gone." [16]And Joseph answered, "Give your cattle, and I will give you food in exchange for your cattle, if your money is

gone." [17]So they brought their cattle to Joseph; and Joseph gave them food in exchange for the horses, the flocks, the herds, and the asses: and he supplied them with food in exchange for all their cattle that year. [18]And when that year was ended, they came to him the following year, and said to him, "We will not hide from my lord that our money is all spent; and the herds of cattle are my lord's; there is nothing left in the sight of my lord but our bodies and our lands. [19]Why should we die before your eyes, both we and our land? Buy us and our land for food, and we with our land will be slaves to Pharaoh; and give us seed, that we may live, and not die, and that the land may not be desolate."

[20]So Joseph bought all the land of Egypt for Pharaoh; for all the Egyptians sold their fields, because the famine was severe upon them. The land became Pharaoh's; [21]and as for the people, he made slaves of them[t] from one end of Egypt to the other. [22]Only the land of the priests he did not buy; for the priests had a fixed allowance from Pharaoh, and lived on the allowance which Pharaoh gave them; therefore they did not sell their land. [23]Then Joseph said to the people, "Behold, I have this day bought you and your land for Pharaoh. Now here is seed for you, and you shall sow the land. [24]And at the harvests you shall give a fifth to Pharaoh, and four fifths shall be your own, as seed for the field and as food for yourselves and your households, and as food for your little ones." [25]And they said, "You have saved our lives; may it please my lord, we will be slaves to Pharaoh." [26]So Joseph made it a statute concerning the land of Egypt, and it stands to this day, that Pharaoh should have the fifth; the land of the priests alone did not become Pharaoh's.

t Sam Gk Compare Vg: Heb *he removed them to the cities*

OVERVIEW: The famine in Egypt becomes the occasion for a meditation on what it means for the famine "to prevail" and how famine never prevails over those whose soul is nourished by the true bread from heaven. Those who gather at the feasts of wisdom drive out the famine that prevails over the land. Likewise the "bondage of the Egyptians" signifies becoming submissive to carnal vices. Similarly the five portions into which the Egyptian harvest is to be divided represent the five bodily senses served by carnal people. In contrast the Israelites honor the number ten, the number of perfection and of the Decalogue. Unlike the priests of Pharaoh, the priests of God have no portion of land, for they cultivate the soul, not the soil, and conform to Christ's counsel to renounce possessions (ORIGEN). In a quite different interpretation of the same text, the portion allotted to the priests of Pharaoh becomes the focus of an exhortation not to neglect the priests of God (CHRYSOSTOM).

47:20 Joseph Buys All the Land

THE FAMINE PREVAILED. ORIGEN: It seems to me that censure of the Egyptians is contained also in this statement. For you would not easily find it written of the Hebrews that "the famine prevailed over them." For although it is written that "the famine prevailed over the land,"[1] nevertheless it is not written that famine prevailed over Jacob or his sons, as it is said of the Egyptians, that "the famine prevailed over them." For although famine should come also to the just, nevertheless it does not prevail over them. For this reason the just glory in famine, as Paul is found to rejoice cheerfully in sufferings of this

[1]Gen 43:1.

kind when he says, "In hunger and thirst, in cold and nakedness."[2] What therefore is an exercise of virtue for the just is a penalty of sin for the unjust.

For it is written also in the times of Abraham that "there came a famine in the country, and Abraham went down to Egypt to dwell there, since the famine prevailed in the land."[3] And certainly if, as some think, the text of the divine Scripture was composed carelessly and awkwardly, it could have said that Abraham went down to Egypt to dwell there because the famine prevailed over him. But observe how great a distinction the divine word uses, how great a caution it employs. When it speaks of the saints it says the famine had prevailed "over the land"; when it speaks of the unjust it says they were held by the famine. Famine therefore prevailed over neither Abraham nor Jacob nor their sons. But also if it should prevail it is said to prevail "over the land." And in the times of Isaac no less it is written: "A famine came in the land, besides that former famine which came in the times of Abraham."[4] But the famine was unable to prevail over Isaac to such an extent that the Lord says to him, "Do not go down into Egypt, but dwell in the land which I shall show you, and dwell in it, and I will be with you."[5]

In accordance with this observation, in my opinion, long after that time the prophet said, "I have been young and now am old, and I have not seen the just forsaken nor his seed seeking bread."[6] And elsewhere: "The Lord will not strike down the just soul with famine."[7] From all these texts it is declared that the earth indeed can suffer famine and those who "mind earthly things."[8] But they can never be oppressed by the fasting of famine whose is that bread that "they should do the will of the Father who is in heaven"[9] and whose soul that "bread which comes down from heaven"[10] nourishes.

For this reason, therefore, the divine Scripture carefully does not say that those were held by famine who it knew possessed knowledge of God and to whom the food of the heavenly wisdom was offered. HOMILIES ON GENESIS 16.3.[11]

FIGURATIVE AND ALLEGORICAL MEANING.

ORIGEN: Since you see, therefore, that an observation of this kind is preserved correctly in almost all the texts of holy Scripture, interpret these words in their figurative and allegorical meaning, which we are taught by the words of the prophets themselves no less. For one of the twelve prophets proclaims clearly and manifestly in a simple statement that a spiritual famine is intended, when he says, "Behold the days come, says the Lord, and I will send forth a famine on the land, not a famine of bread or thirst for water but a famine for hearing the word of the Lord."[12]

Do you see what the famine is which prevails over sinners? Do you see what the famine is which prevails over the land? For they who are of the earth and "mind earthly things "[13] and cannot "perceive what things are of the Spirit of God"[14] suffer "a famine of the word of God." They do not hear the commands of the law; they do not know the reproaches of the prophets. They are ignorant of the apostolic consolations. They do not experience the medicine of the gospel. And for this reason it is said rightly of them: "Famine prevailed over the land."[15]

But for the just and "those who meditate on the law" of the Lord "day and night,"[16] "wisdom prepares her table, she kills her victims, she mixes her wine in the mixing bowl and calls with a loud voice,"[17] not that all may come, not that the abounding, not that the rich or that the wise of this world may turn aside to her. But "if there are those," Scripture says, "who are weak in understanding, let them come to me."[18] That is, if there are those who are "lowly in heart," who have learned from Christ "to be meek and lowly in heart"[19] (which elsewhere is called "poor in spirit")[20] but rich in faith, these gather at the feasts of wisdom and, refreshed by her banquets, they drive out the famine which "prevails over the

---

[2]2 Cor 11:27. [3]Gen 12:10. [4]Gen 26:1. [5]Gen 26:2-3. [6]Ps 37:25 (36:25 LXX). [7]Prov 10:3. [8]Phil 3:19. [9]Mt 7:21. [10]Jn 6:51, 59. [11]FC 71:217-18. [12]Amos 8:11. [13]Phil 3:19. [14]1 Cor 2:14. [15]Gen 43:1. [16]Ps 1:2. [17]Prov 9:2-3. [18]Prov 9:4; Mt 11:25, 28. [19]Mt 11:29. [20]Mt 5:3; Jas 2:5.

land." HOMILIES ON GENESIS 16.4.[21]

47:21 Joseph Makes Slaves of the People

ISRAEL REMAINS FREE. ORIGEN: According to the trustworthiness of Scripture, no Egyptian was free. For "Pharaoh reduced the people to slavery to himself," nor did he leave anyone free within the borders of the Egyptians, but freedom was taken away in all the land of Egypt. And perhaps for this reason it is written, "I am the Lord your God who brought you out of the land of Egypt, out of the house of bondage."[22] Egypt, therefore, became the house of bondage and, what is more unfortunate, of voluntary bondage.

For although it is related of the Hebrews that they were reduced to bondage and that, freedom having been snatched away, they bore the yoke of tyranny, nevertheless they are said to have been brought to this state "violently." For it is written, "The Egyptians abhorred the children of Israel, and with might the Egyptians violently oppressed the sons of Israel and afflicted their life with hard works in mud and brick, and with all the works which were in the plains, in all of which they reduced them to bondage by force."[23] Notice carefully, therefore, how the Hebrews are recorded to have been reduced to bondage "violently." There was a natural freedom in them which was not wrenched away from them easily or by some deception but by force. HOMILIES ON GENESIS 16.1.[24]

THE BONDAGE OF THE EGYPTIANS. ORIGEN: If, therefore, we understand these words spiritually concerning the bondage of the Egyptians, we recognize that to serve the Egyptians is nothing other than to become submissive to carnal vices and to be subjected to demons. At any rate, no necessity coming from without forces anyone into this state. Rather, the sluggishness of the soul and the lust and pleasure of the body overcome each one. The soul, by its own carelessness, subjects itself to this. But one who bears a concern for the free-

dom of the soul and improves the dignity of his mind with thoughts pertaining to heaven belongs to the children of Israel. Although he may be "violently" oppressed for a time, nevertheless he does not lose his freedom forever. For our Savior also, discussing freedom and bondage in the Gospel, speaks thus: "Everyone," he says, "who sins, is a servant of sin."[25] And again he says, "If you continue in my word, you shall know the truth, and the truth shall make you free."[26] HOMILIES ON GENESIS 16.2.[27]

47:24 A Fifth for Pharaoh

THE NUMBER FIVE REPRESENTS THE FIVE SENSES. ORIGEN: Now, if you please, let us compare also the Egyptian people with the Israelite people.

For it is said subsequently that after the famine and bondage the Egyptian people should offer a fifth part to Pharaoh. But on the contrary the Israelite people offer tithes to the priests. Behold also in this that the divine Scripture is supported by remarkable reasonableness. See the Egyptian people weighing out contributions with the number five; for the five senses in the body are designated, which carnal people serve; for the Egyptians always submit to things visible and corporal. But on the other hand the Israelite people honor ten, the number of perfection; for they received the ten words of the law, and, held together by the power of the Decalogue, they entered upon, by the bestowing, divine mysteries unknown to this world. But also in the New Testament likewise ten is venerable as the fruit of the Spirit is explained to sprout forth in ten virtues[28] and the faithful servant offers his lord ten pounds in profits from his business dealings and receives authority over ten cities.[29] . . .

Behold, therefore, from all these things the difference between the Egyptian people and the people of Israel. . . . If you still serve the carnal

---

[21]FC 71:219-20. [22]Ex 20:2. [23]Ex 1:12-14. [24]FC 71:214. [25]Jn 8:34. [26]Jn 8:31-32. [27]FC 71:215-16*. [28]Gal 5:22. [29]Lk 19:16-17.

senses, if you still pay tax with the number five and look to those things which are "visible" and "temporal" and do not look to those things which are "invisible" and "eternal,"[30] know that you belong to the Egyptian people. HOMILIES ON GENESIS 16.6.[31]

47:26 The Priests of Pharaoh

THE DIFFERENCE BETWEEN THE PRIESTS OF GOD AND THE PRIESTS OF PHARAOH. ORIGEN:
Indeed, do you wish to know what the difference is between the priests of God and the priests of Pharaoh? Pharaoh grants lands to his priests. The Lord, on the other hand, does not grant his priests a portion in the land but says to them: "I am your portion."[32] You, therefore, who read these words, observe all the priests of the Lord and notice what difference there is between the priests, lest perhaps they who have a portion in the land and have time for earthly cares and pursuits may appear not so much to be priests of the Lord as priests of Pharaoh. For it is Pharaoh who wishes his priests to have possessions of lands and to work at the cultivation of the soil, not of the soul; to give attention to the fields and not to the law. But let us hear what Christ our Lord admonishes his priests: "He who has not renounced all he possesses," he says, "cannot be my disciple."[33]

I tremble when I speak these words. For I myself am my own, I say, my own accuser first of all. I utter my own condemnations. For Christ denies that that person whom he has seen possessing anything and that one who does not "renounce all that he possesses" is his disciple. And what do we do? How do we, who not only do not renounce these things which we possess but also wish to acquire those things which we never had before we came to Christ, either read these words ourselves or explain them to people? For since conscience rebukes us, are we able to hide and not bring forth the words that are written? I do not wish to be guilty of a double crime. I admit, and I admit openly to the people who are listening, that

these things are written, although I know that I have not yet fulfilled them. But warned from this, let us, at least, hasten to fulfill them, let us hasten to pass over from the priests of Pharaoh, who have an earthly possession, to the priests of the Lord, who have no portion in the earth, whose "portion" is "the Lord."[34] HOMILIES ON GENESIS 16.5.[35]

SHOW REGARD FOR THOSE ENTRUSTED WITH THE SERVICE OF GOD. CHRYSOSTOM: Let people of today take heed of the extent of the privilege enjoyed in antiquity by priests serving idols and learn a lesson to show at least equal regard for those entrusted with the service of the God of all. . . . You see, it is not for [the priest's] sake that you ought take pains but for him who is the object of the priest's service, and so you will gain reward from him in generous measure. Hence Jesus also said, "When you do it to one of these, you do it to me," and, "Whoever receives a prophet in the name of a prophet will receive a prophet's reward."[36] . . . As the respect shown for their sake wins us much confidence (he takes to himself, you see, what is done to his servants), so too neglect of them brings upon us heavy condemnation from above. I mean, as he takes to himself respect for them, so too contempt of them.

Realizing this, let us never neglect attention to the priests of God. I say this not to set such store by them as by your love, and out of a wish for you to be advantaged in every way. What do you give, after all, that is so valuable as what you receive from the Lord? Yet, in return for that token that is expended in the present life, you gain undying reward and blessings beyond telling. With this in mind, let us hasten to render such services, considering not the expense but the gain and the favor arising from this action. If, for example, we had in view some friend of a person highly placed in this world's honors and went out of our way to give him every attention, in the belief that what

---

[30]2 Cor 4:18. [31]FC 71:222-23*. [32]Num 18:20. [33]Lk 14:33. [34]Num 18:20; Ps 119:57 (118:57 LXX). [35]FC 71:221-22. [36]Mt 25:40; 10:41.

was done to him redounded to the credit of his patron and that when this was communicated to the latter it would cause us to enjoy greater favor with him, all the more should this be true of the Lord of all. I mean, if a person shows some friendliness and compassion for some chance acquaintance lying abjectly in a public place, the Lord takes his actions as done to himself and promises to bring into the kingdom those who do any good to such people and to say, "Come, you whom my Father has blessed, because I was hun-

gry and you gave me something to eat."[37] So much more if anyone renders a service to those afflicted for God's sake and carrying the dignity of priesthood, he will not simply enjoy a reward of these proportions but many times more abundant, since the loving God generously surpasses without fail what we do. HOMILIES ON GENESIS 65.15-16.[38]

---

[37]Mt 25:34-35. [38]FC 87:251-53.

47:27-31 THE LAST DAYS OF JACOB

[27]*Thus Israel dwelt in the land of Egypt, in the land of Goshen; and they gained possessions in it, and were fruitful and multiplied exceedingly.* [28]*And Jacob lived in the land of Egypt seventeen years; so the days of Jacob, the years of his life, were a hundred and forty-seven years.*

[29]*And when the time drew near that Israel must die, he called his son Joseph and said to him, "If now I have found favor in your sight, put your hand under my thigh, and promise to deal loyally and truly with me. Do not bury me in Egypt,* [30]*but let me lie with my fathers; carry me out of Egypt and bury me in their burying place." He answered, "I will do as you have said."* [31]*And he said, "Swear to me"; and he swore to him. Then Israel bowed himself upon the head of his bed.*

OVERVIEW: The etymology of the name Gessen (Goshen) forms the basis of an allegorical meditation to the effect that we may be near to God even though we live in the body under harsh conditions as symbolized by Egypt (ORIGEN). Jacob's request not to be buried in Egypt serves as the point of departure for a meditation that the only real death in exile for Christians is to die in sin (CHRYSOSTOM).

47:27 Israel in Goshen

ISRAEL REMAINS NEAR TO GOD WHILE DWELLING IN EGYPT. ORIGEN: Let us see what Moses says after these words: "And Israel dwelt," the text says, "in Egypt, in the land of Goshen."

Now "Goshen" means "proximity" or "nearness." By this it is shown that although Israel dwells in Egypt, it is nevertheless not far from God but is close to him and near, as he himself also says: "I will go down with you into Egypt, and I will be with you."[1]

And therefore, even if we appear to have gone down into Egypt, even if placed in the flesh we undergo the battles and struggles of this world, even if we dwell among those who are subject to Pharaoh, nevertheless if we are near God, if we live in meditation on his commandments and in-

---

[1]Gen 46:4; 26:3.

quire diligently after "his precept and judgments"[2]—for this is what it means to be always near God, to think the things which are of God, "to seek the things which are of God"[3]—God also will always be with us, through Christ Jesus our Lord, "to whom belongs glory forever and ever. Amen."[4] HOMILIES ON GENESIS 16.7.[5]

47:29 Jacob's Final Request

THOSE WHO HAVE PASSED AWAY AFTER A LIFE OF VIRTUE. CHRYSOSTOM: Many mean-spirited people, when we exhort them not to be overly concerned about burial or to give highest priority to having the remains of the dead brought back from foreign parts to their native land, quote this story to us, claiming that the patriarch also gave attention to it. First of all, however, as I said before, it must be remembered that the same set of values is not to be looked for at that time as it is with people of today. Second, the good man wanted this done not without reason but to let his descendants have a glimpse of the real prospect of returning themselves some day to the Promised Land. . . . I mean, for proof that future events become visible to the eyes of faith, listen to Jacob already calling death sleeping; he said, remember, "I want to sleep with my forebears," Hence Paul also said, "By faith these people passed on without having received what was promised but having seen it from afar and greeted it."[6] How? By the eyes of faith. So let no one think Jacob's instruction came from meanness of spirit. It was due to the times and the vision of the return that would be theirs. Acquit the good man of any blame.

I mean, today when there has been a deepening of our values in the wake of Christ's coming, it would be proper for someone to be blamed for worrying about things such as burial. Let him not think it a misfortune for someone to end his days in a foreign land or to pass from this life in solitude. After all, it is not such a person who deserves to be thought unfortunate, but the one who dies in sin, even if he dies in bed, at home, in the bosom of his family. . . .

For proof that nothing of the kind causes any harm to the virtuous person, learn that good people generally—I mean the prophets and the apostles—with few exceptions were buried we know not where. Some, you see, were beheaded; others were stoned and so departed this life; others suffered countless punishments of different kinds for the sake of religion, while all were martyrs for Christ. No one would dare say about such people that their death was without honor; instead, it would be in keeping with those words of sacred Scripture, "Honorable in the sight of the Lord is the death of his holy ones."[7] Just as it called the death of holy people honorable, so listen also to Scripture calling the death of sinners wretched: "The death of sinners is wretched."[8] . . . So even if one ends one's life at home, in the presence of wife and children, with relatives and friends at hand, but in fact one is bereft of virtue, such a person's death would be wretched. . . . Even if the person endowed with virtue falls among brigands, even if he becomes the food of wild beasts, his death would be honorable. Tell me, after all, was not the son of Zacharias beheaded? Was not Stephen the first to be bedecked in the martyr's garland, stoned and so ended his life? Peter and Paul too: was not one beheaded, while the other, on the contrary, underwent the punishment of crucifixion and departed this life in that manner? Are they not for that reason in particular celebrated and eulogized everywhere in the world?

With all this in mind let us neither lament those who meet their end in exile nor declare blessed those who depart this life at home. Instead, following the norm of sacred Scripture, let us declare blessed those who have passed away after a life of virtue and lament those who have died in sin. . . . It behooves us, then, as we ponder these truths, to be attentive to virtue and strive in this present life as though in a gymnasium so that, once the contest is over, we may succeed in

---

[2]Deut 12:1. [3]Phil 2:21. [4]Gal 1:5. [5]FC 71:224. [6]Heb 11:13. [7]Ps 116:15 (115:6 LXX). [8]Ps 33:22 LXX.

donning the bright crown and not have futile re-grets. As long as the contest lasts, you see, it is possible, if we wish it, to shake off indifference and cling to virtue so as to succeed in attaining

the crowns laid up for us. HOMILIES ON GENESIS 66.2-5.[9]

[9]FC 87:255-58.

48:1-7 JACOB MAKES JOSEPH'S SONS HIS OWN

[1]*After this Joseph was told, "Behold, your father is ill"; so he took with him his two sons, Manasseh and Ephraim. 2And it was told to Jacob, "Your son Joseph has come to you"; then Israel summoned his strength, and sat up in bed. 3And Jacob said to Joseph, "God Almightyu appeared to me at Luz in the land of Canaan and blessed me, 4and said to me, 'Behold, I will make you fruit-ful, and multiply you, and I will make of you a company of peoples, and will give this land to your descendants after you for an everlasting possession.' 5And now your two sons, who were born to you in the land of Egypt before I came to you in Egypt, are mine; Ephraim and Manasseh shall be mine, as Reuben and Simeon are. 6And the offspring born to you after them shall be yours; they shall be called by the name of their brothers in their inheritance. 7For when I came from Paddan, Rachel to my sorrow died in the land of Canaan on the way, when there was still some distance to go to Ephrath; and I buried her there on the way to Ephrath (that is, Bethlehem)."*

u Heb *El Shaddai*

OVERVIEW: Jacob's creation of a thirteenth tribe by making Joseph's sons his own foreshadows the calling of Paul as the thirteenth apostle (HIPPOLY-TUS, AMBROSE). In a different allegorical interpre-tation, Jacob's action signifies God the Father's reception of the Gentiles, symbolized by Joseph, who have already become children of Christ (CYRIL OF ALEXANDRIA).

48:5 Ephraim and Manasseh

PAUL'S APOSTOLATE IS ANALOGOUS TO THE THIRTEENTH TRIBE. HIPPOLYTUS: This clearly shows [that Jacob makes Ephraim and Manasseh his own]. Since Jacob had twelve sons, to whom the twelve tribes owed their existence, he distrib-uted the two sons of Joseph into two tribes; and so

the tribes became thirteen as the tribe of Joseph was divided between his two sons. And therefore Paul himself, the apostle, was related to these events. After being chosen among the tribes, he was counted the thirteenth after the apostles, and so he was sent to the Gentiles as apostle. ON THE BLESSINGS OF ISAAC AND JACOB 11.[1]

PAUL IS CHOSEN LATER. AMBROSE: Joseph hur-ried to receive a blessing.[2] Indeed, he presented his sons Manasseh and Ephraim, and Jacob blessed them.[3] Because Jacob had twelve sons, and Paul, as one chosen later, was going to be the thirteenth apostle, a thirteenth tribe would thus be sanctified from the descendants of Manasseh

[1]PO 27:48-50. [2]Gen 48:1. [3]Gen 48:8-20.

and Ephraim, and divided between them both. Thus Paul would not appear outside the enumeration of the tribes of the fathers; as an outstanding preacher of the Old and the New Testaments, he would readily confirm that the inheritance of a father's blessing was of help to himself as well. THE PATRIARCHS 1.2.[4]

JACOB EMBRACES JOSEPH'S SONS AS HIS OWN. CYRIL OF ALEXANDRIA: And we the last became the first through faith,[5] and the nation of the Gentiles inherited the glory of the firstborn. They obtained that honor through obedience and faith. And Christ himself testified about them by saying, "A people whom I did not know served me, with their ear's hearing they obeyed me."[6] Even though we were born from a mother of different kinds, since the church was called among different nations, Christ is sufficient for us as a mediator, who unites us to God the Father, and ascribes some to the lot of the saints, and gives them the right glory and declares us to be a holy generation. But see how through Jacob's love for Joseph he placed the sons of Joseph among his own sons. And so we are also beloved in Christ, and after we were born again through him in a spiritual generation, we are received by the Father, as I have already said, and added to the saints who preceded us. In fact, if we have been called children of God the Father, we also must be under the power and control of the one who led us and united us to him, that is, Christ. See how the holy Jacob received Ephraim and Manasseh among his own sons: "As for the offspring born to you after them, they will be yours." You understand now that even though we are called children of God, nonetheless we will be children of Christ. And this is, I believe, what he says to the Father in another passage: "Those whom you gave me from the world were yours, and you gave them to me, and I have been glorified in them."[7] GLAPHYRA ON GENESIS, 6.2.[8]

---

[4]FC 65:243. [5]Mt 19:30. [6]Ps 17:44-45 LXX. [7]Jn 17:6, 10. [8]PG 69:328-29.

48:8-16 JACOB BLESSES JOSEPH'S SONS

[8]When Israel saw Joseph's sons, he said, "Who are these?" [9]Joseph said to his father, "They are my sons, whom God has given me here." And he said, "Bring them to me, I pray you, that I may bless them." [10]Now the eyes of Israel were dim with age, so that he could not see. So Joseph brought them near him; and he kissed them and embraced them. [11]And Israel said to Joseph, "I had not thought to see your face; and lo, God has let me see your children also." [12]Then Joseph removed them from his knees, and he bowed himself with his face to the earth.* [13]And Joseph took them both, Ephraim in his right hand toward Israel's left hand, and Manasseh in his left hand toward Israel's right hand, and brought them near him. [14]And Israel stretched out his right hand and laid it upon the head of Ephraim, who was the younger, and his left hand upon the head of Manasseh, crossing his hands, for Manasseh was the first-born. [15]And he blessed Joseph, and said,

"The God before whom my fathers Abraham and Isaac walked,

the God who has led me all my life long to this day,

¹⁶the angel who has redeemed me from all evil, bless the lads;

and in them let my name be perpetuated, and the name of my fathers Abraham and Isaac;

and let them grow into a multitude in the midst of the earth."

*LXX, "they prostrated themselves."

Overview: Although Jacob's bodily eyes were weak, the eyes of his mind saw through faith what was to happen. His words manifest his insight and his humility (Chrysostom). Jacob's crossing of his hands signifies the mystery of the cross (Ephrem). The two sons symbolize, as did Esau and Jacob earlier, the people of the Jews and the younger people, the body of Christ (Ambrose).

48:12 Joseph Bows to the Earth

The Eyes of Jacob's Mind Were Strengthened. Chrysostom: See how he also taught his sons from the very beginning to show due respect for the old man. Joseph brought them along according to seniority, the text says, and presented Manasseh and then Ephraim. At this point notice, I ask you, how the good man's bodily eyes were by this time weak through old age ("His eyes had faded with age," remember, "and he could not see"),[1] but the eyes of his mind were strengthened, and by faith Jacob already saw what was going to happen. I mean, instead of heeding Joseph, Jacob crossed his hands over in blessing them and gave precedence to the younger, putting Ephraim ahead of Manasseh. Homilies on Genesis 66.9.[2]

48:14 Israel Places His Hands on Ephraim and Manasseh

The Cross Is Symbolized. Ephrem the Syrian: Here too the cross is clearly symbolized to depict that mystery with which Israel the firstborn departed, just as Manasseh the firstborn, and the peoples increase in the manner of Ephraim the younger. Commentary on Genesis 41.4.[3]

Ephraim Refers to Those to Become the Body of Christ. Ambrose: What extraordinary mysteries there are in this! Joseph took his sons, who were born to him in Egypt, and brought them before his father. He placed Ephraim at his right, but at the left of his father Israel, and Manasseh at his left, but at Israel's right. But Israel, stretching out his right hand, put it on Ephraim's head, although he was the younger son and stood at his grandfather's left. And he put his left hand on Manasseh, who was at his right, and with his hands crossed so, he blessed them.[4] In this Joseph observed the order of nature, to grant more to the elder son. Likewise Isaac also desired to give his blessing to Esau, the first son, but Jacob believed the younger son was to be preferred as a symbol of the younger people, just as he himself had been preferred by his mother.[5] Indeed, in our tongue, Manasseh signifies "out of forgetfulness,"[6] because the people of the Jews forgot their God, who made them,[7] and whoever from out of that people believes is called back, as it were, from forgetfulness. Moreover, Ephraim promises fruitfulness in faith by the meaning of his name, "who made his father to grow," just as Joseph himself says, "because God has made me to grow in the land of my humiliation."[8] This refers especially to the younger people, which are the body of Christ, making its Father to grow and not forsaking its own God. The Patriarchs 1.3-4.[9]

48:16 Israel Blesses Manasseh and Ephraim

---

[1]Gen 48:10. [2]FC 87:260. [3]FC 91:199. [4]Gen 48:13-20. [5]Gen 27:1-40. [6]Gen 41:51. [7]Deut 32:18. [8]Gen 41:52. [9]FC 65:243-44*.

HIS INSIGHT AND HIS HUMILITY. CHRYSOS-
TOM: Words of a grateful heart, of a God-fearing
spirit keeping fresh in his mind God's kindnesses.
He to whom my forebears were pleasing, he is
saying, who reared me from youth to the present,
who from the beginning snatched me from every
trouble, who showed such care for me, he "will
bless these children; my name will be invoked in
them, as also the name of my forebears Abraham
and Isaac, and they will grow into a teeming multitude on the earth." Do you see Jacob's insight

and, at the same time, his humility? His insight,
on the one hand, in foreseeing with the eyes of
faith, and so giving precedence to Ephraim ahead
of Manasseh. And on the other his humility, in
making no mention at all of his own virtue but instead invoking a blessing on them on the basis of
the satisfaction given by his forebears and the
kindnesses done to him. HOMILIES ON GENESIS
66.10.[10]

---

[10]FC 87:261.

48:17-22 JACOB PUTS EPHRAIM AHEAD OF MANASSEH

[17]*When Joseph saw that his father laid his right hand upon the head of Ephraim, it displeased him; and he took his father's hand, to remove it from Ephraim's head to Manasseh's head. [18]And Joseph said to his father, "Not so, my father; for this one is the first-born; put your right hand upon his head." [19]But his father refused, and said, "I know, my son, I know; he also shall become a peo-ple, and he also shall be great; nevertheless his younger brother shall be greater than he, and his descendants shall become a multitude of nations." [20]So he blessed them that day, saying,*

"By you Israel will pronounce blessings, saying,
'God make you as Ephraim and as Manasseh'";

and thus he put Ephraim before Manasseh. [21]Then Israel said to Joseph, "Behold, I am about to die, but God will be with you, and will bring you again to the land of your fathers. [22]Moreover I have given to you rather than to your brothers one mountain slope[v]* which I took from the hand of the Amorites with my sword and with my bow."

v Heb *shekem*, shoulder   *"One mountain slope"; LXX, Sikimes (= Shechem).

OVERVIEW: Jacob's insistence, against Joseph's
objection, in blessing Ephraim before Manasseh
shows clearly that this mystery referred in a spiritual sense to the peoples, that is, the Gentiles
(AMBROSE). A prophetic spirit moved Jacob to
foresee as already present things that would happen long afterward. The text also offers the occasion for a meditation on the importance of

preferring virtue and God's blessing to material
possessions. Jacob's prediction of the future illustrates the general principle that the hope of good
things to come mitigates the troubles of the
present life. The Septuagint variant that introduces Shechem into the text causes a difficulty in
reconciling Jacob's words here with those of Genesis 49:5-7 (CHRYSOSTOM).

48:20 *Ephraim Before Manasseh*

THE YOUNGER BROTHER SHALL BE GREATER.
AMBROSE: Indeed, the old man Jacob stated that this mystery referred in a spiritual sense to the peoples. For since his son Joseph thought that he had made a mistake from a defect in his vision, which was a bit dim, he wanted to change the position of his hands, saying, "'Not so, father, for this is the firstborn; put your right hand on his head.' But he refused and said, 'I know, son, I know. He too shall become a people, he too shall be exalted, but his younger brother shall be greater than he, and his seed will be a multitude of nations.'"[1] Yes, by the order also in which he gave his blessing, Jacob prophesied that Ephraim was to be preferred to the elder brother, for he said, "In you Israel will be blessed, and it will be said, 'May God do to you as to Ephraim and Manasseh.'" And so, although they were grandsons, they were adopted into the place of sons, so that they would not be deprived of their grandfather's blessing. THE PATRIARCHS 1.5.[2]

THE EYES OF FAITH. CHRYSOSTOM: Do you see how God's grace foretold this to him and how, moved by a prophetic spirit, he blessed Joseph's sons in this way, foreseeing as already present and visible to the brothers what would happen so long afterward? This is what prophecy is like, after all. Just as the eyes of the body can form an image of nothing beyond visible things, so the eyes of faith do not see visible things but form an image of things that are due to happen many generations later. You will gain a more precise notion of this from the blessings he bestows on his own sons. HOMILIES ON GENESIS 66.12.[3]

48:21 *The Land of Your Fathers*

TEACH CHILDREN TO PREFER VIRTUE TO ALL

ELSE. CHRYSOSTOM: Let us therefore not be anxious to amass money and bequeath it to our children; rather, let us teach them virtue and call down blessing from God on them. This, you see, this is the greatest wealth; this wealth is beyond counting, proof against consumption, leading to greater wealth as each day passes. Nothing in fact is equal to virtue; nothing more potent than it. Even if you were to mention kingship itself and the wearer of the crown, he would be worse off than any pauper clad in rags if he lacked virtue. What good, after all, could the crown or royal purple be to the man betrayed by his own indifference? I mean, surely the Lord has no respect for distinctions based on externals? Surely he is not moved by the fame of prominent people? One thing is to be sought after with him, to be able to find the door opened to confidence with him on the basis of the operation of virtue. The person who enjoys no such confidence will be among the least respected and least entitled to speak. HOMILIES ON GENESIS 66.14.[4]

48:22 *The Land of the Amorites*

THE HOPE OF GOOD THINGS TO COME. CHRYSOSTOM: After he blessed the sons and promoted the younger ahead of the elder by way of forecasting the future, he wanted to convince Joseph that it was not idly or to no purpose that he had done this but to foretell what was due to happen. So he predicted his own death and the fact that they would return from foreign parts to Canaan, the land of their ancestors, and raised sound hope in them so as to cheer them up with the expectation. The hope of good things to come, after all, always mitigates the troubles of the present life. HOMILIES ON GENESIS 67.2.[5]

---

[1]Gen 48:18-19.   [2]FC 65:244-45.   [3]FC 87:262.   [4]FC 87:262-63.   [5]FC 87:266.

49:1-2 JACOB CALLS HIS SONS

[1]Then Jacob called his sons, and said, "Gather yourselves together, that I may tell you what shall befall you in days to come.*
  [2]Assemble and hear, O sons of Jacob,
    and hearken to Israel your father.

*LXX, "in the last days." This phrase could be understood in a historical, messianic or eschatological sense.

OVERVIEW: This chapter attracted more attention than any other chapter of the patriarchal history because Jacob's blessings to his sons could be interpreted as prophecies of the divine plan of salvation in Jesus Christ as well as of the end of time. They could also be read to refer to the development of the spiritual life. Some commentators attempt to give more that one explanation of the same verse or phrase. The most systematic of these is Rufinus, who often offers an explanation on the historical or literal level, the mystical level and the moral level, comparing these three meanings to the ark with three levels that Noah was commanded to construct.

Jacob's pronouncements are blessings and prophecies, both referring to the future, with blessings falling on the one prefigured by Joseph and the prophecies falling on his enemies (HIPPOLYTUS). Arguably Jacob is the first biblical figure to refer to the final age, to which these prophecies are directed (ORIGEN). In this chapter Jacob is presenting anew his announcement of events to come in later ages (AMBROSE). Under the inspiration of the Spirit, Jacob foretells what will happen in the last days (CHRYSOSTOM).

49:1 Jacob Prepares to Bless His Sons

DISTINGUISHING PROPHECIES FROM BLESSINGS. HIPPOLYTUS: This is a prophecy and not a blessing. In fact, the blessing is concerned with someone who is blessed, while the prophecy is fulfilled when a certain action is accomplished. How will the explanation proposed above agree with these words of the Scripture: "All these are the twelve tribes of Israel; and this is what their father said to them as he blessed them, blessing each with the blessing suitable to him."[1] At one time are they clearly prophecies, at another prophecies called blessings? In this explanation it must be understood that exactly in the things said are the prophecies and the blessings, so that the blessings fall on the one who was born from Judah, on the one who was prefigured by Joseph, on the one who, coming from Levi, finds himself being the priest of the Father, while the prophecies fall on those who acted as enemies and had no consideration for the Son of God. THE BLESSINGS OF THE PATRIARCHS 12.[2]

THE CONSUMMATION OF THE WORLD. ORIGEN: And as for the consummation of the world, Jacob is the first to refer to this when, in giving his testament to his sons he says, "Gather to me, you sons of Jacob, that I may tell you what shall be in the last days," or, "after the last days." If then there are "last days," or a time "after the last days," it follows of necessity that the days that had a beginning also come to an end. ON FIRST PRINCIPLES 3.5.1.[3]

ANNOUNCEMENT OF EVENTS TO COME. AMBROSE: After the joyous conferral of this blessing, Jacob called his sons as well.[4] Whereas before he had preferred the younger to the elder, he begins with the eldest. In the former case he pre-

---

[1]Gen 49:28. [2]PO 27:52. [3]OFP 237*. [4]Gen 49:1-2.

ferred the symbolic gift; in this one he maintains the order of age. Likewise earlier he had blessed all men with all their posterity and offspring of times to come in the persons of the two brothers; a repetition of that blessing of the people might seem superfluous, or the earlier blessing might be considered invalid. And so it is with reason that Jacob says he is presenting anew his announcement of events that were to come in later ages, rather than a blessing. THE PATRIARCHS 2.6.[5]

49:2 Sons of Jacob, Listen!

LEARN WHAT WILL HAPPEN. CHRYSOSTOM: See the good man's shrewdness. Since he foresaw the moment of his death, he summoned his sons and said, "Gather around so that I may predict ahead of time what is in store for you at the end of your days. Come together, and listen to Israel your father." Come along, he says, and learn from me, not the immediate future but what will happen in the last days. This I foretell to you not of myself but under the inspiration of the Spirit; hence I predict ahead of time what will occur after many generations. You see, as I am on the point of departing this life, I want to imprint it on the memory of each of you as if on some bronze pillar.

Now consider how with his sons gathered together the good man follows the order of their birth and in this way bestows curse or blessing appropriate to each, showing by this procedure the extraordinary degree of his own virtue. HOMILIES ON GENESIS 67.4-5.[6]

---

[5]FC 65:245. [6]FC 87:267.

49:3-4 REUBEN

[3]Reuben, you are my first-born,
  my might, and the first fruits of my strength,
  pre-eminent in pride and pre-eminent in power.
[4]Unstable as water, you shall not have pre-eminence
  because you went up to your father's bed;
  then you defiled it—you[w] went up to my couch!

---

w Gk Syr Tg: Heb he

OVERVIEW: Interpreted mystically (allegorically), Reuben may be seen as representing the Jewish people, who, in the light of a series of other texts, can be said to have offended God the Father (RUFINUS). The description of Reuben in these two verses, positive and negative, shows that no profit comes to us from natural advantage unless accompanied by good deeds of free will (CHRYSOSTOM). The words couch and bed refer to the holy flesh of Christ on which the saints enjoy their rest but which was abused by an impious and unbelieving people (HIPPOLYTUS, AMBROSE). In a rather different interpretation, a parallel is drawn between the curse on Reuben, blotted out by Moses, and the decree of death against Adam removed by the promise of resurrection through Christ (EPHREM). Jacob's accusation against Reuben may also be read as an anticipation of the Mosaic legislation forbidding father and son to have relations with the same woman (CHRYSOSTOM).

49:3 Reuben the Firstborn

REUBEN ABUSED HIS STATUS. RUFINUS: It seems to me that, according to the mystical interpretation, Reuben may play the role of the first Jewish people, that is, the firstborn and the beginning of the children, as the prophet says: "Israel is my firstborn."[1] The words of God in fact were first addressed to that people.[2] And the Scriptures relate that that people was hard and reckless. About whom the prophet says, "Whatsoever this people says, is hard."[3] Elsewhere he says again about the Jews, "You stiff-necked people, uncircumcised in heart."[4] And these people offended God the Father when they turned their back to him and not their face. They defiled the concubine's bed into which they got, that is, the law of the Old Testament, which they often stained with their transgressions. Paul teaches us that the concubine symbolically represents the law of the Old Testament by saying, "Abraham had two sons, one by a slave and one by a free woman: these are the two Testaments";[5] and Hagar, who was the concubine, clearly is the figure of the Old Testament.

One indeed was the perfect dove or mother, the church that, as a chaste virgin and as a queen for her bridegroom the king, is united through the gospel to Christ.[6] THE BLESSINGS OF THE PATRIARCHS 2.5.[7]

NATURAL ADVANTAGE, FREELY CHOSEN GOOD DEEDS. CHRYSOSTOM: See the extent of the good man's wisdom. Intending to level a worse accusation against Reuben, he first mentioned the privileges conceded him by nature and the precedence he enjoyed in being the beginning of his line and enjoying the dignity of firstborn. Then he records his sins of free will as if on a bronze pillar to show that no advantage comes to us from natural advantage unless accompanied by good deeds of free will—these, you see, are what bring us com-

mendation or lend us the stigma of blame. "Unyielding in endurance," he says, "unyielding in willfulness": the pride of place accorded you by nature you have forfeited by your own headstrong behavior. HOMILIES ON GENESIS 67.5.[8]

49:4 You Defiled Your Father's Bed

THE HOLY FLESH OF CHRIST. HIPPOLYTUS: He said "couch" and "bed," that is, the holy flesh of Christ, on which the saints are saved while enjoying their rest as on a holy divan. This is the flesh that those outlaws took possession of and then outraged by offering him [Christ] vinegar, by hitting his head with a reed, by flogging him on the back, by spitting on his face, by skinning his cheeks with slaps and by piercing his hands with nails.[9] All these things the impious and unbelieving people did in accordance with the high priests, the scribes and the leaders of the people. That is why the blessed prophet neither has remained silent about their deeds nor wants to be involved in their wickedness and evil decisions. On the contrary, he keeps himself away from their intrigues where such criminal plots are conceived. ON THE BLESSINGS OF ISAAC AND JACOB 13.[10]

JUDGMENT REVERSED. EPHREM THE SYRIAN: Just as the justice of Jacob cursed his firstborn because of his evil deed and this curse of Reuben was blotted out by Moses who was the descendant of Jacob,[11] so too was death decreed by God against Adam when he transgressed the commandment. But the Son of God came and, with the promise of the resurrection that he promised, brought to nought the judgment that accompanied Adam out of paradise. COMMENTARY ON GENESIS 43.2.[12]

A REPROACH RATHER THAN A BLESSING.

---

[1]Ex 4:22. [2]Rom 3:2. [3]Is 8:12. [4]Acts 7:51. [5]Gal 4:22-24. [6]See Song 6:8. [7]SC 140:80-82. [8]FC 87:267-68*. [9]Mt 27:26, 30, 34-35. [10]PO 27:58-60. [11]Moses' father and mother were Levites; see Ex 2:1. [12]FC 91:209.

AMBROSE: Doesn't this seem to be a reproach rather than a blessing? Thus it really is more a prophecy than a blessing. For a prophecy is an announcement of events to come, whereas a blessing is the longed for bestowal of sanctification and of graces.

The Jews suppose that the old man is saying these things to his son Reuben on this account, because the latter lay with Bilhah, his father's concubine, and polluted his father's bed. But they are easily refuted; this had already taken place. Now Jacob is promising that he will speak of events to come in the last days, not what took place before. Therefore the meaning is consistent and in accord with the thought of the patriarch himself: he sees the future passion of the Lord under persecution from the Jews and execrates the boundless audacity of that firstborn people. . . . For Israel itself was called the firstborn and said to be stiff-necked, and of it Moses said, "You are a stiff-necked people."[13] THE PATRIARCHS 2.7-9.[14]

JACOB ANTICIPATES THE LAW. CHRYSOSTOM: See how through the insight granted him by the Spirit Jacob anticipates the legislation of Moses against allowing father and son to have relations with the same woman. Ahead of time he forbids this in censuring his son thus, "You stained the couch" by entering your father's bed. You committed an unlawful act, he says. Hence "you ran riot like water, but you shall not break out again." HOMILIES ON GENESIS 67.6.[15]

---

[13]Ex 33:3. [14]FC 65:245-46. [15]FC 87:268.

49:5-7 SIMEON AND LEVI

[5]*Simeon and Levi are brothers;*
 weapons of violence are their swords.
[6]*O my soul, come not into their council;*
 O my spirit,[x] *be not joined to their company;*
for in their anger they slay men,
 and in their wantonness they hamstring oxen.
[7]*Cursed be their anger, for it is fierce;*
 and their wrath, for it is cruel!
I will divide them in Jacob
 and scatter them in Israel.

x Or *glory*

OVERVIEW: Simeon and Levi are seen as figures for Satan and death, which attacked all flesh, as the brothers had done at Shechem (EPHREM). Since it is the tribes that are meant by the names of the patriarchs, Jacob's condemnation is not to be read so much of the brothers' act of vindication of their sister but rather as a condemnation of the scribes and chief priests later represented by Simeon and Levi (HIPPOLYTUS, AMBROSE). On the literal level, Jacob is seen as dissociating himself from the brothers' anger and desire for vengeance and predicting their dispersal (RUFINUS, CHRYSOSTOM). The same prediction can also be read on another level as a promise of redemption in the gathering together of the nations (Ambrose).

49:5 Weapons of Violence

Figures for Satan and Death. Ephrem the Syrian: These too are figures for Satan and death. For just as Simeon and Levi, in their anger, destroyed a city and, through their greed, plundered its possessions, so also Satan, in his envy, killed the world secretly as Simeon and Levi had killed the sons of Shechem openly, and death fell suddenly upon all flesh as Simeon and Levi did on the possessions of the inhabitants of Shechem. The gospel of our Lord raised up those whom sin had slain in secret, and the blessed promise of the Son raised up the dead upon whom the tyrant Death suddenly fell. Commentary on Genesis 43.3.[1]

With Heavenly Words and the Sword of the Spirit. Ambrose: For the brothers supplied the reasons for their own misfortune when they claimed to their father that they, although young in years, were vindicators and avengers of a wrong done to the sense of respect and of a violation of chastity. Surely the holy Jacob could not have condemned the fact that they did not permit their sister to be unavenged, in the position of a harlot, who had lost her virginity and did not have the consolation of a vindication. This is especially the case, seeing that Jacob himself approved the deed; for when he had possession of Shechem, he gave it at his death to his most beloved son Joseph and said to him, "I give to you above all your brothers Shechem in particular, which I took from the hands of the Amorites with my sword and bow."[2] The act is undeniable; still, we can interpret that by "Shechem" are meant "shoulders" and by "shoulders" are meant "works." Therefore Jacob chose the holy Joseph before the others as heir to his good works, for the other brothers could not match his works. Who indeed could match Christ's deeds? Moreover Christ, being unspotted and chaste, has car-

ried back the spoils of victory from this earthly sojourn and from the instigators of impurity. With heavenly words and the sword of the Spirit he has taken a place that was free of debaucheries and outrages, for a dwelling of the saints. . . .

It is the tribes then that are meant by the names of the patriarchs. From the tribe of Simeon come the scribes, from that of Levi the chief priests, who brought their wickedness to completion and filled up the entire measure of their fathers' unholiness[3] in the passion of the Lord. They took counsel against the Lord Jesus, to kill him, even as Isaiah says, "Alas for their souls! Because they have counseled an evil counsel against themselves, saying, 'Let us bind the just one, for he is profitless to us.' "[4] They killed the prophets and apostles who announced the coming of the Lord of salvation and preached his glorious passion and resurrection. The Patriarchs 3.11-13.[5]

49:6-7 Anger and Wantonness Condemned

The Scribes and High Priests Foreshadowed. Hippolytus: Read the gospel and you will find it written down; the scribes were from the tribe of Simeon, and the high priests from that of Levi. Since the decision to arrest the Christ and to execute him was taken in their council, the prophet foreknowing that said, "O my soul, come not into their council!" In this passage he talks about the council where they took their decisions by searching for a reason through which they might accuse Christ, so that "they took counsel together in order to arrest Jesus by stealth and kill him."[6] And Isaiah says the same: "Woe to their soul, for they have devised an evil counsel against themselves, saying, 'Let us bind the just one, for he is burdensome to us.' "[7] On the Blessings of Isaac and Jacob 14.[8]

Their Evil Intent. Chrysostom: God forbid, Jacob is saying, that I should share their evil

---

[1]FC 91:209. [2]Gen 48:22 LXX. [3]Mt 23:32. [4]Is 3:9-10 LXX. [5]FC 65:247-49. [6]Mt 26:4. [7]Is 3:9-10 LXX. [8]PO 27:64.

intent or associate myself with their unjust doings. "Because in the heat of their passion they slew people"; their rage turned irrational. . . . After all, even if Shechem had sinned,[9] there was no need to turn their thirst for blood against everyone. "And in their fury they cut down a bull"; there is reference here to the son of Hamor,[10] calling him a bull because of his hot-blooded maturity. HOMILIES ON GENESIS 67.7.[11]

ISRAEL CURSES THEIR CRUELTY AND RECKLESSNESS. RUFINUS: As for the historical account, it seems that in this passage [Simeon and Levi] are reproached because, through deceit and fraud, they slaughtered Shechem, the son of Hamor, who after sleeping with their sister had tried to associate himself with the family of Israel. They also destroyed the whole people [of Shechem], so that Israel himself, their father, said to them, "You made me odious in this world."[12] Therefore he curses their cruelty and their recklessness and declares he will scatter them amid the people of Israel, and that from them the Levites and the priests who do not have their own inheritance of land will descend. THE BLESSINGS OF THE PATRIARCHS 2.7.[13]

A SURPRISING MEMBER OF LEVI'S TRIBE. AMBROSE: Likewise, when he said to Simeon and Levi, "I will divide you in Jacob and scatter you in Israel,"[14] he revealed that they were to be redeemed in the gathering together of the nations. For when the shepherd has been struck down, the flock that was previously brought together is scattered;[15] thus one who did not belong could enter in and all Israel could be saved.[16] And we ought in particular to assume this as regards the tribe of Levi, for it appears that the Lord Jesus

traced his origin from that tribe, as concerns his taking on of the body. Of that tribe are the priests Levi and Nathan, and, in the Gospel which he wrote, St. Luke counted them among the ancestors of the Lord.[17] For the Priest of the Father and Chief of all priests, even as it is written, "You are a priest forever,"[18] should have laid claim to succession from a priestly line. On this account also Moses blessed this tribe and said, "Give to Levi the lot of his own approbation, and to the holy man his truth."[19] THE PATRIARCHS 3.14-15.[20]

THE PUNISHMENT THAT AWAITS THEM. CHRYSOSTOM: Then, in a reference to their crimes Jacob applies a curse in the words "Cursed be their rage for its ferocity and their frenzy for its willfulness": this touches on the stratagem they employed in deceiving the inhabitants of Shechem and imposed on them by guile. Their rage was "ferocious," he says, headstrong, irrational. "Their frenzy is cursed for its willfulness." When the Shechemites came to believe they had won great favor with them, then it was that Simeon and Levi vented their baleful frenzy and deployed the tactics of a foe against them. Referring to their exploit as sins, he foretells as well the punishment for it that awaits them: "I will disperse them in Jacob and scatter them in Israel." They will be scattered in all directions so that this very thing will be obvious to everyone, namely, that they had persisted in committing this crime out of bravado. HOMILIES ON GENESIS 67.7.[21]

---

[9]A reference to Shechem's rape of Dinah. [10]Gen 34:2. [11]FC 87:268-69. [12]Gen 34:25-30. [13]SC 140:84. [14]Gen 49:7. [15]Mt 26:31. [16]Rom 11:26. [17]Lk 3:29, 31. [18]Ps 110:4 (109:4 LXX). [19]Deut 33:8 LXX. [20]FC 65:249-50. [21]FC 87:269.

49:8-12 JUDAH

⁸*Judah, your brothers shall praise you;*
   your hand shall be on the neck* of your enemies;
   your father's sons shall bow down before you.
⁹*Judah is a lion's whelp;*
   from the prey,[†] my son, you have gone up.
He stooped down, he couched as a lion,
   and as a lioness; who dares rouse him up?
¹⁰*The scepter shall not depart from Judah,*
   nor the ruler's staff from between his feet,
until he comes to whom it belongs;^y
   and to him shall be the obedience of the peoples.[‡]
¹¹*Binding his foal to the vine*
   and his ass's colt to the choice vine,
he washes his garments in wine
   and his vesture in the blood of grapes;
¹²*his eyes shall be red with wine,*
   and his teeth white with milk.

y Syr Compare Tg: Heb *until Shiloh comes* or *until he comes to Shiloh*   *LXX, "back."   [†]LXX, "bud" or "sprout." This recalls the "shoot" from the rod of Jesse (Is 11:1) and provides the basis for the messianic interpretation.   [‡]LXX, "the expectation of the nations."

OVERVIEW: Within Genesis 49 the early Christian commentators found the verses referring to Judah particularly interesting because of the possibility of reading them in a messianic sense. In blessing Judah, Jacob, knowing future events in their spiritual sense, was blessing David and Christ, who was born according to the flesh from David. The brothers, who praise him, represent the apostles (HIPPOLYTUS).

Jacob appears to be addressing the patriarch Judah, but it is the later Judah, Christ, that is meant. His hands are on the back of his enemies (AMBROSE, RUFINUS). The meaning of the name Judah, understood as "praise" or "celebrated with hymns," shows that the words must be referred to Christ (CYRIL OF ALEXANDRIA). In Genesis 49:9 the "lion" and "lion's whelp" are to be understood as referring to the Father and the Son. The phrase "a shoot" shows the generation of Christ according to the flesh (HIPPOLYTUS, AMBROSE). In a different interpretation of the same verse, Judah, representing Christ, is called a lion to show his kingly nature and in opposition to our adversary (the devil), also called a lion in Scripture (CYRIL OF JERUSALEM). With the aid of a citation from the *Physiologus*,[1] it can be shown that "lion's whelp" symbolically and literally signifies Christ. The "shoot" suggests that he was generated apart from sexual intercourse and without human seed. The same words can also be applied

[1]The name given to collections of questions and answers regarding the wonders of the natural sciences. The *Physiologus* is presumed to be Aristotle, but these collections do not predate the third century A.D. They have been transmitted in various forms in Greek, Latin and the oriental languages and attributed to a variety of authors, including Epiphanius, Basil and Chrysostom.

to the apostle Paul in a different sense (RUFINUS). The reference to the lion sleeping is interpreted as an allusion to the three days that Christ's body lay in the tomb. The reference to waking points to Christ's resurrection (HIPPOLYTUS, AMBROSE, RUFINUS).

The mention of the scepter in Genesis 49:10 is to be interpreted of Christ, the true king, as is the reference to the nations that hope in him (AMBROSE, RUFINUS). On the moral level of interpretation, the nations signify the passions of the soul, which may come under submission through confessing Christ (RUFINUS).

The vine in Genesis 49:11 symbolizes Christ to whom the new people, represented by the ass or colt, is bound (CLEMENT OF ALEXANDRIA, AMBROSE, CHRYSOSTOM, RUFINUS). The verse also refers to Christ's future entrance into Jerusalem on a foal (EPHRAIM). On the moral level, the ass's foal refers to the senses of the soul (RUFINUS). The mention of washing his garments in wine can be interpreted as a reference to Christ's baptism and passion. With many variations, Christ's robe is his flesh and his garments are interpreted to refer to the Gentiles or the church (HIPPOLYTUS, NOVATIAN, AMBROSE, RUFINUS).

The "eyes" mentioned in Genesis 49:12 are interpreted to be the prophets as the eyes of Christ and the "teeth" refer either to the apostles or the commandments of the Lord (HIPPOLYTUS, AMBROSE). All of these things refer to the Word. Even the reference to milk can be understood as a figure of the blood of the Lord (CLEMENT OF ALEXANDRIA). In a different interpretation, the "teeth whiter than milk" refers to the members of Christ's body, who can chew the solid food of the Word of God (RUFINUS).

49:8 Praise from Your Brothers

ACCORDING TO THE SPIRIT AND THE FLESH. HIPPOLYTUS: But, one may say, why did it seem right to the prophet to impose on Judah such a blessing, when he had done nothing like that for the first ones?

Now learn the reason. . . . In fact David had to be born from the tribe of Judah and Christ from David with regard to the flesh. [Therefore] the prophet foreknowing the future events in their spiritual sense has blessed there David, who descended from Judah, and the Christ who, according to the flesh, had to be born from David, so that he might receive from God not only the blessing according to the spirit but also the blessing according to the flesh. ON THE BLESSINGS OF ISAAC AND JACOB 15.[2]

THE BROTHERS ARE THE APOSTLES. HIPPOLYTUS: Who are the brothers who praised and adored him but the apostles, to whom the Lord said, "Are you my brothers and coheirs?"[3] And then to say, "Your hands are on the back of your enemies" can mean either of two things: by simply stretching his hands [on the cross] Christ was able, in the course of the fight against his enemies, to triumph over [invisible] powers.[4] Or he has become the Lord and Master and Judge of all those who were his enemies according to the flesh, after being set in this role by the Father.[5] ON THE BLESSINGS OF ISAAC AND JACOB 16.[6]

JUDAH REPRESENTS THE TRUE CONFESSOR WHO WAS TO COME. AMBROSE: This text appears to be directed to the patriarch Judah, indeed, but more so that later Judah is meant, the true confessor who was born of that tribe and who alone is praised by his brothers; of them he says, "I will declare your name to my brothers."[7] He is the Lord by nature but a brother by grace; his hands, which he stretched out to an unbelieving people,[8] are on the back of his enemies. For with those same hands and by that same passion Christ protected his own, subjugated hostile powers, and made subject to himself all people who were without faith and devotion. Of these the Father says to his Son, "And you will rule in

---

[2]PO 27:70-72. [3]Mt 12:50; Jn 20:17; Rom 8:17. [4]Col 2:15. [5]Jn 5:22. [6]PO 27:74-76. [7]Ps 22:22 (21:23 LXX). [8]Is 65:2; Rom 10:11.

the midst of your enemies."[9] It was their own wickedness that made them enemies, not Christ's will. In this there is a great gift of the Lord. Previously, spiritual wickedness[10] generally used to make our neck bend to the yoke of captivity. Thus even David wrote that he felt in some way the hands of those who triumphed over him, for he said, "Upon my back sinners have wrought."[11] But now spiritual wickedness is subject to the triumph of Christ and to his hands, as it were; that is, wickedness undergoes the affliction of captivity, being subject forever in deeds and in works. And it is he indeed to whom the sons of his Father bow down, when we bow down to him; for he has permitted us to call upon the Father, and to be subject to the Father is to be subject to virtue. THE PATRIARCHS 4.17.[12]

THESE TEXTS CAN FITTINGLY BE REFERRED TO CHRIST. RUFINUS: This can be referred to the historical Judah as well as to those kings who were his descendants. They broke the back of their enemies by administering the kingdom of that people. But this can also be fittingly referred to Christ, who is praised with good reason by his brothers, that is, by the apostles whom he himself called brothers in the Gospel. And his enemies, on whose back is his hand, appear to be those whom the Father promised to place under his feet by saying, "Sit at my right hand until I place your enemies under your feet."[13] They are enemies as long as they are unbelieving and unfaithful, and for that reason they are struck on the back. But after their conversion they become brothers and praise the One who, by summoning them to the adoption of the Father, has made them his coheirs and brothers. It is said correctly that the back of the enemies is struck by Christ. All those who worshiped the idols turned their back to God, as the Lord, through the prophet, accused them by saying, "They turned their backs to me, and not their faces."[14] Therefore he strikes their back so that after being converted they may turn their back to the idols and raise their forehead to God and may accomplish what is written here: "Your

father's sons shall bow down before you." In fact, they adore him when they have become sons of the Father and have received the spirit of adoption in which they cry out, "Abba, Father."[15] No one calls Jesus Christ Lord except those who are in the Holy Spirit.[16] THE BLESSINGS OF THE PATRIARCHS 1.5.[17]

THESE WORDS MUST BE REFERRED TO CHRIST. CYRIL OF ALEXANDRIA: In these blessings, the way that they expressly introduced the listeners to the prophecy concerning the incarnation of our Savior is extremely clear. At the beginning of the blessing the meaning of the name itself is set before the reader's eyes, and also the fact that the tribe of Judah was superior to all the others for its glory. If one wants to interpret the name Judah, it means "praise" or "hymn" or "celebrated with hymns." These words therefore must be referred to Christ, who obviously is from the tribe of Judah according to the flesh. He was born from Judah, Jesse and David and from that virgin who was assumed for the generation of the flesh. . . . You must be praised, and to God you will give back the glory that is due him. No one else is suited to be glorified but only the living and well-known God. Even though you appeared human and emptied yourself,[18] you are known to be holy and eternal. Your brothers according to human nature will not be related to you as man but rather will praise you as Lord, though placed among your brothers, and will glorify you as Creator, though you have placed yourself with them among the creatures. They will recognize you as the Lord and the King, even though you appeared veiled under the "form of a slave."[19] Moreover, he foretold the fact that the Immanuel would have overcome all those who opposed him . . . saying, "Your hands on the back of your enemies." And Christ himself, through the voice of David, foretold the same thing. He said, "I will pursue my

---

[9]Ps 110:2 (109:2 LXX). [10]Eph 6:12. [11]Ps 129:3 (128:3 LXX). [12]FC 65:251*. [13]Ps 110:1 (109:1 LXX). [14]Jer 2:27. [15]Rom 8:15-16. [16]1 Cor 12:3. [17]SC 140:42-44. [18]Phil 2:7. [19]Phil 2:7.

enemies and will take them, and I will not return until they are defeated. I will crush them, and they will not be able to stand but will fall under my feet."[20] Then Jacob said rightly, "His hands will be on the back of his enemies," that is, as those of the one pursuing rather than those of one fleeing, as those of the one striking rather than those of one who is struck. What is declared in the book of the Psalms is true: "The enemy shall have no advantage against him, and the son of iniquity shall not hurt him again."[21] If he gives us the power to "tread upon serpents and scorpions, and over all the power of the enemy,"[22] how can we not be confident that he has under his control those who want to oppose him and to exalt themselves impiously? The divine Jacob foretold that Christ cannot flee but only pursue and that he would defeat everyone effortlessly (in fact, he conquered the world),[23] when he said, "Your hands will be on the back of your enemies, and the children of your father will adore you." GLAPHYRA ON GENESIS, 7.[24]

49:9 Judah Is a Lion's Whelp

HE HAS CLEARLY SHOWN THE FATHER AND THE SON. HIPPOLYTUS: By saying "lion" and "lion's whelp," he has clearly pointed toward the two persons: that of the Father and that of the Son. He said, "From a shoot, my son, you have gone up"[25] in order to show the generation of Christ according to the flesh. Christ, after his incarnation, being conceived by the Holy Spirit in the womb of the Virgin, sprouted in her, and like a flower and a pleasant perfume, once he went out of that womb into the world, he appeared visibly. On the other hand, by saying "whelp of the lion" he indicates Christ's generation according to spirit, through which he appears to come directly from God, as he has shown him like a king born of a king. However, he has not remained silent about his generation according to the flesh but says clearly, "From a shoot, my son, you have gone up." Isaiah says, "And there shall come forth a rod out of the root of Jesse, and a blossom shall come

up from it."[26] The root of Jesse was the stump of the patriarchs, like a root planted in the ground, and the rod coming out of it was Mary, because she was from the house and the family of David.[27] The blossom that had come up from the rod was Christ, the one that Jacob had prophesied by saying, "From a shoot, my son, you have gone up." ON THE BLESSINGS OF ISAAC AND JACOB 16.[28]

HE IS CALLED A LION. CYRIL OF JERUSALEM: Again, he is called a Lion; not a man eater, but, as it were, showing by this title his kingly, strong and resolute nature, Then too, he is called a Lion in opposition to the lion, our adversary who roars and devours those who have been deceived.[29] For the Savior came, not having changed his own gentle nature, and yet as the mighty lion of the tribe of Judah, saving them that believe but trampling upon the adversary. CATECHETICAL LECTURES 10.3.[30]

HE REPRESENTED THE FATHER AND MANIFESTED THE SON. AMBROSE: "A lion's whelp is Judah." Isn't it clear that he represented the Father and manifested the Son? Is there any clearer way to teach that God the Son is of one nature with the Father? The one is the lion, the other the lion's whelp. By this paltry comparison, their unity in the same nature and power is perceived. King proceeds from king, a strong one from one who is strong. Because Jacob foresaw that there would be those to claim that the Son was younger in age, he replied to them by adding, "From my seed you have come up to me. Resting you have slept like a lion and like a whelp." And in a different passage you find that the whelp is himself "the lion of the tribe of Judah."[31] . . . But the Son is not being named in such a way as to be separated from the Father. Jacob, who confesses the Son, also esteems him equal.

Moreover, he represented the Son's incarna-

[20]Ps 18:37-38 (17:38-39 LXX). [21]Ps 88:23 LXX. [22]Lk 10:19. [23]Jn 16:33. [24]PG 69:349-52. [25]LXX. [26]Is 11:1. [27]Lk 2:4. [28]PO 27:76-78. [29]1 Pet 5:8. [30]FC 61:197. [31]Rev 5:5.

tion in a wonderful fashion when he said, "From my seed you have come up to me." For Christ sprouted in the womb of the Virgin like a shrub upon the earth; like a flower of pleasing fragrance, he was sent forth in the splendor of new light and came up from his mother's vitals for the redemption of the entire world. Just so, Isaiah says, "There shall come forth a rod out of the root of Jesse, and a flower shall come up out of the root."[32] The root is the household of the Jews, the rod is Mary, the flower of Mary is Christ. She is rightly called a rod, for she is of royal lineage, of the house and family of David.[33] Her flower is Christ, who destroyed the stench of worldly pollution and poured out the fragrance of eternal life. THE PATRIARCHS 4.18-19.[34]

THE MYSTICAL INTERPRETATION. RUFINUS: The mystical interpretation, according to which the lion's whelp not only symbolically but also literally signifies Christ, is much more suitable to this passage. In fact, the *Physiologus*[35] writes with regard to the lion's whelp that after its birth it sleeps for three days and three nights; then the lair itself awakens the sleeping whelp, as if it was shaken by the noise and the roar of the father. Therefore this whelp rises from the shoot: he was born from the Virgin, not from a seed but from a shoot. So Christ was born without sexual intercourse with a man and without the natural seed, like a bough or a branch. In this manner the reality of the assumption of the flesh from the Virgin is clearly demonstrated, and the contact with human or natural seed is excluded in the holy shoot. THE BLESSINGS OF THE PATRIARCHS 1.6.[36]

PAUL WAS RIGHTLY CONSIDERED TO BE A JUDAH. RUFINUS: "Judah is a lion's whelp: from the shoot, my son, you have gone up." With good reason the one who was crucified and resurrected with Christ[37] is called "young lion," as Paul, who was rightly considered to be a Judah, said when he confessed his sin: "For I am the least of the apostles, unfit to be called an apostle, because I persecuted the church of God."[38] And Paul asserts

that the essence of Christ [lit. "what Christ is"] is in himself when he proclaims, "I have been crucified with Christ; and it is no longer I who live, but it is Christ who lives in me."[39] Therefore a young lion is either the one who sleeps with Christ, because he died for sins, or the one who is resurrected with Christ, because he lives for God.[40]

And the son has sprouted from the shoot. Without doubt the reference here is to the one who, being a wild olive tree, was grafted onto the good olive tree.[41] He rejected the vulgar and gross morals of the carnal nature, remaining in Christ, the true vine, through the spirit of adoption,[42] thereby producing much fruit from his precepts.

And since he is so, reclining, he sleeps like a lion. The wise man has the confidence of the lion,[43] especially when he can assuredly assert, "I can do all things through him who strengthens me."[44] No fear, no threat, no temptation can awaken him; his decisions are firm, and his mind is stable. THE BLESSINGS OF THE PATRIARCHS 1.11.[45]

THE THREE DAYS OF HIS BURIAL. HIPPOLYTUS: He says the words "After stooping down, you slept like a lion and a whelp" in order to show Christ sleeping during the three days of his burial, when he rests in the heart of the earth. And also the Lord himself has testified such when he said, "For as Jonah was three days and three nights in the belly of the whale, so will the Son of man be three days and three nights in the heart of the earth."[46] And David by announcing him in advance said, "I lay down and slept; I awoke for the Lord will help me."[47] Jacob also said, "Who will wake him?" He did not say "Nobody will wake him" but "Who?" in order that we may understand that the Father woke the Son from the dead, as the apostle confirms: "and through God the Father who woke him from the dead."[48] And

[32]Is 11:1. [33]Lk 1:27. [34]FC 65:252-53*. [35]See CPG 3766. For *Physiologus* see p. 325, n.1. [36]SC 140:46. [37]Cf. Gal 2:19. [38]1 Cor 15:9. [39]Gal 2:19-20. [40]Gal 2:19; Rom 6:10. [41]Rom 11:17. [42]Rom 8:15. [43]Prov 28:1. [44]Phil 4:13. [45]SC 140:64-66. [46]Mt 12:40. [47]Ps 3:5 (3:6 LXX). [48]Gal 1:1.

Peter said, "But God raised him up, having loosed the pangs of death, because it was not possible for him to be held by it."[49] ON THE BLESSINGS OF ISAAC AND JACOB 16.[50]

THE AUTHOR OF HIS OWN RESURRECTION.

AMBROSE: Therefore you have become acquainted with the incarnation; learn of the passion. "Resting, you have slept like a lion." When Christ lay at rest in the tomb, it was as if he were in a kind of bodily sleep, as he himself says, "I have slept and have taken my rest and have risen up, because the Lord will sustain me."[51] On this account also Jacob says, "Who will arouse him?" that is, him whom the Lord will take up. Who else is there to rouse him again, unless he rouses himself by his own power and the power of the Father? I see that he was born by his own authority, I see that he died by his own will; I see that he sleeps by his own power. He did all things by his own dominion; will he need the help of someone else to rise again? Therefore he is the author of his own resurrection, he is the judge of his death; he is expected by the nations. THE PATRIARCHS 4.20.[52]

LIKE A WHELP HE WOKE ON THE THIRD DAY.

RUFINUS: "Having crouched, you slept as a lion and as a whelp."[53] It is evident that the actions of crouching and sleeping signify the passion and death. But let us see why he sleeps as a lion and a whelp. With regard to the sleep of the whelp it has been already said above that it can very conveniently be referred to Christ, who, after being buried for three days and three nights in the heart of the earth, completed, as was expected, the sleep of death. But I believe that the expression "as a lion" must be interpreted in this way: the death of Christ marked the defeat and the triumph over the demons. In fact, our lion captured all the prey that the hostile lion had conquered[54] after destroying and crushing the man. Then, by coming back from the underworld and ascending on high, he made slavery his captive.[55] Therefore in his sleep the lion won and defeated every evil

and destroyed the one who had the power of death.[56] And like a whelp he woke up on the third day. THE BLESSINGS OF THE PATRIARCHS 1.6.[57]

49:10 Obedience of the Peoples to Judah

THE HOPE OF THE CHURCH LIES IN CHRIST.

AMBROSE: Yes, because they denied the true king, they began to have false kings. And so the patriarch is saying this: The inheritance of an unblemished line of succession, traced through the kings, will be kept among the judges and kings of the Jews, "until he comes for whom it has been reserved," reserved that he may gather together the church of God out of the assembly of all the nations and the devotion of the Gentile peoples. That is, this awaits him, this is kept for him as his due—the prerogative of such great grace is given to him.

"And he is the expectation of the nations." Jacob spoke more meaningfully than if he had said, "The nations are expecting him," for in Christ lies the entire hope of the church. Therefore it is said to Moses, "Remove the sandals from your feet."[58] Otherwise Moses, who was chosen as leader of the people, might be thought to be the bridegroom of the church. It was for that reason that Joshua, son of Nun, removed his sandals,[59] in order that he also could preserve the gift of so great a function for him who was to come. It is for that reason that John says, "A man is coming after me, the strap of whose sandal I am not worthy to untie."[60] He also says, "He who has the bride is the bridegroom; but the friend of the bridegroom, who stands and hears him, rejoices with joy."[61] This means he alone is the husband of the church, he is the expectation of the nations, and the prophets removed their sandals while offering to him a union of nuptial grace. THE PATRIARCHS 4.21-22.[62]

---

[49]Acts 2:24. [50]PO 27:78. [51]Ps 3:6. [52]FC 65:253. [53]LXX. [54]1 Pet 5:9. [55]Eph 4:8 = Ps 68:18 (67:19 LXX). [56]Heb 2:14. [57]SC 140:46-48. [58]Ex 3:5. [59]Josh 5:15. [60]Jn 1:27. [61]Jn 3:29. [62]FC 65:253-54*.

THE KINGDOM HAS BEEN RESERVED. RUFI-NUS: This passage clearly refers to Judah. It appears that until the birth of Christ there was no lack of princes from the family of Judah or of heads from its sides, until Herod came, who according to the history written by Josephus was a foreigner and usurped the throne of Judea through his plots. As soon as this happened and a head from the sides of Judah was lacking, the one to whom the kingdom had been reserved immediately came. THE BLESSINGS OF THE PATRIARCHS 1.7.[63]

THE PASSIONS OF OUR SOUL. RUFINUS: "And he will be the expectation of nations." Since we propose to investigate once and for all the moral meaning of the text, we need to look inside ourselves for those nations who expect from confession such purification and perfection of the senses. We can certainly see the nations inside ourselves as all the passions of our soul, which are more restless in our youth and, in a sense, act like pagans. THE BLESSINGS OF THE PATRIARCHS 1.11.[64]

49:11 Judah's Foal

THE VINE SIGNIFIES THE WORD. CLEMENT OF ALEXANDRIA: Again, it is said, "He tethers his colt to the vine." This means he united the simple, new people to the Word, whom the vine signifies. For the product of the vine is wine; of the Word, blood. Both are saving potions: wine, for the health of the body; the other, blood, for the salvation of the soul. CHRIST THE EDUCATOR 1.5.15.[65]

HIS FOAL IS BOUND TO THE VINE. EPHREM THE SYRIAN: When our Lord came, he also bound his foal to the true vine. Just as all the symbols are fulfilled by him, he would fulfill in truth even this that was handed down to them in likeness. Either there was a vine in Jerusalem outside of the sanctuary to which he bound his foal when he entered the temple, or in that city from which the foal came it had been bound to a vine. He

said, "If they say to you, 'Why are you untying this foal?' say to them, 'The master requires it.' "[66] COMMENTARY ON GENESIS 42.6.[67]

THE ENTRY INTO JERUSALEM. AMBROSE: Let us be bound with bonds of a faith that is like a fruitful branch and cannot be undone, as it were, to that everlasting vine, that is, to the Lord Jesus, who says, "I am the vine; my Father is the gardener."[68] This explains the mystery that the Lord Jesus in the Gospel ordered an ass's colt to be loosed and himself sat upon it;[69] thus, like one that was bound to a vine, he could find rest in the everlasting goodness of the saints. THE PATRIARCHS 4.23.[70]

THE GENTILES WOULD PROVE MORE RESPONSIVE. CHRYSOSTOM: I mean, since the ass is an unclean animal, hence he says, "Those unclean Gentiles will be introduced with such ease as if someone were to tether the foal to the stem of the vine, referring to the extraordinary degree of his authority and to the great responsiveness of the Gentiles." That is to say, its readiness to be tethered to the stem of the vine is a mark of the ass's gentleness. Now it was to the vine that Jesus compared his own teaching: "I am the true vine," he says, remember, "and my Father is the vinedresser."[71] HOMILIES ON GENESIS 67.9.[72]

HIS FOAL IS THE PEOPLE OF THE NATIONS. RUFINUS: This is appropriately and exclusively said about Christ. He that said, "I am the true vine"[73] bound his foal to the vine. Therefore he binds his foal and his ass's foal to this vine. His foal is the people of the nations, onto whom certainly the burden of the law had never been imposed and among whom no one but he had ever held the first position. His ass's foal are those, who coming from the first people symbolized here by the she-ass, were elected for salvation and

---

[63]SC 140:50. [64]SC 140:68. [65]FC 23:16. [66]Lk 19:31. [67]FC 91:204. [68]Jn 15:1. [69]Mt 21:1-7; Zech 9:9; Is 62:11. [70]FC 65:254-55*. [71]Jn 15:1. [72]FC 87:270*. [73]Jn 15:1.

about whom the prophet says, "If the sons of Israel are like the sand of the sea, the rest shall be saved."[74] After rejecting the she-ass who preferred to wear the yoke of the law in its infidelity, the foal born from it is elected, that is, a new people coming from the old one through faith is adopted and associated to the people of the nations. Therefore Christ is called "vine" because he has received the human nature, to which the Word of God binds his foal, that is, unites his people and associates it with that way of life that he followed in the flesh, so that the foal that has been bound may become with him son of God and coheir of Christ. THE BLESSINGS OF THE PATRIARCHS 1.8.[75]

THE FOAL REPRESENTS THE SENSES OF THE SOUL. RUFINUS: "Binding his foal to the vine." Here we understand "foal" as the sense itself (intelligence, reason) on account of the renewal of life: that same sense which elsewhere the Lord calls "child," when he says, "Truly I tell you, unless you change and become like children, you will never enter the kingdom of heaven."[76] When one unites with the Lord and becomes a single spirit with him,[77] he binds his foal to the vine by saying, "It is good for me to cleave close to God."[78] "And his ass's foal to its branch." That branch or rather that tendril, as we have interpreted it above, can be understood as the subtle and flexible intelligence of knowledge. When the ass's foal, that is, the senses of the soul, are bound to it, they prevent the soul itself from falling. THE BLESSINGS OF THE PATRIARCHS 1.11.[79]

HE HAS MYSTICALLY INDICATED HIS BAPTISM. HIPPOLYTUS: Here Christ has mystically indicated his baptism. After he had come up from the Jordan and had purified its waters (by plunging in them), he received the grace and the gift of the Holy Spirit.[80] ... And since by hanging on the cross he was like a bunch of ripe grapes, after his side was pierced he emitted blood and water:[81] the former for the bath (baptism), the latter for the ransom (redemption), the prophet [Jacob] rightly said, "He shall wash his robe in wine, and

his garment in the blood of ripe grapes." ON THE BLESSINGS OF ISAAC AND JACOB 18.[82]

THE GARMENT AND THE CLOTHING OF THE WORD. NOVATIAN: Therefore it was the Word of God, as we have already stated, who is found to have at one time put on and at another time to have put off the flesh. He even foretold this in the blessing "He shall wash his garment in wine, and his clothing in the blood of the grape." ... It is quite evident to us that the flesh was the garment and the body was the clothing of the Word who washed the substance of his body and the matter of his flesh in the blood, that is, in wine, cleansing by his passion that humanity he had taken upon himself. Therefore, inasmuch as he is washed, he is man, because the garment that is washed is flesh. But he who washed it is the Word of God, who, in order to wash the garment, was made the wearer of the garment. Accordingly he is declared to be man by that substance which was assumed that it might be washed, just as he who washed it is shown to be God, by the authority of the Word. ON THE TRINITY 21.12-16.[83]

THE WATER WASHED US, THE BLOOD REDEEMED US. AMBROSE: "He will wash his robe in wine." The good robe is the flesh of Christ, which has covered the sins of all people, taken up the offenses of all, concealed the misdeeds of all—the good robe which has clothed all people with the garment of rejoicing. He washed this robe in wine at his baptism in the Jordan, when the Holy Spirit came down like a dove and remained upon him.[84] By this, it is indicated that the fullness of the Holy Spirit will be indivisible in him and will not depart. On this account also the Evangelist says, "The Lord Jesus, full of Holy Spirit, returned from the Jordan."[85] Therefore Jesus washed his robe, not to wash away his stain, for he had none, but to wash away the stain

---

[74]Rom 9:27; Is 10:22; Hos 1:10. [75]SC 140:52-54. [76]Mt 18:3. [77]1 Cor 6:17. [78]Ps 73:28 (72:28 LXX). [79]SC 140:68. [80]Mt 3:13-17. [81]Jn 19:34. [82]PO 27:80-82. [83]FC 67:80-81. [84]Jn 1:32. [85]Lk 4:1.

that was ours. Then Jacob continued, "and his mantle in the blood of the grape." This means that in the passion of his body he washed the nations with his blood. Truly the mantle represents the nations, as it is written, "As I live, says the Lord, unless I shall clothe myself with them all, as with a garment,"[86] and in another passage, "Like clothing you will change them, and they will be changed."[87] And so with his own blood he cleansed not his own sins, for there were none, but the offenses that we committed. It was appropriate that Jacob spoke of a grape, because Christ hung on the wood like a grape. He is the vine, he is the grape; he is the vine because he cleaves to the wood and the grape because, when his side was opened by the soldier's lance, he sent forth water and blood. For thus John said that "there came out from him blood and water,"[88] water for baptism, blood for redemption. The water washed us, the blood redeemed us. THE PATRIARCHS 4.24.[89]

CHRIST'S ROBE REPRESENTS THE CHURCH.
RUFINUS: "He shall wash his robe in wine and his garment in the blood of grapes." These words, on the basis of the historical account, will appear to signify a fertile land full of vineyards or, in a hyperbolic manner, the abundance of wine. But the mystical explanation will give them a nobler sense. Christ's robe washed in wine is interpreted with good reason as the church, which he himself has purified in his blood and is spotless and faultless.[90] "You were not redeemed through silver and gold," the apostle says, "but through the precious blood of the only-begotten Son of God."[91] And therefore in the wine of that blood, that is, in the bath of regeneration Christ washes the church.[92] And we are buried with him through baptism in his death and in his blood. . . . But let us see how he will wash his garment in the blood of grapes. The garment appears to be a more intimate cloth, which is closer to the body than the robe. Those who, after they had been washed with the bath and had become his robe, reached the sacrament of the blood of grapes, that is, a more intimate

and more secret mystery; they in a sense participate in his garment. In fact, the soul is washed in the blood of grapes, when it has begun to grasp the meaning of that sacrament. After perceiving and comprehending the virtue of the blood of the Word of God, the soul will become more receptive as it is purer. Each day it is washed in order to improve in its knowledge. THE BLESSINGS OF THE PATRIARCHS 1.9.[93]

49:12 Eyes Red with Wine

THE PROPHETS HAVE BEEN THE EYES OF CHRIST. HIPPOLYTUS: "Eyes" then, the prophets have been the eyes of Christ when they rejoiced in the power of the Spirit, and announced in advance the sufferings which had to rush upon him and which were useful for the generations after him to understand that every person can be saved. Through the words "His teeth (are) whiter than milk" he signified either the apostles sanctified by the Word himself and become like milk, the apostles who have provided us with the spiritual and heavenly nourishment. Or, . . . he means the commandments of the Lord, which were uttered by a holy mouth but remain for us milk, so that by obtaining from them nourishment and growth we may take our part of the heavenly bread. ON THE BLESSINGS OF ISAAC AND JACOB 19.[94]

THE LORD IS ALL THESE THINGS. CLEMENT OF ALEXANDRIA: All these various ways and figures of speech speak of the Word: solid food, flesh, nourishment, bread, blood and milk. The Lord is all these things for the refreshment of us who believe in him. Let no one think it strange, then, that we speak of the blood of the Lord also under the figure of milk. Is it not named wine, metaphorically? "He washes his garment in wine," Scripture says, "and his robe in the blood of the grape."[95] That means he will attire the body of the

---

[86]Is 49:18. [87]Ps 102:26 (101:27 LXX). [88]Jn 19:34. [89]FC 65:255-56*. [90]Eph 5:26-27. [91]1 Pet 1:18-19. [92]Tit 3:5. [93]SC 140:56-58. [94]PO 27:84. [95]Gen 49:11.

Word with his own blood, just as he will nurture those who hunger for the Word with his own Spirit. Christ the Educator 1.6.47.[96]

He Means the Prophets and the Apostles.

Ambrose: And therefore the prophet says, "His eyes are joyful from wine, and his teeth are whiter than milk," for he means the prophets and the apostles. For some, like eyes of Christ, have foreseen and announced his coming, and of them Christ himself says, "Abraham saw my day and he rejoiced,"[97] and one of the prophets says, "I saw the Lord of hosts."[98] Seeing him, they were filled with a spiritual joy. Others, however, that is, the apostles, whom the Lord cleansed from every stain of sin, were made whiter than milk, for no blemish darkened them afterward. Indeed, milk is a temporal thing, but the grace of the apostles remains forever. They provided us with that spiritual sustenance which is of heaven, and they nourished the vitals of the spirit which is within. There are also those who think that the commandments of the Lord, which were revealed from the mouth of God, being clear, have become to us like milk. Nourished upon them, we come to the sustenance of the bread of heaven. On this account also Paul says, "I gave you milk to drink, not solid food; for you were not yet ready."[99] The Corinthian in the beginning of faith is initiated with milk to drink, whereas those saints whose faith is proclaimed in the whole world[100] are strengthened with more solid food, as if they had been weaned. The Patriarchs 4.25.[101]

Like a Wine That Cheers the Human

Heart. Rufinus: And also Christ's eyes will be like this, those eyes which bring the light of knowledge to the whole body, according to what is written in the Gospel: "The lamp of your body is the eye."[102] Therefore these eyes are made graceful: a word of knowledge is seasoned with salt[103] to be pleasing to the audience. The one who proclaims the word of knowledge is not said to be "made graceful" just because he has in

himself the grace but because he also acts in order that his listeners may have the grace. In fact, "after comprehending that, the wise man will become wiser."[104] His eyes are made graceful by wine because nothing is watery, nothing is fluid, nothing is cold in the word of knowledge. It is like a wine that cheers the human heart and is sprinkled on the wounds of the victims of robbers. This means that the wounds of the listeners, their sins, are not only soothed by the sweetness of oil but are also purified by the harshness of wine. The Blessings of the Patriarchs 1.10.[105]

Digest the Solid Food the Scripture

Offers. Rufinus: We have already discussed many times about the nature and quality of Christ's limbs, and it seems to be superfluous to repeat again the same things in this passage. So his teeth whiter than milk are those who can chew and grind with their teeth the strong and solid food of the Word of God to extreme fineness, those about whom the apostle in his epistle to the Hebrews says, "Solid food is for the mature, for those whose faculties have been trained by practice to distinguish good from evil."[106] About the still imperfect Corinthians he says, "I fed you with milk, not solid food, for you were not ready for solid food."[107] Since they are superior to those who live on milk, his teeth are therefore white, that is, those who can take and eat solid food are superior to those who still need milk like babies. That is why in the law those animals which ruminate and bring back to their teeth the food that they had previously eaten, in order to make it very fine for their feeding, are called pure animals.[108] And so in the most consistent manner his teeth are said to be white. All those who are perfect and, by explaining through worthy and proper interpretations the food of the Scripture, administer to the

---

[96]FC 23:44**. [97]Jn 8:56. [98]Is 6:1. [99]1 Cor 3:2. [100]Rom 1:8. [101]FC 65:256. [102]Mt 6:22. [103]Col 4:6. [104]Prov 1:5. [105]SC 140:60. [106]Heb 5:14. [107]1 Cor 3:2. [108]Lev 11:3.

church the subtle and fine intelligence, which is called spiritual, must be pure and free and faultless, so that they may never be told, "You, then, that teach others, will you not teach your-self?"[109] The Blessings of the Patriarchs 1.10.[110]

[109]Rom 2:21. [110]SC 140:60-62.

49:13 ZEBULUN

[13]Zebulun shall dwell at the shore of the sea;
 he shall become a haven for ships,
 and his border shall be at Sidon.

Overview: Zebulun dwelling at the shore of the sea signifies the pagan nations that look for refuge in harbors, that is, the church, a harbor of salvation (Hippolytus, Ambrose). On the moral level, Zebulun is variously interpreted to mean "freedom from things of night" (Ambrose) or "nocturnal flux" (Rufinus).

49:13 Zebulun and the Shore of the Sea

The Pagan Nations Seek Harbor. Hippolytus: Through Zebulun he has metaphorically foretold the pagan nations, who live now in the world along the coast and are tormented by the storm of temptations as if they were in the sea. Therefore they move and look for refuge in harbors, that is, in churches. The Blessings of the Patriarchs 20.[1]

The Church Is Like a Harbor of Salvation. Ambrose: The very interpretation of his name gives promise of better things, since in our tongue it means "freedom from the things of night," which is surely a good, and appropriate to one who trusts in the wings of the Lord. For the truth of the Lord encompasses him, so that he is not afraid of the terror of the night or of the thing that walks about in darkness.[2] Therefore "Zebu-lun shall dwell by the sea." Thus he may look upon the shipwrecks of others while being himself free from danger; he may behold others driven here and there on the sea of this world, those who are borne about by every wind of doctrine, while himself persevering on the ground of an immovable faith.[3] Just so, the most holy church is grounded and founded in faith, as it beholds the tempests of heretics and the shipwrecks of the Jews, because they refused the pilot whom they once had. Therefore [the church] dwells beside the waters, but it is not disturbed by the waters. It is ready to give help rather than being subject to danger. Even so, if anyone have been driven by severe storms and wants to take refuge in the harbor, the church is at hand like a harbor of salvation. Opening its arms, it calls into the lap of its tranquility those who are in danger and shows them a trusty place of anchorage. Therefore, the churches in this world are scattered over the coasts like seaports; they stand to meet the afflicted, and say to them that a refuge has been prepared for believers, where they can beach their wind-battered vessels. The Patriarchs 5.26.[4]

[1]PO 27:84-86. [2]Ps 91:4-6 (90:4-6 LXX). [3]1 Tim 1:19. [4]FC 65:256-57**.

ZEBULUN EXTENDS AS FAR AS SIDON. RUFI-
NUS: But the fact that he extends as far as Sidon,
that is, to the hunters, might mean that this man
also tries to be among those to whom it was said,
"Catch us the little foxes that spoil the vineyards."[5] Therefore Zebulun extends to the hunters, so that he may learn to hunt, in case some
wild animals or cunning foxes, that is, ferocious

demons or damaging thoughts, should enter his
heart and try to destroy the vineyard of the Lord
Sabaoth. In order to catch them, he has become a
good hunter against bad thoughts. THE BLESS-
INGS OF THE PATRIARCHS 2.11.[6]

---

[5]Song 2:15. [6]SC 140:92.

49:14-15 ISSACHAR

[14]*Issachar is a strong ass,*
    crouching between the sheepfolds;
[15]*he saw that a resting place was good,*
    and that the land was pleasant;
so he bowed his shoulder to bear,
    *and became a slave at forced labor.**

*The LXX differs significantly from the Hebrew text: "Issachar has desired that which is good; resting between the inheritances. And having seen the resting place that it was good, and the land that it was fertile, he subjected his shoulder to labor, and became a husbandman."

OVERVIEW: On the moral level of interpretation,
Issachar, whose name means "reward," represents
the person who waits for the reward of his good
works, walks on the right path of virtue and rests
in the midst of his "lots," that is, the commandments of God (RUFINUS). On an allegorical level,
Issachar represents Christ as our "reward," who
rests among the "lots," that is, the Old and New
Testaments and in the midst of the prophets
Moses and Elijah (HIPPOLYTUS). He bowed his
shoulders to the cross (AMBROSE).

49:14 Issachar Is a Strong Ass

**ONE WHO WAITS FOR THE REWARD OF GOOD
WORKS.** RUFINUS: Above we have taken into consideration that one who erred because of the threefold impulse of the soul (as a weakness of the entire
soul), which is divided into carnal passion symbol-

ized by Reuben, into anger symbolized by Simeon
and into ill-directed prudence symbolized by Levi.
But then we have shown this person when he re-
pents in the figure of Judah and is largely converted
in the figure of Zebulun. In Issachar, which means
"reward," we see this man wait for the reward of his
good works; and since he has not only driven away
the evil but has also wished for the good, he rests in
the midst of his lots.[1] In the midst is the one who,
according to the warning of the Wisdom, turns neither to the left nor the right,[2] that is, who stays and
walks on the right path of virtue. Here the "lots"
can be interpreted in this manner: "lot" is understood as that which allows people to obtain a part
of the inheritance. This does not appear to happen

---

[1]Rufinus's interpretation is based on the Old Latin translation (*sors*) of
the Greek *klēros*, which can be translated as "inheritance," "lot" or
"fortune." [2]Prov 4:27.

casually, as the pagans think, but is decreed by the judgment and the division of God. Therefore in this moral explanation we must understand the "lots" to be the commandments of God through which the heavenly inheritance will be obtained. So this already converted man hopes in the reward for his actions and rests in the midst of the lots, that is, in the midst of the commandments of God, "seeing that the rest is good and that the land is fertile." After driving away and suppressing the internal fight of his thoughts,[3] which lasted as long as the flesh in him opposed the desires of the spirit and the spirit those of the flesh,[4] his spirit eventually took rest in God. He has seen that the rest is good, since Jesus could by now say to him, "Come and rest awhile."[5] But he also sees that the land is good. When did he see that the land is good? When he purified his flesh from vices and passions, he saw that the land was fertile and fruitful.... We must consider him to be a farmer of his land. He is the one who constantly breaks and furrows with the plough of the Word of God and with the ploughshare of Scripture the fields of his soul and the fallow lands of his heart, and waters the plantations of faith, of charity, of hope and justice with the springs of Israel, and employs any method of agriculture in the field of his soul. THE BLESSINGS OF THE PATRIARCHS 2.14.[6]

49:15 At Forced Labor

REST IN THE INHERITANCE OF THE PROPHETS. HIPPOLYTUS: The text metaphorically and allegorically signifies the Savior through Issachar. Only this one, in fact, wished for the good since his childhood, as Isaiah confirms: "Before the child learned how to call mother and father, he said no to evil and chose the good."[7] He has found his rest in the inheritance of the prophets, in order to accomplish what they had foretold. On the mountain Moses and Elijah were seen while they talked to him by standing one at his right and the other at his left, in order to demonstrate that the Savior rested between them.[8] ON THE BLESSINGS OF ISAAC AND JACOB 21.[9]

HE RESTED AMONG THE LOTS OF THE OLD TESTAMENT AND THE NEW. AMBROSE: "Issachar desired the good and rested in the midst of lots. And seeing the place of rest that it is good, and the land that it is rich, he bowed his shoulder to labor and became a husbandman."[10] Issachar is called "reward," and therefore he represents Christ, who is our reward, because we buy him for ourselves for the hope of everlasting salvation, not with gold and silver but with faith and devotion.... He is the one who desired the good from the beginning and did not know how to desire what is evil. Of him also Isaiah says, "Before the child knows how to call his father or mother, he does not trust evil, choosing what is good."[11] He rested among the lots of the Old Testament and the New and in the midst of the prophets. And therefore he appeared in the middle between Moses and Elijah,[12] to show us that he had rest through discourse with them, through whom many renounce their sins and believe in the living God, and that they themselves are witnesses of his resurrection and blessed repose. Accordingly, to call the nations to the grace of his resurrection—which is the rich and fertile land that bears everlasting fruits, fruits a hundredfold and sixtyfold[13]—he bowed his shoulder to labor, bowed himself to the cross, to carry our sins. For that reason the prophet says, "whose government is on his shoulder."[14] This means, above the passion of his body is the power of his divinity, or it refers to the cross that towers above his body. Therefore he bowed his shoulder, applying himself to the plow, patient in the endurance of all insults, and so subject to affliction that he was wounded on account of our iniquities and weakened on account of our sins.[15] "And he became a gardener," for he knew how to sow his own land with good grain and to plant fruitful trees with deep roots. THE PATRIARCHS 6.30-31.[16]

---

[3]Rom 2:15. [4]Gal 5:17. [5]Mk 6:31. [6]SC 140:96-100. [7]Is 7:16. [8]Mt 17:3. [9]PO 27:88. [10]Gen 49:14-15 LXX. [11]Is 8:4; 7:16. [12]Mt 17:3. [13]Mt 13:8; Mk 4:8. [14]Is 9:6. [15]Is 53:3-5. [16]FC 65:258-59*.

49:16-18 DAN

> [16]Dan shall judge his people
>   as one of the tribes of Israel.
> [17]Dan shall be a serpent in the way,
>   a viper by the path,
> that bites the horse's heels
>   so that his rider falls backward.
> [18]I wait for thy salvation, O LORD.

OVERVIEW: The reference to Dan as a judge prompts the observation that the One from the tribe of Judah will judge all the nations, who is a serpent to the first serpent, Satan (EPHREM). The prophecy may refer to the Antichrist, a cruel judge who tries to throw down those who walk in the way of truth (AMBROSE). The phrase "biting the heel of the horse" signifies the testing of those who announce the way of truth and salvation (HIPPOLYTUS, AMBROSE). In the moral interpretation, Dan represents the person who continues to make moral progress. The "path" indicates the narrow way of salvation, and the serpent signifies ascetical discipline (RUFINUS).

49:16 Dan Shall Judge

JUDGING ALL THE NATIONS. EPHREM THE SYRIAN: If one from Dan judges his people, how much more will that one from Judah, to whom the kingdom belongs, judge all the nations? For our Lord became a serpent to that first serpent and a viper to Satan, just like the serpent of bronze that countered the snakes.[1] COMMENTARY ON GENESIS 43.6.[2]

THE PROPHECY FORETELLS THE ANTICHRIST. AMBROSE: The simple interpretation is this, that the tribe of Dan also supplied the judge in Israel. Granted, after Joshua the son of Nun, the judges of the people were from various tribes. However,

Samson was from the tribe of Dan,[3] and he judged for twenty years.[4] But the prophecy does not refer to him but the Antichrist, a cruel judge and savage tyrant who will come from the tribe of Dan and will judge the people. Like a serpent sitting in the way, he will try to throw down those who walk in the way of truth, for he desires to overthrow the truth. Indeed, this is to bite the horse's heel, so that the horse, injured by the infusion of poison and wounded by the serpent's tooth, lifts up his heel. Just so the betrayer Judas, when tempted by the devil, lifted up his heel[5] upon the Lord Jesus to throw down the rider who threw himself down to lift up all people. THE PATRIARCHS 7.32.[6]

49:17 A Serpent

TESTING THOSE WHO ANNOUNCE TRUTH. HIPPOLYTUS: The fact that the prophet says "biting the heel of the horse" signifies that Christ will test those who announce the way of the truth and salvation. So he also tested the apostles, cheated Judas and took hold of him; he took hold of him as of a horse and threw the rider who was on it to death. ON THE BLESSINGS OF ISAAC AND JACOB 22.[7]

SHUN THE BITES OF THE SERPENT. AMBROSE: On this account, when we run well[8] in the way,

---

[1]Num 21:4-9. [2]FC 91:210. [3]Judg 13:2. [4]Judg 15:20. [5]Ps 41:9 (40:10 LXX); Jn 13:18. [6]FC 65:260**. [7]PO 27:90-92. [8]Gal 5:7.

let us beware that the serpent may not lie hid anywhere in the path and undermine the footstep of the horse—that is, of our body—and suddenly throw the sleeping rider. For if we are vigilant, we ought to be on our guard in some measure and shun the bites of the serpent. Therefore let the sleep of neglect, the sleep of the world, not overwhelm us. Let the sleep of wealth not overwhelm us, lest it be said of us also, "They have slept their sleep, and all the men of riches have found nothing."[9] But there are indeed riders who sleep, of whom it is written, "They have slumbered who mounted on horses."[10] Should avarice wound your heart, should lust inflame it, you are a sleeping rider. . . . Judas was sleeping; therefore he did not hear the words of Christ. Judas was sleeping, yes, sleeping the sleep of wealth, for he sought recompense from his betrayal.[11] The devil saw that he was sleeping, yes, buried in the deep sleep of avarice. He let himself into Judas's heart,[12] wounded the horse and threw the rider, whom he separated from Christ. THE PATRIARCHS 7.33.[13]

THE PATH INDICATES A NARROW WAY. RUFI-NUS: The path indicates a more narrow way, which demonstrates that he does not walk along that wide and spacious way leading to death but along that narrow way full of obstacles leading to life.[14] He bites the heel of the horse and so does what the apostle Paul said: "I pommel my body and subdue it, lest after preaching to others I myself should be disqualified."[15] He acts in this manner so that the rider may fall backwards. He always fears elations and heights and prefers his soul to fall from an evil height to an honest humility, in order to learn from Christ, who is modest and gentle in his heart.[16] It is typical of those who progress to fear elation. And finally a very important apostle like Paul said, "A thorn was given me in the flesh, a messenger of Satan, to keep me from being too elated."[17] And so the soul, after being recalled from elation and led back to the humility of Christ, waits for the salvation of the Lord. THE BLESSINGS OF THE PATRIARCHS 2.17.[18]

[9]Ps 75:6 LXX. [10]Ps 75:7 LXX. [11]Mt 26:15. [12]Lk 22:3. [13]FC 65:260-61. [14]Mt 7:13-14. [15]1 Cor 9:27. [16]Mt 11:29. [17]2 Cor 12:7. [18]SC 140:106-8.

49:19 GAD

[19]Raiders[z] shall raid Gad,
  but he shall raid at their heels.[*]

[z] Heb gedud, a raiding troop [*]LXX, "Gad, trial shall try him, and he shall try them at their heels." In Greek, peiratērion can be read as "trial, testing" or "gang of robbers."

OVERVIEW: According to Hippolytus and Ambrose, Gad represents the Savior, tried by the Sanhedrin or the assembly of scribes and priests, who seek to entrap him. On the moral level, Gad represents the person who has made progress but continues to be tested by temptations (RUFINUS).

49:19 Raiding at the Raiders' Heels

THE PROPHET SIGNIFIES THE EVIL SANHE-DRIN. HIPPOLYTUS: Through the expression "a gang of enemies" (or "a place of trial") the prophet signifies the evil Sanhedrin of the high priests and scribes, who tested the Savior with different pretenses in order to find some ground to move accusations against him and then take hold of him and execute him.[1] But he, knowing their intentions, put them to test in his justice and delivered them to death for their sin.[2] ON THE BLESSINGS OF ISAAC AND JACOB 23.[3]

THIS PROPHECY REFERS TO CHRIST.

AMBROSE: "Gad, trial shall try him, and he shall try them at their heels." The trial is the cunning assembly of scribes and priests who tried the Lord Jesus about Caesar's tribute[4] and John's baptism,[5] as Scripture teaches. In his holiness, Jesus turned the trial back upon them. "At their heels," that is, replying immediately without any deliberation, so that he might rather corner those trying him. For when they said, "By what authority do you do these things?" Christ did not respond to their inquiries but rather he himself inquired, saying, "I also will ask you one question, and if you answer me this, I in turn will tell you by what authority I do these things."[6] Again, when they said, "Is it lawful to give tribute to Caesar, or not?" he said, "Why do you try me, you hypocrites? Show me the coin of the tribute." And when they offered it, again he asked, "Whose are the image and inscription?" They said to him, "Caesar's." And thereupon he bound them in their own words and tied them in their own entanglement. For then he said to them, "Render to Caesar the things that are Caesar's and to God

the things that are God's,"[7] so that they could not contradict their own words. Indeed they marveled and departed from him. . . . Moses explained clearly that this prophecy of holy Jacob was in reference to Christ, for he spoke thus: "Blessed is he who enlarged Gad. He has rested like a lion, breaking arms and chiefs. And he saw from his beginning that the land of the chiefs assembled with the leaders of the tribes was there divided; the Lord executed justice and judgment for Israel."[8] Consequently we recognize him who rested like a lion, when he broke the arms of the powerful, because he saw from the beginning the divisions among those who were trying him. THE PATRIARCHS 8.35-37.[9]

MATURITY COMES FROM TESTING.

RUFINUS: And therefore, according to a similar process, the moral sense develops: that man of ours, after confessing his error, by his repentance turns out to be converted through knowledge and shows a significant progress, so that he is tempted by the enemy and the strength of his soul and the soundness of his intentions are tested. In fact, the Scripture says, "The one who is not tempted is not credible."[10] No one will ever reach perfection if he is not first tested in temptations. THE BLESSINGS OF THE PATRIARCHS 2.20.[11]

---

[1]Mt 26:4; Jn 8:6. [2]Jn 8:24. [3]PO 27:92-94. [4]Mt 22:15-22. [5]Mt 21:25. [6]Mt 21:23-24. [7]Mt 22:17-21. [8]Deut 33:20-21 (LXX). [9]FC 65:262-63**. [10]Sir 34:10 LXX. [11]SC 140:110-12.

49:20 ASHER

[20]*Asher's food shall be rich,*
and he shall yield royal dainties.[*]

*The LXX reads "Asher, his bread shall be fat; and he shall yield dainties to princes."

OVERVIEW: The description of Asher's bread as rich or fat can be interpreted as a reference to Christ, who is the bread from heaven and the food of the saints (HIPPOLYTUS, AMBROSE). On the moral level, Asher, which means "blessed," refers to the person who, after victory over temptations, eats the bread from heaven (RUFINUS).

49:20 Rich Food

THE PROPHET SPEAKS OBSCURELY. HIPPOLYTUS: Here the prophet speaks obscurely either about the apostles, who had the duty to provide and distribute the bread of life, or about the Savior himself, since he foretells and let us know the bread descending from heaven, which is food and drink for the saints. In fact, Asher is interpreted as "richness," as he alone was so rich that he might satiate all those who came to him. And Christ also testified about himself by saying, "I am the bread that came down from heaven. Your ancestors ate the manna in the wilderness, and they died; but whoever eats of my bread will never see eternal death."[1] ON THE BLESSINGS OF ISAAC AND JACOB 24.[2]

WHO IS RICH BUT THE LORD JESUS? AMBROSE: "Asher, his bread is rich, and he will furnish food to princes."[3] Asher in our tongue means "riches." Who then is rich except where there is the depth of the riches of the wisdom and knowledge of God?[4] Who is rich but the Lord Jesus, who always abounds and never fails? He came into this world a poor man and abounds in all things; he has filled all people. How mighty he is in riches, for he has made all people rich by his poverty! But Christ was poor for our sakes, and rich with the Father. He was poor to deliver us from want, as the apostle teaches when he says, "Being rich, he became poor for your sakes, that by his poverty you might become rich."[5] His poverty enriches, the fringe of his garment heals,[6] his hunger satisfies, his death gives life, his burial gives resurrection. Therefore he is a rich treasure,

for his bread is rich. And "rich" is apt, for one who has eaten this bread will be unable to feel hunger.[7] He gave it to the apostles to distribute to a believing people,[8] and today Christ gives it to us, for he, as a priest, daily consecrates it with his own words. Therefore this bread has become the food of the saints.

Likewise we can take the Lord himself, who has given us his own flesh, just as he said, "I am the bread of life. Your fathers ate the manna in the desert and have died. But this is the bread that comes down from heaven, so that if anyone eat of it he will not die."[9] . . . Moses too delivered a very appropriate prophecy when he said, in his blessings, "Asher is blessed with children and will be acceptable to his brothers, and he shall dip his foot in oil. His shoe shall be iron and brass, and as your days are, so will your powers be. There is not anyone as is your God in heaven, your helper and the mighty Lord of the firmament and the God of the highest, protecting you, and through the strength of his powerful arms he casts out your enemy from your presence, saying, 'Let him perish.' And Israel shall dwell securely alone upon the land, Jacob in grain and wine, and heaven shall be misty with dew for you."[10] THE PATRIARCHS 9.38-40.[11]

THE BREAD FROM HEAVEN. RUFINUS: Since Asher means "blessed," the bread of that one whom, after being recalled from error to penitence, we lead step by step to the present state of blessedness, after his conversion, after the spiritual knowledge, after the victory over temptations, is, to be sure, called "fat." He eats that bread "which comes down from heaven and gives life to the world,"[12] and that bread is fat for him. THE BLESSINGS OF THE PATRIARCHS 2.21.[13]

---

[1]Jn 6:48-49, 51; 8:51. [2]PO 27:96. [3]LXX. [4]Rom 11:33. [5]2 Cor 8:9. [6]Mt 9:20-22; 14:34-36. [7]Jn 6:35. [8]Mt 15:36. [9]Jn 6:48-50. [10]Deut 33:24-28. The translation of this passage is based on the text of PL 14:686-87. [11]FC 65:263-64*. [12]Jn 6:33. [13]SC 140:112.

49:21 NAPHTALI

21Naphtali is a hind let loose,
*   that bears comely fawns.*a*

a Or *who gives beautiful words*   *The LXX differs notably from the Hebrew: "Nephthalim is a spreading stem, bestowing beauty on its fruit."

OVERVIEW: On the basis of the Septuagint reading, Naphthali as "a spreading vine branch" represents the people called to freedom through faith and to the fullness of grace in the church (HIPPOLYTUS, AMBROSE). On the moral level, the name Naphthali, interpreted to mean "vine" or "leafy tree," signifies the person who has made such progress as to be worthy of the priesthood or who manifests the wisdom of God (RUFINUS).

49:21 A Hind Let Loose

PEOPLE CALLED TO FREEDOM THROUGH
FAITH. HIPPOLYTUS: "A spreading vine branch" signifies the people that are called to freedom through faith, so that all may bring fruits to God. In fact, the Savior was the spiritual vine, its branches and trunks are the saints who believe in him. Its bunches of grapes are the martyrs; the trunks of wood which are bound to vines indicate the passion. The grape pickers are the angels; the baskets where the fruits of the vine are gathered are the apostles. The winepress is the church; the wine is the power of the Holy Spirit. Therefore the words "spreading vine branch" signify those who have been freed from the chains of death, as Isaiah [actually Malachi] himself says, "You shall go forth and rejoice as young calves let loose from bonds."[1] On the other hand, the sentence "bestowing beauty on its fruits" means that in the regeneration through water they receive the grace and beauty of the Word, who was richer than the sons of men in beauty.[2] ON THE BLESSINGS OF ISAAC AND JACOB 25.[3]

THE PEOPLE OF GOD FORESHADOWED. AM-

BROSE: "Naphtali is a spreading vine, putting forth beauty in its shoot."[4] One branch of the vine is cut off, because it seems useless, so that the vine may not run wild in the profusion of its branches and be unfruitful. Another is cut back only for a little while and is permitted to grow so that it may produce fruit. Its beauty is in its product. While it rises to things that are above, it embraces the vine; mounting to the top, it clothes the necks of the crossbeam, as it were, with a necklace of precious vine shoots. There is also such beauty in its product, because it pours forth many fruits from full shoots. This branch is beautiful, but it is a far fairer thing that the reference is to a shoot clinging to a spiritual vine, of which we are the branch and can bear fruit, if we remain on the vine; but otherwise we are cut off. The holy patriarch Naphtali was an abundant shoot. For this reason Moses says, "Naphtali is the abundance of those that receive; he shall be filled with a blessing from the Lord, he shall possess the sea and the south."[5] This is in explanation of that which Jacob had said, that he is a spreading vine. That is, through the grace of faith he was stripped of the bonds of death, and in him there is foreshadowed the people of God, called to the liberty of faith and to the fullness of grace and spread over the whole world. It clothes the crossbeam of Christ with good fruit and encompasses the wood of that true vine, that is, the mysteries of the Lord's cross; it does not fear the danger of acknowledging him, but rather, even amid persecutions, it glories in the

---

[1]Mal 4:2 (3:20 LXX). [2]Ps 45:2 (44:3 LXX). [3]PO 27:98-100. [4]LXX.
[5]Deut 33:23.

name of Christ. THE PATRIARCHS 10.41-43.[6]

SPLENDID FRUIT. RUFINUS: With regard to the third[7] explanation, the interpretation of the name Naphtali is that indicated by his father when he blesses him, that is, "leafy tree" or "vine." There was that man of ours, who a bit earlier fed on fat bread and offered food to princes (that bread that comforts the heart of people[8]). Now, as a second phase, Christ, the true vine,[9] has shown for him a splendid fruit through which he may now cheer with wine the heart that he had comforted before with bread.[10] In both cases it seems to me that he

has reached such a stage of progress that he may even obtain the sacraments of priesthood. But if we prefer to interpret Nephthalim as "tree," which shows its beauty in its fruits, instead of "leafy vine," what will ever be the tree showing its beauty in the fruits but the Wisdom of God? About her Solomon says, "She is a tree of life to those who lay hold of her."[11] THE BLESSINGS OF THE PATRIARCHS 2.24.[12]

---

[6]FC 65:264-65. [7]For Rufinus, the "third" explanation is the moral sense of the passage. [8]Ps 104:15 (103:15 LXX). [9]Jn 15:1. [10]Ps 104:15 (103:15 LXX). [11]Prov 3:18. [12]SC 140:116.

49:22-26 JOSEPH

[22]*Joseph is a fruitful bough,*
a fruitful bough by a spring;
his branches run over the wall.
[23]*The archers fiercely attacked him,*
shot at him, and harassed him sorely;
[24]*yet his bow remained unmoved,*
his arms[b] were made agile
by the hands of the Mighty One of Jacob
(by the name of the Shepherd, the Rock of Israel),
[25]*by the God of your father who will help you,*
by God Almighty[u] who will bless you
with blessings of heaven above,
blessings of the deep that couches beneath,
blessings of the breasts and of the womb.
[26]*The blessings of your father*
are mighty beyond the blessings of the eternal mountains,[c]
the bounties of the everlasting hills;
may they be on the head of Joseph,
*and on the brow of him who was separate from his brothers.**

b Heb *the arms of his hands*   **u** Heb *El Shaddai*   **c** Compare Gk: Heb *of my progenitors to*   *The verses concerning Joseph are notably different in the LXX: "[22]Joseph is a son increased; my dearly loved son is increased; my youngest son, turn to me. [23]Against whom men taking evil counsel reproached him, and the archers pressed hard upon him. [24]But their bow and arrows were mightily consumed, and the sinews of their arms were slackened by the hand of the mighty one of Jacob; thence is he that strengthened Israel from the God of your father; [25]and my God helped you, and he blessed you with the blessing of heaven from above, and the blessing of the earth possessing all things, because of the blessing of the breasts and of the womb, [26]the blessings of your father and your mother—it has prevailed above the blessing of the lasting mountains, and beyond the blessings of the everlasting hills; they shall be upon the head of Joseph, and upon the head of the brothers of whom he took the lead."

OVERVIEW: Jacob blessed Joseph more than all his brothers, because Jacob saw prefigured in him the mysteries that would be fulfilled in Christ (HIPPOLYTUS, AMBROSE). As Jacob depended on Joseph instead of Reuben his firstborn, so the world depends on Christ instead of Adam, the firstborn and rebellious one. As Joseph was a son of Jacob's old age, so Christ came late to a world growing old (EPHREM, AMBROSE). The "blessing of the breasts" can be understood to refer to the two Testaments or to the breasts of Mary. The phrase "the blessing of the womb of your father and mother" may allude to the divine and human origin of Christ (HIPPOLYTUS, AMBROSE). The believer is called "son" three times referring to birth according to the flesh, birth through conversion and baptism and birth through regeneration, that is, the resurrection of the dead (RUFINUS).

49:22 A Fruitful Bough

JOSEPH'S FRUITFULNESS INCREASES. HIPPOLYTUS: The prophet has blessed Joseph more than all his brothers, because he contemplated the mysteries which, having been prefigured in him, would be fulfilled in Christ. Therefore Jacob did not praise Joseph but the one who was symbolized by Joseph. In fact, he says to him, "My son is increased, Joseph," because thanks to his[1] kingly and perfect name the grace of Christ has increased and has become abundant in the world. ON THE BLESSINGS OF ISAAC AND JACOB 26.[2]

THE SON OF OLD AGE. EPHREM THE SYRIAN: Just as Jacob depended on Joseph instead of Reuben the firstborn, so also instead of Adam, the firstborn and rebellious one, the world had one Son of old age, in the latter days of the world, so that the whole world might stand and lean on him as if on a pillar. "Rise up, O spring, O build-

ing supported" by brothers and sons. Through the power of our Lord the world is supported on the prophets and on the apostles. Joseph became a wall of plenty to his brothers in the time of famine, and our Lord became the wall of knowledge to the world in the time of error. COMMENTARY ON GENESIS 43.10.[3]

THE GRACE GIVEN TO JOSEPH INCREASES ABUNDANTLY. AMBROSE: What is the reason why the father honored his son Joseph more abundantly than all his sons? Only because he saw in him the mysteries prefiguring Christ. On this account he blessed him who was awaited rather than him who was seen and said, "My son Joseph is to be increased." Who is to be increased but Christ, whose grace is always increased, for his glory does not have an end to its advance? Of him also John says, "He must increase, but I must decrease,"[4] because, through that perfect and saving name of his, grace was piled up and abounded in this world—"My son is to be increased." And so, because his brothers saw that he was growing, they began to envy him; moreover, he whom Joseph prefigured also met with envy from those whom he loved more. In fact he said, "I have not come except to the lost sheep of the house of Israel."[5] And they said, "We do not know where he is from."[6] He had care for them, and they denied him. THE PATRIARCHS 11.47.[7]

THE SON CAME LATE TO A WORLD GROWING OLD. AMBROSE: "My young son"—in truth he was young, for he was almost the last to be born. Indeed, Scripture also says, "Jacob loved him, because he was the son of his old age."[8] This has ref-

---

[1]Joseph's name in Hebrew, *ysp*, means "add," "increase." This meaning is found in Philo *De Somniis* 2:47. [2]PO 27:102. [3]FC 91:211. [4]Jn 3:30. [5]Mt 15:24. [6]Jn 9:29. [7]FC 65:266-67. [8]Gen 37:3.

erence likewise to Christ. For the Son of God, rising like the dawn through his birth from the Virgin Mary, came late to a world that was growing old and on the point of perishing. As a son of old age, he took on a body according to the mystery, while before the ages he was always with his Father. For this reason the Father says to him, "Return to me," calling forth from earth to heaven the one whom he had sent for our salvation. And so, raising up his only-begotten Son, he made vain the counsel of those who spoke evil. THE PATRIARCHS 11.48-49.[9]

WHY IS JOSEPH CALLED A SON THREE TIMES? RUFINUS: What is the significance of the fact that only Joseph among all the brothers is called son three times? In accordance with the limits of my point of view, I understand that the first time Joseph was born [to his father] as a son, because he was born of Rachel when his father did not hope any longer to obtain an offspring.[10] But then Joseph was, in a sense, born to his father a second time as a son, because it was announced to Jacob that he was alive, when he was by now convinced of his death.[11] And finally he becomes his son for the third time when, by instructing [Joseph] and educating him with doctrine and erudition and all the virtues through which he was able to see God, he had begotten him also in the spirit. On the other hand, it would not be correct for Jacob to call Joseph the youngest son, since he is older than Benjamin, unless we must understand that he is the youngest in the teaching of his father. THE BLESSINGS OF THE PATRIARCHS 2.25.[12]

49:25 More Blessings for Joseph

THE BLESSING OF BREASTS AND WOMB. AMBROSE: And therefore, in that contemptible body, so to speak, "You prevailed by reason of the blessing of breasts and womb, the blessings of your father and mother." Jacob spoke of the breasts, or the two Testaments, in one of which Christ was foretold and in the other revealed. And he did well to say "breasts," because the Son

nurtured us and offered us to the Father as people nourished on a kind of spiritual milk. Or else he is speaking of Mary's breasts, which were truly blessed, for with them the holy Virgin gave milk to drink to the people of the Lord. This is the reason the woman in the Gospel says, "Blessed is the womb that bore you and the breasts that nursed you."[13] THE PATRIARCHS 11.51.[14]

THE WOMB OF YOUR FATHER AND MOTHER CHRISTOLOGICALLY UNDERSTOOD. HIPPOLYTUS: By adding and saying "Because of the blessing of the womb of your father and your mother" the prophet proclaims in advance a spiritual mystery. He could have said, "Because of the blessing of the womb of your mother," in order to indicate with this expression Mary, in whose womb the Word was borne for nine months. Well, this is not what he said; on the contrary he said, "Because of the blessing of the womb of your father and your mother." By uniting these two things, he made them one, in order that it might be clearly understood that to this person belongs what is according to spirit and what is according to flesh. The Word took his origin from a father's heart; ... rightly the Father said through the prophet, "My heart has uttered a good Word."[15] On the other hand, according to flesh he took his origin in the latter times from a virginal womb after he was borne in it for nine months, so that he might appear to be visible as he was born a second time from a mother's womb. And therefore he himself said through the prophet, "And thus said the Lord that formed me from the womb to be his own servant."[16] And through Jeremiah [the Father] said, "Before I formed you in the womb [of your mother], I knew you, and before you came forth from the womb, I sanctified you."[17] Since the Word was begotten both according to spirit and flesh and was actually both God and man, with good reason the prophet [Jacob] has used the word *womb* for a father and a mother; and this might seem to

---

[9]FC 65:267. [10]Gen 30:22-24. [11]Gen 45:26. [12]SC 140:118-20. [13]Lk 11:27. [14]FC 65:268*. [15]Ps 45:1 (44:2 LXX). [16]Is 49:5. [17]Jer 1:5.

be ridiculous to somebody, if it were not understood this way. In fact, the term *womb* can be suitably referred only to the female nature. But here he has said, "Because of the blessing of the womb of your father and mother," so that you might correctly understand that the Word is begotten from two substances, that of God and that of the Virgin. ON THE BLESSINGS OF ISAAC AND JACOB 27.[18]

ANTICIPATING THE INCARNATE LORD'S DIVINITY AND HUMANITY. AMBROSE: But as to what Jacob says, "the blessing of the womb, the blessing of your father and mother," if we should choose to interpret it as the womb only of Mary, the reason why he coupled the two blessings will escape our notice, for he could have spoken of the womb only of the mother. But I think it more appropriate that we should take it, according to the spiritual mystery, as the two begettings of the Lord Jesus, that according to the divinity and that according to the flesh, because he was begotten from the Father before all ages. For this reason also the Father says, "My heart has uttered a good Word,"[19] because the Son has proceeded from the most profound and incomprehensible substance of the Father and is always in him. For this reason also the Evangelist says, "No one has at any time seen God, except the only-begotten Son, who is in the bosom of the Father, he has revealed him."[20] "The bosom of the Father," then, is to be understood in a spiritual sense, as a kind of innermost dwelling of the Father's love and of his nature, in which the Son always dwells. Even so, the Father's womb is the spiritual womb of an inner sanctuary, from which the Son has proceeded just as from a generative womb. To be sure, we read in different versions, now that it was the Father's womb, again that it was his heart, with which he uttered the Word, and again that it was his mouth from which justice proceeded and from which Wisdom came forth, as Wisdom herself says, "From the mouth of the Most High I came forth."[21] Thus, since the One is not limited and all things declare the One, the blessing refers rather to the spiritual mystery of generation from the

Father than to some part of the body. But just as we interpret it to mean that generation from the Father, likewise let us interpret it to mean the generation from Mary unto the completion of faith, when the mother's womb is blessed, that virginal womb of Mary which brought forth for us the Lord Jesus. The Father speaks of that womb through the prophet Jeremiah, "Before I formed you in the womb, I knew you, and before you came forth from your mother's womb, I sanctified you."[22] Therefore the prophet showed that there was a twofold nature in Christ, the divine and the fleshly, the former from the Father, the latter from a virgin, but in such a way that Christ was not deprived of his divinity when he was born from a virgin and was in the body. THE PATRIARCHS 11.51.[23]

49:26 Mighty Blessings

THE STRENGTH OF JOSEPH. AMBROSE: From here "he grew strong over all the mountains and the desires of the everlasting hills." For he shone forth like a heavenly light above all those men of exalted merit, patriarchs and prophets and apostles, and beyond the sun and moon and archangels as well, even as he says, "No disciple is above his teacher, nor is the servant above his master."[24] Who indeed among them was there to whom all things were subject? Rather, Christ gave to them their nature. In him all his saints are blessed, because he is the head of all, above the heads of all[25]—for "the head of the woman is the man, the head of the man is Christ"[26]—and above the crowns of the heads of all men, because he is the surpassing crown of the whole of humanity. But the highest crown belongs to the just, because he won them through grace and through a sharing of his resurrection, as it were, and calls them brothers.[27] On this account also we understand by the brothers of Joseph those brothers, rather, of

---

[18]PO 27:108-12. [19]Ps 45:1 (44:2 LXX); cf. 110:3 (109:3 LXX). [20]Jn 1:18. [21]Sir 24:3. [22]Jer 1:5. [23]FC 65:268-69. [24]Mt 10:24. [25]Eph 1:22; 4:15. [26]1 Cor 11:3; cf. Eph 5:23. [27]Mt 12:49-50.

whom the psalmist says, "I will proclaim your name to my brothers; in the midst of the assembly I will sing your praises."[28] THE PATRIARCHS 11.52.[29]

THE BELIEVER'S STANDING MANIFESTED IN THREE WAYS. RUFINUS: Now then, with regard to the third sense, that man, being renewed and increased through the spiritual steps, ascends to the greatness of Joseph, who, thanks to the progress of his faith and the gifts of the Holy Spirit, rose to such an extent that he became the victim of envy. Therefore by what garlands braided by our words will that man be crowned for whom, after fighting, and completing his race and preserving his faith, God, the just Judge, keeps in store the crown of justice?[30] About him the father says, "Joseph is a son increased."[31] And who is so increased as that one who, after his errors and fall, is renewed and returned through the different stages of virtue to such a degree that he reaches the greatest victory? But since he rises little by little, for this reason he is said to be increased in the single stages. In fact, first he began to be increased in Judah through confession. Then he is increased again in Zebulun because he dispelled the obscurity of darkness.[32] Then he is increased again in Issachar because the reward for his works was increased. He is increased again in Dan when he began to keep a correct capacity of judgment in the context of his free will. He is increased again in Gad because he resisted temptation. He is finally increased in Asher when he reached beatitude. In an appropriate manner Joseph also is called "increased son," because he obtains already the goods to come. But he is also called "envied son,"[33] that is, the one who is set as a model to be imitated by the righteous and will receive the zeal of envy and hatred from the wicked. Also the apostle speaks about the good and the bad zeal and with regard to the evil zeal of the Jews says, "They make much of you, but for no good purpose."[34] And with regard to the good zeal, he says about himself, "I feel a divine jealousy for you."[35] But he is also called "the youngest son."[36] Why should not that one who put off the old man with his actions, resurrected in Christ and walking in the renewal of life,[37] be called the youngest son? And this new man will be called "son" three times. The first was his birth according to the flesh, the second the birth through conversion and baptism. The third is the birth also defined as regeneration, which is the resurrection of the dead. THE BLESSINGS OF THE PATRIARCHS 2.27.[38]

---

[28]Ps 22:22 (21:23 LXX). [29]FC 65:269-70*. [30]2 Tim 4:7-8. [31]Gen 49:22 LXX. [32]Rom 13:12. [33]Gen 49:22 LXX. [34]Gal 4:17. [35]2 Cor 11:2. [36]Gen 49:22 LXX. [37]Rom 6:4. [38]SC 140:130-32.

49:27 BENJAMIN

---

[27]*Benjamin is a ravenous wolf,*
      in the morning devouring the prey,
      and at even dividing the spoil."

OVERVIEW: The description of Benjamin as a "ravenous wolf" is to be understood of the apostle Paul, who persecuted the church before his conversion and who was from the tribe of Benjamin

(HIPPOLYTUS, EPHREM, AMBROSE). The reference to "dividing the spoil"[1] in the evening can be understood also of Paul separating the spiritual and corporeal aspects of the law after his conversion (RUFINUS).

49:27 A Ravenous Wolf

PAUL WAS A WOLF. EPHREM THE SYRIAN: [This refers to] Paul, who was a wolf to the wolves and snatched all souls away from the evil one. And "in the evening he will divide what he seizes," that is, at the end of the world he will also rest with a reward greater than his labors. COMMENTARY ON GENESIS 43.11.[2]

HE WHO HAD BEEN A WOLF BECAME A SHEPHERD. AMBROSE: The devil has very many wolves that he sends against the sheep of Christ. And therefore he whom Joseph prefigured, in order to protect his own sheep, seized the very enemy that was coming to plunder the sheep, the wolf Paul, and from a persecutor turned him into a teacher. Of him Jacob says, just as it is written, "Benjamin is a ravenous wolf; in the morning he shall still be eating, and for the evening he shall distribute food among chiefs." He was a wolf when he scattered and devoured the sheep of the church; but he who had been a wolf became a shepherd. He was a wolf when he was Saul, when he would go into houses and drag men and women off to prison. He was a wolf when he breathed threats of murder against the disciples of the Lord and asked for letters from the chief priests to seize the humble servants of Christ.[3] Jesus blinded him with an outpouring of light,[4] as if he were a wolf roaming abroad in the darkness of night. And so, when Rachel gave birth to Benjamin, she called his name "son of my sorrow,"[5] as a prophecy that from that tribe Paul would come, to afflict the sons of the church in the time of his persecution and to trouble their mother with a grievous sorrow. But nonetheless, at a later time, the same Paul distributed food among chiefs when he preached the word of God to the Gentiles and stirred very many to faith, for they received the grace of the Lord through his preaching, as did the deputy of the proconsul Paulus[6] and the chief Publius.[7] Moreover, when Moses blessed the tribe of Benjamin, he also said aptly, "The beloved of the Lord shall dwell confidently, and God shall overshadow him all the days, and the beloved of the Lord shall rest between his shoulders."[8] Paul was also made a vessel of election,[9] for he was converted only through the Lord's compassionate love. For this reason he attributes nothing to his own merit but assigns everything to Christ and says, "For I am the least of the apostles and am not worthy to be called an apostle, because I persecuted the church of God. But by the grace of God I am what I am, and his grace in me has not been to no effect."[10] He dwelt confidently in the house that he used to empty of its inhabitants; he dwelt in the habitations of Christ, whereas before he used to roam in the woods like a wolf. And God overshadowed him when Christ appeared to him. Although he saw nothing when his eyes were opened,[11] still he saw Christ. And it was fitting that he saw Christ present and also heard him speaking. That overshadowing is not the overshadowing of blindness but of grace. Indeed, it is said to Mary: "The Holy Spirit shall come upon you, and the power of the Most High shall overshadow you."[12] THE PATRIARCHS 12.57-58.[13]

SEPARATING SPIRITUAL REALITIES FROM CORPOREAL ONES. RUFINUS: "At evening he will divide the food." The evening is that final time when Paul is converted. Thus we also call evening the time of our conversion in which we are now. Then he will divide the food, then he understands that in the law it is necessary to divide the letter from the spirit and will know that "the letter kills, but the Spirit gives life."[14] Since after being enlightened by the grace of the Lord, Paul

---

[1]LXX, "food." [2]FC 91:211. [3]Acts 9:1-2. [4]Acts 9:3-9. [5]Gen 35:18. [6]Acts 13:7-12. In most versions it is the proconsul Paulus who is converted, not a deputy. [7]Acts 28:7-10. [8]Deut 33:12. [9]Acts 9:15. [10]1 Cor 15:9-10. [11]Acts 9:8. [12]Lk 1:35. [13]FC 65:273-75*. [14]2 Cor 3:6.

begins to divide and separate in the law the spiritual realities from the corporeal ones, he is said to divide the food at evening. In fact, although meditating all day long on the law, he had not done

that before. The Blessings of the Patriarchs 2.29.[15]

[15]SC 140:138.

[49:28-33 THE DEATH OF JACOB]

50:1-14 JACOB'S BURIAL IN THE LAND OF CANAAN

[1]Then Joseph fell on his father's face, and wept over him, and kissed him. [2]And Joseph commanded his servants the physicians to embalm his father. So the physicians embalmed Israel; [3]forty days were required for it, for so many are required for embalming. And the Egyptians wept for him seventy days.

[4]And when the days of weeping for him were past, Joseph spoke to the household of Pharaoh, saying, "If now I have found favor in your eyes, speak, I pray you, in the ears of Pharaoh, saying, [5]My father made me swear, saying, 'I am about to die: in my tomb which I hewed out for myself in the land of Canaan, there shall you bury me.' Now therefore let me go up, I pray you, and bury my father; then I will return." [6]And Pharaoh answered, "Go up, and bury your father, as he made you swear." [7]So Joseph went up to bury his father; and with him went up all the servants of Pharaoh, the elders of his household, and all the elders of the land of Egypt, [8]as well as all the household of Joseph, his brothers, and his father's household; only their children, their flocks, and their herds were left in the land of Goshen. [9]And there went up with him both chariots and horsemen; it was a very great company. [10]When they came to the threshing floor of Atad, which is beyond the Jordan, they lamented there with a very great and sorrowful lamentation; and he made a mourning for his father seven days. [11]When the inhabitants of the land, the Canaanites, saw the mourning on the threshing floor of Atad, they said, "This is a grievous mourning to the Egyptians." Therefore the place was named Abel-mizraim;[d] it is beyond the Jordan. [12]Thus his sons did for him as he had commanded them; [13]for his sons carried him to the land of Canaan, and buried him in the cave of the field at Mach-pelah, to the east of Mamre, which Abraham bought with the field from Ephron the Hittite, to possess as a burying place. [14]After he had buried his father, Joseph returned to Egypt with his brothers and all who had gone up with him to bury his father.

d That is meadow (or mourning) of Egypt

OVERVIEW: By comparison with Genesis 49, which was interpreted to speak of the future, this chapter seemed somewhat anticlimactic and thus did not attract much comment from patristic authors. Joseph is not to be blamed for the lengthy mourning for his father, because the gates of the underworld had not yet been broken. We, on the contrary, can rejoice at death, for we have the certitude of resurrection (CHRYSOSTOM).

50:10 Joseph Mourns for Seven Days

THE GATES OF THE UNDERWORLD WERE STILL NOT BROKEN. CHRYSOSTOM: For your part, however, dearly beloved, don't simply pass this by on hearing it; instead, consider the time when it happened and absolve Joseph of all blame. I mean, the gates of the underworld were still not broken or the bonds of death loosed. Nor was death yet called sleep. Hence, because they feared death, they acted this way; today, on the contrary, thanks to the grace of God, since death has been turned into slumber and life's end into repose and since there is great certitude of resurrection, we rejoice and exult at death like people moving from one life to another. Why do I say from one life to another? From a worse to a better, from a temporary to an eternal, from an earthly to a heavenly. HOMILIES ON GENESIS 67.17.[1]

---

[1]FC 87:274-75*.

50:15-21 JOSEPH FORGIVES HIS BROTHERS

[15]When Joseph's brothers saw that their father was dead, they said, "It may be that Joseph will hate us and pay us back for all the evil which we did to him." [16]So they sent a message to Joseph, saying, "Your father gave this command before he died, [17]'Say to Joseph, Forgive, I pray you, the transgression of your brothers and their sin, because they did evil to you.' And now, we pray you, forgive the transgression of the servants of the God of your father." Joseph wept when they spoke to him. [18]His brothers also came and fell down before him, and said, "Behold, we are your servants." [19]But Joseph said to them, "Fear not, for am I in the place of God?* [20]As for you, you meant evil against me; but God meant it for good, to bring it about that many people should be kept alive, as they are today. [21]So do not fear; I will provide for you and your little ones." Thus he reassured them and comforted them.

*LXX, "I belong to God."

OVERVIEW: With Jacob gone, Joseph's brothers have renewed cause for fear of him and beg to be his servants, which manifests the greatness of his virtue. Joseph calms their fears, insisting on the role of the creative wisdom of God in all that had taken place (EPHREM, CHRYSOSTOM).

50:17 Joseph Weeps When His Brothers Speak

GOD TRANSFORMED EVIL INTO GOOD. EPHREM THE SYRIAN: Joseph wept and said, "Do not be afraid of me, for although your father has died, the God of your father, on account of whom I will never strike you, is still alive. Because he turned the evil that you did to me to my good and he placed many people in my hands, God forbid that I do any evil to those who thus became the cause of life for many. But, just as I did not kill you in Egypt, do not leave my bones in Egypt." He made them swear to this and said, "God will indeed remember you and will bring you up to the land which he swore to Abraham. Bring my bones up to there, so that even if I do not inherit the land with you, I may be raised up with you from that land." COMMENTARY ON GENESIS 44.2.[1]

50:18 *We Are Your Servants*

HOW GREAT A THING VIRTUE IS. CHRYSOSTOM: See how great a thing virtue is, how powerful and invincible, and how profound the weakness of evil. I mean, look, the one who endured such suffering reigns as king whereas those who submitted their brother to such indignities beg to be slaves of the one given by them into servitude. HOMILIES ON GENESIS 67.19.[2]

50:20 *God Turned Evil to Good*

GOD'S WISDOM TRANSFORMS ALL THEIR WICKEDNESS. CHRYSOSTOM: "Don't be apprehensive or anxious," Jacob says. "I belong to God," and in imitation of my Lord I strive to reward with kindness those who are maliciously disposed to me—"I belong to God," after all. Then to show how great is the favor he enjoys from God Joseph says, You acted against me with evil intent, but God turned everything to good for me. Hence Paul also said, "For those who love God all things work together for good."[3] "All things," he says. What is meant by "all things"? Opposition and apparent disappointment—even these things are turned into good, which is exactly what happened with this remarkable man. In fact, what was done by his brothers had the particular effect of bringing him the kingship, thanks to the creative God's wisdom transforming all their wickedness into good. HOMILIES ON GENESIS 67.19.[4]

---

[1]FC 91:212. [2]FC 87:275-76. [3]Rom 8:28. [4]FC 87:276*.

50:22-26 JOSEPH'S LAST DAYS AND DEATH

[22]*So Joseph dwelt in Egypt, he and his father's house; and Joseph lived a hundred and ten years.* [23]*And Joseph saw Ephraim's children of the third generation; the children also of Machir the son of Manasseh were born upon Joseph's knees.* [24]*And Joseph said to his brothers, "I am about to die; but God will visit you, and bring you up out of this land to the land which he swore to Abraham, to Isaac, and to Jacob."* [25]*Then Joseph took an oath of the sons of Israel, saying, "God will visit you, and you shall carry up my bones from here."* [26]*So Joseph died, being a hundred and ten years old; and they embalmed him, and he was put in a coffin in Egypt.*

OVERVIEW: Joseph's age is mentioned in the text in order to indicate that he had control of Egypt for eighty years and thus demonstrate how much greater were the rewards than the hardships he endured. The directions he gave concerning his bones were a sign of faith, as already indicated by the interpretation of the letter to the Hebrews (Chrysostom).

50:26 Joseph's Death

By Faith He Did All This. Chrysostom: The text goes on: "Joseph passed away at one hundred and ten."[1] Why did it indicate to us his age too? For you to learn how long he had been entrusted with the control of Egypt. He was seventeen when he went down to Egypt, and it was when he reached the age of thirty that he appeared before Pharaoh and interpreted his dreams. Joseph then held complete control of Egypt for eighty years. Do you see how the rewards were greater than the hardships and the recompense manifold? For thirteen years he struggled with temptations, suffering servitude, that illicit accusation, ill treatment in prison. Since he nobly bore everything with thankfulness, accordingly he attained generous rewards even in the present life. Consider, after all, I ask you, that as a result of that short period that he endured servitude and imprisonment Joseph occupied a royal position for eighty years. For proof that it was by faith that he did all this and for the same motive gave directions about the transfer of his bones, listen to Paul's words: "It was by faith that at the point of death Joseph gave a reminder about the exodus of the sons of Israel."[2] Homilies on Genesis 67.22.[3]

---

[1]Gen 50:25. [2]Heb 11:22. [3]FC 87:277-78*.

APPENDIX
Early Christian Writers and the Documents Cited

The following table lists all the early Christian documents cited in this volume by author, if known, or by the title of the work. The English title used in this commentary is followed in parentheses with the Latin designation and, where available, the Thesaurus Linguae Graecae (=TLG) digital referenences or Cetedoc Clavis numbers. Printed sources of original language versions may be found in the bibliography.

Ambrose

Flight from the World (*De fuga saeculi*)	Cetedoc 0133
Isaac, or the Soul (*De Isaac vel anima*)	Cetedoc 0128
Jacob and the Happy Life (*De Jacob et vita beata*)	Cetedoc 0130
Joseph (*De Joseph*)	Cetedoc 0131
Letters (*Epistulae*)	Cetedoc 0160
Letters to Bishops	
Letters to Laymen	
On Abraham (*De Abraham*)	Cetedoc 0127
On His Brother Satyrus (*De excessu fratris Satyri*)	Cetedoc 0157
On the Death of Theodosius (*De obitu Theodosii*)	Cetedoc 0159
Patriarchs (*De patriarchis*)	Cetedoc 0132

Antony the Great

Letter

Aphrahat

On Prayer

Athanasius

Festal Letters (*Epistulae festales*)	TLG 2035.x01

Augustine

Against Lying (*Contra mendacium*)	Cetedoc 0304
Christian Instruction (*De doctrina christiana*)	Cetedoc 0263
City of God (*De civitate Dei*)	Cetedoc 0313
Confessions (*Confessionum libri tredecim*)	Cetedoc 0251
Letters (*Epistulae*)	Cetedoc 0262
On Patience (*De patientia*)	Cetedoc 0308

On the Trinity (*De Trinitate*)   Cetedoc 0329
Sermons (*Sermones*)   Cetedoc 0284
   Sermons on the Liturgical Season
The Care to Be Taken for the Dead (*De cura pro mortuis gerenda*)   Cetedoc 0307
The Good of Marriage (*De bono conjugali*)   Cetedoc 0299
Tractates on the Gospel of John (*In Johannis evangelium tractatus*)   Cetedoc 0278

Basil the Great
On Renunciation of the World (*Sermo 11 [sermo asceticus et exhortatio*
  de renunciation mundi])   TLG 2040.041

Bede the Venerable
Homilies on the Gospels (*Homiliarum evangelii libri ii*)   Cetedoc 1367
On Genesis (*In principium Genesis usque ad nativitatem Isaac etc.*)   Cetedoc 1344
On the Tabernacle (*De tabernaculo et vasis eius ac vestibus sacerdotum libri iii*)   Cetedoc 1345

Caesarius of Arles
Sermon (*Sermones*)   Cetedoc 1008

Chromatius
Sermons (*Sermones*)   Cetedoc 0217

Clement of Alexandria
Christ the Educator (*Paedagogus*)   TLG 0555.002
Stromateis (*Stromata*)   TLG 0555.004

Clement of Rome
1 Clement (*Epistula i ad Corinthios*)   TLG 1271.001

Cyprian
Letters (*Epistulae*)   Cetedoc 0050

Cyril of Alexandria
Glaphyra on Genesis (*Glaphyra in Pentateuchum*)   TLG 4090.097
Letters (See *Commentarii in Lucam*)   TLG 4090.108

Cyril of Jerusalem
Catechetical Lectures (*Catecheses ad illuminados*)   TLG 2110.003

Didymus the Blind
On Genesis (*In Genesim*)   TLG 2102.041

Ephrem the Syrian
Commentary on Genesis

Eusebius of Caesarea
History of the Church (*Historia ecclesiastica*)   TLG 2018.002

Eusebius of Emesa
Catena on Genesis

Gregory of Nyssa
On Perfection (*De perfectione Christiana ad Olympium monachum*) TLG 2017.026
On Virginity (*De virginitate*)   TLG 2017.043

Hilary of Poitiers
On the Trinity (*De Trinitate*)   Cetedoc 0433

Hippolytus
On the Benedictions of Isaac and Jacob (*De benedictionibus Isaaci et Jacobi*) TLG 2115.033

Irenaeus
Against Heresies (*Adversus haereses*)   TLG 1447.007

Jerome
Homilies on the Psalms (*Tractatus lix in psalmos*)   Cetedoc 0592
Letters (*Epistulae*)   Cetedoc 0620

John Chrysostom
Do Not Despair (*Non esse desperandum*)   TLG 2062.083
Homilies on Genesis (*In Genesim [homiliae 1-67]*)   TLG 2062.112

Justin Martyr
Dialogue with Trypho (*Dialogus cum Tryphone*)   TLG 0645.003

Martin of Braga
Sayings of the Egyptian Fathers (*Sententiae Patrum Aegyptiorum*)

Novatian
On the Trinity (*De Trinitate*)   Cetedoc 0071

Origen
Selections on Genesis (*Selecta in Genesim [fragmenta e catenis]*) TLG 2042.048
Commentary on John (*Commentarii in evangelium Joannis*) TLG 2042.005, 079
Homilies on Genesis (*In Genesim homiliae*) Cetedoc 0198 6 (A)
Homilies on Luke (*Homiliae in Lucam*)   TLG 2042.016
On First Principles (*De principiis*) Cetedoc 0198 E (A)
On First Principles (Fragments) (*Fragmenta de principiis*) TLG 2042.003

Paulinus of Nola
Poems (*Carmina*)   Cetedoc 0203

Peter Chrysologus
Sermons (*Collectio sermonum*)   Cetedoc 0227

Philo of Alexandria
Questions on Genesis (*Quaestiones in Genesim*)   TLG 0018.034

Prudentius
Scenes from Sacred History (*Tituli historiarum siue Dittochaeon*)   Cetedoc 1444

Pseudo-Barnabas
Epistle of Barnabas (*Barnabae epistula*)   TLG 1216.001

Quodvultdeus
 The Book of Promises and Predictions of God (*Liber promissionum et praedictorum Dei*)   Cetedoc 0413

Rufinus of Aquileia
The Blessings of the Patriarchs (*De benedictionibus patriarcharum*)   Cetedoc 0195

Salvian the Presbyter
The Governance of God (*De gubernatione Dei*)   Cetedoc 0485

Severian of Gabala
Catena on Genesis

Tertullian
On Patience (*De patientia*)   Cetedoc 0009
On Prayer (*De oratione*)   Cetedoc 0007
On the Soul (*De anima*)   Cetedoc 0017

Theodore of Mopsuestia
Catena on Genesis

BIOGRAPHICAL SKETCHES & SHORT DESCRIPTIONS OF SELECT ANONYMOUS WORKS

This listing is cumulative, including all the authors and works cited in this series to date.

Acacius of Caesarea (d. c. 365). Pro-Arian bishop of Caesarea in Palestine, disciple and biographer of Eusebius of Caesarea, the historian. He was a man of great learning and authored a treatise on Ecclesiastes.

Alexander of Alexandria (fl. 312-328). Bishop of Alexandria and predecessor of Athanasius, upon whom he asserted considerable theological influence during the rise of Arianism. Alexander excommunicated Arius, whom he had appointed to the parish of Baucalis, in 319. His teaching regarding the eternal generation and divine substantial union of the Son with the Father was eventually confirmed at the Council of Nicaea (325).

Ambrose of Milan (c. 333-397; fl. 374-397). Bishop of Milan and teacher of Augustine who defended the divinity of the Holy Spirit and the perpetual virginity of Mary.

Ambrosiaster (fl. c. 366-384). Name given by Erasmus to the author of a work once thought to have been composed by Ambrose.

Ammonius (c. fifth century). An Aristotelian commentator and teacher in Alexandria, where he was born and of whose school he became head. Also an exegete of Plato, he enjoyed fame among his contemporaries and successors, although modern critics accuse him of pedantry and banality.

Andreas (c. seventh century). Monk who collected commentary from earlier writers to form a catena on various biblical books.

Antony (or Anthony) the Great (c. 251-c. 356). An anchorite of the Egyptian desert, well-known as a monastic father. Athanasius regarded him as the ideal of monastic life, and he has become a model for Christian hagiography.

Aphrahat (c. 270-350 fl. 337-345). "The Persian Sage" and first major Syriac writer whose work survives. He is also known by his Greek name Aphraates.

Apollinaris of Laodicea (310-c. 392). Bishop of Laodicea who was attacked by Gregory of Nazianzus, Gregory of Nyssa and Theodore for denying that Christ had a human mind.

Apostolic Constitutions (c. 381-394). Also known as *Constitutions of the Holy Apostles* and thought to be the work of the Arian bishop Julian of Neapolis. The work is divided into eight books, and is primarily a collection of and expansion on previous works such as the *Didache* (c. 140) and the *Apostolic Traditions*. Book 8 ends with eighty-five canons from various sources and is elsewhere known as the *Apostolic Canons*.

Arius (fl. c. 320). Heretic condemned at the Council of Nicaea (325) for refusing to accept that the Son was not a creature but was God by nature like the Father.

Athanasius of Alexandria (c. 295-373; fl. 325-373). Bishop of Alexandria from 328, though often in exile. He wrote his classic polemics against the Arians while most of the eastern bishops were against him.

Athenagoras (fl. 176-180). Early Christian philosopher and apologist from Athens, whose only authenticated writing, *A Plea Regarding Christians*, is addressed to the emperors Marcus Aurelius and Commodius, and defends Christians from the common accusations of atheism, incest and cannibalism.

Augustine of Hippo (354-430). Bishop of Hippo and a voluminous writer on philosophical, exegetical, theological and ecclesiological topics. He formulated the Western doctrines of predestination and original sin in his writings against the Pelagians.

Babai the Great (d. 628). Syriac monk who founded a monastery and school in his region of Beth Zabday and later served as third superior at the Great Convent of Mount Izla during a period of crisis in the Nestorian church.

Basil the Great (b. c. 330; fl. 357-379). One of the Cappadocian fathers, bishop of Caesarea and champion of the teaching on the Trinity propounded at Nicaea in 325. He was a great administrator and founded a monastic rule.

Basil of Seleucia (fl. 444-468). Bishop of Seleucia in Isauria and ecclesiastical writer. He took part in the Synod of Constantinople in 448 for the condemnation of the Eutychian errors and the deposition of their great champion, Dioscurus of Alexandria.

Basilides (fl. second century). Alexandrian heretic of the early second century who is said to have believed that souls migrate from body to body and that we do not sin if we lie to protect the body from martyrdom.

Bede the Venerable (c. 672/673-735). Born in Northumbria, at the age of seven he was put under the care of the Benedictine monks of Saints Peter and Paul at Jarrow and given a broad classical education in the monastic tradition. Considered one of the most learned men of his age, he is the author of *An Ecclesiastical History of the English People*.

Benedict of Nursia (c. 480-547). Considered the most important figure in the history of Western monasticism. Benedict founded many monasteries, the most notable found at Montecassino, but his lasting influence lay in his famous Rule. The Rule outlines the theological and inspirational foundation of the monastic ideal while also legislating the shape and organization of the coenobitic life.

Book of Steps (c. 400). Written by an anonymous Syriac author, this work consists of thirty homilies or discourses which specifically deal with the more advanced stages of growth in the spiritual life.

Braulio of Saragossa (c. 585-651). Bishop of Saragossa (631-651) and noted writer of the Visigothic renaissance. His *Life* of St. Aemilianus is his crowning literary achievement.

Caesarius of Arles (c. 470-543). Bishop of Arles renowned for his attention to his pastoral duties. Among his surviving works the most important is a collection of some 238 sermons that display an ability to preach Christian doctrine to a variety of audiences.

Callistus of Rome (d. 222). Pope (217-222) who excommunicated Sabellius for heresy. It is very probable that he suffered martyrdom.

Cassian, John (360-432). Author of a the *Institutes* and the *Conferences*, works purporting to relay the teachings of he Egyptian monastic fathers on the nature of the spiritual life which were highly influential in the development of Western monasticism.

Cassiodorus (c. 485-c. 540). Founder of Western monasticism whose writings include valuable histories and less valuable commentaries.

Chromatius (fl. 400). Bishop of Aquileia, friend of Rufinus and Jerome and author of tracts and sermons.

Clement of Alexandria (c. 150-215). A highly educated Christian convert from paganism, head of the catechetical school in Alexandria and pioneer of Christian scholarship. His major works,

Protrepticus, Paedagogus and the *Stromata*, bring Christian doctrine face to face with the ideas and achievements of his time.

Clement of Rome (fl. c. 92-101). Pope whose *Epistle to the Corinthians* is one of the most important documents of subapostolic times.

Commodian (c. third or fifth century). Poet of unknown origin (possibly Syrian?) whose two surviving works focus on the Apocalypse and Christian apologetics.

Constitutions of the Holy Apostles. *See Apostolic Constitutions.*

Cyprian of Carthage (fl. 248-258). Martyred bishop of Carthage who maintained that those baptized by schismatics and heretics had no share in the blessings of the church.

Cyril of Alexandria (375-444; fl. 412-444). Patriarch of Alexandria whose strong espousal of the unity of Christ led to the condemnation of Nestorius in 431.

Cyril of Jerusalem (c. 315-386; fl. c. 348). Bishop of Jerusalem after 350 and author of *Catechetical Homilies*.

Cyril of Scythopolis (b. c. 525; d. after 557). Palestinian monk and author of biographies of famous Palestinian monks. Because of him we have precise knowledge of monastic life in the fifth and sixth centuries and a description of the Origenist crisis and its suppression in the mid-sixth century.

Diadochus of Photice (c. 400-474). Antimonophysite bishop of Epirus Vetus whose work *Discourse on the Ascension of Our Lord Jesus Christ* exerted influence in both the East and West through its Chalcedonian Christology. He is also the subject of the mystical *Vision of St. Diadochus Bishop of Photice in Epirus.*

Didache (c. 140). Of unknown authorship, this text intertwines Jewish ethics with Christian liturgical practice to form a whole discourse on the "way of life." It exerted an enormous amount of influence in the patristic period and was especially used in the training of catechumen.

Didymus the Blind (c. 313-398). Alexandrian exegete who was much influenced by Origen and admired by Jerome.

Diodore of Tarsus (d. c. 394). Bishop of Tarsus and Antiochene theologian. He authored a great scope of exegetical, doctrinal and apologetic works, which come to us mostly in fragments because of his condemnation as the predecessor of Nestorianism. Diodore was a teacher of John Chrysostom and Theodore of Mopsuestia.

Dionysius of Alexandria (d. c. 264). Bishop of Alexandria and student of Origen. Dionysius actively engaged in the theological disputes of his day, opposed Sabellianism, defended himself against accusations of tritheism and wrote the earliest extant Christian refutation of Epicureanism. His writings have survived mainly in extracts preserved by other early Christian authors.

Dorotheus of Gaza (fl. c. 525-540). Member of Abbot Seridos's monastery and later leader of a monastery where he wrote *Spiritual Instructions.* He also wrote a work on traditions of Palestinian monasticism.

Epiphanius of Salamis (c. 315-403). Bishop of Salamis in Cyprus, author of a refutation of eighty heresies (the *Panarion*) and instrumental in the condemnation of Origen.

Epiphanius the Latin. Author of the late fifth-century or early sixth century Latin text *Interpretation of the Gospels.* He was possibly a bishop of Benevento or Seville.

Ephrem the Syrian (b. c. 306; fl. 363-373). Syrian writer of commentaries and devotional hymns which are sometimes regarded as the greatest specimens of Christian poetry prior to Dante.

Eucherius of Lyons (fl. 420-449). Bishop of Lyons c. 435-449. Born into an aristocratic family, he, along with his wife and sons, joined the monastery at Lérins soon after its founding.

Eunomius (d. 393). Bishop of Cyzicyus who was attacked by Basil and Gregory of Nyssa for maintaining that the Father and the Son were of different natures, one ingenerate, one generate.

Eusebius of Caesarea (c. 260/263-340). Bishop of Caesarea, partisan of the Emperor Constantine and first historian of the Christian church. He argued that the truth of the gospel had been foreshadowed in pagan writings but had to defend his own doctrine against suspicion of Arian sympathies.

Eusebius of Emesa (c. 300-c. 359). Bishop of Emesa from c. 339. A biblical exegete and writer on doctrinal subjects, he displays some semi-Arian tendencies of his mentor Eusebius of Caesarea.

Eusebius of Vercelli (fl. c. 360). Bishop of Vercelli who supported the trinitarian teaching of Nicaea (325) when it was being undermined by compromise in the West.

Euthymius (377-473). A native of Melitene and influential monk. He was educated by Bishop Otreius of Melitene, who ordained him priest and placed him in charge of all the monasteries in his diocese. When the Council of Chalcedon (451) condemned the errors of Eutyches, it was greatly due to the authority of Euthymius that most of the Eastern recluses accepted its decrees. The empress Eudoxia returned to Chalcedonian orthodoxy through his efforts.

Evagrius of Pontus (c. 345-399). Disciple and teacher of ascetic life who astutely absorbed and creatively transmitted the spirituality of Egyptian and Palestinian monasticism of the late fourth century. Although Origenist elements of his writings were formally condemned by the Fifth Ecumenical Council (Constantinople II, A.D. 553), his literary corpus continued to influence the tradition of the church.

Fastidius (c. fourth-fifth centuries). British author of *On the Christian Life*. He is believed to have written some works attributed to Pelagius.

Faustinus (fl. 380). A priest in Rome and supporter of Lucifer and author of a treatise on the Trinity.

Filastrius (fl. 380). Bishop of Brescia and author of a compilation against all heresies.

Fulgentius of Ruspe (c. 467-532). Bishop of Ruspe and author of many orthodox sermons and tracts under the influence of Augustine.

Gaudentius of Brescia (fl. 395). Successor of Filastrius as bishop of Brescia and author of numerous tracts.

Gennadius of Constantinople (d. 471). Patriarch of Constantinople, author of numerous commentaries and an opponent of the Christology of Cyril of Alexandria.

Gnostics. Name now given generally to followers of Basilides, Marcion, Valentinus, Mani and others. The characteristic belief is that matter is a prison made for the spirit by an evil or ignorant creator, and that redemption depends on fate, not on free will.

Gregory of Elvira (fl. 359-385). Bishop of Elvira who wrote allegorical treatises in the style of Origen and defended the Nicene faith against the Arians.

Gregory of Nazianzus (b. 329/330; fl. 372-389). Bishop of Nazianzus and friend of

Basil and Gregory of Nyssa. He is famous for maintaining the humanity of Christ as well as the orthodox doctrine of the Trinity.

Gregory of Nyssa (c. 335-394). Bishop of Nyssa and brother of Basil, he is famous for maintaining the equality in unity of the Father, Son and Holy Spirit.

Gregory Thaumaturgus (fl. c. 248-264). Bishop of Neocaesarea and a disciple of Origen. There are at least five legendary *Lives* that recount the events and miracles which led to his being called "the wonder worker." His most important work was the *Address of Thanks to Origen*, which is a rhetorically structured panegyric to Origen and an outline of his teaching.

Gregory the Great (c. 540-604). Pope from 590, the fourth and last of the Latin "Doctors of the Church." He was a prolific author and a powerful unifying force within the Latin Church, initiating the liturgical reform that brought about the Gregorian Sacramentary and Gregorian chant.

Hesychius of Jerusalem (fl. 412-450). Presbyter and exegete, thought to have commented on the whole of Scripture.

Hilary of Arles (c. 401-449). Archbishop of Arles and leader of the Semi-Pelagian party. Hilary incurred the wrath of Pope Leo I when he removed a bishop from his see and appointed a new bishop. Leo demoted Arles from a metropolitan see to a bishopric to assert papal power over the church in Gaul.

Hilary of Poitiers (c. 315-367). Bishop of Poitiers and called the "Athanasius of the West" because of his defense (against the Arians) of the common nature of Father and Son.

Hippolytus (fl. 222-245). Recent scholarship places Hippolytus in a Palestinian context, personally familiar with Origen. Though he is known mostly for *The Refutation of All Heresies,* he was primarily a commentator on Scripture (especially the Old Testament) and other sacred texts.

Ignatius of Antioch (c. 35-107/112). Bishop of Antioch who wrote several letters to local churches while being taken from Antioch to Rome to be martyred. In the letters, which warn against heresy, he stresses orthodox Christology, the centrality of the Eucharist and unique role of the bishop in preserving the unity of the church.

Irenaeus of Lyons (c. 135-c. 202). Bishop of Lyons who published the most famous and influential refutation of Gnostic thought.

Isaac of Nineveh (d. c. 700). Also known as Isaac the Syrian or Isaac Syrus, this monastic writer served for a short while as bishop of Nineveh before retiring to live a secluded monastic life. His writings on ascetic subjects survive in the form of numerous homilies.

Isho'dad of Merv (fl. c. 850). Nestorian commentator of the ninth century. He wrote especially on James, 1 Peter and 1 John.

Isidore of Seville (c. 560-636). Youngest of a family of monks and clerics, including sister Florentina and brothers Leander and Fulgentius. He was an erudite author of comprehensive scale in matters both religious and sacred, including his encyclopedic *Etymologies.*

Jacob of Nisibis (d. 338). Bishop of Nisibis. He was present at the council of Nicaea in 325 and took an active part in the opposition to Arius.

Jacob of Sarug (c. 450-c. 520). Syriac ecclesiastical writer. Jacob received his education at Edessa. At the end of his life he was ordained bishop of Sarug. His principal writing was a long series of metrical homilies, earning him the title "The Flute of the Holy Spirit." His theological views are not certain, but it seems that he expressed a moderate monophysite position.

Jerome (c. 347-420). Gifted exegete and exponent of a classical Latin style, now best known as the translator of the Latin Vulgate. He defended the perpetual virginity of Mary, attacked Origen and Pelagius and supported extreme ascetic practices.

John Chrysostom (344/354-407; fl. 386-407). Bishop of Constantinople who was famous for his orthodoxy, his eloquence and his attacks on Christian laxity in high places.

John of Damascus (c. 650-750). Arab monastic and theologian whose writings enjoyed great influence in both the Eastern and Western Churches. His most famous writing was the *Orthodox Faith.*

John the Elder (c. eighth century) A Syriac author who belonged to monastic circles of the Church of the East and lived in the region of Mount Qardu (northern Iraq). His most important writings are twenty-two homilies and a collection of fifty-one short letters in which he describes the mystical life as an anticipatory experience of the resurrection life, the fruit of the sacraments of baptism and the Eucharist.

Josephus, Flavius (c. 37-c. 101). Jewish historian from a distinguished priestly family. Acquainted with the Essenes and Sadducees, he himself became a Pharisee. He joined the great Jewish revolt that broke out in 66 and was chosen by the Sanhedrin at Jerusalem to be commander-in-chief in Galilee. Showing great shrewdness to ingratiate himself with Vespasian by foretelling his elevation and that of his son Titus to the imperial dignity, Josephus was restored his liberty after 69 when Vespasian became emperor.

Justin Martyr (c. 100/110-165; fl. c. 148-161). Palestinian philosopher who was converted to Christianity, "the only sure and worthy philosophy." He traveled to Rome where he wrote several apologies against both pagans and Jews, combining Greek philosophy and Christian theology; he was eventually martyred.

Lactantius (c. 260-c. 330). An eloquent writer known to us through Jerome. He is acknowledged more for his technical writing skills than for his theological thought.

Leander (c. 545-c. 600). Latin ecclesiastical writer, of whose works only two survive. He was instrumental in spreading Christianity among the Visigoths, gaining significant historical influence in Spain in his time.

Leo the Great (regn. 440-461). Bishop of Rome whose *Tome to Flavian* helped to strike a balance between Nestorian and Cyrilline positions at the Council of Chalcedon in 451.

Letter of Barnabas (c. 130). An allegorical and typological interpretation of the Old Testament with a decidedly anti-Jewish tone. It was included with other New Testament works as a "Catholic epistle" at least until Eusebius of Caesarea (c. 260/263-340) questioned its authenticity.

Letter to Diognetus (c. third century). A refutation of paganism and an exposition of the Christian life and faith. The author of this letter is unknown, and the exact identity of its recipient, Diognetus, continues to elude patristic scholars.

Lucifer (d. 370/371). Bishop of Cagliari and vigorous supporter of Athanasius and the Nicene Creed. He and his followers entered into schism after refusing to acknowledge less orthodox bishops appointed by the emperor Constantius.

Luculentius (fifth century). Unknown author of a group of short commentaries on the New Testament, especially Pauline passages. His exegesis is mainly literal and relies mostly on earlier authors such as Jerome and Augustine. The content of his writing may place it in the fifth century.

Macarius of Egypt (c. 300-c. 390). One of the Desert Fathers. Accused of supporting Athanasius, Macarius was exiled c. 374 to an island in the Nile by Lucius, the Arian successor of Athanasius. Macarius continued his teaching of monastic theology until his death.

Macrina the Younger (c. 327-379). The elder sister of Basil the Great and Gregory of Nyssa, she is known as "the Younger" to distinguish her from her paternal grandmother. She had a powerful influence on her younger brothers, especially on Gregory, who called her his teacher and relates her teaching in *On the Soul and the Resurrection*.

Manichaeans. A religious movement that originated circa 241 in Persia under the leadership of Mani but was apparently of complex Christian origin. It is said to have denied free will and the universal sovereignty of God, teaching that kingdoms of light and darkness are coeternal and that the redeemed are particles of a spiritual man of light held captive in the darkness of matter (*see* Gnostics).

Marcion (fl. 144). Heretic of the mid-second century who rejected the Old Testament and much of the New Testament, claiming that the Father of Jesus Christ was other than the Creator God (*see* Gnostics).

Marius Victorinus (b. c. 280/285; fl. c. 355-363). Grammarian who translated works of Platonists and, after his late conversion (c. 355), used them against the Arians.

Mark the Hermit (c. sixth century). Monk who lived near Tarsus and produced works on ascetic practices as well as christological issues.

Martin of Braga (fl. c. 568-579). Anti-Arian metropolitan of Braga on the Iberian peninsula. He was highly educated and presided over the provincial council of Braga in 572.

Maximus of Turin (d. 408/423). Bishop of Turin who died during the reigns of Honorius and Theodosius the Younger (408-423). Over one hundred of his sermons survive.

Maximus the Confessor (c. 580-662). Greek theologian and ascetic writer. Fleeing the Arab invasion of Jerusalem in 614, he took refuge in Constantinople and later Africa. He died near the Black Sea after imprisonment and severe suffering. His thought centered on the humanity of Christ.

Methodius of Olympus (d. 311). Bishop of Olympus who celebrated virginity in a *Symposium* partly modeled on Plato's dialogue of that name.

Minucius Felix of Rome (second or third century). Christian apologist who flourished between 160 and 300 (the exact dates are not known). His *Octavius* agrees at numerous points with the *Apologeticum* of Tertullian. His birthplace is believed to be in Africa.

Montanist Oracles. Montanism was an apocalyptic and strictly ascetic movement begun in the latter half of the second century by a certain Montanus in Phrygia, who, along with certain of his followers, uttered oracles they claimed were inspired by the Holy Spirit. Little of the authentic oracles remains and most of what is known of Montanism comes from the authors who wrote against the movement. Montanism was formally condemned as a heresy before by Asiatic synods.

Nemesius of Emesa (fl. late fourth century). Bishop of Emesa in Syria whose most important work, *Of the Nature of Man*, draws on several theological and philosophical sources and is the first exposition of a Christian anthropology.

Nestorius (c. 381-c. 451). Patriarch of Constantinople 428-431 and credited with the foundation of the heresy which says that the divine and human natures were associated, rather than truly united, in the incarnation of Christ.

Nicetas of Remesiana (fl. second half of fourth century). Bishop of Remesiana in Serbia, whose works affirm the consubstantiality of the Son and the deity of the Holy Spirit.

Novatian of Rome (fl. 235-258). Roman theologian, otherwise orthodox, who formed a schismatic church after failing to become pope. His treatise on the Trinity states the classic western doctrine.

Oecumenius (sixth century). Called the Rhetor or the Philosopher, Oecumenius wrote the earliest extant Greek commentary on Revelation. Scholia by Oecumenius on some of John Chrysostom's commentaries on the Pauline Epistles are still extant.

Origen of Alexandria (b. 185; fl. c. 200-254). Influential exegete and systematic theologian. He was condemned (perhaps unfairly) for maintaining the preexistence of souls while denying the resurrection of the body, the literal truth of Scripture and the equality of the Father and the Son in the Trinity.

Pachomius (c. 292-347). Founder of cenobitic monasticism. A gifted group leader and author of a set of rules, he was defended after his death by Athanasius of Alexandria.

Pacian of Barcelona (c. fourth century). Bishop of Barcelona whose writings polemicize against popular pagan festivals as well as Novatian schismatics.

Palladius of Helenopolis (c. 363/364-c. 431). Bishop of Helenopolis (400-417) and then Aspuna in Galatia. A disciple of Evagrius of Pontus and admirer of Origen, Palladius became a zealous adherent of John Chrysostom and shared his troubles in 403. His *Dialogus de vita S. Johannis* is essentially a work of edification, stressing the spiritual value of the life of the desert, where he spent a number of years as a monk.

Paschasius of Dumium (c. 515-c. 580). Translator of sentences of the Desert Fathers from Greek into Latin while a monk in Dumium.

Paterius (c. sixth-seventh century). Disciple of Gregory the Great who is primarily responsible for the transmission of Gregory's works to many later medieval authors.

Paulinus of Nola (355-431). Roman senator and distinguished Latin poet whose frequent encounters with Ambrose of Milan (c. 333-397) led to his eventual conversion and baptism in 389. He eventually renounced his wealth and influential position and took up his pen to write poetry in service of Christ. He also wrote many letters to, among others, Augustine, Jerome and Rufinus.

Paulus Orosius (b. c. 380). An outspoken critic of Pelagius, mentored by Augustine. His *Seven Books of History Against the Pagans* was perhaps the first history of Christianity.

Pelagius (c. 354-c. 420). Christian teacher whose followers were condemned in 418 and 431 for maintaining that a Christian could be perfect and that salvation depended on free will.

Peter of Alexandria (d. c. 311). Bishop of Alexandria. He marked (and very probably initiated) the reaction at Alexandria against extreme doctrines of Origen. During the persecution of Christians in Alexandria, Peter was arrested and beheaded by Roman officials. Eusebius of Caesarea described him as "a model bishop, remarkable for his virtuous life and his ardent study of the Scriptures."

Peter Chrysologus (c. 380-450). Latin archbishop of Ravenna whose teachings included arguments for the supremacy of the papacy and the relationship between grace and Christian living.

Philo of Alexandria (c. 20 B.C.-c. A.D. 50). Jewish-born exegete who greatly influenced Christian patristic interpretation of the Old Testament. Born to a rich family in Alexandria, Philo was a contemporary of Jesus and lived an ascetic and contemplative life that makes some believe he was a rabbi. His interpretation of Scripture based the spiritual sense on the literal. Although influenced by Hellenism, Philo's theology remains thoroughly Jewish.

Philoxenus of Mabbug (c. 440-523). Bishop of Mabbug (Hierapolis) and a leading thinker in the early Syrian Orthodox Church. His extensive writings in Syriac include a set of thirteen *Discourses on the Christian Life*, several works on the incarnation and a number of exegetical works.

Poemen (c. fifth century). One-seventh of the sayings in the *Sayings of the Desert Fathers* are attributed to Poemen, which is Greek for shepherd. Poemen was a common title among early Egyptian desert ascetics, and it is unknown whether all of the sayings come from one person.

Polycarp of Smyrna (c. 69-155). Bishop of Smyrna who vigorously fought heretics such as the Marcionites and Valentinians. He was the leading Christian figure in Roman Asia in the middle of the second century.

Potamius of Lisbon (fl. c. 350-360). Bishop of Lisbon who joined the Arian party in 357, but later returned to the Catholic faith (c. 359?). His works from both periods are concerned with the larger Trinitarian debates of his time.

Procopius of Gaza (c. 465-c. 530). A Christian Sophist educated in Alexandria. He wrote numerous theological works and commentaries on Scripture (particularly the Hebrew Bible), the latter marked by the allegorical exegesis for which the Alexandrian school was known.

Prudentius (c. 348-c. 410). Latin poet and hymn-writer who devoted his later life to Christian writing. He wrote didactic poems on the theology of the incarnation, against the heretic Marcion and against the resurgence of paganism.

Pseudo-Dionysius the Areopagite (fl. c. 500). Author who assumed the name of Dionysius the Areopagite mentioned in Acts 17:34, and who composed the works known as the *Corpus Areopagiticum* (or *Dionysiacum*). These writings were the foundation of the apophatic school of mysticism in their denial that anything can be truly predicated of God.

Pseudo-Macarius (fl. c. 390). An imaginative writer and ascetic from Mesopotamia to eastern Asia Minor with keen insight into human nature and clear articulation of the theology of the Trinity. His work includes some one hundred discourses and homilies.

Quodvultdeus (fl. 430). Carthaginian deacon and friend of Augustine who endeavored to show at length how the New Testament fulfilled the Old Testament.

Rufinus of Aquileia (c. 345-411). Orthodox Christian thinker and historian who nonetheless translated Origen and defended him against the strictures of Jerome and Epiphanius.

Sabellius (fl. 200). Allegedly the author of the heresy which maintains that the Father and Son are a single person. The patripassian variant of this heresy states that the Father suffered on the cross.

Sahdona (fl. 635-640). Known in Greek as Martyrius, this Syriac author was bishop of Beth Garmai for a short time. His most important work is the deeply scriptural *Book of Perfection* which ranks as one of the masterpieces of Syriac monastic literature.

Salvian the Presbyter of Marseilles (c. 400-c. 480). An important author for the history of his own time. He saw the fall of Roman civilization to the barbarians as a consequence of the reprehensible conduct of Roman Christians.

Second Letter of Clement (c. 150). The so-called *Second Letter of Clement* is the earliest surviving Christian sermon probably written by a Corinthian author, though some scholars have assigned it to a Roman or Alexandrian author.

Severian of Gabala (fl. c. 400). A contemporary

of John Chrysostom, he was a highly regarded preacher in Constantinople, particularly at the imperial court, and ultimately sided with Chrysostom's accusers. His sermons are dominated by antiheretical concerns.

Severus of Antioch (fl. 488-538). A monophysite theologian, consecrated bishop of Antioch in 522. Severus believed that Christ's human nature was an annex to his divine nature and argued that if Christ were both divine and human, he would necessarily have been two persons.

***Shepherd* of Hermas** (second century). Divided into five *Visions*, twelve *Mandates* and ten *Similitudes*, this Christian apocalypse was written by a former slave and named for the form of the second angel said to have granted him his visions. This work was highly esteemed for its moral value and was used as a textbook for catechumens in the early church.

Sulpicius Severus (c. 360-c. 420). An ecclesiastical writer born of noble parents. Devoting himself to monastic retirement, he became a personal friend and enthusiastic disciple of St. Martin of Tours. His ordination to the priesthood is vouched for by Gennadius, but no details of his priestly activity have reached us.

Symeon the New Theologian (c. 949-1022). Compassionate spiritual leader known for his strict rule. He believed that the divine light could be perceived and received through the practice of mental prayer.

Tertullian of Carthage (c. 155/160-225/250; fl. c. 197-222). Brilliant Carthaginian apologist and polemicist who laid the foundations of Christology and trinitarian orthodoxy in the West, though he himself was estranged from the main church by its laxity.

Theodore of Heraclea (d. c. 355). An anti-Nicene bishop of Thrace. He was part of a team seeking reconciliation between Eastern and Western Christianity. In 343 he was excommunicated at the council of Sardica. His writings focus on a literal interpretation of Scripture.

Theodore of Mopsuestia (c. 350-428). Bishop of Mopsuestia, founder of the Antiochene, or literalistic, school of exegesis. A great man in his day, he was later condemned as a precursor of Nestorius.

Theodoret of Cyr (c. 393-466). Bishop of Cyr (Cyrrhus), he was an opponent of Cyril, whose doctrine of Christ's person was finally vindicated in 451 at the Council of Chalcedon.

Theophilus of Antioch (late second century). Bishop of Antioch. His only surviving work is *Ad Autholycum*, where we find the first Christian commentary on Genesis and the first use of the term *Trinity*. Theophilus's apologetic literary heritage had influence on Irenaeus and possibly Tertullian.

Theophylact of Ohrid (c. 1050-c. 1108). Byzantine archbishop of Ohrid (or Achrida) in what is now Bulgaria. Drawing on earlier works, he wrote commentaries on several Old Testament books and all of the New Testament except for Revelation.

Valentinus (fl. c. 140). Alexandrian heretic of the mid-second century who taught that the material world was created by the transgression of God's Wisdom, or Sophia (*see* Gnostics).

Valerian of Cimiez (fl. c. 422-439). Bishop of Cimiez. He participated in the councils of Riez (439) and Vaison (422) with a view to strengthening church discipline. He supported Hilary of Arles in quarrels with Pope Leo I.

Victorius of Petovium (d. c. 304). Latin biblical exegete. With multiple works attributed to him, his sole surviving work is the *Commentary on the Apocalypse* and perhaps some fragments from *Commentary on Matthew*. Victorinus expressed strong millenarianism in his writing, though his was less materialistic than the millenarianism of Papias or Irenaeus. In his allegorical approach he could be called a spiritual disciple of Origen. Victorinus died during the first year of Diocletian's persecution, probably in 304.

Vincent of Lérins (d. 435). Monk who has exerted considerable influence through his writings on orthodox dogmatic theological method, as contrasted with the theological methodologies of the heresies.

Timeline of Writers of the Patristic Period

Location Period	British Isles	Gaul	Spain, Portugal	Italy	Africa
Period					Philo of Alexandria, c. 20 B.C.—c. A.D. 50 (Greek)
2nd century		Irenaeus of Lyons, c. 135-c. 202 (Greek)		Clement of Rome, fl. c. 92-101 (Greek) Justin Martyr (Ephesus, Rome), c. 100/110-165 (Greek) Valentinus the Gnostic, fl. c. 140, (Greek) Marcion, fl. 144 (Greek)	
3rd century		Lactantius, c. 260- c. 330 (Latin)		Callistus of Rome, regn. 217-222 (Latin) Minucius Felix of Rome, fl. c. 218-235 (Latin) Novatian of Rome, fl. 235-258 (Latin)	Clement of Alexandria, c. 150-215 (Latin) Tertullian of Carthage, c. 155/160-225/250 (Latin) Origen (Alexandria, Caesaria of Palestine), 185-254 (Greek) Cyprian of Carthage, fl. 248-258 (Latin) Dionysius of Alexandria, d. c. 264 (Latin) Antony the Great, c. 251-c. 355 (Greek) Arius (Alexandria), fl. c. 320 (Greek)
4th century		Hilary of Poitiers, c. 315-367 (Latin)	Potamius of Lisbon, fl. c. 350-360 (Latin) Gregory of Elvira, fl. 359-385 (Latin) Prudentius, c. 348-c. 410 (Latin)	Marius Victorinus (Rome), fl. 355-363 (Latin) Eusebius of Vercelli, fl. c. 360 (Latin) Lucifer of Cagliari (Sardinia), d. 370/371 (Latin) Faustinus (Rome), fl. 380 (Latin) Filastrius of Brescia, fl. 380 (Latin) Ambrosiaster (Italy?), fl. c. 366-384 (Latin) Gaudentius of Brescia, fl. 395 (Latin) Ambrose of Milan, c. 333-397; fl. 374-397 (Latin) Rufinus of Aquileia, c. 345-411 (Latin)	Alexander of Alexandria, fl. 312-328 (Greek) Pachomius (Egypt), c. 292-347 (Coptic/Greek?) Athanasius of Alexandria, c. 295-373; fl. 325-373 (Greek) Macarius of Egypt, c. 300-c. 390 (Greek) Didymus (the Blind) of Alexandria, c. 313-398 (Greek) Augustine of Hippo, 354-430 (Latin)

Greece	Asia Minor	Syria	Mesopotamia, Persia	Palestine	Location Unknown
	Polycarp of Smyrna, c. 69-155 (Greek)	Ignatius of Antioch, c. 35-107/112 (Greek)			
Athenagoras, fl. 176-180 (Greek)		Theophilus of Antioch, c. late 2nd cent. (Greek)			
				Hippolytus (Palestine?), fl. 222-245 (Greek)	
	Gregory Thaumaturgus (Neocaesarea), fl. c. 248-264 (Greek)				
	Methodius of Olympus (Lycia), d. 311 (Greek)		Aphrahat c. 270-350 (Syriac)	Eusebius of Caesarea (Palestine), c. 260/263-340 (Greek)	Commodian, c. 3rd or 5th cent. (Latin)
Epiphanius of Salamis (Cyprus), c. 315-403 (Greek)		Eusebius of Emesa, c. 300-c. 359 (Greek)		Acacius of Caesarea (Palestine), d. c. 365 (Greek)	
	Basil the Great, b. c. 330; fl. 357-379 (Greek)	Ephrem the Syrian, c. 306-373 (Syriac)		Cyril of Jerusalem, c. 315-386 (Greek)	
	Macrina the Younger, c. 327-379 (Greek)				
	Apollinaris of Laodicea, 310-c. 392 (Greek)				
John Chrysostom (Antioch, Constantinople), 344/354-407 (Greek)	Gregory of Nazianzus, b. 329/330; fl. 372-389 (Greek)				
	Gregory of Nyssa, c. 335-394 (Greek)				
	Evagrius of Pontus, c. 345-399 (Greek)	Nemesius of Emesa (Syria), fl. late 4th cent. (Greek)		Diodore of Tarsus, d. c. 394 (Greek)	
				Jerome (Rome, Antioch, Bethlehem), c. 347-420 (Latin)	
	Theodore of Mopsuestia, c. 350-428 (Greek)				

Timeline of Writers of the Patristic Period

Location / Period	British Isles	Gaul	Spain, Portugal	Italy	Africa
5th century	Fastidius, c. 4th-5th cent. (Latin)	John Cassian (Palestine, Egypt, Constantinople, Rome, Marseilles), 360-432 (Latin)		Chromatius (Aquileia), fl. 400 (Latin)	Cyril of Alexandria, 375-444 (Greek)
		Sulpicius Severus, c. 360-c. 420 (Latin)		Pelagius (Britain, Rome), c. 354-c. 420 (Greek)	Quodvultdeus (Carthage), fl. 430 (Latin)
		Vincent of Lérins, d. 435 (Latin)		Maximus of Turin, d. 408/423 (Latin)	Palladius of Helenopolis, c. 363/364-c. 431 (Greek)
		Valerian of Cimiez, fl. c. 422-439 (Latin)		Paulinus of Nola, 355-431 (Latin)	Ammonius of Alexandria, 5th cent. (Greek)
		Eucherius of Lyons, fl. 420-449 (Latin)		Peter Chrysologus (Ravenna), c. 380-450 (Latin)	
		Hilary of Arles, c. 401-449 (Latin)		Leo the Great (Rome), regn. 440-461 (Latin)	
		Salvian the Presbyter of Marseilles, c. 400-c. 480 (Latin)			
6th century		Caesarius of Arles, c. 470-543 (Latin)	Paschasius of Dumium (Portugal), c. 515-c. 580 (Latin)	Benedict of Nursia, c. 480-547 (Latin)	
			Leander of Seville, c. 545-c. 600 (Latin)	Cassiodorus (Calabria), c. 485-c. 540 (Latin)	Fulgentius of Ruspe, c. 467-532 (Latin)
			Isidore of Seville, c. 560-636 (Latin)	Gregory the Great, c. 540-604 (Latin)	
			Martin of Braga, fl. c. 568-579 (Latin)		
7th century			Braulio of Saragossa, c. 585-651 (Latin)		
8th century	Bede the Venerable, c. 672/673-735 (Latin)				

Greece	Asia Minor	Syria	Mesopotamia, Persia	Palestine	Location Unknown
Nestorius (Constantinople), c. 381-c. 451 (Greek)	Basil of Seleucia, fl. 444-468 (Greek)	Severian of Gabala, fl. c. 400 (Greek)		Hesychius of Jerusalem, fl. 412-450 (Greek)	
		Theodoret of Cyr, c. 393-466 (Greek)			
	Diadochus of Photice, c. 400-474 (Greek)				
Gennadius of Constantinople, d. 471 (Greek)					
		Philoxenus of Mabbug, c. 440-523 (Syriac)			
			Jacob of Sarug, c. 450-c. 520 (Syriac)		
				Procopius of Gaza (Palestine), c. 465-c. 530 (Greek)	
		Severus of Antioch, fl. 488-538 (Greek)			
	Mark the Hermit (Tarsus), c. 6th cent. (Greek)			Dorotheus of Gaza, fl. c. 525-540 (Greek)	Pseudo-Dionysius the Areopagite, fl. c. 500 (Greek)
	Oecumenius (Isauria), 6th cent. (Greek)			Cyril of Scythopolis, b. c. 525; d. after 557 (Greek)	
					(Pseudo-) Constantius, before 7th cent. ? (Greek)
Maximus the Confessor (Constantinople), c. 580-662 (Greek)					Andreas, c. 7th cent. (Greek)
		Sahdona, fl. 635-640 (Syriac)			
		John of Damascus, c. 650-750 (Greek)	Isaac of Nineveh, d. c. 700 (Syriac)		
			John the Elder, 8th cent. (Syriac)		

Ambrose. "De Abraham." In *Sancti Ambrosii opera*. Edited by Karl Schenkl. Corpus Scriptorum Ecclesiasticorum Latinorum, vol. 32, pt. 1, pp. 501-638. Vienna, Austria: F. Tempsky; Leipzig, Germany: G. Freytag, 1896.

———. "De excessu fratris Satyri." In *Sancti Ambrosii opera*. Edited by O. Faller. Corpus Scriptorum Ecclesiasticorum Latinorum, vol. 73, pp. 209-325. Vienna, Austria: F. Tempsky, 1955.

———. "De fuga saeculi." In *Sancti Ambrosii opera*. Edited by Karl Schenkl. Corpus Scriptorum Ecclesiasticorum Latinorum, vol. 32, pt. 2, pp. 163-207. Vienna, Austria: F. Tempsky; Lipzig: G. Freytag, 1897.

———. "De Isaac vel anima." In *Sancti Ambrosii opera*. Edited by Karl Schenkl. Corpus Scriptorum Ecclesiasticorum Latinorum, vol. 32, pt. 1, pp. 641-700. Vienna, Austria: F. Tempsky; Leipzig, Germany: G. Freytag, 1896.

———. "De Jacob et vita beata." In *Sancti Ambrosii opera*. Edited by Karl Schenkl. Corpus Scriptorum Ecclesiasticorum Latinorum, vol. 32, pt. 2, pp. 3-70. Vienna, Austria: F. Tempsky; Leipzig, Germany: G. Freytag, 1897.

———. "De Joseph." In *Sancti Ambrosii opera*. Edited by Karl Schenkl. Corpus Scriptorum Ecclesiasticorum Latinorum, vol. 32, pt. 2, pp. 73-122. Vienna, Austria: F. Tempsky; Leipzig, Germany: G. Freytag, 1897.

———. "De obitu Theodosii." In *Sancti Ambrosii opera*. Edited by O. Faller. Corpus Scriptorum Ecllesiasticorum Latinorum, vol. 73, pp. 371-401. Turnhout, Belgium: Brepols, 1955.

———. "De patriarchis." In *Sancti Ambrosii opera*. Edited by Karl Schenkl. Corpus Scriptorum Ecclesiasticorum Latinorum, vol. 32, pt. 2, pp. 123-60. Vienna, Austria: F. Tempsky; Leipzig, Germany: G. Freytag, 1897.

———. "Epistulae." In *Sancti Ambrosii opera*. Edited by O. Faller and M. Zelzer. Corpus Scriptorum Ecclesiasticorum Latinorum, vol. 82 pt. 1, pt. 2 and pt. 3. Vienna, Austria: F. Tempsky, 1968-1990.

Antony the Great. *Epistolae sanctissimorum*. Patrologiae Cursus Completus, Series Graeca, vol. 40, cols. 977-1000. Edited by J.-P. Migne. Paris: Migne, 1857-1886.

Aphrahat. "Demonstrationes (IV)." In *Patrologia Syriaca*, vol. 1, cols. 137-82. Edited by R. Graffin. Paris: Firmin-Didot et socii, 1910.

Athanasius. "Epistulae festales." In *Opera omnia*. Patrologiae Cursus Completus, Series Graeca, vol. 26. Edited by J.-P. Migne. Paris: Migne, 1857-1886.

Augustine. *Confessionum libri tredecim*. Edited by L. Verheijen. Corpus Christianorum, Series Latina, vol. 27. Turnhout, Belgium: Brepols, 1981.

———. "Contra mendacium." In *Opera*. Edited by J. Zycha. Corpus Christianorum, Series Latina, vol. 41, pp. 469-528. Vienna, Austria: F. Tempsky, 1900.

———. "De bono coniugali." In *Opera*. Edited by J. Zycha. Corpus Christianorum, Series Latina, vol.

41, pp. 187-230. Vienna, Austria: F. Tempsky, 1900.

———. *De civitate Dei*. In *Opera*. Edited by B. Dombart and A. Kalb. Corpus Christianorum, Series Latina, vols. 47-48. Turnhout, Belgium: Brepols, 1955.

———. "De cura pro mortuis gerenda." In *Opera*. Edited by J. Zycha. Corpus Christianorum, Series Latina, vol. 41, pp. 621-59. Vienna, Austria: F. Tempsky, 1900.

———. "De doctrina christiana." In *Opera*. Edited by J. Martin. Corpus Christianorum, Series Latina, vol. 32, pp. 1-167. Turnhout, Belgium: Brepols, 1962.

———. "De patientia." In *Opera*. Edited by J. Zycha. Corpus Christianorum, Series Latina, vol. 41, pp. 663-91. Vienna, Austria: F. Tempsky, 1900.

———. *De Trinitate*. Edited by W. J. Mountain. Corpus Christianorum, Series Latinia, vols. 50-50a. Turnhout, Belgium: Brepols, 1968.

———. "Epistuale." In *Sancti Augustii opera*. Edited by A. Goldbacher. Corpus Scriptorum Ecclesiasticorum Latinorum, vol. 34 pts. 1, 2; vol. 44; vol. 57; vol. 58. Vienna, Austria: F. Tempsky, 1895-1898.

———. *In Johannis evangelium tractatus*. Edited by R. Willems. Corpus Christianorum, Series Latina, vol. 36. Turnhout, Belgium: Brepols, 1954.

———. *Sermones*. Patrologiae Cursus Completus, Series Latina, vols. 38-39. Edited by J.-P. Migne. Paris: Migne, 1844-1864.

Basil the Great. "Sermo 11: sermo asceticus et exhortatio de renunciation mundi." In *Opera omnia*. Patrologiae Cursus Completus, Series Graeca, vol. 31, cols. 625-48. Edited by J.-P. Migne. Paris: Migne, 1857-1886.

Bede the Venerable. *De tabernaculo et vasis eius ac vestibus sacerdotum libri iii*. In *Opera*. Edited by D. Hurst. Corpus Christianorum, Series Latina, vol. 119a. Turnhout, Belgium: Brepols, 1969.

———. *Homiliarum evangelii lib. ii*. In *Opera*. Edited by D. Hurst. Corpus Christianorum, Series Latina, vol. 122. Turnhout, Belgium: Brepols, 1955.

———. *In principium Genesis usque ad nativitatem Isaac etc*. In *Opera exegetica*. Edited by C. W. Jones. Corpus Christianorum, Series Latina, vol. 118a. Turnhout, Belgium: Brepols, 1967.

Caesarius of Arles. *Sermones*. Edited by G. Morin. Corpus Christianorum, Series Latina, vols. 103-4. Turnhout, Belgium: Brepols, 1953.

Chromatius. "Sermones." In *Opera*. Edited by J. Lemarié. Corpus Christianorum, Series Latina, vol. 9a, pp. 3-182; and vol. 9a supplementum, pp. 616-17. Turnhout, Belgium: Brepols, 1974.

Clement of Alexandria. *Clement d'Alexandrie: Le pédagogue*. 3 vols. Edited by H.-I. Marrou, M. Harl, C. Mondésert and C. Matray, 1:108-294; 2:10-242; 3:12-190. Sources chrétiennes, vols. 70, 108, 158. Paris: Cerf, 1960-1970.

———. "Stromata." In *Clemens Alexandrinus*, vol. 2, 3d ed., and vol. 3, 2d ed. Edited by O. Stählin, L. Früchtel, U. Treu. *Die griechischen christlichen Schriftsteller*, vols. 52 (15), 17. Berlin: Akademie-Verlag, 1960-1970.

Clement of Rome. "Epistula i ad Corinthios." In *Clément de Rome: Épitre aux Corinthiens*, pp. 98-204. Edited by A. Jaubert. Sources chrétiennes, vol. 167. Paris: Cerf, 1971.

Cyprian. *Sancti Cypriani episcopi epistularium*. 2 vols. Edited by G. F. Diercks. Corpus Christianorum, Series Latina, vols. 3b-3c. Turnhout, Belgium: Brepols, 1994-1996.

Cyril of Alexandria. "Commentarii in Lucam (in catenis)." In *Opera Omnia*. Patrologiae Cursus Completus, Series Graeca, vol. 72, cols. 476-949. Edited by J.-P. Migne. Paris: Migne, 1857-1886.

———. "Glaphyra in pentateuchum." In *Opera Omnia*. Patrologiae Cursus Completus, Series Graeca, vol. 69, cols. 9-677. Edited by J.-P. Migne. Paris: Migne, 1857-1886.

Cyril of Jerusalem. "Catecheses ad illuminandos 1-18." In *Cyrilli Hierosolymorum archiepiscopi opera quae supersunt omnia*, 1:28-320; 2:2-342. 2 vols. Edited by W. C. Reischl and J. Rupp. Munich: Lentner, 1860 (repr. Hildesheim: Olms, 1967).

Didymus the Blind. *Didyme l'Aveugle: Sur la Genèse*, 1:32-322; 2:8-238. 2 vols. Edited by P. Nautin and L. Doutreleau. Sources chrétiennes, vols. 233, 244. Paris: Cerf, 1976, 1978.

Ephrem the Syrian. *Sancti Ephraem Syri in Genesim et in Exodum commentarii*. Corpus Scriptorum Christianorum Orientalium, vols. 152, 153. Louvain, 1955.

Eusebius of Caesarea. *Eusèbe de Césarée: Histoire ecclésiastique*. 3 vols. Edited by G. Bardy. Sources chrétiennes, 31, 41, 55. Paris: Cerf, 1952-1958.

Eusebius of Emesa. "Catena on Genesis." *La chaîne sur la Genèse*. Edited by F. Petit. Traditio Exegetica Graeca, vols. 3-4. Louvain: Peeters, 1991.

Gregory of Nyssa. "De perfectione Christiana ad Olympium monachum." In *Gregorii Nysseni opera* 8.1:173-214. Edited by W. Jaeger. Leiden: Brill, 1963.

———. *Grégoire de Nyssé: Traité de la virginité*. Edited by M. Aubineau. Sources chrétiennes, vol. 119. Paris: Cerf, 1966.

Hilary of Poitiers. "De trinitate." In *Opera*. Edited by P. Smulders. Corpus Christianorum, Series Latina, vols. 62-62a. Turnhout, Belgium: Brepols, 1979-1980.

Hippolytus. *Hippolyte de Rome: Sur les bénédictions d'Isaac, de Jacob et de Moïse*. Patrologia Orientalis, vol. 27, pp. 2-114. Paris: Firmin-Didot, 1954.

Irenaeus. *Irénée de Lyon: Contre les hérésies, Livre 4*. Edited by A. Rousseau, B. Hemmerdinger, L. Doutreleau and C. Mercier. Sources chrétiennes, vol. 100. Paris: Cerf, 1965.

Jerome. "Epistulae." In *Opera*. Edited by I. Hilberg, J. Divjak and C. Moreschini. Corpus Scriptorum Ecclesiasticorum Latinorum, vols. 54, 55, 56, 88. Vienna, Austria: F. Tempsky, 1910-1918, 1981.

———. "Tractatus lix in psalmos." In *Opera*. Edited by G. Morin, Corpus Christianorum, Series Latina, vol. 78, pp. 3-352. Turnhout, Belgium: Brepols, 1958.

John Chrysostom. "In Genesim (homiliae 1-67)." In *Opera omnia*. Patrologiae Cursus Completus, Series Graeca, vol. 54, cols. 385-580. Edited by J. -P. Migne. Paris: Migne, 1857-1886.

———. "Non esse desperandum." In *Opera omina*. Patrologiae Cursus Completus, Series Graeca, vol. 51, cols. 363-72. Edited by J.-P. Migne. Paris: Migne, 1857-1886.

Justin Martyr. "Dialogus cum Tryphone." In *Die altesten Apologeten*, pp. 90-265. Edited by E. J. Goodspeed. Göttingen: Vandenhoeck & Ruprecht, 1915.

Martin of Braga. "Sententiae Patrum Aegyptiorum." In *Martini Episcopi Bracarensis opera omnia*. Edited by C. W. Barlow. Papers and Monographs of the American Academy in Rome, vol. 12. New Haven, 1950.

Novation. "De trinitate." In *Opera*. Edited by G. F. Diercks. Corpus Christianorum, Series Latina, vol. 4, pp. 11-78. Turnhout, Belgium: Brepols, 1972.

Origen. "Commentarii in evangelium Joannis (lib. 1, 2, 4, 5, 6, 10, 13)." In *Origène: Commentaire sur saint Jean*. 3 vols. Edited by C. Blanc. Sources chrétiennes, vols. 120, 157, 222. Paris: Cerf, 1966-1975.

———. "Commentarii in evangelium Joannis (lib. 19, 20, 28, 32)." In *Origenes Werke*, vol. 4, pp. 298-480. Edited by E. Preuschen. Die griechischen christlichen Schriftsteller, vol. 10. Leipzig: Hinrichs, 1903.

———. "De principiis (Periarchon)." In *Origenes secundum translationem quam fecit Rufinus*, pp. 7-364. Edited by P. Koetschau. Corpus Berolinense, vol. 22. Paris, 1913.

———. "Fragmenta de principiis." In *Origenes vier Bücher von den Prinzipien*. Edited by H. Görgemanns and H. Karpp. Darmstadt, Germany: Wissenschaftliche Buchgesellschaft, 1976.

———. "Homiliae in Lucam." In *Opera omnia*. Patrologiae Cursus Completus, Series Graeca, vol. 13, cols. 1799-1902. Edited by J.-P. Migne. Paris: Migne, 1857-1886.

———. "In Genesim homiliae." In *Origenes secundum translationem quam fecit Rufinus*, pp. 1-144. Edited by W. A. Baerhens. Corpus Berolinense, vol. 29. Paris, 1920.

————. "Selecta in Genesim (fragmenta e catenis)." In *Opera omnia*. Patrologiae Cursus Completus, Series Graeca, vol. 12, cols. 92-145. Edited by J.-P. Migne. Paris: Migne, 1857-1886.

Paulinus of Nola. *Carmina*. Edited by W. Hartel. Corpus Scriptorum Ecclesiasticorum Latinorum, vol. 30. Vienna, 1894.

Peter Chrysologus. "Collectio Sermonum." In *Opera*. Edited by A. Olivar. Corpus Christianorum, Series Latina, vols. 24, 24a, 24b. Turnhout, Belgium: Brepols, 1975.

Philo of Alexandria. "Quaestiones in Genesim." In *Quaestiones in Genesim et in Exodum: Fragmenta Graeca [Les oeuvres de Philon d'Alexandrie]*. Edited by F. Petit. Paris: Cerf, 1978.

Prudentius. "Tituli historiarum." In *Opera*. Edited by M. P. Cunningham. Corpus Christianorum, Series Latina, vol. 126, pp. 390-400. Turnhout, Belgium: Brepols, 1966.

Pseudo-Barnabas. *Épître de Barnabé*. Edited by R. A. Kraft. Sources chrétiennes, vol. 172. Paris: Cerf, 1971.

Quodvultdeus. "Liber promissionum et praedictorum Dei." In *Opera Quodvulteo Carhaginiensi episcopo tributa*. Edited by R. Braun. Corpus Christianorum, Series Latina, vol. 60. Turnhout, Belgium: Brepols, 1976.

Rufinus of Aquileia. "De benedictionibus patriarcharum." In Corpus Christianorum, Series Latina, vol. 20, pp. 189-228. Edited by M. Simonetti. Turnhout, Belgium: Brepols, 1961.

Salvian the Presbyter. "De gubernatione Dei." In *Ouvres*, vol. 2, pp. 95-527. Edited by G. Lagarrigue. Sources chrétiennes, vol. 220. Paris: Cerf, 1975.

Severian of Gabala. "Catena on Genesis." In *La chaîne sur la Genèse*. Edited by F. Petit. Traditio Exegetica Graeca, vol. 3. Louvain: Peeters, 1991.

Tertullian. "De anima." In *Opera*. Edited by J. H. Waszink. Corpus Christianorum, Series Latina, vol. 2, pp. 781-869. Turnhout, Belgium: Brepols, 1954.

————. "De oratione." In *Opera*. Edited by G. F. Diercks. Corpus Christianorum, Series Latina, vol. 1, pp. 257-74. Turnhout, Belgium: Brepols, 1954.

————. "De patientia." In *Opera*. Edited by J. G. Ph. Borleffs. Corpus Christianorum, Series Latina, vol. 1, pp. 299-317. Turnhout, Belgium: Brepols, 1954.

Theodore of Mopsuestia. "Catena on Genesis." In *La chaîne sur la Genèse*. Edited by F. Petit. Traditio Exegetica Graeca, vol. 3. Louvain: Peeters, 1991.

Bibliography of Works in English Translation

Ambrose. "Flight from the World." In *Saint Ambrose: Seven Exegetical Works*, pp. 281-323. Translated by Michael P. McHugh. FC 65. Washington, D.C.: The Catholic University of America Press, 1972.

———. "Isaac, or the Soul." In *Saint Ambrose: Seven Exegetical Works*, pp. 10-65. Translated by Michael P. McHugh. FC 65. Washington, D.C.: The Catholic University of America Press, 1972.

———. "Jacob and the Happy Life." In *Saint Ambrose: Seven Exegetical Works*, pp. 119-84. Translated by Michael P. McHugh. FC 65. Washington, D.C.: The Catholic University of America Press, 1972.

———. "Joseph." In *Saint Ambrose: Seven Exegetical Works*, pp. 189-237. Translated by Michael P. McHugh. FC 65. Washington, D.C.: The Catholic University of America Press, 1972.

———. "Letters to Bishops." In *Saint Ambrose Letters*. Translated by Sister Mary Melchior Beyenka, O.P. FC 26. Washington, D.C.: The Catholic University of America Press, 1954.

———. "Letters to Laymen." In *Saint Ambrose Letters*. Translated by Sister Mary Melchior Beyenka, O.P. FC 26. Washington, D.C.: The Catholic University of America Press, 1954.

———. "On His Brother Satyrus." In *Funeral Orations by Saint Gregory Nazianzen and Saint Ambrose*, pp. 197-259. Translated by John J. Sullivan and Marin R. P. McGuire. FC 22. Washington, D.C.: The Catholic University of America Press, 1953.

———. "On the Death of Theodosius." In *Funeral Orations by Saint Gregory Nazianzen and Saint Ambrose*, pp. 307-32. Translated by Roy J. Deferrari. FC 22. Washington, D.C.: The Catholic University of America Press, 1953.

———. "Patriarchs." In *Saint Ambrose: Seven Exegetical Works*, pp. 243-75. Translated by Michael P. McHugh. FC 65. Washington, D.C.: The Catholic University of America Press, 1972.

Antony the Great. *The Letters of St. Antony: Origenist Theology, Monastic Tradition and the Making of a Saint.* Studies in Antiquity and Christianity. Minneapolis: Fortress Press, 1995.

Aphrahat. "On Prayer." In *The Syriac Fathers on Prayer and the Spiritual Life*, pp. 5-25. Translated and introduced by Sebastian Brock. CS 101. Kalamazoo, Mich.: Cistercian Publications Inc., 1987.

Athanasius. *The Resurrection Letters* ("Festal Letters"). Paraphrased and introduced by Jack N. Sparks. Nashville, Tenn.: Thomas Nelson, 1979.

Augustine. "Against Lying." In *Saint Augustine: Treatises on Various Subjects*, pp. 125-79. Translated by Harold B. Jaffee. FC 16. Washington, D.C.: The Catholic University of America Press, 1952.

———. "The Care to Be Taken for the Dead." In *Saint Augustine: Treatises on Marriage and Other Subjects*, pp. 351-84. Translated by John A. Lacy. FC 27. Washington, D.C.: The Catholic University of America Press, 1955.

———. "Christian Instruction." In *Saint Augustine*, pp. 19-235. Translated by John J. Gavigan. FC 2. Washington, D.C.: The Catholic University of America Press, 1947.

———. *The City of God*. Translated by Henry Bettenson, New York: Penguin, 1984.

———. *The City of God Books 8-16*. Translated by Gerald G. Walsh and Mother Grace Monahan. FC 14.

Washington, D.C.: The Catholic University of America Press, 1952.

———. *City of God, Christian Doctrine.* Translated by Marcus Dods. NPNF, vol. 2. Series 1. Edited by Philip Schaff. 1886-1889. 14 vols. Repr. Peabody, Mass.: Hendrickson, 1994.

———. *Confessions and Enchiridion*, pp. 31-333. Edited and translated by Albert C. Outler. LCC, vol. 7. London: SCM Press, 1955.

———. "The Good of Marriage." In *Saint Augustine: Treatises on Marriage and Other Subjects*, pp. 9-59. Translated by Charles T. Wilcox. FC 27. Edited by Roy J. Deferrari. New York: Fathers of the Church, Inc., 1955.

———. "Letters." In *Saint Augustine: Letters Volume 4 (165-203).* Translated by Sister Wilfrid Parsons. FC 30. Washington, D.C.: The Catholic University of America Press, 1955.

———. "On Patience." In *Saint Augustine: Treatises on Various Subjects*, pp. 237-64. Translated by Sister Luanne Meagher. FC 16. Washington, D.C.: The Catholic University of America Press, 1952.

———. *Sermons on the New Testament (94a-147a).* Edited by John E. Rotelle. Translated by Edmund Hill. Introduction by Cardinal Michele Pellegrino. WSA, part 3, vol. 1. Brooklyn, N.Y.: New City Press, 1990.

———. *Sermons on the Old Testament (1-19).* Edited by John E. Rotelle. Translated by Edmund Hill. Introduction by Cardinal Michele Pellegrino. WSA, part 3, vol. 1. Brooklyn, N.Y.: New City Press, 1990.

———. *Sermons on the Liturgical Seasons (184-229z).* Edited by John E. Rotelle. Translated by Edmund Hill. Introduction by Cardinal Michele Pellegrino. WSA, part 3, vol. 1. Brooklyn, N.Y.: New City Press, 1990.

———. *Sermons on the Liturgical Seasons.* Translated by Sister Mary Sarah Muldowney. FC 38. Washington, D.C.: The Catholic University of America Press, 1959.

———. *Tractates on the Gospel of John 1-10.* Translated by John W. Rettig. FC 78. Washington, D.C.: The Catholic University of America Press, 1988.

———. *Tractates on the Gospel of John 28-54.* Translated by John W. Rettig. FC 88. Washington, D.C.: The Catholic University of America Press, 1993.

———. *The Trinity.* Translated by Edmund Hill. WSA, part 1, vol. 5. Brooklyn, N.Y.: New City Press, 1991.

Basil the Great. "On Renunciation of the World." In *Saint Basil: Ascetical Works*, pp. 15-31. Translated by Sister M. Monica Wagner. FC 9. New York: Fathers of the Church, Inc., 1950.

Bede the Venerable. *Homilies on the Gospels, Book One: Advent to Lent.* Translated by Lawrence T. Martin and David Hurst. Preface by Benedicta Ward. Introduction by Lawrence T. Martin. CS, vol. 110. Kalamazoo, Mich.: Cistercian Publications, 1991.

———. "On the Tabernacle." In *Bede: On the Tabernacle.* Translated with notes and introduction by Arthur G. Holder. TTH 18. Liverpool: Liverpool University Press, 1994.

Caesarius of Arles. *Sermons Volume 2: 81-186.* Translated by Sister Mary Magdeleine Mueller. FC 47. Washington, D.C.: The Catholic University of America Press, 1964.

Clement of Alexandria. *Christ the Educator.* Translated by Simon P. Wood. FC 23. Washington, D.C.: The Catholic University of America Press, 1954.

———. *Stromateis Books 1-3.* Translated by John Ferguson. FC 85. Washington, D.C.: The Catholic University of America Press, 1991.

Clement of Rome. "First Letter to the Corinthians." In *The Apostlic Fathers*, pp. 9-58. Translated by Francis X. Glimm. FC 1. New York: Christian Heritage, Inc., 1947.

Cyprian. *Letters 1-81.* Translated by Sister Rose Bernard Donna. FC 51. Washington, D.C.: The Catholic University of America Press, 1964.

Cyril of Alexandria. *Letters 1-50.* Translated by John I. McEnerney. FC 76. Washington, D.C.: The Catholic University of America Press, 1987.

Cyril of Jerusalem. "Catechetical Lectures." In *The Works of Saint Cyril of Jerusalem*, pp. 91-249. Translated by Leo P. McCauley. FC 61. Washington, D.C.: The Catholic University of America Press, 1969.

Ephrem the Syrian. "Commentary on Genesis." In *St. Ephrem the Syrian: Selected Prose Works*, pp. 67-213. Translated by Edward G. Mathews Jr. and Joseph P. Amar. FC 91. Edited by Kathleen McVey. Washington, D.C.: The Catholic University of America Press, 1994.

Eusebius of Caesarea. *Ecclesiastical History, Books 1-5.* Translated by Roy J. Deferrari. FC 19. Washington, D.C.: The Catholic University of America Press, 1953.

Gregory of Nyssa. "On Perfection." In *Saint Gregory of Nyssa: Ascetical Works*, pp. 95-122. Translated by Virginia Woods Callahan. FC 58. Washington, D.C.: The Catholic University of America Press, 1967.

———. "On Virginity." In *Saint Gregory of Nyssa: Ascetical Works*, pp. 6-75. Translated by Virginia Woods Callahan. FC 58. Washington, D.C.: The Catholic University of America Press, 1967.

Hilary of Poitiers. *The Trinity.* Translated by Stephen McKenna. FC 25. Washington, D.C.: The Catholic University of America Press, 1954.

Jerome. *Homilies Volume 1 (1-59 On the Psalms).* Translated by Sister Marie Liguori Ewald. FC 48. Washington, D.C.: The Catholic University of America Press, 1964.

John Chrysostom. *Homilies on Genesis 18-45.* Translated by Robert C. Hill. FC 82. Washington, D.C.: The Catholic University of America Press, 1990.

Justin Martyr. "Dialogue with Trypho." In *Writings of Saint Justin Martyr*, pp. 147-366. Translated by Thomas B. Falls. FC 6. New York: Christian Heritage, Inc., 1948.

Martin of Braga. "Sayings of the Egyptian Fathers." In *Iberian Fathers Volume 1: Martin of Braga, Paschasius of Dumium, Leander of Seville*, pp. 17-34. Translated by Claude W. Barlow. FC 62. Washington, D.C.: The Catholic University of America Press, 1969.

Novatian. "On the Trinity." In *Novatian: The Writings*, pp. 23-111. Translated by Russell J. DeSimone. FC 67. Washington, D.C.: The Catholic University of America Press, 1974.

Origen. "Commentary on John." In *Origen: Commentary on the Gospel According to John, Books 13-32.* Translated by Ronald E. Heine. FC 89. Washington, D.C.: The Catholic University of America Press, 1993.

———. "Homilies on Genesis." In *Origen: Homilies on Genesis and Exodus*, pp. 47-224. Translated by Ronald E. Heine. FC 71. Washington, D.C.: The Catholic University of America Press, 1982.

———. *Homilies on Luke, Fragments on Luke*, pp. 5-162. Translated by Joseph T. Lienhard. FC 94. Washington, D.C.: The Catholic University of America Press, 1996.

———. "On First Principles (Book 4)." In *Origen: Selected Writings*, pp. 171-216. Translated by Rowan A. Greer. Classics of Western Spirituality: A Library of the Great Spiritual Masters. Mahwah, N.J.: Paulist, 1979.

Paulinus of Nola. "Poem." In *The Poems of St. Paulinus of Nola.* Translated and annotated by P. G. Walsh. ACW 40. New York: Newman Press, 1975.

Peter Chrysologus. "Sermon." In *Saint Peter Chrysologus: Selected Sermons and Saint Valerian: Homilies*, pp. 25-282. Translated by George E. Ganss. FC 17. Washington, D.C.: The Catholic University of America Press, 1953.

Prudentius. "Scenes from Sacred History." In *The Poems of Prudentius, Volume 2*, pp. 179-95. Translated by Sister M. Clement Eagan. FC 52. Washington, D.C.: The Catholic University of America Press, 1965.

Pseudo-Barnabas. "Epistle of Barnabas." In *The Apostolic Fathers*, pp. 335-409. Translated by Kirsopp

Lake. LCL 24. London: Heinemann, 1912.

Salvian the Presbyter. "The Governance of God." In *The Writings of Salvian, The Presbyter*, pp. 25-232. Translated by Jeremiah F. O'Sullivan. FC 3. Washington, D.C.: The Catholic University of America Press, 1962.

Tertullian. "On Patience." In *Tertullian: Disciplinary, Moral and Ascetical Works*, pp. 193-222. Translated by Sister Emily Joseph Daly. FC 40. Washington, D.C.: The Catholic University of America Press, 1959.

———. "On Prayer." In *Tertullian: Disciplinary, Moral and Ascetical Works*, pp. 157-88. Translated by Sister Emily Joseph Daly. FC 40. Washington, D.C.: The Catholic University of America Press, 1959.

———. "On the Soul." In *Tertullian: Apologetical Works and Minucius Felix: Octavius*, pp. 179-309. Translated by Edwin A. Quain. FC 10. Washington, D.C.: The Catholic University of America Press, 1950.